IRELAND

FÁILTE

www.marco-polo.com

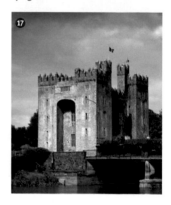

⑱ ✴✴ Kilkenny

A lovely little town with medieval houses and alleyways. the Kilkenny Design Centre is not to be missed.
page 396

⑲ ✴✴ Rock of Cashel

Once the seat of the kings of Munster, Cashel was the political and religious centre of the region.
page 244

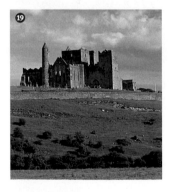

⑳ ✴✴ Irish National Heritage Park

This open-air museum conveys a vivid impression of 9,000 years of Irish history. It is especially popular with children.
page 512

㉑ ✴✴ Killarney Area

Great scenic beauty, with lakes embedded in a landscape of mountains and hills. One of the most popular tourist regions in Ireland.
page 406

㉒ ✴✴ Ring of Kerry

This coastal route of 200 km/125 miles around the Iveragh peninsula is famed for its wonderful views, wild moors and hilly landscape. Set aside a full day to see it!
page 460

㉓ ✴✴ Garinish Island

The creation of gardens between 1910 and 1920 made Garinish into an island of flowers. In good weather seals can be seen from the ferry.
page 194

㉔ ✴✴ Skellig Islands

These two awe-inspiring rocky islands are bird reserves. Skellig Michael is not to be missed.
page 478

Do You Feel Like

home-made Irish stew, modern Irish art, literary masterpieces, historic sites with a mythical atmosphere or wonderful parks and gardens in stunning scenery? Then Ireland is the place for you.

GARDENS AND PARKS

LITERATURE

MODERN ART

HISTORIC SITES

COUNTRY COOKING

BACKGROUND

ENJOY IRELAND

Traditional Irish garb for Heritage Day in Ballina

TOURS

SIGHTS
FROM A TO Z

PRICE CATEGORIES
Restaurants
(main course)
€€€€ = over 25 € (20 £)
€€€ = 20–25 € (16–20 £)
€€ = 10–20 € (8–16 £)
€ = below 10 € (8 £)
Hotels (double room
including breakfast)
€€€€ = über 130 € (105 £)
€€€ = 100–130 € (80–105 £)
€€ = 80–100 € (65–80 £)
€ = below 80 € (65 £)

Note
Billable service telephone
numbers are marked with an
asterisk: *0180....

The basalt columns of Giant's Causeway

PRACTICAL INFORMATION

BACKGROUND

What do you need to know and more about the Emerald Isle: the countryside and its people, the chequered history and its rich and varied culture.

The Emerald Isle

»Forty shades of green«, as the famous song goes. Well, green is indeed the dominant colour in this country, its many variations sustained by the gentle, moist climate. Meadows, pastures and hedgerows are offset by glorious touches of colour provided by rhododendron bushes and fuchsia hedges in lavish bloom.

The beauty of the landscape has to be the main attraction for anybody visiting Ireland. And of course most people would hope to enjoy the island in sunshine. But even if it does rain frequently, **the weather changes reliably fast**, and you can find all four seasons in one day; after a pelting shower the sky clears up quickly, the mild Irish sun bathing the undulating landscape in a beautifully soft light.

MIND AND BODY

Alongside its magnificent natural beauty, Ireland has plenty of art and culture to offer. The bizarre shapes and figures of the country's Celtic prehistory, and the early Christian monuments, monasteries and high crosses, are highlights of any trip to Ireland. Another striking feature of the landscape are the **round towers**, found nowhere else in the world. For many visitors, a trip to Ireland provides a great opportunity for an active holiday. Top of the list is golf – in Ireland, a sport for everyone. There are some 183,000 members of over 300 clubs, including one third of the world's links courses, and more are being built all the time. Many tourists also appreciate the opportunity to explore the country on horse-

Thatched cottages were a common type of dwelling for centuries, but their numbers are dwindling

back or by bike, taking advantage of the attractive, varied landscape and the relatively low volume of traffic on the roads. But beware, bike tours in Ireland are a relentless up-and-down and do require a bit of stamina. The island is a paradise for anglers too, drawn by the numerous unpolluted inland waterways and lakes teeming with shoals of fish, as well as by the rich fishing grounds of the coast, fed by the mild Gulf Stream. This **classic fishing country** offers the advanced angler plenty of opportunities for coarse fishing, game fishing and deep-sea angling.

ADVENTURES ON THE WATER

For a particularly rewarding experience, consider a holiday on a house-boat and discover Ireland on the Shannon and its tributaries – no boatman's license necessary! The Shannon-Erne canal connects Ireland's longest river with the scenic Erne Lakes in Northern Ireland, and, with the successful peace process, crossing the border is no longer an issue. In the past, Belfast and Derry used to be ghost towns come evening; today the restaurants, cinemas, theatres and of course, pubs, attract a lively crowd.

BEYOND PUB CULTURE

Education has always been important to the Irish. Literature and teachers have been held in high regard since the times when Irish schools were prohibited and »hedge school masters« used to illegally teach the countryside's children for a penny per week. The hedge school masters are said to have carried their ink well on a chain around their neck, and their copy of Virgil as well as an Irish primer in their pocket. Once Irish schools were allowed again, education and teaching passed mostly into the hands of religious teaching orders and lay priests. Today, school is compulsory from ages six to fifteen. The »Celtic Tiger«, the economic boom of the 1990s, would not have been possible without Ireland's highly qualified workforce. Despite the emigration of young people in recent years, Ireland will overcome the crisis that affected the financial sector after 2008.

WELCOME TO IRELAND

Visitors who want to get to know the Irish should try the pub, where a pint of Guinness is the perfect accompaniment to stories, debates and songs. Strangers are usually invited to join the conversation, which is why the first word that the visitor learns in the old Gaelic tongue is nearly always »Fáilte« – »Welcome«!

Facts

Natural Environment

Geographically, there are two sides to Ireland: a low-lying centre is accompanied by mountain ranges. One characteristic unites almost all regions of the Ireland: the dominance of the colour green, in every variation.

The interior of the island is dominated by extensive limestone plains with peat bogs, low hills and large and small lakes. About a fifth of the country is covered by the Shannon's extensive network of rivers and lakes. The central lowlands only extend to the coast in the Dublin area.

Central lowlands

Mountain ranges near the coast are characteristic of Ireland's landscape. One of the best examples is the Macgillycuddy's Reeks in the southwest, which reach up to 1,041m/3,415ft at Carrantuohill, the highest peak in Ireland. The mountains in the south are mainly comprised of red sandstone, those in Connemara, Donegal and Mayo mainly of granite and quartzite. Single conical, bare peaks jutting out of the plain are a typical feature of this type of landscape. Most of the northeast is covered by a basalt plateau, whilst the predominant rock in the Wicklow Mountains is granite. Of particular interest for geologists and botanists is the karst area of the Burren, on the western coast of County Clare. Ireland has experienced at least two **ice ages**; both left their traces in smoothly polished rocks and dark mountain lakes, and in the course of many valleys and numerous sediments, such as the drumlins (round low hillocks) between Sligo and Belfast. The coastline is a steady succession of steep cliffs and sandy bays, often with dunes. The most spectacular coastal scenery can be found at the Cliffs of Moher, Slieve League and the cliffs of Achill Island.

Mountains

Across large swaths of the »Emerald Isle«, nature remains intact. In sparsely populated areas where organic agriculture – mainly cattle rearing – is practised, there are few problems. Over recent years however, in the wake of increasing industrial activity, much has changed, with important environmental legislation subservient to economic survival. The consequences have been water and air pollution, overfishing and the destruction of the peat eco-system through unregulated exploitation. However, an awareness of green issues has gained ground, and the Irish tourist industry understands the importance of safeguarding the natural environment as the resource which makes the island attractive to visitors.

Natural environment

Many parts of the west coast of Ireland are rugged and inhospitable

FLORA AND FAUNA

Low level of biodiversity
Ireland's flora and fauna is unusually poor in biodiversity. During the last Ice Age, the country was nearly completely covered by ice, allowing only a few Arctic plants to survive. When Ireland became an island at the end of the last Ice Age, the plants and animals struggled to take root here again. Only half of the flowering plants that visitors would expect to see in a country with Ireland's latitude and climate are actually found here. On the other hand, Ireland presents all shades of the colour green – depending on the weather, cloud formation, amount of rain, direction of the wind and type of soil. This rich palette of greens has earned the island the nickname »Emerald Isle«.

No snakes
In the animal kingdom, the situation is similar: Ireland has **55 different species of mammal**, of which 26 are thought to be native, and no snakes at all. The reptile family is only represented by the common lizard. Extinct species include the Irish elk, the great auk, the wildcat, the European beaver and since 1786 the wolf, Many kinds of bird, for example the golden eagle, have been reintroduced.

PLANTS

Forests
Of the **forests** that once covered the whole island – made up of oak, holly, birch, ash and hazel – only a few remnants are left. A state reforestation programme is trying to reverse this trend by using, amongst others, the Sitka spruce; however, this species does not always thrive in Ireland. Today 12.6% of the land surface is forest.

? MARCO ⊕ POLO INSIGHT

Endangered peat bogs

Extraction of peat and the expansion of agriculture have had a severe effect on the peat bogs. Since 2005 the EU has supported the activities of the irish Peatland Conservation Council. This programme fences off threatened areas, preserves ecological variety and promotes sustainable tourism (www.ipcc.ie).

Almost **one fifth of the land surface** of Ireland is covered in peat bog. There are three different types: highland peat bog (c4%), reaching a depth of 7m/23ft, blanket bogs (c11%), only going down to a depth of 3.5m/11ft and covering both mountains and valleys, with the remainder made up of lowland peat bog. All types of bog are home to various species of bog moss, whilst heather, cotton grass, broom heather, bell heather and bog asphodel thrive on highland and blanket bog.

Imported plants
Tropical and subtropical shrubs that once used to be planted in the parks and gardens of stately homes have today spread over the whole

country. In the warm southwest in particular, you frequently see palm trees and evergreen plants. Huge **broom and rhododendron bushes**, as well as fuchsia hedges in bloom, add touches of colour to all that green. In the nature reserves the spread of these plants is not always greeted with enthusiasm, as they often stifle the endemic vegetation. The foxglove and bluebell thrive in Ireland.

In the southwest of the country and in the Burren, subtropical and **arctic or alpine vegetation** can be found within a confined space, as plants managed to survive here due to the cool summers following the last Ice Age.

In the southwest

ANIMALS

The island is rich in birdlife, with some **250 migratory bird**s joining **135 local species**. Many songbirds nest in hedges, and the bogs are home to larks, curlews and common snipe. In wetland areas, oyster-

Birds

Puffins on the bird island of Little Skellig

Ireland

Republic of Ireland
Northern Ireland

Derry
DONEGAL   DERRY   ANTRIM
            TYRONE
U L S T E R   BELFAST
    FERMANAGH   DOWN
                ARMAGH
        Sligo   MONAGHAN
    SLIGO   LEITRIM CAVAN
MAYO
    ROSCOMMON LONG-   LOUTH
CONNAUGHT   FORD
            WEST-   MEATH
            MEATH   DUBLIN
    Athlone
Galway   DUBLIN
    GALWAY   OFFALY   KILDARE
            LEINSTER
CLARE   LAOIS   WICKLOW
                CARLOW
        KILKENNY
Limerick TIPPERARY
    LIMERICK   WEXFORD
    MUNSTER   Waterford
KERRY   WATERFORD
    CORK
Killarney
    Cork
©BAEDEKER

state border
province border
county border

catchers – although, like puffins, they are coastal birds – may be seen
inland. On the rugged Atlantic coast nest seagulls, guillemots, cormorants, and the agile gannets, dive-bombing their prey in the sea
from great heights. The fulmar and the tern are less frequently seen.

Fish, marine life The water of the Irish lakes, rivers and brooks is often peaty brown,
but clean and therefore rich in fish. About **40 species of freshwater
fish** are currently recorded. Salmon and trout are the anglers' favourite prey, with pike and rainbow trout only recently established here.
Irish **coastal waters** are home to some 375 fish species; of importance for the fishing industry are herring, sprat, cod, mackerel, plaice,
haddock, sole and monkfish. Various species of seal live on the coast
and around the islands.

Population · Politics · Economy

The Irish Republic is one of the least-populated regions in Europe. As nearly a third of the country's population lives in Greater Dublin, vast areas can appear practically deserted.

POPULATION

In the first half of the 19th century, Ireland was one of the most densely populated countries in Europe. However, a wave of emigration started in the second decade, culminating in a veritable exodus during the Great Famine of 1845–52 (►History, Potato blight). About **1 million Irish left their home country** and tried to make a new life for themselves in the USA or in Britain. The population declined from 8.5 million in 1845 to less than 5 million in 1900. Another marked wave of emigration started after the Second World War as, between 1951 and 1961, over 40,000 Irish emigrated every year. In 1961 a mere 3 million lived in the Republic of Ireland, and a further 1.5 million in Northern Ireland.

Emigration

Improved economic conditions then encouraged people to stay, or even return, and led to an increase in population of 15.6% (Northern Ireland only 1.7%) between 1970 and 1980. High unemployment in the following decade again boosted emigration, before the years of plenty of the »Celtic tiger« followed in the 1990s. The exodus then started again in the wake of the financial crisis: in both 2010 and 2011, some 50,000 well-educated Irish citizens left the country. Countries outside the European Union, especially, Canada, New Zealand and the USA, were the most popular destinations.

In the mid- 1990s, a **massive economic boom** reversed the old trends. Many citizens from other European countries came to Ireland, and immigrants from Asia, Africa and South America, too, took advantage of the good job opportunities. Despite the economic crisis beginning in 2008, between 2007 and 2011 a total of 125,000 immigrants arrived in the country. Ireland has the highest birth rate in the EU, 16.1 births per 1000 inhabitants.

Immigration

The Irish emigrating to the US mostly settled in the large cities of the north. Soon, unskilled Irish workers dominated the canal and railway construction sector, and turned into a political force to be reckoned with. In the years between 1870 and 1920, in every US city with a sizable Irish population, the Irish had their own political leader, often

The Irish in the US

Facts and Figures

Location:
Northwest Europe

← **290km/
180mi** →

**466km/
290mi**

IRL   NIR

Dublin

Area:
**84,430 sq km/
32,588 sq mi**, of which
13,843 sq km/ 5,340 sq mi
is Northern Ireland

51°30' – 55°30
north latitud

**465km/
289mi**

Length of coast:
3700km/2300mi

■ London

Population (2013):
4.64 Mio. IRL
1.84 Mio. NIR

Population density:
65 persons per sq km/168 per sq mi, IRL
122 per sq km/316 per sq mi, NIR

©BAEDEKER

▶ Population

Largest cities:
Dublin: 1.10 mil.
(Greater Dublin 1.81 mil.)
Belfast: 267,500
(Greater Belfast: 641,600)

▶ Religion

	IRL %	NIR %
Roman Catholic	86,6	40,3
Church of Ireland	3,0	15,3
Other	3,1	6,4
Not religion	6,4	13,9
Presbyterian		20,7
Methodist		3,5

▶ Symbols

The golden harp stands
for the great tradition
of singers and bards.
The three-leafed clover
represents the Holy
Trinity, a reference to
St Patrick's teaching.

▶ Flag

Republic of Ireland:
Green stands for the Catholic
orange for the Protestants
(derived from the colours of William of
Orange), white for peace between the two
parts of the population.

▶ Northern Ireland

The Union Jack flies in the part of Ireland
that belongs to the United Kingdom. Its
symbol is the red hand of Ulster on a white
background, deriving from Viking times an
representing a territorial claim.

▶ Language

Irish (official language), **English** (linga
franca), **Scots** (regional)

▶ State

Republic (Poblacht na h'Éireann, Republic o
Ireland), **parliamentary democracy**.
Head of state: directly elected president
with ceremonial duties, elected for seven
years, two terms max.
Executive: prime minister (Taoiseach)
and ministers.
Parliament: two chambers: the **Dáil Éireann**
and the **Senate** (Seanad Éireann)

Administration

Four historic provinces:
Leinster, Munster, Ulster,
Connacht

32 historisc counties:
26 in IRL, **6** in NIR

Since 2001 in Ireland
34 Councils, of which **29** Land
Councils and **5** City Councils.

Economy

Gross domestic product
2015, per capita:
IRL 45770 €
NIR 32 170 £ (2014)
2014, by sector
agriculture/fishery **1.56%**
industry **25.62%**
services **72.82%**

Unemployment (2015):
IRL **8.9%**,
NIR **6.5 %**

Climate in Dublin

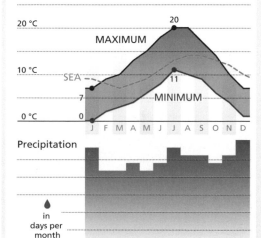

Emigration

During the Great **Famine of 1845–55**, caused by potato blight and restrictions on the availability of food, approximately **2 million** Irish emigrated to the **USA**, **British North America** (Canada), **Great Britain** and **Australia**.

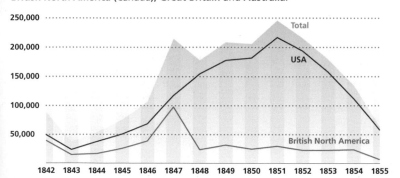

Cities that still celebrate St Patrick's Day:
New York, Boston, New Orleans, Chicago

Welcome to Everyday Life!

Get to know Ireland off the tourist trail and meet »normal« people. Here are some tips from the Marco Polo team.

ORGANIC HOLIDAY?

WWOOF (Worldwide Opportunities on Organic Farms) organizes stays at 362 organic farms in the Republic of Ireland and Northern Ireland. Free board and lodging is offered in exchange for work on the farm – for example at Turcarra Farm in Co. Armagh, at Mulligan's in Co. Donegal, at the Jaguar Organic Farm in West Connemara, Co. Galway, and also in the sunny south of the island. Minimum age: 16 years.
WWOOF Ireland
Coomhola, Bantry, Co. Cork
Tel. 027 5 12 54 (Annie or Rob, only Wed, 9.30am to 1pm)
www.wwoof.ie.

COUCH SURFING

A cheap way to travel, especially popular amongst the young, is couch surfing. Visitors are accommodated in private homes. This can be much more than just a low-cost bed for the night – depending on the host, it can be an excellent entrée to local life and culture. The biggest range of addresses is in the major cities, especially in Dublin and Belfast.
www.couchsurfing.org

SLAINTE!

Since the start of the city of Dublin's welcome programme in summer 2011, 1,000 guests have been greeted. The »Rolls Royce of city welcome programmes« (Sidney Morning Herald, Australia) is unique worldwide, and it works! Visitors arriving in Dublin can meet one of 3,000 Dublin ambassadors, volunteers who know their home district well, for a cup of tea or a glass of Guinness, and talk about the weather, Ireland and the Irish, the eurozone crisis, gardens or their families. A free pint is provided at the cost of sponsors the Dublin City Council, the Dublin Regional Authority and Fáilte Ireland. The service can be booked through the internet site of the association City of a Thousand Welcomes, based in the Little Museum, where every meeting begins, thus providing a guarantee of safety. The organizers say »We are celebrating Dublin as a place where get a warm welcome, and where good conversation is part of the culture.«
City of a Thousand Welcomes (CTW)
St. Steven's Green 15, 1. Stock
Dublin 2, Tel. 01 6 61 10 00
www.cityofathousandwelcomes.com

LEARN GAELIC!

The organization Oideas Gael in Glencolumbkille, Co. Donegal, runs courses in Irish Gaelic and many other subjects, such as playing the whistle, harp or bodhran, and the craft of traditional tapestry. Gael Linn runs courses in Irish language and sports in Dublin and in the Gaeltacht.
www.oideasgael.ie

VOLUNTEERING

Volunteer Ireland is an organization formed from a merger of Volunteer Centres Ireland and Volunteering Ireland. It looks for people willing to help at, for example, a volunteer centre in north Dublin, finds placements at institutions such as the Chester Beatty Library, assists at the Spraoi Festival in Waterford (300 volunteers), organizes summer work camps and sets up contacts to Sea Shepherd Ireland in Sligo, which has dedicated itself since 1977 to protecting the marine environment and saving whales (www.seashepherd.org).
Volunteer Ireland
18 Eustace Street
Dublin 2 (Temple Bar)
Tel. 01 6 36 94 46
www.volunteeringireland.ie.

the mayor, and large numbers of Irish immigrants worked in the police force and as firefighters. One famous American of Irish descent was playwright **Eugene O'Neill** (1888–1953), who in 1936 was awarded the Nobel Prize for Literature.

Travellers, Tinkers

One underprivileged marginalized group in Ireland are the **Travellers**, also derogatorily called **Tinkers**. Similarly to the Roma, though not related to them ethnically, the Travellers have a semi-nomadic lifestyle. In the past, they earned their living mainly repairing pots and pans. They have their own language too; however, it is now proven that the Travellers did not immigrate from elsewhere but are in fact Irish in origin. These days they have long swapped their brightly painted horse-drawn carts, popular with tourists today, for modern mobile homes.

Anglo-Irish

Anglo-Irish is the name given to those families whose English ancestors from around the 17th century were given the lands and properties of dispossessed Irish. Where earlier English settlers had learned Gaelic and adopted the lifestyle of the native population, the new rulers kept themselves to themselves. They continued to speak English, held on to their religion and shut themselves off from their Catholic Irish neighbours behind high walls. In the worst cases, they saw their lands purely as an asset to be exploited, hardly visiting Ireland and leaving their agents to collect the rents. Later, the Anglo-Irish landed gentry, as the ruling class, became the repository of cultural life in Ireland, building fine houses and laying out large landscaped parks with many exotic plants.

Dwellings

In Ireland, most people usually live in their own home, even if it is humble. It is only in the cities that more people rent their homes. The traditional type of house in rural areas is a **cottage** with a thatched roof. In the past, a cottage often comprised just one big room, with a smaller room each side., accommodating families of six or more - not a romantic way to live in those days.

The **property boom** around the turn of the millennium and the ready availability of credit was followed by the financial crisis, when the bubble burst. In 2012 the value of newly built housing fell by 48%, a situation that left many families with negative equity or forced them to leave their homes. A new phenomenon appeared: »**ghost es-tates**«, of which by early2012 there were 2881, with a total of 300,000 empty homes. Many of them lie close to cottages that were abandoned around 1850 during the Great Famine.

STATE AND SOCIETY

The two major parties in Ireland, **Fianna Fáil/FF** (»Soldiers of Fate«, founded in 1926) and **Fine Gael/FG** (»Family of the Irish«, founded in 1933), have their roots in the Irish independence movement Sinn Féin. They have alternated in power since the founding of the state. Parliamentary elections are held every five years.

Political parties

Since 2011 the head of state, and ninth president of Ireland, has been the widely admired writer and former minister of culture **Michael Daniel Higgins**. In 2011 **Enda Kenny** became the new prime minister following the resignation of the previous government in the banking crisis. His party Fine Gael with 36.1% of the votes and 72 seats in the Dáil formed a coalition with the Labour Party (19.5%, 37

Romantic, at least to look at: a typical cottage in County Galway

seats). The opposition consists of Fianna Fáil (17.5% and 20 seats following dramatic loss of 24.2% of the vote), Sinn Féin (9.9%, 14 seats), the Socialist Party (1.1%, 2 seats), the new People Before Profit party (PBPA, 1.0%, 2 seats), the Workers and Unemployed Action Group (WUAG, 0.4%, 1 seat) and 14 independents. The Green Party is no longer represented.

Military   There is **no conscription** in Ireland. The Defence Force has a strength of 8,500, the Air Corps 939, the Irish Naval Service with its eight vessels 1,144. The Defence Force has proved its worth in UN peace-keeping missions in many parts of the globe.

ECONOMY

Develop-   After Ireland became a Free State in 1922, most of the capital re-
ments up to   mained in the hands of wealthy Anglo-Irish families. In 1932, Fianna
1945   Fáil, led by Eamon de Valera, came to power, establishing a **policy of economic self-sufficiency** and favouring manufacturing industry through protective tariffs. Furthermore, the new Irish government

Lush meadows and herds of sheep are a common sight right across the island

refused to pay the British government's land annuities, a provision of the treaty of 1921. An economic war ensued, with the British government placing a 40% import duty on imports from Ireland, resulting in a dramatic downturn for the Irish export industry. The consequences of this »war« were softened by an agreement; as long as Ireland kept importing its coal from Britain, Britain would in turn import a large number of Irish cattle. The Anglo-Irish economic conflict only ended in 1938, when Britain dismantled its military installations in Ireland.

Up to the Second World War, the government's top priority was boosting the economy through the creation of numerous semi-state institutions such as the Agricultural Credit Corporation or the Electricity Supply Board, amongst others. Leaving the Commonwealth (1949) gave Ireland more economic freedom. From the late 1950s government support was given to establishing new industries. Today the tool-making, electrical, electronics and chemical industries are the principal manufactured goods and exports. A quarter of the export volume consists of pharmaceuticals, medical instruments and orthopaedic aids.

Boom at turn of the millennium

The late 1990s and the first years of the new millennium saw an economic boom that gave Ireland the name »**Celtic tiger**«. The judicious use of EU subsidies gave a competitive infrastructure to an island that had always been regarded as poor. Inflation stayed low, economic growth was high, unemployment declined and Ireland attracted immigration for the first time ever.

Banking and financial crisis

The construction boom that began around 2000 ended abruptly with the banking crisis of 2008. By nationalizing and providing guarantees for the four major Irish banks, especially to the Anglo Irish Bank, which was merged with the Irish Nationwide Building Society in July 2011 to form the Irish Bank Resolution Company, the Irish state took over responsibility. Its exposure in the case of the Anglo Irish Bank amounts to 34.5 billion €.

State support

Between 2009 and 2011, the Irish state seriously contravened the terms of the Maastricht Treaty for a budget deficit of maximum 3% of GDP (2010: -31.3%). **State debt** mushroomed from 65.2% of GDP in 2009 to 108.1% in 2011, which represented a debt per person of 100,000 €. From 2009 the Irish government pursued a **severe austerity policy** which met with international approval and had consequences for economic growth: the recession years 2008 (-3.0%) and 2009 (-7.0%) were followed by better figures in 2010 (-0.4%) and 2011 (0.9%), partly thanks to financial support amounting to 85 billion € from the EU, the crisis fund named European Financial Stability Facility (EFSF) and the International Monetary Fund.

?

The Billion Euro House

The artist Frank Buckley, who bought a house for 365,000 € in 2006 and then became unemployed on support payments of 188 € per week, received 1.4 billion euros from the Irish state bank to adorn three of his rooms. The downside: the banknotes had been shredded, and were normally used in this state as heating material for the poor. Buckley recycled them to bricks worth 50,000 € each and opened a gallery under the name Billion €uro House in 2012. Here art lovers can admire his euro paintings and the foundation stone of Bailout Day (Coke Lane, Smithfield, Dublin 7; daily 9 am - 5 pm; admission free; http://billioneurohouse.com

Although acceptance of the emergency plan was criticised as an abandonment of national sovereignty, in June 2012 60% of Irish voters agreed to the EU package, which includes a limit on state debts. Cuts in social security payments and the high level of unemployment, which reached 14.7% in 2012 before falling to 8.8% in 2015, were major problems. Ireland has been successful in attracting foreign companies, especially from the USA, UK and EU. Exports have increased, partly owing to Europe's biggest zinc mine (Tara Mine, Mavan, Co. Meath) and discoveries of natural gas reserves.

Some 70% of the country's surface is used for **agriculture**, mostly as pasture. The **rearing of cattle** is concentrated on meat production in the Midlands, and on dairy farming in the south. Alongside cattle, sheep, pigs and poultry are kept. Good pastures are used for breeding racehorses. The **main crop is barley**, used for beer brewing and as animal feed; other crops cultivated in Ireland are potatoes, sugar beet, wheat and oats. Agriculture accounts for 5% of Irish exports.

Fisheries   The country's rivers, lakes and bays, by and large still very unpolluted, are an important asset for the economy as well as for tourism. Here, over recent years, more **fish farms** have been set up, breeding game fish. Annual production exceeds 60,000 tons with a value of 100 billion €. The catch of the ocean fisheries amounts to 530,000 tons, worth 7 billion €. The fishing industry in Northern Ireland (23,600 tons) is worth 33.6 billion €.

Energy   Roughly a third of energy demand is covered by production from hydraulic power and peat, some 60% by imported fossil fuels such as coal and petroleum. The power plant on the River Shannon is the largest of those working on a good number of the country's rivers. Recently, larger **offshore wind farms** have been set up. The huge bogs covering large parts of Ireland's central plain and the northern, western and southern coastline, provide a seemingly unlimited supply of peat. Peat has always been and still is the main Irish domestic fuel. Since 1946 it has been extracted mechanically. The government

A peat cutter at work

organization Bord na Móna is in charge of the extraction, processing and use of the **peat in power plants.** This is a limited resource, however. Large-scale peat extraction may come to an end after 2020. Since 2005, with EU support, measures to **save the peat bogs** have been underway. Only 30% of the worked land can be used for agriculture, a further 22% for forestry. The remaining half is bog without economic benefit that has to be returned to its natural state at great cost.

Despite its many ancient art treasures and monuments, picturesque landscape and friendly people, for a long time Ireland stayed a well-kept secret for a small number of **travellers who wanted something different**. However, by 1988 the government was trying to change this and a five-year plan was issued aiming to significantly improve the tourist infrastructure, both in numbers and in quality. This concept paid off, even during the financial crisis, when numbers declined only slightly. from the previous best total of 8.01 million visitors in 2007. The reduction of VAT for many tourist services from 13.5% to 9% and lower hotel prices helped to create employment in a sector that accounts for around 6% of GDP.

Tourism

Tourism in Northern Ireland The outbreak of the Troubles in Northern Ireland in the late 1960s hit tourism badly. After 25 years of a downhill trend, the mid-1990s marked a turning point. Along the coast in particular, the owners of B&Bs and small rural hotels are benefiting from unified efforts to market the tourist attractions of the whole island. In the »Titanic year« of 2012 more tourists than ever visited the north.

Language

In the Republic of Ireland, Irish is the country's official language. The language of daily life, however, is English.

Official texts, documents and road signs are bilingual. In the Irish parliament, the Dáil, deputies (TDs) often start their speeches with a few words of Irish, but usually continue in English.

In some regions, called Gaeltacht, Irish is still the mother tongue of most inhabitants. Various institutions try to keep Irish from dying out. A **Gaeltacht ministry** is charged with protection of the minority language. Tax breaks and subsidies are in place to support the Gaeltacht areas.

IRISH/GAELIC

The Irish language, often called »Gaelic«, belongs to the **Celtic language family**, and within that family, to the branch of island-Celtic languages. Alongside Irish, the Gaelic family of languages comprises Scottish Gaelic.

History of the language Originally, Celtic was spoken all over the British Isles. Invasion by Germanic tribes in the 5th century brought Germanic languages into the region. The English languages that developed out of those Germanic tongues put so much pressure on the old language that it was only able to survive in remote regions – such as Ireland. From the time of English rule up to the establishment of the independent Republic of Ireland, Irish was more than just a means of communication – it signalled a commitment to national unity. The late 18th century saw a euphoric, often romantically-tinged revival of the Irish language. With increasing Irish confidence, the language gained in importance in terms of culture and history, to the extent that by the end of the 19th century it had become the expression of national identity and autonomy.

From the 4th to the 7th century, the Ogham alphabet (▶ MARCO POLO Insight, p. 34) was used for writing in Ireland and in some parts of western Scotland and Britain.

Ogham alphabet

CHARACTERISTICS OF THE LANGUAGE

To most people, the Irish language will initially seem completely foreign and unintelligible. There are few parallels to familiar structures or concepts. There is no such thing as national standards; the three main regional dialects have equal status.

GAELTACHT

The areas where the language is spoken are shrinking, despite conscious efforts to preserve Irish over the last 200 years. Between 1851 and 1961, in a matter of about a century, the area where Irish was spoken decreased by nearly 80 per cent. Efforts are being made to preserve the language from extinction. **Irish is compulsory** at all schools for pupils between the ages of six and fifteen. In some 30 28 secondary schools teaching is completely or partly in Irish, According to the census of 2011 in the Republic of Ireland, 94,000 people actively speak Irish. 1.7 million understand it, and use the language sometimes. There are also a few thousand speakers of Irish Gaelic in Northern Ireland. In the **St Andrews Agreement** of 2006, the British government agreed to promote the use of the Irish language in Northern Ireland. Since 2007 it has been an official language of the EU, and is used during debates in the European Parliament. Enclaves of native speakers exist in North America, New Zealand, Australia and Argentina.

An endangered language

Religion

Ireland became Christian as early as the 5th century. To this day the Roman Catholic Church, to which 86% of Irish citizens belong, plays an important role in the Republic of Ireland. In Northern Ireland, by contrast, Protestantism is much stronger.

CELTIC CHRISTIANITY

Over the course of the 5th century, the Celtic Irish took on the Christian faith. The teachings of the early missionaries **St Brendan and St**

Christianization

Irish-Gaelic Culture

The Celtic Gaels arrived on the island from 400 BC on and brought along their own culture, which mingled with Irish culture. This cultural heritage is still being cultivated in Ireland.

Amazing Grace in Gaelic
www.youtube.com

▶ **Irish-Gaelic language**
Along with Scots, Breton, and Welsh, Irish is one of he island Celtic languages. During British rule it was only spoken in inaccessible western parts of the island. Today irish is being promoted in kindergartens and schools.

Irish is on the rise
Acccording to the 2011 census more than 1.7 mil. professed some ability in the Irish, which corresponds to 41.4% of the entire population.

1.7
1.5 mil.
1.1
1 mil.
0.54
0.5 mil.
0 mil.

1861   1911   1961   2011

©BAEDEKER

Current use
of Irish as first
language (Gaeltacht)

Gaelic alphabet
The letters »j k q v w x y« do not occur
in the Gaelic alphabet:

ᴀ ᴃ ᴄ ᴅ ᴇ ғ ᴦ ʜ ɪ ʟ ᴍ ɴ ᴏ ᴩ ᴙ s ᴛ ᴜ

A	B	C	D	E	F	G	H	I	L	M	N	O	P	R	S	T	U
aw	*bay*	*kay*	*dhay*	*ey*	*eff*	*gay*	*hh*	*ee*	*ell*	*emm*	*nn*	*oh*	*pay*	*arr*	*es*	*thay*	*ou*

Some consonants are aspirated. When they occur at the beginning of a word they are marked with a dot above the letter.

ḃ ċ ḋ ḟ ġ ṁ ṗ ṡ ṫ

Written	bh	ch	dh	fh	gh	mh	ph	sh	th
Pronounced	[w], [v]	[x]	[ɣ]	[Ø]	[ɣ]	[w], [v]	[f]	[h]	[h]

Gaelic	Pronunciation	English
aimsir	*ämaßier*	time
ceann-bhaile	*kjanna-wahlje*	capital city
airgiod	*ärragött*	money
àrmhach	*ahrawach*	battlefield
dorch	*doroch*	dark
seanmhathair	*schjanawahär*	grandmother
inghean	*inichjan*	daughter

aelic sports
ports with Celtic roots are promoted and
pervised by the Gaelic Athletic Association
ww.gaa.ie).

urling is a team sport with
players. The ball is hit
with a bat called a hurling...

Gaelic Football
is a mixture of football
and rugby. A team
consists of 15 players.

Irish Handball
is like squash but without
a racket. It is played in
singles or doubles.

Camogie is what
women's hurling is
called. A team has
12 players. The bats
are a little smaller
and body contact
is not allowed.

ounders
like baseball.

▶ Ogham script
This script was used in Ireland,
Scotland, Wales and Cornwall in
the 4th – 6th cent. for short
messages or to inscribe names in
menhirs. The sounds are based on
the Latin alphabet, but the letters
are completely different. In Ireland
more than 300 Ogham stones are
known to exist.

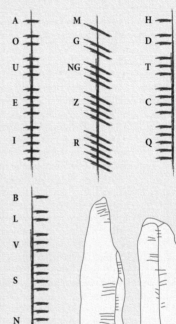

A	M	H
O	G	D
U	NG	T
E	Z	C
I	R	Q

B
L
V
S
N

Midnight Court
Cúirt an Mheon Oíche

»There stood the mountains,
the head of one lay on the shoulder
of the other.
All sadness was gone.
II forgot exhaustion, my suffering.«

Patrick were adopted without bloodshed; there were no martyrs. Often, whole clans decided to lead the monastic life, the leader founding a monastery and proclaiming himself abbot. His family, followers and charges took his example and submitted to the strict discipline of monastic life. Books of penitence and copies of monastic regulations tell of the hard life in the early monasteries.

Monasteries Alongside a church and cells, monasteries comprised a refectory, guest quarters, a scriptorium and workshops. People from England and the Continent as well as people fleeing the fallout from the great migrations came here. Latin was spoken alongside Gaelic, and the writings of Virgil, Cicero and Ovid read alongside religious texts.

Green and white martyrdom As the faithful were denied the »red martyrdom« (laying down their life), many of them took on the »green martyrdom« of **voluntary exile** into remote areas. Whilst the hermits of the Middle East retreated into the desert, the Irish chose outlying small islands in the Atlantic that were difficult to reach. Visitors to Ireland can see what such hermitages would have looked like in the 8th-century monastic settlement of Skellig Michael; the tiny churches and stone cells reminiscent of beehives on the top rungs of this bare rock have survived to this day. Alongside the »green« martyrdom, a »white« martyrdom began – the »peregrinatio pro Christo«: leaving your home country behind for Christ. In light wooden boats tarred with animal pelts, Irish monks ventured into the »pathless« sea. Crossing England and France as itinerant penance preachers, they came to numerous European countries. Alongside a strong faith, they brought humanist learning; in their leather satchels they carried valuable manuscripts and codices (books). They established new religious and cultural centres in places that had bee devastated by war.

From the 9th century, when conversion of mainland Europe to Christianity had been completed, Irish monks reached the Continent as **scholars and advisers** to rulers.

Irish saints Amongst the **saints** of the early Celtic church, some personalities stand out, with their names cropping up again and again in Ireland. One of them is the nation's patron saint Patrick, who came to Ireland in 432 and whose life gave rise to numerous legends (▶MARCO POLO Insight p.38).

In 490, Saint Enda was one of the first to retreat to a remote and lonely place to dedicate his life as a hermit to study and renunciation. Soon, numerous students followed him to the Aran Island of Inishmór, establishing a large monastic settlement there. Its fame reached across the sea to the European continent.

Of those men who came to join Enda, many went on to found monasteries themselves. One of those was St Ciarán , who settled in 548 on the Shannon. ►Clonmacnoise, which to this day continues to leave visitors spellbound, was soon called the »university of the west« thanks to its monks' erudition.

St Kevin, born around the year 618, chose the hermit's life, retreating into the mountains and forests of Wicklow. His monastery in ►Glendalough went on to draw a large number of students, being equal in size and prominence to Clonmacnoise.

Amongst the women, St Brigid is the most important. She founded a large double monastery for monks and nuns in Kildare, probably around 468. Following a pre-Christian ritual, an eternal flame burned there. The archbishop of Dublin ordered it to be extinguished in 1220. Today still, a St Brigid's cross woven from straw or rushes can be found in many Irish houses as a protective symbol.

St Brendan first founded a monastery in Clonfert, which was to attract many monks (►Ballinasloe), around the year 563. This saint became an inspiration for all who left their home to become a missionary and ventured out to sea, with an unknown destination (►Famous People).

> ### ? Shamrock Trinity
>
> MARCO ⊕ POLO INSIGHT
>
> Using the three-leafed clover (shamrock), St Patrick is said to have explained the doctrine of the Holy Trinity. Today the shamrock, a national symbol of Ireland, can be found everywhere: made of fabric plastic or dough, in the form of a bouquet, etc. On St Patrick's Day the Irish pin a shamrock on their chest.

Columba the Elder (521/522–597), called Columcille (»dove of the churches«), was, like St Kevin, of royal descent. He caused his own exile; born in Gartan in Ireland, Columba had secretly copied a book of psalms belonging to St Finian, who jealously guarded his books and claimed the copy for himself alone. As the two men could not come to an amicable agreement, Finian took the argument to the High King. The king ruled in favour of Finian, saying that a copy belonged with the book as a calf belongs to the cow. However, Columba and his followers were not prepared to accept the ruling, and Benbulben Mountain, north of Sligo, became the site of their battle against the king. Columba's victory resulted in the death of 3,000 people. In order to do penance for these deaths, Columba left his home country. Landing in 563 with twelve companions on the Hebridean island of Hy (today Iona), he founded a monastery there that became the base for his missionary activities. Despite his rigid faith, Columcille is said to have been a likeable person who loved nature, and animals.

Columba the Younger, also called Saint Columbanus, was born in 540. He lived as a pupil of Comgall in the famous monastery of Bangor. Only when he had reached the age of 50 did Columba set off on a missionary voyage to the continent, taking twelve companions with

Ireland's Patron

Ireland is said to be the only country where conversion to Christianity was not accompanied by bloodshed. This peaceful Christianization was by and large the work of Saint Patrick (387-461), apostle and patron saint of Ireland.

Ireland's patron saint was born in a place called Banna Venta Berniae in Roman Britannia, according to a letter written by Patrick himself. Less reliable sources give his birthplace as Scotland (Old Kilpatrick) or Wales. HIs name was probably Patricius originally, and his father was a Roman officer and deacon called Caponius. At the age of 16, Patrick was captured by slave traders and sold in the region that is now Ulster., but managed to escape. In Gaul, probably Auxerre, he was trained as a priest. In the year 432 Pope Celestine sent him on a mission to Ireland.

This richly decorated bell shrine is attributed to the saint and kept in the National Museum in Dublin.

Though not the first, he was seemingly the most successful priest of the first generation. He founded schools, churches and monasteries all over Ireland. Establishing his episcopal see in Armagh, he was able to win over many Celtic tribal lords to the Christian faith. When Patrick died, the whole of Ireland had been converted. Many legends surround this successful missionary.

St Patrick's Day

The cult of St Patrick is part of Irish identity. Since the 17th century at the latest, St Patrick's Day has been celebrated on 17 March. It is said that wherever in the world three Irish people are together, they celebrated this feast day. In New York there is a big parade on 5th Avenue, and each year some 300,000 people come to Dublin for a festival and parade, contribution 50 million € or more to the economy. In rural areas, people wear a ribbon or shamrock on their clothing.

On Northern Ireland's new St Patrick's Trail, the saint is present all year round. A 149km/93 mile route connects 15 places, including Bangor, Newtownards, Downpatrick and Newry, around the bishop's seat of Armagh.

The statue of St Patrick at the foot of Croagh Patrick is gleaming white and marks the beginning of the pilgrimage path

Pilgrimages

Every year, on the last Sunday in July, tens of thousands of people, some of them barefoot, climb the rocky summit of Croagh Patrick. This rocky mountain is said to be the site of a 40-day penance that the saint undertook in 411. The bare quartzite cone with its sharp scree on steep slops makes the climb hard work.

Station Island in Lough Derg (Co. Donegal), near the border with Northern Ireland, is also the site of an important pilgrimage. Back in pagan times, a cave on this island was thought to be the entrance to the underworld. The cave became famous all over Europe as »St Patrick's Purgatory«, the site where St Patrick is said to have had a vision of purgatory after 40 days of fasting. Erasmus, Rabelais, Dante and Calderón took inspiration from reports of vision of hell that were glimpsed there. The »hardest pilgrimage in Christendom« is undertaken between mid-June and mid-August, almost exclusively by the Irish. Alongside Mass and prayers during their three-day stay on the island, the pilgrims have to perform numerous penances, mainly consisting of vigils and fasting. During the pilgrimage season, the island may be visited only by the faithful.

him. At the Burgundian court, he became very influential, founding the monasteries of Annegrey and Luxueil. Columba is described as being strong in faith and charismatic, but also as irascible. Following a falling-out with the Burgundian king, Columba went up the Rhine via Lake Constance and the Alps to Italy, founding his last monastery in Italy and dying in Bobbio in 615. Through his monastic foundations, Columba acquired followers all over Europe. His monastic rules were a decisive influence on Western monasticism.

Irish missionaries Some Irish missionaries , who were active abroad, are less known in their home country. Their tonsure – on the forehead rather than at the back of the head as was the custom in Europe – as well as their language, distinguished them from the other monks. Many came to Europe via monasteries in Scotland. The influence of Hiberno-Scottish missionaries extended far, as evidenced by the so-called **Scottish monasteries** of Regensburg and Vienna.

Gallus, one of Columba's companions, stayed at Lake Constance. The former monastery of St Gallen owns a number of beautiful manuscripts from the heyday of Irish book illumination. »Look how green and lovely this land is!«, the monk Kilian, apostle of Franconia, is said to have called when he reached the river Main with his companions Kolonat and Totnan. There they remained as missionaries and suffered a martyr's death.

Learned monks Later, when the Vikings were already ravaging their island, Irish monks could be found as renowned scholars at many courts in Europe. »Irish« (»Scotus«) became an honorary title. Clemens Scotus followed Alcuin as head of the famous palace school at the court of Charlemagne, where Dicuil (grammarian, geographer and astronomer) also taught. Sedulius Scotus, who was highly regarded for his learning, came to Cologne via Metz. John Scotus Eriugena (»born in Ireland«), a towering mind of his era, belonged to the court of Charles II (the Bald) around 845.

CHURCH AND POPULAR FAITH

Tradition of faith No other people in Europe have so held on to the tradition of their faith as the Irish have – despite or maybe because of the religious conflicts of past centuries. As long as Catholics were banned from religious practice, the faithful celebrated Mass in secret, often outdoors at hidden rocks (Mass Rocks). Young men wanting to enter the priesthood had to travel abroad for training and ordination, to France or Spain. And once the building of churches was allowed again, their construction was initially only allowed in inconspicuous side streets.

Today, the influence of the Catholic church, which around 85% of the population profess to belong to, is evident in all areas of Irish life. On a Sunday, the many churches holding Mass are full to the brim, and the names of Irish saints remain popular as Christian names, nowadays often for reasons of tradition. Couples get married in church in the presence of extended family; there are very few registry office weddings. **Divorce has only been legal since 1995**, and abortion in Ireland is only possible when the life of the mother is in danger; at a referendum conducted in November 1992 (and confirmed in 2002), the majority voted for freedom of information in matters of abortion and the freedom to travel of pregnant women, i.e. to terminate the pregnancy abroad, but rejected any amendment of the core legislation.

Influence of the church

In large Irish families there was often a son or daughter who would decide to join the clergy or a religious order. Priests are still an integral part of Irish daily life, and clerics and nuns from Ireland can be found all over the developing world working as teachers, nurses and in other social sectors. The ethics of Christian welfare dominate daily life in Ireland, but these positive aspects have had a dark side too: **censorship**, for instance, used to be so strict that writers such as James Joyce and Sean O'Casey turned their backs on their home country.

Clergy

Since 1992 scandals have rocked the Catholic Church in Ireland. The issues are both sexual abuse and the treatment of vulnerable persons such as orphans and unmarried mothers in residential In 2009 a state commission of inquiry, having heard 2,000 witnesses, published an 2,600-page report that made serious accusations. In 2010 Pope Benedict XVI made an apology and ordered a papal visitation. After publication of the Cloyne Report, in 2011 Prime Minister Kenny attacked the Vatican for playing down cases of rape and mistreatment of Irish children. The Vatican then recalled its ambassador, and the Republic of Ireland closed its representation at the Holy See. A new law imposes on obligation on all persons, including clergy, to report cases of child abuse. Some priests oppose this, citing the confidentiality of confession, but the law provides for prison sentences of up to ten years.

Scandals

Knock in County Mayo, site of an apparition of the Virgin Mary in the last century, draws many pilgrims. Of the many sick coming to look for a cure, few are from abroad.

Knock

Alongside the major pilgrimages, several local feast days are celebrated in the honour of a saint's anniversary (Pattern Day). For instance, on Inisheer, the smallest of the Aran Islands, every year on 14th June,

Pattern Days

the local population gathers together in order to dig out the church of St Cavan, which is under constant threat of being engulfed by the sand dunes, and celebrate Mass there.

At many road intersections, Lourdes grottoes have been set up or built into the rock. Occasionally the visitor might stumble across wells with rosaries and coins, but also items of daily life placed on the ground around them. Bits of clothing are hung on shrubs or wooden posts standing close to each other. The water of such holy wells is credited with curative powers for certain diseases.

Holy wells

In the same way that monks were the first to write down the ancient folk tales, helping to preserve them, the Celtic church tolerated animist concepts. In Ireland, part of the »half-world of the spirits« were the »**sidhe**« (fairies), dwelling in tree-covered hills, whilst the »**leprechauns**«, or »little people«, live under hawthorn bushes. According to popular belief in the west of Ireland, cutting down a hawthorn bush would carry dire consequences. A black animal called »**pooka**« frightens lonely wanderers, and the wailing call of the »**banshee**« announces the impending death of a relative of a long-established local family.

Belief in spirits

At St Patrick's Well near Ballyshannon (Co. Donegal), the faithful hang up strips of cloth to honour Ireland's patron saint

History

The Long Fight for Freedom

Ireland has many remains from the Stone Age and from long-lost civilizations. The Irish, initiators of peaceful Christianization in Europe, were themselves again and again overrun by violent waves of conquest. In recent decades they have been able to determine their own fate, and do this with great self-confidence.

HUMANS BETWEEN ICE AND SEA, STONE AND METAL

6600 BC	First settlements in County Derry (Londonderry)
4500 BC	Wave of migration brings agriculture to Ireland, cairn and passage tombs appear
1750–500 BC	Ireland is famous for its metalwork
400 BC	Conquest by the Celtic Gaels, rise of Tara to a political and cultural centre
from 300 AD	Ireland extends its influence to Wales and Scotland

During the Ice Age, the whole of Ireland was covered in ice, making the region uninhabitable. Only with the melting of the glaciers did people, animals and plants from Scotland start arriving across the land bridge that still existed at the time. Around 6600 BC, the inhabitants of the first settlements in County Derry lived off hunting and fishing.

Ice and stone

Some 2,000 years later, a new wave of migration brought agriculture to the land. Alongside wood, stone became an important material, as evidenced by stone axes, house foundations and the famous cairn and passage tombs.

Agriculture

Once, Ireland was rich in mineral resources. Gold, silver, and copper deposits enabled metallurgy to flourish from 1750 to 500 BC, with the necessary know-how brought to the island by migrants. The half-moon-shaped »torc« collar became a popular export all over Europe.

Mineral resources

The Celts owed their victory over the indigenous population to their better military equipment, their iron weapons proving superior to

Celts

Ardmore monastery, with one of the most beautiful round towers in Ireland

Celtic heritage

Druids were Celtic priests who fore-cast the future, cured the sick, read the stars and sat in judgment. They were held in great esteem by the common people. The word »druid« comes from the Gaelic, meaning »the one who knows the oak«. In today's Ireland, only a few keep the memory of the Celtic rites alive, congregating in secret at dusk to celebrate pre-Christian rites.

the Irish bronze swords and shields. From 400 BC, the Gaels, a Celtic tribe, started to subjugate almost the whole island. For nearly 800 years, Celtic culture dominated the country, with High Kings ruling over 150 kingdoms, grouped together in provinces. During this time, **Tara** rose to be a centre of political power and the arts, ring forts secured the country, and druids, priests and legal scholars were held in high esteem.

Romans   For centuries, it was claimed that the **Romans** never set foot on Ireland (as opposed to England). Archaeological finds, however, disprove this; settlers from the Roman province of Britannia did come to Ireland, gaining a foothold in some places near the coast. Whilst the Roman influence was limited both in duration and in geographical extent, after the fall of the Roman Empire, from AD 300 onwards, Ireland was able to extend its influence to Wales and Scotland.

CHRISTIANS

from 432	Christianization by St Patrick
461	Death of St Patrick, Ireland is Catholic
from 500	Irish missionaries are active on the European continent

Pirates and   It was a pirate raid that made Ireland one of the most Catholic coun-
saints   tries in the world – the kidnapping of St Patrick. (▶MARCO POLO Insight, p.38) The kidnapping gave rise to the Christianization of Ireland; St Patrick's main achievement was to peacefully convert the Celtic chieftains and to integrate pre-Christian myths, customs and structures into Christian daily life.

»Scots«   By the time of St Patrick's death in 461, the entire island had been largely converted to Christianity (▶Religion, Christianization). Over subsequent centuries Ireland developed its own characteristic religious institutions and customs. Monasteries were established on the basis of Celtic tribal structures and headed by abbots of noble birth. The country experienced peaceful times, staying untouched by enemy incursions as well as by the developments of the Roman Catholic church. Keeping their maxim of non-violent proselytizing, the Irish took their faith first to northern England and Scotland, later also to the Continent, where they were often erroneously called »Scots«. Their ecclesiastical foundations are today still called **»Scots« churches or monasteries**. The most famous Irish monasteries on the European continent were established in St Gallen, Luxeuil, Bobbio, Regensburg and Vienna.

»NORSEMEN AND NORMANS«

from 795	Raids by Norwegian Vikings
from 840	The Vikings establish settlements
1014	Viking rule ends with the Battle of Clontarf
1172	Henry II of England claims Ireland
till 1250	The Normans conquer the country
1366	Statutes of Kilkenny: the Irish language and intermarriage between Irish and Anglo-Irish are banned

Around 800, the northern Irish coast saw frequent raids by Norwegian Vikings. The belligerent and violent **»Norsemen« first founded settlements** in Ireland in 840. Of particular strategic importance were the estuaries on the east coast; Dublin, Wexford and Waterford, for instance, were founded by Vikings. From there, they sailed up the rivers, sowing fear and terror amongst the monasteries in particular, and slowly conquering the interior of the country. However, the monasteries were not just plundered by the Vikings, but also by the equally greedy Celtic tribal lords. Over time, the Vikings settled and converted to Christianity, whilst the Irish adopted improvements in shipbuilding, the military use of fleet and cavalry, as well as monetary commerce.

Viking influence

As the tribal lords lost influence and the regional lords gained, a power struggle for domination of the country broke out. In 1014, Brian Boru led an army against the Vikings in the legendary battle of Clontarf. His victory, whilst paid for with his life, marked the end of the Viking era in Ireland.

Battle of Clontarf

The subjugation of Ireland under Anglo-Norman rule was a **political coup for the Vatican**; the independence of the Irish monasteries had long been a thorn in the side of Rome. After the Cluniac reforms tightened ecclesiastical hierarchies all over Europe and strengthened the influence of the pope on the monasteries, in the early 12th century these trends came to Ireland too, bringing new architectural styles and a new ecclesiastical philosophy. In order to tie the Irish church quickly and more permanently to Rome, the pope gave the English king Henry II the right to reform it, and thus the opportu-

Between the Normans and Rome

The Normans' armour and weapons made them far superior to the Irish in battle

nity to intervene in Ireland. In 1172, Henry II gained confirmation of his authority over the Irish.

Anglo-Nor-mans In 1066, under **William the Conqueror**, the Normans had taken power in England. From 1169 onwards, they used Wales as a base to carry out raids in Ireland. Yet again, the Irish were defeated due to their inferior weaponry, facing Norman swordsmen and archers – kitted out in chain mail and iron helmets – in cotton tunics, wielding axes and stone slings. By 1250, the Normans had conquered 75 % of the country. Imposing fortresses secured their rule, many new settlements were established, as well as churches and monasteries in the new Hiberno-Romanesque style. The arrival of the mendicant and preaching orders gave the church a new lease of life, establishing the church's closeness to the people that still endures today.

Within just 150 years, the Normans in Ireland were nearly completely assimilated. Fearing a loss of power, in 1366 the English Crown tried to secure its influence with the **Statutes of Kilkenny**, strictly banning mixed marriages and the Irish language. The **plague of 1348** was especially severe in the towns, mainly claiming victims among the Normans and English. The Irish peasantry, and their language, were little affected. English influence was largely limited to Dublin. **Anglo-Irish**

THE ENGLISH CROWN – COLONIALIZATION AND CONFLICT

1541	Henry VIII becomes King of Ireland, implements the Reformation and dissolves some 400 monasteries
1607	Battle of Kinsale: the Catholics are defeated by the Protestants, and by 1607 their leaders leave the country.
till 1641	»Plantations«: lands are transferred to English ownership; resistance forms in the Confederation of Kilkenny
1649	Cromwell puts a bloody end to Irish resistance
1690	The Battle of the Boyne ends the bloody war of succession fought between James II and William III of Orange in Ireland
1695	»Penal laws«: Catholics lose their civil rights
1699	Economic and political colonization: installation of a viceroy, export bans
1740–41	In the Irish Famine, two winters of starvation, 400,000 die and 150,000 emigrate.
1801	Act of Union: Ireland becomes part of the United Kingdom and no longer has a separate parliament.

Only in Henry VIII's violent reign did England, from 1536 onwards, put its sights on Ireland again. Irish princes, who submitted to English sovereignty and English law, received privileges and estates. Henry VIII crowned himself King of Ireland in 1541, introducing the Reformation and dissolving some 400 monasteries. **Henry VIII**

In subsequent years, the Irish made several unsuccessful attempts to shake off the English yoke, finding support among anti-English and **Flight of the Earls**

Counter-Reformation forces on the Continent. The decisive **Battle of Kinsale** was won by the English, however, in 1601. In 1607, after the subjugation of more and more provinces, the leaders of the insurrections left the country. The »Flight of the Earls« has since become a symbol of defeat, but also of preferring emigration to a life without freedom.

Land ownership

The English strategy of **»plantations«** marked the beginning of a creeping colonization. Large estates were given to English and Scottish settlers. As the owners often preferred to stay in their English homelands, they installed agents on their new estates. Pushing for maximum profits, the absentee landlords rented out the land to Irish farmers for high rents. Over the coming centuries, this system was to drag Ireland down until it became the poorhouse of Europe.

Cromwell

In 1641 an army formed around the remaining Catholic landowners in Ulster. In October that year, some 4,000 Protestant English and Scottish colonists were massacred. 8,000 settlers fled from Ulster, which meant the failure of the »plantations«. In 1642 the kingdom of Scotland sent an army of 10,000 men to suppress the rebellion, and up to 1650 many bloody skirmishes followed.

Following the end of the English civil war in 1649, Oliver Cromwell with an army of 12,000 attacked both the Irish rebels and confederates, and also the Scottish troops. Battles and massacres took place in Drogheda and Wexford, while there was great loss of life in, for example, the siege of Clonmel in 1650. By 1653 Ireland had been **completely subjugated**. In the following years, Cromwell ruthlessly implemented the plantations and confiscations. By 1652 300,000 Irish, including 100,000 children, had been sold as slaves to the Caribbean, Virginia and New England. In 1655, the Irish only owned 25% of the land.

Jacobites and Orangemen

The trigger for the final **colonization of Ireland** was the succession dispute between James II and William III of Orange. The Catholic James had been driven from the English throne and replaced by his Protestant son-in-law. Following this, James left his French exile in 1689 to take an army to Ireland, which called William III into action in 1690. The Catholic Irish supported James II, resisting the Protestant Orangemen until 1691. After the Protestants' victory at the Battle of the Boyne, the **Treaty of Limerick** was negotiated, designed to grant Ireland freedom of religion. However, this apparent success proved deceptive, as the treaty was never ratified by the English parliament.

Colonization and revolts

In 1695, the **»penal laws«** came into force, banning Catholics from having their own schools and universities, from voting or holding higher office as well as from bearing arms. In the years to come, these segregation laws were implemented with the utmost rigidity. Meanwhile, Irish culture, religion and traditions survived underground, strengthening the sense of national identity. The proportion of land owned by the Irish themselves fell to 5%. In the **Irish Famine** of 1740–41, two hard winters forced 150,000 to emigrate and cost 400,000 lives.

However, in the 18th century neither Catholics nor Protestants were prepared to accept the status quo. The Anglo-Irish Patriotic Party advocated the model of an Irish-English dual monarchy and a relaxation of the anti-Catholic laws. Inspired by the autonomy movement of the American Revolution and by the French Revolution, the United Irishmen formed, under Wolfe Tone. When, in 1796, the French and Spanish wanted to lend armed support, the landing of their troops was foiled by the rough Irish Sea. England's reaction was unequivocal: with the **Act of Union** of 1801, Ireland became part of the United Kingdom and the parliament in Dublin, which had shown itself to be independent-minded, was dissolved. `Wolfe Tone`

THE FIGHT FOR SURVIVAL

1829	Anti-Catholic laws repealed after mass protests led by O'Connell
1845–1849	Potato blight leading to the Great Famine; around one million Irish starve to death, another million emigrate
1870	»Home Rule« movement led by Charles Stewart Parnell
1880	First »boycott«; isolation of the English agent Boycott

Over the following years, Irish resistance carried on unbroken, finding charismatic leaders in Robert Emmet and Daniel O'Connell. The founder of the **Catholic Association** in 1823, O'Connell used mass meetings to call for non-violent protest. In 1829, unable to continue resisting this pressure, England repealed the anti-Catholic laws. O'Connell became the first Catholic to take a seat in the English parliament. A revival of Irish arts and culture boosted the country's sense of **national identity**. However, this political and cultural success did little to improve the daily life for the majority of Ireland's impoverished rural population. `First steps`

However, the biggest blow to Ireland was dealt not by wars, colonialism or repression, but by the potato blight that came from America and struck across Europe in the mid-19th century. In the wet climate of Ireland, the impact of the disease was devastating, leading, in 1845–49 to a **massive famine**. Underlying this desperate situation was terrible poverty: Irish leaseholders were pushed from the fertile `Potato blight` east to the barren west while English estate owners switched much of the agricultural land to pastures, exporting grain and cattle to England on a large scale.

Invention of the »boycott« The fallout from the European revolutions of 1848 also reached Ireland. The protest movement even spread to the rural population: in 1880, their anger found a target in an English agent called Boycott (►Captain Boycott, Lough Corrib, Lough Mask), who despite terrible harvests insisted on collecting inflated rents from tenant farmers for the landowner, Lord Erne, in Ballinrobe, Co. Mayo. The tenants isolated Boycott, refusing to speak to him or to sit near him in church. This form of **peaceful resistance** attracted attention in London, and was associated with the agent's name.

Home Rule The era of large estate owners was coming to an end. In 1869, discriminatory laws against the Catholic Church were also repealed. The call for Irish autonomy was becoming louder, and in 1870 became organized as the Home Rule movement under the leadership of **Charles Stewart Parnell** (►Famous People). As leader of the Irish Parliamentary Party, Parnell was able to push through land and social reform at Westminster. The northeastern province of Ulster, however, was strictly opposed to the reforms and Republican aims and wanted to remain part of the United Kingdom instead. Before Parnell's private life – he had a long-term affair with the wife of a party colleague – caused his downfall in 1890, he carried the hopes of independence on his shoulders. His fall paved the way for more radical and nationalist factions, who rejected parliamentarianism.

TOWARDS THE REPUBLIC

1914	»Home Rule« suspended at the start of the First World War
1916	Easter Rising quashed by British troops
1918	Election victory for banned Sinn Féin party
1920	Establishment of two Irish parliaments in Dublin and Belfast
1921	Ireland – excluding Northern Ireland – becomes a Free State; end of British rule

Northern Ireland breaks away When the three Home Rule laws passed Parliament in 1910–14, Irish independence seemed to be within reach. However, the six northern counties continued to reject the Home Rule legislation, wishing to remain in the United Kingdom. At the start of the First World War in 1914 these laws were suspended. Volunteer corps were formed in the British army. In opposition to the royalist Ulster Volunteers were the Irish Volunteers. The political separation of Northern Ireland was beginning.

Connemara at the time of the Great Hunger

For Ireland, the outbreak of the First World War initially meant a pause in the fight for national self-determination. The Irish did not want to stab England in the back when the country was busy fighting a war. However, various factions, parties and brotherhoods were becoming more radical, with their different philosophies and goals hampering the emergence of a united leadership. Before the **Easter Rising of 1916**, Irish Republicans had already made a pact with Germany: Irish prisoners of war were to side with the Germans. In exchange, Germany would supply the revolution in Ireland with modern weaponry. The Germans did indeed send a shipload of arms to Ireland, but as a result of storms the ship »Libau« was not able to reach Tralee Bay in Co. Kerry until 23 April 1916, was discovered and escorted into Cork harbour, and was scuttled by its crew. Without these weapons the Irish stood no chance and Britain quashed the revolt. Most of the leaders of the Easter Rising were executed. Eamon de Valera, who was born in America, was only spared because of confusion about his citizenship. The executed leaders of the insurrection became idols of the independence movement. Ultimately, the Easter Rising meant the beginning of the end of British rule in Ireland.

The road to the Republic

The 1918 elections were won by the banned Sinn Féin party. However, the party's deputies refused to take their seats in Westminster, setting up an Irish national assembly in Dublin instead. Compounded by bloody clashes in Northern Ireland, the situation escalated into civil war. In 1920, with victory by military means appearing impossible and likely to cause great bloodshed, the British government gave in and established two Irish parliaments: one in Dublin, another in Belfast. In 1921, a treaty gave Ireland the status of a **Free State**. This spelled the end of British colonial rule, but at a price: the separation of Northern Ireland.

Civil war

Reconciliation at Last!

The conflict in Northern Ireland, »The Troubles«, claimed exactly 3,526 lives, including those of 1,855 civilians, between 1968 and 2001 (MARCO POLO Insight, p. 288). In June 2010 the presentation of the Saville Report in the British Parliament was a milestone in ending the conflict. The four-day visit of Queen Elizabeth II to Ireland in 2011, the first by a British monarch since the 1920s, was a conspicuous symbol of reconciliation.

In 2010 Prime Minister David Cameron made an apology for the shootings by British soldiers in Derry on »Bloody Sunday« in 1972. Their actions were »unjustified and indefensible«, said Cameron. Deeply moved, many Irish people accepted the apology. The subsequent visit of the Queen to Croke Park in Dublin on 18 May 2011 can be described as historic: the stadium was the scene of the first »Bloody Sunday« in 1920.

Historic Days

Of greater political importance than the Queen's well-received gestures was the presentation of Lord Saville's report in 2010 after a twelve-year inquiry by a tribunal in Derry that cost over 200 million pounds. After 434 days of evidence, Lord Saville expressed the hope that »healing of the history in Derry and Ireland« could be achieved. In ten files with a total of over 5,000 pages, the Saville Report documented a culmination of the Troubles, the second »Bloody Sunday« on 30 January 1972, and partly cleared the names of the 14 victims of the shootings. Lord Saville stated that »the British army, British judiciary, British government and the Stormont government must all take responsibility for »Bloody Sunday« and its consequences.

This day in 1972 was a turning point in conflicts that had continued since the 1960s. When Catholics, inspired by the international movement for civil rights, demonstrated in Dungannon for the first time in March 1967 for democratic rights (»one man, one vote«), the conflict escalated. The second demonstration on 5 October 1967 was stopped police violence. Further demonstrations came to a bloody end. From 14 August 1969 the British army was called in to restore order. Initially it was welcomed by the Catholics as a neutral protector.

However, »Bloody Sunday« 1972 changed all of this. In Derry paratroops opened fire on protestors, and 14 unarmed persons were killed. From that time many Catholics regarded the British army as its enemy, and at the same time a process of radicalization and the formation of paramilitary groups took place on both sides. 1972 was the peak of the Troubles: more than 500 persons died violently.

21 July 1972 was an equally black day. The Catholic IRA (Irish Republican Army) carried out acts of re-

The occupation of the General Post Office in Dublin on 24 April 1916, Easter Monday, was the start of the Easter Rising against British rule

venge. 22 bombs were detonated in Belfast, with nine deaths. Further series of bombings and arson attacks followed, with both military and civilian victims. Attacks were also carried out in London, and in 1984 there was an attempt to assassinate Margaret Thatcher.

No Surrender

The implacable attitudes in the Troubles had historical precedents such as the Easter Rising of 1916 and above all 21 November 1920. On the previous day Michael Collins, leader of the movement for Irish independence, had ordered the murder of the so-called Cairo Gang, consisting of twelve British secret agents. On the following day came the response in the form of killings in Dublin's Croke Park stadium. British soldiers opened fire during a Gaelic football match attended by 10,000 spectators. 14 died and 65 were injured. High-ranking IRA officers were arrested,

and later were shot »while trying to flee«.

However, the first violent conflicts took place much earlier, for example in the bloody suppression of revolts in 1649 by Oliver Cromwell. Fuel was added to the flames by the struggle for the British throne between the Catholic James II and William of Orange in the late 17th century. At that time Derry was besieged by Catholic forces for 105 days, but the supporters of William of Orange did not give up. »No surrender« was their watchword, and this motto can be heard to this day at memorial days in Derry and on 12 July, when the Orangemen march to commemorate victory in the Battle of the Boyne in 1691. The defeat and subsequent repression of Catholic Ireland was sealed by this battle.

Parallel Societies

The smouldering conflict came to a head in the northern province of Ulster after the partition of Ireland in 1921. There was a deep divide along religious lines, and violence ruled. The Ulster Protestants rejected the independence of Ireland,

A mural stating the Republicans' demand

fearing that they would be subjected to Roman Catholic hegemony and lose their position of economic dominance. They looked to support from Britain and introduced restrictions on Catholics in Northern Ireland by controlling jobs and housing, and by linking the right to vote in local elections to earnings and property. The result was the emergence of parallel societies of Catholics and Protestants. No dialogue about disputes took place. The poet and holder of the Nobel Prize for Literature, Seamus Heaney, summarized the situation in the words »Whatever you say, say nothing.«

Ulster was a political issue that had wider ramifications, as both British governments and Irish republicans took sides. Attempts to mediate in the 1950s and 1960s failed to overcome hardline positions. Political support turned into financial, then military assistance. The Troubles had begun.

An Eye for an Eye

Terrorist attacks by the IRA were countered by house searches and from 1971 by arrests, often without trial. Hunger strikes were held to protest against the conditions of imprisonment. In 1981 Bobby Sands died in Maze Prison after refusing food for 66 days. The IRA had its first martyr, and nine more followed before the hunger strikes ended in October 1981. The IRA recommenced bombings. Accusations were made that the SAS (Special Air Service, a unit of the British army) had a shoot-to-kill policy against members of the IRA. Militant Protestant groups, the Ulster Volunteer Force and the Ulster Freedom Fighters, carried out attacks on Catholics who were suspected of IRA membership. Bloody assassinations and attacks on pubs were carried out.

Search for a Solution

Violence, patrols and street barricades were part of everyday life in Northern Ireland in the 1970s and 1980s. More and more citizens, both Catholics and Protestants, had had enough. Their views were represented by Betty Williams and Mairead Corrigan, the founders of the Community of Peace People, which received the Nobel Peace Prize in 1976.

but major breakthrough such as the IRA's renunciation of armed struggle in July 2005 and its surrender of weapons the following September. In 2007 the Northern Irish parliament, Stormont, reopened.

Violent times in Belfast after the death of hunger striker Bobby Sands

From 1985 the peace process officially restarted. An armistice in 1994 was followed in 1998 by the Good Friday Agreement, a milestone for which the politicians David Trimble and John Hume were awarded the Nobel Peace Prize. There were setbacks such as the resignation of Trimble in 2001 with subsequent unrest and the suspension of regional elections in 2003,

Two former mortal enemies, Ian Paisley, the aged leader of the Democratic Unionist Party, and Martin McGuinness of Sinn Fein jointly led the government of the province. This arrangement proved to be stable: in January 2016 Arlene Foster became the new First Minister of Northern Ireland, with McGuinness remaining in his role as Deputy First Minister.

THE YOUNG REPUBLIC

1937	Constitution makes Ireland a de facto republic
1939–1945	In World War II, Ireland remains neutral; air raids on Belfast
1949	Proclamation of the Republic of Ireland (ROI)
1955	ROI joins the United Nations
1968	Start of the »Troubles«, unrest in Northern Ireland
1973	ROI joins the European Union (EU)
1993 onwards	Peace initiatives for Northern Ireland
1998	Good Friday Agreement: semi-autonomous status for Northern Ireland
1999	ROI changes its constitution, renouncing its claim on Northern Ireland
2007	End of armed conflict in Northern Ireland, government by a coalition of Protestants and Catholics
2008–10	The property bubble bursts, the global financial crisis takes the Irish Republic to the verge of bankruptcy
2010	The British prime minister Cameron makes an apology for the events of Bloody Sunday.
2010	Bailout day: Ireland signs the EU fiscal agreement and gets access to 85 billion € of funds.

De Valera Eamon de Valera became the father of Ireland's statehood and neutrality (▶Famous People). De Valera was to shape the young republic as its prime minister and president, amongst other roles, until 1973. He founded Fianna Fáil in 1926. This political party and its competitor Fine Gael, established in 1933, were to dominate Irish politics. When de Valera took office as prime minister in 1932, he was an advocate of severing ties with Britain. The **constitution of 1937** effectively made Ireland a republic. The outbreak of the Second World War hindered its implementation: Ireland, strictly neutral, kept out of the war. Belfast though, due to its strategic shipyards and port, became the target of German air raids from 1941, whilst numerous Northern Irish fought on the side of the Allies.

»Special relationship« After effectively breaking away from Great Britain, Ireland took the final official steps towards independence by proclaiming the Republic and **leaving the Commonwealth** in 1949. In the same year, the British »Ireland Act« sealed the special relationship between the two countries, cementing Northern Ireland's status as part of the United Kingdom, whilst at the same time allowing citizens of the Republic unrestricted entry to Britain.

Efforts for peace The election of women to the office of president brought a breath of fresh air to Irish politics: **Mary Robinson** was elected in 1990, and succeeded by **Mary McAleese**, who was born in Northern Ireland.

Mary Robinson pushed through social improvements, worked on behalf of Irish emigrants, and contributed to a resolution of the conflict in Northern Ireland. Negotiations during her term of office brought about an IRA ceasefire from 1994 to 1996. From 1997, **Bertie Ahern**, »taoiseach« and head of the government, worked with his British counterpart **Tony Blair** towards resolving the conflict in Northern Ireland. With the changing of the constitution in 1999, the Republic renounced its claim to Northern Ireland, enabling the implementation of the 1998 Good Friday Agreement. The commitment of the Northern Irish politicians David Trimble (Protestant) and John Hume (Catholic) was rewarded with the Nobel Peace Prize.

Progress was slow, violence flared up again and again, and ceasefires by the IRA were undermined by its own members. However, in 2005 the IRA renounced armed conflict. In 2007 the Northern Ireland parliament was reinstated at Stormont **under the Unionist first minister Ian Paisley and the Republican deputy first minister Martin McGuinness**. In 2008 the British Army officially ended its operations in Northern Ireland, although 5,000 soldiers are still stationed there

End of the Troubles

Ireland, although it is a beneficiary of the European Union, voted against the **Treaty of Nice**, about the admission of new members to the EU, in a referendum in 2001. The treaty was approved only at the second attempt. It also took two votes to gain acceptance of the **Lisbon Treaties** about European constitutional arrangements, which had been rejected in France and the Netherlands.
During the years of the economic boom, Irish property prices rose by a factor of ten. The bursting of the bubble and the **global financial crisis** in 2008 had a severe effect on the Irish banking sector. In 2010 Ireland agreed terms for financial rescue by the EU. In June 2010 the publication of the Saville Report and the apology by the British prime minister David Cameron for Bloody Sunday were further steps to overcoming the »Troubles«. Two visits in 2011, by President Barack Obama and the British Queen, attracted a great deal of international attention.

From past to present

Arts and Culture

Art History

Ireland possesses a wealth of treasures from pre-Christian times; flourishing Celtic art and culture reached a peak in Ireland. From tombs, high crosses, monasteries and castles to illuminated manuscripts and literature: the breadth of Irish art and culture delights every visitor.

In Ireland, Celtic art and culture flourished in a way unrivalled elsewhere in the world. The island remained largely untouched by Roman influences, meaning that today's visitors find Celtic monasteries and high crosses, metalwork and book illuminations of unique beauty here. However, through a lack of patrons and art-loving rulers, nothing similar has been achieved since the Middle Ages. From the 18th century onwards, the wealthy Anglo-Irish classes did leave their mark with classical country castles and Georgian houses. However, while in most European countries such buildings were altered several times, in Ireland they mostly remained untouched – often there was simply not the money. Many ruins have been left as they stand, although in recent years some churches and castles have been restored and revived.

PRE-CHRISTIAN PERIOD

During the Stone Age (c7000–2000 BC) megalithic tombs, shaped from large rough boulders, sprang up all over the island.   Megalithic tombs

Dolmens are some of the earliest megalithic tombs: several upright boulders form a narrow space covered by an extremely heavy cap stone, its lower end sloping downwards towards the back end of the burial chamber. One of the largest dolmens can be admired in the grounds of Browne's Hill near Carlow (MARCO POLO Insight, p. 236).

Passage tombs feature a passage between high boulders to a central burial chamber. Earth was tipped over boulders decorated with spirals, zigzag lines and other ornamental designs. Often, these graves also have a cruciform ground plan, with three side chambers branching off from the main passage. The most famous passage tombs are situated in the Boyne Valley.

By contrast, passage and chamber are not separated in a **gallery grave.** Wedge-shaped gallery graves have a burial chamber which is

A prehistoric monument in The Burren.
There are many such ancient stones in Ireland.

broader on one side than the other, surrounded by upright standing stones in a horse-shoe formation. These are the most common tombs in Ireland and one can be seen in Ballyedmonduff near Dublin. **Court cairns** »Court cairns« (cairn = mound of stones), are burial mounds with a semicircular or oval forecourt and serving ritual purposes. One example can be admired north of Sligo, at Creevykeel.

Stone circles
Stone circles, today preserved as impressive remains, were in use during the **Bronze Age** (c2000–500 BC). They probably served religious purposes. A good example is the Drombeg Stone Circle in County Cork. There are also single standing stones (Irish: gallain), called »menhirs« in Brittany.

Jewellery
Gold from the Wicklow Mountains gave rise to the production of valuable ornaments such as »lunulae« (crescent-shaped collars made from sheet gold). During the Iron Age, the Irish imported the art of **enamelling**, probably from the Roman provinces, and used it brilliantly to decorate jewellery and everyday items.

Fortifications
In the Iron Age and the subsequent Christian period, c500 BC–400 AD, **ring forts** were built. Ireland is believed to have over 40,000 ring forts; built from soil or stone, their Irish name is »rath«. Some were erected on an elevation. One such **hill fort** (Irish: lis) is Dún Aenghus on the Aran Island of lnishmór.
Promontory forts (Irish: dún) are stone ring fortifications situated on steep cliffs or promontories jutting out to sea. One of these is on the promontory at Dunbeg on the southwestern coast of the Dingle Peninsula. A »crannóg«, an artificial island erected on piles – though sometimes natural islands were used – served as served as the equivalent of a moated castle. Some of these were inhabited well into the Middle Ages.

EARLY CHRISTIAN PERIOD

The early Christian period (400–1170 AD) was the heyday of Irish arts. This was a time of **lavishly illuminated manuscripts** and carved high crosses. Only a few stone buildings remain from this period, as wattle-and-daub construction was dominant.

Beehive huts
Beehive huts (Irish: clochán) are one of the most interesting architectural features of this period. The walls of these circular buildings are formed by corbelled stones stacked up without mortar. The top of the »false vault« is formed by a large keystone. Probably the most famous beehive huts are those built by the monks of Skellig Michael at the top of six hundred steps hewn into the rock.

The first small churches were known as oratories. With two of the walls angled together to form a roof, an oratory chapel is shaped like an upturned boat. Apart from the door aperture, and later a narrow window above the altar, the interior is unlit.

Oratories

The tomb slabs found in monastery grounds reveal an artistic evolution from simple to ornate decoration. In Clonmacnoise, an impressive selection of slabs and fragments has been set together into a wall. The four tips of the cross at the centre are finished with rich ornamental decoration. Standing stones from pagan times were »baptized«, by having a cross carved into them.

Tomb slabs

Tomb slabs are probably the precursors of the famous Irish high crosses. In Fahan and Carndonagh on the Inishowen Peninsula there are stones dating back to the 7th century bearing a cruciform outline, on which interlacing patterns and primitive figurative relief can be made out. By contrast, the crosses of Ahenny feature a slim shaft rising from the base, with a stone ring connecting the shaft and arms. The surface of these crosses is divided into individual panels and entirely covered in geometric patterns. The bases feature figurative representations; evidently scenes from monastic life. Given the stylistic similarities of their geometric motifs with those found in the Book of Kells, the Ahenny crosses probably date back to the 8th century. In the following century, the ornamentation on high crosses is replaced by figurative decorations: Daniel in the lion's den, the boys in the fiery furnace, Abraham and Isaac, David and Goliath. St Paul and St Anthony are references to the role models of Irish hermits, while animal figures on the sides have an oriental appearance. This change marks the dawning of the heyday of **biblical crosses**: as visible signs of piety and in the interests of instruction they are set up in monastic grounds. Their exquisitely carved figures, grouped inside rectangular panels, depict scenes from the Old and New Testament. In nearly all cases, a message of redemption lies at the centre of the imagery. High crosses were mainly made from local, fine-grained sandstone; examples can be seen at Kells and Monasterboice (Muiredach Cross, early 9th century). If no sandstone was available, then granite was used, such as in the Colum-

High crosses

Beehive huts on Skellig Michael

Testimony to Irish Piety

Imposing monasteries dating back to the 8th or 9th century are unique to Ireland. With their round towers and high crosses, these witnesses to the past contribute to the special atmosphere of the country.

❶ Round towers

The round tower, or bell tower, is an elegant structure tapering to its conical stone roof at a height of 20-30 metres / 65-100 feet. Light entered only through a small window, used to spot enemies coming.

❷ High crosses

Up to the 8th century, high crosses were decorated with ornaments. After that, they tended to feature figures. The centre is almost always occupied by representations of Christ on the Cross or Christ in Glory. The top of the cross is often a small stone house with a shingle roof in the shape of a shrine.

High Crosses in Ireland

1 Clonca
2 Carndonagh
3 Fahan
4 Ardboe
5 Donaghmore
6 Drumcliffe
7 Tynan
8 Termonfeckin
9 Monasterboice
10 Kells
11 Duleek
12 Tuam
13 Bealin
14 Clonmacnoise
15 Durrow
16 Kilcullen
17 Glendalough
18 Moone
19 Castledermot
20 Kilfenora
21 Dysert O'Dea/Ennis
22 Graiguenamanagh
23 Kilree
24 Killamery
25 St Mullins
26 Ahenny
27 Kilkeeran

© BAEDEKER

ban monastery of Moone in the southeast of Ireland, although the harder material required simplification that sometimes bordered on abstraction. The figures on the High Cross of Moone appear schematic, but their faces are not without expression. From around the 11th century onwards, the representation of biblical scenes, with the exception of Christ on the cross, was largely abandoned. Ornamental decorations covering the crosses were again favoured. Often, individual figures rise in high relief from a ring-less, limestone cross with shortened arms, such as those seen in County Clare. In Dysert O'Dea, the centre of the cross is dominated by Christ in a long gown; below him is the dignified figure of a bishop with his crozier.

Round towers

Round towers, **only found in Ireland**, have become a symbol of the country. Originally they all stood in monastic grounds, having probably been built after the first Viking incursions, when they served as a place of refuge and safety. The entrance was several metres above the ground. In peaceful times, the ringing of a handbell from this position called the monks to prayer. Around 50 Irish round towers are preserved completely or in part. While the first towers were built from rough blocks and without decorations, later examples show ornate stone friezes and decorated archways. Some round towers, for instance the one at Monasterboice, are only accessible via ladders, just as in the olden days. The most beautiful example of its kind is said to be the round tower of Ardmore in County Waterford.

Metalwork and artefacts

Alongside sculpture and book illumination, **enamel craft and metalwork** also flourished in the pre-Christian period. Older techniques, patterns and forms were refined. Exquisite pieces of jewellery were crafted, such as the Tara Brooch, while liturgical objects were also given splendid decorations. Depending on the wealth of the monasteries, chalices, ornate book covers, croziers or reliquaries were created. Even the containers for such objects were richly decorated; finely wrought bronze containers for wooden croziers, decorated with animal figures, are still preserved. St Patrick's own abbot's bell was kept in a bronze case lavishly set with precious stones and featuring gold and silver filigree work. Most commonly preserved are small reliquary shrines in the shape of a house, inspired by early Christian churches and carried on a band around the neck. They were usually worked in wood, then coated with bronze plate and decorated. Through Viking raids and looting, many of these artefacts ended up in Norway. They were popular burial objects, for women in particular. The **Cross of Cong**, made around 1123 in luminous gold and blue, and decorated with animals and mythical beasts, now in the National Museum in Dublin, can be seen as the last great masterpiece of Irish metalwork.

To this day, **Irish manuscripts** and book illuminations are considered unique evidence of the art form's highest stage of evolution. The script developed by monks is particularly impressive: the interaction of the lettering and the decorative imagery puts Irish book illumination on a par with the highest achievements of Chinese or Arabic calligraphy.

Book illumination

The beginnings are shown by the Cathach (c600), the psalter of St Columba, which features **initials** comprising flourishes and spiral patterns, but only in red and black ink. Later manuscripts are illuminated in purple, light red, emerald green, dark blue and yellow. In the individual chapters of the Gospels, the initials interlace and end in the heads of humans and animals; sometimes human bodies form the letter. Later, such initials fill entire pages of books. Countless bizarre creatures populate the pages of the Holy Scriptures: cats, mice, chickens, birds and fish appear above and below the lines. Entire ornamental pages with elaborate decorations or representations from the story of Christian salvation show Irish book illumination at its peak. The similarities with motifs visible in metalwork and on wooden crosses are unmistakable. The four Evangelists, or their symbols, are a favourite theme. Here too, the artists were quite liberal in the implementation of their ideas: figures have their feet turned sideways, with two sets of hands, harlequin-like gowns, or blue hair. In Dublin, the Royal Irish Academy exhibits St Columba's 6th-century Cathach (mentioned above), as well as the early 9th-century Stowe Missal. The Old Library at Trinity College possesses the 7th-century Book of Durrow (its earliest manuscript), the 8th-century Book of Dimma, the Book of Ardagh (dating from c807; with all four Gospels) and, of course, the undisputed masterpiece of Irish book illumination: the **Book of Kells** (▶ MARCO POLO Insight p.68).

The Cathach and other famous manuscripts

Thanks to missions by Irish monks, their manuscripts travelled to Britain and on to the Continent. Magnificent **libraries and scriptoria** were set up in the monasteries they founded. Many of the codices that subsequently emerged were written in a script that had originally evolved in Ireland. Occasionally, Irish scribes added personal notes in the margins of their work: poetry, observations of nature, pious (and sometimes less pious) thoughts. The fear of the Vikings is also expressed; and the raids of these Norsemen eventually did put an end to this flourishing period for the arts.

ROMANESQUE STYLE

Ireland had to wait for the ecclesiastical reforms of the 12th century before the building of more monumental churches. Cormac's Chapel, on the Rock of Cashel, is a masterpiece of the emerging and dis-

Ecclesiastical architecture

Book of Kells

On display in the library of Trinity College Dublin is one of humankind's greatest works of art in history: the Book of Kells. Since 1953 the book has been bound in four volumes. In alternation two of these volumes are on display, one with a decorated page, the other with a double page of text. Pages of the Book of Armagh and the Book of Durrow are on show for comparison. With some 470,000 visitors in 2011, the Book of Kells is one of Ireland's top visitor attractions and Dublin's greatest cultural visit after the National Gallery.

Origin and Wanderings

To this day it is not known exactly when and where this marvel was produced. The most probable scenario is that the Book of Kells was written by monks towards the end of the 8th century on Iona, a barren island off the west coast of Scotland. In 791, the Irish **abbot Connachtach** assembled the best artists and calligraphers in Europe in his monastery, founded by Columbkille (St Columba) in 563. This was the mother house for monks travelling to the European mainland to leave their mark by founding monasteries in Würzburg/Germany, in Luxeuil/France, Bobbio/Italy and St Gallen/Switzerland. Another pointer towards Iona as the probable place of origin for the Book of Kells is an illustration showing the Evangelist Luke, on page 201. In his right hand, the top part of the word »Jonas« can be made out, another name for the island of Iona. In 806, Vikings landed on the island to plunder and pillage. The abbot of the monastery and 86 of his monks died. But research suggests that precautions had already been taken for the book following the first Viking raid

on Iona in 794. Shortly before their second attack, the book, still incomplete, is thought to have been shipped to the safe Irish monastery of Kells (Ceananus Mor), where it was completed in the early 9th century. It was stolen in the 11th century, but found again three months later – missing only its gilded cover. According to a different theory, the book was produced in Ireland. In any case, the 12th century finds it at Kells monastery. We know this from the statutes of the monastic community, written on the white empty pages of this masterpiece. When Oliver Cromwell's marauding army came to attack Ireland, the book was taken to Trinity College Dublin for safekeeping.

Translation and Material

The text of the Book of Kells is based on the Vulgate, the Latin translation of the Bible executed by Saint Jerome/Hieronymus in the 4th century. The Book of Kells does not, however, follow this translation of the Bible word for word. The reason for this might be that several different sources were used in its production. Some say that this work of art was originally meant to be a **magnificent altar book**. This would explain the extraordinary degree of illumination and its format, which is larger than the other Gospel Books produced between the 7th and 9th centuries. No expense was spared in the making of the Book of Kells. The hides of hundreds of calves were used for the fine soft vellum for the pages. The colour pigments were brought in from all over the world: ultramarine (via Persia and Constantinople) from the Hindu Kush mountains, carmine red from the south of France, purple and yellow orpiment from Spain. The variety of artistic styles points to the fact that several artists – probably four – worked on the book.

Illuminated Initials

Every paragraph of the four Gospels starts with an **illuminated initial**. There are over 2,000 of these and they are all different. Between the exquisitely illuminated ornamentation, surprisingly well-drawn human and animal figures can be made out. The artistic work on the book page illustrated above is reminiscent of the most exquisite piece of goldsmith's work. The viewer cannot help but be fascinated by this blend of almost orien-

tal and, at the same time, typically Celtic style elements. The interaction of decorative and figurative representation indisputably places the Book of Kells at the pinnacle of book illumination in Ireland or anywhere else.

The chi-rho monogram at the beginning of the Gospel of St Matthew combines the first two Greek letters of the name »Christos« – the »X« (chi) runs diagonally over the whole page, the »P« (rho) is at the right on the bottom.

tinctive **Hiberno-Romanesque** style. Consecrated in 1134, this was the first time that the nave of an Irish church was given a tunnel vault and the choir a rib vault. Two square towers also form part of the structure. A steep-pitched stone roof is typical of Irish Celtic design, as are vividly carved mythical beasts and human heads. In Dysert O'Dea, for instance, moustached faces frame the main entrance. At Clonfert Cathedral the ornate main entrance is topped by an extraordinary triangular tympanum featuring human heads. Zigzag bands around doorways and ornately carved chancel arches characterize other Romanesque churches on the island. In Mellifont, a master builder from Burgundy was responsible for a new type of monastery, which was to become a model for numerous other new buildings. After their conquests, the Anglo-Normans erected various **fortifications**. A good example is the motte, a wooden tower on a hill, surrounded by a forecourt protected by palisades. Remains of the almost impregnable keep have often survived.

Rectangular towers with extremely thick walls usually form the centrepiece of large fortifications. Over time, following English models, castles fortified by corner towers appeared, along with mighty crenellated stone walls.

GOTHIC STYLE

The Gothic style is not typical for Ireland. It was brought over to the island from the 13th century onwards by Norman settlers or new monastic orders, but uncertain times and limited means meant that Gothic cathedrals and monasteries appear rather modest. Rosserilly, for example, with its tower and cloister, refectory with niche for a reader, bakery and fish pond, appears like a Franciscan monastery in miniature.

Sculpture

The Irish tombs of the Middle Ages, in common with their precursors, occupy a special place in the history of art. Rory O'Tunney was one of the most gifted stonemasons from the area around Kilkenny. Figures executed by him can be admired in the cloister of Jerpoint Abbey, on sarcophagi in the monasteries of Jerpoint and Kilcooley (near Urlingford) and also in Kilkenny Cathedral. In sculpted recesses, the likenesses of the dead in full armour rest on a stone sarcophagus. Particular attention was paid to hair and gowns, whilst the inscrutable gaze of the subject seems to be turned towards the hereafter.

Another typical feature of Irish art are **sheela-na-gigs**. These small, obscene figures are probably fertility symbols or were used to ward

An example of the late Norman style: Clonfert Cathedral

off evil. Carved from stone, they were mounted in discreet places in some churches. A list of all surviving sheela-na-gigs can be found at www.irelands-sheelanagigs.org.

STYLES UP TO THE PRESENT DAY

Due to the poor economic situation in Ireland, there are few outstanding examples of architecture or fine art.

18th century   In the 18th century, the wealthy Anglo-Irish built houses and mansions to reflect their social standing, mostly in the classical style and following the Italian architect **Palladio** and the Englishman **Inigo Jones**. Castletown House near Dublin is an example. This house, featuring wings and curved colonnades, was built for the speaker of the Irish parliament, William Connolly, between 1722 and 1732 by Alessandro Galilei and Sir Edward Lovett Pearce. The stucco work was carried out by the Francini brothers. However, estate owners were usually more interested in laying out and landscaping parks than furnishing their living quarters. Exotic trees, immaculate lawns and terraces (as in the park of Powerscourt) were more important than paintings, furniture or carpets. Some patrons realized their eccentric ideas in **follies**, enhancing their parks with Greek or Egyptian temples, obelisks or artificial ruins.

Dublin   Mid-17th-century Dublin saw the beginning of a **construction boom**. Within 100 years, this fairly insignificant town was transformed into the second-biggest city in the British Empire. Four new bridges spanned the Liffey, quays lined its banks. Broader streets and planted squares framed the city centre. As early as 1670, architect Sir William Robinson was building the Royal Hospital as a home for retired soldiers, following the French model of the Invalides church in Paris. The construction activity reached a peak in the 18th century: Dublin Castle and Trinity College were redesigned, while Edward Lovett Pearce built a parliamentary building (today the Bank of Ireland). Architects from other countries also left their mark in Ireland and Dublin: Richard Castle (or Cassels, 1690–1751), a German, built Tyrone House and Leinster House, today the home of the Irish parliament. James Gandon (1743–1823), an Englishmen of Huguenot descent, built King's Inns in the north of Dublin, as well as the Custom House and the Four Courts, two conspicuous landmarks on the north bank of the Liffey. Francis Johnston (1761–1829), a champion of the classical and neo-Gothic styles, was responsible for the chapel in Dublin Castle, as well as the General Post Office building, which was to be at the centre of heavy fighting in 1916 and was rebuilt as a symbol of the struggle for independence.

Brightly painted Georgian doorways in Dublin

Alongside the large public buildings, imposing residences were built   Georgian
for aristocrats and wealthy merchants, with stylish façades and front   style
gardens behind cast-iron railings. This Georgian style takes its name
from the rulers on the English throne at that time. High windows
structure the well-proportioned brick façades of these Georgian
houses; the only decorations are the numerous varieties of colourful
painted doors with their shiny polished brass plates. The doors are
framed by pillars or columns with an architrave and a semicircular
fanlight with lantern and house number. The interior of these houses
was often decorated by leading stucco craftsmen such as the Francini
brothers. Unfortunately, many individual houses or whole blocks
have since been demolished to make way for modern housing. Only
in recent times have conservation projects successfully preserved or
skilfully restored some of the most beautiful streets and squares. The
area around St Stephen's Green, Merrion Square and Fitzwilliam
Square provides a **cohesive ensemble of Georgian façades**. In
other cities too, Limerick and Cork in particular, three-storey and
four-storey brick houses with their colourful doors catch the eye.

Stained glass   In the 19th century, under the influence of Catholicism, numerous new churches were built, fostering stained-glass of exceptional quality. The first workshops were soon turned into schools; artists experimented with new techniques and established connections to the continent, with **Art Nouveau** playing a significant role. Leading stained glass artists included Michael Healy, Harry Clarke, Sarah Purser and Evie Hone.

Painting   Irish painting evolved mostly under the influence of international movements without producing really major artists. In the second half of the 18th century, portrait painter Robert Hunter (1748–1803) and James Barry (1741–1806) acquired national fame, the latter making his name with historical paintings, allegorical representations and etchings. The painters of the 19th century, such as Nathaniel Hone (1831–1917) and William Mulready (1786–1863), dedicated themselves primarily to landscape, history and genre painting. Around the turn of the century, Naturalism and Impressionism became the dominant styles in Ireland. William Orpen (1878–1931) was probably the most popular English society painter of his time. The works of Jack Butler Yeats (1871–1957) became successively more abstract (►Famous People). Paintings by Roderic O'Connor (1860–1940) are reminiscent of the Expressionists. The Dubliner Louis de Brocquy (1916–2012), who employed a variety of painting techniques, is regarded as the most important Irish painter of the 20th century. Sean Scully (born 1945) is among the finest contemporary abstract artists.

Contemporary art and architecture   Today's architecture and fine art increasingly references **style elements of the early period**. Round churches are built with a layout reminiscent of prehistoric stone forts, for example in Liam McCormick's **St Aengus Church** in Burt, Co. Donegal (1967), which was voted Ireland's most significant building of the 20th century. The windows are the work of Helen Moloney, while the altar, font and crucifix were made by Imogen Stuart. Of particular interest are the secular buildings of architect Michael Scott, who designed Dublin's Abbey Theatre (1959) and the Bank of Ireland building (1973). The new library of Trinity College Dublin by Ahrends, Burton & Koralek (1963–1967) also merits a closer look. Completely new developments were revealed at Dublin's **Grand Canal Docks** by the Dublin-born American Kevin Roche (Dublin Convention Centre, 2010) and by Santiago Calatrava's Samuel Beckett Bridge (2009). In Northern Ireland the

! *Modern Art* **Insider Tip**

MARCO ⊕ POLO TIP   The best place for gaining an impression of the variety and attractiveness of modern Irish art is the Irish Museum of Modern Art (IMMA) in Dublin. With over 400,000 visitors annually, it is among the top ten visitor destinations in Ireland.

architectural practices Civic Arts (London) and Todd (Belfast) set down markers for the 21st century with their Belfast Titanic (2012). The futuristic interior design is the work of Kay Elliott, and Todd architects continue to work on completion of the Titanic Quarter. Smaller bronze sculptures (by Edward Delaney and Oisin Kelly, amongst others) can be seen in public spaces; developed from works of early Celtic history, these have a style all of their own. They do however seem to share something with the brush drawings by Louis le Brocquy, Ireland's most expensive living painter, who has illustrated Thomas Kinsella's modern version of the Cattle-Raid saga (The Táin).

Irish Literature

Ireland's literature, like its people, is bilingual. Whereas writing in Irish dominated in the MIddle Ages, since the 17th century English has been the main language. Works of the most famous Irish authors, including James Joyce, Oscar Wilde and Samuel Beckett, are among the classics of world literature.

From the archaic epoch, some 360 short inscriptions (basically consisting of people's names) in the Ogham alphabet (►Language) have survived, mostly on tombstones or boundary stones. The poets and singers of pre-Christian times, known as *filid*, had a high standing. As chroniclers they preserved the oral traditions of their tribes and ruling families. For their patrons, they would write songs of praise and laments, whilst composing insulting jibes against their protectors' enemies. The early period of Irish literature is the great age of **heroic sagas**. The oldest written records of these prose epics have been handed down as manuscripts from the 12th and 13th centuries. However, they still preserve the linguistic form of centuries earlier and reveal a pagan world still untouched by Christianity. The Irish heroic sagas are classified in cycles. The Ulster Cycle, with its central story *The Cattle Raid of Cooley*, comprises, amongst other elements, the story of the tragic love of Deirdre (the *Tristan and Isolde* theme) and many archaic elements such as chariot battles, enemies' heads as trophies and the workings of the supernatural. The cycle describes the battle of mythical supernatural creatures, the Tuatha Dé Danann, and their king Dagdá against gods and demons. The Tuatha Dé Danann are probably meant to represent the native inhabitants of Ireland. The legends and tales collected in the *Cycle of the Kings* are stories about individual historic kings, for instance Cath Almain (The Battle of Allen) or Buile Suibhne (The Madness of Sweeney).Among

Archaic and early periods

survivals from the **poetry of the early period**, in addition to historical poems and the more political poems of the filid, are religious poems such as the *Festology of the Saints of Ireland* (*Félire*, around 800) by Óengus mac Óengobann. This was also a time of saint's legends and gospel books such as the Book of Kells, an Irish national treasure (▶MARCO POLO Insight, p.68), and medicinal as well as legal treatises (the *Séanchas Mar* Irish legal corpus). The *Dindshenchas*, a form of topography of Ireland that combines individually described locations with short stories and legends, encapsulates examples of evolving religious and scholarly prose.

Middle period

During the course of the Anglo-Norman invasion in 1171, bards at the newly established princely courts replaced the filid as court poets, even though the filid had previously had a high social status. Bards such as Muireadhach Albanach Ó Dálaigh, who lived in the first half of the 13th century, would mainly write songs of praise or satirical songs making fun of their patrons' enemies. Prose from the middle period is mainly represented by the fairy-tale folklore of the *Finn Cycle*, the fourth great Irish cycle of sagas, centring around the *Acallam na senórach* (*Colloquy of the Old Men*) story.

Late period

The suppression of the Irish language led to the disintegration of a unified literary language into various dialects. As the English prohibited the printing of Irish-language books, Irish literature became available only handwritten with a limited distribution. In the 17th and 18th centuries, **folk poetry** written by farmers and craftsmen flourished, particularly in the southern Irish province of Munster. One of the most significant works of this Munster poetry is T*he Midnight Court (Cúirt an mhéanoiche)* by Brian Merriman (1740–1808).

English as literary language

Since the 17th century, Irish writers have also written in English. The satirist **Jonathan Swift** (1667–1745) produced his masterpiece *Gulliver's Travels* (1726). In later centuries, selective editing reduced the book to its fantastic, adventurous storyline until it was finally misinterpreted as a children's book. Wit, humour and the joy of telling wonderful stories characterize both the content and style of the works of **Laurence Sterne** (1713–68). The masterpiece of this rural clergyman is the comic novel *The Life and Opinions of Tristram Shandy*, published 1760–67, a biography of the protagonist, embellished with digressions and ramblings.

Modern period

The »Gaelic Revival« kicked off a renewal of the Irish language and culture, triggered by the founding of the Gaelic League in 1893 by Douglas Hyde (1860–1949), who later became the first president of the Republic of Ireland. In his novels, James Stephens (1882–1950), one of the most popular prose writers of the Gaelic Revival, referenced the world of Irish legends. The first Irish national theatre, the **Irish Literary Theatre**, was founded in 1899 by Lady Augusta Gregory and WB Yeats (1865–1939), who also drew on Irish legend for the themes and plots of his plays ("Famous People). In 1901, the theatre premiered the first Irish-language stage play. With his realistic poetic tragedies and comedies in stylised Irish language, JM Synge (1871–1909) is considered the strongest dramatic force of the time. Sean O'Casey (1884–1964) and Brendan Behan (1923–1964) used their plays and short stories to tell the story of the miserable social conditions in their home country and the ongoing Irish liberation struggle. Irish theatre has produced a whole range of remarkable authors, including four Nobel Prize winners (▶Famous People): **WB Yeats** in 1923, **George Bernard Shaw** in 1925, **Samuel Beckett** in 1969 and **Seamus Heaney** in 1995, as well as the world-class playwright and author **Oscar Wilde**.

James Joyce (1882–1941, ▶Famous People) is considered the most important novelist Ireland has produced. His novel *Ulysses* (1921) portrays Dublin and Ireland in the early 20th century (▶MARCO POLO Insight p.320). With the novels, short stories and satires of Frank O'Connor (1903–66), Seán O'Faoláin (1900–91), Liam O'Flaherty (1897–1984) and M Ó Cadhain (1905–70), whose work points to the increasing social ills and religious problems in Ireland, the spotlight of Irish literature turned increasingly towards political and social issues. The poet Máirtín Ó Diréan (1910–88), who writes of the beauty of his native Aran Islands, at the same time criticised Irish society.

One of the most popular works of world literature was penned by **Abraham (Bram) Stoker** (1847–1912): *Dracula* (1897). In this sensationalist novel, set far away from Ireland in the Transylvanian region of Romania, Stoker borrowed the name of his protagonist from the Romanian Count Vlad Tepes. Infamous with his enemies because of his cruelty, the count, dubbed Dracula, lived in the 15th century. In Dracula, Bram Stoker used old Romanian myths and legends as well as the interest in vampirism and supernatural phenomena widespread in Europe in the second half of the 19th century. Bram Stoker did not live to see his work become one of the most popular novels of the 20th century. It was the screen adaptations of the vampire story – around 100 to date – that ensured world fame for the novel, the character of Count Dracula and, thereby, for its author.

Bram Stoker

In **Flann O'Brien**, real name Brian O'Nolan (1911–66), Ireland boasts a writer whose work is a veritable firework display of comic wit. From 1929 to 1935, O'Brien studied Irish, English and German literature at University College Dublin. After spending 1934–1935 in

Contemporary literature

A Place to Sing

Packed to the doors every evening, a terrific atmosphere every evening. Why does Irish beer taste so good? And why are the pubs such wonderful places for having a conversation? It must be something to do with the music. There seems to be magic in the air.

The Irish have always loved singing. In Celtic times, the bards had an important role. They passed on language, culture and history, and became advisors to rulers. To accompany singing, the most important instruments were the harp and the bodhrán drum. The musical tradition seemed subversive to English colonizers in the 17th century. They saw danger in the ideas of the singers. Cromwell had harps burned and harpists executed. Today the Celtic harp is a national symbol that appears on the coat of arms of Ireland.

Out into the World

Music has always been a solace for homesickness. For the Irish who emigrated, making music together in their new homeland was important. Their influence in the USA and Canada is evident to this day, as Irish elements in pop, rock and folk music are still unmistakeable. Traditional music was a means of establishing identity in the years of struggle for independence. Since 1950 the organization Comhaltas Ceoltióri Éirann has promoted Irish music with increasing success. Open-air festivals in summer, especially Fleadh Cheoil in August, have become great attractions. In addition to the official programme, the laid-back atmosphere is a big draw: people come to meet friends, camp in tents or sleeping bags beneath the stars and, if they are not on stage themselves, many make music in pub or some other venue.

Pub People

Infectious rhythms and melodious ballads have made Irish music popular all over the world. Visitors to the island can experience the roots of this music for themselves in »singing pubs«, when musicians turn up to play the tin whistle, fiddle, guitar, banjo, uillean pipes (a kind of bagpipe) or accordion. Everyone joins in the refrain of well-known songs, and sometimes the lyrics are adapted in accordance with current events.

Bands such as the Dubliners and the Pogues became well-known far beyond the borders of Ireland. While the Dubliners represent a mainstream tradition, the Pogues always seemed to have imbibed plenty of the beer and whiskey that they liked to sing about. In the 1960s Christy Moore started his career as a songwriter and musician of the »traditional folk« style. Among the classic representatives of Irish instrumental music are the Chieftains. Back in the 1960s they paved the way for the worldwide revival of Irish folk. The group Clannad, singing in Gaelic, produced wonderful a capella music.

A singing pub in Doolin, a centre for Irish folk music

Music in their Blood

In comparison to the population of the island, Ireland has brought forth a disproportionate number of prominent musicians. Gary Moore and Roger Gallagher are two big names in the world of blues, Chris de Burgh a highly successful singer-songwriter. Innovative groups included Them and Thin Lizzy, the latter famous for their version of the folk song Whiskey in the Jar. A member of Them, Van Morrison, started his solo career in 1967 and became a cult figure, as did Gilbert O'Sullivan. The Boomtown Rats only made their breakthrough when they moved to London, and their front man Bob Geldof became a kind of »pop-music saint« in the 1980s for his commitment to social causes. He helped to organize charity concerts such as Band Aid. In international terms, the most successful Irish band of all was U2. Here the producer Brian Eno sensed the potential of the combination of good lyrics and the charismatic voice of front man Bono. The Cranberries and Sinéad O' Connor were also influenced by the tradition of Irish pop music. All those who have irish ancestry can count their lucky stars in at least one respect: they have music in their blood!

Famous People

SAMUEL BECKETT (1906 – 89)

Samuel Beckett became world-famous as one of the main exponents   Writer
of the Theatre of the Absurd. Born and bred in Dublin, he studied
Romance languages and literature at Trinity College from 1923 to
1927, going on to teach English in Paris. There, Beckett met James
Joyce and the Existentialists. Beckett moved to London in 1933, and
started writing his first poems, short stories and essays in English. In
1937, he moved back to Paris, writing subsequent works in French
and translating them into English himself. Beckett had to wait a little
longer for his breakthrough; but the novel »Molloy« (1951) made his
name known, and his first stage play, »Waiting for Godot« (1952)
caused a major stir. All his work shows a break with traditional form;
the action is reduced to a minimum. Using grotesque and burlesque
elements, Beckett draws a pessimistic picture of the absurdity of human existence. In 1969, Beckett was awarded the Nobel Prize for Literature.

ST BRENDAN (C484–C578)

Published around the year 900, The Voyage of St Brendan was trans-   Monk
lated into many western European languages and became a bestseller
in medieval Europe. The Voyage describes how the 6th-century Irish
abbot Brendan »the Navigator« discovers the »Promised Land« beyond the Atlantic. The Irish saint Brendan founded several monasteries in Ireland, including Clonfert in County Galway. Driven by missionary zeal, he travelled through the Scottish isles and Wales.
According to legend, he took to sea between 512 and 530 with 17
companions (according to some sources, with 60 pilgrims) and a
well-equipped boat after hearing of a »Promised Land« beyond the
ocean, inhabited by saints. It took him seven years to return. In 1976,
Timothy Severin proved that crossing the Atlantic in a leather boat
of the type common in Brendan's time was possible. Inspired by the
similarity of place names in the book and the actual topography on
Labrador, Severin sailed in a reconstruction of an early boat from
Ireland to Canada.

ST BRIGID OF KILDARE (451 – 525)

The beautiful daughter of a nobleman and a slave woman, Brigid,   Writer
whose Celtic name means »the sublime one«, became a nun at the
age of 14. Close to her parents' house she established a cell beneath

A statue of James Joyce on O'Connell Street in Dublin

an oak tree, which evolved into a nunnery and then into the double monastery of Kildare for monks and nuns. News of her piety and charity spread quickly. Biographers describe her as a highly educated and resolute woman. Along with St Patrick and St Columba, Brigid is one of the three patron saints of Ireland. She is commemorated on 1 February, previously the day of the Celtic mother goddess Brighid, seen as the date when spring begins. This is the origin of the word »bright«.

ROGER CASEMENT (1864 – 1916)

Rebel On 3 August 1916 Sir Roger Casement was hanged for conspiracy with the German war enemy and for preparing an Irish rebellion. Born in Dublin, by the age of 20 Roger Casement was already travelling in Africa. From 1900, he was commissioned by the British government to investigate conditions in the Belgian Congo and Peru. Casement confirmed rumours of mistreatment at the hands of white colonialists, bringing them to world-wide attention. From then on, Casement was considered an advocate of the poor, consequently held in high esteem internationally and given a knighthood. Having damaged his health through his long stay in the tropics, Casement left the British civil service in 1913. From then on he dedicated himself to the fight for Ireland's independence. Shortly after the outbreak of the First World War, he made contact with the German government in Berlin. The German Reich agreed to smuggle 20,000 guns along with ammunition on board the ship »Libau« to the Irish coast. When the ship was discovered by the British Navy, the captain scuttled it. Casement was taken by submarine to a nearby place in Ireland, where he was immediately arrested. The Dublin Easter Rising of 1916 was defeated after only four days by British armed forces. Casement was regarded as the chief responsible person, and condemned to death for high treason, sabotage and espionage, and hanged on 13 August 1916. In 1965 his mortal remains were transferred from England to Dublin and laid to rest in Glasnevin Cemetery in a ceremony attended by 30,000 people.

JAMES JOYCE (1882 – 1941)

Novelist While few will have read this world-famous author's masterpiece »Ulysses«, published in 1922, in its entirety, this book is the reason behind Bloomsday, celebrated by fans every year on 16 June in Dublin (▶MARCO POLO Insight, p.320). After an education at Jesuit schools and at University College Dublin, Joyce went to Paris in 1902 to study medicine. From 1904 onwards, he lived in self-chosen exile

The literary works of James Joyce are ever-present in Dublin

in Trieste, Rome, Zurich and Paris, amongst other places. Ten years later, »Dubliners« was published: 15 short stories in which Joyce depicts Dublin society through different ages of life. The autobiographical novel »Portrait of the Artist as a Young Man« (1916) uses interior monologue to show the tensions between a young artist and his environment. In his last work, »Finnegan's Wake« (1939), Joyce tried – as in »Ulysses« – to harness the subconscious to language. Joyce's works owe much to the atmosphere of his home city of Dublin and, despite the many difficulties of interpretation, they were a significant influence on 20th-century literature. In 1940, Joyce fled with his family from Paris to Zurich, where he died on 13 January 1941 following a serious illness. He lies buried in Fluntern cemetery.

CONSTANCE MARKIEVICZ (1868 – 1927)

Born in London, the daughter of the Anglo-Irish landowner Sir Henry Booth-Gore, she grew up in Co. Sligo and was a friend of W.B.

Patriot

Yeats in her youth. She met her Polish husband while staying in Paris as a student of painting. They later moved to Dublin, where Constance joined the Daughters of Ireland, a society founded in 1900 that supported Irish independence. In 1908 she became a member of Sinn Féin and co-founded a militant IRA women's league. In 1916 she was sentenced to death for her active role in the fighting during the Easter Rising. The sentence was commuted to life imprisonment, and Markievicz was freed in a general amnesty of 1917. In 1918, back in prison, she became the only woman to be elected to the British Parliament for Sinn Féin, but instead entered the Irish parliament following her release in 1919, becoming minister of labour in Eamon de Valera's shadow cabinet. During the civil war she joined in the fighting, and was elected to Parliament for Fianna Fáil in 1923 and again in 1927, in which year she died in Dublin, probably from tuberculosis.

DANIEL O'CONNELL (1775 – 1847)

Resistance
leader

Daniel O'Connell was one of the best-known leaders of the Irish resistance against the English Crown. In the early 19th century, O'Connell was known as »Ireland's uncrowned king« but was ultimately defeated by the political realities. As the son of a relatively wealthy Catholic estate owner, O'Connell was able to study in France, where he witnessed the French Revolution. O'Connell set up as a lawyer in Dublin, and took an increasingly active part in politics. He pursued two goals: equal rights for Irish Catholics and the protection of small Irish tenants against injustice by English owners of large estates. With this in mind, O'Connell founded the Catholic Association in 1823. Soon the association numbered over a million members from all social classes. With their help, O'Connell won the County Clare election to become MP, but it took an amendment of the English law to allow him, as a non-Anglican, to take his seat at Westminster. When the Conservatives returned to power in England, O'Connell's political influence waned. The situation escalated when the English lord lieutenant proposed using the military to prevent a planned mass rally near Dublin. O'Connell cancelled the rally the evening before to avoid violence; most of his young supporters felt let down and turned their backs on him. Already in declining health, O'Connell went to Italy to recuperate, but died in Genoa in 1847.

CHARLES STEWART PARNELL (1846 – 1891)

Politician

Born into a Protestant Anglo-Irish family, Charles Stewart Parnell became a figurehead for the Irish national movement. Parnell started his political career in the Home Rule League, a party founded in 1870 that demanded the independence of the Irish parliament but rejected violence against British supremacy. Parnell soon became party leader and the most important Irish politician, using peaceful means to fight the British government for concessions. The first boycott in world history ensured his popularity. Parnell particularly detested British landowners who exploited the destitute rural population by using unscrupulous agents. It was against such an agent, Captain Charles Boycott, that Parnell instigated an action of completely refusing cooperation with him (►Boycott, Lough Corrib, Lough Mask). However, Parnell's policy of peaceful rapprochement towards the liberal Home Rule policy of British prime minister Gladstone made him enemies. As it became apparent that Irish independence was unachievable within the framework of the constitution, his political opponents began a campaign against him. Parnell's affair with Katherine (Kitty) O'Shea, a married woman separated from her husband, was pilloried as »immoral behaviour«. Marrying Kitty O'Shea did not protect Parnell from being voted out as head of the party – and he died a few months after his deposition.

MARY ROBINSON (BORN 1944)

A lawyer born in Ballina, Mary Robinson became Professor of Criminal Law at Trinity College, Dublin at the age of only 25. From 1969 to 1989 she was a member of the Senate. In 1990, representing the Labour Party, she won the presidential election, becoming the first woman to hold the position. After that she pursued an international career, becoming UN High Commissioner for Human Rights and later honorary president of Oxfam. In 2009 she was awarded the highest civilian honour of the USA, the Presidential Medal of Freedom. Her memoirs, »Everybody Matters«, were published in 2012.

Irish president

GEORGE BERNARD SHAW (1856 – 1950)

Cynicism, mockery and humour made George Bernard Shaw famous beyond his literary creations. Shaw was born in Dublin, the son of an English father and Irish mother. In 1876, Shaw moved to London, where he wrote reviews of theatre, music and art that were admired as much as they were feared. Eight years later he co-found the Fabian Society., which supported evolutionary socialism rather than Marxist revolutionary ideals. From 1891, Shaw turned to writing plays, which heaped scorn on conventions and well-loved clichés in polished dialogues and witty punch lines. His most famous plays include Pygmalion (1912) and Saint Joan (1923). In 1925, Shaw was awarded the

Author and critic

Shaw maintained his intellectual activity to a ripe old age

Nobel Prize for Literature, but refused a knighthood. With Al Gore, he is the only person to have won both a Nobel Prize (for Literature in 1925) and an Oscar (for his screenplay for a film version of »Pygmalion«, 1939). Shaw's views of Ireland found expression in »John Bull's Other Island« (1904): »Ireland cannot be compared to any other country, in what's good and in what's bad; and nobody can touch its soil or breathe its air without becoming better or worse.«

JONATHAN SWIFT (1667 – 1745)

Satirist   «Gulliver's Travels« is one of the most popular children's books in world literature. However, this adventure story, written in 1726 by Jonathan Swift, is much more than just a children's book. Swift describes the exploits of his protagonist Gulliver in different worlds: the land of Lilliput, the land of giants, the country where eternal life is possible, and in the realm of the horses endowed with reason who have created an ideal society with humans as servants. The book is a biting satire on contemporary English society, human stupidity and malice, as well as social ills. Irony is the hallmark of Swift's literary

work; he is considered the most important satirist in English literature, world literature even. In 1713, Swift returned to Dublin, holding
the deanery of St Patrick's Cathedral up to his death. In 1729, he was
given the freedom of the city, but when his companion Stella died,
Swift's tone became more and more cynical; his contemporaries considered him to be disturbed. Jonathan Swift lies buried next to Stella
in Dublin's St Patrick's Cathedral.

JOHN MILLINGTON SYNGE (1871 – 1909)

Born into an Anglo-Irish lawyer's family, the writer John Millington   Writer
Synge studied at Trinity College Dublin. Travelling in Germany and
Italy in 1892, he spent most of the years 1893–98 in Paris. There, he
met William B Yeats, who recommended a stay on the Aran Islands
on the west coast of Ireland to study the way of life and the language
of the islanders. Initially Synge only stayed for six weeks but in the
following years he returned time and again, immortalizing the landscape and its people in »The Aran Islands« (1907). In 1904, Synge,
who had settled in Dublin in 1902, became director of the newly
founded Abbey Theatre, which he managed up to his death. In his
works, Synge dealt with themes from the world of Irish peasants and
fishermen. »Riders to the Sea«, one of his most important works, presents a fisherman's watery grave as inevitable. The black comedy »The
Playboy of the Western World« (1907) is also famous as homage to
the islanders' rough but warm turn of phrase.

EAMON DE VALERA (1882 – 1975)

Eamon de Valera is the most important personality of Irish 20th-   Politician
century history. For six decades (1913–73), de Valera dominated
politics on the »Emerald Isle«; the Irish owe the creation of the Republic of Ireland first and foremost to him. Born in New York on 14
October 1882, the son of a Spaniard and an Irishwoman, he grew up
in Ireland with his grandmother, following the early death of his father. De Valera studied mathematics in Dublin and became a teacher.
His political career started in 1913 as a member of the recently
founded Irish Volunteers, who demanded more autonomy for Ireland. As one of the leaders of the Easter Rising in 1916, de Valera was
sentenced to death – but the sentence was not carried out. After being released, he stood for the British House of Commons and was
elected. In May 1918, the English government had de Valera arrested
again and interned in England, but he managed to flee to the United
States. Whilst still in exile, de Valera became party chief of Sinn Féin,
founded in 1918. Aiming for Irish independence, the party wanted

to win the majority of the Irish mandates in the British House of Commons. However, instead of taking their seats in Westminster, they founded the illegal Council of Ireland (Dáil Eireann) in 1919 under the presidency of de Valera, who returned to Ireland in 1920. De Valera's goal was still the same: full independence for Ireland. In protest against the Anglo-Irish Treaty, which created the Irish Free State as a dominion of the British Empire but allowed Northern Ireland to opt out, he stood down from parliament. During the civil war of 1922-23, he opposed the government. In 1926, de Valera founded the Fianna Fáil party, winning the 1932 elections as their candidate. Under his government, Ireland became a de facto republic, on the basis of the constitution of 1937, which he helped to draw up. During the Second World War, de Valera strictly maintained Ireland's neutrality, surviving a tricky time with a state that was not yet consolidated. Voted out of office in 1948 by his fellow Irish, he was nevertheless recalled to be »Taoiseach« (head of government) in the years 1951–54 and 1957–59. From 1959 to 1973, he represented his country as president. Eamon de Valera (known as »Dev« to his supporters and also as the »Long Fellow«) died on 29 August 1975, aged 93.

JACK BUTLER YEATS (1871 – 1957)

Painter   Jack Butler Yeats , the brother of writer William, dedicated himself to painting as his father had before him. Born in London, he spent his childhood in Sligo, returning there for his studies. Throughout his life, J B Yeats painted Irish landscapes and daily life, such as scenes from the pub, variety theatre or the racecourse.

WILLIAM BUTLER YEATS (1865 – 1939)

Poet   The writer William Butler Yeats was the founder and guiding spirit of the Gaelic Revival. This movement, closely linked to the struggle for Irish independence, aimed to revive Irish-Celtic traditions in the arts and culture. Yeats spent his childhood in Dublin, London and Sligo, remaining strongly attached to the landscapes of the west coast of Ireland, its legends and folktales, all his life. From 1884 to 1886, Yeats attended art college with a view to becoming a painter. However, from 1886 onwards he dedicated himself to literature, becoming, in 1899, one of the founders of the Irish National Theatre. After the proclamation of the Irish Free State, Yeats became senator and used his term in office (1922 – 28) to propose the decoration of Irish coins with animals mentioned in the Book of Kells: hare, dog, fish and bird. Yeats' entire oeuvre is suffused with Irish Celtic legends, fairytales and myths. Whilst his early work still shows the influence of French symbolism and »fin-de-siècle« aesthetics, the author later became interested in magic and occultism, rites and symbols. His plays resemble epic poems, with a symbolic plot and protagonists representing types rather than individuals. Yeats' most beautiful poems are collected in two volumes of poetry: »The Tower« (1928) and »The Winding Stair and Other Poems« (1933). Yeats was awarded the 1923 Nobel Prize for Literature.

ENJOY IRELAND

Where are the best places to go fishing? Which are the finest festivals and sporting events? What should you expect from new irish cuisine? Read on to find answers to these and many other questions.

Accommodation

A Bed for Every Budget

Whether your preferences or financial means point to a country house hotel, B & B, a cottage, a campsite or a hostel, you will find the right accommodation in Ireland. Thanks the reduction of VAT during the financial crisis, prices have remained stable or even fallen.

Hotels are officially categorized into five groups, from luxury hotels with five stars and standard hotels with two or three stars, to simple accommodation with one star. In Northern Ireland there are only four categories. Small guesthouses get between one and four stars, while in Northern Ireland they are simply categorized as A or B. Hotel prices in Dublin and other cities are significantly higher than in the country. **Hotels**

?	*Price categories*
MARCO ⊕ POLO INSIGHT	Hotels (double room including breakfast):
	€ € € € over 130 € (105 £)
	€ € € 100 – 130 € (80 – 105 £)
	€ € 80 – 100 € (65 – 80 £)
	€ below 80 € (65 £)

Many fine **country houses** have been converted into hotels and restaurants, and the country house food served there is the basis of new Irish cuisine. Ireland`s Blue Book and Tourism Ireland are good sources of addresses. Luxurious country house accommodation can be booked through Hidden Ireland. Holiday cottages and apartments are abundant in both rural and urban areas. A traditional Irish cottage, ideally with a thatched roof, is one of the most charming alternatives – for information refer to Tourism Ireland and Self-Catering Ireland.

There are approximately 140 officially recognized camping and caravanning sites in the Republic of Ireland, graded according to their facilities. The best have four stars, the most basic have one star. Northern Ireland, too, is well provided with campsites. Camping wild or unofficially is generally prohibited. **Others**

Old-style youth hostels now face a lot of competition from newer backpacker hostels, especially in cities. Couchsurfing (www.couchsurfing.org) is also well established on the island, with over 2,000 hosts in Dublin.

A lot of B & B accommodation is available, especially in the country

Like Staying with Friends

The advantages of B & Bs are obvious, especially in rural areas: personal atmosphere and service, sometimes in a family environment, contact to locals, a typical Irish breakfast that is sometimes outstandingly good, normally no problems finding somewhere to park the car – and all of this for a fair price. The arguments speak for themselves.

Not even the financial crisis affected the situation: bed and breakfast is one of the most popular types of accommodation in Ireland. Those who have to keep an eye on how much they spend will find reasonably priced accommodation in every corner of the island in homes that are often lovingly cared for.

But it is not only travellers on a limited budget who appreciate B & Bs. In contrast to the hotels, where conversation rarely goes beyond some small talk at the reception, real contact to the hosts is possible. Around the fireplace or on the garden terrace, tourists have the chance to hear news about life in Ireland and get valuable tips on what to see in the surrounding area. This kind of knowledge is exclusive to B & Bs, emphasizes Margaret Cahill, chair of B & B Ireland. For travellers engaged in an active holiday, many B & Bs have an attractive location, with wonderful walking trails and bike routes on the doorstep. Some places can rent out bikes, and if not will often know where to go for bike hire. Others cater specifically for the needs of walkers on long-distance trails, golfers, anglers or aficionados of adventurous sports. More over, some 200 B & Bs are farmhouses, even equestrian centres with their own programme of activities.

Useful Information

The comprehensive, annually published brochure Bed & Breakfast Ireland (www.bandireland.com) lists what is on offer. It tells you, for example, which B & Bs accept pets. They are regularly inspected and categorized in five classes. Almost all addresses are easy to find, especially as the brochure states their GPS coordinates. What could go wrong?

A cosy B & B

Useful Addresses

INFORMATION
Tourism Ireland
Tel. 353 1 476 3400
www.discoverireland.com

www.goireland.com
An online database for hotels,
guesthouses, hostels, etc.

BED & BREAKFAST
B & B Ireland
Tel. 719 82 22 22
www.bandireland.com
Here you can find 1,000 B & B
addresses.

COUNTRY HOUSES
Ireland's Blue Book
 www.irelands-blue-book.com
Tel. (01) 6769914
An exquisite selection of country
house hotels and restaurants

The Hidden Ireland
Tel. (098) 6 6650 (Westport)
(01) 6 627166 (Dublin)
www.hidden-ireland.com
High-class, privately owned historic houses.

HOLIDAY HOUSES
**Irish Cottage Holiday Homes
Association**
Tel. (01) 205 27 77
www.irishcottageholidays.com
Historic and modern holiday ho-
mes in the Irish Republic

Self Catering Ireland
Tel 053 917 81 00
www.selfcatering-ireland.com
Properties in all counties of the
Irish Republic

CAMPING
AND CARAVANNING
**Irish Caravan & Camping
Council**
www.camping-ireland.ie
An excellent presentation of Irish
campsites

HOSTELS
**AN ÓIGE Irish Youth Hostel
Association**
Tel. 01 8 304555
www.anoige.ie
21 hostels in the Republic, seven
in Northern Ireland. Special offers
for groups and tourists.

**Hostelling International
Northern Ireland (HINI)**
Tel. 0 28 90324733
www.hini.org.uk
Six hostels in Northern Ireland,
special offers for groups and families.

Travelling with Children

Fun and Excitement are Guaranteed

Ireland is different from many countries in one way: its birth rate is among the highest in Europe. So many Irish people come from large families, and it is no surprise that they are pleased to see children.

You don't have to pay for everything: one of the great attractions of the Emerald Isle, its magnificent scenery, amounts to one huge adventure playground for children. They can look at Europe's highest cliffs, Slieve League in Donegal, explore the flora and fauna on beach walks or go swimming in one of the many lakes. Trips by bike and kayak enable active kids to work off energy and see a lot at the same time.

Various attractions

And there are many other reasons not to be bored. If the family is not attracted by a tour of the ancient monuments on the Hill of Tara or Glendalough Abbey, there are plenty of swimming pools and water parks, even in small towns. For children who like an adventure or something a bit scary, Ireland is full of pirate and vampire stories, castles with ghosts and dark dungeons.

MARCO POLO TIP

Insider Tip

A true treasure chest ...

... for families travelling to Ireland is the website www.familyfun.ie with everything from visits to castles to child-friendly restaurants, from summer camps to children's parties in fun parks -- hundreds of tips!

The availability of numerous discounts also helps to make ireland a popular destination for a family holiday. Many hotels have special offers for families, and B & Bs are inexpensive places to stay. Reduced prices are offered for kids on public transport, in museums and in galleries, as well as in publicly run attractions such as zoos.

Good to know

Note the rules on the times when minors may be in places that serve alcohol: children below the age of 16 are allowed in pubs and bars only when accompanied by an adult, up to 9pm or, from May to September, until 10pm. In Northern Ireland the official minimum age for entering a pub is 21 years; when accompanied by someone aged over 21, they may stay until 9.30pm.

In Ireland's magnificent outdoors, nothing stops kids from working off their energy

Attractions for Children

MUSEUMS
Dublinia
p. 327
This look at Dublin in the Middle Ages is lots of fun for young and old, and a good history lesson into the bargain. It's a real experience to learn about the Vikings and the work of »history hunters« (archaeologists).

Imaginosity
The Plaza
Beacon South Quarter
Sandyford, Dublin 18
Tel. 01 217 61 30
www.imaginosity.ie
Mo 1.30–5.30pm, Tue–Fri 9.30am–5.30pm, Sat–Sun 10am–6pm, admission 8 €.
Dublin's children's museum has a varied programme for kids up to the age of nine. In Dr Apple-a-day's office, for example, they learn about healthy eating.

Titanic Belfast
p. 204
A must-see, and very exciting for children. The car ride on the fourth floor, for example, shows the world of work at the shipyards that built Titanic.

ARTS & CRAFTS
The Ark
p. 325
Europe's first arts centre for children is an attraction in Dublin's Temple Bar district. Its aim is to develop creativity through fun in age groups from toddlers to 12-year-olds. There are new workshops every day, for example in summer making masks that the children can take home, and children's theatre.

Wallcandies in Ennis
Ennis is an ideal small town for families. Children love the treasure trail leading to 18 hidden wallcandies, little works of art on the walls in the old quarter, made by street artists. The wallcandy map (www.wallcandy.ie/map.html) is helpful. It is also worth taking the 4km/2.5-mile trip to Ballyalla Lake, home to 5,000 birds and the Clare Equestrian Centre in Doora, where adults and children can ride.

NATURE
Atlantaquaria in Galway
p. 378
Ireland's national aquarium has a touch pool, where children can stroke the fish. Touch pool tours are held at weekends at 12 noon, 2pm and 5pm. Of course feeding time is also entertaining (daily 1pm, 3pm, 4pm).

Brigit's Garden
Children can have fun while learning about Celtic culture and nature in the discovery centre and in the gardens that symbolize the four seasons and the old festivals Samhain (Hallowe'en), Imbolc, Bealtaine and Lughnasa. There is also a nature trail and a children's discovery trail. In July and August summer camps are organized (Mon–Fri 10am–1pm, 60 €) on themes such as fun in nature and survival games.

Ancient Irish myths live on at Giant's Causeway

ADVENTURE/ACTIVITIES
Giant's Causeway
p. 250

The causeway made of basalt and the Finn McCool Trail are a must for all age groups. Family activities, including excursions for kids, include butterfly hunts, a trip on a train from and to Bushmills and the suspension bridge at Carrick-a-Reed in Ballintoy (admission 5.60 €), www.nationaltrust.org.uk/carrick-a-rede).

Shannon Houseboat Tour
c/o Shannon Cruisers /
Shannon Castle Line
Williamstown Harbour
Whitegate, Co. Clare
Tel. 061 92 7042
www.shannoncruisers.com

Excellent infrastructure, a low level of risk, few locks (six on the Shannon, one on Erne, 16 automatic lifts on the Shannon-Erne Waterway), nature and lots of sights to see. Hiring a houseboat is an ideal family holiday.

Lough Key Forest Park
p. 223

Zip It Forest Adventurers: children taller than one metre and over seven years old, accompanied by an adult, can swing through the treetops in the Lough Key Forest Park. There are four tours with different levels of difficulty, between 1 and 20 metres in height. There is also an Adventure Play Kingdom for small children. The treetop walkway and Boda Borg are also top attractions.

Festivals, Holidays and Events

Lots of Variety

Between April and September there are many festivals and public holidays in Ireland that attract thousands of locals and tourists from all over the world. Music, art and culture are at the centre of many events. And as far as parties are concerned, whether in pubs, on the beach or at a festival, the Irish certainly know how to celebrate.

If the Irish are asked what is the most important feast day in the calendar, then the answer in unanimous: St Patrick's Day, 17 March, is celebrated in Ireland with big parades, and almost everywhere else where an Irish community exists. Patrick and other saints play a major role in the annual round. On Reek Sunday in July, pilgrims set out for Croagh Patrick, the island's holy mountain, many feast days relate to patron saints. Historical events, too, are celebrated: in Northern Ireland the Protestants commemorate the victory of King William III over the forces of the Catholic James II at the Battle of the Boyne with their parades on Orangemen's Day (12 July). | Traditional events

Honouring writers is typical of Ireland. This happens at festivals such as Writers' Week in Listowel (late May/early June) and on Bloomsday in Dublin (16 June). For more than 60 years a major opera festival has been held in Wexford. The East Cork Early Music Festival in the second week of October is devoted to music composed before 1750. Lighter music and operettas feature strongly in the International Festival of Light Music in Waterford (early May). The Dublin Theatre Festival (late September to mid-October) has a high international reputation. Belfast in autumn is enlivened by the varied cultural programme of the Festival at Queen's, which has now taken place for more than 50 years (www.belfastfestival.com). Ireland's Celtic musical heritage is celebrated in August at the Flead Cheoil na hÉireann, held in a different place each year. | Cultural events

The Dublin Horse Show in August is more than just an equestrian competition – it is an event for high society. The best-dressed lady is chosen each year on Ladies' Day. Top sporting events in September are the finals of the hurling and Gaelic football competitions at Croke Park in Dublin, which holds 83,000 spectators. The home of football, rugby (e.g. the Six Nations Cup) and American football (here Notre Dame versus Navy is the classic fixture) is the modern Aviva Stadium in Dublin, the successor to the legendary Lansdowne Road | Sport events

All Ireland wears green on St Patrick's Day

In Dublin a colourful parade commemorates St Patrick

stadium, which was demolished in 2007. The stadium is also used for big pop and rock concerts.

Culinary events

Ireland`s history is regularly celebrated in medieval banquets, for example at Bunratty Castle in County Clare and Dunvair Castle in Kinvara (Co. Galway). Food festivals are also highly popular events. At the best-known of these, the Galway Oyster Festival in late September, the world championships in oyster-shucking are held. The oyster festival in Hillsborough, Northern Ireland, in early September is a rival event. Adherents of the Slow Food movement go to Waterford at harvest time in mid-September. For beer drinkers there are events such as the festival at the Hilden Brewery in Lisburn (Co. Antrim) in August. On 22 September the Guinness Brewery holds Arthur`s Day in honour of its founder, an occasion at which millions of people all over the world drink a celebratory pint.

Public Holidays

1 January
1 New Year's Day

17 March
St Patrick's Day

March/April
Good Friday, Easter Monday

May
Labour Day on first Monday; in Northern Ireland also late May

bank holiday on last Monday of the month

June
First Monday of the month in the Republic

July
Orangemen's Day on 12 July in Northern Ireland

August
First Monday in the Republic of Ireland, last Monday in Northern Ireland

October
Autumn Bank Holiday on last Monday (only in Republic of Ireland)

December
Christmas Day and Boxing Day

Festivals

JANUARY
Temple Bar Trad Fest
The biggest Irish music festival in late January consists of more than 200 events in Dublin.

MARCH/APRIL
Fairyhouse Easter Festival
In the village of Fairyhouse, Co. Meath, the horse-racing season starts. The Irish Grand National is held on Easter Monday.

JUNE
Cork Midsummer Festival
High-calibre cultural festival with dance and music

JULY
Galway Arts Festival
This is Ireland's leading festival for visual and performing arts.

AUGUST
Killorglin Puck Fair
At Ireland's oldest traditional fair in Co. Kerry, a goat is crowned.

Auld (Oul') Lammas Fair
Another fair with a long tradition, held in Ballycastle, Co. Antrim.

Appalachina and Bluegrass Festival
In late August and early September, bluegrass fans meet for a weekend of live music sessions in the Ulster American Folk Park.

SEPTEMBER
Lisdoonvarna Matchmaking Festival
One of the world's biggest rendezvous for singles.

Absolutely Fringe
A 16-day festival that draws many thousands of spectators.

OCTOBER
Ballinasloe Horse Fair
One of the oldest events of this kind in Europe

Rose of Tralee Festival
Internationally famous beauty contest

NOVEMBER
Cork International Film Festival
A week of high-class cinema

Treats for Foodies

Once a year the small town of Kinsale goes mad. Guests at the local gourmet festival move from one culinary hotspot to the next and thoroughly enjoy themselves. An eye-witness report.

Maria O'Mahony, the organizer of the festival, slips into the role of Alice in Wonderland: a light-blue dress, a white apron, hooped stockings and a whistle. With a short acoustic blast she directs her flock of 125 well-tended fans through the Mad Hatter's Taste, which takes place on the Saturday of the 40-year-old Kinsale Gourmet Festival, and is also its climax. She is joined on this sunny October day by further characters from Alice in Wonderland to lead the Mad Hatter's Parade, which brings traffic to a halt in this seaside village south of Cork. Queues of cars form when the participants proudly parade their head gear – hats extravagantly adorned with pheasant and ostrich feathers, with artistically arranged playing cards. Mrs Minihane, later to receive the »Hat of the Year« award, balances a Victorian cup on her head. Alongside the Mad Hatters there is the personification of Lewis Carroll's March Hare: Jerry Hurley, with enormous ears on his top hat.

The expression »mad as a hatter« in truth derives from the occupational hazard of hat makers in the 19th century, who inhaled mercury fumes as part of their work, with resultant brain damage. But this doesn't bother David McGrain, a cheerful 39-year-old whose purple hat on an orange wig, black-and-red waistcoat and blaring post horn help to create a merry mood.

Some things are worth waiting for: queuing up outside The White Lady

There are plenty of jokers among the 500 who join the parade, and a number of them have come from the European Continent for the occasion. Some people are wearing a roast turkey – in the form of a soft toy – on their head, others have tweed kilts and Viking helmets, piratical three-cornered hats or wizards' caps in the style of the Harry Potter films.

Culinary Delights

Until late into the afternoon they pass around Kinsale to sample three gigantic buffets at every stop, and make the acquaintance of the best chefs in town. Olivier Queva, for example, who cooks in a French-Irish style and runs Max's along with his wife Anne-Marie. Long queues form up to try quails with warm potato salad, oysters, chutney and walnut bread. Opposite this, Martin Shanahan is at the stove. His restaurant, Fishy Fishy, is famous all over Ireland thanks to a TV show called »Martin's mad about fish«. His cookery books are bestsellers, and of course he serves fish today, in every imaginable way. Paul McBride, chef at the Captain's Table restaurant in Actons Hotel, dishes up goose liver and duck sausage with pear chutney – after all, he has his reputation to think of.

To the sound of Arlo Guthrie's hit *You can get anything you want at Alice's restaurant*, the crowd, no longer so hungry, follows Alice to the second stop – at the end of the world. To be precise, this is the Trident Hotel, World's End. Along the way, the Dormouse appears. For more than 15 years Charles Henderson has played this role in a whole-body costume. He used to be the mayor of Kinsale, standing as an independent. At Pier One Frank O'Reilly takes care of the seafood paté, the crew at the Crack Pot serve almond lollipops with chilli, and David Peare from the Quay Food Company provides delicious cheese. At Man Friday, Philip Morgan opts to serve lamb.

The third stop is the ballroom at The White Lady, where the in-house restaurant triumphs with plaice, chilli and oyster sauce. But the honours go to Pearse and Mary O'Sullivan, whose restaurant Toddies at the Bulman wins the gastronomic prize. Their suppliers are listed to ensure top quality. This is a clinching argument for Elizabeth Creed, a member of the jury, who is committed to sustainability.

At 4 pm the parade moves on to the last stop. In the courtyard of Hamlets Café Bar in the Blue Haven Hotel, steaks and fruit desserts are served. Once more alcoholic drinks are on offer, so the guests need stamina. The party continues with a ball. And on the following day, a seafood buffet is on the programme. The guiding principles are: don't lose your hat, never mislay your sense of humour – and don't even think about the calorie count.

INFORMATION
Kinsale Good Food Circle
71 Main Street, Kinsale, Co. Cork
Tel. 021 477 35 71
www.kinsalerestaurants.com
Tickets: 240 € for all events, Fri 85 € (including dinner), Sat 90 € (including ball), Sun 75 € (with seafood buffet).

Food and Drink

Traditional and Modern

The years when Ireland was the Celtic Tiger gave an innovative shot in the arm to Irish food, helping creative, fresh and healthy dishes to get established and extending the range beyond staples such as Irish stew. New Irish cuisine is characterized by sustainability, an emphasis on regional and local products and outstanding quality, partly thanks to organic ingredients.

This new style of eating, which has already brought forth a number of Michelin-starred chefs, is based on the work of Irish producers. Despite the years of austerity, the trend continues. Cookery schools that specialize in »country house kitchen« are thriving, and the restaurants are full. Gourmet festivals, guided tours or holidays with a culinary theme and food trails demonstrate the quality of Irish cuisine, trends that have created much employment, especially in rural areas. Organic and vegetarian foods are part of the trend, as well as meat production that takes account of animal welfare and sustainable fishing. Good Food Ireland (www.goodfoodireland.ie) has addresses of restaurants and producers.

No need to fear Irish cooking!

Note
Charged service numbers are marked with an asterisk: *0180.

Alongside lamb, beef and poultry, important ingredients are salmon and trout, oysters, lobster and other seafood. A full Irish breakfast consists of cereal or porridge followed by eggs, bacon, sausage, baked beans and a grilled tomato, perhaps with black pudding and accompanied by Irish soda bread, and the obligatory toast and marmalade to round things off. At lunchtime many restaurants have special offers, though a pub lunch is usually cheaper. Afternoon tea may not be in fashion everywhere, but in good hotels and in Dublin there are enough places that serve scones and sandwiches at this time of day. To save money on an evening meal, look out for pre-theatre or early bird menus, usually available between approximately 5 pm and 7 pm.

From breakfast to dinner

? MARCO ⊕ POLO INSIGHT

Price categories

Restaurants (main course)

€€€€ over 25 € (20 £)
€€€ 20–25 € (16–20 £)
€€ 10–20€ (8–16 £)
€ below 10 € (8 £)

Perhaps not to everyone's taste: oysters and a pint of Guinness

Green Grass, Yellow Butter

Where would Irish agriculture be without its prize product – butter? The cows of County Cork and Kerry supply the milk for the world's second-largest producer after the Netherlands.

There is no talk of a crisis in the butter business: through the Irish Dairy Board, products worth 1.8 billion euros are exported annually to Britain, the European Union and the USA. Brand names like Kerrygold (www.kerrygold.com) are known the world over. 100 years ago, the view from the summit of Ireland's »butter mountain« was even better. This was the top of the hill in Shandon, a district in Cork, where the international Butter Exchange opened its doors in 1770 every morning a 6 o'clock on the dot. Until 1900 it was the world's largest butter exchange.

Salted butter was transported from the surrounding area in oak barrels called firkins – a name derived from Danish, meaning a quarter-barrel. Coopers made these barrels in the circular Firkin Crane Building opposite the exchange. Lined up in rows, the quality and quantity of the contents meticulously examined, they were auctioned to be sold on every continent. On maritime routes known as the Butter Roads, the products were taken to ports in Europe, the Caribbean and Australia. The golden age came to an end after the First World War, and the Butter Exchange was converted to a hat factory in 1925.

A common sight in Ireland: happy cows on lush green meadows

Golden yellow and full of flavour:
unsalted Irish butter

Products with a History

A man who knows everything about Irish butter is Peter Foynes, director of the Cork Butter Museum (www.corkbuttermuseum.ie) on O'Connell Square, to the left of the old Butter Exchange building. He keeps the most valuable butter up on the first floor: 1,000-year-old bog butter, a loan from the National Museum in Dublin, where more barrels of butter are exhibited alongside Clonycavan Man, who was discovered in Ballivor (Co. Meath) in 2003. The barrel that has inventory number NMI 1970:31 was buried in a bog near Barownstown West, Rosbarry (Co. Kildare) in about 400–350 BC.

Thanks to the barrels of bog butter, we know about the endlessly long history of Irish butter. In 2004 the veil of mystery that lay over bog butter was finally removed. Since 1857 it has been found in Ireland, Scotland, Norway, the Netherlands and northern Germany. The wax-like, white or yellowish substance was first interred in peat in wooden barrels, baskets and animal hides in Ireland during the Bronze Age (1000 BC), as shown by a discovery in Giltown, Co. Kildare. This was a natural means of preserving foodstuffs in an age without refrigerators. Why were some of the barrels, which weighed up to 35 kg and contained up to 15% fat and lard, never retrieved? This remains an enigma. Were they simply forgotten, or were religious beliefs about offerings involved? The tradition of burying butter in peat continued until the 17th century. Seven years of ripening in the peat improved the taste, making bog butter into rancid »strong butter«. Its aroma was the occasion for all kinds of literary jokes at the expense of the Irish, but butter from the island nevertheless conquered markets across the globe.

From Green to Yellow

Irish butter and other dairy products (milk, yoghurt, cheese, cream, ice-cream) are prized in many countries. What is the secret of this success? No-one who travels in the Emerald Isle can fail to notice: it is the grass! Irish cows are not kept in sheds, eating fodder such as maize, but graze in the lush pastures. The grass that they eat contains the carotene that gives Irish butter its yellow colour. The short-chained fats from this grass also lend a creamy texture to the butter.

The best place to explore the wonderful taste of Irish butter is on the spot, by buying it from Irish shops or paying a visit to the Buttercup Café on O`Connell Square, for example by ordering a sandwich made with O'Keefe's home-made white or brown bread.

Guiness is Good for You

The heart of Ireland beats at St James's Gate in Dublin – the place whe-re Guinness is brewed. Every Irish person knows the »wine of life«, as James Joyce calls the dark beer in his Ulysses, as a medicine, staple food and mood enhancer. But it is not the only kind of beer that gets poured into Irish glasses.

Seen in the cold light of day, Guinness is a dark, top-fermented beer brewed in a special way. For their beer mash the brewers on the River Liffey use, apart from roasted malt, a little grain roasted over beech-wood logs but not malted, to get the dark colour. Hops are then added, the liquor is heated and filtered, then yeast goes into the liquid to do its work. After removal of the yeast, the mixture is called green beer. A few days of storage turn it into a »bright beer«, and the final result is an »Extra Stout« which, despite its name, only has an alcoholic content of 4.3%. Specialist tasters ensure that the taste remains constant. In Ireland, Draught Guinness has the most intensive and fresh taste, as the rapid turnover means the beer does not have to be pasteurized. If you have tried Guinness at home, you will be surprised not just at the taste, but also at the colour of the original version of the beverage: it is much darker, with a nearly white head. Depending on the country where it is to be sold, Guinness is brewed to a different recipe, the strongest selling as »Foreign Extra Stout« in the tropics (see MARCO POLO Insight, p. 332).

A Family Business

However, Guinness is much more than just a beer and the national tipple; it is also the success story of one family and its product, beco-ming a worldwide brand and le-gend. In 1759, Arthur Guinness I came to Dublin from Celbridge, Co. Kildare, with 100 pounds he had inherited. He leased the brewery at St James's Gate for 9,000 years at a rent of 45 pounds per annum. Only until 1799 did he brew light-colou-red beers, as the success of the dark »entire« beer, a blend of seve-ral mashes, began in 1788. As this strong beer was a favourite with porters, it soon came to be called by that name. When Arthur Guin-ness I handed over the brewery to his son, also called Arthur of course, he already dominated the Irish beer and grain market – at one time, nearly the entire Irish grain harvest ended up in the Guinness Brewery. Arthur Guinness II started wooing English beer drin-kers, and soon even the British up-per class partook of the former proletarians' brew.

The population's increasing thirst for Guinness increased the family's fame and wealth. Benjamin Lee, the third in the dynasty, even beca-me mayor of Dublin, was a patron of the arts, and – his most impor-tant deed in a global context – int-roduced bottled Guinness. His suc-cessor Edward Cecil who, in 1899, floated what was by that stage the largest brewery in the world on the stock market, was made a peer.

Since then, the head of the Guinness dynasty has been styled Earl of Iveagh. The fame of the family even extended to literature: James Joyce immortalized Edward Cecil as Noble Buniveagh in *Ulysses*! Cecil also gave the Australian South Pole explorer Douglas Mawson a few bottles of Guinness to leave behind in the ice. Naturally, when the bottles were found again 18 years later, they were perfectly drinkable. On his estate in Phoenix Park, Edward Cecil had a tower built next to his mansion, climbing it every morning after his early-morning tea. The idea was to check whether the chimneys of his brewery at the other end of town were still smoking. To this day, every member of the Guinness family would be able to climb down again, reassured, if the estate had not been sold to the Irish government in 1999. The family seat is now Elveden in Suffolk, England. Edward Cecil was a hard act to follow; his successor Rupert only took to the limelight once as a member of parliament, in an issue regarding his own company. When the disfigurement of the landscape by

All over the world, Guinness is associated with the warm spirit of Ireland

Guinness billboards proclaiming »Guinness is Good for You« was debated, Sir Rupert stood up to reply »But Guinness **Is** Good For You!«

Publicity

This advertising slogan, originally conceived by the crime writer Dorothy Sayers, stands for the hugely successful Guinness publicity in the 1920s and 1940s. Alongside well-known writers, no less famous artists such as Rex Whistler, H M Bateman and the cartoonist Vicky worked for Guinness, illustrating the advertising slogans. The most popular was a series about a zookeeper who recovers with a glass of porter from the surprises the animals constantly hold in store for him (»My Goodness – My Guinness«). This campaign was so successful that in 1953 Guinness had publicity posters printed for the coronation of Elizabeth II, with no slogan and no mention of beer, just a sea lion, a toucan and a kangaroo – everybody knew the story.

Guinness Today

Over time, porter lost its popularity, and was not brewed in England or Ireland after 1973. The last barrel was drunk in a mourning ceremony in a Belfast pub in May 1973. However, Guinness had started to back the stronger stout in good time, to fill the gap left by the demise of porter. Today, Guinness is not only the largest brewery in Europe, but also a multinational group with interests in the car and food industry, a company that owns chains of stores, runs a fleet of cabin cruisers on the lakes and

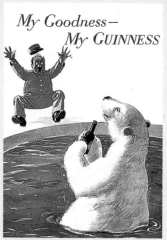

Stories from the zoo – a poster from a famous Guinness advertising campaign

rivers of Ireland and operates a visitor centre, Guinness Storehouse, on the site of the brewery that is second only to Dublin Zoo as the most-visited tourist attraction in Ireland. Even Queen Elizabeth II paid a visit to the Storehouse to enjoy the fantastic view of Dublin from the Gravity Bar. Family members have married into the European aristocracy and have not had to deal with money worries for a long time. Many simple Irish folk, at least the males, still harbour a desire for a dream job: taster at Guinness – they do exist (www.guinness.com)

Small is Beautiful

Beer lovers don't have to drink Guinness when they are in Ireland. Many small breweries have been founded and met with an enthusiastic reception.   Ireland's oldest independent brewer is the HIlden Brewery in Lisburn, Northern Ireland (www.hildenbrewery.co.uk). Porterhouse (www.porterhouse-brewco.com) in Dublin is the second-oldest microbrewery in the country, after the legendary Biddy Early Brewery in Inagh (Co. Clare), which has unfortunately closed down again. Under the management of Oliver Hughes, Porterhouse produces Tempel Bräu, Brainblasta, Plain, Red, Hop Head, Stout, a blond Hersbrucker Pilsner and a true rarity, Oyster Beer. This smooth beer is made with real oysters added to the wort. These treats can be sampled in Temple Bar in Dublin, in Porterhouse North in Dublin, and at the Porterhouse Inn in Bray (Co. Wicklow).

The rival Messrs. Maguire Microbrewery has set up shop very close to Porterhouse. This award-winning brewpub is a Mecca for sports fans (www.messrsmaguire.ie/). Cork's drinkers have the local Murphy's stout, but also the Franciscan Well Brewery (www.franciscanwellbrewery.com). The tradition of brewing at Bunratty Castle, home of Bunratty Mead (www.bunrattymead.net) goes back to the Middle Ages. To go with this old-style Celtic drink, potcheen is distilled here, a spirit officially banned in 1760, produced in a pot still.

Luxury restaurants have begun to serve their own brew. At Acton's Country Pub in Macredin Village (Co. Wicklow), an organic wheat beer, organic stout and organic lager, made on site, flow from the taps. Since 2011, on the upper floor of the Roadside Tavern (www.roadsidetavern.ie), Peter

Crutin has been making his Burren Gold, Red and Black, an excellent choice for washing down smoked fish with potato salad. The small breweries are well able to provide an alternative to Guinness in terms of quality, but on one point they cannot live up to the standards of their big brother: no-one else can offer the panorama from the bar at the top of the Guinness Storehouse in Dublin.

ADDRESSES
Guinness Storehouse
St James Gate, Dublin 8
Tel. 01 453 83 64
www.guinness-storehouse.com
Daily 9.30am– 5pm (July and Aug until 7pm)
Admission: 16.50 € (including one pint of Guinness)

The Porterhouse Temple Bar
16– 18 Parliament Street
Dublin 2
Tel. 01 679 88 47

Porterhouse North
Cross Guns Bridge
Glasnevin, Dublin 9
Tel. 01 830 98 84

Messr Maguire Micro Brewery
O'Connell Bridge
Burgh Quay, Dublin 2
Tel. 01 670 57 77

Franciscan Well Brewery
14b North Mall
Cork
Tel. 021 421 01 30

Roadside Tavern
Lisdoonvarna, Co. Clare
Tel. 065 707 40 84.

Warming and Hearty

Many people think that Irish cooking is potatoes, meat, butter and cabbage – and are not far off. The traditional dishes are experiencing a renaissance in many places.

Boxty and Potato Cake: The potato has long been a staple of the Irish diet, and it is still part of various basic dishes. Boxty (the name comes from the Gaelic »bocht ti«, meaning »poorhouse bread«) is a pancake made from raw potatoes. It is served with pumpkin and sauce, and is especially popular in the counties Mayo, Sligo and Donegal. and the province of Ulster. Potato cakes are made from boiled potatoes and baking soda, and sometimes served at breakfast.

One and One: Like the British, the Irish consume great quantities of fish and chips, known in Dublin slang as »one and one«. The origin of this is said to be an Italian named Giuseppe Cervi, who opened the city's first fish and chip shop in 1885. His wife would ask customers »Uno di questa, uno di quella?« (»one of this, one of the other?«). Since 2003 the kind of fish has to be specified, so instead of plain fish and chips, the outlet has to offer cod and chips or haddock and chips.

Black Pudding: Black pudding often features in the Irish breakfast, sometimes known in Northern Ireland as the Ulster fry. The Black Pudding Company in Clonakilty has been in business since 1880, and modern cuisine combines the product with modish ingredients such as scallops and goat's cheese.

Humble Pie: The name derives from the French word »nomble«, meaning the inner organs of deer. In its finest form the pie contains the heart, liver and kidneys of a stag, with mint added. The name is also used to describe a vegetable hotpot, and even a dessert made with apples.

Irish Stew: A dish famous beyond the shores of Ireland, this casserole of mutton, potatoes, onions and herbs is simmered for several hours. Although it is the Irish classic, it is not often eaten by the Irish themselves, being regarded as a poor man's meal. However, it does feature in new Irish cuisine, sometimes in variations using poultry or beef instead of lamb.

Dublin Lawyer: This is a characteristic dish of new Irish cuisine. Lobster or some other shellfish is lightly braised in butter, then flambéed in whiskey and cooked in double cream with lemon juice and mustard. Potatoes and salad go well with it. There is even an option for following a seafood main course with a dessert that has marine ingredients: carageen moss jelly« is made from edible seaweed, milk, sugar and lemon zest.

Coddle and Colcannon: Colcannon is another example of poor man's fare and therefore rarely found today. It consists of cabbage, mashed potatoes, carrots and turnips is to this day considered poor man's fare. Coddle, too, is a stew, usually made with potatoes, bacon and sausage..

The Irish are great tea drinkers. Where alcoholic drinks are concerned, the best-known beer is of course Guinness, and the leading brand of whiskey is Bushmills. Irish orchards produce the apples for excellent cider, for example the Magner brand.

Drinks

A restaurant with a full licence can serve all alcoholic drinks, while some only have a wine licence. The minimum legal age for buying alcoholic drinks is 18, and even in the company of adults, minors are not officially allowed to stay in pubs later than 9 pm. Be aware also of the ban on drinking in public places, especially in Northern Ireland. In certain places heavy fines have to be paid for disregarding the regulation.

Pubs, especially the famous singing pubs, are an important part of the Irish way of life, despite the smoking ban and high prices. Most pubs are open from 12 noon until about 11 pm, or longer on Fridays and Saturdays. Tourism Ireland certifies pubs, awarding them the title of »quality assured pubs«.

MARCO ⊕ POLO TIP

 How to make Irish coffee

In order to make a proper Irish coffee or Gaelic coffee, firstly a tall glass needs to be rinsed in hot water, then real Irish whiskey is added to a little sugar, followed by hot strong black coffee. The whole thing is then stirred and topped by a generous portion of fresh cream or whipped cream. Irish Mist – made on a similar basis to Irish whiskey – is a liquor supposedly from Tullamore, where they add heather honey to the whiskey.

Tips of 5% or 10% in restaurants are normal, either in cash or by adding an amount to the credit card payment.

Tipping

Shopping

Ireland to Take Home

Ireland has a host of attractive souvenirs to keep memories alive after your trip has ended. Classics such as Irish whiskey can, of course, be bought at home or ordered online. This does not apply to craft products, by contrast, or to increasingly popular, high-quality Irish foods, which are a good way to put the tastes of the island on your dining table.

Traditional craft work is still done all over Ireland. Potters, weavers, basket makers and glass blowers: all of these handmade products have their fans. Visitors who want to be creative themselves have the opportunity in countless workshops, and the results are fine souvenirs to take home. An Grianán (www.an-grianan.ie) and the Crafts Council of Ireland (ccoi.ie) provide information about such courses. The National Craft Gallery in Kilkenny (www.nationalcraftgallery.ie) is a source for finding craft exhibitions.

Craft work

> **? MARCO POLO INSIGHT**
>
> *Opening times*
>
> Most shops open from 9am to 6pm (in Northern Ireland until 5.30pm), and larger stores stay open on Thursdays until 8pm or 9pm (on other days, too, in Northern Ireland). Some places have Sunday opening from 12 noon to 5pm (1pm to 5pm in Northern Ireland).

Typical Irish products, often of excellent quality, include hand-woven tweed, fine lace, pullovers, pipes, porcelain and earthenware, musical instruments, silver, jewellery and hand-polished crystal. Smoked salmon and hand-knitted Aran sweaters are popular items to take home, and there is no shortage of antique shops.

All sorts of weird and wonderful things can be found on fleamarkets such as the one that takes place every Friday in Limerick, which conveys a good impression of everyday life in Ireland, or the Dublin Flea Market at Newmarket Square, where at least 60 stalls, protected from the vagaries of the Irish weather, can be found on the last Sunday in the month.

Fleamarkets

The cheapest sources for designer and brand products are the outlet centres in Blarney, Killarney and Banbridge (Northern Ireland), where you can often get up to 70% reduction on the list price. Dublin, Belfast, Cork and Galway also have a wide selection of shops.

Outlet centres

Culinary treats on a Dublin market

From Farm to Fork

Organic food produced locally is in increasing demand in Ireland, and more and more of it is being supplied. The motto »from farm to fork«, which promotes both quality and sustainability, has been adopted by hundreds of Irish producers, large and small. Their produce can be purchased at many farmers' markets.

The new local »food heroes« supply nutritious, healthy and above all delicious foodstuffs. They are apple growers and trout farmers, owners of smokehouses, makers of jam and chutney, meat producers, wheat farmers and processors of food. There are bakeries that make excellent bread, producers of organic cheese and country butchers, often family companies, that gain an international reputation. This has not escaped the notice of the restaurant owners and hoteliers, who carefully note on their menus the provenance of the food and its characteristics.

Impressive Quality

This verifiable supply chain from producer to consumer works well. It is monitored and supported by organizations such as Good Food Ireland, the Organic Trust Ireland (www.organic-trust.org) and Slow Food Ireland (www.slowfoodireland.com). Local and regional initiatives also promote quality assurance. All of this is boosting and reviving rural areas and creating jobs, even in times of economic crisis.

Visitors to Ireland can find out for themselves by sampling products on the spot – Gubbeen or Durrus organic cheese, home-baked soda bread, cheese from the Ardsallagh Goat Farm (Carrighwohill, Co. Cork) or organically reared duck from the Silver Hill Foods Farm in Emyvale (Co. Monaghan).

Many products can also be bought online, for example via Good Food Ireland. Other suppliers such as the Burren Smoke House have a delivery service. But the most enjoyable way to try these foods is to look for them at source: dried seaweed from the west coast, organic rapeseed oil from Newgrange, or oysters from Oysterhaven near Kinsale.

Good Food Ireland, founded in 2006 by Margaret Jeffares, has lists of all participating producers and processors, restaurants and hotels, organizes gourmet tours and advertises food festivals. GFI also sets up direct contact to accommodation, producers, shops and cookery schools, provides gastronomic news from Ireland, wine and restaurant reviews and a host of wonderful recipes. Real foodies like to shop at farmers' markets or country markets, as well as in farm shops. The Irish Ministry of Agriculture promotes such markets and the Irish Food Board (Bord Biá) has lists of all markets, from Carlow to Wicklow, some of which are linked musical or other cultural events (www.bordbia.ie/farmersmarkets). Food trails such as those in Dublin (www.fabfoodtrails.com) and Cork are a good way to find little-known markets and suppliers. Items to watch out for in Ireland are organic cheese, smoked fish, chutney and rapeseed oil.

ADDRESSES
Good Food Ireland (GFI)
Ballykelly House, Drinagh, Wexford
Tel. 053 915 86 93
www.goodfoodireland.ie

Dungarvan Farmers' Market
Grattan Square, Dungarvan
Co. Waterford
Tel. 086 394 05 64
www.dungarvanfarmersmarket.com
Thu 9.30am–2pm
One of the most interesting and lively markets in Ireland.

Naas Farmers' Market
Friary Lane (Trax Brasserie)
Naas, Co. Kildare, tel. 087 608 01 19
www.naasfarmersmarket.com
Sat 10am–3pm
A colourful market with lots of live music, and crafts too on the first Saturday in the month.

Temple Bar Food Market
Meeting House Square
Temple Bar, Dublin
Tel. 01 677 22 55, www.templebar.ie
Sat 10am–4.30pm
Fresh produce, including plenty of organic foodstuffs. You can plan your own three-course menus (see information online) which are then prepared on Meeting House Square.

First taste, then buy – this is not a problem at a farmers' market

Sport and Outdoors

A Sports-Loving Island

Almost everyone in Ireland is involved in sport in one way or another, as an active participant or as a spectator. The importance of sports is demonstrated by high TV ratings and the Irish love of betting. From A for angling to Z for zip-wires in the treetops of adventure parks, there is every opportunity for holidaymakers to share in the Irish love of sports. Even in the pub, where snooker and darts are played. As spectators, the Irish are enthusiastic, well-informed, fair and peaceful.

ON AND AROUND WATER

Swimmers find good conditions on the south coast, which is lapped by the warm Gulf Stream. Many sandy beaches have received a Blue Flag award, and have lifeguards. Be aware of the local rules and advice, as sea currents and the Atlantic waves hold dangers. Many lakes are also suitable for swimming.

Swimmig and bathing

The Atlantic Ocean and the Irish Sea are excellent sailing territory. For longer jaunts, the southwest of Ireland is especially popular, but many yachts can also be seen on Ireland's lakes. The Royal Cork Yacht Club, founded in 1720, is thought to be the world's oldest. Various sailing schools and centres offer courses for beginners and experienced sailors.

Sailing

Thanks to steady winds, Ireland's coasts are paradise for windsurfers. Sandhill near Sligo attracts advanced practitioners, and other good locations are Kinsale, Killaloe, Rosslare, Caherdaniel, Schull and Carlingford.

Other water sports

There are good opportunities for water skiing and wakeboarding on rivers and lakes, and especially along the flat coastal areas. Necessary equipment and boats can be rented at, among other places, the Blessington Lakes, the Craigavon Lakes and Lough Muckno.

The country's numerous rivers and lakes are ideal for rowing and the use of inflatables. Information is available from the Irish Amateur Rowing Union.

Rowing, canoeing and kayaking are possible on many waterways. Furthermore, white water is found on the Liffey, Barrow, Nore, Boyne, Slaney, Lee, Shannon and Suir.

The Irish landscape is perfect for riding

»It was this big!«

Numerous rivers and a long coastline make Ireland a classic destination for anglers. Fish are caught on Irish streams and rivers with a total length of 26,000km/16,000 miles, on lakes with a total surface area of 200,000 hectares (770 sq miles), and not least in the seas around the island.

Fishing, according to Kevin Crowley from the Galway-based Inland Fisheries Ireland, is much more important for Irish tourism than golf. Thousands of anglers from many different countries come to Ireland every year for the fishing. No wonder: Crowley says that Ireland is number one in Europe for trout, and is one of the world's best countries for salmon fishing. On the Ferguson River in County Clare, brown trout weighing 5kg (over 10lb) are caught, and sometimes lucky anglers land a specimen weighing 10kg (over 20lb).

What to Catch Where?

The situation on the high seas has also improved. Many salmon farmers have ceased business, for ecological reasons. They were an indirect cause of the parasites that infested sea trout, and are now much less of a problem. Moreover, since 2006 drift-net fishing has been prohibited. Since then the stocks of salmon in rivers such as the Erriff in Connemara have increased significantly. Despite this, the best spots for fishing are not overcrowded. Usually no more than two rods per site are to be seen: there are 150 salmon rivers in Ireland. Thanks to the construction of fish ladders, the ecological damage that arose when hydroelectric plants were built in the 1930s and

1940s has now long been eliminated.

Most visitors come for the game fishing, i.e. trout and salmon. The best places for this are in the west of the country, for example on Lough Corrib and in County Mayo. The noble art of fly fishing is cultivated here. Those who go to Delphi Lodge (www.delphilodge.ie), Ireland's institution for fly fishing, may be lucky enough to meet Peter O'Reilly. Peter is no longer young, but he still gives courses at the Fly Fishing School, and is regarded as the Irish guru of the sport. Beginners start off with »dry fishing«, practice at casting the rod on a lawn. Peter's books on the subject are holy writ for anglers (http://oreillyflyfishing.com).

Ireland's predatory fish is the pike, which can grew to be 20kg/45lb. The Shannon-Erne Waterway connects the main pike-fishing regions: Cavan, Leitrim and Shannon. In Cavan alone there are 365 lakes. Pike can be caught all year round in the larger lakes, although the chances are higher in the winter months.

The Irish coast is 5,600km/3,500 miles long. Outstandingly good grounds for deep-sea fishing can be found here. Sharks, rays, haddock, cod, mullet, hake, sea bream and other species are caught from spring until autumn.

What You Need to Know

It is important to respect the closed season from late August to early January (for trout from November to January) and other regulations. Ireland Fisheries provides detailed brochures for all regions and fish species, and also operates and extremely useful website at www.fisheriesireland. ie. To fish for salmon and sea trout, you require a licence. The regulations, which change from year to year, can be read online. There is a maximum catch per angler per season per place of ten salmon. From 12 May to 31 August, a daily limit of three salmon or sea trout (longer than 40cm/16in) applies. Often only »catch and release« is permitted. Furthermore, blue marker tapes must be installed and catches have to be recorded in a catch book.

Licences are not needed for catching trout, but it goes without saying that day or season licences have to be purchased and a fee paid per catch. This, and the size of the catch, are monitored. It is therefore also important to know how the fish are measured: in Ireland the lower, shorter fin is taken for measurement. It is not unusual for a blind eye to be turned as long as the angler seems to have no malicious intent. For fishing on the Atlantic coast, too, it is necessary to be appraised of the regulations. Licences are obtainable from Ireland Fisheries, at specialist anglers' shops and online at www. salmonlicences.ie. On unknown waters it is recommended to employ a ghillie. If you charter a boat for sea fishing, beware of treacherous shallows, reefs and rocks – care is required.

A peaceful idyll on Lough Muckno

More than Sports

Irish culture preserves many kinds of sport, some of which can be traced back to prehistoric times. 800,000 Irish people, almost 20 per cent of the population, are members of 2,800 sports clubs that keep this heritage alive. The Gaelic Athletic Association (GAA), one of the world's biggest associations for amateur sports, organizes these games.

The sacred site for spectators and active participants is Dublin's Croke Park Stadium, which for a long time was used exclusively for Gaelic sports. The GAA Museum at the stadium preserves the history and documents the connected issue of national identity since the 19th century. Until 1972 Irish sports fans who merely attended a game of an »English« sport such as rugby or football faced the threat of expulsion from the GAA. Since 2001 British nationals have been permitted to join, and in 2007 the first games of rugby and football were staged at Croke Park.

Hurling and Camogie

The earliest descriptions of hurling, which is among the fastest of team sports, go back to the mythical hero Cóchulainn and the Battle of Moytura in the 14th century BC. It seems likely that hurling originated in martial arts, but this can only be speculation.

A match is played between two sides of 15 »hurlers« each. They carry a hurley (or camán), a stick between 64cm/25in and 97cm/38in in length, wider at the end. The leather ball (sliotar) weighs 120g/4oz, has a diameter of 69–72cm (approx. 2.75in), and flies around at speeds of up to 150kmh/95mph. Since 2011 the wearing of helmets has been compulsory, and body-

checking is not allowed. As in rugby, at each end of the pitch is a goal, 6.5m/21ft wide with posts 7m/23ft high that are connected by a crossbar at a height of 2.5m(8ft. When the ball goes under the crossbar, a goal has been scored; if it goes above, a point is awarded. Two halves of 30 minutes, in county games 35 minutes, each are played. The highlights of the season are the all-Ireland finals at Croke Park. The best hurling teams are from Kilkenny (34 championships), Tipperary, Limerick, Waterford and Wexford. More than 100,000 players are registered in Ireland, and hurling was an unofficial Olympic sport in 1904.

Camogie, the women's version, is equally popular. 100,000 Irishwomen play the game in 550 clubs. The rules are the same as for hurling, but a team has only 12 players, the stick is smaller, and physical contact is not allowed.

Gaelic Football

A sport with even greater popularity than hurling is Gaelic football (also called peil, peil ghaelach or caid), which 34 per cent of all sports fans watch and 180,000 people organized in 2,500 clubs actively play. The two sports together mobilize more people than football and rugby. Gaelic football is played on a field with posts like that used for hurling, also with 15 players in each team. The match consists of two halves of 35 minutes each. The ball, made from 18 strips of leather, looks like a volleyball, weights 370–425g/13–15oz and is 69–74cm/27–29in in circumference. The earliest mention of the game dates from 1308. Those who looked down on this wild Gaelic game used to refer to it as bogball. The eagerly awaited climax of the season is the all-Ireland final on the third or fourth Sunday in September, held at Croke Park.

Gaelic Handball

In the Irish version of handball (liathróid láimhe), the players throw or hit the ball against a wall using their hand or fist, aiming to do so in such a way that the opponent does not reach it – rather like squash without a racquet. Singles and doubles are played. The court measures 12.2 x 6.1m/40 x 20 ft, and the wall is 6.1m/20ft high. Only the player who serves can score a point. The annual championships take place in Castlebar (www.gaahandball.ie).

Road Bowling

On Sunday mornings it is better not to drive along country roads, especially in County Armagh and County Cork. Many roads are then closed to hold road bowling (ból an bhóthair) competitions between village teams, individuals and club teams. This game is like golf without a club, and the ball is propelled along a rural road. The ball is made of iron, weighs 800g/28oz, and resembles a tennis ball in size and shape. The course has a length of at least 4m/2.5 miles, and the winner is the person or team that covers the distance with the smallest number of throws. The contests attract a lot of knowledgeable spectators, bets are placed, and honour is at stake. »Road showers«, who have a role like caddies, show the way for the players. Others shout »Fág a bealach!«, »Clear the way!«. This call was once a feared battle cry, and now keeps the spectators in a safe position behind the players. It has sufficient similarities with a game played in Frisia to permit a European championship to be held every four years.

Road Bowling in 1936

At Clew Bay, one of the most beautiful golf courses in Ireland

NORTHERN IRELAND
Ardglass Golf Club
Castle Place Ardglass
Tel. 028 44841219
www.ardglassgolfclub.com
Course of the year in 2011, set in a natural landscape, and challenging

City of Derry Golf Club
Victoria Road, Londonderry
Tel. 028 71 346369
www.cityofderrygolfclub.com
18-hole and 9-hole course. Visitors welcome on weekdays before 4.30pm

Clandeboye Golf Club
Conlig, Newtownards, Co. Down
Tel. 028 91271767
Two 18-hole courses in a park and heath landscape. Afternoon tea can be booked online..

Foyle Golf Centre
12-14 Alder Road, Londonderry
Tel. 028 71352222
www.foylegolfcentre.co.uk
18-hole and 9-hole courses. The 15th is by far the most difficult hole.

Massereene Golf Club
51 Lough Road, Antrim
Tel. 028 94428096
www.massereene.com
A wonderful and varied course on Lough Neagh, with a stunning view from the 7th tee.

Royal Portrush
Dunluce Road, Portrush
Tel. (028) 70822311
www.royalportrushgolfclub.com
Two of the world's best and most difficult courses. The Valley Link (18 holes, par 70) is a hidden gem.

Right by the sea: Royal Portrush Golf Club

Further addresses

CANOEING AND ROWING
Irish Canoe Union
Tel. 01 6 251105
www.canoe.ie

Rowing Ireland
Tel. 021 6 251105
www.canoe.ie

HORSE-DRAWN CARAVANS
Irish Horse Drawn Caravans
www.irishhorsedrawncaravans.
com
Here you can read everything you
need to know about these trips.

IRELAND BY BICYCLE
Raleigh Rent-a-Bike
www.raleigh.ie
A database with hire points all
over Ireland

Dublin City Cycling
www.dublincitycycling.ie
www.dublinbikes.ie (bookings)
500 bikes can be hired at 40 different places across Dublin. Membership for 3 days costs 2 €, hire
for 3 hours also 2 €

Dublin City Bike Tours
Raleigh House
Kylemore Road, Dublin 10
Tel (01) 6 261333
www.raleigh.ie

Raleigh Rent-a-Bike
Meeting point: Isaac's Hostel
2-5 Frenchman's Lane, Dublin 1
Tel 087 134 18 66
www.dublincitybiketours.com
Tours start daily at 10am (24 €),
arrive 30 minutes earlier. From
May to mid-September, afternoon

tours are held at 2pm at weekends.

Cycle NI
www.cycleni.com
The bike network in Northern Ireland

Explore Ireland Tours
Tel. 087 250 19 83
www.exploreirelandtours.com
A tip: Sabine Murphy shows you
the real Ireland. Reasonable prices
and a good mix of activity and
culture. Many tours go along the
coast, with options for kayaking,
horse riding, surfing and whale
watching.

SAILING AND
WINDSURFING
Irish Sailing Association
Tel. 01 2 800239
www.sailing.ie

**Irish Windsurfing
Association**
www.windsurfing.ie

SCUBA DIVING
Irish Underwater Council
Tel. 01 2 844601
http://diving.ie/site

WALKING
Walk Northern Ireland
www.walkni.com

WATER SKIING
**Irish Waterski and Wake-
board Federation**
Tel. 01 285 52 05
www.irishwwf.ie

TOURS

Nature trips along coasts warmed by the Gulf Stream, art and culture in the interior, quiet fishing villages, gardens and parks – a holiday on the Emerald Isle is unforgettable.

Tours of Ireland

The road network in Ireland has improved greatly, making exploration of the island a wonderful experience. The five routes suggested here show different aspects of the country.

Tour 1   **Trail of the Stones**
From Dublin, the route goes to Newgrange and up to Armagh and Belfast in Northern Ireland. The Causeway Coastal Road then leads across to Derry.
►page 141

Tour 2   **Forests, Monks, Long Beaches**
Starting from Dublin and sights on the edge of the city, the tour goes to the Wicklow Mountains, an area settled for over 7,000 years whose natural and cultural attractions were discovered long ago for Hollywood films. On the way south to Wexford, the centre of the south-eastern region, lie coastal towns with spas and sandy beaches.
►page 144

Tour 3   **Culinary Treats, Cliffs and Heritage**
Cork, for many the alternative capital of Ireland, is the starting point for a culinary trip through delightful scenery on the »Irish Riviera«. The route passes along a coast pampered by the Gulf Stream with lush vegetation to the Killarney National Park and back to Cork.
►page 147

Tour 4   **Whiskey, Salmon and the Wild West**
This is an ideal tour for those who are new to Ireland. Distilleries, the river Shannon, monasteries and the family-friendly town of Ennis give an impression of Irish life. The Burren, Galway and Connemara possess both natural and urban charm, and the Aran Islands are a real highlight.
►page 150

Tour 5   **From Sea to Sea**
This route connects Dublin on the Irish Sea with Sligo on the Atlantic Ocean, then follows the wild, rugged coast of Donegal to the north and to Derry.
►page 150

ATLANTIC OCEAN

Inishowen Peninsula

Dunfanaghy

** Giant's Causeway

Fair Head

* Gleanveagh National Park

* Grianán of Aileach

* Derry/ Londonderry

* Glens of Antrim

Larne

* Belfast

Donegal Town

Enniskillen

* Armagh

TOUR 1

Banbridge

Céide Fields

Ballina

* Sligo

TOUR 5

** Monasterboice

* Boyle

Carrick-on-Shannon

** Newgrange

Kells

Irish Sea

** Connemara

* Lough Corrib

Athlone

* Hill of Tara

** DUBLIN

* Clifden

* Galway

TOUR 4

** Clonmacnoise

Naas

Bray

** Aran Islands

Ballyvaughan

Loughrea

** Powerscourt Estate

TOUR 2

Lisdoonvarna

Gort

Portlaoise

** Glendalough

Wicklow

** Cliffs of Moher

Roscrea

Carlow

Macreddin

Avoca Village

Ennistymon

Ennis

Arklow

* Limerick

** Kilkenny

* Adare

Cashel

Enniscorthy

Tipperary

Saint George's Channel

* Wexford

* Dingle Peninsula

Waterford

Rosslare

* Killarney

Youghal

* Ring of Kerry

TOUR 3

* Cork

* Kenmare

Celtic Sea

* Glengariff

* Bantry

* Kinsale

Drombeg Stone Circle

50 km
31 mi

© BAEDEKER

Travelling in Ireland

Driving There are many ways to explore the Emerald Isle: by car, motorbike, bike, by houseboat, kayak or horse-drawn caravan. You can cross the island on long-distance walking trails or sail around its coasts. A car trip is ideal for exploring the southwest, or the south and southeast coast. In the barren west and northwest, too, a car is the best way to get around. The east coast of the Republic of Ireland and Northern Ireland has many cultural attractions and vibrant urban life.

As in Britain, in Ireland people **drive on the left**. The years of economic growth up to 2008 gave the country many new roads in all categories, wider roads, improvements to the surface of existing roads and better signposting. It is still helpful to have a satnav device with software for the Irish road system. Potholes are less of a problem nowadays than **dips and rises**, where it is advisable to go slowly, and there are still country routes where sheep or cows regularly block the way. There is so much to see along the way that it is sensible not to plan long stretches of driving each day. If you have not booked accommodation, look out for a B & B in the early afternoon at the latest, especially in the high season.

Monasterboice is famous for its spectacular high crosses

Dublin, Belfast, Cork and Galway have excellent, low-cost systems of **local transport** (buses, in Dublin trams and local trains too). Tourist travel passes are available in Belfast and Dublin. Coach services connect these two cities with all other counties. Round trips with bus passes are possible, and the **coaches** also transport bicycles. Ireland's international airports all have bus connections. The **Irish railways** move at a leisurely pace, but the routes are attractive, e.g. between Dublin and Cork, are scenically attractive. The service, including refreshments on board, is good. Tickets can be purchased online, and the ticket machines at stations are easy to operate.

Public transport

Trail of the Stones   Tour 1

Start: Dublin   **Length of Tour:** approx.
End: Derry/Londonderry   320km/200 miles
                                 Duration: at least four days

An ideal tour for fans of ancient stones of every kind, such as the Newgrange megaliths with their spiral decorations , the delicately worked high crosses and the round tower of Monasterboice, the buildings of Belfast or the 40,000 basalt pillars of the spectacular Giant's Causeway up on the wild north coast in the Antrim Coast and Glens region, where nature itself was the creator. The tour ends in Derry/Londonderry with its 400-year-old city wall.

The starting point is ❶** **Dublin** , the capital of the Republic of Ireland, where the wealth of attractions makes a stay of several days worthwhile. If you have little time, take a day at least to get to know the charm of the city.

The tour begins by crossing the Beckett Bridge and passing through the tunnel of the M1, heading for Belfast. In the Boyne Valley stop to admire a UNESCO World Heritage site that was not excavated until the 1970s, the 5,200-year-old burial mounds of ❷** **Newgrange**. Do not be deterred by the crowds of visitors here, as Newgrange is an outstanding sight. Continuing the drive, it is worth the detour to Beaulieu House a short distance northeast of Drogheda to see the museum of sports cars. At Oldbridge the Battle of the Boyne Visitor Centre, to the west of Drogheda and the M1, brings the military events of 1690 to life.
Take the Drogheda North exit to reach the former monastic settlement of ❸** **Monasterboice**, which is famous for its spectacular

high crosses with imagery that takes visitors back to early Christian times.

The route continues to Northern Ireland. Near Newry the A28 forks off to beautiful ❸∗**Armagh**, whose surrounding area is well-known for its apple trees. The planetarium and its astropark are also worth a visit. Café Rumour (Marketplace, www.rumourcoffee.com) is a good place to take a break. The status of Armagh as a religious centre is evident not only at St Patrick's Cathedral but also in the prohibition on alcoholic drinks on church land. Take heed of this, as the penalty for breaching the rule is a fine of £ 500.

If you are not in a hurry, follow the St Patrick Trail from Armagh via Downpatrick to Bangor. The country road to ❺**Banbridge** passes through lush green Ulster scenery. At the edge of town on the road to Newry is a visitor centre with the studio of the sculptor F.E. McWillian (1909–92). In the garden here, note the impressive works »Legs Static« (1978) and the bronze »Woman in a Bomb Blast No. 1« (1974).

In 30 minutes the A1 takes you to the southern suburbs of ❻∗**Belfast**, where the Queen's Quarter is a recommended place to visit. Beyond this, the dominant theme in the city is the Titanic – even when enjoying an evening pint in Robinson's Pub, where a glass case displays the doll Philomena, rescued from the waters of the Atlantic.

North of Belfast, the A2 is the well-signposted, 200km/125-mile Causeway Coastal Route. The holiday experience starts beyond ❼**Larne**, but before that it is worth stopping to admire the views of Belfast Lough in Newtownabbey and at the mighty Carrickfergus Castle, 15km/10mi northeast of Belfast. If you have time, consider a detour to Island Magee, a peninsula.

On the north side of Larne (expect diversions here due to long-term bridge construction), the Carnfunnock Country Park holds attractions for the whole family, including a miniature railway and three treasure trails.

The route now follows an excellent road, popular with bike tourists and motorcyclists. There are lots of laybys and picnic spots with views of the Irish Sea. Magnificent palm trees grow along the bay at Ballygally. At various points, a side trip is possible heading inland along panoramic roads into the ❽∗**Glens of Antrim**, nine lovely valleys. leading inland.

For a breathtaking drive, closed to buses and campervans, take the steep, narrow coastal road to the viewing points at ❾**Fair Head,** northeast of Ballycastle. This is Ireland at its finest.

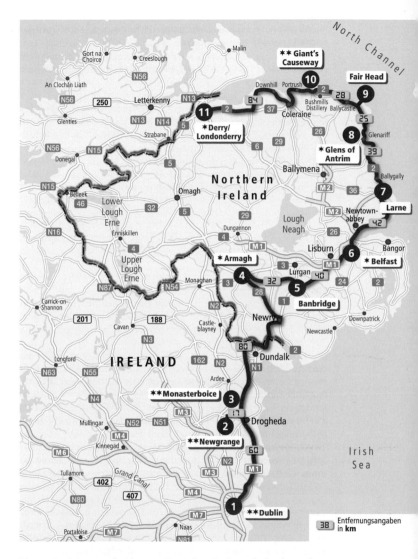

The swinging rope bridge at Carrick-a-Rede and the legendary
⑩**Giant's Causeway with its bizarrely formed basalt pillars are
highlights for visitors of all ages. The same does not apply to Bushmills Distillery, which whiskey fans can visit in the town of the same
name, almost 20km/13 miles west of Ballycastle. At the ruins of Dun-

luce Castle begins the western section of the Causeway Coastal Route. Places to stop here are the beaches at Portrush and Port Stewart, but the true highlight here is a visit to Mussenden Temple followed by the beach at Downhill, perhaps the most beautiful on the north coast.

The tour reaches its destination in ⑪***Derry**, the second-largest city in the north of Ireland and worth a full day's visit to see its massive and exceptionally well-preserved town walls alone. The first British city to be named European Capital of Culture, Derry on the east bank of the river Foyle has a great deal of charm. A walk along the new promenade and across the Peace Bridge leads to Ebrington Square and the Mute Meadow art installation.

Tour 2 Forests, Monks and Long Beaches

Start: Dublin
End: Rosslare

Length of Tour: approx. 240km/150 miles
Duration: at least two days

Deep forests, often mysteriously shrouded in mist, and endless sandy beaches characterize the quiet, idyllic southeast of Ireland. And a culinary garden of Eden lies practically on Dublin's doorstep.

The N11 and M11 take you out of ❶**** Dublin** quickly, but a more scenic route goes through Dun Laoghaire to the Martello Tower in Sandycove and the Joyce Museum. Perhaps the weather is fair enough for a dip in the Irish Sea at Forty Foot Cove, a famous bathing spot. It is only 12km/8 miles from the centre of Dublin, easily reached with the DART local train. The place is described in »Ulysses«, and also by Flann O'Brian in »At Swim-Two-Birds«.

Two attractions for children are the programme of drama at Dalkey Castle, 18km/11 miles southeast of Dublin, and the National Sealife Centre in ❷**Bray** one of Ireland's largest seaside resorts. Hiring a bike is a good way to explore Bray.

It is not far from here to Enniskerry to visit the beautiful ❸**** Powerscourt Estate**. You can spend a whole day here, looking at the house and park, picnicing in the Japanese Garden and admiring the rare plants that are on sale in the garden centre.

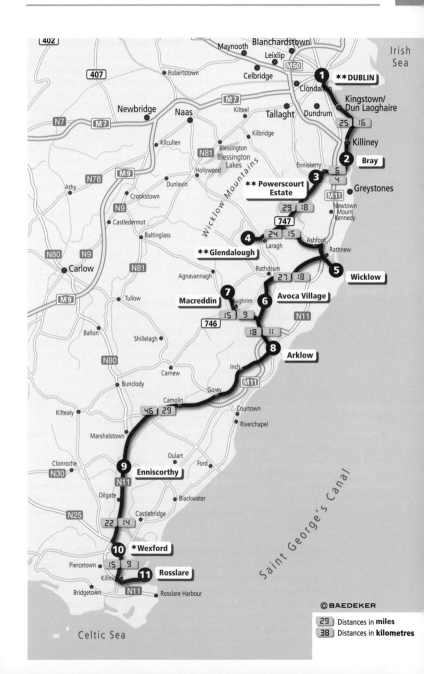

402
407
Maynooth Blanchardstown
Leixlip
Robertstown Celbridge **M50**
1 **DUBLIN**
Clondalkin
Kingstown/
Dun Laoghaire
M7
Newbridge Naas Kilteel Tallaght Dundrum
25 **16**
N7 **M7**
Kilcullen Kilbridge
Killiney
N81
Blessington **2** **Bray**
Blessington
Lakes
Enniskerry **6**
N78 **M9**
Hollywood **Powerscourt** **3** **4**
Athy
Dunlavin **Estate** Greystones
Crookstown **M11**
Castledermot Newtown
Mount
Kennedy
Baltinglass **747**
N80 **N9**
4 **24** **15**
Carlow **N81**
Laragh Ashford
Agnavannagh Rathdrum Rathnew
M9 Tullow **5**
Glendalough **Wicklow**
7 **27** **18**
Ballon Oughrim **6** **Avoca Village**
Macreddin
Shillelagh **15** **9**
N80 **N11**
Carnew **746**
Bunclody **18** **11**
Kiltealy Camolin **8** **Arklow**
46 **29** Courtown
Marshalstown Riverchapel
Oulart **M11**
Gorey
Clonroche Ford Inch
N30 **9** **Enniscorthy**
N11
Oilgate Blackwater
N25 Castlebridge
22 **14**
10 **Wexford**
Piercetown **15** **9**
Killinick **11** **Rosslare**
Bridgetown **N11** Rosslare Harbour

Irish
Sea

Wicklow Mountains

Saint George's Canal

Celtic Sea

© BAEDEKER

29 Distances in **miles**
38 Distances in **kilometres**

The legendary monastic ruins of ❹** **Glendalough** are reached on magnificent roads through the Wicklow Mountains. The hiking trails all around are terrific! Those with a car can do a circuit taking in the Blessington Lakes and the village of Hollywood. The association with the Californian movie industry does not deceive: famous films such as »Michael Collins« and »Excalibur« were made in the Wicklow Mountains. Via Rathnew the R763 goes back to the coast at Wicklow, which is not only a good base for a few days' walking, but also has sights that are worth half a day or more, for example Mount Usher Gardens, Wicklow Gaol and the view from the lighthouses at Wicklow Head.

South of Rathdrum there is an opportunity to relax in tranquil surroundings in Avondale Forest Park, with a visit to Avondale House and the enchanting Meeting of the Waters.

At the ❻ **Avoca Village** you can buy woollens. The hit BBC series Ballykissangel was filmed here, although in fact the original scene of the stories is Killorglin in County Kerry. However, Avoca and Enniskerry were a better match for melodramas in Baile Coisc Aingeal, the »town of the fallen angels«.

From the church in Aughrim, a signed path leads to the village of ❼ **Macreddin**, which was abandoned in the 19th century. Pretty modern cottages can be hired in Macreddin Village. For a little bit of luxury, stay at Ireland's top organic hotel, the Brook Lodge & Wells Spa. Golf, horse riding and bike tours are activities that make it worth staying longer in this region.

After a visit to the Maritime Museum in ❽ * **Arklow**, where the yacht paintings by Ruben Chappell are a highlight, drive south to Gorey. Here Nóirin's Bakehouse & Café in McDermott Street elevates baking to an art form. The cakes, tarts and quiches are irresistible. For outdoor activity, head to the Gravity Forest Adventure Park near Gorey. If you are well equipped for walking, go south along the beaches.

Next stop is ❾ **Enniscorthy**, an attractive little town on the banks of the Slaney. The museum in Enniscorthy Castle is dedicated to the Easter Rising of 1916. Here the long-established potteries have an excellent reputation – for example the renowned Hillview Pottery and Carleys Bridge Pottery, founded in 1654 and the oldest in Ireland.

The attractions around the picturesque coastal town of ❿ * **Wexford**, where the Slaney runs into the sea, are the Irish National Heritage Park and the wild geese at the Wexford Wildlife Reserve. Harbour Thrills runs boat trips to Ireland's largest colony of seals.

South of Wexford the tour reaches the resort of ⓫ **Rosslare**, situated on a wide bay with a sandy beach 8km/5 miles long, where Kelly's Resort Hotel & Spa has been indulging its guests since 1895.

Culinary Treats, Cliffs and Heritage

Tour 3

Start: Cork
End: Cork

Length of Tour: approx. 290km/180 miles
Duration: at least two days

Stunningly beautiful roads cross the wild, lonely southwest, warmed by the Gulf Stream. West Cork is Ireland's garden of Eden, a culinary paradise. There are no less than 16 opportunities to visit parks and gardens. No doubt about it: a tour of the »real Ireland«, the land of national heroes such as Michael Collins, is full of spectacular attractions.

A great start to the tour in ❶ ***Cork** is a hearty breakfast at the Farmgate Café in the English Market, where delicious produce is sold in a

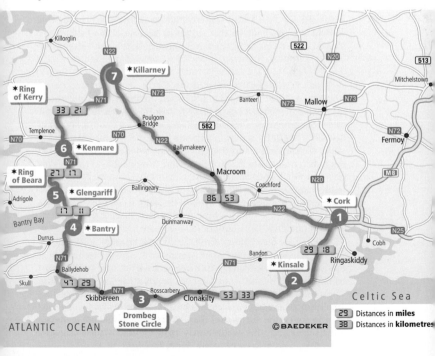

setting of handsome Victorian architecture. Further sights are the museums and Colman's Cathedral, the Lifetime Lab, the Glucksman Gallery on the university campus, and perhaps a trip to Cobb, 24km/15 miles southeast. When this town was still called Queens-town, the Titanic put in – her last port of call before sinking. An exhibition commemorates the event.

Follow the N71 25km/16 miles south to the appealing port of ❷* **Kinsale** for a pit stop, not least because the local restaurants such as Fishy Fishy and Max offer fine dining, and the oysters from nearby Oysterhaven are guaranteed to be good. There is an impressive panoramic view from the Garden of Remembrance for the New York firemen who were in action on 11 September 2001, about 1km/0.5 miles above the Trident Hotel. By contrast, busts of the two Antarctic pioneers Timothy and Mortimer McCarthy on Pier Road with their big ears are more likely to raise a smile.

No-one who is interested in environmental issues should fail to visit the farm Gort na Nain in Ballyherkin, Nohoval, east of Kinsale on the L 3215. The Lisselan Estate Gardens at Clonakilty are in the Victorian style, and the local Model Railway Village is a treat for children. A walk in late afternoon on the two sandy beaches of the Inchydoney Island Lodge & Spa, frequented by windsurfers, is highly recommended.

A detour to the ❸***Drombeg Stone Circle** , one of Ireland's best-preserved megalithic stone circles, is well worthwhile. An alternative is to visit Ballydehop, once a village for drop-outs, where are strange, huge monument for a wrestling champion who was born here is to be seen. The effects of the Gulf Stream can especially be noted in the parks of Skibbereen and the lush meadows of Schull, the source of the milk for Gubbeen Farm cheese. Here it is possible to see the dairy, herb garden and smokehouse.
Bantry House and Gardens near ❹* **Bantry** demonstrate the astonishing results of the mild climate in this region (www.bantryhouse. ie).

From here it is only 20km/13 miles to ❺ **Glengarriff**, undoubtedly one of the highlights of the southwest coast. Fresh mussels are sold at the harbour. In the Glengarriff Bamboo Park, 38 different kinds of bamboo are cultivated, as well as orchids, rhododendrons, roses and various floral rarities. The charms of Bantry Bay can also be seen on a boat trip to Ilnocullen, also known as **Garinish Island**, where sea lions are often spotted. A tour of the Ring of Beara to the northwest, for which at least a full day should be planned, reveals fuchsia hedges in glowing colours and wonderful natural sights.

The wild and rugged beauty of the coast on the Ring of Beara

The N71 then heads straight for ❻ *Kenmare. This is the start of a famous panoramic highway, the **Ring of Kerry**, which largely follows the coast and offers any number of viewpoints, This tour takes two to three days. The nougat bars of the Lorge chocolate shop in Bonane, Kenmare, have gained the acclaim of gourmets.

Continue through the Killarney National Park to ❼ **Killarney**, the capital of tourism in the beautiful **Killarney Area**. Thanks to a mild climate and lush vegetation, this is one of Ireland's top tourist regions. Magnificent hiking tours, the Killarney Cycling Trail and the Gap of Dunloe are good reasons to spend time her before returning to Cork, where the treats sold in the English Market make a fine conclusion to the tour.

Tour 4 # Whiskey, Salmon and the Wild West

Start: Dublin
End: Clifden (Connemara)

Length of Tour: approx.
480km/300 miles
Duration: at least three days

This tour travels along the west coast, to the friendly town of Ennis, to the cultural and natural treasures of the Burren, to lively Galway and finally to romantic Connemara. The crowning glory is a visit to the Aran Islands , where Gaelic is still spoken.

For a break on the 100km/60 miles of motorway from ❶****Dublin**, the Kilbeggan Distillery Experience in the town of the same name and a short detour to Tullamore are good options. The Tullamore Dew Heritage Centre, refurbished in 2013, has a modern exhibition about the history of whiskey (www.tullamore-dew.org).
❷ **Athlone**, where the River Shannon flows out of Lough Ree, is dominated by its castle. The Athlone Gallery in Grace Street presents modern art and an exhibition about the opera tenor John Count McCormack. Garden lovers should drive out to Glasson, the village or roses northeast of Athlone.

There now follows a leisurely drive through idyllic countryside to the ruins of the famous monastic settlement of ❸****Clonmacnoise** on a bend in the river Shannon. After admiring the famous high crosses and round towers, you can stop at the café or buy souvenirs in the craft shop. Shannonbridge is the starting point for boat trips, and a detour goes south along the Shannon to the Grand Canal and on to Clonfert with its cathedral.
The attraction in ❹ **Loughrea** is St Brenda's Cathedral, where the stained glass windows and stations of the cross are notable.

If you are short of time, from here head straight to Galway Bay. However, a more interesting route is to take a loop south to the typically Irish provincial town of ❺ **Gort**. The ruined manor in Coole Park in the north of the town was once the home of the author Lady Gregory, where many Irish writers came to stay. This is also a station on the Yeats Trail, coming down from Sligo.

The next destination is ❻**Ennis**, a real Irish small town with a relaxed atmosphere, a high quality of life, good food, an excellent music scene and many attractions, for example the recently restored Old Ennis Friary. To delight children, there is a trail of »wall candies«, murals in the historic part of town (www.wallcandies.ie). Ennis has even erected a monument to the greatest-ever boxer, Mohamed Ali (Cassius Clay). To drink a pint of Guinness in traditional surroundings, go to the Poet's Corner pub in the Old Ground Hotel.

Allow a full day to explore the natural and cultural treasures of the Burren, which is reached via Inagh and the market town of **7 Ennistymon**. Exhibitions on the subject of »salmon poetry« are held in the Courthouse Gallery. The background to this is the »Salmon of Knowledge« of Celtic mythology, which is also the subject of the murals on gables and in the Burren Smoke House, seen when returning north to **8 Lisdoonvarna**, Ireland's only health spa. Here, too, the Roadside Tavern presents an opportunity to sample specialities from the Burren, including wild salmon, mackerel, seaweed and rapeseed oil. At the Cliffs of Moher, a UNESCO geopark on the coast between Ennistymon and Lisdoonvarna, and in the Burren Interpretative Centre in Kilfenora, to the east of the route, you can learn about the region. For an enchanting scented souvenir, go to the Burren Perfumery in Carren, where the fruits of a wildflower and herb garden are preserved in aromatic soaps, oils, salts and creams.

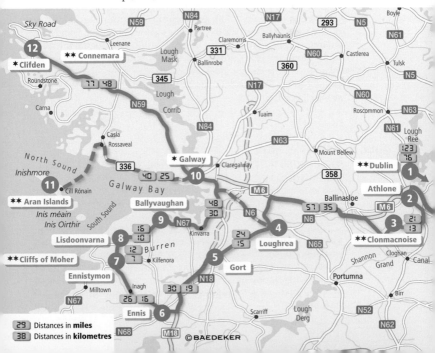

In ❾**Ballyvaughan** the tour has reached Galway Bay. Educational entertainment for the whole family can be found at Ailwee Cave and the Birds of Prey Centre, where demonstrations of the flight of eagles, hawks and owls are on the programme. The Burren, and to be precise the longest cave in Ireland, Pollnagollum Cave, provided J.R.R. Tolkien with inspiration for his figure of Gollum in »Lord of the Rings«.

❿**Galway**, the gateway to the west of Ireland, has a vibrant urban atmosphere, especially in the student district, known as the Latin Quarter, with its shops, pubs and restaurants. The most notable sights are the cathedral, the Claddagh love rings in Thomas Dillon's Claddagh Gold Museum on Quay Street, and Atlantaquaria, the national aquarium in the suburb of Salthill.

From Rossaveal, almost 40km/25 miles west of Galway, ferries set off for the ⓫****Aran Islands**. The three rocky islands are largely barren, exposed to the wind and waves of the Atlantic. The islanders practise agriculture on a few sheltered patches of land, but mainly live from tourism and fishing.

From Galway the journey continues to the far west of Ireland. Lough Corrib, north of Galway, attracts anglers. Celtic magic comes alive in Brigit's Garden in Roscahill, and then the wild, romantic landscape of Connemara never fails to captivate visitors. There are wonderful Atlantic beaches, both rocky and sandy, around the coastal towns of Roundstone and ⓬***Clifden**, which lies at the end of a long, narrow inlet. To see the deeply indented coastline in all its glory, take the 15km/10-mile Sky Road northwest of Clifden – though in the high season it is rather busy.

Tour 5 # From Sea to Sea

Start: Dublin	**Length of Tour:** approx.
End: Derry/Londonderry	440km/275 miles
	Duration: at least three days

The tour starts with two of Ireland's leading attractions, Kells and the Hill of Tara, going on to the moors and table mountains of County Sligo. The breathtaking coastal roads of Donegal, wide sandy beaches and a sunny castle in the north lie on the route, which finishes in the vibrant city of Derry/Londonderry.

The M 3 and N 3 lead from ❶**Dublin** to the ❷*Hill of Tara, once seat of the Irish High Kings, a distance of 37km/22 miles. There are few physical remains of what was the navel of the Irish Celtic world, but its mystic aura can be sensed to this day. The visit could be combined with the nearby Trim Castle, the largest Norman fortification in Ireland.

The early medieval Book of Kells is now in the library of Trinity College, Dublin, while in the little village of ❸ Kells itself, where the famous illustrated manuscript was once kept in the monastery, eleven medieval buildings, including a round tower and high crosses, can be admired on the Kells Heritage Trail. Only a few miles north, in Mullagh, the St Kilian's Heritage Centre is dedicated to the missionary known as the Apostle of the Franks.

Via the N51 and N52, it is worth taking the detour to **Mullingar**, where two wonderful mosaics by the Russian artist Boris Anrep can be seen in the Cathedral of Christ the King. Continue north on the N4, to ❹ **Carrick-on-Shannon**, the departure point for cabin cruises on the Shannon or Shannon-Erne Waterway and for excursions to the poets' country of Turlough O'Carolan. It is also worth making a stop-over in ❺*Boyle for the sake of the beautiful Cistercian Abbey and – for walkers – for the sake of the Lough Key Forest Park. The eponymous lake is beloved of anglers and rowers.

The sea is reached at last at ❻*Sligo. The beautiful birthplace of W. B. Yeats, whose literary work is honoured in the Yeats Memorial Building, is also worth a visit because of the many pubs. For art lovers there are the Niland Collection in a new gallery called The Model and wooden sculptures by Michael Quirke in Wine Street. The surfing and beach scene is in Strandhill. Anglers and boat trippers can go to Lough Gill, admirers of W.B. Yeats to the poet's grave in the cemetery of Drumcliff, 6km/3.5 miles north of Sligo.

The N15 then follows the storm-battered coast past several resorts to ❼*Donegal Town, a centre of the tweed industry where plenty of activities are on offer: boat trips to Donegal Bay, walks on the 65km/40-mile Blue Stack Way from Donegal across country to Ardara. From here the onward route remains extremely appealing – on the coast road to the cliffs of Slieve League, and to the Folk Village and pilgrim centre for St Columba at Glencolumbkille. The Ardara Heritage Centre has demonstrations how tweed is woven by hand.

If time is short, take the direct road from Ardara to Letterkenny. If you prefer to follow the coastline, small roads lead in many places to stunning rock formations north of Donegal Town, an excellent way to spend the third day of the tour.

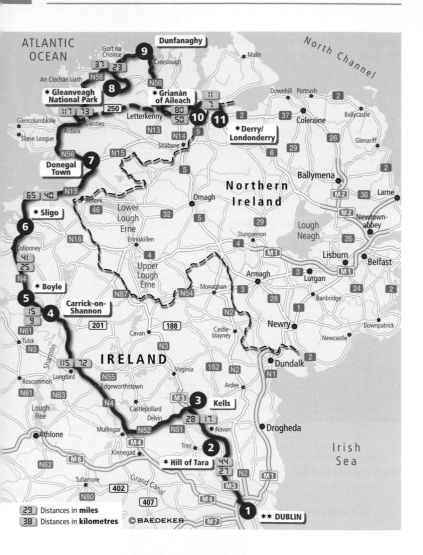

Impressive and varied scenery is protected by the ❽*Glean-veagh National Park**, the largest of the six national parks in Ireland, around Mount Errigal. The bare summit regions are home to an Arctic and Alpine flora and fauna, while Atlantic moorland lies below. The lakes are full of trout and eel, salmon and Arctic char.

Via the windswept landscape of the Bloody Forelands, continue north to **Horn Head**, and the beautifully situated holiday resort ❾＊**Dunfanagy** with its wonderful sandy beaches. Shortly before reaching the open border to Northern Ireland, you will reach ❿＊**G-rianán of Aileach** (»sun palace«), a round stone fort from the early Christian era, shrouded in mystery, with a fantastic view. across green countryside and the inlet of Lough Swilly.

From here it is not far to ⓫＊**Derry** (Tour 1), a port on Lough Foyle, with a walled historic centre, a vibrant Northern Irish city.

SIGHTS FROM
A TO Z

Breathtaking landscapes, mysterious ruins, magnificent art treasures, cosy pubs. The Emerald Isle delights visitors with many highlights.

Achill Island (Oiléan Acaill)

✳ **B/C 1/2**

Republic of Ireland, province: Connacht
County: Mayo
Population: 2,700   **Information:** www.visitachill.com

With a surface area of 148 sq km/57 sq miles, Achill Island is the largest island off the Irish coast. The narrow Achill Sound, spanned by a swing bridge, separates it from the mainland. Almost entirely covered with heather and bog, the island is popular for cycling, horse riding, sailing, windsurfing and diving.

Europe's highest cliffs

For splendid cliff scenery, head to the northern and western coast: the **Cathedral Rock Cliffs** in the west rise up to 670m/2,200ft, making them the highest cliffs in Europe. A spin on the scenic Atlantic Drive reveals the island's most beautiful viewpoints, walkers love the 14 hiking trails, and the loveliest of the Blue Flag beaches is **Keem Bay**.

A DRIVE AROUND ACHILL ISLAND

Achill Sound

Not far from the bridge, Achill Sound village is the island's main shopping centre, where you can swim, hire canoes and sailing boats, and start out on a diving or deep-sea fishing expedition. Take the **Atlantic Drive** around the southern tip of the island, to see the 12m/39ft-high Kildavnet Tower, which was built in 1429 and later belonged to the pirate Grace O'Malley (►MARCO POLO Insight p.509). On Atlantic Drive the Dutchman Willem von Goor and his wife Doutsje Nauta admit visitors to the floral splendour of their **Achill Secret Garden**, which belonged to Sir Anthony Bevir, private secretary to Winston Churchill, from 1970 to 1980.

❶ March-May, Sept, Mo, Wed, Fri 10am-5pm, June and Aug daily 10am-5pm, admission 8 €, http://achillsecretgarden.com

Dugort

11km/7 miles northwest of Achill Sound, on the northern coast of the island, lies Dugort. Standing on the main road is the house where Heinrich Böll and his family used to live, intermittently, from the 1955 onwards. The cottage was already little used in the last years of the German writer's life; today, writers and artists can use it as part of a scholarship programme. Dugort also boasts a fine sandy beach, and, nearby, some remains of megalithic graves (cairns) and dolmens.

**Feel the force of the roaring sea all around
the circular Atlantic Drive**

Slievemore

A climb or hike around Slievemore (661m/2,169ft), is well worth the effort, rewarded by wonderful views. Passing the deserted village of Slievemore, spare a thought for its inhabitants who abandoned it in the mid-19th century, during the Great Famine. The seal caves below the mountain are accessible by sea and in good weather; ask experienced boatsmen to take you there from Dugort.

Keel

Situated 6km/3.5 miles southwest of Dugort, Keel is an attractive holiday resort with a sandy beach stretching 3km/2 miles southeast to the foot of the steep Minaun Cliffs. In 2001 a circular building of pre-cast concrete parts was built near Keel in only one day. It is modelled on megalithic structures such as Stonehenge. **Achill Henge** was put up without planning permission, but its builder, Joe McNamara, refuses to demolish it. A megalithic site is said to exist in the bog close by.

Dooagh   5km/3 miles to the west of Keel, Dooagh, with its white thatched houses, is a pretty village in which the writer Graham Greene lived in the 1940s. The **Achill Archaeology Centre** runs courses and fascinating day trips to excavations (www.achill-fieldschool.com).

* Adare (Áth Dara)

—————————————————— ✶ D 3

Republic of Ireland, province: Munster
County: Limerick
Population: 2,650   **Information:** www.adarevillage.com

This well-kept if fairly touristy village in the southwest has a reputation as »Ireland's most beautiful village«. Its name means »oak ford«. On the forested western shores of the River Maigue, the Earl of Dunraven built picturesque thatched houses built in the 19th century. There are three abbeys in the surrounding area.

German refugees   In the early 18th century, German refugees from the Palatinate region were settled between Adare and Rathkeale, earning the area the name of »Palatine«. German traditions were upheld for a long time, and today still, German names can be encountered here.

Desmond Castle   The village bridge, washing pond and park set the scene. The restored ruins of the late 12th-century Desmond Castle can be visited on tours from the Adare Heritage Centre.
   ❶ Daily June-Sept, admission 6 €

Adare Heritage Centre   The Adare Heritage Centre, also the tourist office, has information on the history of the village, Models explain the arrival of the Normans and life in the abbeys.
   ❶ Main Street, daily 9am–6pm, admission 5 €, www.adareheritagecentre.ie

*Adare Manor   Adare Manor, the former manor house of the Dunraven family, has for several years been run as a **luxury castle hotel** with restaurant (www.adaremanor.com). The park surrounding the neo-Gothic building today serves as a golf course, but visitors who come for lunch or afternoon tea can look around the estate. The historical tour is only for hotel guests. Also in the park, look for the relics of a Franciscan friary of 1464. In the cemetery by the golf course stands the Church of St Nicholas (13th-16th century).

Adare

INFORMATION
See Adare Heritage Centre

WHERE TO EAT
Wild Geese €€€€
Rose Cottage, Tel. (061) 396451
www.thewild-geese.com
Julie Randles and David Foley serve exquisite new Irish cuisine. The early bird menu offers three courses for 35 €, Sunday brunch costs 25 €.

Blue Door €€€
Main Street
Tel. (061) 396481
www.bluedooradare.com
In a thatched cottage dating from 1830. Try cod in Chardonnay sauce or duck with orange and sesame dressing.

WHERE TO STAY
Dunraven Arms €€€€
Tel. (061) 605900
www.dunravenhotel.com
90 rooms and suites
Stylishly furnished rooms with antique furniture, a good restaurant, as well as a fine garden with stables and a spa with 17m/55ft pool.

Oakwood House €€   Insider Tip
Ballingarry Road (N21)
Tel. (061) 396075
An award-winning B & B, two minutes by car from Adare on the R 519 and 500m/550yd from the N 21. Excellent breakfast

---

The Catholic Holy Trinity Church in the village used to belong to the **only Trinitarian monastery in Ireland**. Dating from the 13th century, it took on its current size and shape in the 19th century. At the eastern end of Adare, near the bridge over the River Maigue, stands the 14th-century Augustinian abbey, used since the 19th century as the Protestant church and school.

Churches in Adare

AROUND ADARE

Some 11km/7 miles southwest of Adare, this museum in the old railway station of the little market town of Rathkeale commemorates the immigration of Germans from the Palatinate in 1709, displaying historic clothing, pipes and branding irons.

Irish Palatine Heritage Centre

❶ Mid-June-Aug Sun-Fri 2-5pm, otherwise on appointment, admission 5 €, www.irishpalatines.org

The Celtic Park & Garden was established on the site of a former Celtic settlement in what is today Kilcornan, 7km/4.5 miles northwest of Adare. Reproductions of a stone circle, a dolmen, and a holy well aim to make the past come alive.

Celtic Park & Garden

❶ Mid-March-Oct daily 9.30am-6pm, admission 6 €

★★ **Antrim Coast & Glens**

───────────── ✳ **A/ B 5/6**

Northern Ireland, province: Ulster
County: Antrim

North of Belfast, one of the most beautiful roads in Ireland hugs the coast, past the famous Glens of Antrim up 90km/55 miles to the ►Causeway Coast.

The Glens of Antrim lie between Larne and Ballycastle, with every one of the narrow valleys having its own character and its own coastal village. From south to north these are: Ballygally, Glenarm, Carnlough, Cushendall and Ballyvoy. All in all, this is a **wild and romantic area shrouded in legend**, with murmuring brooks and waterfalls, wooded mountain slopes and small villages.

> **MARCO ⊕ POLO** TIP
>
> *Panoramic view* **Insider Tip**
>
> For particularly fine panoramic views, go to Torr Head and Fair Head, accessible from a narrow country road between Cushendun and Ballycastle. From the viewpoints you can see Rathlin Island, sometimes even the outline of the Isle of Arran in Scotland. The route leads past Lough na Cranagh, with an old Crannóg at its centre, but is closed to campervans and caravans.

Coming from Red Bay, a coastal strip with spectacular sandstone cliffs, the scenic valley of Glenariff branches off just before Cushendall. The visitors' car park at **Glenariff Forest Park** is the starting point for various signposted trails; the 5km/3-mile Waterfall Trail is particularly beautiful. The visitor centre with its tea room, gift shop, exhibition and camp site is open daily from Easter to October. The coastal village of Glenariff is known for its Feis na NGleann, a summer festival with music, dance and the **Irish national sport: hurling**.

Ossian's Grave Past the village of Cushendall, some 1km/0.6 miles to the north, lie the ruins of Layde Old Church, originally founded by Franciscans. Following the A2 inland (approx. 5km/3 miles south of Cushendun) and taking a left turn, small backroads lead to Ossian's Grave on the slopes of Tievebulliagh Mountain. According to local legend, the **megalithic burial site** (approx. 800 BC) holds the grave of the poet-warrior Ossian, son of Finn MacCool.

Cushendun The pretty village of Cushendun, nestling among fuchsia and honeysuckle hedges, is famous for the houses designed by Clough Williams Ellis (1883–1977) for Lord Cushendun. Also, the village is a popular stop with hikers, lying on the route of the Ulster Way, which runs

northwards inland before Murlough Bay and then along the coast to
Ballycastle, southwards towards Cushendall (www.walkni.com/ul-
sterway).

Murlough Bay is often called the loveliest of all the bays on the   ***Murlough
Antrim coast; on clear days, the view stretches all the way to the Mull   Bay**
of Kintyre in Scotland. The best thing to do is leave the car in one of
the three car parks and take a walk to really appreciate the landscape
in peace and quiet. From the second car park, the remains of a cross
commemorating Sir Roger Casement (▶Famous People) are visible.
Casement's family came from this area; shortly before his execution
in 1916 in London he asked to be buried at Murlough Bay.

Antrim Coast & Glens

INFORMATION
www.northantrim.com
www.causewaycoastalroute.com

WHERE TO STAY
Londonderry Arms Hotel ££££
20 Harbour Road Carnlough Co. Antrim
Tel. (0 28) 28885255

www.glensofantrim.com
Built in 1847, this pretty Georgian ivy-
clad house used to belong to Sir Winston Churchill. There are fireplaces in the
cosy Arkle Bar and elsewhere, the
award-winning restaurant Frances Anne
and the Coach House Bistro.

The glen at Cushendall

Ballycastle A picturesque port surrounded by forests is Ballycastle (pop. 4,000), where **the Atlantic and the Irish Sea meet**. Ballycastle is a practical base for bike trips around the area (www.ballycastletown.co.uk). In the park between the harbour and the attractive sandy beach is the local park with a large-scale sculpture representing flying swans.

From Ballycastle, it is a 25-minute ferry trip to **Rathlin Island**. This small island, inhabited by around 100 people, lies 9km/5.5 miles off the coast of Ballycastle. At the harbour, there is a pub, a restaurant, shops and accommodation. Photos and artefacts in the **Boathouse Visitor Centre** explain the history, flora and fauna of the island. A local caves was made famous by Robert the Bruce. In 1306, he is said to have hidden here to regroup for a counter-attack after his defeat at the hands of the English.

Kebble Nature Reserve A walk of 4.6km/3 miles or a trip by minibus or bike takes visitors to the Kebble Nature Reserve and a new **Seabird Centre** by the western lighthouse. To reach the viewpoint, descend 84 steps at the cliffs. Thousands of seabirds live here, especially in the nesting season from May to July. Paul Quinn is a guide on three spectacular island walks (www.rathlinwalkingtours.com).

Boathouse Visitor Centre: May-Sept daily 91m-5.30pm; free admission
Seabird Centre: April to end of Aug, daily 10am-4pm; donation requested

** **Aran Islands (Oileáin Árainn)**

✦ C 2

Republic of Ireland, province: Connacht
County: Galway
Population (in total): 1,200   **Information:** www.aranislands.ie

The main draw of the three Aran Islands, jutting out of the Atlantic Ocean southwest of Galway, is their wind-torn aspect and barren, untouched natural environment. The inhabitants hang on to many elements of Irish culture which have disappeared in other places, and the majority continue to speak Irish.

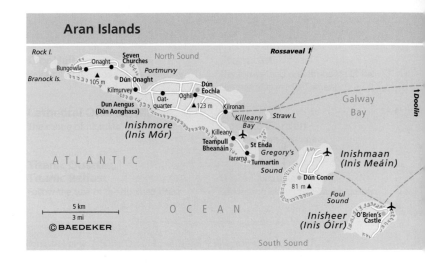

The Aran Islands consist of the three rocky islands of Inishmór, Inishmaan and Inisheer, as well as four tiny uninhabited islets. In order to make the karst ground yield anything at all, the inhabitants of the islands have collected sand and seaweed and laid it down layer by layer on small plots of land protected by dry-stone walls. Locally, these man-made patches of soil are called »gardens«. Towards the sea, the rocky coast descends in terraces; there are few beaches. As with the Burren, various rare plant species have survived here.

Barren islands

Whilst tourism has continued to gain in importance over recent years – several private rooms, holiday homes and small B&Bs are available – the inhabitants have held on to many old traditions. Numerous writers have portrayed the islands' tough fishing folk. Up to this day, fishing and lobster fishing is the second-most important source of income after tourism. For this, the locals still sometimes use the curraghs, light boats made from wooden laths covered with tarred canvas.

Old traditions

The Aran Islands are accessible by plane or boat. Aer Arann flies several times daily from the Connemara Regional Airport at Inverin (38km/24 miles west of Galway) to all three islands (www.aerarann.com). There are ferry connections to Inishmór from Rossaveal, as well as in the summer months once daily from Doolin (www.aran-islandferries.com).

Getting there

A walk along the dramatic cliffs of Inishmore reveals the barren splendour of the island

Inishmór Today, some 800 people live on Inishmór island, 12km/7.5 miles long and up to 3km/1.8 miles wide; a hundred years ago it was twice as many. Life focuses on the island capital **Kilronan**, where the ferries put in. Long footpaths lead to some 50 sights from pre-Christian and Christian times. Minibuses, horse-drawn coaches and bikes, which can be hired on the island, are also good ways of getting around.

The main sight of the Aran Islands is the **stone fort** Dún Aenghus   ****Dún**
on the southwestern coast of Inishmór. This is one of the mightiest   **Aenghus**
prehistoric fortifications in Europe, three semi-circular stone walls
and a fourth (nearly completely destroyed) outer wall enclosing a
space of 45m/50yd diameter immediately at the edge of the vertical
sea cliffs. A defensive belt made
from thousands of spiky stones set
upright and close together into the
ground **in the style of today's an-
ti-tank defences** (»chevaux-de-
frise«), was intended to deter attackers. 900m/1,000yd from the fort is a
visitor centre with a small museum.
❶ March, Nov, Dec daily 9.30am-4pm,
April-Oct 9.45am-6pm, Jan, Feb
Wed-Sun 9.30am-4pm; admission 3 €

> ! **MARCO ⊕ POLO** TIP
>
> *Aran sweaters*   **Insider Tip**
>
> ... are one of the favourite souve-
> nirs from Ireland. On the islands,
> the fancifully patterned garments
> can be found on every corner.
> The story goes that the fishermen
> were able to identify the drow-
> ned by their family knitting pat-
> tern, but this is all it is: a story. In
> fact, the »typical« sweaters were
> only introduced here at the end
> of the 19th century. Out of
> season is the right time for a bar-
> gain!

North of Dún Aenghus, near the
hamlet of Kilmurvey, stand the
churches of St Brecan, dating back
to the 9th century, and Temple Mac-
Duagh. There is a fine beach here
too. On a ridge to the northwest ri-
ses the stone fort of Dún Eoghanachta. On the way back to Kilronan,
watch out for seals in the sheltered bay of Port Chorrúch. Further east
stands Dún Eochla (Oghil Fort), a stone fort with two circular walls,
as well as the Early Christian church of Teampall Chiaráin with a
high cross.

Some 3km/1.8 miles south of Kilronan, the area around **Killeany**   **Killeany**
contains numerous sacred sites, amongst them Tighlagh Eany, the
remains of a monastic settlement. Its church holds a particularly
beautiful cross shaft with interlacing and a horseman in relief.
This area also boasts **one of the smallest churches in the
world**, St Benan's Church (Teampull Bheanáin, 3.2 x 2.1 m/10ft 6
in x 7ft).

Standing on high, steep ground on Inismaan, **Fort Dún Conor** has   **Inismaan**
some stone huts within its grounds and good views from the walls.
Also worth seeing are Cill Cheannannach church and Dún Fearb-
haigh fort. The house where poet and playwright John Millington
Synge spent some holidays is lovingly kept. His book, »The Aran
Islands« (1907) caused a sensation. He spent much time on a cliff in
the west of the island, at a place now called **Synge's Chair** (signposted).
Synge's Cottage: May-Sept daily at varying times; admission 3 €

Inisheer At 3km/1.8 miles in diameter, is the smallest of the Aran Islands. However, it has several monuments of interest to the visitor: O'Brien's Castle, a medieval structure with a tower visible from afar, St Gobnet's church (Cill Gobnet), with the characteristic features of early Irish architecture, and St Cavan church. Every year on 14 June, shovels are taken to this church, to free it from the sand threatening to bury it.

Ardara (Árd na Rátha)
—————————————————————— ✦ **B 3**

Republic of Ireland, province: Ulster
County: Donegal
Population: 580   **Information:** www.ardara.ie

Ardara, near Loughros More Bay, is famous for tweed fabrics and knitwear. »Nancy's« is said to be one of the best pubs in all Donegal. Nearby, enjoy lakes with fish aplenty and great hiking territory.

All about In most cases, today's tweed fabrics are no longer spun on the loom
tweed at home, but some factories encourage visitors to watch tweed being made and buy it at much lower prices than in the shops in the towns and cities. The **Ardara Heritage Centre** with its theatre, cinema, tourist office and café has further information on the history of Donegal and tweed. Hand-weaving of tweed is demonstrated by Eddie Doherty in his little shop on Front Street (www.handwoventweed.com).
❶ Tel. 074 954 1704, admission 2.50 €

AROUND ARDARA

Glenties Around 11km/7 miles northeast of Ardara, on the Owenea River amidst a forested region of lakes with plenty of fish and fine hiking trails, lies the village of Glenties. To the northeast, Aghla Mountain rises 589m/1,932ft above long Lough Finn, source of the Finn River. Some 3km/1.8 miles southwest of Ardara, a road turns off to the west, winding its way in narrow bends through a landscape of impressive and barren heights up to the **Glengesh Pass** and on to ▶Glencolumbkille.

Loughros West of Ardara, the long narrow Loughros Peninsula is great for
Peninsula walks or bike tours. There are splendid views from its western tip, Loughros Point . From the northern shore of Loughros Beg Bay, the **Maghera Caves** are accessible at low tide. Footpaths lead from the

point along the coast or via the heights of Slievetooey (460m/1,509ft) to ►Glencolumbkille.

North of Ardara it is worth making an excursion to Narin and Portnoo, two holiday villages in a sheltered position on the southern shore of Gweebarra Bay. Narin has an 18-hole golf links and a sandy beach. 1.5km/1 mile south of Narin, the **Dolmen Eco-Tourism Centre** is devoted to the flora and fauna of the area and to its archaeology and geology. Activities such as cliff walks, riding, golf, angling, whale and dolphin watching are on offer here. Archaeological excursions go to the dolmen and multi-chamber tomb in Kilclooney (3000-2000 BC), to the Drumboghill stone fort (1600 BC) and the 6th-century Celtic chapel on the islet of Inishkeel, which can be reached on foot at low tide.

Narin and Portnoo

The quiet seaside resort of **Rosbeg**, 5km/3 miles south of Portnoo, boasts a sandy beach and trout fishing.

Ardmore (Aird Mhór)

✦ E 4

Republic of Ireland, province: Munster
County: Waterford
Population: 410
Information: www.dungarvantourism.com

Looking for old buildings and modern villas, as well as beaches and steep cliffs? The popular beach resort of Ardmore, halfway along the southern coast of Ireland, fits the bill.

The 12th-century round tower of Ardmore is **one of the best-preserved in Ireland** and very photogenic. Inside the tower, which is nearly 29m/95ft high, look out for corbelled stones with grotesque faces. In 1642 Irish rebels were holed up here. They eventually surrendered, but 117 were hanged by the English forces.

*Round tower

Next to the tower stand the ruins of a 13th-century cathedral. The Romanesque reliefs on the west gable are particularly impressive. Despite the damage wrought by the elements, it is possible to make out, in the top row, Archangel Michael Weighing the Souls, below Adam and Eve, the Judgment of Solomon, as well as the Adoration of the Magi. The choir has two Ogham stones. The church was named after bishop St Declan who is said to have founded a Christian congregation here before the arrival of St Patrick.

*Cathedral

St Declan's Well Some 800m/900yd east of the cluster of buildings stands the ruined Dysert Church, formerly of great size. Close by, pilgrims used to take a bath in St Declan's holy well. **St Declan's Stone** The erratic (boulder) lying at the southern tip of the beach is St Declan's Stone. The story goes that sufferers of rheumatism who crawl under it will be cured – if they are free of sin.

Cliff walks There are various cliff walks to choose from: to the sea caves of Ardmore Head and Ram Head to the east and south of the town, also to Whiting Bay (west of Ardmore) and the bay of Monatray.

✳ Ards Peninsula (Ain Aird)
✳ B 6

Northern Ireland, province: Ulster
County: Down

In the northeast of County Down, large Strangford Lough divides the Ards Peninsula from the Irish Sea. The quiet peninsula, an hour's drive from Belfast, boasts beautiful beaches.

Tower houses and ostrich farms This 35km/22-mile-long peninsula has different faces: the Strangford Lough is sheltered, whereas the sea coast is wind-ravaged. What strikes the visitor is the wealth of tower houses, of which, however, only remains are left today. In the 15th and 16th centuries, numerous buildings of this type were erected, as King Henry VI, in 1429, offered a reward to everyone building this kind of fortification to protect the borders. The Ards Peninsula is an agricultural region; in recent times, traditional farming methods have diversified to include **ostrich rearing and daffodil cultivation**.

Newtownards A starting point for a drive around the Ards Peninsula is the nice market town of (population: 27,800). The top of the 41m/134ft **Scrabo Tower**, standing 2km/1.2 miles southwest in Scrabo Hill County Park, offers a wonderful view of Strangford Lough. The tower was erected in 1857 in honour of the third Marquess of Londonderry. In the **Ards Art Centre** on Conway Square there are two galleries for changing exhibitions and a theatre.
Scrabo Tower: March–May and Oct Sat–Sun 1–5pm, June–Sept daily 10am–5pm, Nov–Feb Sun 12 noon–4pm; free admission

Somme Heritage Centre Some 3km/1.8 miles north of Newtownards on the A21, the Somme Heritage Centre commemorates the Battle of the Somme (1916), in which many Irishmen died. The historical events of the First World War are presented from the perspective of soldiers from Ireland and

Ulster. Close by, the Ark Open Farm is open to the public, displaying its rare breeds of sheep, cattle and poultry.

Somme Heritage Centre: 233 Bangor Road; April–June and Sept Mon–Thu 10am–4pm, Sat 11am–4pm, July–Aug Mon–Fri 10am–4pm, Sat until 5pm, Oct–March Mon–Thu 10am–4pm: admission 5.75 £; www.irishsoldier.org
Ark Open Farm: April–Oct Mon–Sat 10am–6pm, Sun 2–6pm, Nov–March Mon–Sat 10am–5pm, Sun 2–5pm; admission 5 £; www.thearkopenfarm.co.uk

Mount Stewart House and Gardens lie 8km/4.8 miles south of New-townards on the A21. The splendid 18th-century manor house boasts an important art collection, but the real attraction are the **imaginative gardens**, which were in large part laid out in the 1920s according to the ideas of Lady Edith, the wife of the 7th Marquess of Londonderry. Divided into 17 different sectors, the garden shows a varied range of landscapes, comprising a natural-looking parkscape with many exotic trees and shrubs, a bizarre border featuring the Red Hand of Ulster, as well as a yew tree pruned into the shape of an Irish harp. Also fairly unusual are the statues of dinosaurs and mermaids. The octagonal »Temple of the Winds« banqueting house with views of Strangford Lough was erected in 1780. | ***Mount Stewart House and Gardens**

Portaferry Road; Lakeside Gardens: daily 10am–6pm, Formal Gardens mid-March–Oct daily 10am–6pm
House: mid-March–Oct Thu–Tue 10am–6pm
Temple of the Winds: mid-March–Oct Sun 2–5pm; information: www.nationaltrust.org.uk.

Only 1.5km/1 mile southeast of here lies the village of Greyabbey, with the ruins of the old **Grey Abbey** amidst a fine park. Founded in 1193 by John de Courcey, his wife Affreca, daughter of the King of the Isle of Man, gifted it to the Welsh Cistercian monastery Holm Cultram. In 1572 the abbey was destroyed, but the church was restored and remained in use until the construction of a new building in 1778. Look out for the three-light lancet windows, very reminiscent of English cathedrals, and the preserved western doorway. Also of interest are the **medieval monastery gardens**, with over 50 different medicinal and culinary herbs. | **Grey Abbey**

❶ March, Oct Tues–Sun 1–5pm, April, May Tues–Sun 10am–5pm, June–Sept daily 10am–5pm, Nov–Feb Sun 2–4pm; free admission

In the quiet town of Portaferry (pop 2,450), on the furthest tip of the peninsula, the A20 ends. From here, a ferry takes five minutes to cross over to Strangford on the western shore (►Downpatrick, Around) for some diving, fishing or to continue the tour following the eastern route. | **Portaferry**

The names of Strangford Lough describe its character: the Old Norse »Strangford« refers to the strong current of the narrows, the Irish | **Strangford Lough** name »Loch Cuan« to the calm waters of the mud flats. The lough is said to be one of the maritime areas of Europe with the most **biodiversity**, as the current brings huge amounts of plankton into this deep inlet on a daily basis. This is an opportunity to spot rare waterbirds, seals and sometimes even whales and sharks. Thanks to this wealth of interesting wildlife, the famous marine biology station likes to use the shore region as a field lab; the Strangford Lough Wildlife Scheme runs boat tours and ornithological excursions. Large flocks of wild geese regularly spend the winter in this bird and wildlife reserve; greylags and Greenland white-fronted geese cackle, various birds roam the mudflats, and seagulls and sea swifts spend the summer here (www.strangfordlough.org).

Exploris The diverse fauna of Strangford Lough and the Irish Sea is also explored in the Exploris Aquarium in Portaferry, situated near the small 16th-century tower house. Children in particular enjoy the various tanks, where they can touch sea urchins, sea anemones and other animals. There is also an orphanage for **baby seals**.

❶ April–Aug Mon–Fri 10am–6pm, Sat 11am–6pm, Sun 12 noon–6pm; Sept–March only to 5pm; admission 7.50 £; www.exploris.co.uk

Millisle The stone wall leading out to sea at Millisle (approx. 20km/12 miles north of Portaferry and 12km/7.5 miles east of Newtownards), is a good vantage point for spotting eider ducks and wild geese. The popular coastal resort has an amusement park, shops, pubs, a swimming pool and campsites.

Ballycopeland Windmill Standing only 1.5km/1 mile to the northwest, on Moss Road (B172 towards Newtownards), the late 18th-century Ballycopeland Windmill is a popular subject for holiday snaps and **one of the last two working windmills in Ireland**. Take a guided tour to learn about flour production and what the miller's work involves.

❶ Windmill Road, Millisle, tel. 028 91 81 1491, only July–Aug daily 10am–5pm

! *Grace Neill's* **Insider Tip**

MARCO ⬤ POLO TIP

Peter the Great of Russia is said to have had a drink here during his tour of Europe in 1697. Grace Neill's (33 High Street) in Donaghadee is Ireland's oldest pub, opened in 1611. Mon–Fri 12 noon–3pm and 5.30–9pm, Sat 12 noon–9.30pm, Sun 12.30–8pm: www.graceneills.com

A bit further north, the nice port of **Donaghadee** is the point of embarkation, in summer, for boats to the three Copeland Islands. For nearly 50 years, seabirds have been the islands' only inhabitants.

The emblem of Donaghadee is its charming little harbour, built at the same time as the lighthouse in 1821

Arklow
(An tInbhear Mór)

◆ D 5

Republic of Ireland, province: Leinster
County: Wicklow
Population: 12,800   **Information:** arklow.ie

It is said that Saint Patrick chose Arklow to come ashore. To-day, the town attracts visitors with pleasing sandy bays and charming potteries. In spring, the nearby Vale of Avoca is transformed into a dream of cherry blossoms.

History At Arklow, the Avoca River, which gave the valley its name, flows into the Irish Sea. Over the course of history, the town has changed owners several times. A monument in front of the Catholic parish church commemorates the last battles that took place during the rebellion of 1798.

Sights Arklow has few sights. The **Arklow Maritime Museum** in the Bridgwater Centre possesses a few treasures, including models of shops and eight paintings by the famous maritime artist Ruben Chappell. The **farmers' market** in Abbey Lane and the **country market** in Pigeon House, Castlepark, are worth a look.

Arklow Maritime Museum: Tue–Sat 10am–1pm, 2–5pm,; free admission; www.arklowmaritimemuseum.com

Farmers' market: Friday 10am–1pm
Country market: Sat 10.30am–12 noon

MARCO ⊕ POLO TIP

! *Avoca handweavers* **Insider Tip**

A trip to Avoca in the south of the Wicklow Mountains is well worth making: visit Ireland's oldest hand-weaving mill, buy nice textiles, enjoy the good restaurant, and visit the factory (daily 9.30am–6pm; free admission). The whole country has branches of Avoca Handweavers (www.avoca.ie).

AROUND ARKLOW

From Woodenbridge, the R752 leads north to the **Vale of Avoca**, a valley much praised for its scenic beauty. The springtime wild cherry blossom is stunning. However, as various industries have now established themselves in the region, some parts of the Vale of Avoca have lost their charm.

Meeting of the Waters Some 5km/3 miles upriver, Castle Howard looks down from a cliff onto the famous **Meeting of the Waters**, where the Avonmore and Avonbeg become the Avoca River. Lion's Bridge is a particularly good vantage point to watch the two rivers converge.

Another 3km/1.8 miles further along, Avondale Forest Park is an extensive forest park, with the **birthplace of Charles Stewart Parnell** (►Famous People) open to the public. The interior of the building, built in 1779 to plans by James Wyatt, is beautiful, and a video provides information on the life of the Irish freedom fighter.

❶ Rathdrum, Co. Wicklow, Easter–Oct Tue–Sun 11am–4pm; admission 7.50 €; www.coillteoutdoors.ie.

✱ Armagh (Ard Mhacha)

── ✳ B 5

Northern Ireland, province: Ulster
District: Armagh
Population: 14,600

Armagh, one of the most interesting towns in Northern Ireland, lies amidst the Garden of Ulster, southwest of ►Lough Neagh. The countryside is particularly attractive during Apple Blossom Time in May. A signposted Apple Blossom Trail begins and ends in Armagh.

Armagh is the seat of a Protestant and a Catholic archbishop and holds great significance for the ecclesiastical life of the province. Many buildings are in pink, yellow or reddish limestone called »Armagh Marble«. The material was very popular with local architect Francis Johnston (1761–1829), who designed several public buildings and Georgian town houses along the Mall, Armagh's main street. The Irish name for the town is Ard Macha (»Macha's Hill«), as in the 3rd century BC, the legendary Queen Macha had a fort built on a hill some 3km/1.8 miles west of Armagh (see Navan Fort, p.179). The place became important in early Christian times, when St Patrick had a monastery and a church built here around 445, laying the foundation for Armagh to become a centre of missionary activity. The famous **Book of Armagh** manuscript was written in the monastery in around the year 807.

Religious centre of Ireland

The town is therefore the starting and finishing point of the 149km/93-mile St Patrick's Trail, which follows the saint's footsteps through Northern Ireland to such highlights as the North Down Museum and Bangor Castle, to Bangor Abbey, Grey Abbey, Downpatrick and Bagenal's Castle in Newry.

Armagh

INFORMATION
Market Place Theatre and Arts Centre
Market Street
Tel. (028) 37521800
www.armagh.gov.uk

SIGHTS IN ARMAGH

Protestant St Patrick's Cathedral

The Protestant St Patrick's Cathedral (Vicar's Hill) stands on the site where St Patrick founded a church in the 5th century. This Church of Ireland cathedral owes its current appearance to a restoration carried out in the 19th century by Lewis Cottingham. Inside, the original crypt and several monuments – for Sir Thomas Molyneux, amongst others – are worth seeing, as well as a bust of Archbishop Richard Robinson. On the outer wall, a plaque records that in 1004 the Irish king Brian Boru, after his death at the Battle of Clontarf, was buried in the grounds of the cathedral, according to his wishes.

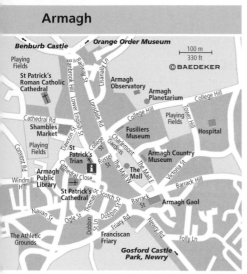

Armagh

Benburb Castle · Orange Order Museum
100 m
330 ft
©BAEDEKER
Playing Fields
St Patrick's Roman Catholic Cathedral
Barnbrook Hill · Lower English St · Railway St · Lisanally Ln
Armagh Observatory
Armagh Planetarium
College Hill
Cathedral Rd
Shambles Market
College Hill
Playing Fields
Lonsdale Rd
Fusiliers Museum
Tower Hill
Hospital
Convent Rd
Playing Fields
Dawson St
College St
Charlemont Gardens
Russel St
The Mall N
Armagh Country Museum
St Patrick's Trian
Armagh Public Library
Cathedral Close
The Mall E
Windmill Hill
St Patrick's Cathedral
Scotch St
The Mall S
Victoria St
Barrack Hill
Navan St
Ogle St
Dobbin St
Thomas St Ln
Dobbin St
Barrack St
Friary Rd
Armagh Gaol
The Athletic Grounds
Franciscan Friary
Newry Rd
Folly Ln
Gosford Castle Park, Newry

❶ April–Oct daily 9am–5pm, Nov–March 9am–4pm; admission 3 £ (minimum donation); wwwstpatricks-cathedral.org

When the Armagh Public Library (Robinson Library) was founded nearby in 1771, it was the first public library outside Dublin. An inscription above the main entrance calls it »**the medicine shop of the mind**«. The library comprises a valuable collection of books, mainly from the fields of theology, sciences and archaeology. The institution also possesses the »Claims of the Innocents« (petitions addressed to Oliver Cromwell), some wood engravings by the English painter and engraver William Hogarth (1697– 1764), as well as a copy of Jonathan Swift's »Gulliver's Travels« with handwritten annotations by the author.

❶ 43 Abbey Street, Mon–Fri 10am–1pm, 2-4pm; free admission, guided tour 2 £; http://armaghpubliclibrary.arm.ac.uk)

St Patrick's Roman Catholic Cathedral

In the northwest of town, St Patrick's Roman Catholic Cathedral, a neo-Gothic building (1840–73) with mosaics, stained glass windows and marble panelling executed by Italian artists, occupies a commanding position. During modernization works in 1981, Liam Mc-Cormick redesigned the chancel, including a tabernacle and crucifix made from a light polished stone. Both seem strangely out of place in this otherwise lavishly decorated church.

In the centre of town, 150m/150yd from the oldest Presbyterian church in Armagh, stands St Patrick's Trian, a visitor centre presenting three exhibitions: The Armagh Story looks at the pre-Christian period until the arrival of St Patrick, Patrick's Testament is mainly about the Book of Armagh, and The Land of Lilliput, where children enjoy climbing over a huge model of Gulliver tied to the floor, is about Gulliver's Travels.

St Patrick's Trian

❶ 40 English Street; currently undergoing renovation, opening times normally Mon–Sat 10am–5pm, Sun 2–5p; admission to one exhibition 4.25 £, combined ticket 6 £

The Mall is a finely laid-out park, where horse races and cockfights used to take place. Today, war memorials appear to stand guard over the flower beds. Standing at the northwestern end of the Mall, the Court House was built between 1805 and 1809 by Francis Johnston. Today however, the visitor encounters a reconstruction, as the original building was destroyed by a bomb in 1993.

The Mall

A former school house on the Mall houses the County Museum, boasting interesting exhibits on archaeological, natural and local history of the region, as well as an excellent library. One gruesome feature is the cast-iron skull that used to adorn the Armagh gallows. The museum also has paintings by George Russell (1867–1935) and James Sleator (1889–1950), who portrayed numerous important Armagh personalities.

County Museum

❶ The Mall East; Mon–Fri 10am–5pm, Sat 10am-1pm and 2–5pm; free admission

The Royal Irish Fusiliers Museum in Old Sovereign's House shows military artefacts and commemorates historic battles in which the fusiliers took part.

Royal Irish Fusiliers Museum

❶ Mon–Fri 10am–12.30pm, 1.30–4pm; free admission

From the Court House, College Hill leads past the Royal School, founded by James I in 1608, on the right-hand side, to reach the Armagh Observatory and its Planetarium with the Hall of Astronomy, displaying astronomical instruments (touching allowed!). Furthermore, there is a replica of the Gemini rocket, spacesuits worn by American astronauts, models of the Space Shuttle and Voyager, as well as various telescopes. The guided tours are highly informative, and a walk through the Astropark (free admission) illustrates the dimensions of the solar system and the universe and even allows a walk up Infinity Hill.

Armagh Observatory

Armagh Observatory: Mon–Fri 9.30am–4.30pm; admission free; http://star.arm.ac.uk

Armagh Planetarium: Mon–Sat 10am–5pm, shows on weekdays 2pm, Sat hourly from 11am to 4pm; admission 6 £; www.armaghplanet.com

Franciscan friary

To the south of town, the grounds of the former archbishop's palace (Friary Road) hold the remains of a Franciscan friary founded in 1266. With a length of nearly 40m/130ft, the church is said to be the longest Franciscan church in the country. Today, the monastic buildings house the municipal administration.

Gargoyles and angels

A new **art trail** named Gargoyles and Angels, suitable for both children and adults, takes in 22 hidden miniature bronze statues, the work of a German sculptor resident in Ireland, Holger Lönze.

Navan Fort is quiet, hilly country today

AROUND ARMAGH (NORTHWEST)

On the A28, some 3km/1.8 miles west of Armagh, the tree-lined grass mound of Navan Fort (Emain Macha) occupies the centre of a 7ha/17-acre area of mysterious hill forts and holy lakes from the Bronze and Iron Ages. According to legend, the destiny of Navan Fort was decided around 300 BC, when the mythical **Queen Macha** is said to have built a wooden palace here, serving as the base for the Red Branch Knights. Around AD 450, the palace and the surrounding town were destroyed by looters from Connacht. Walk ***Visitor centre** for only five minutes to reach the award-winning visitor centre, which is designed to look like a green hill, blending in wonderfully with the landscape. The centre has information on the history of the town, explaining the archaeology and introducing the visitor to the **Celtic myths** and the epic literature of Ulster.

Navan Centre & Fort

> **MARCO POLO INSIGHT**
>
> ### Irish Camelot
>
> For over six centuries, Navan Fort was the seat of the Kings of Ulster – an Irish Camelot, which the geographer Ptolemy called »Isamnium« when he drew up his map of the world as early as the 2nd century. It is said that Queen Macha gave birth to twins here after a horse race; hence the name Emain Macha, meaning »Twins of Macha«.

❶ April-Sept daily except Christmas: Mon–Fri 10am–5pm, Oct–March daily 10am–4pm

Benburb Valley Park, approx. 11km/7 miles northwest of Armagh, cuts through the Blackwater, which is very popular with anglers (salmon) and kayakers. Lying within the park, Benburb Castle was used by US troops during World War II as a hospital. 800m/0.5 miles away, a former linen mill houses the Benburb Valley Heritage Centre.

Benburb Valley Park

❶ 89 Milltown Road, Benburb; park open daily, castle and heritage centre Easter to Sept. daily 10am–5pm; admission to park free, castle and heritage centre 2 £

In the village of Loughgall, 10km/6 miles north of Armagh, it is worth visiting the country park and its golf course. The village is, however, known for a different reason: **Orange Museum** a skirmish that took place in 1795 between Catholics and Protestants around 5km/3 miles northeast at Diamond Hill. Subsequently, the Protestant farmers in the area decided, in the Loughgall pub, to found an order taking its name from William of Orange: the Orange Order. Its first secretary, James Sloan, lived at Sloan House, where there is a small Orange Museum and a heritage centre is planned.

Loughgall

❶ Visits by appointment, tel. 077 6739 3090

Ardress House   5km/3 miles northeast of Loughgall (14.5km/9 miles from Armagh), Ardress House was a modest manor house until 1760, when it was converted into an imposing stately home. Look out for the classical stucco work in the drawing room and the precious 18th-century furniture. The farm belonging to the estate, with pig breeding and a smithy, is still working; the garden has been planted with various traditional apple varieties, and there are **old varieties of Irish roses** in a small rose garden.

❶ Park daily until dusk, house March–June, Sept and Oct Sat and Sun 1–6pm, July–Aug Thu-Sun 1–6pm; admission from 3 £; www.nationaltrust.org.uk

The Argory   Further north, on Derrycaw Road (off the B28, 3.5km/2.2 miles northwest of Moy), on a hill overlooking the Blackwater, look out for The Argory, a pretty **country house**. The furnishings, original murals and an organ – dating from 1824 and still used – are very well-preserved. The rose garden is a marvel.

❶ Grounds daily 10am–6pm, house March–June Wed–Mon 12 noon–5pm, July–Aug daily; admission to grounds 3 £, with tour of house 5 £

AROUND ARMAGH (SOUTH)

Gosford Castle Forest Park   Children in particular will love a trip to Gosford Castle Forest Park near Markethill (approx. 10km/6 miles southeast of Armagh) to see red deer and other animals; there are also nice **nature trails and places for a picnic**. Jonathan Swift is said to have stayed at Gosford Castle several times.

❶ Daily 10am until dusk; free admission, parking 4.50 £; www.gosford.co.uk

Milford   The model village for linen weavers, dating from the 19th century, is now in a state of disrepair. Milford supplied linen for the *Titanic* in 1912. The **Milford House Museum** displays 1940s furniture.

❶ April–Sept Sat and Sun 2–6pm; admission 3.50 £; www.milfordhouse.org.uk

A trip into »Bandit Country«   Southern Armagh, alleged hideout for smugglers and partisan fighters, is also known as Bandit Country. It is true that the armed battles between the IRA and the British army were particularly fierce here. From Armagh, take the A28 south and drive some 20km/12 miles on the A25 to Camlough, where a sign points south to the remains of the two **Killevy Churches**, 5km/3 miles away. Here, medieval Augustinian nuns erected a new convent on top of the ruins of a convent founded in the 5th century and destroyed in 923 by the Vikings. The eastern church dates from the

15th century, the western one is some 300 years older. The western door's solid lintel is even said to date back to around 900.

Slieve Gullion Forest Park

Only a few miles further west, Slieve Gullion Forest Park (577m/1,893ft) lies at the centre of the Ring of Gullion, a particularly scenic landscape in the hills and mountains of south Armagh. Legend has it that it was here that the Irish hero Cú Chulainn stopped the armies of Queen Maeve. The area abounds in **legends**; the southern cairn on the mountain summit is said to be the house of Caillech Bhérri, the huge old witch and incarnation of the winter and death aspects of the Irish mother goddess. Nearby, the northern cairn has two Bronze Age cists. This area is ideal for cycling and walking. A panoramic road lead through the conifer forest on the southern slopes of the park.

Slieve Gullion Forest Park: Easter to mid-Sept daily, 8am–dusk; free admission

Music at its best

Discover traditional music in the **Thí Chulainn Cultural Centre** in the village of Mullach Ban, west of Slieve Gullion. Here, and in neighbouring Forkhill, regular folk music sessions are held. Reasonably priced accommodation is also available at Tí Chulainn (www.tichulainn.com)

Crossmaglen

Another place known for its music is Crossmaglen (pop. 1,450), approx. 5km/3 miles southwest; a horse fair also takes place here in early September. During the Troubles, over 20 British soldiers were killed by Provisional IRA bombs and attacks in and around the town.

Athlone (Baile Átha Luain)

✴ C 4

Republic of Ireland, province: Leinster
County: Westmeath
Population: 15,550

Athlone lies close to the geographical centre of the island, on the shores of the Shannon. The town is a lively rail and road hub, as well as featuring a marina for the sailing and nature paradise of the Shannon and Lough Ree.

Disputed bridgehead

The Shannon crossing at Athlone has been of strategic significance since time immemorial. A wattle bridge stood here as early as the end of the first millennium. In the 13th century, a bridge-

Athlone

INFORMATION
Tourist Information
Civic Centre, Grace Road
Tel. 090 64946 30
www.athloneartandtourism.ie

WHERE TO EAT **Insider Tip**
The Olive Grove Restaurant €€
Custume Pier
Tel. (0 901) 647 69 46
www.theolivegrove.ie
Gale and Gerry service delicious new
Irish cuisine in a lounge atmosphere.
There is seating for 50 in the open air
right above the Shannon. Low-priced
dishes for children.

WHERE TO STAY
Hodson Bay Hotel
Roscommon Road,
Tel. (0 90) 644 2000
www.hodsonbayhotel.com
This hotel on Lough Ree is for lovers
of golf, and tennis. Indoor pool and gym

Shamrock Lodge €€€€
Clonown Road
Tel. (0 90) 649 26 01
www.shamrocklodge.ie
68 doubles, 2 suites
Illustrious guests such as Prince Rainier
and Princess Grace have stayed here.
The hotel has a spa and beauty rooms.

head was established, with a castle and shore fortifications that
through the centuries were to be fought over, destroyed and rebuilt again. North of Athlone, the ►Shannon flows through the
large Lough Ree.

Athlone Castle & Museum
In 1210, King John of England commissioned the building of Athlone
Castle. King John's Castle took on most of its current aspect in the
early 19th century. Today, the group of buildings houses a visitor cen-
tre documenting the history of the castle and town, including The
Siege Experience in the upper keep, with a 360° that brings to life the
siege of 1690. At Athlone Arts and Tourism in Grace Road, the Luan
Gallery is devoted to exhibitions of modern and contemporary art.
The tourist information centre is also here.
Athlone Castle Visitor Centre: March–May Tue–Sat 11am-5pm, Sun 12
noon–5pm, June–Aug Mon–Sat 10am–6pm, Sun 12 noon–6pm, Nov–Feb
Wed–Sat 11am–5pm, Sun 12 noon–5pm; 8 €;
www.athloneartsandtourism.ie
Luan Gallery: Tue–Sat 11am–5pm, Sun 12 noon–5pm; free admission

AROUND ATHLONE

Lough Ree
No visit to Athlone would be complete without a boat trip on the
Shannon or, north of the town, large, reed-lined Lough Ree, famous

for the early Christian monastery ruins on its many islets, and for excellent trout fishing. Many migrating birds nest here, mainly swans, mallards and curlews. There is also very good sailing to be had here.

Goldsmith Country

Northeast of Athlone, the N55 leads through Goldsmith Country, the **literary landscape** of Oliver Goldsmith and John K Casey. Goldsmith was born and bred in Lissoy. **Glasson**, northeast of Athlone, has been known since the 19th century as a village of roses, and now also for the Oliver International Literary Festival. The work on display at the Irish Designer Craft Village in **Balli-nahown** has won numerous prizes. The area is also very well suited to bike rides, in particular the route along the »Lough Ree Trail«.

Moate

At Moate, half-way between Athlone and Kilbeggan on the N6, lies the **Dún na Sí Heritage Park** which aims to give visitors the experience of life on a 19th-century farm. On the first Friday each months, and every Friday in July and August, traditional Irish evenings are held here with music, dance and storytelling.
❶ Mon-Thu 9am-5pm, Fri 9am-4pm; admission 3.50 €

Athy (Baile Áth Í)

✦ **D 5**

Republic of Ireland, province: Leinster
County: Kildare
Population: 10,500   **Information:** www.athy.ie

Athy occupies a scenic position on the shores of the gently flowing River Barrow. The town's most conspicuous building is its bulky 15th-century tower. Visible from afar, it signals the end of this particular leg of the journey to all hungry and thirsty houseboat skippers.

Important ford

The fact that the ford of the River Barrow has been of significance for Athy since time immemorial is shown by the Irish name for the town, meaning »town of the ford of I«. One branch of the ►Grand Canal joins the river here. Athy lies in the east of Ireland, southwest of Dublin and south of Portlaoise. The most notable building in Athy is **White's Castle**, a bulky rectangle with corner towers, built by the Earl of Kildare in the 15th century to protect the bridge over the River Barrow. The bridge has the unusual name of Crom-a-boo, derived from the war cry of Desmond's followers (one earl of Desmond was English governor around 1420).

**Athy Herita-
ge Centre
Museum**
The museum in the old town hall has an exhibition about the Arctic explorer Ernest Shackleton, who was born in Kilkea House near Athy in 1874. Other sections are devoted to motor sports, local history and Gordon Bennett, once owner of the New York Herald.

● Mon–Fri 10am–5pm, admission 3 €, www.athyheritagecentre-museum.ie

AROUND ATHY

Ballitore
10km/6 miles further east, Ballitore was once a vibrant Quaker settlement with a school whose fame extended beyond the region. A reminder of this time is the **Quaker Meeting House**, housing a small museum. **Rath of Mullagast**, an Iron Age fort, lies only 2km/1.2 miles to the west. One of the legendary »monster meetings« led by the Catholic freedom fighter Daniel O'Connell is said to have taken place here in 1843.

● Quaker Meeting House: Tue–Sat 12 noon–5pm, July–Aug also Sun 2–6pm; free admission; www.quakersinireland.ie

Look out for the harps depicted on the high crosses of Castledermot

South of Ballitore, near the N9 at Moone (coming from Dublin, to the right-hand side of the road) stands a ruined church. Here, the visitor finds a slim Celtic high cross, at nearly 6m/20ft high the second-tallest in Ireland. Its stylized bas-reliefs have a strong visual impact, showing scenes from the Bible, such as the Sacrifice of Abraham, the Twelve Apostles and the Flight to Egypt.

*High Cross of Moone

East of Moone, Baltinglass, situated on the N81, houses the remains of the 12th-century Cistercian monastery **Valle Salutis**. Its stonemasonry works (nave and choir) display a mix of Hiberno-Romanesque and Cistercian forms. Parts of the cloister are more recent, while the tower and east window are 19th century.

Baltinglass

Northeast of the village rises Baltinglass Hill (377m/1,237ft). On its summit stand the stone walls of a hill fort enclosing **Neolithic passage tombs**. A pleasant panoramic view can be enjoyed from here.

Baltinglass Hill

Take the N9 south from Moone to reach, after 8km/5 miles, **Castledermot**. Look out for the remains of a very ancient monastery, (9th century), amongst them a Romanesque archway, a round tower and two granite high crosses. The scene with David playing the harp is of particular interest, being one of the few representations of an Irish harp. In the southern part of the village, the remains of a 13th-century Franciscan monastery are all that survived its dissolution in the 16th century.

Castledermot

On the way back to Athy (driving northwest from Castledermot), after 5km/3 miles the road passes Kilkea Castle, which was built in 1180, but suffered extensive alterations in the 19th century.

Kilkea Castle

Ballina (Béal an Átha)

B 2

Republic of Ireland, province: Connacht
County: Mayo
Population: 11,100
Information: www.northmayo.ie

Ballina, the largest town in County Mayo, is an ideal base for anglers. Those who are not in the mood for salmon and trout fishing can try the friendly town's cosy pubs and good restaurants.

Ballina lies far in the northwest of Ireland, in the boggy terrain on the River Moy, where the river widens into its Atlantic estuary at Killala

Paradise for anglers

Bay. In this fishing paradise, keen anglers flock first and foremost to the River Moy, as well as to the fish-rich lakes of Lough Conn and Lough Cullin.

Cathedral The stained glass in the 20th-century Catholic cathedral are worth a brief visit. Nearby stand the remains of a 15th-century Augustinian abbey. The **Ballina Arts Centre** runs a year-round programme of art and events. there aren't that many sights around here.

Jackie Clarke Museum The new Jackie Clarke Museum, housed in the former Provincial Bank, holds a huge collection of documents and items illustrating 400 years of Irish history, gathered by the local businessman Jackie Clarke (1927–2000).

Not far from the railway station, a **dolmen** serves as tomb for four brothers said to have murdered their foster father, a bishop, in the 6th century.

Ballina Arts Centre: Barrett St., Mon–Fri 10am–5pm, Sat 10am–3pm.
Jackie Clarke Museum: Pearse St., Tue–Sat 10am–5pm; free admission; www.clarkecollection.ie

AROUND BALLINA

Rosserk Abbey Take the R314 until, after approx. 6km/3.5 miles, you reach a sign. Follow this and turn left at the next crossroads to reach 15th-century Rosserk Abbey. The lavishly sculpted western doorway of this Franciscan abbey leads into the single-aisled church, with one south chapel. The choir features a double piscina (baptismal font), with a round tower and a square tower carved into one of its columns.

Ballina

INFORMATION
Tourist Information Office
Cathedral Road
Tel. (0 96) 70848

WHERE TO STAY
Downhill Inn €€€
Sligo Road, Tel. (0 96) 7 3444
www.downhillinn.ie
45 rooms
Angling, golf, swimming pool, squash, sauna, tennis – all these options and freshly cooked meals in the restaurant

are on offer at this comfortable establishment

Diamond Coast Hotel €€€
Enniscrone, Co. Sligo
Tel. (0 96) 2 60 00
www.diamondcoast.ie
92 rooms
Many rooms have a spectacular view across the Enniscrone golf course and dunes. The Golden Beach (Blue Flag) is nearby. Restaurant, club for kids and family activities.

Back on the main road, take a left-hand turn after another 3km/2miles just past the village; this side road leads southwest to the 15th-century Moyne Abbey right on the seaside. Many parts of this Franciscan abbey are preserved if only as ruins.

*Moyne Abbey

Another 6km/3.5 miles to the north, in Killala (pop. 570), a 26m/85 ft well-preserved round tower stands opposite a small 17th-century church. French forces who landed in Kilcummin Bay in 1798 to support the rebels, held on to Killala for a while as a bulwark against the British.

Killala

Past Ballycastle (▶p.164), it is worth taking the east coast by road via Rathlackan; take a right turn in Carrowmore towards Lackan Bay. The road leads past the remains of Rathfran Friary; a signposted path points to the 2.5m/8 ft Breastagh Ogham Stone.

Breastagh Ogham Stone

The R314 leads northwest to Ballycastle; however, the drive along the coast via Downpatrick Head is also very scenic, with its shore rocks, shaped into bizarre formations by the sea. Jets of water gush up where the surf pushes the seawater through narrow openings.

Downpatrick Head

At 10 sq km/4 sq miles, Céide Fields is **the largest Neolithic archaeological site in the world**. The village, 5,000 years old, lies 8km/5 miles west of Ballycastle on the R314. The settlers cleared the forest, laid out pastures and lived in free-standing farmsteads, with walls dividing the plots of land from each other. The remains of walls excavated from under a thick layer of turf may not seem impressive to the lay visitor, but a visitor centre provides the necessary background to the sensational discoveries made here.

**Céide Fields

Visitor centre: Easter–Oct daily 10am– 5pm, June–Sept until 6pm; admission 4 €; www.museumofmayo.com

MARCO POLO TIP

Insider Tip

Tír Sáile

The North Mayo Sculpture Trail (Tír Sáile) runs along the coast, from Ballina via Killala, Ballycastle, Belderrig and Belmullet to finish in Blacksod. For the celebrations of Mayo's 5,000 year-history, 15 international artists were commissioned to create sculptures reflecting the wild beauty of the region. For more information, see www.ballina.mayo-ireland.ie.

At Enniscrone, **Kilcullen's Bath House** is a restorative trip down memory lane. In addition to steam baths and a massage, visitors can enjoy the 100-year-old »hot sea water bath and seaweed bath« with its Art Nouveau tiles and porcelain tubs.

Enniscrone

❶ June–Sept daily 10am–8pm, Oct–May Mon–Fri 12 noon–8pm; Sat and Sun 10–8pm; admission 25 €; www.kilcullenseaweedbaths.com

Foxford It is a quick 16km/10-mile drive on the N57 to reach **Foxford** south of Ballina. In the past century, the hydropower of the River Moy, snaking through the little town, was harnessed to power mills for spinning wool. The **Foxford Woollen Mills Visitor Centre** shows wool production then and now.

❶ Mon–Sat 10am–5pm, Sun 12 noon–5pm; free admission; www. foxfordwollenmills.com

Angling The River Moy is considered **one of the most salmon-rich rivers in Europe**. Going south, the R310 leads to the narrow strait between Lough Conn (famous for its trout and pike) and Lough Cullin. Over-fishing has led to restrictions on angling at the popular Pontoon Bridge between the two lakes.

Ballinasloe (Béal Átha na Sluaighe)

✦ C 3

Republic of Ireland, province: Connacht
County: Galway
Population: 6,450

Ballinasloe is a busy commercial town, famous for its horse, cattle and sheep fairs. The October Fair is the largest in Ireland

Terminal of the Grand Canal Once, Ballinasloe – in the heart of Ireland, southwest of Lough Ree, on the N6 – had a significant strategic position. Ballinasloe is also the western terminal of the ▶Grand Canal, which is, however, not navigable on its last stretch. Above the River Suck, 19th-century Ivy Castle stands on earlier defensive structures.

AROUND BALLINASLOE

Clontuskert Abbey On the R355, 8km/5 miles south of town lies the ruined Augustinian monastery of Clontuskert Abbey. The western entrance of the church, erected in 1471, is worth seeing for its ornate carvings: St Michael weighing the souls, saints, a pelican, and a mermaid holding a mirror amongst others.

Clonfert Abbey From the monastery, take a byroad via Laurencetown to reach Clonfert Abbey, 21km/13 miles southeast of Ballinasloe. The former abbey's famous main doorway, dating from the 12th century and sumptuously carved with human heads and triangles, is considered the peak of Hiberno-Romanesque sculpture. The eastern choir windows count among the most important examples of late-Romanesque art in Ireland. Inside, look out for the decorations of later sections – the supporting arches of the tower, featuring angels and a mermaid, the chancel arch and the 15th-century window.

The small diocesan museum of Clonfert in Loughrea (St Brendan's Cathedral) has a fine collection of sculpture from the 15th to 18th centuries and the famous Kilcorban Madonna, dating from 1180 (www.clonfertdiocese.ie).

Loughrea

Ballinasloe

INFORMATION
Ballinasloe Visitor Information Point
c/o Society Travel, Society Street
Tel. (090) 961 5350
www.ballinasloe.com

Ballybunion (Baile an Bhuinneánaigh)

✦ D 2

Republic of Ireland, province: Munster
County: Kerry
Population: 1,370

Sea caves, jagged cliffs, bays, little hideouts and a seemingly endless sandy beach offer a varied and attractive holiday experience in and around Ballybunion. Many tourists come just for the golf – even US president Bill Clinton was here in 1998, his visit commemorated by a sculpture outside the Garda (police) Station.

This popular family resort lies in the southwest of Ireland, where the Shannon meets the Atlantic. The northern coastal strip has many caves that are accessible from the sea, some of them by boat, others, at low tide, on foot. A path of approx. 5km/3 miles leads along the top of the cliffs between Doon Cove and Doon Point, both with remains of promontory forts, and past the old fortress of Lick Castle. East of Ballybunion rises **Knockamore Hill** (264m/866ft), which offers a magnificent panoramic view.

Coastal caves

AROUND BALLYBUNION

Northeast, the R551 leads to Ballylongford . On the western side of the narrow inlet stands **Carrigafoyle Castle**, dating from the 15th

Ballylongford

century; there are splendid views from the top of the 26m/85ft tower. East of the town lie the ruins of the Franciscan **Lisloughtin Abbey**, also dating from the 15th century. Note, in particular, the west window of the church. The Ballylongford Cross, today kept in the National Museum in Dublin, is from this monastery.

Tarbert Continue on the R551 from Ballylongford for 8km/5 miles to reach Tarbert (pop. 810), the embarkation point for a car ferry to Killimer (►Kilkee), crossing the Shannon. The **Tarbert Bridewell Courthouse & Jail** of 1831 highlights the harsh criminal justice system in the 19th century. There is also an exhibition about the Talbert poet Thomas McGreevey. Musical evenings are held here. Tarbert Island has a lighthouse and an old gun battery.

ℹ April–Sept daily 10am–6pm, Oct–March Mon–Fri 10am–4pm; admission 5 €

Listowel Some 14km/9 miles southeast of Ballybunion, Listowel (pop. 4,340) is an up-and-coming town, with, some say, more pubs than residential buildings! Listowel became famous for its **Writers' Week** (www.writersweek.ie) taking place every year in June. Another event is the harvest festival at the end of September, which to this day serves simultaneously as a **marriage fair**.

*Rattoo Round Tower A good 12km/7.5-mile drive west of Listowel, in the grounds of the early monastic foundation of Rattoo, stand a 15th-century church and the very well-preserved 28m/92ft Rattoo Round Tower.

* Bantry (Beanntrai)

✦ E 2

Republic of Ireland, province: Munster
County: Cork
Population: 3,350

Giant fuchsia hedges and palm trees are a common sight in the famously beautiful Bantry Bay in the furthest southwestern corner of Ireland, as the influence of the Gulf Stream can indeed be felt here.

Lively holiday resort Bantry itself is fairly busy if not that attractive – not helped by the **oil terminal** on Whiddy Island, with facilities for supertankers. French fleets invaded the bay twice: in 1689, to support James II, and in 1796, to help the Irish rebels. They failed, however, on both accounts. Conscientious visitors may prepare their visit to Bantry House by following the Bantry Heritage Trail to the **Bantry Museum**, located behind the fire station. Market day is Friday.

Bantry Museum: Wolfe Tone Square, June, Aug Tue, Thu 10am–1pm, Wed, Fri 2pm–5pm, free admission, www.bantry.ie

On the southern edge of town, in a magnificent park, Bantry House awaits. This Georgian building, begun in 1740, was extended in 1840 by two wings to form a harmonious broad ensemble. Bantry House boasts a **valuable art collection** with exhibits from all over Europe, including icons, tapestries and French furniture, and mosaics from Pompeii adorning the hall. The pretty tearoom is a good place to linger. The most beautiful feature though is the park with its Italianate terraces and sculptures seemingly leaning against the ascending slopes.

*Bantry House & Gardens

❶ Early April–Oct, daily 10am–6pm; admission 11 €; www.bantryhouse.com

Opposite Bantry House, visit the 1796 French Armada Exhibition Centre. In the **winter of 1796**, a French fleet of 43 ships with 16,000 men aboard sailed to Ireland to support the United Irishmen in their insurrection against the British. However, as only 16 ships reached Bantry Bay, the French had to retreat after only a few skirmishes. Unfavourable winds prevented the larger part of the force from landing, although it was in Tone's words »close enough to toss a biscuit ashore«. A model of the sunk French frigate »La Surveillante« is on display at the Armada Museum.

1796 French Armada Exhibition Centre

❶ April–Oct 10am–6pm; admission 5 €

Feel like an earl for once – a wing of Bantry House is used for affordable accommodation

Bantry

INFORMATION
Tel. (027) 50229
www.bantry.ie
Open June to Sept

WHERE TO STAY
Westlodge Hotel €€€
Tel. (0 27) 5 0360
www.westlodgehotel.ie
90 rooms, 1 suite
A family-friendly hotel with restaurant,
9-hole golf, swimming pools, squash,
gym, tennis, leisure centre and kids' club

Gougane Barra Hotel €€€

Insider Tip

Gougane Barra
Ballingeary
Tel. (0 26) 4 70 69
www.gouganebarrahotel.com 26 rooms
A quiet, idyllic spot on Gougane Barra
Lake, with performances at the Theatre
by the Lake in July and August. Walking,
riding, cycling and angling are the activities here. Restaurant for lunch and dinner.

AROUND BANTRY

Stones and waterfalls

Around Bantry, there are several nice options for tours to explore the scenic area. One route leads to the **Kilnaurane Pillar Stone**, featuring one of the rare representations of the boat allegedly used by **St Brendan** to sail to America in the 6th century. To find the stone, take the N71 in the direction of Cork. At the Westlodge Hotel, 2km/1.2 miles out of town, turn left; after 800m/0.5 miles, you will pass a sign pointing to a gate.

Cousane Pass

Particularly nice roads to explore are the routes to Macroom (▶Cork, Around) and on to Glengarriff (▶Beara Peninsula) along the coast, with **beautiful vistas** of the sea and mountains.

Donemare Waterfalls

North of the town, on the road to Glengarriff, visit the impressive Donemare Waterfalls of Mealagh River, which, together with Drombrow Lough above, and Lough Bofinna, offers anglers good fishing grounds. Continuing to Glengariff, it is worth stopping at **Ballylickey**, where Manning's Emporium, a gourmet shop with café, has good wine and Irish specialities.

Sheep's Head Peninsula

Stretching southwest from Bantry, the long, scenic Sheep's Head Peninsula has attractive beaches on its southern coast, at Kilcrohane and Ahakista. It is worth driving all around the peninsula, pushing on as far as Sheep's Head. The road from Kilcrohane to Gouladoo runs below Seefin mountain (340m/1,115ft), with particularly fine views.

To reach one of the loveliest mountain lakes in Ireland, only 16km/10 miles east of Bantry, take the R584 towards Macroom. Situated at the end of a cul-de-sac, the lonely dark Gougane Barra Lake has an islet where St Finbarr is said to have set up his first hermitage at the end of the 6th-century. Every year in late autumn, pilgrims visit the holy site. Behind the lake begins **Gougane Barra Forest Park**, a 150ha/370-acre forest with hiking trails, picnic sites and beautiful viewpoints.

Gougane Barra Lake

✴ Beara Peninsula

✳ E 1 / 2

Republic of Ireland, province: Munster
County: Cork

The Beara Peninsula in the southwest of Ireland, with its many small lakes, has a unique wild beauty. Jutting out some 60km/40 miles to sea between the bays of ▸Bantry and the Kenmare River, it is strewn with great viewpoints.

On the Beara Peninsula, the coast road (Ring of Beara) winds its way behind Bantry Bay around rocky bays and promontories, past beautiful sandy beaches and charming fishing villages, whilst the inland route leads through barren mountain scenery.

Peninsula with varied scenery

✴ RING OF BEARA

Glengarriff, in Irish An Gleann Garb (»the barren valley«), is a small village in the southwest of Ireland at the end of a 10km/6-mile valley, where the Glengarriff River flows into Bantry Bay. The village (pop. 800) is **completely given over to tourism**, with numerous guesthouses and B&Bs and Ireland's only interactive sculpture park, The Ewe Gallery and Sculpture Garden, 4.5km/3 miles north on Kenmare Road. Day trippers mainly come here to visit **Garinish Island** just offshore or to start their drive around the Ring of Beara. Due to the favourable climate nurtured by the warm Gulf Stream, an almost tropical vegetation of fuchsia, yew trees, holly and strawberry trees (arbutus) covers the rocky slopes down to the sea. Also recommended is a visit to Glengarriff Woods, a huge oak and pine forest, the entrance to which lies about 1km/0.6 miles north of town.
It is well worth visiting the **Bamboo Park**, where palms, ferns, fuchsias and eucalyptus can be admired, as well as bamboo.

Glengarriff

Ewe Gallery and Sculpture Garden: Easter–Sept daily 10am–6pm, admission 6.50 €, www.theewe.com
Bamboo Park: daily 9am–7pm, admission 6 €, www.bamboo-park.com

Garinish, a garden island with subtropical plants

Garinish Island Of the many small islands in the bay, Garinish Island (Ilnacullin), east of the R572, is most worth a visit. During the 15-minute trip out to the island, the boat passes a rock with seals basking in the sun. The **fine gardens on Garinish Island, with magnolias, rhododendrons, camellias and many exotic trees, were only laid out between 1910 and 1920. All other buildings on the islands, blending in well with the park landscape, were built at the same time – apart from one Martello tower from the Napoleonic era. The gardens inspired George Bernard Shaw, who wrote much of his play »Saint Joan« on the island in 1923.

❶ April Mon–Sat 10am–5.30pm, Sun 3–6pm, May and Sept Mon–Sat 10am–6pm, Sun 12 noon–6pm, June Mon–Sat 10am–6pm, Sun 11am–6pm, July–Aug Mon–Sat 9.30am–6pm, Sun 11am–6pm; Oct Mon–Sat 10am–4pm, Sun 1–5pm; admission 4 €, www.garinishisland.com; ferry tel. 021 631 16, www.harbourqueenferry.com

Drive around the peninsula From Glengarriff, start exploring the peninsula jutting out west into the sea, the Ring of Beara. This stretch of approx. 135km/85 miles offers spectacular scenery. The interior of the peninsula is traversed by the bleak ranges of the Caha and Slieve Miskish mountains (400m/1,300ft to 700m/2,300ft). The R572 initially wends its way between the Caha Mountains and the sea along Bantry Bay, around the bay of Adrigole Harbour, to the fishing village of Castletownbere (pop. 870). Lying off the shore of Castletownbere, **Bere Island** has an interesting shape and boasts a sailing school and good hiking. Some 3km/2 miles to the southeast, visit the picturesque ruins of **Dunboy Castle**, the former residence of the O'Sullivans, which burned out in 1602. Close by, look for the remains of the **mansion of the Puxleys**, who prospered here in the 19th century by exploiting the local copper mines. Daphne du Maurier, in her novel »Hungry Hill«, allegedly based her protagonists on individual members of this family. Dursey Sound separates the furthest point of the peninsula from the island of the same name. Only a dozen people live on **Dursey Island**. Daring visitors can take the Dursey Cable Car, **the only cable car in Ireland**. A short ride in this tiny tin cab dangling between two masts will leave lasting memories.

Between 1810 and 1962, the small village of Allihies was a centre for copper mining ; the **Copper Mine Trail** leads to stone cottages and chimneys, reminders of the time when almost 1,300 men, women and children worked here. The **Allihies Coppermine Museum** in the old mine chapel of 1845 was opened by President Mary McAleese in 2007. Industrial archaeology and 3,500 years of mining history are presented here. **Allihies**

❶ April-Oct daily 10am–6pm; admission 5 €; www.acmm.ie

Follow the road northeast for 12km/7.5 miles to the prettily situated village of Eyeries, where a sign points to the **Ardgroom Stone Circle**, dating from the Bronze Age. From Eyeries, the road runs northeast across the border with County Kerry to Lauragh, where the **Derreen Gardens**, featuring a 100-year-old jungle of tree ferns, are a must-see. Mossy paths lead through a forest landscape, past tall rhododendron, eucalyptus and bamboo groves, yielding splendid vistas of the sea. From Lauragh, one option is to drive south to return to Glengarriff via Healy Pass (325m/1,066ft) and Adrigole. **Eyeries and Lauragh**

❶ Derreen Garden: daily 10am–6pm, Aug only Fri–Sun; admission 7 €

Beara Peninsula

WHERE TO STAY

Glengarriff Eccles Hotel €€€€
Glengarriff
Tel. (0 27) 6 3003
www.ecceshotel.com, 65 rooms
Recently restored, this hotel on Bantry Bay is one of the oldest in Ireland. Writers such as Yeats and Shaw stayed here. Restaurant, hotel terrace, and many special offers.

Foley's Shamrock €€€
Henry Street, Kenmare
Tel. (0 87) 234 62 82
www.foleyskenmare.com, 10 rooms
This guesthouse in the centre of Kenmare has a good restaurant and an award-winning pub with frequent live music, also self-catering accommodation.

** Belfast (Beál Feirste)

— ☀ B 5/6

Northern Ireland, province: Ulster
District: Belfast
Population: 267,500 (Greater Belfast 579,300)

Belfast has been the capital of Northern Ireland since 1920 – nearly a third of all the inhabitants of the province live here. As the Troubles came to an end, the city began to prosper. Belfast »reinvented« itself with new technology businesses, a construction boom and not least an ever increasing number of visitors as a result of the 100th anniversary of the »Titanic'» in 1912.

Capital of Northern Ireland

Belfast (Béal Feirste means »sandy ford at the river mouth«), with its position on the estuary of the Lagan, is an important industrial and port city. The most attractive districts are the city centre, the cathedral quarter on the western shore of the River Lagan, and on its east

The City Hall is a Belfast landmark

Belfast Highlights

► **City Hall**
Belfast's emblem on Donegall Square
►page 200

► **Cathedral Quarter, MAC**
The centre of nightlife
►page 202

► **Titanic Quarter, Titanic Belfast**
Follow the trail of the doomed liner
►page 204

► **Stormont**
The former and present home of the Northern Ireland Parliament
►page 207

► **Botanic Garden**
Relax beneath palm trees
►page 209

► **Ulster Museum**
Last resting place of a Spanish galleon
►page 210

bank the new Titanic Quarter with numerous attractions on the site of the old shipyards. There is plenty of atmosphere in the Queen's Quarter and, in south Belfast, the area of the Queen's University, the Botanical Gardens and narrow, quiet streets with old trees, small Victorian houses, little shops and galleries. The highlights of north Belfast are Belfast Castle and the zoo in Cave Hill Park. The Gaeltacht Quarter in West Belfast, once renowned for the Troubles and its murals on houses, now increasingly attracts tourists.

Take a bike Many places to visit, for example the Lagan Valley Regional Park in the south and the Crawfordsburn Country Park in the east, can be reached by bike from the city centre. The dense network of Northern Irish **bike paths** is being constantly improved and expanded for the purposes of natural, sustainable recreation (www.cycleni.com).

Festivals Outstanding events in the packed calendar of festivals (www.belfastfestival.com) are the Belfast Summer City Fest, the Belfast City Folk Festival featuring local and international stars, and the Féile an Phobail in the Gaeltacht Quarter. High-calibre artistic offerings are found in the Festival at Queen's (mid-Oct to late Nov) and the Cathedral Quarter Arts Festival in early May (►Events).

History Belfast already had a fortress in the early Middle Ages, but by 1177 it was destroyed. The castle erected subsequently was much fought over between the English conquerors and Irish owners. From the early days, linen production played an important role in Belfast; the sector was boosted significantly with the arrival of the Huguenots fleeing France in the late 17th century. These immigrants not only introduced better methods of production, but also gave »**Linenopo-**

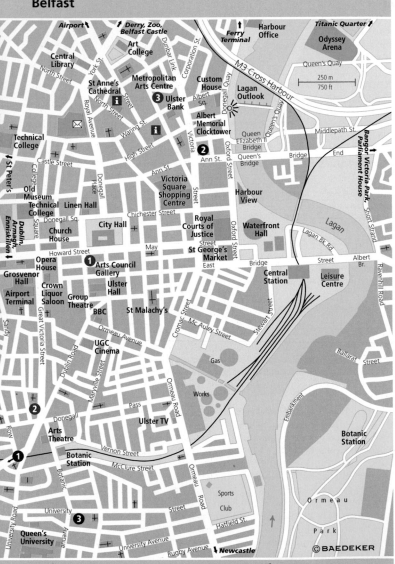

Belfast

Where to stay
1 Malone Lodge
2 The Belfast Mall
3 Dukes Hotel

Where to eat
1 Deane's Restaurant
2 Cayenne
3 Nick's Warehouse

©BAEDEKER

Belfast

INFORMATION
Belfast Welcome Centre
47 Donegall Place
Tel. 028 90 24 66 09
www.gotobelfast.com
June–Sept Mon–Sat 9am–7pm, Sun
11am–4pm, Oct–May Mon–Sat 9am–
5.30pm, Sun 11–4pm. Come here to get
the Belfast Visitor Pass (valid for 1–3
days, 6.50 £, 10 £ or 14 £), which provides many discounts and free use of public transport.

WHERE TO EAT
To find out the latest on Belfast's lively
gastronomic scene, see www.greatfood-
belfast.com

❶ *Deane's Restaurant* £££££
36–40 Howard Street
Tel. (0 28) 90 33 11 34
www.michaeldeane.co.uk
Closed Sun.
A top restaurant with seafood bar. The
menu includes the dishes served to first-
class passengers on the Titanic. The
group includes Deane's Deli/Vin Café (44
Bedford St.), Deane's at Queen's (1 College Gardens) and Simply Deane's (Outlet Centre, Dublin Road near Banbridge).

❷ *Cayenne* £££
7 Ascot House, Shaftesbury Square
Tel. (0 28) 19 33 15 32
www.cayennerestaurant.co.uk

Closed Mon, Tue
Fine dining, Asian-inspired, with a reasonably priced lunch (3 courses 16.95 £

❸ *Nick's Warehouse* ££
35–39 Hill Street
Tel. (0 28) 90 43 96 90
www.nickswarehouse.co.uk
Closed Mon, Tue
An institution in the Cathedral Quarter,
always, busy. Nibbles are served Mon–
Sat 12 noon–10pm, a low-priced theatre menu in the evenings.

WHERE TO STAY
❶ *Malone Lodge Hotel* ££££
60 Eglantine Avenue
Tel. (0 28) 90 38 80 607
www.malonelodgehotelbelfast.com
111 rooms and suites, 23 apartments
A Victorian town house in the university
quarter amongst parks

❷ *The Belfast Mall* £££
34–38 Victoria Street
Tel. (0 845) 365 42 47
www.malmaison.com/hotels
62 rooms
The hotel has a gym and a brasserie serving modern Irish cuisine.

❸ *Dukes Hotel* £££
65–67 University Street
Tel. (0 28) 90 23 66 66
www.dukesatqueens.com
32 rooms
A Victorian building near Queen's University with a shuttle to the Titanic Belfast. Dinner is served in Claudine's Cock-
tail bar from Mon to Wed, lunch from
Thu to Sun.

lis« a little French flair and enriched it culturally. After the union with England (1800), Belfast grew to be a major industrial city, its magnificent 19th-century buildings earning it the epithet of »**Athens of the North**«. Alongside linen weaving, rope manufacture, shipbuilding and the tobacco industry rang in Belfast's economic heyday. Belfast suffered severely in the economic crisis between the two world wars.

The close proximity of Catholic and Protestant districts made Belfast one of the main scene of the Troubles. Since the beginning of the »peace process« in 1994, what was once the »**European Beirut**« has prospered, and a construction boom has changed the face of the city.

CITY CENTRE

The hub of the city centre is **Donegall Square**. At the north end of the square lies the shopping zone Donegall Place, where the Belfast Welcome Centre can be found (►p. 199). The landmarks on Donegall Place are eight large, new copper pillars by Dennis Gilloway, a reference to great vessels such as the »Titanic« that came from Belfast's shipyards. From here, it is a five-minute walk to The Entries, an old commercial quarter with narrow streets and plenty of atmosphere. Along the shopping mile of Royal Avenue lies the city's biggest shopping mall, Castlecourt Centre. Further north, reaching as far as the Central Library and Dunbar Link, lies the transformed **Cathedral Quarter**. The cathedral itself, the 76m/250ft-high St Anne's, now lies in the shadow of surrounding high-rises.

To the east of Donegall Square, Chichester Street leads to **Victoria Square**. Here stand the Jaffe Fountain, erected in 1870 to honour Mayor Otto Jaffe, and the enormous **Victoria Square Shopping Centre** (www.victoriasquare.com). From the glass dome above its atrium, the view across the city is wonderful. On level one there is a Titanic exhibition with original prints from 100 years of maritime history.

*Donegall Square and City Hall

Unmissable on Donegall Square, City Hall is an imposing building with four towers and an enormous dome, erected 1898–1906 in the Neorenaissance style after designs by Sir Brumwell Thomas. Worth seeing in particular are the 50m/164ft-long, splendidly furnished **banqueting hall**, the marble-lined entrance hall, as well as the wall painting by John Luke (1951) showing important trades that played a major role in the development of the city: rope-making, shipbuilding, weaving and spinning. Two exhibitions can be seen in the **Bobeen Coffee Shop**: the industrial history of Belfast is presented in »Walking the Giant«, and 68 citizens are portrayed in photographs in »No Mean City.

In front of City Hall stand statues, including Queen Victoria. To the east is the **Titanic Memorial Garden**, opened in 2012. At its centre is the restored Titanic Monument, made of Carrara marble in 1920 by Sir Thomas Brock, behind which a new memorial stone lists the names of all victims of the disaster. City Hall is also the starting point for the Titanic Trail, leading to Sinclair's Seaman's Church (see tip p.204) and the footbridge at the former Lagan Lookout Visitor Centre before continuing to the Titanic Quarter.

❶ City Hall: Mon–Thu 8.30am–5pm, Fri 8.30am–4.30pm; free admission; free guided tours: Mon–Fri 11am, 2pm and 3pm, Sat 2pm, 3pm;

MARCO POLO TIP

The Red Hand Insider Tip

Above the entrance to the Linen Hall Library, look out for the symbol of Ulster, the Red Hand. It is said to go back to Viking days, when one band of Vikings had already settled and a rival group tried to dispossess them. The leader of the settlers declared that the land should belong to the first who could lay a hand on it. He then cut of his hand and cast it on the ground, thus thwarting the attackers.

Situated on the northwestern corner of Donegall Square, the Linen Hall Library (1788) is **Belfast's oldest library**. Irish literature occupies the whole of the first floor. Unusual here is the **Political Collection**, containing over 100,000 works dealing with different aspects of political life in Northern Ireland since 1966. Moreover, some of the first books to be printed in Belfast belong to the Linen Hall Library, for instance »Paddy's Resource« (1796), an early collection of patriotic Irish songs. The first librarian here, Thomas Russell, was a founding member of the United Irishmen and a close friend of Wolfe Tone's; after Robert Emmet's failed rebellion, Russell was hanged in 1803.

Linen Hall Library

❶ Mon–Fri 9.30am–5.30pm, Sat 9.30am–4pm; free admission, donation requested; www.linenhall.com

The oldest part of Belfast suffered extensive damage during the Second World War. In pedestrian zones between Castle Street and College Street is a new cultural quarter with galleries.
Narrow alleyways, called »Entries« branch off from High Street and Ann Street. There are **some fine old pubs and bars** here, such as the Morning Star in Pottinger's Entry, which also serves good food, The Globe in Joy's Entry and **the oldest pub in Belfast**, The White Tavern in Winecellar Entry. The United Irishmen, led by the Protestants Wolfe Tone, McCracken and Samuel Nielson, were founded in 1791 in Peggy Barlay's Tavern in Crown Entry. In the area, Samuel Nielson also published the »Northern Star«, a magazine dedicated to the

The Entries & High Street

revolutionary ideals of freedom, equality and brotherhood. On Queen's Square, where High Street and Victoria Street meet, stands the **Albert Memorial Clocktower**, 34.4m/112ft high, which was erected in 1869 in memory of Albert, consort of Queen Victoria. Due to its similarity to the famous Big Ben in London, the tower is often called »Big Ben of Belfast«.

✳ CATHEDRAL QUARTER AND LAGANSIDE

New art quarter
The Cathedral Quarter, the district between Royal Avenue, the Central Library and Dunbar Link, has undergone a far-reaching transformation. Back in the 1970s, North Street was the centre of the punk scene. The Art College of the University of Ulster was home to the avant-garde. Now this area is characterized by a mixture of art, media and entertainment venues.

St Anne's Cathedral
The quarter centres around St Anne's Cathedral, begun in 1898 to designs by Sir Thomas Drew and now the main church of the Anglican Church of Ireland. The building, in the style of a neo-Romanesque basilica, has three notable western doorways with archways and sculptures. The mosaic ceiling in the baptismal chapel consists of hundreds of thousands of small glass stones. The only tomb in the cathedral is that of Lord Carson, the redoubtable opponent of Home Rule and leader of the Irish Unionist Party (died 1935). St Anne's is famous for its youth choir and its evening and lunchtime concerts.

Writers' Square
On Writers' Square by the cathedral, paving stones bear quotes from the writings of 27 writers from Northern Ireland. To the right of the cathedral the **War Memorial Gallery** commemorates 900 victims of the Belfast Blitz in 1941, when the city was bombarded by the German Luftwaffe, and the US troops who were stationed here in the war. The window dedicated to the fallen of both world wars is the work of Stanley Scott.
  ❶ St Anne's Cathedral: 8am–4pm; admission 2 £; www.belfastcathedral.org
  ❶ War Memorial Gallery: Mon–Fri 10.30am–4.30pm, June–Sept also Sun 11am–1pm; www.niwarmemorial.org

✳Metropolitan Arts Centre
The new cultural highlight of the district is the Metropolitan Arts Centre (MAC), opened in 2012. It is home to three galleries, two theatres and a dance studio.
  ❶ 10 Exchange Street West; daily 10am–7pm; free admission; http://themaclive.com

Ulster Bank
The Ulster Bank of 1860 with its the fluted pillars, Greek urns and female warriors on the balustrade has been converted into the elegant

Merchant Hotel. The Red Hand of Ulster adorns the gilded railings. The café in the lobby is a favourite rendezvous, for example for afternoon tea. Bert's Jazz Bar has a bit of New York atmosphere in the evenings, when good food is served to the sounds of live jazz.

Directly opposite, the Belfast Print Workshop, with a gallery and atelier for producing art prints, is a reminder of the press and printing tradition of the area.

Belfast Print Workshop

❶ Cotton Court, 30–42 Waring Street; Tue–Fri 10am–5pm, Sat 12 noon-4pm; http://bpw.org.uk

To the east, beyond Oxford Street and the Royal Court of Justice, lies the Belfast Waterfront, site of the **Waterfront Hall**, a concert and congress venue built in 1997 (www.waterfront.co.uk). The **Riverside Walk** behind the hall goes north from the Hilton Hotel on the west bank of the Lagan River. This is high-rise Belfast. There is also a footpath on the east bank. Three **Laganside Art Trails** to 30 works of art follow the riverbank paths (www.laganside.com).

Belfast Waterfront

Just before reaching the **Queen's Bridge**, by the architect Sir Charles Lanyon, with its ornate lamps and the large, Celtic-inspired female figure of ***Harmony** (by Andy Scott, 2005), you reach Thanksgiving Square, where the MV Confiance is at anchor. The ship, known as the **Belfast Barge**, houses a film and photographic exhibition entitled The Greatest Story Never Told« about the Lagan River and the maritime past of the city. There is also a stage for live theatre.

Boat trips leave from the pier behind the Queen Elizabeth Bridge, which was renovated for the diamond jubilee of the Queen in 2012. Opposite, on busy Custom House Square, stands the **Custom House**, completed in 1857 in the Corinthian style by Sir Charles Lanyon. The **Obel Tower** (an abbreviation of obelisk«) is an apartment building on Donegall Quay on the west bank of the Lagan, at 87m/285ft the tallest building in Belfast.

> **!** *Maritime Church* **Insider Tip**
>
> MARCO POLO TIP
>
> Sinclair's Seaman's Church was made to make sailors feel at home. Built in 1857 near the harbour office, it has a pulpit made from a ship's bows. The bell comes from HMS Hood and the impression of a maritime cabinet of curiosities is heightened by the presence of ships lamps and other maritime paraphernalia (open Wed 2–4.30pm; Sunday services at 11am and 6.30pm

Between the Lagan Lookout Visitor Centre, now closed, and the ***Big Fish** by John Kindness (1999), a 10m/33ft-long ceramic mosaic of a salmon that shimmers blue and bears texts from city history, is the snail-shaped ramp leading up to the new footbridge leading to the Titanic Quarter. This is the start of the Titanic Trail.

Belfast Barge: daily 10am–4pm, admission 4 £; www.laganlegacy.com

** TITANIC QUARTER

A major project The Civic Arts architectural practice has converted part of the Harland and Wolff shipyards into an industrial monument and the Titanic Quarter (www.titanic-quarter.com). Construction work continues, with plans for 7,500 new apartments and some 25,000 jobs.

Hamilton Graving Dock In 1861 James Harland (1831–95) and Gustav Wilhelm Wolff (1834–1913), an engineer from Hamburg, founded the shipyard that bore their name. A relic of those early years on the west bank of the Lagan is Hamilton Graving Dock (1863–67), now a protected monument, at which imported coal was landed for many decades. Today it is home to the ***SS Nomadic**, a ship of the White Star Line. She was built by Harland & Wolff in 1910–11, serving as a tender until 1968 (including service for the Titanic) and from 1970 until 1999 as a restaurant ship by the Eiffel Tower in Paris. In 2009 she came back to Belfast for restoration. The story of the ship is told on board in an interactive exhibition covering its role for the Titanic and its work in wartime and peace.

> **MARCO POLO TIP**
>
> **!** *Titanic tours* Insider Tip
>
> Individual tours of the quarter are given by Susie Millar, the great-granddaughter of Thomas Millar, the engineer of the Titanic, who went down with the ship on its maiden voyage. She has written a book about the family history of the Titanic (»The Two Pennies«, 9.95 £. Contact details: Titanic Tours Belfast, tel. (078) 52 71 66 55; 30 £; www.titanictours-belfast.co.uk.

❶ April–Sept daily 9am–6pm (July–Aug until 7pm), Oct–March daily 10am–5pm; admission 4 £, www.nomadicbelfast.com

Odyssey Complex Plaques in the ground on the east bank path relate to the Titanic and the fast clipper Star of Russia, a three-master built in Belfast in 1874. Right by the river stands the huge Odyssey Complex, with an indoor arena seating 10,000, cinemas, bars, restaurants and shops, as well as the ***W5 Science Centre**, which provides answers to the questions who? what? when? where? and why? with the help of 250 interactive exhibits. Visitors can try out a lie detector or look through a scientific microscope.

❶ 2 Queens Quay; Mon–Fri 10am–5pm, Sat 10am–6pm, Sun 12 noon–6pm; admission 7.90 £; www.w5online.co.uk

PRONI It is just a few steps from the Odyssey Arena to PRONI (Public Record Office of Northern Ireland), where exhibitions about life in the province can be viewed.

❶ 2 Titanic Boulevard; Mon–Fri 9am–4.5pm, Thu until 8.45am; free admission; www.proni.gov.uk

The main attraction of the quarter opened in 2012, in time for the centenary of the Titanic disaster. In nine galleries on four floors of a building designed to resemble the bows of a great ship, Titanic Belfast draws on all the resources of modern museum technology to depict life in a shipyard, the construction and sinking of the great liner, the passengers who went down with her and the treatment of the story in Hollywood films. The Ocean Exploration Centre takes visitors on an expedition to the wreck on the submarine Nautilus. Note: the

**Titanic Belfast

The new flagship museum in the capital of Northern Ireland, Titanic Belfast, has the largest exhibition anywhere about the doomed liner

timed tickets should be booked in advance. Behind the building are the **slipways** on which the hulls of the Titanic and Olympic were launched.

❶ Queen's Road; April, June–Aug daily 9am–7pm, May and Sept until 6pm, Oct–March daily 10am–5pm; admission 15.50 £, www.titanicbelfast.com

H & W Headquarters To the right of Titanic Belfast are the historic buildings of the Titanic Quarter. In the Drawing Offices of the H & W Headquarters, built between 1900 and 1919, in use until 1989, ships were designed. The plans for Titanic were drawn up in the two oldest offices, on the ground floor. They are listed for protection and may be used as a museum. To the right are car parks and the Harland & Wolff Shipyards (www.harland-wolff.com). In the early 20th century, H & W had a workforce numbering tens of thousands, some 30,000 of them in Belfast. Today there are only 500 jobs here, most of them connected with offshore wind power generation. The Titanic Film Studios in the Paint Hall stand alongside the office buildings.

Workers' meals **Insider Tip**

MARCO ⊕ POLO TIP

On the right-hand side of Queen's Road, the Crane View Kitchens in the T-13 complex serve the food that workers ate 100 years ago: stew and the legendary Belfast Bap, a crusty, round roll with a sandwich filling; Queen's Road, Mon–Sat 12 noon–3pm, on Sat also open in the evenings; www.t13.tv.

Alexandra Graving Dock Further along Queen's Road is the Alexandra Graving Dock, built in 1885–89 and 253m/275yd long. Here **HMS Caroline**, the sixth-oldest ship of the Royal Navy, lies at anchor. The flagship for a flotilla of six light cruisers, she was launched in 1914 and saw service at the Battle of Jutland in 1916, then came to Belfast in 1924.

Pumphouse There is a good view of the ship from the courtyard by the visitor centre of the Pumphouse, which was built in 1911 between the Alexandra Graving Dock and the Thompson Graving Dock. The latter was the world's largest dry dock in its day. The Pumphouse is still in working order. Its pumps could empty the dock in 110 minutes. The shipyard workers reached the docks through tunnels.

❶ Queen's Road; daily 10.30am–5pm, Fri from 9.30am; admission 5 £; www.titanicsdock.com

Musgrave Channel Road On the opposite side of the island, on Musgrave Channel Road, are two yellow **cranes**, among the largest in the world, called Samson and Goliath. They were built in the 1960s and can each lift 840 t. At Victoria Yard there are still three cranes that were once powered by steam. H & W once had 50 such steam cranes.

EAST BELFAST

Belfast's Modern Art Gallery has gained a reputation for innovative work. It promotes talent from the region, organizes auctions and has an emphasis on modern photography.

Modern Art Gallery

❶ 92 Castlereagh Road; Mon–Sat 10am–pm;
www.themodernartgallery.co.uk

The **Northern Irish Parliament** is located 9km/5.6 miles east of the city in Stormont. Approaching by road, the classical white building (1928–1932) catches the eye amidst extensive parkland. The Parliament of Northern Ireland sat here until 1972. Following the Good Friday Agreement in 1998, work recommenced, and the assembly has met here again since 2007, since 2010 with full legislative powers for the 108 deputies.

*Stormont

❶ Mon–Fri 9am–4pm; visitors are admitted to parliamentary sessions Mon from 12 noon, Tue from 10.30 am; free guided tours Mon–Fri 10am and 3pm, bookings tel. 028 90 52 18 02; www.niassembly.gov.uk

QUEEN'S QUARTER AND SOUTH BELFAST

The Golden Mile is the area between Great Victoria Street and Dublin Road, ending at Bradbury Place to the south. Two striking sights are situated on Great Victoria Street: the fine **Grand Opera House** of 1895 (www.goh.co.uk) and the only pub owned by the National Trust, the Crown Liquor Saloon (▶p 208). Titanic fans head for ***Robinsons Saloon** (38–42 Great Victoria Street) to talk about its construction and sinking, poor rivets and dents instead of cracks in the hull. A large number of original items are on display in glass cases, e.g. the doll Philomena, which miraculously rose to the surface and was kept for many years in a chapel in Belfast.

*Golden Mile

The **Europa Hotel**, opened in 1971 on Great Victoria Street, holds a sorry record: it was the target of 27 bombings during the Troubles .The cultural showpiece of the Golden Mile is the **Ulster Hall** in Bedford Street, which was renovated in 2009 and celebrated its 150th anniversary in 2012. It is home to the highly respected Ulster Orchestra, and possesses one of the biggest organs in the world. Enrico Caruso, the Rolling Stones and the Dalai Lama have all taken the stage at a venue that was renowned in the Second World War for its wild dance parties. In a new gallery, 13 oil paintings by Joseph W. Carey (1902) on the history of Belfast are on show (www.ulsterhall.co.uk). Two blocks away, at the corner of Russel Street and Alfred Street, it is worth taking a look at the Catholic **St Malachy's Church**, built in 1841–44 in the Tudor Revival style, and unique in Ireland.

❶ Robinsons Saloon: Mon–Sat 11.30am–1am, Sun 11am–midnight,
www.robinsonsbar.co.uk

Donegall Pass   To the southeast lies the old quarter of the linen weavers, Donegall Pass. The Ormeau Bath Gallery (OBG) in a restored public bath house is Belfast's leading gallery for contemporary art. The political agreements on Northern Ireland included clauses on promotion of the Irish language. The courses and musical, dance and literary events at the **An Droichead** arts centre reflect this.

❶ Ormeau Bath Gallery: 18A Ormeau Avenue, Tue–Sun 10amö5pm; www.ormeaubaths.co.uk

❶ An Droichead: 20 Cook Street; tickets 12.50 £; www.androichead.com

> **MARCO POLO TIP**
>
> ! *Crown Liquor Saloon* **Insider Tip**
>
> The Crown Liquor Saloon opposite the Europa Hotel must be the best-known pub in Belfast. The exterior is lavishly decorated with tiles, while inside it gains its atmosphere from gas lamps, a marble-topped bar and lots of mahogany. The excellent food consists of typical Ulster dishes, sometimes oysters. For the quiet Crown Liquor Restaurant, walk around the corner, continued 20 metres and go up the steps (46 Great Victoria Street, Mon–Thu 11.30am–11pm, Thu–Sat 11.30am–midnight, Sun 12.30–10pm; www.crownbar.com.

West of the Golden Mile and Great Victoria Street, along Sandy Row, discover a **Protestant working-class neighbourhood**. It was long the heartland of the Ulster Defence Association (UDA) and the Orange Order. The district, also known as the Royal Mile or Carr's Row, can be recognized from Loyalist **murals** and kerbstones painted in red-white-blue. Its most famous resident was snooker world champion Alex »Hurricane« Higgins (1949–2010), who is commemorated by a wall portrait at the corner of Abingdon Drive and Donegall Road. Fans of Van Morrison are bound to remember the line from his album »Astral Weeks« (1968), where he sings about roaming »up and down the Sandy Row«.

*University Area   South of Bradbury Place, University Road leads to the Queen's University, passing the late 19th-century **Crescent Church**, with its skeletal bell tower. The university (1845–1894) was built in red-brick Tudor-style to designs by Charles Lanyon. On the left in the Tudor-style red-brick ***Lanyon Building**, the Northern Ireland Tourist Board runs the Queen's Welcome Centre. The central tower of the Lanyon Building is reminiscent of the Founder's Tower of the more famous Magdalen College in Oxford. The first floor above the Welcome Centre is occupied by Belfast's most exciting art space, the ***Naughton Gallery**, home to high-calibre changing exhibitions and the portrait collection from the ***Great Hall**. Many cafés and bars can be found in the smaller streets around the campus.

Crescent Church: Tue–Fri 10am–4pm, www.crescentchurch.org

Lanyon Building: Mon–Fri 9.30am–4.30pm; free admission, tours 3.50 £; www.queensevents.com

Naughton Gallery: Tue–Sun 11am–4pm; free admission; www.naughtongallery.org

A thorough restoration completed in 2002 returned the Lanyon
Building to its former glory

On College Park, Botanic Avenue, the nicely laid-out, popular Bo- ***Botanic**
tanic Gardens are a good place to take a breather from the city. At the **Gardens**
gate stands a statue of Lord Kelvin, who was born in Belfast and developed the Kelvin scale for measuring temperatures. No alcohol
may be consumed in the park. There are frequent events here. Sir
Charles Lanyon designed the ***Palm House**, a Victorian glass palace
erected in 1852. The glasshouse above the **Tropical Ravine**, with ex-
otics such as orchids or banana plants, dates from 1889.

Gardens: daily 7.30am–dusk, in summer until 9pm
Palm House and Tropical Ravine: April-Sept daily Fri 10am–noon and
1–5pm, winter 4pm; free admission

*Ulster Museum To the south of the Kelvin Monument stands **Ulster's most important museum**. The Ulster Museum shows finds from the Celtic and early Christian period. Look out for the gold and silver treasures salvaged in 1968 from the Girona, a Spanish galleon sunk in the 16th century off the Northern Irish coast. The art gallery shows European painters of the 17th and 18th centuries and Irish artists of different periods. Art from Africa, Asia and the Pacific region is also on display.

❶ Tue–Sun 10am–5pm; free admission, free tours Tue–Fri 2.30pm Sun 1.30pm; www.nmni.com/um

Southern periphery At the Stranmillis Embankment on the west bank of the Lagan, the **Lyric Theatre** opened in 2011 (www.lyrictheatre.co.uk). A 15-minute stroll from the Botanic Gardens along Strandmillis Road leads to the river and the start of the 24km/15-mile **Lagan Towpath**, which passes through the Lagan Valley Regional Park and along the 18th-century canal system as far as Lisburn (www.walkni.com). A popular spot for lunch is Cutter's Wharf in Lockview Road (www.cutterswharf.co.uk). Head out of town on Milltown Road to the entrance to the **Barnett Demesne** park near Shaw's Bridge (metro line 8 A-C; get off at Dublin Lane).

There are many paths, connecting to the Lagan Towpath, an arboretum In **Malone House**, a late-Georgian manor house in the grounds of the Barnett Demesne, receptions and readings are often held, and the **Higgin Gallery** puts on temporary exhibitions.

Higgin Gallery: Mon–Sat 9am–5pm, Sun 12 noon–4.30pm; free admission

NORTH BELFAST

Crumlin Road Gaol Since 2012 the Crumlin Road Gaol, widely known as The Crum, has been open as a museum. It was built with four wings within a five-sided wall from black basalt in 1843–45 by Sir Charles Lanyon. A tunnel through which prisoners were taken leads to the courthouse opposite. In 150 years of operation until 1996, 25,000 persons, including suffragettes, Eamon de Valera and Ian Paisley, were imprisoned here. It was the first prison to introduce solitary confinement. Between 1901 and 1961, 17 executions were carried out at the end of C Wing.

❶ Guided tours only; mid-June–mid-Sept, Fri, Sat and Sun, booking via Belfast Welcome Centre: admission 5 £

Cave Hill Country Park Cave Hill Country Park takes up nearly 300ha/750 acres of space near Belfast Lough. This is a great place for long walks, visits to Belfast Zoo and Castle, or to climb Cave Hill itself (360m/1,180ft), also called »Napoleon's Profile« due to a passing resemblance to the profile of the French emperor. On a clear day, the hill offers a fantastic view over the city, across to Lough Neagh to the west and towards the coast, and the Isle of Man to the east. In 1795, Wolfe Tone and the northern Irish leaders of the United Irishmen met here to join forces, plotting a rebellion against England. Three paths, also used

MARCO POLO TIP

Insider Tip

Lucky cats

According to a legend, fortune will smile on the residents of Belfast Castle only if a white cat lives there. This is the reason for the large number of cats depicted in the garden on mosaics or paintings and even as sculptures and furnishings.

for cycling, lead out to the Belfast Hills (www.belfasthills.org; get here Mon-Sat by metro lines 1 A–H, Sun by lines 1 C–E or 1 H).
Belfast Castle Halfway up Cave Hill rises **Belfast Castle** (1870), the former manor of the Earl of Shaftesbury. Today, the second floor houses the Cave Hill Visitor Centre.
Cave Hill Country Park: daily 7.30am–dusk, in summer until 10pm; free admission
Belfast Castle: Mon–Sat 9am–10pm, Sun 9am–5.30pm; free admission; www.belfastcastle.co.uk

Belfast Zoo is home to 150 species and 1,000 animals. Particularly popular with children are the baby chimps, sea lions, kangaroos and the Sumatra tiger. **Belfast Zoo**
❶ Entrance: Antrim Road; April–Sept daily 10am–6pm, Oct–March daily 10am–4pm; admission 11 £, www.belfastzoo.co.uk

WEST BELFAST

When the Troubles started in Northern Ireland (Troubles, ▶Insight p.46) in 1968, murals sprang up in the Catholic Falls Road and the Protestant Shankill Road in order to document allegiance to political groups. Kerbs, posts and gates, among other things, were painted in the colours of Ireland (green, white, orange) or the British Union Jack (red, white, blue). Public institutions and shops were protected with walls and barbed wire. Around 100 of these »**Peace Walls**« or »**Peace Lines**« still exist as testimony to the years of conflict. Slowly West Belfast, especially the area around Falls Road, is attracting tourists as the Irish Gaeltacht Quarter. The group **Coiste Political Tours** takes groups around Shankill and the Gaeltacht Quarter. The guides are former prisoners who can tell about the Troubles from first-hand experience. **Murals**
Coiste Political Tours: Mon–Sat 11am, Sun 4pm from Divis Towers, Falls Road, 8 £; www.visitwestbelfast.com

Shankill Road   The 2.4km/1.5-mile-long Shankill Road, which takes its name from »Seankill«, meaning »old church«, starts near St Anne's Cathedral and runs west. Numerous Protestant murals show that »The Shankill« is a stronghold of Unionism. Not all of them murals are political. Themes such as boxing matches are also depicted; the most interesting shows how the Apprentice Boys of Derry locked the city gates in 1689. The first murals were painted as early as 1908 by Loyalists to celebrate the anniversary of the Battle of the Boyne (1690). Later, too, they continued using militaristic motifs to express their belief in Northern Ireland's role as a part of the United Kingdom. Most of their murals feature masked members of the Ulster Volunteer Force in black battle gear, armed with machine guns, and the vow »No Surrender«. Often they also show the Red Hand of Ulster or the British Union Jack.

> **MARCO ☉ POLO TIP**
>
> **!** *Black Cab Tours, Taxi Trax* **Insider Tip**
>
> Now that former enemies are working together in government and parliament, tours of once-opposed working-class districts in West Belfast explain the history of the Troubles. The drivers of black cabs take passengers to the political murals and other places in the areas. Information: www.belfast-tours.com and www.taxitrax.com.

Falls Road   West of the city centre of Belfast, Castle Street becomes Divis Street and then Falls Road. To the southwest lies Lower Falls. Newly installed plaques on Falls Road explain the Troubles. On its upper section, the **International Wall** has murals devoted to a wide range of Irish and international topical themes. The renovated **Conway Mill,** built in 1842 for spinning flax, houses 20 artists' studios and the **Irish Republican Museum**.

Back on Falls Road note the fine blue and gold railings of the **Royal Hospital**, which played a major role in the Troubles. The railings incorporate portraits of senior citizens, cleverly created in a grid pattern. Murals on Falls Road refer to the Republican support for a united Ireland. The most famous of those murals relates to Bobby Sands, who was the first to die in the hunger strike of 1981. At the corner of Rock Street is an image of the »Blanket Man«, depicting a prisoner who refused to wear regulation prison clothing.

A Presbyterian church at 216 Falls Road has been converted to the **Cultúrlann McAdam O'Faich** arts centre, with a bookshop, performances of Irish music, the Gerard Dillon Gallery presenting Irish art, and a café. **Clonard Monastery** on Clonard Gardens, and its Church of the Holy Redeemer, built in 1911, is the destination for a major pilgrimage in June to a shrine of the Virgin Mary. Further south on Falls Road, a new symbol of the district was unveiled in 2011: the large-scale sculpture **Aisling an Phobail** (The People's Dream) resembles St Brigid's Cross, a symbol of peace.

Beyond Lower Falls lies **Milltown Cemetery Milltown Cemetery**, with the graves of Republicans who died during the Troubles, 1,000 victims of the Belfast Blitz and 80,000 who died in the influenza epidemic on 1918–19 (www.milltowncemetery.com).

Irish Republican History Museum: 5–7 Conway Street, Tue–Sat 10am–2pm; free admission; www.conwaymill.org

Cultúrlann McAdam O'Faich: Mon, Fri, Sat 9am–6pm, Tue–Tue 9am–9pm, Sun 11am–4pm; free admission; www.culturlann.ie

A mural commemorating the hunger striker Bobby Sands

AROUND BELFAST

Some 5km/3 miles north of West Belfast, near Cultra, is the Ulster Folk & Transport Museum, also known as the Cultra Museum. The open-air zone called Ballycultra Town is an entire Irish village with shops, workshops, a school and church, showcasing traditional crafts and agricultural methods all year round. A new permanent exhibition called TITANIC – The People's Story brings to life the conditions of the population of Belfast at the time when the Titanic was built. A shuttle bus (daily 10.20am–5.20pm) runs between the Folk Museum and the Transport Museum, where a further impressive Titanic exhibition can be seen: **TITANICa – The Exhibition** presents a well-researched history of the luxury liner with 500 original artefacts. The museum also houses one of the largest railway collections in existence. The Road Galleries display an abundance of cars, trucks, motorbikes and bicycles, and there is also an aviation collection, including a flight simulator.

*Ulster Folk & Transport Museum

❶ March–Sept Tue–Sun 10am–5pm, Oct–Feb Mon–Fri 10am–4pm, Sat, Sun 11am–4pm; admission 8 £ per museum, combined ticket 9.50 €; www.nmni.com

To the north and south of Belfast Lough, the wide bay forming the estuary of the River Lagan, the coast boasts several popular seaside resorts. The northern coast is particularly beautiful. (►Antrim Coast & Glens).

Belfast Lough

11km/7 miles north of Belfast, Carrickfergus was an important seaport before Belfast took its place. It is famous for its very well pre-

*Carrickfergus Castle

Carrickfergus Castle

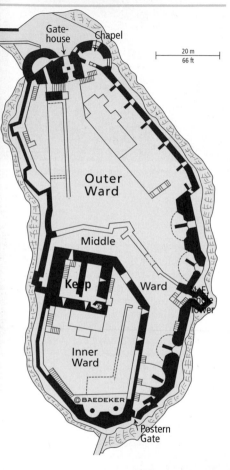

20 m
66 ft

Gate-house

Chapel

Outer Ward

Middle

Keep

Ward

Half-moon tower

Inner Ward

©BAEDEKER

Postern Gate

served Norman castle on a rocky outcrop which was originally surrounded by water on all sides except the north. This position lent it **strategic significance** for nearly 750 years. The Norman John de Courcy began the building between 1180 and 1204, and King John captured it in 1210 after a near year-long siege. In 1316, the castle fell into the hands of the Scottish, and the French were the last to capture it in 1760. In the 18th century, Carrickfergus Castle served as a prison, later as an army depot and armoury (up to 1928). The **main sights** are the bulky keep housing a small museum of military history, and on the third floor a magnificent Norman hall, with nice views from the top, a twin-turreted gatehouse, and in the eastern tower a room called »chapel« for its unusual window, as well as several cannons dating from the 16th–19th centuries.

❶ March–Oct 10am–6pm, Nov–Feb 10am–4pm, admission 5 £

A very romantic and attractive proposition is the **coast road leading from Larne to Cushendun**. First, drive through the Black Cave Tunnel, then round Ballygalley Head with its mighty basalt rocks. **Ballygalley** is a popular spa resort, with the former castle turned into a hotel. White limestone cliffs line the road to Glenarm. The next resort along is Carnlough, where a small harbour and pleasant sandy beach provide a good place to stop. The village of **Waterfoot** occupies a charming position close to the shoreline of Red Bay on the Antrim coast. Its sandstone cliffs resemble an amphitheatre. From there, one of the most beautiful glens of Antrim, Glenariff, stretches southwest. Drive north from Waterfoot to discover Cushendall and Cushendun (▶Antrim Coast)

Greater Belfast

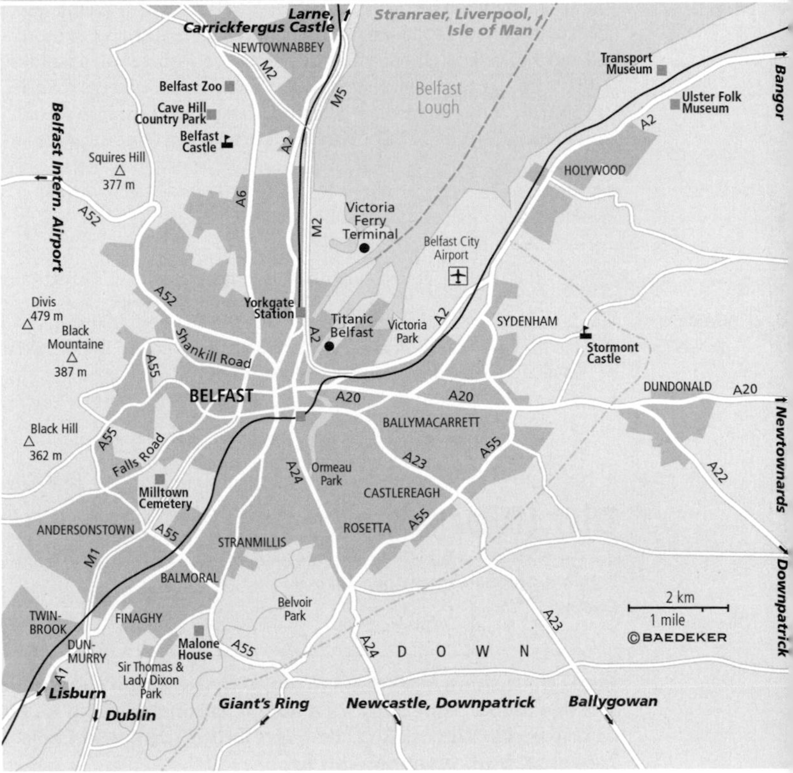

Holywood

Via Holywood, where there are remains of the 12th-century Franciscan friary of Sanctus Boscus (»holy wood«), you reach Crawfordsburn and the popular **Crawfordsburn Country Park** on Helen's Bay. Four walking trails go through the woods and past a beach populated by seals. On the bay stands **Greypoint Fort**, which was built in 1907 and played a leading role in the Belfast Blitz in 1941. Volunteers have created an interesting little museum here, unsurprisingly including artefacts from the Titanic, and give tours.

Crawfordsburn Country Park: visitor centre March–Oct 10am–7pm, Nov–Feb until 4.30pm

Greypoint Fort: Oct–Oct Sun 12 noon–4pm, April and June–Sept daily 10am–9pm; admission free

Bangor Bangor is the most popular seaside resort in Northern Ireland, with many options for entertainment and sports, long sandy beaches and fine promenades. The castle and Castle Park are worth seeing. Here the **North Down Museum** presents the history of the area, a monk's cell and a Viking longhouse. **Bangor Abbey**, a 19th-century building with a 15th-century tower, stands on the site of a monastery founded in 555 with connections to St Columba. There is an attractive excursion to the 300-year-old **Cockle Row Cottages** in Groomsport Harbour.

❶ North Down Museum: Mon–Sat 10am–4.30pm, Sun 12 noon–4.30pm, closed Sun from Sept to June; free admission
Cockle Row Cottages: April and May Sat–Sun 11am–5pm, June–Aug daily; free admission

*Gardens of Rowallane Garden lovers should ignore the route along the Lough and instead choose the one taking in the village of Saintfield, where the Gardens of Rowallane display **a wealth of rare plants**.

❶ Feb, Nov, Dec daily 10am–4pm, March, April, Sept, Oct until 6pm, May–Aug until 8pm; admission 5.70 £.

* Birr (Biorra)

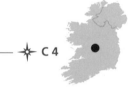

C 4

Republic of Ireland, province: Leinster
County: Offaly
Population: 5,800

Birr, a flourishing market town in the centre of the country, is worth a detour, especially for amateur astronomers and lovers of fine parks. West of Birr, the rivers Little Brosna and Camcor converge, both teeming with fish.

Provincial town with astronomer Four main roads, starting from Emmet Square, form the basic layout of Birr. The attractive street façades are dominated by buildings from the 17th and 18th centuries, particularly in Oxmanlown Mall and St John's Mall. This is also the site of a monument to **William Parsons**, third Earl of Rosse, a famous astronomer who studied spiral nebula in the 1840s.

*Birr Castle Birr Castle, built in the early 17th century by Sir Laurence Parsons, suffered various sieges and was altered and enlarged several times. The castle is not open to the public, but the magnificent park, laid out in the mid-18th century on the Camcor River, is. Over 1,000 different species of trees and shrubs thrive here. A particular source of pride are the approx. 12m/40ft-**high box tree hedges** said to be over 200

Birr

INFORMATION
Birr Tourist Office
Wilmer Road, tel. 057 921 10 10
Mid-May to mid-September

WHERE TO STAY
County Arms €€€
Station Road
el. (0 57) 912 07 91
www.countyarmshotel.com
70 rooms, 2 suites
A relaxing place to stay with wonderful
Georgian architecture, gardens and a
modern spa with a 20m/70ft pool. The
Trilogy Restaurant is known for its leg of
lamb and duck.

**A delightful bower in the garden of
Birr Castle**

years old. To find the sculpture of »Sweeney«, the very well hidden
figure of a Celtic king, amongst them, follow the Sweeney Trail. The
best times to visit are spring when the magnolias are in bloom, or
autumn when the trees glow in a blaze of colours. Around 1840, William Parsons, the third Earl of Rosse, designed and built a **huge telescope**, setting it up in his park. Until 1917 Leviathan was the biggest
telescope in the world, and Parsons used it to discover the spiral
structures in galaxies. The restored telescope may still be admired
today; there is also an exhibition of optical devices and drawings.
❶ Mid-March–Oct daily 9am–6pm, Nov–Feb daily 10am–4pm; admission 9 €;
www.birrcastle.com

AROUND BIRR

Some 13km/8 miles northwest of Birr, on an elevation on the eastern **Banagher**
shore of the Shannon, lies Banagher (pop. 1,640). The English gun
batteries opposite date from the 17th century. 8km/5 miles northeast
of Banagher stand the impressive ruins of 16th-century **Clonony
Castle**. The road there passes Shannon Harbour, where the ▶Shan-
non and ▶Grand Canal meet. Old warehouses and a hotel dating
from 1806 are evidence of the former importance of the place.

East of Birr rise the Slieve Bloom Mountains, with, at their foot, the **Kinnitty**
pretty village of Kinnitty. Continuing southwest from here, look out

for **St Ciaran's Bush**, a hawthorn growing in the middle of the road just past the Clareen crossroads. This is the site where the saint founded a monastery in the 5th century.

* Blarney (An Bhlarna)

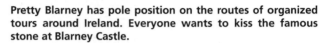

E 3

Republic of Ireland, province: Munster
County: Cork
Population: 5,200

Pretty Blarney has pole position on the routes of organized tours around Ireland. Everyone wants to kiss the famous stone at Blarney Castle.

Wool and crafts

Blarney, 8km/5 miles northwest of ▶Cork, near the south coast, is one of the most popular tourist destinations in Ireland. The town once lived from the wool industry, and a crafts centre (Blarney Woollen Mills) has opened in a restored mill dating from 1824. With an area of 30,000 sq m/320,000 sq ft for selling clothing, crystal glass and crafts, as well as a large visitor information centre, it is Ireland's largest tourist complex.
 Mon–Sat 9.30am–6pm, Sun 10am–6pm: www.blarney.com

Blarney Castle

Blarney Castle is a 15th-century romantic castle set in an extensive park. With its walls 5.5m/18ft thick and a 25m/82ft-high tower, this was the best-fortified castle in the province of Munster. A part of the park, Rock Close, features boulders in interesting shapes, as well as a stone circle set up in the 18th century. It is said that kissing the Blarney Stone confers the gift of eloquence, or the famous Irish »gift of

Blarney

INFORMATION
Tourist Information Office
Tel. 021 438 1624

WHERE TO STAY
Blarney Woollen Mills Hotel €€€
Tel. (0 21) 438 2000
www.blarneywoollenmillshotel.com
48 rooms

A high-class hotel with restaurant for lunch and dinner

Blarney Castle Hotel €€
Tel. (0 21) 438 5116
www.blarneycastlehotel.com
Family-run since 1837, with live music in Johnny's Bar and the Lemon Tree Restaurant

Blarney House can be visited on a guided tour in summer

the gab«. And sure enough, today visitors queue to kiss the stone set in the battlements. To do this, lie on your back, helped by a guard, bend your upper body downwards above the abyss (covered by a gate) and try to kiss the underside of the Blarney Stone.

»Talking Blarney« means something like »flattering talk« or »blah-blah«. The expression was coined by Queen Elizabeth I. She had asked the Lord of Blarney to stop getting himself elected by the chief-

»Talking Blarney«

tains and have his lands granted to him as a Crown fiefdom instead. Lord Cormac McCarthy, pretending to accept this demand, kept coming up with excuses to delay complying with it, until the Queen called out in anger: »This is all Blarney; what he says, he never means!«

Bloody Foreland (Cnoc Fola)

✳ A 3

Republic of Ireland, province: Ulster
County: Donegal

Bloody Foreland, in Irish Cnoc Fola (»bloody mountain«), the broad headland high up north, takes its name from the red colour of the rocky coastline at sunset. The waters also take on a rosy hue, and Tory Island off the coast turns into a glowing dream island.

Stone walls divide up the fields in the Bloody Foreland

Bloody Foreland, the area between Ballyness Bay in the north and Gweedore in the south, is one of the Gaeltacht regions of Ireland where **Irish is still the main language**. It is taught at two Irish summer schools, at Bunbeg and Gloghanheely.

Irish schools

In the southeast of the area, on salmon-rich Lough Dunlewy, lies the village of the same name. Study traditional **wool production** at the Lakeside Centre – the region is famous for its sheep farming and its tweed and woollens.

Dunlewy

❶ April–Oct Mon–Sat 10.30am–6pm, Sun 11am–6pm; www.dunleweycentre.com

Climbing Mount Errigal (740m/2,428ft), north of the lake does not take an experienced mountaineer (ascent: 1½–2 hours). The marked path from the east starts at a car park on the R251. There is a magnificent view from the top: north towards the wild and lonely Altan Lough, with Mount Aglamore rising up over 400m/1,300ft, east to the Derryveagh Mountains, south to the rocky canyon of Poisoned Glen (named after the spurge growing there) and west to the Atlantic coast.

Mount Errigal & The Poisoned Glen

From Bunbeg, boat trips run to the islands off Gweedore Bay: Innishinny, Gola and others; with their rocks and cliffs, all have scenic appeal. There are fine beaches along the coast too, such as the extensive Magheraclogher Strand.

Gweedore Bay

In the north of Bloody Foreland, Gortahork and Falcarragh on Ballyness Bay are starting points for climbing Mount Muckish (670m/ 2,198ft). The steep climb is rewarded by a splendid view.

Mount Muckish

AROUND BLOODY FORELAND

Between April and October there are daily ferry connections to Tory Island (www.toryislandferry.com) from Bunbeg and Maheraroarty From Portnablagh and Downings, and in the winter months, ferries are less frequent. Often the crossing cannot be made due to rough seas, and in the winter months there are fewer boats. Despite its barrenness, Tory Island, north of Bloody Foreland, has been **settled for over 4,000 years**. For the 160 inhabitants, the highlight of the week is the ceilidh, an evening of music and dance put on every Saturday night in the two villages on the island. Apart from a few scant remains of buildings, there are not many sights on Tory Island, but local painters have created powerful works portraying life on the island. View or buy them in the Dixon Gallery (www.oileanthorei. com) at the harbour.

Tory Island

✴ Boyle (Mainistir na Búille)
✦ C 3

Republic of Ireland, province: Connacht
County: Roscommon
Population: 2,600   **Information:** www.realboyle.com

The Irish name for Boyle, Mainistir na Búille, means »monastery of the pasture river«. Today, the ruins of the former Cistercian abbey are the main sights in town. Children will be thrilled with King House.

Market town in the northwest
Boyle lies in the northwest of Ireland on the northern banks of the Boyle River, which connects Lough Gara with Lough Key, and is known for its farmers market. The tourist cooperative Una Bhán on Main Street (www.unabhan.net) runs guided tours. 3km/2 miles north of the town, the impressive metal sculpture entitled **Gaelic Chieftain** (1999) by Maurice Harron commemorates a battle on the Curlow Pass on 15 August, 1599, in which 500 English soldiers were killed.

*Boyle Abbey
At the northern end of Boyle stand the ruins of Boyle Abbey, founded in 1161 as a Cistercian daughter house of Mellifont Abbey. Of the roofless cruciform church, the nave, choir and transepts are well-preserved, as are the guesthouse and kitchen of the monastic buildings. Particularly fine are the capitals with figurative and foliage decorations, amongst them the representation of a cockfight, dogs and two men holding a tree.
❶ April–Sept 10am–6pm, admission 3 €

The ruins of Boyle Abbey

In the centre of Boyle stands the lavishly restoredKing House. Built in 1730, this was the country seat of the Kings, Protestant lords of the manor who made themselves unpopular with the Irish through their harshness, but who were elevated to Earls of Kingston by King George III in 1768. Later, the building was used by the Irish Army. Today, the visitor centre is a lot of fun for the kids too, offering interactive features alongside interesting audiovisual exhibitions on the history of the region. Children can, for instance, learn to write using a quill, or try on old Irish capes, brooches and leather shoes.

King House

❶ April–Sept Tue–Sat 11am–5pm, admission 5 €

Impressive Frybrook House (1750) in the town centre near Shambles Yard was once known for its luxurious furnishings and the hospitality of its owners. It is said that a bell was rung daily to invite everybody who wanted to share food. Due to the huge demand, a tent was specially erected in the garden.

Frybrook House

❶ June–Aug Mon–Sat 2–6pm

AROUND BOYLE

Northeast of town lies Lough Key, lined by forest and featuring many small bays, peninsulas and islets. Along its southern shore stretches Lough Key Forest and Activity Park. The Lock Key Experience takes visitors through a tunnel built for servants, up the Morlog Tower and along Ireland's only treetop walk at a height of 9m/30ft. Nature trails, a bog garden and the Boda Borg Adventure House round off the amenities, but the biggest attraction is the Zipit Forest Adventure Aerial Trail, 1.7km/1 mile long, with four routes and many challenges.

*Lough Key Forest Park

Lough Key Forest and Activity Park: open all year, visitor centre Nov–Feb Fri–Sun 10am–5pm, March until 6pm, April–Aug daily 10am–6pm, Sept–Oct Wed–Sun 10am–6pm, daily pass 20 €, tickets for individual attraction from 7.50 €, www.loughkey.ie

Zipit Forest Aerial Trail: Feb–May, Sept–Nov Sat–Sun 10am–5pm, June–Aug daily 10am–6pm; admission 27 €; www.zipit.ie

Strokestown (approx. 28km/17 miles southeast of Boyle) is a little town laid out around the year 1800 along a central axis with workshops showcasing old Irish crafts. In the middle of an extensive park stands Lord Hartland's wonderful manor house **Strokestown Park House**, the home of the Mahon family until 1979. A guided tour of the estate gives interesting insights into the world of the rich landed gentry. The disused church today houses the Heritage & Genealogical Centre where visitors can search for their Irish ancestors. (Opening times: June–Aug Tues–Sun 11am to 5.30pm.) The former stables of Strokestown Park House

Strokestown

MARCO ● POLO TIP

!

Drumanone Dolmen **Insider Tip**

Experts and tourists agree that one of the finest dolmen monuments in Ireland is the one at Drumanone near Boyle, reached by following Patrick Street out of town westwards. After 2km/1.2 miles a signpost points the way left to Ballina. Shortly after passing under a railway bridge, cross the tracks to the meadow on which the dolmen stands.

today house the **Irish National Famine Museum**, which poignantly shows the terrible consequences of the potato blight in Ireland: photographs, documents and furnishings recall the Great Famine (1845–1849) and the involvement of the local land-owning family Mahon. At the same time, parallels are drawn to hunger in the developing world.

Strokestown Park and Irish National Famine Museum: 10.30am–5.30pm, in winter until 4pm, combined ticket 12 €, www.strokestownpark.ie

Douglas Hyde Interpretative Centre
Some 15km/9 miles southwest of Boyle, in Frenchpark on the R361, the Douglas Hyde Interpretative Centre commemorates the first President of the Republic of Ireland.
❶ May, June by appointment, tel. 087 78237 51, July–Aug Mon–Fri 11am–5pm, Sat–Sun 2–6pm, Sept Tue–Fri 2–5pm, Sat–Sun 2–6pm, free admission

Monasteraden
West of Lough Gara, already in County Sligo, at Monasteraden stands the most famous of the many holy wells of the region; this one is dedicated to St Attracta. The well is lined on three sides by walls; one of them shows a relief of Christ on the Cross.

Boyne Valley

※ C 5

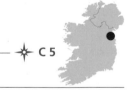

Republic of Ireland, province: Leinster
County: Meath

On the east coast of Ireland, between Belfast and Dublin, in the valley of the River Boyne, lies the cradle of Irish civilization. Archaeologists reckon that the royal tombs in the Boyne Valley are around 5,000 years old. The magnificent megalithic site of Newgrange is world-famous; there are others at Knowth and Dowth.

✶✶ Newgrange
Newgrange, which is only accessible as part of a guided tour, is **the largest of the three burial sites**. Up to 1962 however, it was hidden by an earth mound that could hardly be distinguished from its surroundings. The excavations were completed in the late 1970s, followed by an extensive restoration of the grounds on the basis of the findings.

The megalithic complex consists of a heart-shaped stone-and-earth mound of over 90m/100yd diameter and a height of nearly 11m/36ft. The foot of the mound is formed by reclining stones that stop the roof cover from slipping; the kerb is a reconstruction: all around, there used to stand 97 boulders. The entrance, marked by a stone with spiral decorations, is formed by 43 orthostats (upright stones) between 1.5m/ 5ft and

Boyne Valley

INFORMATION
Newgrange Tourist Office and Visitor Centre
Daily 9.30am-5pm or longer
Knowth closed Oct–Easter
Admission: combined ticket 11€, individual ticket from 3 €

2.4m/8ft high and topped by capstones. A passage leads to the splendid main chamber, with a vault of some 6m/19ft in height. Three side chambers branch off from the main chamber, forming a cruciform ground plan. In the shallow stone bowls of the side chambers, traces of ash and bone have been found. Many of the stones are decorated with impressive carved spirals, lozenges, wavy lines or zigzag ornaments. A path to the coffee shop and archaeological park of **Newgrange Farm** is signposted.

❶ Newgrange Farm: mid-March to mid-Sept 10am-6pm; admission with farm tour 9€; www.newgrangefarm.com

OTHER SIGHTS

Knowth

Whilst the excavations in Knowth still continue, the complex of 18 tombs and 124 kerbstones may be visited. In Knowth, a mound, 10m/33ft high and with a diameter of approx. 85m/95yd covers two passage tombs. As on the site of Newgrange, this main cairn was the last resting place for a leader or king with his extended family. 18 smaller tumuli arranged around the main tomb were intended for the mortal remains of less important persons. Knowth continued to be in use as a burial and religious site well into early Christian times.

❶ Guided tours from Easter to Oct from the visitor centre, admission 5 €

Dowth

In the tomb of Dowth, with very limited access to the public, an 8m/26ft passage leads to one of the two chambers. Several side chambers branch off from this round burial chamber.

Slane

North of Slane, on Slane Hill (158m/518ft), St Patrick is said to have proclaimed the **victory of Christianity in Ireland** in 433 by lighting an Easter fire visible from afar, in the face of a royal ban. The hill has the remains of a 16th-century Franciscan monastery.

** *The Realm of the Dead*

Around 150 prehistoric passage tombs are known to exist in Ireland. The most famous of them all is the 5,000-year-old mausoleum at Newgrange in the Boyne Valley. This complex has been restored to show what the burial mound (cairn) originally looked like. It is 11m/36ft high, and its front is clad with shining white quartz stones.

Newgrange

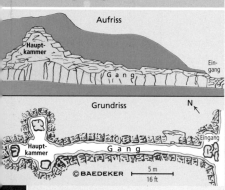

Aufriss

Haupt-kammer · Gang · Eingang

Grundriss · N

Haupt-kammer · Gang · Eingang

© BAEDEKER · 5 m / 16 ft

❶ Entrance

On the southeast side, the entrance leads into a passage, 19m/62ft long and only 1m/3ft wide. 43 upright stones, between 1.5m/5ft and 2.4m/8ft high, covered by capstones, form this passage. One of Newgrange's secrets was discovered in 1969: at the winter solstice, sunlight enters the burial chamber through a small slit in the rectangular »box« above the entrance.

❷ Burial Chamber

In the earliest Irish literature Newgrange, once called »An Brug« (dwelling), is considered the home of the most ancient gods. When light shines into the chamber for 17 minutes at the winter solstice, the decorations on the stones shine, the light is reflected onto the floor and penetrates every last corner. On guided tours, this spectacle is recreated using artificial light.

❸ Vault

The vault of the magnificent main chamber is about 6m/20ft high. It is a corbelled dome built around 3200 BC that has lasted to the present day and does not let in any water, even during periods of prolonged rain.

❹ Side Chambers

Three side chambers branch off from the main chamber, forming a cruciform plan. In shallow stone basins, traces of ash and bones have been found, deriving from five people. Their status – kings, priests? – is not known. Many of the stones are decorated with impressive spirals and lozenges. Wavy lines or zig-zag patterns.

About 38 undressed menhirs surrounded the cairn in a large circle.

Slane Castle (2km/1.2 miles west of Slane) is open to individual visitors only from June to August. The castle park is the venue for the big annual Slane Concert, where musicians of the calibre of David Bowie and U2 have performed.

Slane Mill was the biggest corn mill in Ireland from 1766. Later is was used to mill flax. The Georgian manager's house has now become the exclusive Millhouse Hotel (www.themillhouse.ie).

Slane Castle: June–Aug Sun–Thu 12 noon–5pm, admission 7 €, www.slanecastle.ie

Bray (Bré)

✳ C 5

Republic of Ireland, province: Leinster
County: Wicklow:
Population: 31,900   **Information:** Tel. (01) 286 6796

Bray, previously called Bri Cualann in Irish, is one of the biggest and oldest seaside resorts in Ireland, lying 19km/12 miles south of Dublin in a sheltered bay of the Irish Sea. There are tennis courts and golf links, swimming, motor-boating and sailing, and the National Sealife Centre.

Pleasures of the beach
The social hub of Bray is formed by the **Esplanade**, a broad promenade on the mile-long bay, where in summer, visitors can listen to the beach band or play mini golf. At the northern end is the marina, to the south, Bray Head (240m/787ft) juts up sharply from the shore. A footpath (The Great White Way) leads from the southern end of the Esplanade up the hill past a small ruined church (there and back should take 1½ hours).

Heritage Centre
The Heritage Centre next to the tourist office in the courthouse dating from 1841 has information on the history of the town from the Cambrian era to the present. The National Sealife Centre draws many visitors. Bray is also home to the only film studios in Ireland. Movies such as »Excalibur« (1981), »Braveheart« (1995) and »King Arthur« (2004) were made here (www.ardmore.ie). The annual jazz festival in May is well-known, and the Harbour Bar in Strand Road is famous, having once been voted the best bar in the world (www.harbourbarbray.com).

Heritage Centre: usually Mon–Fri 9.30am–1pm, 2–4.30pm, Sat 10am–3pm, longer hours in July and Aug; admission 3 €
National Sealife Centre: 10am–6pm,; admission 12.50 €

Kilruddery
To the right of the R761 leading south from Bray stands the former manor of Kilruddery (1820), featuring **ornamental gardens** that

are well worth seeing. Small canals snake through the park that was laid out in the late 17th century and has managed to hang on to most of its original character to the present day. The winter garden was added in the 19th century. (Opening times: May, June and Sept daily 1–5pm.) Some 4km/2.5 miles west of town, the River Dargle forms a **romantic valley** with dense forest and wild rock formations. A narrow path follows the river.

❶ House: July–Sept daily 1–5pm, garden April–Oct daily 9.30am–5pm; April and Oct only Sat and Sun; admission 11 €; www.killruddery.com

AROUND BRAY

8km/5 miles south of Bray, in a forested area, the seaside resort of Greystones is attractive for tennis, golf and boat trips.

Greystones

South of Bray, a hiker's paradise stretches around the Great Sugar Loaf Mountains. The summits of both Little Sugar Loaf (337m/ 1,105ft) and the Great Sugar Loaf (496m/1,627ft) offer fine views. On the way there is the shop of Avoca Handweavers in Kilmacanogue (www.avoca.ie).

Great Sugar Loaf Mountains

Bundoran (Bun Dobhráin)

✳ **B 3**

Republic of Ireland, province: Ulster
County: Donegal
Population: 1,970   **Information:** (071) 984 13 50

Surfers appreciate the lively seaside resort of Bundoran on the northern Irish Atlantic coast on Donegal Bay. Visitors have the opportunity to watch china being manufactured nearby.

The main attractions of the resort are its fine sandy beach and the first indoor aquapark in Ireland, **Waterworld**. There is a **sculpture trail**, to which nine artists have contributed. Bundoran is a base for various walks: a good one leads north to the cliffs and caves of Aughrus Head; the **Puffing Hole** blowhole is only one of the interesting features. From there, carry on to Tullan Strand, which has a cairn, dolmen and a stone circle.

Fine sandy beach

❶ Waterworld: April, May and Sept Sat and Sun 12 noon–6pm, June daily 12 noon–6pm, July and Aug daily 10am–7pm; admission 12.50 €, www. waterworldbundoran.com

AROUND BUNDORAN

Ballyshannon The busy town of Ballyshannon (pop. 3,500) is regarded as the oldest town in Ireland, and has had a municipal charter since 1613. The poet **William Allingham** (1824–89) was born here and lies buried in Ballyshannon churchyard. Allingham is best known for his lines »Up the airy mountains/Down the rushy glen« from »The Fairies«. The most famous son of the town is, however, the guitarist Rory Gallagher (1948–95). A plaque, a mural and a statue commemorate him, and a three-day Rory Gallagher Festival is held in early June. The big musical event in August is the Traditional Folk Festival, one of the biggest in Ireland (www.ballyshannonfolkfestival.com).

On Rossnowlagh Road close to the ruined Cistercian abbey of **Assaroe** stands the Abbey Mill & House of Crafts, with a café and craft shop. Nearby, a sign points to **Patrick's Well**, a popular pilgrimage site. Look out for the strips of fabric blowing in the breeze; they are fastened all year round to the hedges surrounding the well to honour the saint. The ruins of **Kilbarron Castle** were once the seat of Michael O'Clery, the principal of the Four Masters (▶Donegal) and co-author of the famous »Annals« chronicling the history of Ireland.

> **!** MARCO POLO TIP
>
> *China's porcelain on Ireland's coastline*
>
> **Insider Tip**
>
> Anyone interested in watching how Chinese porcelain is made, or maybe acquiring one of the delicate beauties should visit the Donegal Parian China Pottery on the road between Ballyshannon and Bundoran. Guided tours through the workshops are free of charge (Mon – Fri 9am – 6pm, Sat, Sun 10am – 8pm).

✳ Burren (Boireann)

✳ C/D 2/3

Republic of Ireland, province: Munster
County: Clare

Burren (Boireann) means »stony place«. Thanks to its green tourism infrastructure, this strange karst landscape together with the Cliffs of Moher was made a UNESCO geopark in 2011. Into this grey desert of rock, the water has dug bizarre holes and grooves where rare flowers thrive.

Bizarre karst landscape The Burren, this **landscape unique in Europe**, roughly at the centre of the Irish west coast, is dominated by hill tops of porous grey rock and bare terraces, brooks that disappear into the cracked earth, and subterranean streams, caves and holes. Lakes that fill up today may

The Burren makes an impression of barrenness

be drained empty tomorrow, but the nooks and crannies with rich soil shelter a unique flora. Seeing this area for the first time, Cromwell's officers are said to have exclaimed: »Too few trees to hang a man, too little water to drown them, too little soil to bury them in.« Many walking trails, for example the **Burren Way** (23km/14 miles), pass through the landscape. The best starting point for activities is the **Burren Interpretive Centre** in Kilfenora, where the exhibition is modern and highly informative. The 12th-century cathedral in Kilfenora is worth a stop for its fine tombstones (13th and 14th century). 100m/100yd away on a pasture stands a lavishly ornamented high cross with a crucifixion scene. The Doorty High Cross in front of the west facade of the cathedral is even finer.

❶ Burren Interpretive Centre: mid-March to Oct daily 10am–5pm, June–Aug daily 9.30am–5.30pm; admission 6 ; www.theburrencentre.ie

A DRIVE THROUGH THE BURREN

There are three different routes through the area: the N67 running straight from **Ballyvaughan** in the north east to Lisdoonvarna in the south west, the R480/R476 running east or the R477 (recommended for travelling back from Lisdoonvarna to Ballyvaughan) running mostly along the coast.
In the fishing village of Ballyvaughan it is worth stopping at the Burren Exposure in Galway Road (4km/2.5miles north) for information

To Lisdoonvarna

MARCO ⊕ POLO TIP

> ! *Mystic Landscape* **Insider Tip**
>
> A good option for getting a better understanding of the bare Burren landscape is to buy Tim Robinson's lovingly designed map entitled »Folding Landscape« in one of the information centres. It marks even the forgotten ruins, holy wells and healing rock chairs.

about regional geology, flora and fauna, and at O`Brien Castle, site of the Burren College of Art.

The ruins of **Corcomroe Abbey**, formerly a Cistercian abbey, founded in 1180, are situated in a peaceful, green valley. The church with its cruciform ground plan possesses rich decoration and a fine vault. A few miles south of Ballyvaughan, look out for the unusual tower of **Newtown Castle**, a cylindrical body rising from a pyramid-shaped foundation. After a steep climb, the road then reaches its highest point, Corkscrew Road (220m/722ft). To the west rises **Slieve Elva** (340m/1,115ft), boasting the **longest cave in Ireland**, Pollnagollum Cave. Shortly before reaching Lisdoonvarna lies the stone fort of **Cahermacnaghten** with a ring wall of 31m/34yd diameter and the remains of a castle.

Ailwee Cave 2km/1.2 miles south of Ballyvaughan, the R480 turns off south from the Corkscrew Road. This road leads to Ailwee Cave. Of the miles of cave passages, a small part is accessible to visitors, who see impressively illuminated stalactites and stalagmites and a subterranean river. The shows evidence of the presence of bears hibernating before the last Ice Age in this cave, which holds a constant temperature of 10°C/50°F.

❶ March-June, Sept and Oct daily 10am–5.30pm, July–Aug 10am–6.30pm, Nov–Feb daily 10am–5pm; admission 12 €; www.ailweecave.ie

Burren Bird of Prey Centre The Burren Bird of Prey Centre is all about eagles, hawks and owls. Up to 200 guests at a time can watch them fly from a stand, and individual trips with hawks and their handlers can be booked.

Gleninsheen Wedge Tomb The R480 also passes the **Gleninsheen Wedge Tomb** (also called »Druid's Altar«). This is where, in 1930, one of the most beautiful examples of prehistoric Irish craftsmanship was found: a golden torc, today in the National Museum in Dublin.

❶ March-June, Sept and Oct daily 10am–5.30pm, July–Aug 10am–6.30pm, Nov–Feb daily 10am–5pm; admission 8 €; www.birdofpreycentre.com

*Poulnabrone Dolmen To the left of the road, after 800m/0.5 miles, look for the impressive Poulnabrone Dolmen, a **mighty megalithic tomb** and one of the most popular holiday snaps in Ireland. The tomb was erected around 3000 BC; excavations have yielded the bones of 16–22 adults and six children.

A favourite photo motif of the Burren: the Poulnabrone dolmen

Some 5km/3 miles east of there, **Carran** (Carron) is famous for its aromatic essences derived from wild flowers. Here, a minor sign-posted road turns off towards Temple Cronan, a small early Christian church approx. 2km/1.2 miles away, with grotesque Romanesque heads in the exterior walls.

Carran

About 1km/0.5 miles south of the Poulnabrone Dolmen, the visitor centre at Caherconnell Fort, which was occupied between 400 and 1200, presents a short audio-show about the tomb. The main attraction, however, is the perfect fort itself with its walls 3m/10ft thick. In 2008 archaeologists found iron arrow-heads and a prehistoric chamber tomb with skeletons from the 15th and 16th centuries.

Caherconnell Fort

At the foot of the Burren, 7km/4.5 miles northwest of Kilfenora, **Lisdoonvarna** (pop. 820) is the only spa in Ireland and a popular holiday destination with the Irish, offering tennis, mini golf, a fun fair and more. The town is also famous for its springs containing sulphur, magnesium, iron and iodine. The Spa Wells Health Centre is open from June to October. However, Lisdoonvarna is most famous for its traditional Matchmaking Festival in September, a kind of marriage fair where lonely hearts meet. This derives from the meetings of farming families after the harvest festival.

Around Kilfenora

In **Killinaboy**, 10km/6 miles to the east, a well-preserved sheela-na-gig can be seen above the south entrance to the ruins of an interesting

> ! **Insider Tip**
>
> *Burren Smokehouse*
>
> Queen Elizabeth enjoyed the taste of the fine, oak-smoked salmon from the Burren Smokehouse on Doolin Road (with visitor centre, audio show, delicatessen; daily 10am–4pm or longer; www.burrensmokehouse. com). Wall mosaics illustrate the legend of the Salmon of Knowledge. 50m/50yd further, Peter Curtin's Roadside Tavern serves salmon and mackerel at reasonable prices, washed down with good stout and ale from the in-house brewery.

church, possibly dating from the 16th century. A sheela-na-gig, a naked woman openly showing her genitals, is a Celtic fertility goddess that survived the coming of Christianity and usually appeared above a church door.

Some 8km/5 miles west of Lisdoonvarna, the fishing village of **Doolin** (pop. 200) offers swimming and angling. In good weather, several boats a day leave from Doolin Pier to the ▶Aran Islands. However, Doolin is most famous for its pubs, playing Irish folk music every night in the summer months.
The drive from Lisdoonvarna along the coast is rewarding. The R477 initially winds northwest, past Ballynalackan Castle, towards the coast and then northwards.

The most northerly point of the coastal route affords a sweeping view over Galway Bay from windswept Black Head, before the route follows the coast west to Ballyvaughan.

∗ Cahir (An Cathair)

✦ **D 4**

Republic of Ireland, province: Munster
County: Tipperary
Population: 3,400

The former garrison town of Cahir in the south of Ireland is today a lively market town. The splendidly restored Cahir Castle makes visiting the town an attractive proposition. Castle Street, lined with pubs, leads to the River Suir, Cahir Castle and the thatched Swiss Cottage. To the west, the Galtee Mountains rise to a height of 900m/2,950ft.

∗Cahir Castle Cahir Castle, one of the largest castles in the country, was built in the mid-12th century and has repeatedly been used as a **backdrop for films**. The current building dates mainly from the 15th and 16th centuries. Following a chequered history of destruction and rebuilding, the castle has been extensively restored over past decades. It consists

of the bulky three-storey tower house with hall, and a further hall building; both are surrounded by tall strong curtain walls, fortified by towers. The living quarters of the fortification are furnished to look as they would have done 500 years ago.
❶ Oct–Feb 9.30am–4.30pm, March–mid-June and Sept–Oct daily 9.30am–5.30pm, mid-June–Aug 9am–6.30pm; admission 3 €

Cahir

INFORMATION
Tourist Office, Castle Car Park
Tel. 052 744 1453
www.visitcahir.ie

Amidst Cahir Park, situated in a pretty location by the water, stands Swiss Cottage, which got its name through a remote resemblance to a Swiss chalet. The small reed-thatched rustic house was built in 1810 by John Nash, the architect of English royalty in the Regency period.
❶ Apr–mid-Oct 10am–6pm; admission 3 €, with guided tour only

Swiss Cottage

AROUND CAHIR

6km/3.5 miles north of Cahir stands a cluster of notable medieval buildings: the Knockgraffon Motte, a 12th-century Anglo-Norman fortress guarding the ford crossing the Suir, as well as the ruins of a church and a 16th-century castle. The lovely Glen of Aherlow northwest of Cahir offers good hiking country. Between Cahir and Michelstown, south of the N8 at Burncourt, visit the **Mitchelstown Caves**, three caves with impressive limestone formations.
❶ Mitchelstown Caves: March–Oct 10am–5pm, in other months until 4pm; admission 9 €, www.mitchelstowncave.com

Knockgraffon Motte

Carlow (Ceatharlach)
✴ D 5

Republic of Ireland, province: Leinster
County: Carlow:
Population: 16,150
Information: www.carlowtourism.com

Due to its strategic position on the River Barrow, Carlow was for a long time a fortified Anglo-Norman base. Today, the town has little for tourists, who usually only pass through on their way to Browne's Hill Dolmen.

Carlow, at the junction of the N9 and the N80, lies southwest of Dublin. The capital of the County Carlow is today considered the

Market and industrial centre

Megalith Cultures

Between 4000 and 500 BC, large stone structures such as dolmens, passage graves and stone circles were built in Ireland. In other places too, within and beyond Europe, megalithic cultures emerged during the Neolithic period and the Bronze Age. Today they are thought to have developed independently of each other.

Browne's Hill dolmen, Ireland
Capstone: 100 t
Length: 6.1m/20ft, width: 4.7m/15ft
up to 2m/6ft 6" thick

Dolmen
A grave chamber consisting of large, upright stones and a capstone

Stonehenge, England
Diameter: 115m/125yd

Stone circles
Round or oval arrangements of menhirs or erratic boulders, often connected with graves

Alignements of Carnac
In Brittany there are 56 rows of stone, called alignements. The most impressive of them, at Carnac, consists of 2,800 menhirs in a 4km/2.5-mile line.

4500	4000	3500	30

Megalith cultures	Sieben Steinhäuser
	Browne´s Hill dolmen
Pyramids	Alignements of Carnac
	Mastabas, predecessor of pyramids
Other stone buildingss	
	Haġar Qim

NEOLITHIC PERIOD

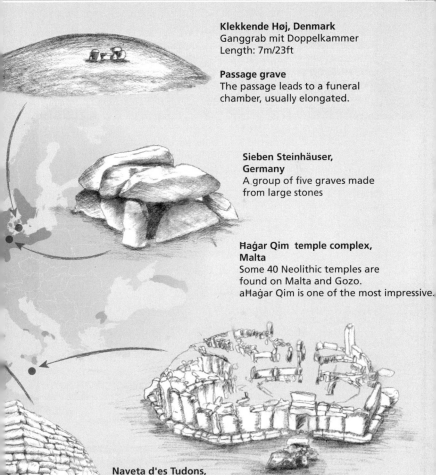

Klekkende Høj, Denmark
Ganggrab mit Doppelkammer
Length: 7m/23ft

Passage grave
The passage leads to a funeral
chamber, usually elongated.

**Sieben Steinhäuser,
Germany**
A group of five graves made
from large stones

**Ħaġar Qim temple complex,
Malta**
Some 40 Neolithic temples are
found on Malta and Gozo.
aĦaġar Qim is one of the most impressive.

**Naveta d'es Tudons,
Menorca**
Grave
Lenght: 13m/43ft, width: 6m/20ft, height: 3m/10ft

2500	2000	1500	1000

Stonehenge

Naveta d'es Tudons

kkendehøj

Naos, predecessor of Greek temples

Ziggurat, terraced step pyramids, Mesopotamia

Pyramids

©BAEDEKER

EGYPT

EGALITH CULTURES

IRON AGE

BRONZE AGE

market and industrial centre of the region. In 1361 Carlow was walled, and since then has been heavily fought over, the last time in 1798 when 640 Irish rebels died. A monument in the shape of **a modern Celtic-style high cross** on Church Street commemorates the dead.

Carlow Castle Castle Hill Street leads to Carlow Castle. Of the core building, only the eastern side with two strong round 13th-century corner towers survives. The interior is currently not open to the public. At the junction of Athy Road and Dublin Road, look out for the splendid Court House, built in 1830 in the classical style.

Carlow County Museum The Carlow County Museum in a former convent in College Street provides insights into the history of the town and the sugar industry. The tourist office is also located here.
❶ June–Aug Mon–Sat 10am–5pm, Sun 2–4.30pm, Sept–May Mon–Sat 10am–4.30pm; free admission

The marina at Carrick-on-Shannon

AROUND CARLOW

4km/2.5 miles west of Carlow, in the cemetery of the village of   **Killeshin**
Killeshin stands a Romanesque 12th-century church; its doorway is
worth seeing for its sculptures and pointed gable top.
The **Tullow Museum** in Bridge Street displays personal items
that belonged to the Antarctic explorer Sir Ernest Shackleton and
to F.M. Murphy, one of the rebels of 1798, who was executed in
Tullow.

Carrick-on-Shannon (Cora Droma Rúisc)

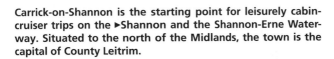

✳ C 3

Republic of Ireland, province: Connacht
County: Leitrim
Population: 3,200
Information: www.carrickonshannon.ie

**Carrick-on-Shannon is the starting point for leisurely cabin-
cruiser trips on the ▶Shannon and the Shannon-Erne Waterway. Situated to the north of the Midlands, the town is the
capital of County Leitrim.**

In Carrick-on-Shannon, not much remains of the buildings from   **Tiny chapel**
previous centuries. Look out for the Courthouse and Costello Memorial Chapel, measuring only 5 x 3.6m/16 x 12ft, at the end of Bridge
Street.

AROUND CARRICK-ON-SHANNON

A few miles north of Carrick-on-Shannon, the Shannon-Erne Water-   **Shannon-**
way branches off from the Shannon. This waterway connects **two of**   **Erne**
the most popular European boating grounds: the Shannon and   **Waterway**
the Erne Lake Area in Northern Ireland. The canal, inaugurated in
1860, turned out to be an economic failure and was closed again in
1869. After extensive repairs, it is now everywhere at least 1.5m/5 ft
deep, making it a very attractive playground for amateur skippers.
With an average house boat, the 78km/49-mile stretch from Carrick
to Belturbet (▶Cavan) takes a good 16 hours.

The R280 leads northwards via the picturesque village of Leitrim,   **Drumshanbo**
which gave the county its name, to Drumshanbo, a holiday resort

for anglers at the southern tip of **Lough Allen**. Driving on along the western shore, the road passes the quarry area of Arigna.

Turlough O'Carolan Country	Near Carrick-on-Shannon, three places are closely associated with **the last and most famous Irish bard**, Turlough O'Carolan (1674–1738). Having spent most of his life in Mohill, the bard lies buried in Kilronan Church, whilst Keadue celebrates the O'Carolan Harp Festival every year in early August in his honour. To get to Mohill, take the N4 towards Dublin from Carrick-on-Shannon and turn off east just past Drumsna, taking the R201. To get to Kilronan Church, take the R280 northwards, turning west in Leitrim on the R284 to Keadue and from there head west in the direction of Sligo.
Lough Rynn	A good 15km/9 miles southeast of Carrick-on-Shannon lies Lough Rynn; on the lake's northeastern shore, an attractive park surrounds the 19th-century **Lough Rynn House**. Today the mansion is occupied by a **luxury hotel** with one of the best restaurants in Ireland ❶ www.oughrynn.ie

Carrick-on-Suir (Carrarig na Siúire)

✳ D 4

Republic of Ireland, province: Munster
County: Tipperary
Population: 8,000
Information: www.carrickonsuir,info

Thanks to its brewery and wool production, the market town of Carrick-on-Suir, 20km/12 east of Clonmel, rose to prominence in the Middle Ages. The town lies near the Irish southern coast on the River Suir, which marks the county border between Tipperary and Waterford.

History	After Henry VIII in 1541 took on the title of King of Ireland, England (under Elizabeth I in particular) tried to claim Ireland once and for all through the settlement of English estate owners. Thanks to their construction activity during the course of the 16th and 17th centuries, **Tudor mansions** appeared, the most important example being Ormond Castle in Carrick-on-Suir.
Ormond Castle	Today's Ormond Castle, the former seat of the earls Butler of Ormond, consists of a fortification dating from 1450 and a manor house, added in 1568. That house was erected for Queen Elizabeth I

of England, but she never stayed there. The manor house gives an idea of what an **Elizabethan mansion** looked like: broad, gabled on the outside, with on the inside a long hall and gallery containing stucco portraits.

❶ April–Sept Wed–Sun 10am–6pm; free admission

AROUND CARRICK-ON-SUIR

North of Carrick-on-Suir, on the border between the counties of Kilkenny and Tipperary, two places with important high crosses are Kilkeeran (8km/5 miles) and Ahenny (10 km/6 miles). Of the three crosses in the churchyard of Kilkeeran, the western cross, dating from the 9th century, is worth seeing. Its base shows eight horsemen, with interlacing geometric motifs. The lower part of the cross shaft, for instance, shows intertwined goose-like animals. In Ahenny, also in a churchyard, stand two especially impressive crosses. These feature figurative carvings on the bases only; on the northern cross, for instance, cross-bearing monks and a pony carrying a headless man can be seen. Both crosses are covered in skilfully carved geometric patterns such as spirals, braiding and rosettes. In their style, the carvings so resemble those of the »Book of Kells« that they can be dated to around the 8th century.

*High crosses in Kilkeeran and Ahenny

Cashel (Caiseal Mumhan)

✦ **D 4**

Republic of Ireland, province: Munster
County: Tipperary
Population: 300

The small town of Cashel, which emerged during construction of the cathedral, seems to be completely in the shadow of the magnificent Rock of Cashel. Apart from this impressive structure, the Folk Village is also worth a visit.

There is more to Cashel than the Rock, with its many pubs, restaurants and shops. A visit to the **Cashel Folk Village** in Dominic Street is very interesting. This recreated Irish village shows the tough daily life of the peasants next to such a towering structure.

The Rock village

❶ Jan to mid-March and mid-Oct to mid-Dec 9.30am-4.30pm,, mid-May to mid-June and mid-Sept to mid-Oct 9.30am-5.30pm, mid-June to mid-Sept 9am-7.30pm; admission 5 €; www.cashelfolkvillage.ie

** *As if Raised to the Heavens ...*

this great 13th-century church stands on the Rock of Cashel. It still emanates the power and aura of a medieval cathedral. A stone fort occupied the site as early as the 5th century, and Brian Ború was crowned High King of Ireland here in 977. Squatting in the shadow of the cathedral, Cormac's Chapel, built between 1127 and 1134, is considered by many to be the most interesting Norman building in Ireland.

❶ Porch
This is the entrance to the cathedral.

❷ Tower house
This massive, laterally placed building with its battlements, a residence for the archbishop dating from the 15th century, looks more like a castle than a dwelling.

❸ Spiral stairs
Within the two towers in the corners of the nave and transepts are stairs.

❹ Crossing tower
This tower was one of the last parts of the cathedral to be completed, in the 14th century. The choir, dating from 1230, is the oldest part, followed by the nave, transepts and crossing.

❺ Round tower
With a height of just under 28m/92ft, this tower was erected at the same time as Cormac's Chapel.

❻ Cormac's Chapel
A masterpiece of Norman architecture. Note the square towers in two different styles. The chapel has no side aisles, and the roof has a strikingly steep pitch.

❼ Hall of the Vicars' Choral
Visitors enter the walled enclosure here. Constructed in the 15th century as a residential building, it has been converted into a museum and houses St Patrick's Cross. The wooden ceiling is painted.

Rock of Cashel

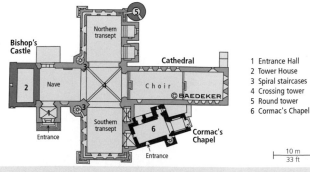

Bishop's Castle

Northern transept

Cathedral

Nave

Choir

©BAEDEKER

Southern transept

Entrance

Cormac's Chapel

Entrance

1 Entrance Hall
2 Tower House
3 Spiral staircases
4 Crossing tower
5 Round tower
6 Cormac's Chapel

10 m
33 ft

History

As early as the 4th century, the rock was fortified by the kings of Munster. After St Patrick baptized King Aengus there in 450, elevating Cashel to a bishopric, several subsequent kings held ecclesiastical office. The famous King **Brian Ború** was crowned here, making Cashel his main seat in 977. One of the O'Brien family gifted the rock to the church, and in 1127 Bishop Cormac MacCarthy started building Cormac's Chapel. In 1152, the bishopric was elevated to an archbishopric. The 13th-century cathedral was damaged by fire in 1495 and 1647, only restored in 1686 and abandoned in 1749. It fell into disrepair until the Rock of Cashel was taken over by the state in 1874 and declared a national monument.

**Rock of Cashel

Rock of Cashel, **one of the greatest cultural treasures of Ireland**, rises 60m/200ft from the plain. It can get very busy here, so try to visit in the morning. Visitors enter the enclosed wall courtyard through the Hall of the Vicar's Choral, the 15th-century former servants' quarters. Today it has been turned into a small museum; the upper floor has been furnished with contemporary furniture. This is where **St Patrick's Cross** is kept, showing the Crucifixion of Christ and St Patrick. The base, decorated with geometric patterns, is said to have been the ancient coronation stone of the kings of Cashel and Munster. Legend has it that St Patrick, whilst baptizing King Aengus, by mistake stabbed the king's foot with his crozier. Aengus did not show anything was amiss, believing this to be part of the holy ritual. A copy of the cross has been set up on the original site in front of the cathedral. The choir and transepts of the cathedral are longer than the – probably unfinished – nave. The transepts still have their gables, in three sections with outer corner turrets. In the intersections between nave and transepts, the round towers' spiral staircases lead up to the massive square tower above the crossing and the walkways on the church walls. They are connected, by corridors and little staircases in the thick walls, with each other and with the round tower (see below) in an elaborate defensive complex. The tomb of Archbishop Myler MacGrath, who died in 1622 at a hundred years of age, is located in the choir. As he was not called to step down from his office in Rome, the clergyman who had converted to Protestantism was for several years archbishop in the service of England as well as a Catholic archbishop. On the western side of the cathedral stands the archbishop's residence, a massive 15th-century rectangular tower.

The cathedral's northern transept is joined to a nearly 28m/92ft-high **round tower** dating from the time of Cormac's Chapel. The entrance of the tower is 3.6m/12ft above ground.

Of particular interest is **Cormac's Chapel** (1127–32). Architecture and sculptural works show the influence of German and English

Cashel

INFORMATION
Heritage Centre & Tourist Office
Main Street
Tel. 062 625 11, www.cashel.ie
Daily 9.30am–5.30pm, Nov-Feb closed
Sat and Sun

WHERE TO EAT
Chez Hans €€€€
Moor Lane
Tel. (0 62) 611 77, www.chezhans.net
Chez Hans in a converted church is
famous for its seafood and more. Try
giant quails with potatoes, beans, chilli
and coriander dress (26 €).

WHERE TO STAY
Cashel Palace €€€€
Main Street

Tel. (0 62) 627 07
www.cashel-palace.ie
23 rooms and suites
A luxury hotel in an 18th-century
bishop's palace. The trees in the park
were planted at the coronation of
Queen Anne. Riding, angling in the
hotel's own fishing grounds, excellent
food, self-catering also available..

Bailey's of Cashel €€
Main Street
Tel. (0 62) 619 37
www.baileyshotelcashel.com
A townhouse built in 1709 with a cellar
bar serving food (daily 12 noon–9.30pm)
as well as a good Restaurant 42 (Thu–
Sat 6–9.30pm, Sun 12 noon–2.30pm)

master builders, without losing its Irish character, still evident, for instance, in the pitched stone roof. The transepts resemble towers, and three-dimensional motifs liven up the walls. The former main entrance (north doorway) has an ornate sectionalized design; its features include a fine tympanum showing a centaur hunting a lion with bow and arrow. Inside, look for the impressive, beautiful sarcophagus from the 12th century, ornately decorated with Scandinavian ornaments.

Hore Abbey

A short walk leads from the foot of the rock to the nearby ruins of the former Benedictine Hore Abbey with its bulky crossing tower. In 1272 the archbishop handed it over to the Cistercians of Mellifont, as he had been told in a dream that the Benedictines were out to kill him.

BrúBorú arts centre

At the car park for Cashel Rock, the BrúBorú arts centre puts on traditional Irish dance, song, storytelling and theatre. 7m/23ft below ground, the **Sounds of History** exhibition presents an introduction to Irish history. In summer a show of music and dance, lasting 2.5 hours, is staged.

❶ Mid-June to mid-Aug daily 9am–11.30pm, at other times Mon–Fri 9am–1pm and 2–7pm; exhibition 5 €; http//comhaltas.ie

*Bolton Library St John's Cathedral (1750–1783) on John Street was built as a replacement for the cathedral on the Rock. It is home to the collection of early manuscripts and valuable early prints of the Bolton Library, including works by Dante, Swift and Calvin, medieval chronicles and historic maps, was assemble between 1730 and 1744.

❶ Mon–Wed 10am–3pm, Thu 10am–2.30pm; admission 2 €

Castlebar (Caisleán an Bharraigh)

✳ C 2

Republic of Ireland, province: Connacht
County: Mayo
Population: 10,650

Castlebar, in the northwest of Ireland, is the capital of County Mayo and boasts the international airport of Knock. Anglers come here, drawn by the lakes south of Castlebar: Lough Mallard, Castlebar Lough and Islanddeady Lough.

Castlebar Races The centre of today's market town with small industries is the Mall, a pretty square planted with lime trees. The main cultural attraction is the Linenhall Arts Centre (www.thelinenhall.com) in a building dating from 1790. In 1798 the French General Humbert celebrated victory after the **Castlebar Races** when an English unit took flight.

Castlebar

INFORMATION
Linenhall Street
Tel. (094) 902 1207
www.castlebar.ie

AROUND CASTLEBAR

The award-winning ***National Museum of Country Life** occupies spectacular new buildings in the wonderful Turlough Park on the N 5 between Castlebar and Dublin. The museum is devoted to rural life in the 19th and 20th centuries. The everyday life of farming people is shown on four levels and in, for example, a reconstructed thatched cottage. Turlough Park House in the Gothic Revival style and the fine park with its lake and glasshouse are also open to visitors.

❶ Tue–Sat 10am–5pm, Sun 12 noon–5pm; free admission

*Straide Take the N5 northeast, in the direction of Foxford, to reach Straide. The ruined church of a former abbey boasts fine sculptures and tombs. One tomb carved around 1475 is considered the most splendid example of the Flamboyant style in Ireland. For reasons unknown, the saints are represented engaged in **hearty laughter**. A small museum commemorates the **Michael Davitt Memorial Museum** Fenian and founding member of the Irish National Land League, Michael Davitt (1846–1906).

❶ 10am–4.30pm, Sun from 2pm; admission 3.20 €; www.michaeldavitt-museum.com

After Fatima and Lourdes, **Knock** (pop. 590) is Europe's third most popular site for **pilgrimage to a shrine of the Virgin Mary**. Over a million pilgrims come every year to Knock Shrine and the basilica of Our Lady of Knock, which holds a congregation of 12,000. The fame of Knock stems from an apparition of

MARCO POLO TIP

Treats from Castlebar — Insider Tip

Excellent agricultural products come from around Castlebar. In 1990 Sheila and Tom Butler started the Cuinneog Irish Farmhouse in Shraheen's about 16km/10mi east of Castlebar; in 2011 it won the Taste Award for milk, country butter and butter milk and was featured on the menu of the State Banquet for Queen Elizabeth II's visit to Ireland (www.cuinneog.com).

the Virgin Mary in 1879, when the Mother of God, accompanied by Saint Joseph and John the Evangelist, allegedly appeared to 15 locals at the back of the old parish church (www.knock-shrine.ie). The **Knock Museum** illuminates local history and the life of Monsignor James Horan, who successfully campaigned for construction of the airport.

Today Ireland West Knock Airport handles 700,000 passengers annually and even has its own anthem, the Knock Song, first performed by the folk singer Christy Moore in Castlebar in 2010.

✳ Causeway Coast   ✦ A 5

Northern Ireland, province: Ulster
Counties: Antrim and Derry

The Causeway Coast is the most beautiful stretch of coast in Northern Ireland. The signposted Causeway Coastal Route leads from Derry to splendid beaches, romantic castles and the Glens of Antrim, ending at the gates of Belfast. The 40,000 basalt pillars of the Giant's Causeway are the highlight.

In 1774, the **eccentric Bishop of Derry** and 4th Earl of Bristol, Frederick Augustus Hervey, had a splendid palace built at Downhill, of which only the outer walls survive. The real attraction in the grounds is the small Mussenden Temple, standing close to the cliff edge. One

Downhill & Mussenden Temple

theory says that Hervey had the structure built in 1783 after the death of his cousin Mrs Mussenden, to whom he was very close. Others claim the clergyman used the temple as a library. In summer Mussenden Temple now forms a romantic backdrop for classical concerts and readings. Walks in the surrounding countryside yield wonderful views of the coast. Directly below Mussenden Temple, Downhill Strand used to be the setting for horse races organized by the bishop, with lucrative parishes the coveted »prize money« for participating clergy. In Hezlett House, once the bishops' residence, everyday life in the 18th century is presented.

❶ Grounds open during daylight hours; Hezlett House 10am–5pm; admission 4.50 £

The Mussenden Temple is modelled on the Temple of the Vestals in Rome

The Victorian charm of the popular holiday resorts of Portstewart and Portrush has faded, but the beaches are wonderful. In Portstewart the **Flowerfield Arts Centre** draws many visitors., while in Portrush the enormous **Dunluce Centre** has family attractions such as a 4D simulator and the Dark Light Laser Dome. To the east of Portrush lie a 5km/3-mile sandy beach and the White Rocks.

Portstewart
Portrush

Flowerfield Arts Centre: 185 Coleraine Road, Mon–Fri 9am–5pm, Sat 10am–1pm; www.flowerfield.org

Dunluce Centre: April–June, Sept and Oct Sat, Sun 12 noon–5pm, July and Aug daily 10.30am–5.30pm; admission 4.75 £; www.dunlucecentre.co.uk

Coleraine, a lively town on the River Bann, used to be known mainly for its salmon, distilleries and linen production. The excavations of **Mountsandel Fort** (12th century) south of Coleraine uncovered the oldest traces of human settlement in Ireland, dating back to between 7900 and 7600 BC.

Coleraine

❶ Open during daylight hours; free admission

When passing the limestone cliffs known as the White Rocks, with the beautiful Curran Strand, don't miss Dunluce Castle, in Irish Dún Libhse, a romantically ruined castle, built in the 14th century on a rocky ledge and subsequently altered several times. In 1584 it was conquered by the MacDonnells, the lords of Antrim, and restored six years later. The money for this came from the gold treasure salvaged from the Spanish galleon »Girona«, shipwrecked in 1588 off the coast. Parts of the treasure can be seen in the Ulster Museum in ▶Belfast. The castle occupies a relatively exposed position on a high cliff; the kitchen crashed into the sea during a storm in 1693.

*Dunluce
Castle

❶ 10am–6pm, Nov–Feb until 4pm; grounds admission, exhibition 5 £

During a visit to Bushmills Distillery, a film tells visitors that apart from the spelling, there are two significant differences in the production of Bushmills malt whiskey and Scottish malt whisky. In Scotland, the malted barley is dried over a turf fire, which lends the whisky a smoky note. Conversely, the Bushmills product is characterized by a milder, honeyed flavour. Here, the malted barley is dried in sealed ovens, without being exposed to smoke. At Bushmills, the whiskey is distilled three times, in Scotland usually only twice. Visitors can see the working distillery and afterwards sample a whiskey at the bar, have a bite to eat or browse in one of the shops.

Bushmills
Distillery

? *Did you know?*

MARCO ⊕ POLO INSIGHT

Bushmills boasts the oldest licensed whiskey distillery in the world. Irish monks are said to have produced the »water of life« here as early as the 13th century, and in 1608 the distillery was granted a licence by James I. Today it belongs to the British Diageo group.

MARCO ⊕ POLO TIP

Special editions Insider Tip

The whiskey shops at Bushmills and other Irish distilleries sell special editions known as distillery reserve that cannot be purchased elsewhere. For a comparison with Scottish varieties, the Scotch House Tavern on Main Street in Bushmills is the place to go.

❶ 2 Distillery Road, April–Oct daily 12 noon–5pm, July and Sept from 11am, Nov–March Mon–Fri 9.15am–5pm, Sat and Sun 12.30-5pm; admission 7 £; www.bushmills.com

Take the historic **narrow gauge railway** between Bushmills and the Giant's Causeway. The trip takes around 15 minutes.
❶ Easter/late April to Oct, Sat and Sun 10am–5pm, July–Aug daily; return ticket 7.50 €

The visitor centre at the ****Giant's Causeway**, a UNESCO World Heritage site. opened in 2012 at a cost of some 18.5 million pounds (▶ photo p. 11). The site can be explored on marked trails and in the Giant's Causeway Experience. The 38,000 basalt pillars of different heights and diameter are volcanic in origin. Following a subterranean eruption around 60 million years ago, the cooling lava formed into the prismatic shapes tourists admire today. Some of the conspicuous rock formations have names, for instance the Camel, the Granny, the Wishing Chair, the Chimney Tops, the Giant's Boot and the Organ. According to one legend, the Causeway was the work of Finn McCool, Ulster warlord and commander-in-chief of the King of Ireland's army. All the outrageous stories involving Finn McCool make him a giant. The story goes that he fell in love with a giantess living on the Hebridean island of Staffa and started the construction of a path to safely bring his lover across to Ulster. **Shuttle buses** run daily from 10am every ten minutes from the visitor centre to the Giant's Causeway, costing 1 £. An alternative is to take the park & ride service from Bushmills Distillery for 1.75 £.
❶ Coastal path and Causeway stones open during daylight hours; visitor centre 9.30am–6pm, Sat and Sun until 6.30pm; parking 6 £

Causeway School Museum The superb school museum above the car park at Giant's Causeway is a work of the architect Sir Clough Williams-Ellis (1873–1978). It houses an exhibition with historic school furnishings, teaching material and the Sculpture of a Child by Rosamund Praeger.
❶ Easter and July–Sept daily 11am–5pm, at other times Mon–Fri 2–5pm; admission 2 £

The remains of Dunseverick Castle above a spectacular inlet of the sea can be admired from a layby. The wonderful atmosphere of the place evokes something of the former importance of Dunseverick; when it was the capital of the Kingdom of Dalriada, one of the royal roads from Tara, seat of the Kings of Ireland, ended here. **Dunseverick Castle**

With its wonderful beach and a youth hostel in a fantastic location, Whitepark Bay mainly draws backpackers. From the bay, a narrow **Whitepark Bay**

Causeway Coast

WHERE TO STAY
Bushmills Inn £££
9 Dunluce Road, Bushmills
Tel. (0 28) 2073 3000
www.bushmillsinn.com

8 rooms and 1 suite
A hotel to promote the well-being of guests, with an open peat fire, gas lamps, massages and an award-winning hotel (Sun–Thu, 3 courses 20 €).

A toll has to be paid to use the Carrick-a-Rede rope bridge

road leads to the tiny but incredibly scenic harbour of Ballintoy. In summer, there are boat trips all around Sheep Island, a rocky island with a colony of cormorants.

*Carrick-a-rede Rope Bridge For anybody who has always wanted to play at being Indiana Jones, the Carrick-a-rede Rope Bridge provides a suitable challenge. From mid-March to September, an 18m/20-yard rope bridge spans a chasm east of the village. The bridge gives salmon fishers access to the fish grounds, but crossing the swaying contraption has now become a **popular dare** with tourists.

❶ Nov, Dec 10.30am–3.30pm, at other times 10am–6pm or 7pm; admission 5.60 £

Cavan (An Cabhán)

✳ C 4

Republic of Ireland, province: Ulster
County: Cavan
Population: 7,950

Nestling amidst hills and lakes, the county capital of Cavan is not far from the southern border of Northern Ireland. Traditionally, Cavan's main importance lay in crystal manufacture. Horses are also important here; nearly every weekend there are showjumping events or auctions. Megalithic tombs, ruined churches and sizeable pikes are the main attractions of the surrounding countryside.

AROUND CAVAN

Kilmore Cathedral West of Cavan, some 5km/3 miles west of the R198 leading from Crossdoney to Killykeen Forest Park, have a look at the 19th-century Kilmore Cathedral. The first cathedral here was built in 885. The remarkable late-Romanesque doorway came from a monastery on Trinity Island (Lough Oughter). In the churchyard lies the tomb of the English bishop William Bedell (1571–1642), who was the first to translate the Bible into Irish. Further northwest, the winding bays of Lough Oughter snake their way into the countryside; the lake is traversed by the Erne River and resembles a water maze. The forest and lake area

Cavan

AUSKUNFT
Farnham Street
Tel. 049 4 33 19 42
www.cavantourism.com
April–Sept.

has been declared **Killykeen Forest Park,** offering fine hiking trails, kayaking, angling and horse-riding. A typically Irish round tower castle is the 13th-century ruined **Clough Oughter**. Killeshandra, surrounded by ice-age drumlins, is a mecca for anglers. 1km/0.5 miles south of Milltown lie the beautifully scenic ruins of the monastery **Drumlane**: a round tower and a church, nestling between two lakes. The church dates from the 13th and 15th century, the tower – still 14m/46ft high and featuring heavily weathered bird reliefs – from the 12th century.

East of Cavan, the R 188 leads to **Cootehill**, where the attractions can be explored on a town trail of 1.5 hours taking in St Michael's Church, the birthplace of the writer Mary Anne Sadlier (1820–1903) and the courthouse. On the R192 leading southeast from Cootehill to Sherock, after 5km/3 miles, look out for **Cohaw** and the mound of a megalithic grave with five chambers and a dual court. Lough Sillan near Shercock, which has a campsite, is well-known for the large pikes caught there. Another 13km/8 miles south, in the most easterly corner of the province, lies the little town of **Kingscourt**. In the parish church of St Mary's, don't miss the colourful stained-glass windows designed by Evie Hone in the 1940s. To the northwest stretches the **Dún an Rí Forest Park**, offering good walking trails, picnic sites and a wishing well.

EXCURSIONS INTO COUNTY CAVAN

The N3 goes to **Belturbet,** a departure point for cabin cruisers on the Erne River, with its plentiful fish. In the town centre a heritage trail of 1.5 hours flags up the sights: Turbet Island Motte, the town hall, railway station and the house of William Percy French. The Shannon-Erne Waterway (▶Carrick-on-Shannon) connects with the Shannon. Just before Ballyconnell, the **Bullyhugh Arts and Cultural Centre**, with B&B, is devoted to the culture of western County Cavan.

Heading north

In **Tirnawannagh**, 2km/1.2 miles from Bawnboy, is a teddy-bear museum with shop and teddy-bear hospital in the Bear Essentials & Silver Bear Centre. The Bear Centre lies within the UNESCO-designated Marble Arch Cave Global Geo Park, in the catchment area of the Shannon springs. The park crosses the border into County Fermanagh. Cave tours lasting 75 minutes can be booked.

The Museum of the Master Saddler in **Corlough**, west of Bawnboy, is unique in the world. Here 100-year-old saddles and coaches dating from 1890, 1896 and 1910 can be seen. The museum director collaborates with the Queen's saddler Keith Luxford.

Dowra lies on the upper reaches of the Shannon; between the river and Mt Slievenakilla (545m/1,788ft), a 5km/3-mile section of the mysterious **Black Pig's Dyke**, an ancient earth wall guarding the borders of Ulster, winds its way. The 17km/10.5-mile Cavan Way hiking trail runs between Dowra and Blacklion, situated 10km/6 miles northeast. Blacklion is also the final stop on the Ulster Way.

Bear Essentials & Silver Bear Centre: Mon–Sat 9.30am–6pm, Sun 11am–6pm; www.bearessentials.ie

Marble Arch Cave Global Geo Park: mid-March to Sept 10am–4.30pm, July and Aug until 5pm; admission 8.75 €; www,marblearchcavesgeopark.com, www.marblearchcaves.net

Museum of the Master Saddler: by appointment, tel. (086) 394 64 67; free admission; www.museumofthe mastersaddler.com

South of Cavan

Almost 20km/13 miles from Cavan, the ***Cavan County Museum** in Ballyjamesduff has an impressive collection of sheela-na-gigs and is dedicated to 6,000 years of local history, the Great Famine of 1850 and hurling. 10km/6 miles further south, in Montnugent, visitors to **Carraig Craft Centre** can make baskets themselves and admire the professional work in the **Basketry Museum**. Situated on the wooded slopes of Lough Ramor, the pleasant town of **Virginia** offers varied leisure pursuits, including a 9-hole golf course, angling, a swimming beach, and boat hire.

Cavan County Museum: Tue–Sat 10am–5pm, June–Sept also Sun 2–6pm; free admission; www.cavanmuseum.ie

Carraig Craft Centre and Basketry Museum: April–Oct Mon–Fri 10am–6pm, Sun 2–6pm; admission 3.50€

** Cliffs of Moher (Aillte an Mhothair)

✦ D 2

Republic of Ireland, province: Munster
County: Clare

Even shrouded in mist or whipped by storms, the Cliffs of Moher in the west of Ireland, south of Galway Bay, are among the most spectacular sights in the country. At the southern tip of the cliff wall, the sheer cliffs jut 120m/394ft out of the sea, and a breathtaking 200m/656ft at O'Brien's Tower further north.

Ireland's most famous cliffs: the Cliffs of Moher

The spectacular cliffs stretch for a good 8km/5 miles. Seagulls, guillemots and other sea birds nest here, the ocean calls from down below with a thundering voice, while rocky crags rise from the water. A visit to the Cliffs of Moher, which is part of the **Burren and Cliffs of Moher Geopark**, is easily combined with a drive around the ▶Burren.

Magnificent cliffs

The exhibition at the **Cliffs of Moher Visitor Experience** covers the themes of ocean and rock, nature and humankind. The virtual audiovisual theatre Atlantic Edge shows spectacular views of a cliff wall from above and below the water surface. A path leads to a sandstone plateau at the cliff's edge and to **O'Brien's Tower**, which on clear days in particular yields a magnificent view across the sea to the Aran Islands. The viewing tower was erected in 1835 by Sir Cornelius O'Brien.

Visitor centre

Cliffs of Moher Visitor Experience: Nov–Feb daily 9am–5pm, at other times daily 9am–6pm or longer July to mid-Aug until 9pm combined ticket 6 €, individual attractions from 2 €
O'Brien's Tower: summer from 10am, winter from 11am,; admission 2 €

Whilst the fantastic view from O'Brien's Tower usually has to be shared with many other sightseers, visitors walking to Hag's Head at the southern end of the Cliffs of Moher will encounter few people.

A walk to Hag's Head

AROUND THE CLIFFS OF MOHER

East of the cliffs, via the fishing village of Liscannor, past the ruined 15th-century Kilmacreehy Church and along Liscannor Bay, with its

Lahinch

Stud (www.coolmore.com) is one of the world's largest and most successful stud farms. In August a medieval fair is celebrated in Fethard. The **Fethard Folk Museum & Transport Museum** on Cashel Road, 500m/550yd from the town centre, has 1,200 exhibits and is the venue for Sunday markets. in the former railway station.

❶ Mon–Sat 10am–6pm, June–Aug also Sun 2.30–6pm; admission 2 €; www.fethard.com

Cong (Conga)

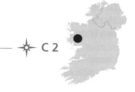

✳ C 2

Republic of Ireland, province: Connacht
County: Mayo
Population: 180
Information: www.congtourism.com

A visit to this beautiful village in the West of Ireland means walking in the footsteps of John Wayne and Maureen O'Hara. This is where in 1198, after spending fifteen years in seclusion, Roderick O'Conor died, the last of the Irish High Kings.

*Cong Abbey — Between Lakes of Lough Mask and ▶Lough Corrib, teeming with fish, lies the pretty, tranquil village of Cong. At the village entrance stand the ruins of Cong Abbey, an Augustinian monastery built in

The cloister of Cong Abbey

the 12th century. The skilfully carved entrance and various capitals of the cloister (dating from the early 13th century) are good examples of Irish Romanesque. Don't miss the restored Monk's Fishing House on the river. An opening in the ground allowed the monks to fish from the comfort of their cottage. This is where the **Cong Cross** was made, a masterpiece of precious metals and enamel work commissioned by King Turlough O'Conor around 1123 and today kept in the National Museum in Dublin.

Ashford Castle — Situated near the monastery, in a park on Lough Corrib, **Ashford Castle** acquired its current aspect in the 19th century, when a member of the Guinness family lived here. Today, it is considered one of the best hotels in the country.

In 1951, **John Wayne and Maureen O'Hara** spent some time in Cong, where the Hollywood classic »The Quiet Man« was filmed. The **Quiet Man Heritage Cottage** on Abbey Street aims to be an exact recreation of John Ford's location. The small house also holds an archaeological and historical exhibition on the history of the town.

Hollywood stars in Cong

❶ April–Oct daily 10am–4pm, guided tours 11am; admission 5 €; www.quietman-cong.com

AROUND CONG

The limestone soil of the landscape between ►Lough Corrib and Lough Mask holds numerous caves. The most interesting are Kelly's Cave – probably established as a burial site in the Bronze Age – and the Pigeon Hole. Pick up the key to Kelly's Cave from Cong's Quiet Man Coffee Shop. Both caves are situated at approx. 1.5km/1 mile from Cong and easily accessible on foot. Near the Pigeon Hole and the Ballymaglancy Cave (3km/2 miles east of Cong), the Giant's Cave, a megalithic burial chamber, is open to the public.

Caves

** Connemara (Conamara)

✳ C 1/2

Republic of Ireland, province: Connacht
County: Galway

The landscape of Connemara is one of the prime sights in the country, with its jagged mountain ranges, barren lone peaks, valleys enfolding dark lakes and a coast where rocky and sandy beaches alternate.

The wild romantic landscape stretches along the heavily indented west coast of Ireland, north of Galway Bay. The region caters to sports fans as well as holidaymakers looking for peace and quiet. The population of Connemara remain **attached to their traditions**, and large parts of the area are still Irish-speaking, evident in Irish-only road signs.

Gaeltacht

The hill village of Cnoc Suain lies 30 minutes by car from Galway. Gaelic cultural events are held here in stone houses dating from the 17th century. Evenings of folklore and the Connemara Gaelic Cultural Experience (www.cnocsuain.com) are part of the programme.

Cnoc Suain

Bittersweet

The Emerald Isle has little truck with movie glamour – but films are another story! After Hollywood, Ireland is American companies' second-favourite location for shooting; both Moby Dick and James Bond fought for their lives on Irish locations. The new Irish cinema, however, offers more than just a scenic backdrop.

James Joyce himself inaugurated Dublin's first cinema in 1909, and the Irish discovered a new passion. They have remained passionate moviegoers ever since. The classic »Man of Aran« by **Robert Flaherty** was awarded the Golden Lion in Venice 1934. As early as 1901, **Sidney Olcott** had started visiting Ireland nearly every year to stage stories from the olden days. Olcott's films, such as »Ireland the Oppressed« delighted Irish emigrants in particular. To this day, the Emerald Isle continues to attract directors who revel in Ireland's landscapes and colours, which are familiar to cinema audiences worldwide.

Whales and »Doppelgangers«

Between 1954 and 1956, **John Huston** shot »Moby Dick« on the Irish coast, falling in love with the country and the people. For several years, he lived near Galway, developing a passionate interest in Irish literature. James Joyce was a particular favourite, and Huston championed the establishment of a Joyce museum at the Martello Tower near Dublin, the original setting of the first chapter of Ulysses. Huston's last film, »The Dead«, is also homage to Joyce, but whilst it was an opulent production, the director had old Dublin Town rebuilt in California.

The Neighbours Come to Visit

Carol Reed, David Lean and Stanley Kubrick came over from England. Reed's collaboration with Graham Greene started in 1947, and »Odd Man Out« was one of Reed's films based on a Graham Greene novel: the portrait of an underground fighter fleeing through the Belfast night after an assassination. In 1970, **David Lean**, a master of big emotions on the big screen, directed »Ryan's Daughter«. In this tragic love story set in 1916, the love of a married Irishwoman (Sarah Miles) to a British officer (Robert Mitchum) is defeated by the historic situation and social conventions. The Dingle Peninsula and the village of Dunquin were given a great boost by the film. To this day, many film buffs make the pilgrimage to the original locations. For »Barry Lyndon«, **Stanley Kubrick** tried to reconstruct the mid-18th century in minute detail, using hundreds of candles to stage night-time banquets and filming the scene with his special lens. In the film, its settings carefully composed like paintings, the erring and wanderings of the Irish rogue take three hours.

Youghal, a sleepy little fishing village, still benefits from memories of the shooting of »Moby Dick«

Up for an Oscar

Irish directors **Neil Jordan** and **Jim Sheridan** have not shied away from tricky subjects, taking political and social issues to the big screen in impressive features from the early 1980s onwards. The two Sheridan films »The Boxer« and »In the Name of the Father« show IRA fighters, court debates and daily life in prison. For his 1983 film on the IRA, »The Crying Game«, Jordan was awarded an Oscar, and the Michael Collins biopic received the Golden Lion in 1996.

Commitments & Co.

The suburbs of Dublin, inhabited by families that argue the hell out of each other but stick together in adversity, their daily grind made bearable by Guinness and humour: this is a common image projected by recent Irish films. »The Commitments« marked the start of a new era. In 1991, **Alan Parker** filmed this first part of Roddy Doyle's tri-

logy, **Stephen Frears** the next two, »The Snapper« and »Fish & Chips«. Using a sharp critical eye for the social scene and good music, the films give authentic insights into contemporary Irish society. Also based on works of literature are Sheridan's »My Left Foot«, which tells the story of a handicapped boy, and »Angela's Ashes«. Films such as »Hear My Song«, on the unintentional comeback of a singer, and »Waking Ned Devine« draw much on the wit of their characters. In the latter film, a whole village joins forces to pocket the lottery winnings of one villager who suffers a fatal cardiac arrest on hearing the happy news. Like other Irish films of recent years, this unspectacular but well-made comedy delights through its fast pace, wit, music and spectacular landscapes. A further big success was Ken Loach's masterpiece about two boys from County Cork in the turbulent events of the civil war in 1920, »The Wind that Shakes the Barley«.

Connemara

INFORMATION
Clifden Tourist Office
Tel. (0 95) 211 63
www.clifden.galway-ireland.ie.

WHERE TO STAY AND EAT
Abbeyglen Castle €€€€
 Sky Road, Clifden
Tel. (0 95) 212 01
 www.abbeyglen.ie
36 rooms and 9 suites
On the Sky Road above the rooftops of
Clifden, with a romantic garden and
waterfall.

Roundstone House Hotel €€
 Roundstone
Tel. (0 95) 358 64
 www.roundstonehousehotel.com
12 rooms
A pleasant hotel in an attractive little
place with the excellent Vaughans Bar,
serving food until 7pm and a high-class
restaurant, known for its seafood. Activities include golf and pony trekking.

Clifden Clifden, a small market town (pop. 1,930) out west, is the main town
of Connemara. It is situated at the end of Clifden Bay, one of the
many narrow inlets that rise eastwards towards the Twelve Bens. In
August, the famous **Connemara Pony Show**, with its diverse folk-
loric contests, attracts many visitors.

Owenglin Below the town, the Owenglin flows down to the valley in beautiful
river cascades. In the right season, at Weir Bridge, situated at the southern
end of Clifden, watch shoals of salmon working against the current.
A bit further south, look for the **remains of the first transatlantic
transmitting station** set up by Guglielmo Marconi (1874–1937), the
Italian radio pioneer who moved to England in 1896.

*Sky Road The promenade on Beach Road in the west of Clifden is popular, but
it is surpassed by the 11km/7-mile Sky Road, which starts at a fork in
the road above the harbour. Walkers and cyclists can round the peninsula, reaching a height of 150m/500ft above the sea.
For an adventure on the **Bog Road**, take the R 341 to wards Ballyconneely, forking left at Ballinaboy to pass through the Roundstone Bog
Conservation Area, then returning from Roundstone to Clifden via
Ballyconneely.

A DRIVE THROUGH CONNEMARA

Cleggan North of Clifden lies the fishing village of Cleggan, whose livelihood
depends on lobster fishing. The top of Cleggan Hill, with a ruined
watchtower, offers a breathtaking view. From Cleggan, boats go to

Inishbofin (pop. 200). The island was settled by monks in the 7th century. A heritage museum outlines the history.

Heritage Museum: Easter and June–Sept daily 12 noon–1.30pm, 2.30–5pm; donation requested

Ferry: Inishbofin Island Discovery, www.inishbofinislanddiscovery; return ticket 20 €

Take the N59 to reach Letterfrack. Thanks to the mild climate, in some places fuchsia hedges grow to great heights in this area. Here is also the visitor centre and thus the main access to the ***Connemara National Park**. The centre has information on flora, fauna and the settlement history of this area, which may be explored on two shorter well-marked trails or on a day trip. (Opening times: park all year round; visitor centre May–Sept daily 10am–6pm.) North of Letterfrack, turn left onto a small road leading to Tully Cross and Renvyle. At the tip of the scenic peninsula, look for the remains of a castle and a church, as well as a dolmen.

Letterfrack

> **!** MARCO ⊕ POLO TIP
>
> *Inishbofin Island*   **Insider Tip**
>
> It is worth visiting Inishbofin only for the sandy beaches and cliffs. Sailing and deep-sea angling are further attractions. The island also has coastal fortifications, stone houses and remains of a barracks from the time of Cromwell, who set up a kind of penal camp for priests and monks.

❶ Park open all year, visitor centre March–Oct daily 9am–5.30pm: free admission: www.connemaranationalpark.ie

From Letterfrack, the N59 runs through the valley of Dawros River to the lakes at Kylemore, nestling between mountains. When the rhododendron and fuchsia blossom, this area displays an overwhelming beauty. To the left, beyond the first lake, rises the palatial Kylemore Abbey, built in the 19th century by a wealthy merchant as a country home and today owned by Irish Benedictines. The church and Victorian walled garden are open to the public; there is also a restaurant and a crafts centre. Walk 1km/0.6 miles from the car park or take the free shuttle bus.

Kylemore Abbey

❶ Jan and Feb daily 11am–4.30pm, March–Oct 9am–5.30pm, July and Aug until 7pm, Nov and Dec 9.30am–4.30pm; admission 13 €, 10% reduction online; www.kylemonastery.com

At the southern shore of Ballynahinch Lough stands the award-winning hotel of the same name (www.ballynahinch-castle.com), a mansion built in the 18th century by the Martin family, who during the Great Famine (1845–49) gave away large parts of their estate to help the poor. A legendary member of the family was Richard »Humanity Dick« Martin, born in 1754, a member of Parliament who campaigned for Catholic emancipation, a keen

Ballynahinch Lough

dueller and also the biggest landowner in Ireland around 1800. He supported the rights of domestic and farm animals, bringing about the Martin Act and earning his nickname given by King George IV. In 1854, 20 years after his death, nothing remained of the family estates.

Follow the road as it winds its way past Kylemore Lough and Lough Fee through a hollow to Killary Harbour, a fjord stretching inland for 16km/10 miles, which once served as a base for the British navy. In the north there is a view of the Valley of Delphi, a rocky valley of impressive beauty. It was given its name by Lord Sligo, who called his fishing cottage there »Delphi«. **Leenane** (pop. 50) is a handy base for anglers and hillwalkers. The museum in the Sheep and Wool Centre is dedicated to the history wool production and processing. There are good walking trails in the surrounding countryside, one of them leading to the Ashleag Waterfall at the eastern tip of Killary Harbour. **Killary Harbour**

❶ Sheep and Wool Centre: mid-March to Oct daily 9.30am–6pm; admission 5 €; www.sheepandwoolcentre.com

Take the R336 via Maam Cross. The road follows the course of the Joyce River to **Joyce's Country**. In Shanafraghaun, Finny, Joe and Mary-Ann Joyce put on sheep-dog demonstrations. At Galway Bay, the works of ten artists are represented at the Spiddal Craft Centre. Stop at the Builí Blasta Café (http://ceardlann.com) for delicious fish-cakes, chowder and brownies. **Carraroe** is famous for the traditional Irish sailing boats, Galway hookers, that are made here. They are celebrated each August at Ireland's leading maritime festival, Féile an Dóilín. A walk on the beach and a look at the Tropical Butterfly Centre round off a visit here. Near Rosmuc on the R340 stands the small cottage **Pearse's Cottage** used by Patrick Pearse (1879–1916) as a summer house. An exhibition commemorates the leader of the 1916 rising. **Onwards via Maam Cross**

Joyce's Country: June–Oct Tue–Sat 11am and 1.30pm; admission 7 €; www.joycecountrysheepdogs.ie
Tropical Butterfly Centre: May–Sept Mon–Sat 10am–6pm, Sun 12 noon–6pm; http://carraroe.galway-ireland.ie
Pearse's Cottage: Easter, end of April–Sept daily 10am–6pm; admission 3 €

Roundstone (pop. 240), was founded in the early 19th century for Scottish fishermen and is popular with artists and for its fine shell beaches. Malachy Kearns, one of the last **traditional instrument makers** in Ireland, lives here. In 2011 Barack and Michelle Obama were presented with a bodhrán, a tambourine-style hand drums cov- **Roundstone**

The landing stage at Killary Harbour

ered with goatskin. Kearns' shop **Roundstone Musical Instruments** in the IDA Craft Centre also sells harps, whistles and fiddles (www.bodhran.com).

Ballyconneely Bay

On Ballyconneely Bay are the ruined Bunowen Castle and the wonderful white sandy beach of Trá Mhóir. For smoked fish, stop at the Connemara Smoke House.

❶ Bunowen Pier, Ballyconneely: Mon–Fri 9am– 1pm and 2–5pm; www.smokehouse.ie

＊ Cork (Corcaigh)

✳ E 3

Republic of Ireland, province: Munster
County: Cork
Population: 119,250

Some consider the university city on the southern coast a »Paris of Ireland«, others detect Dutch atmosphere in Cork. This is due to the many bridges spanning the river and the old canals. The third-largest city in Ireland only became prosperous in the 19th century thanks to the establishment of an international market for butter. In 2005, vibrant Cork was European Capital of Culture.

＊City of bridges

Today still, the River Lee dominates the cityscape. Many canals have been filled in, but the two arms of the river (North Channel and South Channel) enclose the city centre like an island, spanned by bridges. Many of the Quays with their limestone walls are lined by trees. However, visitors may miss the historical ambience, as numerous wars have not left many old buildings. There are only a few notable 18th-century buildings; the Old Town's character around the North Channel and South Channel is dominated mainly by churches from the early 19th century. The main shopping drag is St Patrick's Street with its side streets.

Festivals

Major events in Cork are the **Midsummer Festival** in June (www.corkmidsummer.com), the **International Choral Festival** in May (www.corkchoral.ie) and the **Folk Festival** in early October (www.corkfolkfestival.com).

Two more famous events are **Guinness Cork Jazz** in October (www.guinnessjazzfestival.com) and the film festival in November (www.corkfilmfest.org). All year round performances take place at the Cork Film Centre (►Shandon) and the ►Cork School of Music.

Cork Highlights

▶ **Glucksman Gallery**
Art on the university campus in the west of the city
▶page 276

▶ **English Market**
The huge array of fish and seafood is a sight for sore eyes.
▶page 273

▶ **Crawford Municipal Art Gallery**
Outstanding collections of Irish painting and stained glass.
▶page 273

▶ **St Finbarr's Cathedral**
A neo-Gothic cathedral on the site of a former monastery.
▶page 276

▶ **Cork Butter Museum and St Ann's Shandon**
The story of butter in Cork and the bells of St Ann's Shandon are a must.
▶page 275

▶ **Cork Public Museum**
Exhibitions on the history of the region in a magnificent Georgian house.
▶page 276

▶ **Lifetime Lab**
The city's new attraction is housed in the old waterworks.
▶page 277

Around 650, St Finbarr founded a **monastery** in the marshland of the Lee – the Irish name of Corcaigh (»swamp«) makes reference to this geographical feature. Today, St Finbarr's Cathedral occupies this position. Between the 12th and 17th centuries, the city was conquered, lost again and re-conquered several times by the English or the Irish. It gained its city charter from King John in 1185. During the 18th century, the city was an important commercial centre with its huge **Buttermarket**. During the Great Famine, many citizens left. Nearby, Cobh (or Queenstown) became an embarkation point for America: over 3 million Irish are thought to have emigrated from here between 1815 and 1970. During the **War of Independence** in 1920, two mayors were murdered, large parts of the city suffered fire damage, and the politician Michael Collins was assassinated nearby.

SIGHTS IN CORK

The city centre of Cork lies on a river island. Once, the centre was criss-crossed by canals and bordered by warehouses and residences built by wealthy merchants. Picturesque bridges and quays continue **City on the river island**

Cork

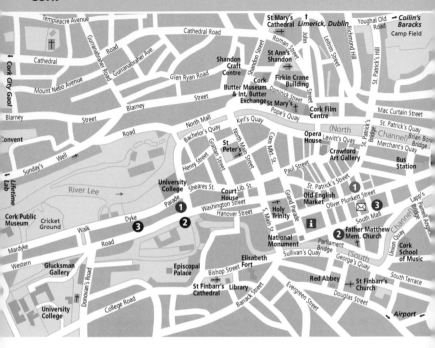

to lend the place a Dutch aura, although today most waterways have
been filled in; only the irregular course of many streets points to what
lies beneath. The streets linking Paul Street, St Patrick's Street and
Oliver Plunkett Street are pedestrian zones. A first port of call for
visitors is the impressive **Cork Vision Centre@St Peter's**. The history of St Peter's goes from 1270 until its deconsecration in 1949. It
has been renovated and now houses a model of the city and a film
show on the history of Cork.

❶ North Main Street; Tue–Sat 10am– 5pm; free admission;
www.corkvisioncentre.com

Grand Parade   Grand Parade today forms the centre of Cork. **National Monument** At its southern end, the **National Monument** commemorates Irish patriots who, in the period 1798–1867, died for their
country. To the east, in Bishop Lucey Park, remains of the old city
wall and the entrance of the old grain market survive. Between
Grand Parade and St Patrick Street, have a good look at the ***English**

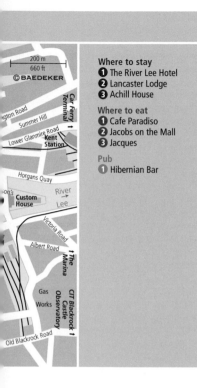

Where to stay
1. The River Lee Hotel
2. Lancaster Lodge
3. Achill House

Where to eat
1. Cafe Paradiso
2. Jacobs on the Mall
3. Jacques

Pub
1. Hibernian Bar

Market, which has been in operation since 1786. In 2011 the Queen visited the market and unveiled the restored fountain on the ground floor. Meat, fish, fruit and organic vegetables are on sale. Moynihans Poultry has a Cork speciality, buttered eggs. Don't miss the Farmgate Café (www.farmgate.ie) on the first floor, where traditional meals are served with the Poetry Wall as a backdrop. The Nobel prize-winner Seamus Heaney added a handwritten poem to the »Great Wall of Cork«.

At the end of St Patrick's Street, near St Patrick's Bridge, the **founder of the teetotal movement, Father Matthew Statue** Father Matthew (1790–1861), has been honoured by a statue. He preached south of South Mall at Holy Trinity Church (1726; also called Christchurch). The church complex, entered from Tobin Street, is home to the **Triskel Christchurch Arts Centre**.

English Market: Mon–Sat 8am–6pm; free admission;
www.corkenglishmarket.ie

Triskel Christchurch Arts Centre: Mon–Sat 10am–5pm, gallery Mon–Sat 12 noon–8pm; free admission; http://trinkelartscentre.ie

The continuations of Grand Parade, Corn Market Street and Paul Street are also good for a leisurely window-shop or stroll. Markets, nice bars, local as well as exotic restaurants and boutiques vie for business. In the Huguenot Quarter at **Rory Gallagher Square** (corner of Paul Street/Careys Lane), an unusual sculpture commemorates the rock musician (1949–1995), who used to live only a few doors down from here. The sculpture features a bent electric guitar, surrounded by flowing notes and lines from Gallagher's lyrics. **Corn Market Street & Paul Street**

One block further west, at Emmet Place, stands the largest art gallery in Cork. Built in 1724 in limestone and red brick, the building first **Crawford Municipal Art Gallery**

Cork

INFORMATION
Cork City, Grand Parade
Tel. (0 21) 425 5100
www.cometocork.com.

WHERE TO STAY
❶ *The River Lee Hotel* €€€€
Western Road
Tel. (0 21) 425 2700
www.doylecollection.com/riverlee
182 rooms
Cork's top design hotel with a great
view of the river, and excellent spa and
fitness facilities. Excellent food is served
in the Weir Bar (Sun, Mon) and the Weir
Bistro (Tue–Sat evenings).

❷ *Lancaster Lodge* €€€
Lancaster Quay, Western Road
Tel. (0 21) 425 1125
www.lancasterlodge.com
48 rooms
Newly renovated, popular hotel five minutes from the city centre. Generous
warm breakfast.

❸ *Achill House* €€
Western Road
Tel. (0 21) 427 9447
www.achillhouse.com
6 rooms
Helena McSweeney ensures that the atmosphere is warm-hearted. The rooms
are luxurious, the breakfast ample.

WHERE TO EAT
❶ *Café Paradiso* €€€€
16 Lancaster Quay, Western Road
Tel. (0 21) 427 7939
www.cafeparadiso.ie
Closed Sun, Mon
An old-established, high-class vegetarian
restaurant. Try the caramelized beetroot
tarts and Bluebell Falls goats cheese with
salsa verde and olive potatoes.

❷ *Jacobs on the Mall* €€€€
30a South Mall, Tel. (0 21) 425 1530
www.jacobsonthemall.com
Closed Sun
Innovative cooking with reasonably priced two- and three-course menus in a
former Turkish bath, where modern Irish
art now hangs.

❸ *Jacques* €€€
Phoenix Street, Tel. (0 21) 427 7387
www.jacquesrestaurant.ie
Closed Mon
The early evening menu for 24 is a good
offer. Try duck breast stuffed with apri-
cots.

PUB ^{Insider Tip}
❶ *Hibernian Bar*
108 Oliver Plunkett Street
Tel. (0 21) 427 2758
www.cafeparadiso.ie
Closed Sun, Mon
A small traditional pub above a pharmacy, with bags of atmosphere and friendly
service.

served as customs office and art college. Today, the Crawford Municipal Art Gallery presents an extraordinary collection of Irish
painting, amongst them works by Jack Yeats (1871–1957). The exhibits include work by international artists such as Miró and Rouault as

well as three windows by the great Irish stained-glass artist Harry Clarke (18891931). Born in Dublin, Clarke made his name as a book illustrator, for example with the works of Hans Christian Andersen and Edgar Allen Poe.

❶ Mon–Sat 10am–5pm; free admission; www.crawfordartgallery.ie

On the northern shore of the River in Shandon district Lee stands the landmark of the city of Cork, St Anne's Church. Crossing the Christy Ring Bridge to Pope's Quay, the portico with Ionic columns belonging to the Dominican church of **St Mary's** (1832–39) catches the eye. A remarkable feature inside is the 14th-century Flemish ivory statue of Our Lady of the Graces on the main altar.

Shandon

Follow Ferry Lane and Dominick Street to get to the **International Butter Exchange** on O`Connell Square. Until 1900 it was the biggest in the world; from 1925 it was a hat factory, and is now unoccupied. Opposite is the circular **Firkin Crane Building** of 1855, designed by Sir John Benson. Here coopers made the barrels (firkins) to transport butter. The name of the imposing building, which has black-and-white representations of different trades on its outer walls, from the hoist that was used to weigh the tarred barrels. Margarine was made here from 1925 until the 1970s. Since 1984 it has housed an internationally respected arts centre (www.firkincrane.ie). To the left of the Butter Exchange stands the **Cork Butter Museum**, where 1,000-year-old bog butter is on display. Only 100m/ 100yd from the Butter Exchange stands *****St Ann's Shandon** (1722), with a fine tower made of natural stone in various colours. Locally, the tower, appearing like a three-fold extended telescope is called »pepperpot«. It is said that

> **MARCO ⊕ POLO TIP** ❗
>
> *Ring the bell* **Insider Tip**
>
> Climb the tower to get a wonderful view of the city and to see the bells, on which visitors themselves can play tunes including Ave Maria, Danny Boy, When Irish Eyes Are Smiling and other Hibernian evergreens.

the monks chose the shape of a salmon for the 3m/10ft weather vane to display their right to fish in the river. The **Cork Film Centre** in the restored Civic Trust House promotes experimental cinema and visual art. In 2012 it opened Ireland's first gallery for video art in the Gunpowdermills Centre in nearby Ballincollig.

Cork Butter Museum: daily March–June, Sept and Oct 10am–5pm, July and Aug 10am–6pm, Nov–Feb Sat–Sun 10am–3.30pm; admission 4 €; http_//corkbutter.museum

St Ann's Shandon: Easter to Nov Mon–Sat 9.30am–5pm, Nov to Easter 10am–3pm; admission to tower and bells 6 €

Cork Film Centre: 50 Pope's Quay, Mon–Fri 10am–6pm; www.corkfilmcentre.com

*St Finbarr's Cathedral The neo-Gothic Anglican St Finbarr's Cathedral (1865–79) occupies a dominating position on the site of an earlier monastery. It was built in 1878 to designs by William Burges in honour of the patron saint of Cork. Notable features are the vaulted ceiling, decorated with paintings and gold leaf and showing Christ surrounded by angels, as well as the fine mosaics and stained-glass windows.

❶ Entrances at Proby's Quay and in Bishop Street; April – Oct Mon – Sat 9.30am – 5.30pm, Sun 1.30pm – 2.30pm & 4.30pm – 6pm; admission 5 €; http://corkcathedral.webs.com

Cork School of Music The new premises of the Cork School of Music on Union Quay are outstanding for their architecture and acoustics. 120 music teachers work here, and the sound of Steinway grand pianos rings from countless rooms. Concerts are held here in the Curtis Auditorium and the Stack Theatre. The free lunchtime concerts of the school's own CSM Jazz Big Band are extremely popular.

❶ Mon–Fri 8.30am–10pm, Sat 9am–5.30pm, Sun 10am–5pm; www.cit.ie

*Cork Public Museum West of the city centre , Fitzgerald Park houses the former prison, the University College Park, as well as the Cork Public Museum. Located in a splendid Georgian house, the latter offers an overview of the history of the region from its early Christian beginnings to today. Find out about the role of the city in the Irish liberation movements, as well as the **crochet and lace work** that Cork was once famous for. (Opening times: Mon–Fri 11am–1pm and 2.15–5pm, Sun 3–5pm.)

❶ Mon–Fri 11am–1pm, 2.15–5pm, Sat 11am–1pm, 2.15–4pm, April Sept also Sun 3–5pm; free admission

University College Washington Road and Western Road lead to University College (founded in 1845) and the award-winning building of the ***Glucksman Gallery**, which holds exhibitions of modern art on three floors. The permanent holdings comprise some 350 exhibits from the university collection, including Ogham stones and early publications from Cork. In the **Honan Chapel**, next to the Gaol Gate (1818), note the stained-glass by Sarah Purser and Harry Clarke. Tours of the campus start from the visitor centre (www.ucc.ie).

Glucksman Gallery: Lower Grounds, University College; Tue–Sat 10am–5pm, Sun 2–5pm; free admission, donation of 5 € requested; www.glucksman.org

> ! **MARCO POLO TIP**
> *Cork City pub crawl* **Insider Tip**
>
> This tour starts every Friday at 8.15pm at the General Post Office in Oliver Plunkett Street. It starts at the Old Oak include an acclaimed microbrewery, the Franciscan Brewery on North Mall (www.franciscanwellbrewery.com). Book with Tim: tel. (087) 760 7151; ticket 10 €; http://corkcitypubcrawl.com.

In **Cork City Jail** on Convent Avenue, guided tours of the former **prison** are highly popular. They are even held at night. A radio museum is attached.

❶ Tour booking tel. (021) 430 5022; March–Oct daily 9.30am–6pm, Nov–Feb 10am–6pm; admission 8 €; www.corkcitygaol.com

The ***Lifetime Lab** in the old waterworks is an attraction for the whole family. Interactive modules are devoted to ecological themes such as water, waste disposal, energy and nature. A visitor centre occupies the coalhouse dating from 1868, and the Steam Centre is also housed in a 19th-century building. Bus no. 8 runs from St Patrick's Street to this attraction

The idyllic University Park

in the west of the city, which can, however, also be reached on foot.

❶ Lee Road; Mon–Fri 9am–5pm, June–Aug also Sat and Sun 10am–5pm; admission 7 €; www.lifetimelab.ie

The universe is the subject of the excellent exhibition entitled Cosmos at the Castle. The 16th-century restored castle lies on the south bank of the Lee, 12 minutes by car from the city centre (or take bus no. 202 from Parnell Place to St Lukes). Here, in Ireland's first interactive theatre, visitors of all ages can play with the Comet Chaser. The exhibition also explains the work of the observatory. Castle tours with a look at the dungeon are included in the admission price.

*CIT Blackrock Castle Observatory

❶ Mon–Fri 10am–5pm, Sat and Sun 11am–5pm, castle tours Mon–Fri on request, Sat and Sun 1.30pm and 3.30pm; admission 6 €; www.bco.ie

AROUND CORK

This pretty country house in Glanmire on the N8 dates from 1602 took on its current aspect in 1745, when the bishop of Cork was residing here. The Francini brothers, famous Italian stucco artists, created extraordinary playful stucco features for the dining hall.

Riverstown House

❶ May–Sept Tue–Sat 2–6pm; tel. (021) 482 1205; admission 5 €

Small Fota Island, east of Cork and connected to the mainland by a bridge, offers several attractions. In **Fota Wildlife Park**, waterfowl,

*Fota Island

The beautiful drive along Lough Allua reveals yellow gorse in spring and white water lilies in summer

giraffes, zebras, antelopes, monkeys and many other animals populate the grounds, a big attraction for children. ***Fota House, Gardens and Arboretum** were renovated by the Irish Heritage Trust, restoring the glory of the architecture and interiors. In the 1820s the 70-room house was converted from a hunting lodge into a fine residence. Sir John Benson added the gallery and billiard room in 1872.

Fota Wildlife Park: Mon–Sat 10am–6pm, Sun 10.30am–6pm; admission 14.50 €; www.fotawildlife.ie

Fota House: only as part of a 60-minute guided tour, Mon–Sat 10am–5pm; Sun 11am–5pm; admission 7 €; www.fotahouse.com

Cobh   The port of Cobh (pop 12,350, formerly called »Queenstown«) used to be the point of departure for thousands of Irish families emigrating to America, and for prisoners being sent to Australia. It was the last port of call of the Titanic before its sinking. The history of the richly decorated neo-Gothic **St Colman's Cathedral** (www.cobhcathedralparish.ie) goes back to the year 560. Since 1916 the church has possessed the largest carillon in the British Isles, consisting of 49 bells weighing 27 tons altogether. From May to September, on Sundays at 4.30pm, recitals by famous carilloneurs from all over the world are held (free admission).

The **Cobh Heritage Centre** in the Victorian railway station documents the town's eventful history: the emigrants to America, the female prisoners sent to Australia, and in The Queenstown Story the fate of the *Titanic* and *Lusitania*. There are spectacular exhibits from the construction of the Titanic and the photos of Father Brown, who was invited aboard for a free voyage but disembarked in Cobh on the orders of his clerical superior. These photos are regarded as the most authentic record of the last days of the doomed liner. In front of the Cobh Heritage Centre, a monument has been erected commemorating **Annie Moore** and her two brothers. Annie Moore was the first immigrant entering the US via Ellis Island on 1 January 1892. The **Cobh Museum** on the High Road tells the social, cultural and commercial history of Cobh and the harbour by orgazizing changing exhibitions.

Cobh Heritage Centre: daily 9.30am–6pm, Nov–April until 5pm; admission 9 €; www.cobheritage.com
Cobh Museum: March–Oct, Mon–Sat 11am–1pm, 2–5pm, Sun 2.30–5.30pm; admission charge; www.cobhmuseum.com

Ballincollig

In 1794, the Royal Gunpowder Mills were founded in the village of Ballincollig, 8km/5 miles west of Cork on the N22 to Killarney, producing gunpowder for the British Army until 1903. This industrial site, part of the **Ballincollig Heritage Park**, can be explored as part of a pleasant walk(access from Inniscarra Bridge, circular walk takes three hours).

Macroom

Macroom (on the N22) owes its fame to its proximity to the place (at Beal-na-Blath) where on 22 August 1922 the Irish politician **Michael Collins** (▶Famous People) was shot dead. Collins was a leader of the rebellion of 1916 and later organised Irish resistance. In the civil war of 1922, he tried to defend the Free State born out of the 1921 peace with England against the radical position of de Valera (▶Famous People). Travelling through west Cork, he was ambushed at a site marked by a memorial stone. Tours are run by the Michael Collins Centre near ▶Clonakilty.

Tips for day trips around Macroom

The roads around Macroom are well-known scenic routes: the R618, for instance, winds its way past Carrighadrohid Castle (on an island) to **Dripsey**, famous for its woollen mills. The R584 leads west to Inehigeelagh, a holiday resort for anglers and artists in a picturesque location on the eastern tip of long **Lough Allua** with its white water lilies.

* Derry/Londonderry (Doire)

—————————————— ✳ A/B 4

Northern Ireland, province: Ulster
District: Derry
Population: 85,000

As the scene of »Bloody Sunday« in 1972, the second-largest city in Northern Ireland entered the history books for its part in the Troubles. However, the recovery of Derry was aided by its role of the first UK City of Culture in 2013, and Derry is now identified with the peace process, of which the visible symbol is the Peace Bridge over the River Foyle, opened in 2011.

City name   Derry is an anglicized version of the Irish »doire«, meaning oak wood. In 1662 the name was changed by royal decree to Londonderry, a reference to its refoundation in 1613 by merchants from London. In 1984 the city council changed its name to Derry City Council, but according to a court ruling of 2007 this has no effect on the official name, which can only be changed by submitting a petition to the Crown. Derry also has nicknames: »Maiden City« refers to the fact that its city wall was never conquered, and the local journalist Gerry Anderson joked that it should be called »Stroke City« to acknowledge the politically correct version that is often used: Derry/Londonderry.

City of transformation   Conspicuous signs of the transformation of Derry over the last decade are the promenades on the river, opened in 2012, and the **Peace Bridge** for pedestrians and cyclists. This link between Harbour Square on the west bank and Ebrington Square on the east bank, the Waterside district occupied by Protestants, bridges the gulf between the two halves of Derry. Bridge and promenade were paid for from the EU Peace Fund. Shopping malls and galleries such as the craft village in the old quarter have appeared, and the **Millennium Forum** (www.millenniumforum.co.uk) is a theatre and congress centre on the west bank.

UK City of Culture 2013   The title of UK City of Culture in 2013 released further sums for investment. although not all residents were pleased with the council's plans, and two attacks were made on the organizing office. However, the great majority of citizens wish to overcome their decades of isolation, and there is a broad agreement that only high employment levels can secure peace in the long term. Large companies such as DuPont, producing Kevlar, and the hard-drive manufacturer Seagate have brought jobs to the city.

According to legend, in 546 St Columba (Colmcille) founded a monastery on the estuary of the Foyle (Lough Foyle) that he called Doire (»oak forest«). Until the 11th century only the monastery existed here. It was repeatedly attacked and destroyed by Vikings. During the course of the colonization of Ulster by James I, 4,000 predominantly Protestant settlers from England and Scotland founded a settlement, which was ended with bloodshed in 1608 by the chieftain of Donegal, Cahir O'Doherty. His warriors came across the marshy land that is now called Bogside. Under the leadership of commercial guilds from London, the settlement was refounded in 1613. The great city wall, 4–12m/13–40ft high, dates from this time. In 1689 the city withstood

History

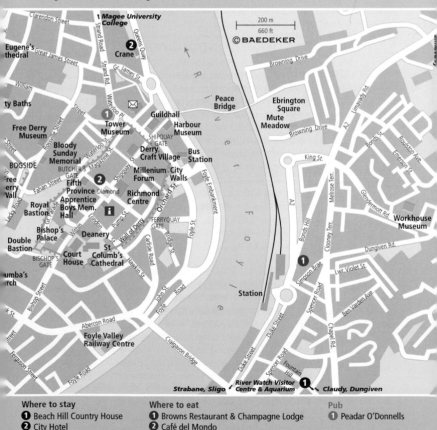

Derry · Londonderry

Where to stay	Where to eat	Pub
❶ Beach Hill Country House	❶ Browns Restaurant & Champagne Lodge	❶ Peadar O'Donnells
❷ City Hotel	❷ Café del Mondo	

a 105-day siege, the longest in British history, by the forces of James II, an event that is commemorated in the annual march of the Apprentice Boys and gave the Northern Irish Unionists their slogan of »**No Surrender**«. In the 18th and 19th centuries Derry was a centre of the textile industry and a port of embarkation for America.

The partition of Ireland in 1921 made Londonderry a **border city.** In the Second World War the port boomed as a base for North Atlantic convoys. In 1945 43 German U-boats surrendered and anchored in the Foyle River.

In the post-war period unemployment and discrimination against Catholic job seekers fuelled the civil rights movement and the Troubles in the Bogside. The violent conflict between Catholics and Protestants culminated in **Bloody Sunday**, 30 January 1972, when British soldiers killed 13 demonstrators. Following the Savile Inquiry, held in the Guildhall of Derry from 1998 to 2004, Prime Minister David Cameron made an official apology in 2010.

SIGHTS IN DERRY/LONDONDERRY

*Harbour Square and west bank
Harbour Square outside the city walls is the historic centre of Derry. Here, in front of the City Hotel, is a statue of the tenor **Joseph Locke** (1917–1999), the son of a butcher who sang in the churches of Bogside at the age of seven and became famous in Blackpool as »the singing Bobby«.

The Harbour Museum has been integrated into the **Foyle Valley Railway Museum** on Foyle Park. Interesting steam and diesel locomotives can be seen here.

A new attraction are canoe tours lasting several days on the River Foyle. Foyle Road leads to a roundabout at the Craigavan Bridge. Here the statue ensemble **Hands Across the Divide** (1992) symbolizes the peace process in Derry.

Foyle Valley Railway Museum: June–Aug Tue–Sat 10am–5pm; free admission

*Peace Bridge and Waterside
The architectural practice Wilson Eyre designed the curving Peace Bridge that crosses the River Foyle to Browning Drive, the underpass leading to ***Ebrington Square**. Once a parade ground and larger than Trafalgar Square in London, it was laid out on the site from which James II's army unsuccessfully besieged Derry in 1689.Later the provisional fort became a barracks and a navy base, which was abandoned in 2004. At great expense, the area surrounded by historic officers' houses was made into a cultural quarter for open-air events. The **hospital** of 1841 is used for changing exhibitions. For a panoramic view of the Peace Bridge and the Walled City, go to the bastion above **Mute Meadow**, Ireland's largest public work of art, an

Derry

INFORMATION
Derry Convention and Visitor Bureau
44 Foyle Street
Tel. (0 28) 7126 7284
www.derryvisitor.com.

WHERE TO STAY
❶ Beech Hill Country House ££££
32 Ardmore Road (Waterside)
Tel. (0 281) 7134 9279
www.beech-hill.com
27 rooms and suites
On the southeastern edge of the city, an elegant and charming hotel in the Georgian style with excellent food. Walking, cycling and golf are among the activities).

❷ City Hotel ££
14-18 Queen' s Quay
Tel. (0 28) 7136 5800

www.cityhotelderry.com
145 rooms and suites
Ideally located for a city break, with 40 parking spaces. Two minutes from the Guildhall and Peace Bridge. Thompson Restaurant, Collins Bar with good bar food in the lobby, gym and pool.

WHERE TO EAT
❶ Browns Restaurant & Champagne Lounge ££££
Bond' s Hill (waterside)
Tel. (0 28) 7134 5180
www.brownsrestaurant.com
Closed Mon
Not to be missed, probably the best restaurant in Northern Ireland. Chef Ian Orr emphasizes dishes made with local ingredients. He gives a cookery demonstration on every first Sat in the month at 4pm, with a three-course menu.

Insider Tip

❷ Café del Mondo ££
1 Shipquay Street (Craft Village)
Tel. (0 28) 7136 6877
www.jacobsonthemall.com
Closed Mon evening
A café by day, a restaurant in the evening, using fresh organic produce for international dishes. There is also a cultural programme in the evenings with live music, storytelling and films.

PUB
❶ Peadar O'Donnell's and Gweedore Bar
63 Waterloo Street
Tel. (0 28) 7137 2318
www.peadars-gweedore.com
Closed Sun, Mon
Three pubs in one, daily live music, night club on the first floor.

The city wall that surrounds Derry is up to 8m/26ft high

installation consisting of 40 double steel masts, designed by Vong Phaophanit and completed in 2011 by Clair Oboussier.

Further attractions of the Waterside are the Waterside Theatre in Glendermott Road and the **Workhouse Museum**, in which up to 800 poor people were housed on two storeys between 1840 and 1948. The museum demonstrations the dreadful conditions that prevailed here and is also a venue for temporary exhibitions.

Upstream, the **River Watch Visitor Centre & Aquarium** is a family attraction with native species of fish in five pools.

Workhouse Museum: 23 Glendermott Road: Mon–Thu and Sat 10am–5pm; free admission
River Watch Visitor Centre & Aquarium: 22 Victoria Street; Mon–Fri 10am–4pm; free admission; www.loughs–agency.org

The stained-glass windows of the Guildhall, built in 1890 in Gothic Revival style on Guildhall Square, depict scenes from city history. Following extensive restoration, the Guildhall now has an exhibition about the Plantations and their historical consequences, interpretation panels about the building, a tourist information point and a café area.

Guildhall

The city walls of Derry are said to be the best-preserved in the United Kingdom. With the exception of three gates added later, they still looks the way they did after completion in 1618. The wall forms a nice promenade; for the best view over the city head for the Walker Monument on the Royal Bastion. Four old gates lead into the city: Butcher's Gate, Shipquay Gate, Ferryquay Gate and, the most beauti-

*City walls

ful, Bishop's Gate. Award-winning tours of the walls are run by **Martin McCrossan City Tours**.

Artillery Street leads up to the **New Gate**. Below it is the Fountain Quarter, where some murals can be seen. The Protestant residents here like to fly the Union Jack. There is a view of the Court House in London Street, once a target for many bombings. It is worth making the short detour to ***St Columb's Cathedral**, built between 1618 and 1633. During the 19th century, it was redesigned in a Gothic revival style. The heads of 16 bishops of the city carry the ceiling as corbelled stones, and worked into the bishop's throne is the armchair of Bishop Bramhall, who consecrated the church in 1633. The chapter house shows documents and exhibits from the time of the Siege of Derry (1688–89), such as the cannon ball that James II had fired into the city, as an exhortation to surrender.

From ***Bishop's Gate** there is a fine view down to the neo-Gothic Anglican St Columba Church, built in 1909. South of the gate, on Bishop Street Without, stands the Heritage Tower, the last remaining tower of a prison built in 1791. The tower dates from 1824, and was used for executions.

Following the dismantling of military installations, the corner house at the Double Bastion is now the **Verbal Arts Centre** (VAC). Storytellers like to meet here in Blooms Café. The Ulysses Art Installation by Colin Darke transcribes James Joyce's masterpiece on three walls. The VAC is a venue for events and for the tradition of storytelling.

The **Double Bastion**, where two cannon serve as reminders of the great siege, is the start of ***Grand Parade**, which leads to the Walker's Plinth. From 1828 a 24m/80ft-high column stood on this plinth, a landmark of Derry and destination for strollers until it was blown up by the IRA in 1971.

In the direction of the town centre is the **Apprentice Boys Memorial Hall**, built in 1873 in the Scottish Baronial style. It commemorates the apprentices who closed the city gates in 1689. The museum here preserves artefacts from those days.

Martin McCrossen City Tours: daily 10am, 12 noon, 2pm; ticket 4 £; www.derrycitytours.com

St Columb's Cathedral: Mon–Sat 9am–5pm, Sun for services; admission 2 £; www.stcolumbscathedral.org;

St Columba Church: Mon–Sat 9.30am–7pm, Sun 7.30am–7pm; free admission, donation requested; www.longtowerchurch.org

Verbal Arts Centre: Mon–Thu 9am–5.30pm, Fri 9am–4pm; free admission; www.verbalartscentre.co.uk

Apprentice Boys Memorial Hall: 13 Society Street; Sat 10am–5pm, Sun 2–5pm; admission 2 £; www.apprenticeboys.co.uk

Historic quarter Close by Magazine Gate stands the excellent ***Tower Museum** with its multimedia exhibitions on the story of Derry and the region.

The Bogside is known for its political murals

Amongst the exhibits, note a well-preserved boat said to date back to the time of St Columba (around 520), as well as the display on La Trinidad Valencera, the largest ship in the Spanish Armada, which sank off the coast in 1588.

At the centre of the old quarter, The Diamond is the site of a war memorial and ***Austin's**, which claims to be the world's oldest department store (1830). The top-floor restaurant is recommended. The Masonic Hall has been used by the Freemasons since 1945; from 1753 it was the bishop's palace.

For **contemporary art**, head to the Craft Village (1 Shipquay Street), the Centre for Contemporary Art Derry-Londonderry (10-12 Artillery Street; http://cca-derry-londonderry.org), the Gordon Gallery (13a Pump Street; www.gordon-gallery.co.uk) or the Nerve Centre (78 Magazine Street).

Tower Museum: Tue–Sat 10am–5pm; admission 4 £

Austins: Mon–Thu, Sat 9.30am–5.30pm, Fri 9.30am–7pm, Sun 1–5pm; www.austinsstore.com

Along Rossville Street is the start of the renovated Bogside Quarter. At the corner of Williams Street is a memorial stone to IRA members. Diagonally opposite is the Pilots Row Community Centre, and next to it the **Bloody Sunday Memorial**. Rossville Street is famous for its **murals** relating to the Troubles. Some of them now have information panels, and can be visited on tours as a kind of "people's gallery" (www.freederrymurals.com). The artists have an international reputation today (www.bogsideartists.com). On an oval traffic island note the **Free Derry Wall**, a house wall bearing the letters »You are now entering Free Derry«. Opposite stands the H-Block Monument, a commemoration of the hunger strikers in Long Kesh prison in the

The Troubles

A term that does not sound especially dramatic refers to decades of conflict fought with great brutality on both sides that claimed thousands of victims. Today the Troubles seem to have been largely overcome.

▶ **Murals**
Across Northern Ireland there are more than 2,000 of these propaganda paintings depicting symbols, persons and activities on both sides. This one, from Derry, refers to the Battle of the Bogside.

▶ **Battle of the Bogside**
One of the first bloody conflicts, between the Catholic DCDA and the Northern Ireland police (RUC)

Wounded
Derry Citizens' Defence Association (DCDA)

> 1000

Royal Ulster Constabulary (RUC)
>350

1919
Foundation of the Catholic Irish Republican Army (IRA)

1966
Foundation of the Protestant Ulster Volunteer Force (UVF)

Dec 1969
Provisional IRA splits from the IRA

30 Jan 1972
Bloody Sunday in Derry; 13 demonstrators shot by British paratroops.

1921
Partition of Ireland; in 1937 proclamation of a republic

12–14 Aug 1969
Street fighting in Derry; the army is called in.

9 Aug 1971
Start of internment of IRA activists

21 July 1972
Bloody Friday; IRA detonates 22 bombs in Belfast.

A war with many victims
Number of dead per county

0–200
300–350
200–250
350–400
250–300
>1000

Deaths outside Northern Ireland

in Ireland
113

in England
125

IRELAND

Derry/
Londonderry

Antrim

NORTHERN IRELAND

Tyrone

Belfast

Down

Fermanagh

Armagh

The fighters
Most of those who died were victims of paramilitary groups on both sides. 82 deaths which have not been explained are not included here..

Republicans | Catholics
Republican paramilitaries
2057

Armed forces of the Republic of Ireland
5

Loyalists | Protestants
Loyalist paramilitaries
1019

British armed forces
363

No one was spared
The victims were not all military or paramilitary personnel.

Military/
paramilitary
killed
1687

Civilians
killed
1842

Wounded
45,000

©BAEDEKER

24 March 1973
Stormont Parliament dissolved, direct rule from Westminster

1976
Nobel Peace Prize for Betty Williams and Mairead Corrigan

From 1988
Secret negotiations between British government and Sinn Féin

2005
IRA ends its armed struggle.

Jan 75–Jan 76
Ceasefire by IRA

1981
Hunger strike by IRA activists; ten die, Sinn Féin becomes a political force.

1994
IIRA ceasefire

1998
Good Friday Agreement; Nobel Peace Prize for John Hume and David Trimble

2007
UVF renounces armed struggle; elections for Stormont

Ernesto Che Guevara Lynch

A mural in the Bogside honours one of the most famous revolutionaries of the 20th century. In the late 19th century, Anna Isabel Lynch emigrated from County Galway to Argentina and married a Basque there. Her famous grandson Ernesto Che Guevara Lynch was thus a direct descendant of the Galway clan that ruled the kingdom of Dalriada (Antrim/Derry) until the Middle Ages. Che's father said, after the death of his son, »The blood of Irish rebels flowed in my son's veins«.

form of an H. A red container houses the **Free Derry Museum**, which is dedicated to the civil rights movement and the Troubles, including the events of Bloody Sunday. This is the starting point of **Free Derry Tours** through the Bogside.

To the south lies Lecky Road in the Brandywell district. Further murals and the **Gasyard Heritage Centre** can be seen here. In the old gas works are displays on the hunger strikes and the position of prisoners up to the start of the peace process in 1994. The exhibition Columba to Conflict presents the history of the Bogside from the first settlements until the Troubles.

Free Derry Museum: 55–61 Glenfada Park; Mon–Fri 9.30am–4.30pm, April–Sept also Sat 1–4pm, July–Sept also Sun 1–4pm; admission 3 £; www.museumoffreederry.org
Free Derry Tours: daily 10am, 2pm, April–Sept also 12 noon, July and Aug also 4pm; ticket 5 £; www.freederry.net
Gasyard Heritage Centre: Mon–Fri 9.30am–5pm; free admission; www.freederry.net

AROUND DERRY

Limavady Limavady in the Roe Valley is the birthplace of one of the most famous Irish songs: in the mid-19th century, Jane Ross was listening to a busker playing the »Londonderry Air«. She noted down the folk melody, originally composed by the bard of the O'Cahan clan, Rory Dall O'Cahan, whose version was a lament for the last clan chieftain. Linda Ross published »Danny Boy« in 1913. A mural and plaque commemorate the event (51 Main Street), and the song is still played today on St Patrick's Day and at funerals.

Roe Valley Country Park Less than 2km/1.2 miles south of town stretches Roe Valley Country Park, good for walking, hiring a canoe, fishing, or visiting old watermills, formerly used in linen production. For further information, head for the visitor centre
❶ 41 Dogleap Road, Limavady; visitor centre March–May and Oct Sat and Sun 1–5pm, June–Sept daily 10am–5pm, Nov–Feb Sun 12 noon–4pm; park open in winter 9am–4.30pm, otherwise until 7 or 9pm; free admission

Around the market town of Dungiven (25km/16 miles southeast of Derry on the A6) a sign on the road leading to Antrim points to the 12th-century Dungiven Priory. There was a ceremonial site here in pre-Norman times; the Augustinian monastery was built later – eventually becoming part of the manor house – and today is a romantic ruin with a wonderful view of the River Roe. The chancel of the church became the burial site of the O'Cahans, featuring an extraordinary and fairly well-preserved tomb dating from the 15th century: the sculpture of an armed man, an O'Cahan chieftain who died in 1385, who seems to be lying beneath a canopy. Below him six nooks are visible, holding small **figures wearing kilts**, probably Scottish mercenaries. The way to Maghera (►Lough Neagh, Around) leads via the A6 over the **Glenshane Pass** (altitude 555m/1,820ft), offering fine views of the ►Sperrin Mountains. Weather conditions can be dangerous here early in the year: in March 2010, 300 drivers were trapped by snowfall and needed medical treatment.

*Dungiven Priory

* Dingle Peninsula

✳ D 1/2

Rep. of Ireland, province: Munster
County: Kerry

Dingle seems to signal the end of the world. This barren but magnificent peninsula attracts artists, photographers and many holidaymakers. Depending on the weather and the season, the landscape is subject to an ongoing change of colour and mood, which has inspired many filmmakers.

Dingle

INFORMATION
Strand Street, Dingle Town
Tel. (0 66) 915 1188
www.dingle-peninsula.ie
April to Oct

WHERE TO STAY
Dingle Benners Hotel ££££
Main Street, Dingle
Tel. (0 66) 915 1638
www.dinglebenners.com
52 rooms

The 300-year-old but modernized building exudes old-world charm, especially in Mrs Benners Bar.

PUB
O'Flaherty's
Bridge Street
Tel. (0 66) 915 1983
The best pub in Dingle for music.
Closed Sun, Mon
Three pubs in one, daily live music, night club on the first floor.

Peninsula of stone monuments	On Dingle, the northernmost peninsula in County Kerry, **nearly 1,500 stone monuments** stand along the coast road, including bee-hive huts, Ogham stones and early churches, as well as several fortifications dating back to the Iron Age. In the west of the peninsula lies one of the seven Irish-language Gaeltacht areas, those parts of Ireland where Irish is the majority language. Old traditions, customs and crafts remain alive here. The impressive landscape has often served as a **backdrop for films**, such as *Ryan's Daughter* (1970) and *Far and Away* (1992) with Tom Cruise and Nicole Kidman.

DRIVE AROUND DINGLE PENINSULA

Inch	Drive west from ▶Tralee along Tralee Bay, to reach Camp. To the southeast of the village rises Caherconree mountain (813m/2,667ft). Below the summit stands the mighty **Caherconree promontory fort**. To the southwest lie the holiday resort Inch and the Inch Peninsula, with a stretch of dunes 5km/3 miles long and a **superb beach**.
*Dingle	Dingle (pop. 1,270), the main town on the peninsula of the same name, lies on a protected bay with fine beaches. Alongside opportunities for deep-sea angling, boating and mini golf, the port with its numerous colourful little houses makes a suitable base to explore the antiquities on the western side of the peninsula. If Fungie doesn't turn up, or the weather is bad, a visit to **Dingle Ocean World**, an aquarium on the harbour displaying fish and other sea-dwelling creatures, is a good idea. The highlights are an **underwater glass tunnel**, a shark pool and »touch pools«.

MARCO ⊕ POLO TIP

‼ *Fungie the Dingle dolphin*   Insider Tip

Since 1984 a 400kg/450lb dolphin has caused excitement among the boat owners and fishermen of Dingle Town. Fungie is a loner, thought he seems to like people, and is often seen in Dingle Bay. He is a very old dolphin now, but visitors can still visit him on tours: tel. 066 15 26 26, www.dingle.dolphin.com.

The chapel of the **Presentation Convent** in Green Street is worth a look for its twelve famous stained-glass windows by Harry Clarke. In one room are paintings and murals by Nano Nagle (1718–1784). The painting of the Last Judgement in what used to be the refectory is by the American artist Eleanor Yates. The convent houses the Diseart Visitor Centre, dedicated to Irish spirituality and culture.

Dingle Ocean World: daily 10am–5pm, July and Aug until 6pm; admission 13 €; www.dingle-oceanworld.ie

Presentation Convent: admission 2 €, garden free admission; www.diseart.ie

Slea Head on the Dingle Peninsula

Near Fahan immediately above the sea lies the fine **promontory fort of Dunbeg**, consisting of four defensive ramparts and a strong stone wall. Inside, look for the remains of a house, laid out round on the outside and square on the inside. A subterranean passage leads to the outer buildings. A few miles further to the west, at Glanfahan, stand groups of beehive huts, all in all 417 buildings, erected in dry-stone, plus 19 souterrains and 18 standing stones.

❶ Visitor centre: March–Nov daily 9am–6pm, in summer until 7pm; admission 3 €; www.dunbegfort.com

Dunbeg Fort & beehive huts

Slea Head is the name of the southwestern point of the peninsula. On the way there, in Kilvicadownig on Ventry Bay, the **Celtic & Prehistoric Museum** displays the only complete skeleton of a woolly mammoth in Ireland, the skeletons of a cave bear and a baby dinosaur, as well as a dinosaur's nest with eggs, and Stone Age artefacts. At Slea Head there is a spectacular view from the narrow road at the foot of Mount Eagle.

❶ March-Oct daily 10am–6pm; admission 4 €

Slea Head

From the small fishing port of Dunquin, take a trip to the Blasket Isles. Basic information on the islands can be picked up from the Blasket Centre at Dunquin. The main island, declared part of the **National Historic Park**, Great Blasket was populated until 1953. It has been said that the people were, in their settled way of life, »the happiest in the world«. At the centre of the island stand the ruins of a church. From the ridge (285m/935ft), look across Blasket Sound towards the rugged coast of Kerry. This is the strait where in 1588 the *Santa Maria de la Rosa* of the Spanish Armada ran aground. On **In-**

Blasket Isles

ishtooskert, the island situated about 6km/3.5 miles northwest of the peninsula, look out for the ruins of a small church, a well-preserved beehive hut and three crosses.

❶ Blasket Centre: Easter–Oct daily 10am–6pm; admission 4 €

Dún an Óir Fort & Riasc Monastic Settlement
Leaving Dunquin in a northerly direction, a visit to the Mulcahy Pottery and its pretty café are recommended (www.louismulcahy.com). After a further 3km/2 miles, a small road turns off to the left to the site where the old Dún an Óir (»gold fort«) castle used to stand; today, the only reminder is a nearby sculpture. In 1580, 600 Spanish and Irish soldiers surrendered here, but were slaughtered.

Ballyferriter
The road leads on to Ballyferriter, where the old schoolhouse is home to the **West Kerry Regional Museum**, which displays archaeological finds and runs Gaelic courses. In Riasc, between the remains of a hermitage, stands a remarkable pillar stone from early Christian times, decorated with a cross and spiral decorations.

❶ Easter and June–Sept daily 10am–5pm; free admission; www.westkerry-museum.com

*Gallarus Oratory
Next stop is Gallarus Oratory, looking like a boat laid upside down onto the ground (Gallarus possibly means »shelter for foreigners«). The walls, over 1m/3ft thick and erected practically without mortar, vault over the 3 x 4.5m(10 x 15ft) floor space; the stones were chosen with such care and laid on top of each other with such precision that the building, despite its advanced age of probably 1,200 years, **remains dry**. A local legend holds that anyone who leaves the oratory through the window is purified of sin. However, the window is only 12cm/5in wide. Visiting the chapel is free; the Visitor Centre charges an entrance fee, but has a tearoom. 1km/0.5 miles to the west are the ruins of the 16th century **Gallarus Castle**, a four-storey tower, with vaulted rooms.

A place for contemplation: Gallarus Oratory

❶ Visitor centre: June–Aug daily 10am–6pm; free admission to oratory, charge for car park

Above Gallarus, **Kilmalkedar Church** is one of the most important sacred sites on the peninsula. A monastery was founded here in the 7th century, but all that survives is a 12th-century Romanesque church with interesting sculptures on the tympanum of the main entrance and on the chancel arch. The whole church shows the influence of Cormac's Chapel in ▶Cashel. In the church stands an **alphabet stone** showing both Ogham markings (see MARCO POLO Insight, p. 34) and Latin letters. In the churchyard, look for an old sundial, whilst close by stands the medieval St Brendan's House.

On Brandon Mountain, the **remains of St Brendan's Oratory** and some stone cottages survive. The climb, on well-marked paths from Cloghane, Faha or from the west, is worth doing because of the magnificent view from up there.

Off the beaten track

Donegal (Dún na nGall)

B 3

Republic of Ireland, province: Ulster
County: Donegal
Population: 2,340

The Irish name Donegal (Dún na nGall, »castle of the strangers«) recalls the Vikings, who in the 9th century established a fortification here. The lively town owes its current appearance to the British, who in the 17th century laid out the diamond-shaped market square. Today still, »The Diamond« is the focal point for numerous pubs, hotels and shops.

In Donegal, the River Eske flows into Donegal Bay. From the quay, with its attractive promenade, boat trips start on the Tipperary (www.donegalbaywaterbus.com). The obelisk on the market square was erected in honour of the Four Masters (see Donegal Abbey). From The Diamond, take a few steps up to St Patrick's Church, built from granite in 1935, and on to the former poorhouse dating from 1841 and the Paupers' Cemetery. Every year, at the end of June/early July, the three-day Donegal Town Summer Festival takes place, celebrated with songs, dances and storytelling.

Waterside town

Donegal

INFORMATION
Donegal Town Tourist Office
The Quay
Tel. (0 74) 972 11 48
www.donegaldirect.com

WHERE TO STAY
Harvey's Point Country Hotel €€€€
Ough Eske, Tel. (0 74) 972 22 08
www.harveyspoint.com
74 rooms
A hotel in a beautiful site with excellent food.

Donegal Castle   Donegal Castle stands as impressive ruins a few paces away from the market square, on a rock on the shore of the River Eske. The castle used to be the seat of the kings of Tir Chonaill from the O'Donnell family. In 1607, the estate fell into English hands. At that time, the exterior of the large square tower (1505) was altered by fitting windows; on the main floor, a splendid fireplace was built, with relief escutcheons. In 1610, a manor house was added.

The remains of the 15th-century Franciscan **Donegal Abbey** occupy a picturesque position on the mouth of the River Eske (reached by taking a little road at the village entrance, coming from Ballyshannon). Here, the **Four Masters**, Michael O'Clery and his three assistants, wrote their famous *Annals of the Four Masters*, a monumental work of historiography.

Donegal Castle: Easter to mid-Sept daily 10am–6pm, at other times Thu–Mon 9.30am–4.30pm

Railway Heritage Centre   Find out more about the history of the **steam engine**, which up to 1959 linked Ballyshannon and Derry, at the Donegal Railway Heritage Centre in the northeast of the town.

❶ Mon–Fri 9am–5pm, July and Aug also Sat and Sun 2–5pm; admission 3.50 €; www.donegalrailway.com

Donegal Craft Village   The area around Donegal is **famous for tweed fabrics** and knitwear. The Donegal Craft Village on the edge of town attracts visitors with stone sculptures, glass and knitwear, as well as the Aroma Café. Tweed fabrics have been at Magee's on The Diamond since 1866. Here, tweed is still produced on the labour-intensive hand loom.

❶ April–Sept Mon–Sat 10am–5pm, Oct–Dec closed Mon; free admission; http://donegalcraftvillage.com

AROUND DONEGAL

Lough Eske and the Blue Stack Mountains   Around 8km/5 miles northeast of town, Lough Eske offers good fishing. Driving around the lake, take a detour to a waterfall, 3km/2 miles further north. The valley carries on into the Blue Stack Mountains, where a pretty little lake, Lough Belshade, is hemmed in by high rock walls. The **Blue Stack Way** from Donegal Town to Ardara is 65km/40 miles long and takes three days to walk.

Lough Derg   The R232 and R233, southeast of Donegal, lead to Lough Derg. At Station Island lies a cave that in pagan times was considered the **entrance to the underworld**; in the Middle Ages, the place came to fame as St Patrick's Purgatory, after a knight errant reported glimpsing the flames there. Every year, the cave is at the centre of an impor-

Peace and quiet on Lough Eske

tant pilgrimage, undertaken nearly exclusively by Irish faithful. During their three-day stay, the pilgrims on the »toughest pilgrimage in Christendom« submit themselves to numerous acts of penitence, vigils and fasting. The pilgrimage was known across Europe, but was suppressed by order of the Privy Council for Ireland in 1632 and remained forbidden in the 18th century. However, in 1813 the three-day order of exercises was established.

The **Lough Derg Visitor Centre** north of Pettigo caters for pilgrims and other visitors.

❶ May, mid-Aug to Sept Mon–Fr 9am–5pm, Sat and Sun 9am–4pm; June to mid-Aug daily 8am–9pm, Oct–April Mon–Fri 9am–5pm; www.loughderg.org

On the Atlantic, 20km/13 miles south of Donegal, lies Rossnowlagh, a holiday resort with a fine sandy beach. The modern Franciscan monastery houses the **Donegal Historical Society Museum**, showing objects from the Stone and Bronze Age, amongst them an exquisitely wrought sword, found during construction works in nearby Ballyshannon.

Rossnowlagh

❶ Daily 9am-6pm; free admission

Downpatrick (Dún Pádraig)

✳ B 6

Northern Ireland, province: Ulster
County: Down
Population: 10,400

Information:
www.visitdownpatrick.com

The county town of Downpatrick, situated amid picturesque landscape, is closely associated with the national saint of Ireland, St Patrick, who in 432 chose this spot to start converting the Irish.

St Patrick's activity was the beginning of the Christianization of the island. (►MARCO POLO Insight p.34) After studying Christian doctrine in France, the saint sailed to Ireland, landing at the village of Saul, situated 3km/2 miles north of Downpatrick. This is where St Patrick built the first church on Irish soil; he is said to have died in this area on **17 March 471**.

In 1177 Downpatrick, in Irish Dún Pádraig (»Patrick's fort«), was conquered by the Norman John de Courcy, who heavily promoted the cult of St Patrick, in order to endow the place with more significance. Distrusting the Augustinians, settled here in 1136 by St Malachy, he replaced them with English Benedictines, for whom he built an abbey church on the cathedral hill.

*Down Cathedral
Started in 1790, today's Down Cathedral was built on the ruins of an earlier church; individual capitals and the baptismal font are parts of the original building. Excavations had revealed the presumed mortal remains of the three great Irish patron saints Patrick, Brigid and Columcille; in reaction to this, de Courcy transferred the seat of the diocese from Bangor to Downpatrick and arranged for the construction of the first cathedral. After its destruction by English soldiers in 1538, it stood empty for over 250 years. Whilst it is unlikely that the actual mortal remains of the three saints are buried here, a granite stone in the churchyard bearing the inscription »Patric« is said to mark the grave of St Patrick. Every year, for St Patrick's Day (17th March), the site on St Patrick's Trail turns into a place of pilgrimage.

❶ Mon–Sat 9.30am–4.30pm, Sun 2–5pm; donation requested; www.downcathedral.org

Down County Museum
The Down County Museum, housed in the former 18th-century prison, tells the story of the county, with a St Patrick's Heritage Centre in the gate house dedicated to **the saint's life and works**, and, at

the far end of the compound, 18th-century cells. From here a sign-posted path branches off to the Norman castle of Mound of Down.

❶ The Mall, English Street: Mon–Fri 10am–5pm, Sat and Sun 12 noon–5pm; free admission; www.downcountymuseum.com

Directly opposite Down County Museum, St Patrick's Centre is the place to get multimedia information on Ireland's national hero and the country's Christianization.

St Patrick's Centre

❶ Mon–Sat 9am–5pm, July and Aug also Sun 1–5pm; admission 4.95 £; www.stpatrickcentre.com

From Strangford Road, take a turn off to the Quoile Countryside Centre, with information on the **animals and plants of the region**.

Quoile Countryside Centre

❶ Visitor centre : March–May and Oct Sat and Sun 1–5pm, June–Sept daily 10am–5pm, Nov–Feb Sun 12 noon–4pm; free admission

In a very idyllic position, on a former marshy island on the Quoyle River, lies Inch Abbey. The Cistercian abbey was founded by de Courcey around 1180, as a penance for the destruction of the monastery at Erenagh.

Inch Abbey

❶ Ruins open all year; free admission; guided tour with Cistercian monk July–Sept Sat and Sun 1.30–5.30pm

Many sites associated with St Patrick are linked by the **St Patrick's Trail** (www.discovernorthernireland.com/stpatrick). A narrow road behind the hospital leads after 2km/1.2 miles to what probably used to be a pagan sacrificial site where the saint was active. It is said the water from the local springs is able to cure various ailments. The site seems to have been particularly popular in the 17th century, when separate bath houses for men and women were erected.

*In the footsteps of St Patrick

AROUND DOWNPATRICK

From Saul, a coastal road leads east to **Strangford** (16km/10miles north-east of Downpatrick). This **old Viking settlement** occupies a picturesque location on the southern tip of Strangford Lough, dominated by a 16th-century tower house, Strangford Castle. Some 3km/2 miles west of Strangford, Castleward House manor was built in 1760. The façade shows both classical and Gothic features – it is said that Lord and Lady Bangor,

> **!** MARCO ⊕ POLO TIP
>
> *Butterfly House* **Insider Tip**
>
> At the Seaforde Tropical Butterfly House, 2km/1.2 miles north of Clough on the A24 near Seaforde, hundreds of butterflies flutter around in a large glasshouse in a park. In addition, many exotic insects and reptiles can be seen behind glass. Easter–Sept Mon–Sat 10am–5pm, Sun 1–6pm; admission 4.70 £; wwwseafordegardens.com.

who built it, were not able to agree on a style. The estate also includes fine parks, a fortified tower house, a laundry, a theatre, a saw mill and a mill, as well as a restaurant and a shop. The park is open all year round. Every summer, events are held in these idyllic surroundings, such as the **Ulster Summer Festival of Opera**.

❶ Garden and park: daily 10am–8pm, house daily 12 noon–5pm; admission 7 £

Killyleagh — A few miles further north the holiday resort of Killyleagh on Strangford Lough is the birthplace of **Sir Hans Sloane**, the founder of the British Museum in London.

Towards Dundrum — Only 4km/2.5 miles south of Strangford, 15th-century Kilclief Castle rises above the strait. No fewer than seven castles used to guard the

The Legananny dolmen is probably about 5,000 years old

fishing village of Ardglass 9km/5.5 miles further south, at the time when Ardglass was an important harbour. One of those, Jordan's Castle, is still partly preserved. West of Killough, situated beyond the bay, look out for a very nice beach. Near St John's Point is the start of probably **the most beautiful coastal drive in Northern Ireland**, leading to Newry (62.5km/39 miles). Via Dundrum Bay, which at low tide is partly exposed, the road carries on in the direction of Newcastle. Dundrum, 4km/2.5 miles south of Clough, is a picturesque fishing village with fine sandy bays and a tower surrounded by a moat which used to belong to a castle. At this site, De Courcy had begun building a fortification in 1177 in order to better guard the road between Drogheda and Downpatrick. In 1210, King John I had the castle confiscated and a tower added, but in 1652, Cromwell's army razed the castle.

Following the road 6km/3.5 miles further south, the seaside resort of Newcastle offers many amenities, amongst them a golf links. Newcastle is situated on the western tip of Dundrum Bay and on the foot of Slieve Donard, at 836m/2,743ft the highest peak in the ►Mourne Mountains. Climbing Slieve Donard takes some 2 hours; the summit offers a spectacular view all the way to the coast of Scotland.

Newcastle

West of Slieve Croob (532m/1,745ft, approx. 20km/12.5 miles west of Downpatrick) stands what is probably **the best-known Stone Age monument in Ulster**: the 2.5m/8-ft Legananny Dolmen. Against the backdrop of the Mourne Mountains, it appears fairly impressive, but not as bulky as other dolmens, as it seems to stand on three »feet«, like a tripod.

*Legananny Dolmen

Drogheda (Droichead Átha)

✳ C 5

Republic of Ireland, province: Leinster
County: Louth
Population: 30,450
Information: www.drogheda.ie

Drogheda, (»bridge over the ford«), was transformed in the decade of the »Celtic tiger« from an industrial town to a place of residence for Dubliners. Its remaining industrial monument is the Boyne Viaduct on the railway from Dublin to Belfast, the seventh-largest bridge in the world when it was completed in 1865.

Chequered history

Drogheda lies north of Dublin on the mouth of the River Boyne. In 911, Vikings expanded the town into a base for their raids. Later, the Anglo-Normans erected a bridge and fortified the town on both banks of the Boyne. In the 14th and 15th centuries, Drogheda was one of the four capitals of Ireland; the town had its own mint, and a university was established in 1465. Parliament met here several times well into the 17th century.

In 1649 Cromwell took the town, and in 1690, after the Battle of the Boyne, Drogheda surrendered to the army of King William III of Orange.

St Peter's Church (Catholic)

St Lawrence's Gate

On the right-hand side of West Street, the Catholic St Peter's Church was built (in the neo-Gothic style) to commemorate the canonized archbishop of Armagh, Oliver Plunkett, executed in 1681 in Tyburn in London. Plunkett's embalmed head is kept as a relic in a shrine in this church. Of the original ten gates the town had, only St Lawrence's Gate on St Lawrence's Street is left. Its two mighty round towers enclose a sturdy gateway. A former Franciscan abbey on St Lawrence's Street houses the **Highlanes Gallery** of modern art.

❶ Mon–Sat 10.30am–5pm; admission free, 2 € donation requested; www.highlanes.ie

Millmount Fort & Museum

On the southern side of the river – behind the bridge following Shop Street – lies Millmount Fort. Originally a passage tomb like Newgrange in the ▶Boyne Valley, it was fortified in the 12th century and used until 1800 as a fortification. Today, the fort houses a museum with exhibits on the history of the town. There is a nice view of Drogheda from the fort.

❶ Mon–Sat 10am–5.30pm, Sun 2–5pm; admission 3.50 € (with tower 5.50 €); www.millmount.net

* Beaulieu House

The estate on the banks of the Boyne River between Drogheda and the Irish Sea belonged to Sir Henry Tichbourne, governor general of the town. Previously the land was owned by the Plunkett family, whose castle stood opposite the present manor house, built in 1722. Today the DeFreitas family, tenth-generation descendants of Tichbourne, occupy the house. Guided tours of the impressive residence give an entertaining account of the history of Beaulieu House and the family. The present (woman) owner had a career as a racing driver in the late 1960s and early 170s. The **Car Museum** presents historic racing cars, including an Austin A40 Farina(1965) and a Blydenstein Vauxhall HC Viva (1979), of which only 25 were ever made.

❶ May to mid–Sept Mon–Fri 11am–5pm, July and Aug also Sat and Sun 1–5pm; admission to all attractions 20 €; www.beaulieu.ie

AROUND DROGHEDA

In the village of Termonfeckin, a 15th-century tower house, Termon-feckin Castle, was restored following damage in the rebellion of 1641. It features a spiral staircase as well as an unusual vaulted roof constructed in the same way as the vault of Newgrange, 4,000 years older (access/admission free). In the graveyard of St Feckin's Church stands a High Cross: covered with geometrical patterns. The crucifixion scene on the base dates from the 16th century.
Clogherhead has good sandy beaches, especially near Port Oriel harbour.

Termonfeckin and Clogherhead

South of Drogheda, in County Meath, the seaside spa resorts of **Bettystown**, which has a golf links, and **Laytown**, both boast beaches nearly 10km/6 miles long. Outside Laytown, in the direction of Julianstown, the **Sonairte National Ecological Centre** has a nature garden, a recommendable walking trail on the river and exhibitions looking at the use of renewable energies. Take the road inland – between the R108 and the R152 – to reach the important burial site of **Fourknocks** (3000–2500 BC) with a large passage tomb and two smaller burial mounds. The key to the grave is kept by Fintan White, who lives 1.5km/1 mile away (signposted). Some 8km/4.5 miles southwest of Drogheda, on the Nanny River lies **Duleek** (pop. 1,730), where monastic life began in the late 5th century. The name means »stone house« or »church«. In the grounds of the priory stand the ruins of a church and a number of high crosses (probably 10th century).

Southwards

❶ Sonairte: Wed–Sun 10.30am–5.30pm; admission 3 €; http://sonairte.ie
Fourknocks: return key by 6pm; deposit required; www.knowth.com/fourknocks.htm

From Drogheda, take the R168 in the direction of Collon; after 4km/2.5 miles, at Tullyallan, take the turn for Mellifont. Here on the Mattoch River, stand the ruins of a once significant Cistercian monastery: Mellifont Abbey, founded in 1142 and built with the help of French monks. By 1272, Mellifont had become the mother house of 24 other monasteries. After its dissolution (1539), the monastery was converted into a fortified manor house. Today, very little remains of the original building: to the north a castle-like gatehouse with a bulky tower, the remarkable crypt of the church, parts of the two-storey, octagonal »lavabo« or washing house adjoining the cloister (with reconstructed arcades) and the vaulted 14th-century chapterhouse, now housing various architectural fragments. Parts of the floor feature glazed tiles from the church. Wall stumps and marks on the ground suggest that the monastery was laid out using Clairvaux as a model. The guest house of the present Mellifont Abbey offers low-priced accommodation.

*Mellifont Abbey

❶ May–Sept daily 10am–6pm; admission 3 €; www.mellifontabbey.ie

✶✶ Dublin (Baile Átha Cliath or Dubhlinn)

✦ C 5

Republic of Ireland, province: Leinster
County: Dublin
Population: 1.8 million

The vibrant city of Dublin is more than just the capital, it is the cultural and economic heart of Ireland, situated in a beautiful position around a wide bay that opens onto the Irish Sea. Visitors experience the expanding city as open and likeable. Since 2010 it has been a UNESCO City of Literature. The »One City, One Book« project honours the four Irish holders of the Nobel Prize for Literature, and each April one book »for everybody« is chosen.

Capital of the Republic of Ireland Nearly a third of all Irish live in Dublin which, since 1990, has experienced rapid growth. In the »Celtic tiger« years at the start of the millennium it became one of the world's top 20 financial centres. Even after the severe hangover that followed, districts such as Temple Bar, Smithfield Market and the Docklands demonstrate the self-confidence of the new Dublin. The classy residential quarters and shopping malls are on the southern shore of the Liffey. The working-class areas on the north bank have partly been revitalized, but still suffer from unemployment. The bursting of the property bubble has unfinished and unoccupied buildings, both in the Docklands and on new residential estates.

> **?**
>
> MARCO ● POLO INSIGHT
>
> *Two Names*
>
> The English name of the city is derived from »Dubhlinn«, meaning »black pool« or »bog«. This was the name of a Viking village, founded in the 9th century close to an older Celtic settlement named »áth Cliath«. From this latter name comes the modern Irish name of the city, Baile Atha Cliath: »town on the fort of hurdles«.

HISTORY

St Patrick is said to have brought Christianity to Dublin in 448. 400 years later the settlement was taken by Danish Vikings. In 1014 High King Brian Boru defeated the Vikings. Following the Norman invasion, Irish chieftains pledged loyalty to King Henry II, and Dublin became the seat of government for »The Pale«, the coastal strip controlled by the English Crown. After 1730 the city, the seat of the Irish parliament, grew to be the second-largest city in the British Empire.

Dublin Highlights

► **Trinity College with Old Library**
The famous Book of Kells is on display in this temple of books.
►page 310, 313

► **Powerscourt House**
Elegant department store with shops and galleries, with the Civic Museum nearby
►page 316

► **National Museum**
Ireland's rich treasure chest
►page 317

► **Merrion Square**
Linger awhile amongst elegant Georgian buildings and a nice park
►page 319

► **National Gallery**
On display are important Irish artists, as well as German and Spanish masters
►page 319

► **Temple Bar District**
Colourful pub and artists' quarter south of the Liffey
►page 324

► **Dublin Castle**
Lavishly furnished state apartments
►page 326

► **St Patrick's Cathedral**
Largest church in Ireland, impressive interior
►page 329

Architecture and the arts flourished, and the Wide Street Commission oversaw the emergence of one of the most spacious and magnificent cities in Europe. With the **Act of Union** in 1801, Ireland's political union with Great Britain, this short period of freedom came to an end. In the following years, resistance against British rule grew; in 1844, Lord Mayor Daniel O'Connell was incarcerated »for incitement of discontent«. A secret brotherhood carried out political murders, and separatist activities increased. During the quashing of the **Easter Rising** and in the ensuing civil war, large parts of the city centre were destroyed. Even after the ratification of the treaty in 1922 which made Ireland a Free State, in fact up to 1927, Dublin still saw internecine fighting, and most public buildings were not restored until 1931. During **World War II** the country remained neutral.

Over subsequent decades, relatively little was done for the city, and there was even some ill-considered demolition of fine Georgian terraces. It was only when Dublin was nominated »European Capital of Culture« in 1991 that a wave of reconstruction and restoration started, improving Dublin's image enormously. Today, the city many restored historic buildings, and the conservation of Dublin's heritage is taken very seriously.

Dublin · City centre

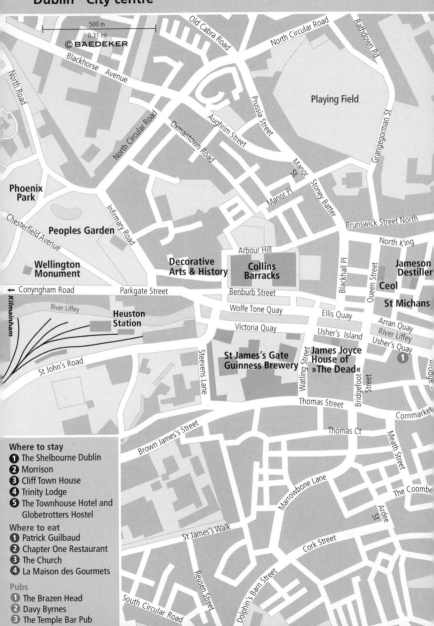

500 m
0.31 mi
© BAEDEKER

North Road

Blackhorse Avenue

Old Cabra Road

North Circular Road

Rathdown Rd

Playing Field

Prussia Street

Aughrim Street

Oxmantown Road

North Circular Road

Grangegorman St

Manor St

Stoney Batter

Manor Pl

Phoenix Park

Peoples Garden

Infirmary Road

Brunswick Street North

North King

Chesterfield Avenue

Arbour Hill

Decorative Arts & History

Collins Barracks

Blackhall Pl

Queen Street

Jameson Destiller

Ceol

St Michans

Wellington Monument

← Conyngham Road

Parkgate Street

Benburb Street

Wolfe Tone Quay

Ellis Quay

Arran Quay

River Liffey

Kilmainham

River Liffey

Heuston Station

Victoria Quay

Usher's Island

Usher's Quay

1

St John's Road

Steevens Lane

St James's Gate Guinness Brewery

Watling Street

James Joyce House of »The Dead«

Bridgefoot Street

Cornmarket

Thomas Street

Thomas Ct

Meath Street

Brown James's Street

Marrowbone Lane

The Coombe

St James's Walk

Cork Street

Ardee St

Reuben Street

Dolphin's Barn Street

South Circular Road

Where to stay
1. The Shelbourne Dublin
2. Morrison
3. Cliff Town House
4. Trinity Lodge
5. The Townhouse Hotel and Globetrotters Hostel

Where to eat
1. Patrick Guilbaud
2. Chapter One Restaurant
3. The Church
4. La Maison des Gourmets

Pubs
1. The Brazen Head
2. Davy Byrnes
3. The Temple Bar Pub

↑ Croke Park

Berkeley Rd
Eccles Street
North Circular Road
Parade
Tolka River

Dorset Street
Temple St
Gardiner St Upr West
Hill Street
Gardiner Street
Summer Hill
Street
Portland Row

Western Way
Dublin City Gallery
Dublin Writers' Museum
James Joyce Centre

Black Church
King's Inns
Constitution

Par. Sq N
Parnell Sq
Garden of Remembrance
Parnell Street
Marlborough Street
O'Connell Street

Connolly Station
Convention Centre Dublin, O2 Theatre

Rotunda Hospital ②
Bolton St
Parnell Street
St Mary's Pro-Cathedral
Street
Talbot Street ⑤
Amiens Street

Street
Joyce Statue
The Spire
Abbey Theatre
Custom House
Famine Memorial

Capel Street
Jervis Street
Henry Street
GPO
Mary Street ③
Abbey St Mid
Eden Quay
Custom House Quay
River Liffey

Mary's Lane
Abbey St Upr
Bachelors Walk
Burgh Qy
Georges Quay
City Quay

ur .ourts ②
Ormond Quay
Halfpenny Bridge
Aston Qy
Tara St
Townsend Street
Tara St Station
City Arts Centre
Samuel Beckett Bridge

nns uay
Merchants Quay
Wood Qy
Essex Qy
Millennium Bridge
Wellington Qy
Temple Bar Gallery + Studios ③
Bank of Ireland
Pearse Street
Lombard St
Grand Canal Docks

Audeon's
Christchurch Cathedral
Irish Film Centre
Dame Street
College Grn
Trinity College

h St
Dublinia
City Hall
Molly Malone
ℹ
Nassau St
Leinster St
Westland Row
Pearse Street Station

Nicholas St
St Werburgh's
Georges St
②④
Civic Museum
Grafton Street
Dawson St
St Anne's
④
Lincoln Pl
Clare Street North

Dublin Castle
South Gt
Royal College of Surgeons
Mansion House
Leinster House
Nat. Library
Nat. Gallery
Merrion Square
Wilde Statue
Holles

rancis St
Patrick St
St Patrick's Cathedral
Aungier St
Little Museum
③ Huguenot Graveyard
St Stephen's Green
National Museum ①
Natural History Museum ①
Merrion Street
Fitzwilliam St
No. 29

Dean St
Kevin St
Kevin St
Cuffe St
Newman House & University Church
Royal Hibernian Academy
Baggot Street
Pembroke Street
Bank of Ireland

New Street
New Bridge St
Wexford Camden Street
Harcourt Street
Marsh's Library
Iveagh Gardens
National Concert Hall
Earlsfort Terrace
Leeson Street
Fitzwilliam Pl
Fitzwilliam Street

Poets, Pubs and Pints

If a vacant position for a poet should be advertised, the story goes, then 10,000 people would put down their glasses in the pubs of Dublin to apply for the job. This is a city with as many writers as pubs – and the number of licensed establishments still runs to around 800. There are no longer 2,500 taverns, as there were in 1750, but James Joyce would nevertheless be content.

»Good puzzle would be cross Dublin without passing a pub«, says Leopold Bloom in Joyce's novel »Ulysses«. For centuries monks and women, who were responsible for brewing, carefully and lovingly established this tradition of beer and inns, which is celebrated in the works and lives of writers such as Joyce, George Bernard Shaw, W.B. Yeats, James Larkin and Flann O`Brien. To follow this literary tradition today on one of the tourist trails, it is necessary to walk many miles, for example on the 14 stages of Stephen Dedalus in »Ulysses« or when walking in the footsteps of Yeats.

An Entertaining Tour

A more relaxed and pleasant way of making a literary pilgrimage is to join Colm Quilligan on his **Literary Pub Crawl**. With his partner Frank, since 1988 he has taken groups on a walk only half a mile long, wearing a bowler hat, pullover and jacket to act the roles, on the trail of hard-drinking authors such as Samuel Beckett and Oscar Wilde. The tour is marked by humour and irony, and never strays far from a pub. In Dublin poets and pints are two sides of a coin, as in the case of **Brendan Behan**, who claimed to be »a drinker with a writing problem«.

Every evening at 7.30, the tour starts on the first floor of The Duke in the snug, once favoured by ladies who wanted to enjoy a tipple without the company of male drinkers. Colm Quilligan's programme takes in four to eight pubs, and lasts two and a half hours. To get in the mood, first of all the 19th-century folk song Waxies` Dargle is played. This was once a hit amongst the Dublin cobblers, whose summer trips out of the city to Dargle never got further than Irishtown, as there were too many pubs along the way. This is followed by an amusing scene from Beckett's »Waiting for Godot«, in which, according to one critic, nothing happens – twice.

Pub Tales

The first pint accompanies anecdotes about James Joyce, and Patrick Kavanagh's lament about »insignificant poets«. But, as the group hears, this applies to all of them since Homer. The second stop is **Trinity College** – for culture but not for a drink. Oscar Wilde (1872) and Samuel Beckett (1920) studied here, and here they learned to drink.

The next pub has no culture, but beer is on tap. At the 300-year-old **O'Neill's**, listeners are regaled by stories of Oscar Wilde's lecture tour of America, where the writer held his own in whiskey sessions with tough miners. Alternative ports of call are the Palace Bar and The Old Stand, where Brendan Behan's bon mot »Drink Canada dry!« is quoted. Behan always held his glass with a purple glove, as he had promised his mother on her deathbed that his hand would never again touch a glass of whiskey. The tour then moves on to **St Andrew's Church**, which stands on the site of the Viking parliament.

The evening comes to a close in **Davy Byrne's**, at 21 Duke Street, where Leopold Bloom orders a glass of burgundy to wash down his gorgonzola sandwich in the wandering rocks chapter of »Ulysses«. The modern version of Bloom's meal would be Guinness with oysters. This pub is an important landmark for Dubliners, as the first provisional Irish government met in the upper room in 1922. Beckett once lived above this pub, and it goes without saying that Behan drank here. He had a sharp tongue, and even as he lay dying said to his nurse, a nun, »God bless you, sister. May you become the mother of a bishop.«

A good place to round off the evening after this pub crawl is a classic pub like Kavanagh's. It used to be called The Gravedigger, as here the money earned from burying the dead was converted into Guinness from 1823 onwards.

The Literary Pub Crawl runs daily from Easter to October, and in the rest of the year from Thursday to Sunday, starting at 7.30pm in The Duke, 9 Duke Street. Tickets cost € 13 and can be bought on the evening (www.dublinpub crawl.com).

A performance of Beckett's »Waiting for Godot« in The Duke

COLLEGE GREEN • TRINITY COLLEGE

College Green was already a place of assembly in Viking times, and later Ireland's centre of power, until the Act of Union. Today, it is the seat of the most prestigious university, in Ireland Trinity College. Opposite **Regent House** on the west side of the college grounds, note the classical façade of the Bank of Ireland – the building where in the 18th century the country's parliament convened.

*Trinity College   The buildings of this university are spread out over a large public park. Founded in 1592 by Elizabeth I, Trinity College was exclusively reserved for Protestants up to 1793. Catholics have only been able to study for a degree and apply for scholarships here since 1873 – women had to wait until 1903. TCD's most famous students include Samuel Beckett, Edmund Burke, Robert Emmet, Oliver Goldsmith, Jonathan Swift, John Millington Synge and Oscar Wilde. Currently, some 16,750 students are enrolled here.

In front of the 90m/100-yd classical façade are statues of the poet and playwright Oliver Goldsmith and the philosopher Edmund Burke (1863–65). In the first courtyard, to the left, stands the **Chapel**, to the right, the **Examination Hall** (1779–91, formerly a theatre), both designed by Sir William Chambers. In the **Dining Hall**, built in 1743 by Richard Cassels behind the chapel, hang paintings of members of the

Trinity College Dublin

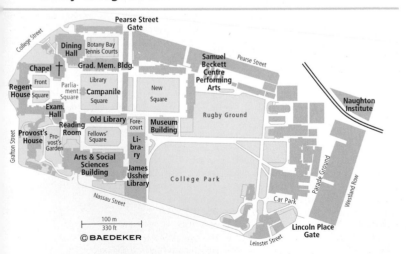

Dublin

INFORMATION
Dublin Tourism Centre
www.visitdublin.com
Suffolk Street, Dublin 2
Tel. 18 50 23 03 30
Mon–Sat 9am–5.30pm, July and Aug
until 7pm, Sun 10.30am–3pm.

PUBLIC TRANSPORT
The DART network of local trains (Dublin
Area Rapid Transit; www.dublin.ie/trans-
port/dart.htm), two tram lines and the
bus network give the city low-cost and
excellent public transport. Taxis (e.g.
Dublin City Cabs, tel. 018 72 72 72,
www.citycabs.ie) can be hard to find on
Friday and Saturday nights. Many sights
in the centre are best explored on foot.
Dublin Bike his bike-hire points all over
the city (www.dublinbikes.ie).

CITY TOURS
The Dublin Tourism Centre has details of
all operators. Bookings can be made at
www.dublinsightseeing.ie

Viking Splash Tours
Daily 10am–5.30pm from St Stephens
Green North, ticket 20 €,
www.vikingsplash.com
Tours in a bright yellow amphibian
vehicle.

SHOPPING
Dublin is a wonderful city for browsing
in shops, with shopping centres and
stores along the main streets, for example Grafton Street, in Temple Bar, and
on Earl Street next to the Dublin Spire. In
the Georges Street Arcades is a fine Victorian market hall. Look for books in
Dawson Street, antiques around Christ-

church Cathedral. Moore Street is
known for its street market (Mon–Sat)
and lots of international shops filled
with knick-knacks.

WHERE TO EAT
❶ Patrick Guilbaud €€€€
21–24 Upper Merrion Street
Dublin 2
Tel. (01) 6 76 41 92
www.restaurantpatrickguilbaud.ie
Closed Sun and Mon
One of the most exclusive restaurants in
Dublin. Imaginative – often innovative –
French cuisine. The lunch menus are rea-
sonably priced.

❷ Chapter One Restaurant €€€€
18/19 Parnell Square North
Tel. (01) 8 73 22 66
www.chapteronerestaurant.com
Michelin-starred restaurant that uses local and seasonal produce in dishes with
strong flavours. The pre-theatre menu is
affordable.

❸ The Church €€€
Jervis Street
Dublin 2
Tel. (01) 8 28 01 02
Five bars and restaurants on four floors.
7,000 guests per year enjoy the high-
class Gallery Restaurant and the Church
Bar on the north bank of the Liffey.

❹ La Maison des Gourmets €€
15 Castlemarket Street
Dublin 2
Tel. (01) 6 72 72 58
www.lamaisonrestaurant.ie
This gem serves delicacies from the
French patisserie and deli below. The

proprietor Olivier Quenet also runs the Schoolhouse Bar for drinks and lower-priced menus at 2–8 Northumberland Road, Dublin 4 (www.schoolhousebar. ie).

PUBS
The Brazen Head
20 Lower Bridge Street, Dublin 8
Tel. 01 677 95 49
www.brazenhead.com
This cosy pub, the oldest in Dublin, has been going since 1198. Good wines, often live music is played after 9pm.

Davy Byrne's
Duke Street, Dublin 2
Tel. 01 677 52 17
www.davybyrnes.com
Famous Dublin pub, which also features in James Joyce's novel *Ulysses* and is

Insider Tip

famous for the sandwich with green cheese and mustard that Mr. Bloom ate with wine. The sandwich is on offer, of course, as well as a reasonably priced lunch menu.

Temple Bar Pub
47 Temple Bar, Dublin 2
Tel. 01 672 5286
www.thetemplebarpub.com
This traditional meeting place in the trendy Temple Bar quarter is popular and noisy. Try Guinness with oysters. Live music every night.

WHERE TO STAY
❶ The Shelbourne Dublin €€€€
27 St Stephen's Green
Dublin 2
Tel. (01) 6 63 45 00
www.marriott.com

Temple Bar and the pub of that name are always busy

243 rooms, 19 suites
The most upmarket hotel in Dublin. The Constitution Suite, where the Irish constitution was signed in 1922, is part of a new museum in the lobby. A good central base, recommended for afternoon tea in the Lord Mayor 's Lounge, also the historic Saddle Room restaurant and two bars. Parking costs 25 € per night.

❷ *Morrison* €€€€
Ormond Quay
Dublin 1
Tel. (01) 8 87 24 00
www.morrisonhotel.ie
138 rooms and suites
One of the most luxurious hotels in Europe and an architectural masterpiece, featuring comfortable rooms and suites with modern furnishings, and a café-bar that is open to non-residents.

❸ *Cliff Town House* €€
22 St Stephens Green
Dublin 2
Tel. (01) 6 38 39 39
www.theclifftownhouse.com

10 rooms
High-class boutique hotel with rooms in Edwardian style and an excellent restaurant that has reasonably priced wines.

❹ *Trinity Lodge* €€€
12 South Frederick Street
Dublin 2
Tel. (01) 6 17 09 00
www.trinitylodge.com
23 rooms
Fine Georgian townhouse in the heart of Dublin, with a restaurant.

❺ *The Townhouse Hotel and Globetrotters Hostel*
47–48 Lower Gardiner Street
Dublin 1
Tel. (01) 8 78 88 08
www.townhouseofdublin.com
80 rooms
Some rooms have a balcony, others a view of the small Japanese garden. The writers Dion Boucicault and Lafcadio Hearn once lived in this Georgian townhouse, a good base in the city centre.

university. In the centre of the square, the **Campanile** (1853) immediately draws attention; nearby, look for a sculpture by Henry Moore.

The most interesting building on campus is the Old Library, built between 1712 and 1732. Since 1801, the library has been a copyright library, i.e. it is entitled to receive a copy of every book printed in Great Britain and Ireland. Around 5,000 manuscripts and nearly three million printed books are held here. Its treasures include manuscripts, incunabula and early prints. On the ground floor, the Colonnades of the Old Library, the famous 8th-century Book of Kells (►MARCO POLO Insight p.68) is on display. The book containing the four gospels has 680 exquisitely illustrated pages, of which a different one is shown every day; the beginnings of the gospels and the individual chapters are particularly beautifully designed. Further valuable manuscripts are the Book of Durrow, the Book of Dimma

**Old Library

The Old Library in Trinity College

and the Book of Armagh (7th–9th century). From the ground floor, a pretty set of stairs leads up to the Long Room, a beautiful library 60m/200ft in length lined with books and the busts of writers and philosophers. Look out for two of the oldest Irish harps.

❶ Mon–Sat 9.30am–5pm, Sun May–Sept 9.30am–4.30pm, Oct–April 12 noon–4.30pm; admission 9 €; www.bookofkells.ie

Campus tours   30-minute campus tours start from the main entrance at the Front Arch. Trinity College also offers accommodation between June and September (www.tcd.ie/accommodation). A number of restaurants and cafés are on side, including the Hamilton Restaurant, the Buttery Food Court (in the main court) and the **Arts Café** in the Arts Building. The same building holds the **Douglas Hyde Gallery**, which shows contemporary Irish art in changing exhibitions in two galleries (entrance on Nassau Street).

On two floors of the Naughton Institute, the ***Science Gallery** presents interactive changing exhibitions. Exhibits from a collection numbering 80,000 items that was started in 1777 are on show in the Story of the Earth in the **Geological Museum** on the top floor of the ***Museum Building** of 1853, which is modelled on Byzantine architecture.

Campus tours: mid-May to Sept daily 10.15, 10.40, 11.05, 11.35am, 12.10, 12.45, 2.15 and 3pm, Mon–Sat also 3.40pm; ticket 10 €

Arts Café: Mon–Fri 7am–4pm, Sat and Sun 9am–3pm; www.tcd.ie/catering

Douglas Hyde Gallery: Mon– Fri 11am–6pm, Thu until 7pm, Sat 11am–4.45pm; free admission; www.douglashydegallery.com

Science Gallery: Tue–Fri 12 noon–8pm, Sat and Sun 12 noon–6pm; free admission; www.sciencegallery.com

Geological Museum: Mon– Fri 10am–5pm; free admission

Opposite, the Bank of Ireland was built in 1729 as a parliament building to a design by Sir Edward Lovett, but sold in 1802 – after the Act of Union – to the Bank of Ireland. Architecturally, the façade, with its various compositions of columns and groups of statues (the result of several alterations), is considered one of the most successful in Dublin. The former House of Commons is now the main banking hall and may be visited during opening hours. The **former House of Lords**, featuring a coffered ceiling and chandeliers, is also open as part of guided tours. The **Bank of Ireland Arts Centre** (entrance on Foster Place) stages art shows, concerts and readings, with regular free recitals at 1.15pm.

*Bank of Ireland

House of Commons: Mon– Fri 10am–4pm, Thu until 5pm, Sat and Sun closed; free admission

House of Lords: 45-minute tour Tue 10.30, 11.30am, 1.45pm; free admission

Bank of Ireland Arts Centre: programme tel. 01 671 1488; Tue–Fri 9.30am–4pm; free admission

> **! MARCO ⊕ POLO TIP**
>
> *Bargains in Dublin* **Insider Tip**
>
> With the Dublin Pass, valid for one to five days, visitors can save up to € 190 in admission charges and avoid queues. The pass is valid for 34 attractions, including museums, the Literary Pub Crawl and the Guinness Store House. Trips on public transport are cheaper, and transfer in the airport bus is free. Price 49 € for one day, 99 € for five days, www.dublin-pass.ie.

BETWEEN GRAFTON STREET AND THE NATIONAL MUSEUM

Grafton Street, one of the main shopping streets in Dublin (pedestrianized), runs south from College Green.

Grafton Street

In the venerable ***Bewley's Café** (1927), with six famous leaded windows made by Harry Clarke in 1931 and many works of art inside, an exhibition illuminates the history of the company since 1835 (free admission). The theatre in the Oriental Room on the second floor is a venue for jazz and cabaret in the evenings and especially at lunchtime.

A narrow street leads to the imposing ***Powerscourt Town House**. Built in 1774, originally as a town house for the Viscount of Powerscourt, it now houses elegant offices and department stores, cafés, exclusive shops and galleries. A few doors further down on William Street South, the **Civic Museum** shows a wealth of exhibits alongside old city maps and models of historic Dublin. At the corner of Suffolk Street, look for the bronze statue of cockle and mussel seller Molly Malone.

The office of the prime minister is in the Government Buildings

Bewley's Café: 78 Grafton Street, Mon-Wed 8am–10pm; Tue–Sat
8am–11pm, Sun 9am–10pm
Oriental Room: admittance 12.50pm, show 1.30–2pm; tickets with light
lunch 8–16 €; www.bewleyscafetheatre.com
Powerscourt Town House: 59 South William Street; Tue and Sat 12 noon
and 2pm; admission 8 €; www.powerscourtcentre.ie
Civic Museum: Tue–Sat 10am–6pm, Sun 11am–2pm; free admission

In Dawson Street , east of Grafton Street, stands **Mansion House**
(1705), which has served as the seat of the lord mayor of Dublin since
1715, and the Royal Irish Academy with its important library holding
manuscripts dating from the 6th to 17th century, amongst them the
Cathach Psalter, written by St Columba. Several exhibitions on Irish
history are held here each year. The **Round Room**, where history has
been made for 200 years, is used for events.

**Dawson
Street**

❶ Mon –Thu 10am –5.30pm, Fri 10am –5pm; free admission;
www.ria.ie/library

Further east stretches the part of Dublin called »Georgian City«.
Monumental **Kildare Street** boasts Leinster House – the parliament
building, seat of the Dáil Éireann (parliament) and Seanad Éireann
(senate). Originally, this solid, somewhat sober building, the work of
Richard Cassels in 1745, was the townhouse of the dukes of Leinster.
Visitors who are not Irish citizens can take part in the so-called **walk-
up tours**, and must bring ID with them.

**Leinster
House**

❶ Tel. 016 18 37 81; tours Mon and Fri 11.30am and 3.30pm; start from
Kildare Street Gate, meet 15 minutes before start of tour; free admission;
www.oireachas.ie

Every Irish writer since James Joyce has spent time in theNational
Library. The episode of Stephen Daedalus' literary debate in Joyce's
novel *Ulysses* also makes a direct reference to this reading room. The
library holds collections of first editions, especially 17th-century
Irish literature, old maps and topographical works. In the exhibition
area, an excellent ***display on W.B. Yeats** can be seen. A book shop
and the Joly Café are also here.

**National
Library**

❶ Mon –Wed 9.30am –7.45pm, Thu and Fri 9.30am –4.45pm, Sat
9.30am –4.30pm, Sun 1 –5pm; free admission; guided tours of Yeats
exhibition Mon 1pm, Sat 3pm, of library Sat 2.30pm; www.nli.ie

The National Museum is a veritable treasure trove for Irish antiquities from prehistory to the late Middle Ages. The Great Hall shows
Irish gold artefacts from different periods. Particularly valuable exhibits are kept in the Treasury next door, amongst them the silver
8th-century Ardagh Chalice, with gilded decorations. One of the
most precious artefacts is the 8th-century **Tara Brooch**. Its intricate

****National
Museum**

decorations are said to have influenced the artists who created the Book of Kells (►MARCO POLO Insight, p.68). Equally impressive is the 12th-century **Cross of Cong**, a processional cross made of oak, with silver and gilded bronze plates in the shape of animals. The most beautiful amongst the reliquary shrines is the 12th-century **Shrine of St Patrick's Bell**, decorated with gilded silver, gold filigree and precious stones. The adjacent **Natural History Museum** (Upper Merrion Street) is dedicated to the flora, fauna and geology of Ireland and the world. The **Decorative Arts & History** department of the National Museum, on a site further west in the city, also displays precious crafts such as silver, furniture, coins, clothing and jewellery, as well as an exhibition on the Easter Rising of 1916 and Irish military history.

Decorative Arts & History: Collins Barracks, Benburg Street, Dublin 7; Tue–Sat 10am–5pm, Sun 2–5pm; free admission

National Museum: Kildare Street; Tue–Sat 10am–5pm, Sun 2–5pm; www.museum.ie; free admission

AROUND ST STEPHEN'S GREEN

St Stephen's Green

Follow Kildare Street on to St Stephen's Green, a 9ha/22-acre park established and paid for by Arthur Guinness in 1880, that has remained popular ever since. In July and August, there are lunchtime concerts with Irish music. There are beautiful gardens, ponds and monuments for famous Irish people. Hiding behind an ornate Victorian façade is the **St Stephen's Green Shopping Centre**. The **Little Museum** presents the history of Dublin in the 20th century, including a growing exhibition about the band U2, with photos, letters and postcards, advertising and various curiosities.

In the 18th and 19th centuries, everybody who was anybody went for a stroll on the northern side of the park, Beaux Walk, and still today, visitors can reside in style at the Shelbourne Hotel (1867). Next to the hotel, in a shady garden, lies the old **Huguenot graveyard** dating from 1693. Many French Huguenots who came to Ireland fleeing persecution from Louis XIV are buried here.

Newman House

The building on the southern side of St Stephen's Green, with the house numbers 85 and 86 is called **Newman House**, in memory of John Henry Newman, the first rector of the Catholic University, the predecessor of University College. Belonging to University College Dublin, it has been lavishly restored and is worth a visit for its elaborate stucco works. No. 85 was built in 1738 for Captain Hugh Montgomery, whilst house no. 86 was begun in 1765 after designs by Robert West.

❶ June–Sept: Mon–Fri noon–4pm, Sat 2pm–4pm, Sun 11am–1pm

Next to Newman House stands the neo-Byzantine Catholic ***Newman University Church**. It has a semi-circular apse and beautiful wall decoration.

In Harcourt Street, branching off from the southwestern corner of St Stephen's Green, there is a good large bar called **Odeon**, which, between 1859 and 1958, was the terminus of the train line between Dublin and Bray. Bram Stoker, the author of Dracula, lived here (at no. 16) as did George Bernard Shaw (no. 61).

Harcourt Street

A veritable jewel in the heart of Dublin are the **Iveagh Gardens**, surrounded by a sturdy wall and hidden behind Newman House. The entrance is reached via Earlsfort Terrace or Clonmel Street, off Harcourt Street. Take Harrington Street to reach Synge Street. No. 33 was the **birthplace of George Bernard Shaw** in 1856. After extensive restoration it now appears again as it did when the Shaw family lived here.

> **MARCO POLO TIP**
>
> **! Dracula fever** Insider Tip
>
> Since 2012, the centenary of the death of Bram Stoker, Dublin has been gripped by Dracula fever. A bus with suitably macabre decorations takes visitors on a Ghost Bus Tour (two hours; Mon–Tue 8pm, Fri–Sat 7pm; tickets 28 €; www.dublinsightseeing.ie/ghostbus). To meet a vampire, buy a ticket to the Secret Castle of Magic (admission 25 €; www.secretcastleofmagic.com). Dracula appears in person in the show at the Wax Museum Plus in Temple Bar.

Little Museum: 15 St Stephen's Green; Fri–Wed 11am–6pm, Thu 11am–8pm; admission 5 €; www.littlemuseum.ie
Newman House: tours June–Aug Tue–Fri 2pm, 3pm, 4pm; admission 5 €
Shaw House: June–Aug Tue–Sat 10am–1pm and 2–5pm, closed Sat morning; admission 6 €

MERRION SQUARE • GEORGIAN DUBLIN

Merrion Square, with its pretty Archbishop Ryan Park and elegant buildings, was built around 1762. Doors in all the colours of the rainbow greet visitors here, with decorated doorknobs and boot scrapers adorning the typical Georgian entrances.

*Merrion Square

An unusual monument in the northwestern corner of the square shows Wilde lounging on a rock. At no. 1, **Oscar Wilde** spent his childhood; he was born, however, in 1854 in nearby 21 Westland Row. Also living here at Merrion Square at one time were politician Daniel O'Connell (no. 58), W B Yeats (no. 82) and the writer Joseph Sheridan Le Fanu (no. 70).

Head for Merrion Street to discover the treasures of the National Gallery, which was inaugurated in 1864. The gallery is divided into four

*National Gallery

A Literary Guidebook

In Dublin, 16 June is not any old day – it's Bloomsday! Every year, hundreds of people wander through the city centre, on their own or in groups, come to a halt at the odd crossroads or building, open a book and look around them. The 800-page work is their guide to the city. It is not a conventional travel guide, however, but a novel: the literary masterpiece of the Irish writer James Joyce (1882–1941).

Ulysses describes the course of one day: 16 June 1904, from eight in the morning to the next morning around 3am, in the life of three inhabitants of Dublin: advertising agent **Leopold Bloom**, **his wife Molly** and the teacher and writer **Stephen Dedalus**. Joyce described the steps taken by Bloom and Dedalus through the Irish capital so faithfully that even today it is possible to use the novel as a guide for a literary pilgrimage through the city centre. *Ulysses* is, in the words of writer Frank Delaney, a »literary Baedeker«. Whilst Joyce was writing his major work, he told a friend: »I want to give a picture of Dublin so complete that if the city one day suddenly disappeared from the earth it could be reconstructed out of my book.« Since 16 June 1954, Bloomsday has become a hit with the tourists: on that day, four Dubliners celebrated the day that Leopold Bloom had crossed Dublin for the first time. During their literary tour, Joyceans mainly use the 8th episode of the novel, which begins in Middle Abbey Street and ends in Kildare Street. Bronze plaques in the pavement show the way and point to the relevant page numbers of the standard English edition. (For more information, pick up a copy of the Ulysses Map of Dublin published by the tourist office.)

The Novel

Ulysses consists of 18 episodes. The focus of the first three is Stephen Dedalus, whilst Leopold Bloom, a modern Everyman, appears in the fourth episode. After breakfast with his wife Molly, Bloom starts his daily odyssey through Dublin: post office, mass, public baths, cemetery (to attend a funeral), publishing house, pub, restaurant, and library. Later, Leopold's path crosses that of Stephen Dedalus'. They first make a detour to a coaching inn before continuing to Bloom's flat at 7 Eccles Street. When Dedalus goes home, Bloom lies down next to Molly to sleep. The 18 episodes of the novel correspond to the 24 cantos of **Homer's Odyssey**. As Odysseus travels through the Greek islands, Bloom travels the streets of Dublin. Part of Joyce's genius lies in the way he challenges traditional narrative structures, with the plot losing its central role. *Ulysses* is one of the first novels to take up the psychoanalytical insights of Sigmund Freud. 20 hours or so in the daily life of three inhabitants of Dublin are portrayed: their actions, their encounters with other citizens of their home town,

It goes without saying that participants in Bloomsday dress fittingly

their thoughts, desires and dreams. The main narrative devices are interior monologue, chains of association, changing points of view, a fragmented chronology and ungrammatical syntax. An easy read this ain't! With new forms of expression, in particular the »«stream of consciousness« narrative technique that he developed further, James Joyce was of decisive influence on the art of the 20th-century novel.

Changing Dublin

In recent decades, Dublin, which so far has largely been spared wars and natural disasters, has experienced radical change. Many streets and lanes were redesigned, and houses torn down. Only the large boulevards have survived, if not always in the shape Joyce knew them. Even Bloom's house is no longer there... Along with many other locations from the novel, the pubs Barney Kieran's and Burke's have disappeared, as has the coaching inn, but at many corners, something of the old Dublin is still there. For instance, the place where the novel kicks off: the **Martello Tower**, in the Dun Laoghaire suburb, today houses the Joyce Museum. **Glasnevin** cemetery is well worth visiting as well as **Bailey's**, today one of Dublin's classiest pubs. Opposite lies **Davy Byrne's** pub, where a hungry Bloom had a gorgonzola sandwich – today on offer on Bloomsday. To purchase a small and cheap souvenir, head for **Sweeney's** on Lincoln Place, where Joyceans come to buy a piece of lemon soap, just as Leopold Bloom did on 16 June 1904.

main departments: Milltown Wing, Dargan Wing, North Wing and the Millennium Wing for international exhibitions in Clare Street.

It is best to start in the Milltown Wing, where works by **Irish artists** are on display; the most famous here is »The Conjurer« by Nathaniel Hone the Elder, believed to show the former president of the Royal Academy, Joshua Reynolds. Many paintings show a romanticized representation of the poor rural population, for instance Augustus Burke's *Connemara Girl*. Irish 20th-century art can be found in rooms 5 and 6; look out for the landscape paintings by Paul Henry (*Connemara Village*) and the portrait of Lady Lavery by her husband John Lavery in particular. The **Yeats Room** in the Dargan Wing is mainly dedicated to the painter Jack B Yeats, brother of the writer WB Yeats. Carry on into the impressive **Shaw Room** with its magnificent Waterford Crystal chandeliers.

In the North Wing, room 32 is the most interesting, showing the famous portraits of James Joyce (by Jacques Blanche) and Sean O'Casey (by Augustus John). Works by British artists are displayed in rooms 33–36; for instance, works by **J M W Turner**. On the second floor of the North Wing (rooms 23 and 24) are some interesting altar paintings and early Renaissance paintings, amongst them a work by **Fra Angelico**. Rooms 26 to 30 show German, Flemish and Dutch art (Vermeer: *A Lady Writing a Letter*). Of particular interest is the Spanish collection (Room 31) with works by **El Greco**, Goya, Velázquez and Picasso. Room 24 houses Italian masters such as Titian and Tintoretto; the undoubted highlight here, however, is **Caravaggio's** *The Taking of Christ*, which for over 60 years hung unnoticed in a Jesuit building in Leeson Street. The most admired Irish painting, ***Hellelil and Hildebrand, the Meeting on the Turret Stairs*** (1864) by Frederic William Burton (1816–1900), has been given its own small room in the Millennium Wing (only Mondays and Wednesdays 11.30am – 12.30pm; limited tickets are available on the day).

❶ Mon–Wed, Fri and Sat 9.30am–5.30pm, Thu 9.30am to 8.30pm, Sun noon – 5.30pm; free admission; www.nationalgallery.ie

29 Merrion Square

On the opposite side of Merrion Square, one of the magnificent Georgian residences has been converted into a museum: no. 29 in **Lower Fitzwilliam Street**. The late 18th-century building has been furnished to look exactly as it did when it was built and the widowed merchant's wife Olivia Beatty moved in here with her three children. Laid out between 1791 and 1825, **Fitzwilliam Square** is arguably the best-preserved square in the Georgian style; the buildings here draw the eye with their beautifully wrought doors and fan lights.

❶ Tue–Sat 10am–5, Sun 12 noon–5pm; admission 6 €; www.esb.ie/no29

The National Gallery started in 1864 with an exhibition of 100 works. Today it is a leading European art gallery

St Stephen's Church
Southeast of Merrion Square, at 2 Mount Street Crescent and the junction with Mount Street Upper, stands **St Stephen's Church**, »The Gem of Dublin«. The church, the last to be built in the city in the Georgian period, takes its name from a hospital for lepers that once stood here and is often the venue for concerts. Its appearance has given it the nickname Peppercanister Church.

❶ Visits only Wed, Thu 12.30–2.30pm; admission free; concert tickets 5 €; www.peppercanister.ie

*Grand Canal Docks
A walk along the south bank of the Liffey leads to the new Grand Canal Docks (start from the DART station of the same name) and the family-friendly **Waterways Visitor Centre** on Grand Canal Quay. A striking building here is the seven-storey **Trinity Design Tower**, housing jewellers and the Digital Dublin gallery, among other things.

The futuristic **Grand Canal Square** is the site of a luxury hotel, shops selling organic products, cafés, restaurants and the ***Grand Canal Theatre** (now called the **Bord Gaís Energy Theatre**, www.bordgais-energytheatre.ie), designed by the American star architect Daniel Libeskind. The landscape architect Martha Schwartz designed the square with its illuminated red stelae.

Cardiff Lane leaks to the south bank of the Liffey and the **Diving Bell** (1866), a reminder of the earliest attempts to dive. Installations and sculptures such as the bronze »Linesman« by Dony MacManus add interest to the area.

A technical sensation that opened in 2009, the **Samuel Beckett Bridge**, spans the river. It is a cable-stayed swing bridge with a pylon in the form of a lying harp. The architect was Santiago Calatrava, who built the James Joyce Bridge upstream in 2003.

Docklands
On the north bank of the Liffey lies the Docklands area, which is in the process of transformation (www.ddda.ie). On Guild Street note the historic Scherzer Bridge (1912) on the Royal Canal and the ***Convention Centre Dublin** on Spencer Dock, a work by the Irish American architect Kevin Roche. To the north is the finance district.

In an easterly direction lie the mouth of the Liffey, the **O2 Theatre** (www.theo2.ie) and the port of Dublin.

Waterways Visitor Centre: Wed–Sun 10am–6pm; admission 4 €; www.waterwaysireland.org

Trinity Design Tower: daily 10am–5pm; www.thedesigntower.com

TEMPLE BAR

Between the southern banks of the Liffey and Dame Street lies the Temple Bar quarter. Once inhabited by workmen and tradespeople, with its 200-year old houses it has become the principal entertainment and artists' district of Dublin. The narrow streets have been pedestrianized and now house small shops, studios, pubs, nightclubs and restaurants, especially in the ***Old City** between Fishamble Street and Parliament Street. A good place to call in is the **Chorus Café** (7 Scarlet Row). Among numerous pubs, the microbrewery **Porterhouse** at 16–18 Parliament Street with nine kinds

of beer is worthy of mention. Of many festivals that are held here, the ***Temple Bar Tradfest**, a folk festival (late January, http://templebar.com) is the biggest. For information about arts in the quarter, go to the Temple Bar Cultural trust Centre at 12 East Essex Street (www.temple-bar.ie) and Temple Bar Traders at 2–5 Wellington Quay (www.visittemplebar.com). The exhibitions at the **Project Arts Centre** have given many young artists a career boost (39 East Essex Street, www.projectartscentre.ie). This is also the venue for the Writers' Festival, the Fringe Festival and other cultural events.

The four floors of the **National Wax Museum Plus** display wax figures and chambers of horrors. An alternative is the **National Photographic Archive**, which holds 600,000 historic photographs and holds temporary exhibitions, as does the **Graphic Studio Gallery** in Cope Street (www.graphicstudiodublin.com). **The Ark** with its rooftop art garden is aimed at children.   **Museums in Temple Bar**

National Wax Museum Plus: 4 Foster Place; daily 10am–7pm; admission 12 €; www.waxmuseumplus.ie
National Photographic Archive: Meeting House square; Mon–Sat 20am–4.45pm, Sun 12 noon–3.45pm; free admission
The Ark: Eustace Street; Mon–Fri 10am–4.30pm; exhibitions Tue–Sun 10am–5pm; admission 4–10 €; httpL//ark.ie

The life of Temple Bar now spills over across the river. **Halfpenny Bridge** is the best crossing. This elegant metal construction was erected in 1816 and financed through a toll fee – hence the name (its official name is Liffey Bridge). It is one of the oldest cast-iron bridges in the world, and was the only pedestrian bridge across the Liffey until 2000. On the north bank, the **National Leprechaun Museum** is devoted to Irish elves. An old literary rendezvous and a good place for a break is **The Winding Stair Book Shop** with its excellent restaurant.   **North of the Liffey**

National Leprechaun Museum: 1 Jervis Street; daily 10am–6.30pm; admission 12 €; www.leprechaunmuseum.ie
The Winding Stair Book Shop: 40 Ormond Quay; Mon–Wed 10am–6pm, Thu–Sat 10am–7pm, Sun 12 noon–6pm; www.winding–stair.com

DUBLIN CASTLE AND SURROUNDINGS

*Dublin Castle

Behind City Hall rises Dublin Castle. This hill already had a Celtic and later a Danish fortification before King John (1204–26) had a castle built here, of which, however, hardly anything remains. Most of today's buildings date from the 18th and 19th centuries. From the time of Elizabeth I to the creation of the Free State in 1921, the castle was the seat of the viceroys and the British administration. On the short eastern side of Upper Yard is an entrance to Lower Yard. To the right is Record Tower, one of the four old corner towers, well preserved, with walls nearly 5m/17ft thick giving an idea of what the medieval castle looked like.

The **Chapel Royal** is a neo-Gothic building (1807–14); its exterior is remarkable for its bizarre decoration: over a hundred carved limestone heads of famous Irishmen.

The State Apartments **State Apartments** are shown to visitors during a half-hour guided tour, unless they are being used for a function (access is opposite the entrance from the street, Cork Hill, in Upper Yard). Look out for the colourful Donegal and Killybegs carpets, as well as the Waterford Crystal chandeliers and the green Connemara marble floor at the entrance.

A guided tour includes **St Patrick's Hall** with its painted ceiling (1778), the Throne Room, lavishly decorated with gold (1740) and a 200-year-old throne, and the State Drawing Room, furnished with original pieces. After the tour of the State Apartments, visitors are shown the remnants of the medieval castle (entrance at the Powder Tower).

The grounds of Dublin Castle also hold the unique collection of the American Chester Beatty . This carefully put together exhibition of books and book art, which received the European Museum of the Year Award in 2002, enchants visitors with its variety, wealth and delight in colours. The exquisite exhibits include manuscripts, early prints and modern art prints, icons, miniatures from Europe, Africa, the Middle East and Asia – not to mention Egyptian papyrus texts, beautifully decorated editions of the Koran and the Bible, Japanese colour woodcuts and Buddhist images.

St Patrick's Hall: entrance next to Powder Tower; Mon–Sat 10am– 4.45pm; June–Aug also Sun 2–4.45pm; admission 4.50 €; www.dublincastle.ie
Chester Beatty Library: daily 10am–5pm, Sat 11am–5pm; Sun 1pm–5pm; Oct–April Mon closed; free admission; www.cbl.ie

Right in front of the castle, on Lord Edward Street stands the town **City Hall**
hall, originally built by Thomas Cooley between 1769 and 1779 as a
Royal Exchange, and today serving as the seat of the municipal authorities. The entrance hall of the imposing domed building is decorated with statues of local celebrities. A multimedia show illuminates
the thousand-year history of Dublin.

❶ Mon–Sat 10am–5.15pm; admission to exhibition 4.50 €;
www.dublincity.ie

West of Dublin Castle runs Werburgh Street, where Dublin's first **St**
theatre used to stand. It is also said that the first church in Dublin was **Werburgh's**
erected on the site of the small St Werburgh's Church. In 1754, the **Church**
building burned down, apart from the tow-
er and the façade. It was, however, rebuilt

> **!** **The world's best fish & chips**
>
> **Insider Tip**
>
> In Werburgh Street, Leo
> Burdock's allegedly serve
> the best fish & chips in the
> world! (www.burdocks.ie)
> There are now branches in
> Temple Bar, Liffey Street,
> Dundrum, Rathmines and
> Phiboro.
>
> **MARCO ⊕ POLO** TIP

only a few years later. From the 18th century it was used as the parish church for the
British lord lieutenants. The interior, with
its Gothic pulpit, is worth seeing (visits by
appointment, tel. 01 478 37 10.

CATHEDRALS

The oldest part of Dublin lies to the west of
Dublin Castle; this is where the Vikings
first founded the city. This is also the site of the original Four Courts.
Today, modern buildings dominate the district, but Christchurch and
St Patrick's, two cathedrals dating from the 12th century, have weath-
ered the times. Both belong to the Church of Ireland.

Christchurch Cathedral owes its current aspect to extensive recon- **Christchurch**
struction between 1871 and 1878. Apart from the crypt running the **Cathedral**
length of the entire nave, only a portal at the southern transept and **and around**
possibly parts of the transepts still date from the 13th-century building. However, there is enough left to get an idea of the former glory
of this church. The **crypt** holds numerous interesting fragments from
various periods, as well as 17th-century statues of Charles II and
James II. In the nave, look for an austere-looking tomb showing a
reclining knight. It is called »Strongbow's Grave« after the Norman
who destroyed the church, only to have it rebuilt in 1172. In 2010
archaeological excavations took place outside the cathedral. The
basement café has lots of atmosphere.

The former Synod Hall, connected with Christchurch Cathedral by a
bridge, shows the **Dublinia exhibition**, looking at the history of
Dublin from the arrival of the Normans in 1170 to the dissolution of
the monasteries in 1540, using videos and many exhibits, amongst

St Patrick's Cathedral is the largest church in the country

them Viking clothes, the chains of slaves, tools and a reconstruction of a Viking house.

❶ Christchurch Cathedral: Oct–March Mon–Sat 9.30am–5pm or longer, Sun 12.30–2.30pm, June–Aug 9.30am–7pm, Sun 12.30–2.30pm and 4.30–6pm; admission 6 €; www.christchurchdublin.ie

Dublinia: daily at least 10am–4.30pm; admission 8.50 €; www.dublinia.ie

St Audoen's Church Close by stands St Audoen's Church, the only church in Dublin that has remained unaltered from the Middle Ages. Of the original building, the 13th-century nave, where Mass is still held today, the choir, the southern transept (both roofless) and two chapels are still standing.

❶ End of April to end of Oct daily 9.30am–5.30pm; free admission

Over the centuries, Christchurch Cathedral has played a leading role in Irish history, even though it was St Patrick's Church that was elevated to cathedral status in the 13th century. When it was founded in the 11th century, the church stood on marshy land outside the city walls. In common with Christchurch Cathedral, the aspect of the church today – at a length of 93m/102yd, the largest in Ireland – is the result of overly rigorous rebuilding (1864–69). The bulky tower on the northwestern corner was erected at the end of the 14th century, its spire dates from 1739. The lofty interior, in sober Early English style, is also impressive. The cathedral has several tombs and numerous monuments. At the second pillar, to the right of the entrance, the graves of **Jonathan Swift** (1667–1745) and Esther Johnson (1681–1728) are marked by bronze plaques. Of the tombs, the

*St Patrick's Cathedral

? *Swift's Epitaph*

At the southwestern entrance of St Patrick's Cathedral, a bust of Jonathan Swift bears a Latin epitaph he wrote for himself, translating as »...where burning indignation can no longer tear at his heart.« Swift, who was dean of St Patrick's Cathedral for 35 years, lies buried here.

following are worth a closer look: to the right of the baptismal chapel (with an old baptismal font), the Boyle Monument of the Earl of Cork (1631) with several figures, of which the child probably represents Robert Boyle, who went on to become a famous physicist; and on the northern wall, opposite the entrance, a monument for **Turlough O'Carolan,** the last of the Irish Bards (1670–1738, ►Carrick-on-Shannon). The choir, which served as a chapel for the Knights of the Order of St Patrick from 1783 to 1869, features their banners, swords and helmets above the stalls. Take a literary walk in the small park of St Patrick's Cathedral: Irish writers are honoured by twelve commemorative plaques set in the wall.

❶ March–Oct Mon–Fri 9am–5pm, Sat 9am–6pm, Sun 9–10.30am, 12.30–6pm, Nov–Feb Mon–Sat 9am–5pm, Sun 9–10.30am, 12.30–2.30pm; admission 5.50 €; www.stpatrickscathedral.ie

Marsh's Library   To the right of St Patrick's, a narrow alleyway swings round to Marsh's Library, the oldest public library in the city, founded by archbishop Marsh and built in 1701 by Sir William Robinson. The library holds 25,000 volumes printed between the 16th and 18th century, maps, many kinds of manuscripts, and some incunabula, i.e. books printed before 1500. The most beautiful and oldest edition in the collection is Cicero's »Letters to Friends« from Milan (1472). During the 1916 Easter Rising the library was shelled. However, its pleasant reading room has remained practically unaltered, including the three »cages«, inside which users wishing to consult valuable books had to work under the watchful eye of the guard.

❶ Mon, Wed–Fri 9.30am–1pm and 2–5pm, Sat 10am–1pm: admission 2.50 €; www.marshlibrary.ie

THE LIBERTIES, GUINNESS BREWERY AND KILMAINHAM

The Liberties   West of St Audoen's, Thomas Street turns into James Street, leading into an area known as the Liberties, as French Huguenots fleeing religious persecution settled here – outside the jurisdiction of the city.

Guinness Brewery   Along James Street stretches the large compound of St James's Gate Brewery, better known as the Guinness Brewery. This is where around 60% of all beer drunk in Ireland is brewed (►MARCO POLO Insight p. 332). The brewery was founded in 1759 by Arthur Guinness. In the 19th century, despite rival beers being imported from England and various economic crises, it became the most important brewery in Ireland. Around 1870, it even became the biggest in the world, with exports rising. In 1936, the brewery founded its first branch abroad in London. Today the company also brews in Nigeria, Ghana, Cameroon and Malaysia. 40% of all beer produced here at the company headquarters is for export.

The **Guinness Store House**, Ireland's biggest visitor attraction, explains all stages of brewing on five floors, ending on the top floor with a panoramic view of Dublin from the ***Gravity Bar** for a tasting. Take bus no. 123 from O'Connell Street to get there.

❶ Daily 9.30am–5pm, July–Aug to 7pm; admission 16.50 €, online cheaper; www.guiness-storehouse.com

Royal Hospital

Nearby, the Royal Hospital today houses the **Irish Museum of Modern Art**. The building, erected between 1680 and 1687 after designs by Sir William Robinson, was intended for invalids and war veterans. No expense or effort was spared during the 1980s restoration of this classical building in the French-Dutch style (the tower dates from 1701). Today, the Great Hall is used for concerts, banquets and conferences. In the chapel, look out for the wood carvings and the Baroque stucco ceiling. Parts of the building were extended to create exhibition space for the Irish Museum of Modern Art. Since 1991, Irish and international 20th-century art, as well as contemporary art, has been presented in fitting surroundings. ❶ Tue and Thu-Sat 10am–5.30pm, Wed 10.30am–5.30pm, Sun 12 noon–5.30pm; free admission; www.imma.ie

Kilmainham

Follow Naas Road into town and cross the Grand Canal to reach the district of Kilmainham. Situated between Emmet Road and Inchicore Road, Kilmainham Jail, built in 1792, was used until 1924 to incarcerate many Irish patriots and rebels, of whom some were executed. The restored compound today houses a museum which keeps their memory alive. Visitors can see the cells, and numerous exhibits give an insight into the darker aspects of Irish history.

❶ April–Sept: daily 9.30am–6pm; Oct–March Mon–Sat 9.30am–5.30pm; admission 6 €

House of The Dead

On the south bank of the Liffey is the famous setting for *The Dead*, the last of the stories in James Joyce's *Dubliners*. His aunts Mrs Lyons and Mrs Callanan lived here, and John Huston filmed the story in the house. There is an exhibition on the theme and dinner parties are held in the style described by Joyce.

❶ 15 Usher's Island; daily 10am–5pm; admission/tours 10 €

My Goodness – My Guinness!

The old slogan holds true far beyond Ireland – in 150 countries across the globe. The colour of dark chocolate, this beer has been brewed in Dublin for 250 years and is a major Irish export, thanks to a consistent brand strategy and brilliant advertising campaigns

▶ Guinness erobert die Welt

Seit 2007 ist das Guinness-Bier in 150 Ländern erhältlich und wird in 50 Ländern gebraut. Eine Auswahl:

1769 **Großbritannien** ❶

1840 **New York** ❹

1801 **Karibik** ❷

1959 **Ghana** ❻ 1949 **Nigeria** ❺

1820 **Sierra Leone** ❸

1970 **Malaysia** ❽ 1965 **Japan** ❼

1973 **Indonesien** ❾

▶ Die Guinness-Dynastie

Eine Erfolgsgeschichte seit mehr als 250 Jahren

1750	1800	1850
1755 Arthur Guinness arbeitet als Brauer im County Kildare.	**1801** Erster Export von West India Porter in die Karibik.	**1850** Sir Benjamin Lee Guinness, Sohn von Arthur Guinness II, übernimmt das Familienunternehmen. Er wird Oberbürgermeister von Dublin.
1759 Arthur Guinness unterzeichnet einen Pachtvertrag über 9000 Jahre für die Dubliner St. James's Gate Brauerei.	**1803** Arthur Guinness stirbt. Sein Sohn Arthur Guinness II. führt die Brauerei weiter.	**1868** Die irische Harfe und die Unterschrift von A. Guinness werden als Markenzeichen eingeführt.
1769 Der erste Export: Sechseinhalb Fass Guinness verlassen Dublin mit einem Schiff in Richtung England.	**1833** Trotz wirtschaftlicher Flaute in der nachnapoleonischen Ära wächst Guinness weiter und wird zum größtem Arbeitgeber für Fassbinder.	**1893** T.B. Case wird der erste Mitarbeiter mit Universitätsabschluss. Bierbrauen wird nun zu einer Wissenschaft.
1799 Guinness braut nur noch Porter.	**1834** Die Glassteuer wird abgeschafft. Fortan wird das Bier in Glasflaschen und nicht in Steingut abgefüllt.	

Guinness worldwide
There is more than one kind of Guinness.
Depending on the local climate and
consumers' tastes, it is brewed with
varying alcoholic strength

Special Export Stout 8%

Foreign Extra Stout 7.5%

Bitter 4,4%

Original/Extra Stout 4.3%

Draught 4,1%

Mid-Strengh 2.8%

► **Beer consumption**
Selected countries,
consumption per head
in litres (2014):

Czech Republic
144

Germany
107

Austria
106

Ireland
81

Luxemburg
83

Lithuania
95

Poland
98

Australia
74

New Zealand
63

Croatia
80

USA
76

United Kingdom
68

1900	1950	2000

1906 sind rund 3240 Mitarbeiter bei Guinness beschäftigt. Mit deren Familien macht das rund 10 000 Menschen. Damit ist einer von 30 Dubliner Bürgern vom Erfolg des Bieres abhängig.

1929 »Guinness Is good for you«! Der auch heute bekannte Slogan taucht zum ersten Mal in einer britischen Tageszeitung auf.

1936 Der Export bleibt trotz des Krieges bis 1944 nahezu aufrechterhalten. Erst gegen Kriegsende bis Juli 1947 muss er eingestellt werden.

1959 200. Jahrestag der Gründung. Die erste Guinness-Zapfsäule wird in den britischen Pubs aufgestellt.

1960 Nigeria erlangt die Unabhängigkeit vom britischen Königreich. Ab 1963 wird Guinness direkt in Nigeria gebraut und ist somit die erste Guinness-Brauerei außerhalb Irlands und Großbritanniens.

2001 2 Milliarden Guinness-Pints werden weltweit getrunken – 1 Million allein auf den Britischen Inseln.

2007 Guinness wird in 150 Ländern getrunken und in 50 Ländern vor Ort gebraut.

2009 Guinness feiert 250 Jahre Brautradition.

250 Jahre Guinness

NORTH DUBLIN: AROUND O'CONNELL STREET

Abbey Theatre O'Connell Street, on the northern bank of the Liffey, is one of the most important thoroughfares in Dublin. To get to the famous Abbey Theatre or the elegant Custom House, follow Eden Quay in an easterly direction. The Abbey Theatre on the corner of Marlborough and Lower Abbey Street opened in 1904. The Irish national theatre, whose first directors were WB Yeats and Lady Gregory, quickly became famous internationally, but many of their performances were controversial to say the least: for instance the first nights of JM Synge's *The Playboy of the Western World* (1907) and Sean O'Casey's *The Plough and the Stars* (1926). In 1951, the theatre burnt down, and it took 15 years for the Abbey Theatre to reopen. More experimental drama is staged in the smaller Peacock Theatre.

> **? MARCO ⊕ POLO INSIGHT**
>
> *Dublin Trams*
>
> After a 55-year wait, Dublin has had a tram again since 2004: LUAS, which in Irish means something like »fast« (www.luas.ie). Both lines run above ground, meaning they have to compete with cars for the limited space on the streets. The green line connects St Stephen's Green with the southern suburb of Sandyford (journey time 22 min), the red line takes 45 minutes from Connolly Station via O'Connell Street and Abbey Street, past the Four Courts, down to the southern suburb of Tallaght.

*Custom House The former customs building is thought to be the masterpiece of the English architect of Huguenot descent James Gandon (1743–1823), who was very active in Dublin. In 1921, during the War of Independence, the Custom House burnt out completely, but the damage to the exterior was repaired according to the original designs. The best view of the long frontage, with its Doric portico and 38m/125ft domed tower above, can be had from opposite the building.

The **Custom House Visitor Centre** is devoted to the work of Gandon and the history of the Custom House.

❶ Mon–Fri 10am–12.30pm, Sat and Sun 2–5pm, Nov to mid-March closed Mon, Tue, Sat; admission 1 €

Famine Memorial Some 200m/200yd east of the Custom House, President Mary Robinson, in 1997, unveiled the Famine Memorial honouring all those who died or were forced to emigrate during the time of the Great Famine (1845–1849). The memorial represents seven life-size, emaciated figures who seem to be dragging themselves along the Quay in the direction of the harbour. The impressive monument was donated by Norma Smurfit, the well-known wife of an Irish entrepreneur. The artist was Rowan Gillespie. The sailing ship moored at Custom House Quay is the **Famine Ship Museum Jeanie John-**

ston, on which the conditions aboard for emigrants are illustrated using life-size figures.

❶ Daily 11am-4pm (admission hourly, tours only); admission 9 €; www.jeaniejohnston.ie

Originally, O'Connell Street was laid out as a wide well-to-do residential street, but it has lost many of its old buildings through the civil wars. Today, the main artery of the city, completely altered in recent years, is a vibrant commercial street with cinemas, restaurants, pubs, snack food joints and amusement arcades. The central reservation boasts statues of Irish patriots, amongst them Daniel O'Connell (near O'Connell Bridge) and Charles Stewart Parnell (both ▶Famous People), as well as the temperance activist Father Matthew. Following the street, note the imposing building of the General Post Office) on the left-hand side. Opened in 1817, it turned into the nerve centre of the 1916 rebellion led by Patrick Pearse and James Connolly. A mon-

O'Connell Street

At the end of O'Connell Street, the bridge of the same name crosses the Liffey

? MARCO ● POLO INSIGHT

The Spire

In the middle of O'Connell Street the Millennium Spire rises to a height of 120m/394ft. This new Dublin landmark had been intended to be up for the Millenium celebrations but was only completed in 2003. Weighing 126 tons and costing four million euros, the steel needle measures three metres/10ft at its base and 15cm/10 inches at its top. The Spike or The Stiletto in the Ghetto, as some Dubliners jokingly call it, stands on the site of Nelson's Column, blasted by the IRA in 1966, and is illuminated at night.

ument in the Great Hall (Death of Cú Chulainn) preserves the memory of the Irish freedom fighters. The Post Museum (access from the right of the hall) has an exhibition entitled »Letters, Lives and Liberty«, displays of stamps and information on the GPO during the Easter Rising of 1916.

❶ Mon-Fri 10am-5pm, Sat 10am-4pm; admission 2 €

The Spire replaced the sculpture of Joyce's **Anna Livia**, thought to symbolise the Liffey. Sharp Irish tongues gave the river goddess the nickname »the floozy in the jacuzzi«. Anna Livia has been installed in her new home in the Croppy Memorial Gardens facing Collins Barracks. A life-like bronze statue of James Joyce stands at the corner of O'Connell St/East Street North.

Moore Street Market
West of the GPO, St Henry Street leads to Moore Street, with colourful fruit and vegetable stalls on the street market.

St Mary's Pro-Cathedral
East of O'Connell Street, at the corner of Marlborough and Cathedral Street, stands Dublin's most important Catholic church, St Mary's Pro-Cathedral. Inspired by the Theseus Temple in Athens, it was consecrated in 1825. Every Sunday at 11am, the well-known Palestrina Choir performs here.
❶ Mon-Fri 7.30am-6.45pm Sat 7.30am-7.15pm, Sun 9am-1.45pm, 5.30-7.45pm; donation requested: www.procathedral.ie, www.palestrinachoir.com

FROM PARNELL SQUARE TO MOUNTJOY SQUARE

Rotunda Maternity Hospital
At the end of O'Connell Street , in Parnell Street, stands the Rotunda Maternity Hospital, founded as early as 1757 as Ireland's first maternity ward to combat the high rate of infant mortality. To pay for its construction, Dr Bartholomew Mosse collected funds at balls, song recital evenings and concerts held especially for this purpose. The main building with its porticos is crowned by a domed tower; an ornate stucco ceiling adorns the chapel. The Rotunda itself houses the Ambassador Cinema. In one part of the building, children are deliv-

ered still, and the Gate Theatre has had its home in the Assembly Rooms since 1929. Behind the Rotunda lies a park, bordering Parnell Square. In 1966, the Garden of Remembrance was laid out here, with the sculpture Children of Lir by Oisin Kelly (1970) dedicated to all who gave their lives for Ireland's freedom.

Since 1927, Charlemont House, built on Parnell Square North by Sir ***Hugh Lane** William Chambers in 1762, has housed the Hugh Lane Municipal **Gallery** Gallery of Modern Art. The gallery, founded in 1908, takes its name from an important member of the Irish artistic and literary scene at the beginning of the 20th century. As an art collector, Lane took an early interest in the Impressionists and subsequent art movements. He acquired an outstanding collection, including, amongst others, Camille Corot, Edgar Degas, Juan Gris, Edouard Manet, Claude Monet, Pablo Picasso, Camille Pissaro and Auguste Renoir. When Lane died, he had just loaned his collection to the Tate Gallery in London; in his will, however, he had bequeathed it to the city of Dublin. Following a lengthy legal battle, the decision was taken to show the 39 paintings alternately in the two museums. The main attraction of the gallery is ****Francis Bacon's studio**, consisting of 2,000 individual items. Left as it was at the artist's death, it was brought from London and installed with archaeological precision, including hundreds of tubes of paint. Bacon was born in 1909 in Lower Baggett Street in Dublin.

❶ Tue–Thu 10am–6pm, Fri and Sat 10am–5pm, Sun 11am–5pm; free admission; www.hughlane.ie

Next to the art gallery, the Dublin Writers' Museum occupies two ***Dublin** 18th-century houses. Whilst no. 18 honours the great Irish writers **Writers'** such as Jonathan Swift, Oscar Wilde, W B Yeats, Bernard Shaw and **Museum** James Joyce, as well as their work, with displays of manuscripts, first editions, letters, photos and the tools of their literary trade, no. 19 serves as a showcase for contemporary writers and their new work. The Chapterhouse Café and portraits of authors round off the attractions.

❶ 18 Parnell Square: Mon–Sat 10am–5pm, Sun 11am–5pm; admission 7.50 €; www.writersmuseum.com 18 Parnell Square: Mon–Sat 10am–5pm, Sun 11am–5pm; admission 7.50 €; www.writersmuseum.com

The recently renovated James Joyce Centre recreates the cramped liv- **James Joyce** ing conditions of the writer's home, with historic theatre posters and **Centre** portraits, including one of Joyce's wife Nora Barnacle, and is the starting point for tours in the footsteps of Leopold Bloom.

❶ North Great George's Street: Tue–Sat 10am–5pm, Sun 12 noon–5pm; admission 5 €; www.jamesjoyce.ie
Tours: Sat 11am, 2pm; April Sept also Tue and Thu; ticket 10 €

Croke Park GAA Museum	Some 2km/1.2 miles east of Mountjoy Square, past the Royal Canal, stands Ireland's biggest sports stadium, holding 83,000 spectators. Croke Park is supposed to host Gaelic sports (hurling, Gaelic football) only, but in recent years it has increasingly been used as a venue for pop and rock concerts. Stadium tours are on offer, including for the daring a **Skyline Tour** over the roofs, lasting two hours, for securely harnessed visitors. The on-site museum examines political aspects of sports

Museum: Mon–Sat 9.30am–5pm, Sun 12 noon–5pm; admission 6 €; www.crokepark.ie
Stadium tour: daily 11am, 1pm, 3pm, Sat and Sun, July and Aug also 12 noon and 2pm; ticket 12 €
Skyline tour: Mon–Fri 10.30, 11.30am, 12.30, 2.30pm, Sat and Sun also 1.30 and 3.30pm; ticket 25 €; www.skylinecrokepark.ie

KING'S INNS, ST MICHAN'S & THE FOUR COURTS

King's Inns Upper Dorset Street (the main arterial road towards the airport) and Bolton Street lead to Henrietta Street, a somewhat neglected dead-end, at the end of which rises the King's Inns on Constitution Hill (designed in 1795 by James Gandon; the two wings on the western façade are later additions). The King's Inns is the headquarters of the supreme Irish jurists' association. During the day, take a stroll through the inner courtyard to Inns Garden, from where there is a very good view of the building. On its western side, take the exit to Constitution Hill, from which St Patrick is said to have looked down on the city.

St Michan's Church From Constitution Hill St Michan's Church, Church Street leads to St Michan's Church, the oldest building north of the Liffey. After several restorations, not much is left of the original church, built as early as 1095: only the tower and some fragments. The church owes its grisly fame to the fact that some mummified bodies are on display in the crypt – due to the tannic acid in the air the corpses do not decompose. The crypt also holds the death mask of Wolfe Tone, one of the leaders of the United Irishmen, as well as the remains of two of his companions. Another extraordinary feature is the carving on the gallery, representing seventeen musical instruments and made from one piece. George Frideric Handel is said to have played the organ, which dates from 1724.

❶ Mid-March to Oct Mon–Fri 10am–12.45pm, 2–4.45pm, Nov to mid-March Mon–Fri 12.30–3.30pm, Sat all year round 10am–12.45pm; admission 4 €

Four Courts Near the banks of the Liffey, on Inns Quay, the Four Courts, seat of the Irish supreme court, are architect James Gandon's masterpiece.

The Four Courts building houses Ireland's highest-ranking court

Gandon built the courts between 1786 and 1802, using an older building (1776–84, by Thomas Cooley). Suffering heavy shelling during the 1922 civil war, by 1931 the building had been restored with few alterations. The river front, 139m/152yd long, with a Corinthian portico, is dwarfed by a domed round structure. In the past, the central hall below gave access to the original four courtrooms giving the building its name: Exchequer (financial matters), Common Pleas (private actions), King's Bench (penal law) and Chancery. The judges still wear black robes and white wigs today. The criminal courts have now moved out, and only civil cases are heard here.

AROUND SMITHFIELD

Head west from the Four Courts to reach cobblestoned Smithfield, an area famous for its horse fairs, held here for the past 300 years, which still take place on every first Sunday of the month. The recently revitalized Smithfield Square is illuminated twelve light masts,

Smithfield Plaza

Shoeing horses at the Smithfield horse market

26.5m/88ft high. They glow green on St Patrick's Day. In 1964 Scenes for *The Spy Who Came in from the Cold* were filmed here with Richard Burton and Oskar Werner. Smithfield is also known for its fruit, vegetable and flower markets.

Old Jameson's Distillery

In 1966, the Jameson Distillery closed its doors, merged with other whiskey producers under the name Irish Distillers and has been blending ever since in huge ultra-modern facilities in Midleton (County Cork). In the warehouse of the former distillery, the Whiskey Corner has been set up: a film tells the 1000-year story of the Irish »water of life« which may be sampled afterwards.

❶ Daily 9am-6pm, Sun from 11am; tours every 20 minutes; ticket 13 €; www.jamesonswhiskey.com

Collins Barracks

A few streets further west, the extensive 18th-century barracks compound of Collins Barracks is today **part of the National Museum**. Its collection includes furniture, glass ware, silver, ceramics and weapons. In the Curator's Choice Room, curators from across Ireland show the 25 most extraordinary and strange objects from their collections.

❶ Tue–Sat 10am–5pm, Sun 2–5pm

BALLSBRIDGE

In the southeast of the city, on the River Dodder, lies the Ballsbridge district of Dublin. To the right, the Royal Dublin Society Showgrounds occupy a large compound on Merrion Road. Well-kept lawns, low white fences, and pretty buildings form the background to the Horse Show, organized annually by the Royal Dublin Society in **Dublin Horse Show** August. This huge horse fair is said to be the largest for Irish thoroughbreds, attracting many overseas buyers (www.dublinhorseshow.com). Races, tournaments, trials, award ceremonies and auctions add to the fun. This is also an important social event, with the big hotels organizing various balls. The Spring Show in early May is dedicated to livestock, agricultural produce and machinery.

Royal Dublin Society

NORTHERN SUBURBS

Thanks to LUAS and the Phoenix Park Shuttle Bus, the largest enclosed park in Europe (800 hectares/2,000 acres) is quickly reached. The bus leaves each hour from 7am to 7pm from Parkgate Street at Heuston Station and stops at all attractions. In the **Phoenix Park Visitor Centre**, bikes can be hired for the 14km/9 miles of cycle paths in the park. It also provides an introduction to 3,500 years of natural and park history. Next door is the restored ***Ashtown Castle**, a tower house dating from the 17th century.

*Phoenix Park

Only in the visitor centre is it possible to buy tickets for ***Áras an Uachtaráin**, the seat of the Irish state president (www.president.ie). Queen Elizabeth I came here in 2011 and planted an Irish oak. Before her, Queen Victoria, George V and Prince Charles had stayed in the 29-room residence. Pope John Paul II, John F. Kennedy, Richard Nixon, Ronald Reagan, Bill Clinton and Barack Obama have also visited. The house (1751–54, by Nathaniel Clements) was previously used by the viceroys and the Apostolic Nunciature. The grounds of Áras an Uachtaráin are notorious for the **Phoenix Park Murders** in 1882, when the British chief minister for Ireland, Lord Frederick Cavendish, and his permanent secretary Thomas Henry Burke were killed using surgical instruments. An unknown group called The Invincibles claimed responsibility. Since 2004 guests have stayed nearby at ***Farmleigh House**, which used to belong to Guinness. It can be visited as part of a tour when no one is in residence.

To the left of Main Road stands a 60m/197ft obelisk, the **Wellington Monument** (1817, by Sir Robert Smirke), an eye-catcher for visitors coming from the city centre; then follow sports fields, a Victorian **walled garden** and children's playgrounds. At the northern end lies the Phoenix Park Race Course. The **Papal Cross** marks the spot where John Paul II held Mass in 1979. There is also a flower garden covering 9 hectares/22 acres and Victorian **tea rooms** on Chesterfield Avenue close to **＊Dublin Zoo**, founded in 1831, which is noted for its successful lion breeding programme and the African Plains enclosure.

Phoenix Park: park open round the clock, visitor centre April–Dec daily 9.30am–5pm; free admission; www.phoenixpark.ie

Ashtown Castle: May–Oct daily 10am–5.45pm, Nov–April Wed–Sun 9.30am–5.30pm; free admission

Áras an Uachtaráin: tours in summer on Sat, 10.15am–4pm, winter 10.30am–3.30pm

Farmleigh House and Estate: Wed–Sun 10am–5pm; free admission; www.farmleigh.ie

Walled garden: daily 10am–4.30pm; free admission

Phoenix Park Tea Rooms: April–Sept daily 10am–5.30pm, Oct–March until 4pm

Dublin Zoo: Nov–Jan daily 9.30am–4pm or longer, Feb until 5pm, March–Oct until 6pm; admission 16.50 €; www.dublinzoo.ie

＊Glasnevin Cemetery (Prospect Cemetery)

This cemetery, opened in 1832 and restored in 2010, houses 1.5 million burials, including many victims of cholera and famine. It is the last resting place of Irish patriots, including Daniel O'Connell, Charles Stewart Parnell and Sir Roger Casement (all ▶Famous People). Its landmark is the **O'Connell Tower**, with a crypt in which Daniel O'Connell's remains lie. In the **museum** and visitor centre the exhibition City of the Dead can be seen, as well as the Milestone Gallery with its 10m/30ft-long time line giving details of some of the persons buried here.

❶ O'Connell Tower: tours Mon–Fri 11.30am, 2.30pm, Sat and Sun also 1pm; ticket 6 €; www.glasnevintrust.ie

Milestone Gallery: Mon–Fri 10am–5pm, Sat and Sun 11am–5pm, admission 6 €, combined ticket with tour 10 €; www.glasnevinmuseum.ie; Tower Café open daily from 10am

＊National Botanic Gardens

The 20-hectare/49-acre Botanic Gardens in Glasnevin are well worth a visit, especially to see the Herbarium and the cast-iron Palm House, erected in 1842–50 by Richard Turner. The visitor centre displays the antlers of a giant deer, a species that died out over 8,000 years ago after the Ice Age.

❶ March–Oct Mon–Fri 9am–5pm, Sat and Sun 10am–6pm, Nov–Feb Mon–Fri 9am–4.30pm, Sat and Sun 10am–4.30pm; free admission: www.botanicgardens.ie

Casino Marino

Some 5km/3 miles out of the city centre, in the suburb of Marino, lies Casino Marino (1765–71, by William Chambers), a summer house for the Earl of Charlemont. The magnificently furnished rooms are open to visitors.

❶ End of April to end of Oct daily 10am–5pm; admission 3 €

Clontarf Road follows the northern bank of the harbour towards Howth. The old part of town lies around the fishing harbour and marina. From here, take a trip to **Ireland's Eye**, an island 2km/1.2 miles offshore (where a small church and a Martello tower are worth seeing). Rising above Howth harbour is the ruin of the collegiate church **St Mary's Church** (14th–15th century) has two naves of different lengths; in the southern nave, look for the fine tomb (approx. 1470) of the Lawrence family. To the west stands **Howth Castle**, a crenellated building dating from the 15th century that has been owned by the Gaisford-St Lawrence family for 800 years. It can be visited by booking a guide and possibly also refreshments (www.

*Howth

Howth is a pretty fishing village, known for its seafood restaurants

! *Along the cliffs* **Insider Tip**

On the eastern and southern side of the Howth peninsula, a scenic cliff walk runs along the cliffs. Take a detour to Baily Lighthouse, dating from 1814, at the southeasterly tip, and past the Chapel of St Fintan, which probably dates back to the 9th century.

howthcastle.ie). The park of the castle is accessible, featuring an 18th-century French garden, bordered by 9m/29-ft hornbeam hedges and glorious rhododendrons. Also in the grounds is the **National Transport Museum**, with historic tractors, double-decker buses, trams, etc. on display.

❶ National Transport Museum: Sat and Sun 2–5pm; admission 3 €; www.nationaltransportmuseum.org

NORTH OF DUBLIN

Newbridge House and Farm

Driving north on the N1, after 3km/2 miles take a right-hand turn (R126) to Donabate. Here, a museum opened in Newbridge House in 1992, shows rural life in 18th-century Ireland. Visitors can see Newbridge House, as well as various workshops, workers' quarters, and a farm with animals and equipment used in the 18th century.

❶ April–Sept daily 10am–5pm, Oct–March Tue–Sun 11am–3.30pm; admission to house 7 €, farm 5 €; www.newbridgehouseandform.com

Ardgillan

North of Skerries, the Ardgillan estate on the road to Balbriggan (R127) has been turned into a family attraction. The manor house, surrounded by a large park, has been restored and may be visited on tours (daily 11.30am, ticket 6.50€). Admission to the rose garden, walled garden, three ornamental gardens and **garden museum** is free. Open-air theatre is staged in the park in summer. Balbriggan itself, on the River Delvin, is a quiet holiday resort with nice sandy beaches and a nine-hole golf links.

❶ House and tea rooms April–Sept Tue–Sun 11am–6pm, July and Aug daily, March and Oct Tue–Sun 11am–4.30pm; park Feb and March 10am–6pm, April and Oct until 7pm, May and Sept until 8pm, June–Aug until 9pm; www.ardgillancastle.ie

NORTHEAST OF DUBLIN

Portmarnock

From the northeastern suburbs or from Howth, via the R106, head for the 3km/2-mile Velvet Strand at Portmarnock. This small holiday resort has a championship golf course.

*St Doulagh's Church

Some 2km/1.2 miles west of town stands the 12th-century St Doulagh's Church, with origins going back to the 5th century. It has the oldest stone roof in Ireland, a chapel and a crenellated 15th-century tower. Rooms in the crypt suggest it was once a hermit's church. The new Gothic Revival church was consecrated in 1865. Bus no. 15, 27, 42, 43 from Dublin. The buildings in the new district **Belmayne**, established in 2007, are evidence of the bursting of the Irish property bubble.

Some 10km/6 miles north of Dublin lies the popular seaside resort of Malahide. On the southwestern edge of town, surrounded by beautiful gardens, stands ***Malahide Castle**. The building features medieval, Georgian and modern elements. Inside, the remarkable great hall with its oak fittings is the only one in Ireland to have preserved its medieval aspect and to have served its original purpose up to 1975. Today, the castle houses the National Portrait Gallery, which forms part of the National Gallery in Dublin. The portraits in this

Malahide

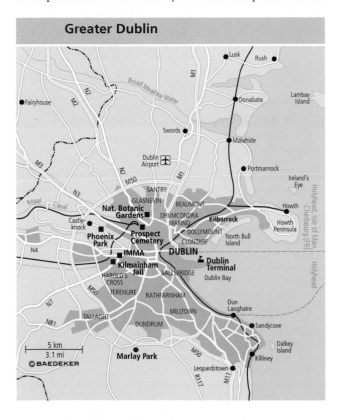

Greater Dublin

At Malahide Castle, you might expect to see a ghost on the battlements

collection are worth seeing, either because of who painted them (William Hogarth, Sir Joshua Reynolds, amongst others) or because of who sat for them (Anne Boleyn, Robert Dudley, James Gandon, Jonathan Swift, Daniel O'Connell, amongst others).

Another attraction in Malahide is the **Fry Model Railway**. It took Irishman Cyril Fry decades of work to create a model railway to a scale of 1:43, which is unrivalled in its originality and detail. Following closure for a number of years, it is due to open in the Casino House.

❶ Malahide Castle: tickets must be booked online 24 hours in advance; admission 12 €; www.malahidecastleandgardens.ie

Skerries   From Lusk, the R127 leads past the ruins of a 15th-century church and castle in Baldongan, to Skerries (good sandy beach and golf links). The **Skerries Mills Heritage Centre** looks after nine windmills and tells the history of mills since the 16th century.

❶ April–Sept daily 10am–5.30pm, Oct–March until 4.30pm; admission 6.50 €; www.skerriesmills.org

WEST OF DUBLIN

Take the R113; 4km/2.5 miles northwest of Tallaght, look for **Clondalkin**
Clondalkin, founded by St Mochuas in the 7th century. Today,
only a 25.5m/84-ft round tower is left; there are also two granite
crosses and a baptismal font in the Church of Ireland graveyard
opposite.

Up the River Liffey, the N4 leads via the suburb of Chapelizod to Lu-   **Lucan**
can, once a popular spa resort, adjoining on its western side the extensive estate of **Lucan House** (1776).
The family-run Lucan Spa Hotel (70 rooms) and the Finnstown
Country House Hotel (www.finnstown-hotel.ie) were both built
shortly after discovery of the healing sulphur springs in 1850.

On the N2 leading northwest, still on the outskirts of Dublin,   **Finglas**
Finglas has the ruins of a medieval church, with a 12th-century
High Cross in the churchyard. 3km/2 miles to the west, slightly
elevated, lies **Dunsink Observatory**, which between 1782 and
1921 was the observatory of Trinity College. Public nights with
demonstrations of the historic Grabb telescope are held on the
first and third Wednesday in the month from October to March
(www.dias.ie).

Approx. 5km/3 miles north of Finglas, to the right of the N2,   ***Dunsoghly**
stands a castle that has preserved its original oak-wood roof –   **Castle**
very rare in Ireland: 15th-century Dunsoghly Castle, a square
tower with small rectangular corner turrets. There is a magnificent view from the connecting galleries. The roof structure was to
serve as the model for the reconstruction of Bunratty Castle (►En-
nis). South of the castle lie the remains of a small chapel (1573).

Dunsoghly Castle was the setting for scenes in the film *Braveheart*
about the Scot William Wallace starring Mel Gibson.

Dundalk (Dún Dealgan)

✳ B 5

Republic of Ireland, province: Leinster
County: Louth
Population: 31,100

**Half-way between Dublin and Belfast, Dundalk is a nice, lively
but modest town, 35km/22 miles north of Drogheda, near the
border with Northern Ireland.**

Industrial town on the east coast
Dundalk has little of interest to offer the visitor but appears a busy and prosperous town thanks to various industries established here. As early as the 10th century, Dundalk saw fights at sea between the Irish and Vikings. The town was fortified in 1185, but burnt down in 1253 and 1315. After that, the town was for 300 years the corner stone of the »English Pale«, as the eastern part of Ireland under English jurisdiction was called. In 1690 King William III of Orange conquered Dundalk. The fortification was razed in 1724.

Sights in Dundalk
In the centre of town, on Crowe Street, lie the pretty court house and the town hall (both dating from the 19th century). In Seatown Place stands a mighty seven-storey old windmill, and on the main road going north the 18th-century Catholic church of St Nicholas (the tower itself is older). St Patrick's Cathedral was built in 1848, taking King's College Chapel in Cambridge as its model.

MARCO ⊕ POLO TIP

! Century Bar *Insider Tip*

The Art Nouveau interior dating from 1902 in the Century Bar creates a cosy atmosphere. On the upper floor is Quaglino's restaurant. 19 Roden Place, tel. 042 933 85 67, www.centurybar.com

The cultural heart of the town is **Dundalk Gaol**, dating from 1853. The Oriel Centre in the former men's prison is used for concerts and exhibitions, the women's prison for the county archive. Executions took place here until 1923. The **Dundalk Train Station Museum** in premises built in 1843 is worth a visit, as is the **County Museum** in the Carrol Centre, the former warehouse of a tobacco factory, where the history of the local tobacco industry is told.

❶ April–Sept daily 10am–5.30pm, Oct–March until 4.30pm; admission 6.50 £; www.skerriesmills.org

AROUND DUNDALK

Towards the Cooley Peninsula
Northeast of town, the pleasant hilly Cooley Peninsula stretches between Dundalk Bay and Carlingford Lough. Follow the N1 to **Faughart** (Foichard), the birthplace of **St Brigid**. The second patron saint of Ireland (alongside St Patrick) is commemorated here with a grotto and a church (St Brigid's Shrine). There is a nice view from the hill with the Old Graveyard; the Irish King Edward Bruce (died 1318) lies buried at its western end. The fabled hero Cu Chulainn is said to have been born nearby.

Proleek Dolmen
Continue on the N1. At Ballymascanlon, in the grounds of the Ballymascanlon Hotel, look for the Proleek Dolmen. Its capstone, weigh-

King John is said to have drafted the opening of Magna Carta in Carlingford Castle

ing some 35 tons, rests on only three legs. Legend has it that if you manage to throw a pebble onto the top of the capstone so that it stays there, a wish will be granted.

Carlingford

On the northeastern side of the peninsula lies the small old town of Carlingford (pop. 650), dominated by the bulky 13th-century King John's Castle. So named because King John stayed here in 1210, it occupies a commanding position on a rock above the harbour.
The Tholsel is a gateway and fortification tower, one of the few that remain in Ireland, that served as a customs post. Just off the Square in the centre of town, a narrow street brings you to **The Mint**, a former mint in a fortified town house that belonged to a rich family of merchants and was built in 1467 at the earliest, when Carlingford was given the right to mint coins. The town wall dates from 1326. **Taaffe's Castle**, opposite the railway station, is a large rectangular tower house with a pretty spiral stair-

case. It belonged to the Taaffe family, who became earls of Carlingford in 1661. **Ghan House** of 1727 is now a highly recommended luxury guest house (www.ghanhouse.com). The south gable of a house in Newry Street bears a curious relief made from medieval stones. It is known as »De Gaulle«, probably because of the »nose«.

Louth Ardee South of Dundalk, the small holiday resort of Blackrock has an 18-hole golf links, tennis courts and opportunities for watersports. Anglers will find plenty of salmon and trout in the River Fane. Another 5km/3 miles south (near the N1), the churchyard of Dromiskin has a round tower and a high cross, and there are several well-preserved castles in the area. Some 2km/1.2 miles south of Dromiskin, in **Castlebellingham**, Bellingham Castle, today a hotel, is located in picturesque scenery.

Dundalk

INFORMATION
Millennium Centre, Dundalk
Tel. (042) 9 33 54 57
www.dunkalk.ie

Southwest of Dundalk, the town of Ardee (pop. 8,300) boasts two town castles: Hatch's Castle and the turreted Ardee Castle, the largest medieval townhouse in Ireland. On the River Dee is a bronze statue of *Cu Chulainn Carrying Ferdia*, an episode from the most famous tale in the Ulster Cycle of sagas. St Mary's (Church of Ireland) was built using parts of an older church, featuring a nicely sculpted baptismal font. Around 3km/2 miles southeast, look out for the remains of the **Jumping Church of Kildemock** (Millockstown Church). Nobody knows why one of the church's walls relocates two or three feet from its foundations The locals claim that the church walls moved in 1715 to exclude the grave of an excommunicated member of the parish.

Louth The town of Louth, north of Ardee, used to be so significant that it gave its name to the county. St Mochta's House is a 12th-century two-storey oratory with a vault and stone roof.

Castletown Castle To the east, on the N53, almost within the town limits of Dundalk still, an earth mound rises over 18m/60ft high. This is said to be the birthplace of the fabled hero Cu Chulainn. Today, there is a nice view from the ruins on top. Nearby Castletown Castle, a four-storey building with flanking towers, dates from the 15th century.

Castleroche The ruins of 13th-century Castle Castleroche stand some 7km/4.5 miles northwest of Dundalk. This triangular building with bastions appears particularly impressive seen from the plains.

Dungarvan (Dún Garbhán)

✴ **D 4**

Republic of Ireland, province: Munster
County: Waterford
Population: 7,800
Information: www.dungarvantourism.com

Dungarvan is a lively coastal town in the centre of the south coast of Ireland. Situated around 40km/25 miles southwest of Waterford, Dungarvan is framed by the Comeragh and Knockmealdon Mountains.

The town offers visitors fine sandy beaches as well as a range of accommodation options and makes an excellent base for day trips. Dungarvan has a famous **farmers market**, held on Thursdays from 9.30am t0 2pm (www.dungarvanfarmersmarket.com), and festivals take place in the course of the year, for example a music festival in May.

Ideal base

The parts of town on either side of the Colligan River are connected by a bridge erected in 1815, spanning the water with a 22.5m/74ft arch. On the right-hand river bank stand the ruins of **King John's Castle** (1185). The historic town hall houses the Waterford County Museum. The arts centre in the 17th-century ***Old Market House** on Lower Main Street is home to changing exhibitions. Look out for a bizarre structure in the churchyard of **St Mary's**: the Old Gable Wall, with round openings that were used to pass food to lepers, but probably derive from an older church. the purpose of which is still a matter of speculation. The Augustinian abbey on the left-hand river bank was established around 1290; its tower, however, was only added in the 15th century. The Tannery Cooking School in Quay Street is a local institution. East of Dungarvan, **Clonea** is a popular small resort with a fine sandy beach and a golf course.

King John's Castle: end of May to Sept daily 10am–6pm; free admission
Waterford County Museum: St Augustine Street, Mon–Fri 10am–5pm, June–Aug also Sat pm; free admission; www.waterfordmuseum.ie
Old Market House: Tue–Fri 11am–5pm, Sat 1–5pm; free admission

? *Four-legged champion*

MARCO POLO INSIGHT

Heading west from Dungarvan, the N72 leads past a monument to a feted greyhound. Master McGrath won the prestigious Waterloo Cup three years on the trot, and in 37 races was only beaten once.

Cunnigar
Peninsula
Pleasant beaches can also be found to the south of Dungarvan town, on the Cunnigar Peninsula, accessible by ferry. Take a hike via the Ring Gaeltacht (An Rinn), famous for its Irish language school, and the old-fashioned fishing village of Ballynagaul, to the foothills of Helvick Head (R674). The walk offers many delightful views of Dungarvan Harbour and the mountains to the north.

Dun Laoghaire

✳ C 5

Republic of Ireland, province: Leinster
County: Dublin
Population: 55,000

At the beginning of the last century, Dun Laoghaire was still a small fishing village. Today, the town is a pretty suburb of Dublin, appreciated by the capital's wealthy inhabitants as a pleasant place to live.

Dun Laoghaire

INFORMATION
Dun Laoghaire
Harbour Company
Tel. (01) 280 1130
www.dharbour.ie

WHERE TO STAY
Royal Marine Hotel €€€€
Marine Road
Tel. (01) 2 30 00 30
www.royalmarine.ie
228 rooms and suites
Set in a magnificent park, this hotel

dating from 1828 has views of Dublin Bay. Amenities include and excellent health club and spa, Laurel and Hardy's Bar and a bistro.

Kingston Hotel €€€
Adelaide St (off Georges St)
Tel. (01) 2 80 18 10,
www.kingstonhotel.com, 52 rooms
With the Oliveto Italian restaurant, Library Bar and weekend offers for walking in the Wicklow Mountains.

WHERE TO EAT
Hartley's
1 Harbour Road
Tel. (01) 2 80 67 67
Closed Mon
Freshly prepared meals and a fine outdoor terrace. Cuban live music and cocktails every Thu from 8pm. The early evening 3-course menu is good value.

Dun Laoghaire (pronounced »Dun Leery«), after a visit of King George IV temporarily named »Kingstown«, had to wait until 1921 to get its old name back. This is the most important passenger port and marina in Dublin Bay. Whilst the town's fashionable residential quarters stretch east into the hills, commercial life takes place in the streets near the harbour.

**Most impor-
tant harbour
of Dublin Bay**

At the time of its construction (1817–21), the large harbour was a major feat of engineering. The eastern pier is popular for a stroll, whilst anglers congregate on the quieter western pier.

Harbour

The National Maritime Museum was set up in **the only seamen's church in Ireland**. The extensive collection highlights Ireland's sea-faring traditions with the Baily Optic whoch was worked from 1902 to 1972 in the Baily Lighthouse in Howth north of Dublin, a model of the *Great Eastern* (the world's biggest ship in 1857: 211m/692 ft long), a large collection of bottle ships, paintings, photographs, documents and much more.

**National
Maritime
Museum**

❶ Tue–Sat 11am–5pm; admission 5 €; www.mariner.ie

Two sculptures catch the eye: directly on the shore, an obelisk rising out of four stone balls was erected in honour of King George IV; one of the balls was damaged by an IRA bomb. On the other side of Queen's Road, the *Christ the King* sculpture, erected in 1926, is a monument for the soldiers who fell in the First World War. The Dominican monastery in Lower George's Street is worth a look, not least for the Celtic symbols in the oratory.

**Sculptures
and symbols**

From the harbour, a minor road runs along the swimming beach in the direction of **Joyce's Tower**. This rocky outcrop offers a sweeping view of Dublin Bay. Martello towers such as these were built to guard against a potential invasion by Napoleonic troops. James Joyce, who in 1904 lived in the tower for a while, describes it in his novel *Ulysses*. Today the ***James Joyce Museum** in the tower displays original manuscripts and rare editions of his works, as well as some of the writer's personal belongings

Imaginosity, The Dublin Children's Museum, reached by LUAS train to Stillorgan or Sandyford, caters for the under-nines with activities such as cooking and making their own TV show.

> **? MARCO ⊕ POLO INSIGHT**
>
> ### A Refreshing Dip
>
> At the foot of Joyce's Tower lies the Forty Foot Pool, where mostly elderly men take to the water in all weathers. This custom goes back to the end of the first chapter of Ulysses, where Buck Mulligan sets out to have his morning swim here. Today, women are also allowed to use the Forty Foot Pool. After 9 am skinny dipping is prohibited!

James Joyce Museum: April–Aug Tue–Sat 10am–1pm, 2–5pm, Sun 2–4pm; admission 6 €

Imaginosity: Beacon South Quarter; Mon 1.30–5.30pm, Tue–Fri 9.30am–5.30pm, Sat and Sun 10am–6pm; admission 8 €; www.imaginosity.ie

AROUND DUN LAOGHAIRE

Dalkey
To the south, merging with Dun Laoghaire, lies the little town of Dalkey, today one of the most expensive residential areas around Dublin. Two medieval fortified houses survive: what is today the town hall and ***Dalkey Castle**. In the heritage centre and museum, Tudor times are vigorously brought back to life on tours led by actors. Art exhibitions are held in the Writers' Gallery.

❶ May–Aug daily 10am–6pm, Sat and Sun from 11am, Sept–April Wed–Mon 10am–5pm, Sat and Sun from 11am; admission 6 €; www.dalkeycastle.com

West of Dun Laoghaire
Near Dundrum the **Airfield Farm and Gardens** are a haven of peace and nature.

In Rockfarnham, don't fail to visit the only pub in Ireland that is run by musicians. The ***Merry Ploughboy Pub**, where music and dance are often performed, can be combined with a visit to **Rockfarnham Castle**, built in 1583 with 18th-century interiors by Sir William Chambers. In St Enda's Park in Grange Road, the **Pearse Museum** in an old school is devoted to the life of the teacher and leader of the 1916 Easter Rising, Patrick Pearse.

In nearby Glencullen, Johnny Fox's Pub, established in 1798 (!), offers lunch from 9.95 € every day between 12.30 and 9pm (www.jfp.ie).

Airfield Farm and Gardens: daily 10am–6pm, admission 10 €; www.airfield.ie

Merry Ploughboy Pub: every evening until at least 11pm; show 20 €, dinner and show 49.50 €; www.MPBpub.com

Rockfarnham Castle: end of May to Oct daily 9.30am–5.30pm; free admission

St Enda's Park and Pearse Museum: park Oct–March daily 9am–4.30pm or longer, April–Sept until 8 or 9pm; museum Nov–Jan Mon–Sat 9.30am–4pm, Feb until 5pm, March–Oct until 5.30pm; free admission

Killiney
South from Sorrento Point stretches Killiney Bay, with a beach and resort of the same name. The garden villas on the slopes exude a distinct Mediterranean atmosphere. Beyond the railway line, which here follows the shore, lies a rocky beach, whilst Killiney Hill Park is a good place for a stroll. To the west of town, near the R117, occupying a most impressive position atop a hill near Kilternan, stands the 4,000-year-old **Kilternan Dolmen**, with its 1.80m/6ft-thick capstone

resting on ten orthostats. The privately-owned **Fernhill Gardens** lie to the north of Kilternan have wonderful old trees, and fine rockery and water gardens

❶ Tue–Sat 11am–5pm, Sun 2–5pm; admission 5.50 €

Ennis (Inis)

✦ **D 3**

Republic of Ireland, province: Munster
County: Clare
Population: 20,200

Real Irish life, and an important traffic hub in the west that is easily reached. This little town is a great place to visit with children, especially during the Flead Nuah music festival in May. Gourmets, too, will like the town.

Ennis is a traditional market town with an attractive farmers market on Friday mornings (car park on Market Street) and a long-established market from Wednesday to Saturday on the Marketplace, where there is a monument in honour of Agriculture. O`Connell

Life on the River Fergus

Ennis

INFORMATION
Arthur's Row
(Merchants Square)
Tel. (065) 6 82 83 66
www.visitennis.ie

WHERE TO STAY
Old Ground €€€€
O'Connell Street
Tel. (065) 6 82 81 27
www.flynnhotels.com
105 rooms and suites
This ivy-clad hotel has a lawn and outdoor terrace, a large car park, the Town Hall Bistro, the Poet`s Corner pub and the O`Brien Dining Room.

Rowan Tree Hostel €
Harmony Row

Tel. (065) 686 86 87
www.rowantreehotel.ie, 29 rooms
In a 17th-century house by the Club Bridge, with good food in the Rowan Tree Bar and a bike shed.

PUBS
Knox's Bar & Bistro
18 Abbey Street
Tel. (065) 682 92 64
www.knoxs.ie
DJ or live music on many evenings, traditional pub atmosphere, restaurant on the upper floor.

Street, where nice shops and ancient pubs line the way up to the O`Connell Monument, is **a wonderful place to stroll**. On the way you pass the Queens Hotel in Abbey Street, mentioned by James Joyce in *Ulysses*, the Club Bridge of 1835 and the courthouse (1850) with a striking statue of the Irish president de Valera (1979). Cornmarket Street leads to a roundabout on Mill Street, where stands a column and a life-size statue of the Maid of Erin, erected in 1881. The weirs and watermills on the River Fergus have been made into parks, and the monument to the famous hurling club of Ennis promises a special place in heaven for hurlers. For a break, try the delightful Gourmet Store in Barrack Street with its street café (www.ennisgourmet.com).

City tours Award-winning guided tours are given from May to October by Jane O`Brien (www.enniswalkingtours.com). For self-guided tours there is the sculpture trail and for children a trail to 18 so-called ***wallcandies**, some of them hidden – little wall paintings and decorative items that beautify the town (www.wallcandy.ie).

*Old Ennis Friary Standing at the end of Abbey Street, the Franciscan Ennis Friary, was founded in 1241. The church, which dates from the time of the friary's founding, was continually extended in subsequent centuries. It features particularly fine statues, amongst them a representation of St Francis with the Stigmata (on the southwestern side of the tower), the McMahon tomb (around 1475, on the southern wall), a royal tomb showing on several panels the Passion of Christ, and a small representation of the Flagellation, complete with a cockerel in the cooking pot (for an explanation of the legend, see ▶Kilkenny, St Canice's Cathedral). In the 14th century, 375 monks and 600 students lived and studied in the monastery, which continued to be inhabited by Franciscan monks until the early 17th century. Since 1892 the new Franciscan abbey has stood in Francis Street

❶ Daily 9.30am–6.30pm

Clare Museum The »Riches of Clare« is an exhibition in the county museum, showing 400 artefacts from all periods, grouped under the themes of earth, power, faith and energy. There is also a display about the healer **Biddy Early** (Bridget Ellen Connors, 1798-1874), who outlived four husbands and was acquitted of a charge of witchcraft.

❶ Arthur's Row; Tue–Sat 9.30am–1pm, 2–4.30pm; free admission; www.clarelibrary.ie

Muhammad Ali Memorial In 2009 Muhammad Ali personally unveiled his monument on Turnpike Road. Round the corner from there he visited descendants of Abe Grady, who emigrated to Kentucky in around 1860 and married a freed slave there. In 1942 his granddaughter Odessa Lee Grady Clay gave birth to Cassius Clay, the legendary boxer later known as Muhammed Ali.

AROUND ENNIS

10km/6 miles southeast of Ennis, on the R469 near Quin, impressive Quin Abbey consists of the well-preserved ruins of a Franciscan friary, erected in 1402 on the foundations of a castle that burned down in 1286. Its bastions are still visible today. The tombs in the church date from the 15th to 19th centuries. The cloister is also well preserved.

*Quin Abbey

❶ Easter–Oct daily 10am–4pm; free admission

Follow the R469 to reach, after 4km/2.5 miles, Knappogue Castle . The tower house, originally built in 1467 by the MacNamara clan and in their possession, with a brief interruption in Cromwell's time, until 1800, has been restored preserving its original style. From April to October, medieval banquets are held daily at 6.30pm

Knappogue Castle

❶ May–Aug daily 10am–4.30pm, admission 6 €

After another 2km/1.2 miles, a little road branches off to the left, leading to the Craggaunowen Project . The art collector John Hunt purchased the grounds in the mid-1960s and restored the 16th-century Craggaunowen Castle. The castle holds a small collection of medieval religious art from the Hunt Collection (►Limerick, National Institute for Higher Education). The gatekeeper's lodge to the left of the castle entrance has been converted into a chapel. Look out for the 15th-century bronze cross. Hunt has created an interesting open-air museum, reconstructing the daily life of Bronze Age man, with a Crannóg (Bronze Age lake dwelling) and a stone ring fort, both with

*Craggaunowen Project

A reconstruction of the leather boat used by St Brendan

huts and tools from that period. The leather boat used by young explorers to retrace the medieval voyage of St Brendan (►Famous People) under 6th-century conditions is on display in a glass house.

❶ Early April–Aug daily 10am–5pm; admission 9 €

Bunratty Castle treats its visitors to medieval banquets

**Bunratty Castle and Folk Park

Bunratty Castle and Folk Park is one of the main tourist attractions in Ireland. Following a chequered history of destruction and reconstruction, the castle, erected in the 15th century, was purchased by Lord Gort in 1954 and beautifully restored. Today, Bunratty Castle and its grounds are managed as a charitable foundation. The entrance hall and banqueting hall, as well as the chapel and living quarters are furnished with exquisite furniture from the late Middle Ages and Early Renaissance. Visitors can attend medieval banquets (►Practicalities) and there is a shop on the lower floor. Behind the castle lies Bunratty Folk Park, an interesting open-air museum. Numerous little houses, workshops and shops, as well as a complete village street, show life as it would have been in late 19th-century Ireland.

❶ Daily 9am–5.30pm, June–Aug Sat and Sun until 6pm; admission 15 €; www.shannonheritage.com

A few miles east of Bunratty, Cratloe Woods House, in the village of Cratloe, is a 17th-century manor. It is the only example of a traditional long house in Ireland, though considerably extended in the 19th century

Cratloe

❶ Mid-June–mid-Sept Mon–Sat 2–6pm; admission 5 €

In the Ballycasey Workshops on the access road to Shannon Airport, visitors are welcome to watch craftspeople at work and purchase their leatherware, jewellery, woollens, ceramics and much more. Gleeson Goldsmiths & Jewellery in Ballycasey House is well known

Ballycasey Workshops

❶ Mon–Fri 9am–5.30pm, Sat 9.30am–5pm; www.gleesongoldsmiths.ie

15km/10 miles south of Ennis, a little way off the N 18, Newmarket on Fergus is a small market town and commercial centre. A bit further north, Dromoland Castle (around 1830), today a luxury hotel with golf course, lies resplendent in extensive parklands. The fine gardens are open to everybody. Carrying on in the direction of Ennis, the village of Clarecastle shares a name with a destroyed castle of the same name in the River Fergus.

Newmarket on Fergus

Take the N85 northwest from Ennis, and the R476 at Fountain Cross, reaching after some 6km/3.5 miles the grounds of Dysert O'Dea. The castle, built in 1480, has been restored at great expense and houses an archaeological museum. From the castle, a 6km/3.5-mile History Trail leads to **25 archaeological sites**, all within a radius of 3km/2 miles. The church of the monastery took on its current aspect towards the end of the 17th century, following the model of the original 12th/13th-century building. The Romanesque archway, with fine geometric patterns, foliage and almost Far Eastern human masks is worth seeing. Near the northwestern corner of the church, the 12m/40ft stump of a round tower is still visible; to the east, look for a high cross in a meadow. The fully clothed figure of Christ on the Cross on the east face is unusual. The other sides are divided into panels with geometrical designs, human figures and animal interlacing.

*Dysert O'Dea

5km/3 miles further on, the award-winning **Clare Heritage Centre** in St Catherine's Church (1719) at Corofin is devoted to the traumatic events of the Great Famine in the 19th century.

Dysert O'Dea: May–Sept daily 10am–6pm; admission 4 €; www.dysertcastle.com

Clare Heritage Centre: April–Oct daily 9.30am–5.30pm; admission 4 €; www.clareroots.com+

Enniscorthy (Inis Coirthaidh)

———————— ✦ **D 5**

Republic of Ireland, province: Leinster
County: Wexford
Population: 10,850

Tranquil Enniscorthy, which celebrated its 1,500th anniversary in 2010, is a small hilly town in the southeast corner of Ireland. The town developed around a Norman castle, which is also its main attraction.

MARCO POLO TIP

United Irishmen **Insider Tip**

The award-winning National 1798 Visitor Centre documents the battle of the United Irishmen against the British on 21 June 1798 on Vinegar Hill. A multimedia presentation takes the visitor back through time, placing the event in the context of today's democracy, explaining weapons and flags, describing the course of battles and introducing the leaders. A multimedia journey through time presents the events as the birth of Irish democracy. (Mon–Fri 9.30am–5pm, Sat and Sun 12 noon–5pm; admission 6 €; www.1798centre.ie

The town lies on the western bank of the River Slaney, rising steeply on both sides, on the main Dublin–Wexford road. The river, navigable up to here, sees much boat traffic with Wexford, some 25km/16 miles further south. In 1798, one of the bloodiest battles against English rule was fought to the east of Enniscorthy.

A market and commercial hub has developed around **Enniscorthy Castle**. Cromwell conquered the castle in 1649, and the rebels who controlled the town in 1798 used it as a prison. Today, the **Wexford County Museum** shows finds from the Stone Age to the present day. The exhibits illuminate the history of the town and castle, the Easter Rising of 1916. The rooms of Henry J. la Roche and his family, who lived here from 1903 to 1951, are on show.

❶ Mon–Fri 9.30am–5pm, Sat and Sun 12 noon–5pm; admission 4 €; www.enniscorthycastle.ie

Enniscorthy

INFORMATION
1798 Visitor Centre
Tel. (053) 923 75 96
www.1798centre.ie

AROUND ENNISCORTHY

Around 13km/8 miles north of Enniscorthy, on the N11, lies **Ferns** (pop. 950), once episcopal see of the county. Three churches and other buildings occupy the grounds of the former monastery, cut in two by the road. The churchyard of the Protestant church has several high crosses. Ferns Castle (around 1200) is a large rectangular keep, reinforced by round towers.

Enniskerry (Ath na Scairbhe)

✳ C 5

Republic of Ireland, province: Leinster
County: Wicklow
Population: 1,810
Information: www.enniskerry.ie

Enniskerry is considered one of the prettiest villages in Ireland and makes a good base for hikes into the mountains.

Enniskerry, founded by the Powerscourt family in the 18th century, lies southwest of Dublin in a hollow in the foothills of the Wicklow Mountains. The entrance to the domain of Powerscourt, with gardens and landscaped park counting amongst the most beautiful in the country, is situated around 800m/0.5 miles south of the village, with a mile-long avenue leading into the estate. The manor house (1731, designed by Richard Cassels) forms the centre of the estate. It burned out completely in 1974 but was rebuilt and reopened in 1997. From the manor house the partly terraced gardens stretch up the slopes, filled with statues, mosaic floors and cast-iron latticework. Other marvels are the artificial pond, small woods with exotic trees, plantations of rhododendron and other flowering shrubs, an Italian and a Japanese garden as well as a red deer park. A relatively new attraction is perhaps the loveliest doll's house in the world: **Tara's Palace and Museum of Childhood**. Adjacent is the upmarket Ritz Carlton Hotel, built in the Palladian style, where afternoon tea in the Sugarloaf Lounge is a highlight.Several films have been shot in the parts of the park left in a more natural state, e. g. John Boorman's *Excalibur* (1980), Stanley Kubrick's *Barry Lyndon* (1975) and Lawrence Olivier's *Henry V* (1943).

**
Powerscourt House and Gardens

It is an hour's hike or a short drive to the famous **Powerscourt Waterfall**, at 120m/394ft the highest in Ireland. Here, the waters of the Dargle plunge down in magnificent cascades, especially after heavy rains.

Powerscourt Gardens: daily 9.30am–5.30pm, in winter until dusk; ballroom Sun 9.30am–1.30pm, May–Sept also Mon; garden pavilion daily 9.30am–5.30pm, Sun from 10am, Tara's Palace daily 10am–5pm, Sun from

12 noon; admission to gardens 8.50 €, Tara's Palace 12 €; www.pow-
erscourt.ie, http://taraspalace.ie
Powerscourt Waterfall: March, April, Sept, Oct daily 10.30am–5.30pm,
May-Aug 9.30am–7pm, Nov–Feb 10.30am-4pm; admission 5.50 €

Some 3km/2 miles above, the Glencree River flows into the Dargle, **Glencree**
on its course through a scenic valley from Glendoo Mountain. At **River**
the end of a rewarding drive up the valley, the road reaches a cluster
of houses called St Kevin's, formerly English barracks protecting
the Military Road. Nearby, in a hollow, lies a **German war cemetery**.

AROUND ENNISKERRY

Some 3km/2 miles north of Enniskerry, the main Dublin road cuts **The Scalp**
through a rocky pass. Between the steep slopes of the Scalp, the glaciers of the last Ice Age cut a deep cleft, depositing massive granite
blocks. The pass is not only impressive to look at, it is also popular
with climbers, offering an ideal terrain with great routes!

Fanad Peninsula

✴ A 4

Republic of Ireland, province: Ulster
County: Donegal

**This peninsula jutting far out into the Atlantic is famous for
its impressive cliffs, hiding a surprising wealth of unspoilt habitats.**

The Fanad peninsula, in the northernmost part of Ireland and Coun- **Fascinating**
ty Donegal, stretches to a length of 20km/12 miles between the nar- **peninsula**
row Mulroy Bay in the west and the broad estuary of Lough Swilly in
the east, to Fanad Head to the north.

DRIVE AROUND FANAD PENINSULA

Drive north from ▶Letterkenny on the N56, to reach Milford, situ- **Milford,**
ated at the southern tip of Mulroy Bay, with the Grey Mare's Tail wa- **Carrowkeel**
terfall nearby. Lough Fern and other smaller lakes make Milford
popular with anglers. Here, the R246 branches off north, leading

The famous Powerscourt waterfall

Arch of Doagh Beg

along the fjord-like bay. Look out for a dolmen with a massive 2 x 4 m(6.5 x 13ft) capstone just before Carrowkeel (Kerrykeel), situated at the foot of the Knockalla Mountains.

Fanad Head At the northern tip of the peninsula, Fanad Head, a large lighthouse has stood since 1817. The peninsula takes its name from High King Congal MacFergus Fanad (700–710), and is the home of famous clans, the Clintons and O'Donnels. Drive along the west coast of Lough Swilly via Portsalon to get to the **unique cliff tunnels**: most famous are the Seven Arches (up to 90m/300ft long) and the Great Arch of Doagh Beg. The village itself has a pretty harbour and an 18-hole golf links.

The R247 leads to Rathmullan (pop. 530), an attractive holiday resort with a sandy beach. The ruins of a 15th-century Carmelite friary hold a church converted into a residence by a 17th century bishop. Near the port, The Battery Visitor Centre was established in a gun battery erected in the early 19th century. The exhibition is mainly dedicated to the Flight of the Earls: following the failed uprising against the English in 1607, the local earls O'Donnell and O'Neill fled to France from Rathmullan. Their extensive estates were confiscated and handed over to English and Scottish settlers.

Rathmullan

❶ Easter–June 10am–6pm, Sun 12.30–6pm, July–Sept daily 10am–6pm, Sun from 12.30pm; admission 2 £

✶✶ Fermanagh Lakelands

✳ B 3 / 4

Northern Ireland, province: Ulster
County: Fermanagh
Information: www.fermanaghlakelands.com

A third of County Fermanagh in the west of Northern Ireland is covered by water. At the heart of the region, the lively holiday resort of Enniskillen is situated exactly between Lower and Upper Lough Erne.

Lough Erne, a maze of waterways, inlets and islands around 32km/20 miles long and up to 9.5km/6 miles wide, is considered the most beautiful lake in Ireland and a paradise for water sports and angling. In the summer, it is popular with motorboats. The lake's southern part, Upper Lough Erne, is dotted with a multitude of islets and has a more indented shoreline than Lower Lough Erne to the north. The western shore runs near the border with the Republic of Ireland.

Lake scenery with countless islets

Visitors can explore the area by land, on foot, by bike and by car along the roads that wind their way along the shore, or hire a boat in Belleek and cruise in peace and quiet between over 200 islands. Since the opening of the 61km/38-mile Shannon-Erne-Waterway (between Lough Erne and Shannon), the 360km/224 miles between Belleek and Killaloe may be covered in comfort on inland waters.

Rowing and hiking

The county town of Enniskillen is a pleasant lively place (pop. 13,600). The centre of town is situated on an islet, with the River Erne here connecting both parts of the lake. Portora Royal School, founded by James I in the early 17th century, counts both Oscar Wilde and Samuel Beckett amongst its pupils. Enniskillen has a Catholic majority. The Butter Market (1835) is now a craft centre with small shops

Enniskillen

Fermanagh Lakelands

WHERE TO STAY
Hotel Carlton ££
2 Main Street
Belleek
Tel. (028) 68 65 82 82

www.hotelcarlton.co.uk, 35 rooms
At the heart of the lakes with a wonderful view of the River Erne from the excellent Waterways Restaurant (daily from 6pm). Spa and gym.

and a café. The town hall (1857) has carved oak doors. The Clinton Centre in Main Road, with its art gallery, is the peaceful response to the IRA bomb attack of 1987, when eleven people died at a Remembrance Day religious service.

Enniskillen Castle houses the Fermanagh History Heritage Centre, as well as the museum of the Royal Inniskilling Fusiliers, which has interesting displays on the early history of Fermanagh and some reproductions of the stone statues on White Island. The military museum shows uniforms, weapons and medals. Standing on a small hill amidst a Victorian-style park, **Cole's Monument** is a tall Doric column erected in honour of Galbraith Lowry Cole (1772–1842), who was born here and served as general under the Duke of Wellington. 180 steps lead to the top of the monument.

*Castle Coole, the seat of the earls of Balmore southwest of the town centre, is now in the care of the National Trust. It is a neoclassical house dating from 1798 with fine Regency furniture and a servants' tunnel.

Enniskillen Castle: Mon 2–5pm, Tue–Fri 10am–5pm, Sat only April–Oct 2–5pm, Sun only July–Aug 2–5pm; admission 4 £

Cole's Monument: mid-April to Sept daily 1.30–3pm; free admission

Castle Coole: house daily 11am–5pm, garden daily 10am–7pm, admission 5 £

** DRIVE AROUND LOWER LOUGH ERNE

*Devenish Island

At the southern tip of Lower Lough Erne, not far from Enniskillen, lies Devenish Island . The island has the ruins of a monastery founded in the 6th century by St Molaise, including a completely preserved round tower that tapers towards the top. Some original parts of the 12th-century St Mary's Abbey and Great Church are still standing; particularly impressive is a cross of nearly 2m/6ft 6 in height. In the summer, there is a ferry to and from Trory Point (6 £). Tours of the lake with a visit to Devenish Island and its monastery start from Enniskillen, Round O and the Manor House Hotel, Killedeas.

Visitor centre and monastery: April–Sept daily 10am–5pm, Oct and March only Sat and Sun; admission included in ferry price

In the old **Killadeas Churchyard**, hewn stones dating back to the 7th and 8th centuries are considered evidence of the transition from the pagan to the Christian worldview. One of them, the **Bishop's Stone**, shows on one side a clergyman with cross and bell, on the other a grotesque **moonface** (see photo). Take the B82 along the river in the direction of Kesh to reach Killadeas Churchyard, following the sign for the Manor House Country Hotel and carrying on for 6km/3.7 miles to Killadeas. The churchyard is located past the entrance to the village, after approx. 1km/0.6 miles, on the left-hand side.

From Castle Archdale Marina there are crossings to **White Island**. On the island, a path from the pier leads to a ruined 12th-century church. Looking through the late-Romanesque doorway, stone figures come into view. Probably erected in the 7th and 9th centuries, they predate the church by a few hundred years. From left to right, there are: a Sheela-na-gig (woman with crossed legs in a provocative pose), an abbot and abbess with a priest's bell and crozier, a clergyman scratching his chin, a man holding a pair of griffins by the scruff of their necks, warriors with sword and shield, and one incomplete figure. To this day, it has not been ascertained whether these are pagan representations or the incarnation of the seven deadly sins, or indeed whether the eighth figure – a face reminiscent of a death mask – really belongs to the series.

❶ Ferry April–Sept daily each hour from 11am; 3 £

MARCO ⊕ POLO TIP

!

For mind, body and environment **Insider Tip**

At Orchard Acre Farm in Lisnarick near Irvinestown (36 Moynaghan North Road) Teresa O'Hare runs Eco Tipi Holidays, with a green cookery school. Pauline Corrigan teaches guests how to make organic cosmetics. There are also weaving courses, yoga and massages (www.orchardacrefarm.com). The garden is open free of charge for visits daily from 2pm to 5pm.

The former Royal Air Force base at Castle Archdale is part of the Castle Archdale Country Park in Lisnarick. Thanks to a secret agreement with the Republic of Ireland, British amphibious aircraft took off from here in the Second World War to hunt German U-boats in the North Atlantic. **The battleship *Bismarck*** was found by one of the Catalina patrol aircraft of No. 209 Squadron RAF stationed here. Exhibits in the visitor centre refer to these events. A butterfly garden and flower meadow are also part of the park.   **Castle Archdale Country Park**

❶ April, May and Oct Sat and Sun 1-5pm, June-Sept daily 10am–5pm, Nov-March Sun 12 noon-4pm; free admission

At Kesh (A35), it is well worth making a detour northeast to ▶Omagh, an ideal base for angling, as well as for hikes into the ▶Sperrin Mountains. On the A32, after a few miles, the road branches off towards the   **Detour to Drumskinny Stone Circle**

Boating on Lough Erne

Bronze Age Drumskinny Stone Circle (7km/4.5 miles northeast of Kesh). This circle, comprised of 39 stones, also includes a small stone cairn and a row built from twelve other stones.

Boa Island
At the northern tip of Lower Lough Erne, narrow Boa Island may be approached from both directions by a bridge connected with the shore. Stone figures, nearly 2,000 years old, lend the Christian graveyard of Caldragh a pagan air. The 73cm/29-inch Caldragh Idol, has a double head with large mouths. The long hair interlaces, with the crossed arms and the belt only hinted at. There are various interpretations of the slightly smaller Lusty Man on the neighbouring island of Lustymore, with one theory claiming it as an Iron Age goddess.

Castle Cald-well Forest Park
Some 5km/3 miles west of Boa Island, on the A47, lies Castle Caldwell Forest Park. The Fiddler's Stone at its entrance is a memorial to a drowned musician. Of the castle, only some ruins are left. Today, the park, with its pleasant walking trail, is a bird sanctuary.

The village of Belleek (pop. 830), on the border between Northern **Belleek**
Ireland and the Republic of Ireland, has been famous since 1857 for
its **porcelain manufactory**, established by a landowner who inherited the estate and wished to improve its condition and provide employment. The museum and visitor centre here attract 2.5 million
visitors yearly, making the site one of the major tourist sights in Ireland.

The Explore Erne Exhibition gives a good overview of the region
and the origins of Lough Erne.

Porcelain factory: Jan and Feb Mon–Fri 9am–5.30pm, March–June and
Oct–Dec Mon–Fri 9am–5.30pm, Sat 10am–5.30pm, Sun 2–5pm, July–Sept
Mon–Sat 10am–6pm, Sun 12 noon–5.30pm; tours every 30 minutes
Mon–Fri 9.30am–12.15pm and 1–45–4pm, June–Sept also Sat 10.30am–
12.15pm, 2–5pm; ticket 3.50 £; www.belleek.ie
Explore Erne Exhibition: July–Sept daily 10am–5pm

After a few miles' drive through Lough Navar Forest (back on the **Lough Navar**
road leading south on the western shore), a viewpoint high up on the **Forest Drive**
Cliffs of Magho offers a wonderful view over the lake. Many hiking
trails lead through the conifer forest. Comprising a few small lakes,
the forest also forms part of the Ulster Way running all the way
around Northern Ireland.

Some 5km/3 miles further on, take a detour to Tully Castle, a fortified **Tully Castle**
Plantation House with a well-preserved protective wall. The gardens,
laid out in the style of the 17th century, are exquisite, the herb garden
in particular.

❶ April–May Sun 12 noon–4pm, June–Sept daily 10am–5pm; free admission

Monea Castle, the best-preserved Plantation Castle in Ireland, stands **Monea Castle**
a little apart from the lake on a rock. Built in 1618 by Protestant immigrants, its style (the towers, in particular) is reminiscent of Scottish
castles.

✳ DRIVE AROUND UPPER LOUGH ERNE

Heading southwest from Enniskillen, a 8km/5-mile drive leads to the **Sheelin**
popular holiday resort of **Bellanaleck**. Lacemaking has a long tradi- **Antique Lace**
tion in Fermanagh; the local museum has a fine collection from the **Museum**
period between 1850 and 1900. Lace, linen and oil lamps can be purchased here.

For taking a break, the Sheeling Tea Shop and its restaurant are recommended.

❶ Shop all year Mon–Sat 10am–6pm, museum only April–Oct; admission to
museum 2.50 £; http://irishlacemuseum.com

Florence Court   West of the A32 (heading for Swanlibar), a byroad leads to Florence Court. Dating from the 18th century, this is one of the finest manor houses in the region. The exquisite rococo stucco above the stairs and the collection of Meissen porcelain and copperplate engravings are particularly worth seeing. In the park, look for the original Florence Court Oak, said to be the ancestor of the Irish oak.

❶ April and Oct Sat and Sun 11am–5pm, May and Sept Sat–Thu 11am–5pm, June–Aug daily 11am–5pm; admission to garden and park 4.50 £, house 4 £

Marble Arch Caves   Continuing on the byroad, visit the Marble Arch Caves, situated on the northern flank of the Cuticagh Mountains: a cave system with lakes and waterfalls, 700m/800yd of which have been made accessible to visitors. The guided tour starts with a subterranean boat trip past impressive stalactites and stalagmites. The caves are part of the new Global Geopark.

❶ Mid-March to June and Sept daily 10am–4.30pm, July and Aug until 5pm; admission 8.75 £: www.marblearchcavesgeopark.com

Crom Estate   Back on the A509, cross the Upper Lough Erne at Derrylin. To the south stretches the 760ha/1,878-acre Crom Estate, with woods, parks and marshland. Of the castle, only some ruins are left, but the area is excellent for hiking, boating, biking or camping. The **Belle Isle Cookery School** in nearby Lisbellaw (www.irishcookeryschool.com) has an outstanding reputation. Day-long and even month-long courses on new Irish cuisine are on offer.

Crom Estate: mid-March to Oct, grounds daily 10am–7pm, visitor centre daily 11am–5pm; admission 3.50 £

Fermoy (Mainistir Fhear Muighe)

✳ D 3

Republic of Ireland, province: Munster
County: Cork
Population: 5,880

Information: http://fermoy.ie/tourism

Amongst sports anglers, Fermoy is considered the most important fishing centre in the south of Ireland. Regular championships are held in and around Fermoy.

Angling centre in the south   The Blackwater river flowing through Fermoy is particularly rich in salmon. Its tributaries are good for river trout fishing and roach, not found elsewhere in Ireland.

AROUND FERMOY

In County Tipperary, a good 25km/16 miles north-east of Fermoy, Mitchelstown Caves is an extensive **system of stalagmites and stalactites**, including Desmond's Cave, named after a 16th-century earl of Desmond who had a high price on his head and used the cave as a hiding place. The New Cave, also boasting fine stalactite and stalagmite formations, was only discovered in 1833. At 120m/130yd long and 12m/39ft high, the New Cave can claim to be the largest cave in the British Isles.

Mitchelstown Caves

❶ Daily April–Sept 10am–5.30pm, Oct from 10am with variable closing time; admission 7 €; www.mitchelstowncave.com

The drive west on the N 72 passes the village of **Killavullen** and, to the west on a cliff above the River Blackwater, the home of the Hennessy family, whose cognac distilled in France is world-famous today. The town of **Mallow**, 30km/19 miles west of Fermoy, in the wooded valley of the River Blackwater (good fishing), has an important sugar industry and was a popular spa in the 18th and 19th centuries. Alongside the Courthouse and the Market House, look out for a pic-

West of Fermoy

The picturesque ruins of Mallow Castle

turesque bell tower, 18th-century residential houses and reminders of the town's heyday: the old Spa House, the race course and Spa Glen, with three bubbling wells on Fermoy Road. At the southeastern end of town, next to a small museum, the turreted ruins of Mallow Castle date from the 16th century. The Rebel Trail, which links places related to Irish independence and the civil war, passes through Mallow.

* Galway (Gaillimh)

✦ C 2

Republic of Ireland, province: Connacht
County: Galway
Population: 76,800

In summer holidaymakers from all over the world join the Irish in the largest city in the west of Ireland. Galway is the seat of a bilingual university, contributing to the city's young atmosphere. Over half of »Galwegians« are between 14 and 44 years old.

Gateway to the wild west of Ireland

In the past 30 years, Galway has experienced a big economic boom and substantial increase in population (over 40 %) rivalled by few other European cities. At the same time, the cultural importance of the city has increased, and tourism is booming too. Situated in a picturesque location on the northeastern tip of Galway Bay, where the plentiful waters of the River Corrib empty into the Atlantic, Galway is a good base for exploring ▶Connemara. As the capital of the county of the same name, it is an episcopal see and has a university (part of the National University of Ireland), where most lectures are held in Irish. The Taebhdhearc na Gaillimhe theatre also keeps Gaelic culture and language alive.

History

There has been a settlement at this site since prehistoric times. The building of the castle (1124) and its conquest by Richard de Burgo (1232) marked the fast rise of Galway to a booming Anglo-Norman town. Fourteen families of noble merchants (»Tribes«) turned Galway into a kind of city-state, loyal to England despite several attacks by the Irish – who were not allowed into the town. In 1473, a big fire destroyed the town, rebuilt subsequently. Trade with western European countries, including Spain, made Galway wealthy. In the 16th and 17th centuries a Free School famous for its scholarship is said to have had 1,200 pupils, but as the town sided with the Irish, large parts were razed by Cromwell's army. During its conquest by the forces of King William III (1691) Galway suffered further damage.

Numerous festivals and fairs are held, e. g. a jazz festival (February), a literature festival (April) and a film festival (early July). The **Galway Arts Festival** lasts for two weeks (end of July / early August), with theatre, art and music events, as well as a parade.

At the end of July, **Galway Race Week** involves a typically Irish fair at the race course in Ballybrit (3km/2 miles to the east). A high-

Festivals

Galway

Where to stay
1. Hotel Meyrick
2. Spanish Arch Hotel
3. Adare Guesthouse

Where to eat
1. Viña Mara
2. The Seafood Bar@Kirwan's Lane
3. Mc Donagh's Seafood Bar

Pub
1. Tigh Neachtain

Galway

INFORMATION
Galway City Aras Failte
Forster Street
Tel. (0 91) 53 77 00
http://galwaycity.galway-ireland.ie

SHOPPING AND GOING OUT
Latin Quarter
The student district of Galway, a pedestrian zone, has lots of entertainment in summer. There are shops, hostels, pubs, restaurants and the Druid Theatre (www.druid.ie), with street performances and music on every corner (www.thelatinquarter.ie).

WHERE TO EAT
❶ Viña Mara €€€
19 Middle Street
Tel. (0 91) 56 16 10
www.vinamara.com

Closed Sun evening
Chic but relaxed, with attentive service. The dishes are Mediterranean, with Irish and other influences. Brunch on Sat and Sun from 12.30pm is reasonably priced.

❷ The Seafood Bar @Kirwan's Lane €€€
Kirwan's Lane
Tel. (0 91) 56 82 66
http://kirwanslane.com
Closed Sun midday
Galway lobster salad is a real treat. Oysters, salmon and dishes from the grill are also good.

❸ McDonagh's Seafood Bar €€€
22 Quay Street
Tel. (0 91) 56 50 01

light of the year however is the **Galway International Oyster Festival** in late September, with the World Oyster Eating championships.

SIGHTS IN GALWAY

John F. Kennedy Memorial Park
The centre of town since 1710, **Eyre Square** was renamed John F Kennedy Memorial Park following the visit of the US president in 1963, but both names are used today. The memorial park is the green campus with a bust of Kennedy, the Browne's Doorway and the Quincentennial Fountain. A row of flagpoles on the square commemorates the great writers who were associated with Galway, including Joyce and Beckett. The statue of the Gaelic-language poet Pádraic O'Conaire (1882–1923) has been taken to the new City Museum at the Spanish Arch.

Hall of the Red Earl
The oldest medieval building in Galway, the Hall of the Red Earl (Halla an Iarla Rua), can be seen through glass on Flood Street. It was built by the De Burgo family in the 13th century.

www.mcdonaghs.net
Closed Sun
A fine, traditional, award-winning
seafood joint. Fish and chips in the bar,
dishes such as mussels with black pudding, bacon and balsamico reduction in
the restaurant.

PUB
❶ Tigh Neaachtain
17 Cross Street
Tel. (0 91) 56 88 20   **Insider Tip**
www.tighneachtain.com
A great choice of whiskeys, live music
every Sunday from 9pm. Bar food, and
upstairs the excellent Artisan Restaurant
(www.artisangalway.com)..

WHERE TO STAY
❶ Hotel Meyrick €€€€
Eyre Square
Tel. (0 91) 56 40 41
www.hotelmeyrick.ie

99 rooms and suites
Imposing Victorian hotel in the city centre, elegantly furnished, with a spa and
a rooftop swimming pool.

❷ Spanish Arch Hotel €€€
Quay Street
Tel. (0 91) 56 96 00
www.spanisharchhotel.ie
20 rooms
Modern rooms in the heart of the Latin
Quarter. Inexpensive restaurant serving
lunch and dinner, parking spaces 8 € per
day.

❸ Adare Guest House €
9 Father Griffin Place
Tel. (0 91) 58 26 38
www.adareguesthouse.ie
11 rooms
The oldest guesthouse in Ireland, familyrun, with an excellent breakfast.

From Eyre Square, Williamsgate Street, one of the city's main shopping streets, leads to 16th-century Lynch's Castle. The grey building, decorated with coats-of-arms is today occupied by the Allied Irish Bank, which was rescued by the state in 2010. It was much altered during restoration works in the 1960s. The castle was once the residence of the Lynchs, a noble family that provided several mayors. ***Lynch's Castle**

James Lynch, an incorruptible mayor dedicated to the common good, condemned his own for the murder of a Spanish sailor and carried out the hanging himself, as no-one else was willing to do the deed. Then he retired to a monastery. The event is commemorated by Lynch's Window on Market Street, said to be the place where the execution took place. The expression »to lynch somebody« is said to have its roots in this story. **Lynch's Window**

St Nicholas Church (Collegiate Church of St Nicholas of Myra), also on Market Street, was built in the 14th century. Altered several times, it still looks like a medieval parish church. Look out for the three-gabled western façade, the gargoyles (rare in Ireland), as well as ***St Nicholas Church**

A sunny alley in the old quarter of Galway

tombs and a lectern inside. The noticeable feature of the church clock is that it only has three clock faces. The northern side is empty

❶ Daily 9am–7pm, Jan and Feb until 5pm; free admission (donation requested); www.stnicholas.ie

Nora Barnac-le birthplace

The birthplace of Nora Barnacle, the wife of James Joyce, is a few steps from the church (no. 8 Bowling Green). Here, in the smallest museum in Ireland, there are literary evenings on Wednesdays in summer.

❶ June to mid-Sept daily 10am–1pm, 2–5pm; admission 2.50 €; www.norabarnacle.com

On Kirwan's Lane there are still many traces of the 16th and 17th centuries to discover. Fourteen Norman merchant families, the Tribes of Galway, shared all commerce in Galway between themselves. The fourteen medieval lanes that bear their names form the core of the old town. After its redevelopment, the quarter is now buzzing with life, many cafés, good restaurants and shops.

Kirwan's Lane

Built in 1594, the Spanish Arch city gate, on the left bank of the Corrib, is all that remains of a bastion that was part of the city walls, designed to protect the ships of the mostly Spanish merchants from looting. The newly built **Galway City Museum** next door is dedicated to the history of the city since prehistoric times and shows modern art in changing exhibitions.
On **Spanish Parade**, a sculpture presented by the city of Genoa commemorates the visit of Christopher Columbus to Galway in 1477.

Spanish Arch

Galway City Museum: Tue–Sat 10am–5pm, Sun 12 noon–5pm; free admission; www.galwaycitymuseum.ie

On the other side of the Wolfe Tone Bridge lies the old fishing village of Claddagh. For centuries, it harboured an independent cooperative of fishermen, until it had to make way for modern buildings. Claddagh was immortalized in the song Galway Bay and its Claddagh Ring.

Claddagh

Further north, **Salmon Weir Bridge**, built in 1818, spans the River Corrib. In the spring, this is a good spot to watch thousands of salmon congregating on the river bed before starting their trek upriver. From the sea to ▶Lough Corrib they only have to clear 6km/3.5 miles.

The **Cathedral of St Nicholas** on the right bank of the river was consecrated in 1965. Its limestone façade and interior with Connemara marble are impressive. dimensions – 100m/330ft long and 47m/155ft wide – make it one of the largest churches in Ireland. Note also the rose windows and mosaics in the side chapels. The organ was made by the Irish organ maker Trevor Crown. The famous cathedral choir

MARCO POLO TIP

! *Claddagh Ring* Insider Tip

The Claddagh Ring can be seen all over the world where there is Irish influence. It shows a heart held by two hands topped by a crown, and stands for friendship, loyalty and love. If the tip of the heart points towards the hand, the wearer's heart is taken; if it points to the fingertips, the wearer's heart is still free. The ring has been worn since the middle of the 18th century. Today, it is more popular than ever, mostly bought as a souvenir. The oldest Claddagh rings can be seen in a display at the jeweller Thomas Dillon's Claddagh Gold in Quay Street.

sings during Mass on Sundays at 11.15am. In July and August, concerts are given on Thursdays at 8pm by international performers. The cathedral stands on the site of a former prison, remembered by the **Gaol Memorial** behind the car park. Northwest of the cathedral stand university buildings. The gardens on the river island are a pleasant place for a stroll.

❶ Daily 8.30am–6.30pm; free admission (donation requested); www.galwaycathedral.ie

Salthill, Claregalway

The beach of Salthill can be reached on foot from the city centre. The national aquarium **Atlantaquaria** shows the marine life of the west coast of Ireland in the Splash Tank, where an artificial wave breaks every 40 seconds, and the Ocean tank, which hold 120,00 litres of sea water. Northeast of the city, on the N17, lies the village of Claregalway with the ruins of a Franciscan friary founded in 1290. In the church, a tomb features the representation of a primitive plough.

Atlantaquaria: Mon–Fri 10am–5pm, Sat and Sun 10am–6pm; feeding time 1pm, 3pm, 4pm; admission 11.50 €; www.nationalaquarium.ie

AROUND GALWAY

Clarinbridge and Kilcolgan

Driving south from Carnmore via Oranmore on the N18 brings the visitor to Clarinbridge, a pretty little village famous for its excellent oysters and mussels. Some 2km/1.2 miles further on, in **Kilcolgan**, the N67 turns off to the right. Around 1km/0.6 miles west of the main road lie the ruins of Drumacoo Church, with fine sculptures on window and portal walls. Also look out for the impressive holy well associated with St Surney.

Dunguaire Castle

Drive further southwest on the N67 to reach .the fully restored Dunguaire Castle. This is a fortified 16th-century tower house, named after Guaire, King of Connacht. From April to October **medieval banquets** are held in the hall with readings from the works of Synge, Joyce and Gogarty.

❶ Early April to early Oct daily 10am–5pm, banquets Mon-Sat 5.30 and 8.45pm, Sun 5.15 and 7.45pm, booking required by tel. 061 36 0788; admission 6 €, banquet 56 €

Brigit's Garden

Northwest of Galway, shortly before reaching Oughterard, lies Brigit's Garden, in Roscahill. Four beautiful gardens are related to themes in Celtic culture. There are activities for children, a round house, a ring fort, nature trails and a café.

❶ Feb–Oct daily 10am–5.30pm; admission 7.50 €; www.brigitsgarden.ie

Glencolumbkille (Gleann Cholm Cille)

—————————— ✳ B 3

Republic of Ireland, province: Ulster
County: Donegal
Population: 720

Information:
www.gleanncholmcille.ie

Glencolumbkille, Irish Gleann Cholm Cille (St Columcille's Valley), is a picturesque holiday resort at the most westerly point of County Donegal in a valley that opens up towards the Atlantic on Glen Bay.

The area boasts a sandy bay and splendid sections of cliff, reached via a boggy treeless upland valley, following the dark-brown Owenwee River. The area around Glencolumbkille is one of the Irish-speaking parts of Donegal. St Columba/Columcille lived and meditated at this lonely spot. According to a legend, Bonnie Prince Charlie, the last Stuart pretender to the thrones of Scotland and England, spent time here whilst on the run. When Glencolumbkille was threatened in the mid-20th century by the lack of employment, Father James McDyer founded a cooperative in order to optimize agricultural production. Successfully harnessing the locals' craftmaking skills, McDyer was able to create better markets for their produce. Thatched cottages were built for holidaymakers, whilst the Folk Museum attracts daytrippers.

Picturesque holiday resort

MARCO ⊕ POLO TIP

Insider Tip
Summer courses

In order to preserve the cultural heritage of the region, the Ulster Cultural Foundation (Foras Cultúir Uladh) offers various courses between March and October, teaching Irish, the dances of Donegal or the fiddle, harp or bodhrán drum, tapestry weaving or painting (the shoreline and seascapes). On offer are also group hikes and archaeological workshops (for more information, call 073/30248 or email oifig@oideas-gael.com).

This open-air museum can claim to be one of the best folk village museums in the country. Situated at the western end of the village, it consists of four thatched houses with furnishings and equipment that represent different periods of Irish life between 1700 and 1900, as well as a school building. Two newer cottages demonstrate the work of cobblers and fishermen. There are also exhibits about the American painter Rockwell Kent and the Welsh writer Dylan Thomas. The museum shop has local produce for sale and the tea shop offers tasty home-made snacks.

Folk Village & Museum

❶ April–Sept Mon–Sat 10am – 6pm, Sun noon – 6pm; admission 4.50 £; www.glenfolkvillage.com

Every year, on 9 June (St Columcille's feast day), a **pilgrimage** takes place, with the pilgrims obliged to walk around the 15 stations in the valley three or seven times (by sunrise). They also lay down a pebble at the foot of the standing stones and pray. Southwest of Glencolumb-kille, **Malinmore** is a pretty holiday resort around a bay lined by pic-turesque cliffs, offering diving, snorkelling and fishing. At Cloghan-more, look for a approx. 3,500 year-old court cairn. **Rathlin O'Birne** The coastal waters around the island of Rathlin O'Birne offer rich fishing. The island has some antiquities as well as a lighthouse.

★★ Glendalough (Gleann dá Loch)

✦ C 5

Republic of Ireland, province: Leinster
County: Wicklow

Nestling in a romantic valley with two lakes, the monastic settlement of Glendalough has retained its magic to this day.

Splendid location
This once very important holy site, founded by St Kevin in the 6th century, lies inland from the east coast of Ireland, just under 40km/25 miles south of Dublin. On the main R755 road leading south from Bray, through the mountains to Arklow, a wooded valley opens up to the west at Laragh. After passing it, a further 2km/1.2-mile-drive brings you to the village famous both for its architectural monuments and its beautiful scenery: the ruins of the monastic town of Glendal-ough (Gleann dá Loch means »valley of the two lakes«). In the sum-mer months at weekends, many daytrippers come to visit; it is qui-eter during the week. The valley belongs to the Glendalough Forest Park, part of the ▶Wicklow Mountains, offering many opportunities for hiking, hillwalking and climbing.

History
St Kevin started out living here as a hermit, but his pious erudition attracted so many students that he founded a monastery. When the saint died at a very old age, in 618, the monastery was just begin-ning to flourish. Later, over a thousand pupils are said to have lived there. The annals report Viking attacks and several fires in the 12th century, whilst in 1163, Abbot Laurence O'Toole was anointed archbishop of Dublin. In 1214, the Normans assigned the monas-tery to the episcopal see, and another fire in 1398 marked the be-ginning of a slow but definite decline. The buildings were restored in 1875–80; since then, their architectural fabric has been well preserved.

The monastic site is open at any time. Parking is available at the visitor centre. The best thing to do is to begin with the informative video in the visitor centre and then to start the tour through the grounds from the Upper Lake, where the nucleus of the site was located. The pretty Green Road leads from the Upper Lake to the remains of the monastic settlement: alongside a model of the monastery, there are various tomb slabs, capitals and other finds from the monastic site. Look out for a 12th-century high cross (market cross), showing a Crucifixion, an abbot, and interlacing ornaments. This cross probably used to stand on the pilgrimage route to Glendalough.

Visitor centre

❶ Mid-March to mid-October daily 9.30am–6pm; at other times until 5pm; admission 3 €; www.heritageireland.ie

The well-preserved round tower dates from the 10th century

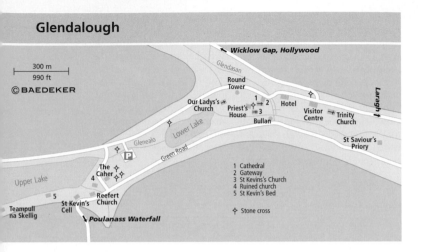

Glendalough

Wicklow Gap, Hollywood

Glendasan

300 m
990 ft
© BAEDEKER

Round Tower

Our Ladys's Church
Priest's House
Bullan

1 → 2   Hotel
→ 3

Visitor Centre
Trinity Church

Laragh

St Saviour's Priory

Glenealo
Lower Lake

Green Road

Upper Lake

P
The Caher

1 Cathedral
2 Gateway
3 St Kevins's Church
4 Ruined church
5 St Kevin's Bed

Reefert Church

⚹ Stone cross

4

5
St Kevin's Cell

Teampull na Skellig

Poulanass Waterfall

Upper Lake The small rectangular **Teampull na Skellig church**, built on a rock, is only accessible by boat. The oldest parts of the partly restored church date back to the late 7th century. Steep steps carved into the rock lead to a small cave known as **St Kevin's Bed**. In the Bronze Age, this rock cave probably served as a burial site. **St Kevin's Cell** – a beehive hut where the saint is said to have lived, is easier to access. Near a small bridge stands the 11th-century **Reefert Church**, with a choir and nave.

To the right of the car park, between the Upper and Lower Lakes, the remains of an ancient stone fort (the Caher) as well as three stone crosses are visible. They probably served as boundary markers and were later used as stations on the pilgrimage route.

Lower Lake The main cluster of monastic buildings stands downriver, near the visitor centre. They date from the time of the monastery's heyday and were accessed through the gateway. The nearby round tower, with a height of 31m/102ft and a diameter of 5m/16ft, is preserved in its original state, apart from the top of its cap, restored using old stones. Its entrance is situated over 3m/10ft above ground.

Next door, at St **Mary's Church**, erected in the 10th century from granite blocks, the faithful worshipped at the tomb of St Kevin well into the 18th century. The **Priest's House** is a 12th-century Hiberno-Romanesque building, with a much older lintel relief above the entrance door. The largest church in the grounds of Glendalough is the **cathedral**, with choir, nave and sacristy (11th and 12th century). It lost its cathedral status in the early 13th century.

A most remarkable architectural monument in Glendalough is **St Kevin's Church**, erroneously called »Kitchen« because of its chimney-like bell tower. St Kevin's was built in the 11th/12th century, of hard mica schist, with a pitched roof. The interior still holds a few stone masonry finds from the region.

On the right-hand side of the road leading to Laragh stands the 11/12th-century **Trinity Church**, which preserves its original granite chancel arch.

To the east, beyond the river, the most recent cluster of buildings, the 12th-century **St Saviour's Priory**, was restored around 1875. There are some very good examples of Romanesque stonemasonry on the chancel arch and windows, as well as some outbuildings.

Gort
(Gort Jase Guaire)

✴ C 3

Republic of Ireland, province: Connacht
County: Galway
Population: 2,640
Information: www.gortonline.com

The little market town of Gort lies far out to the west of Ireland, south of Galway Bay – an ideal base for exploring the sights of the area!

The broad through road of this pleasant town is lined by 18th-century houses. Typical for an Irish provincial town are the tall chimneys, the grey, unadorned façades and large market square.

Typical provincial town

AROUND GORT

To the north of town, west of the N18, lies Coole Park. Many Irish writers used to visit this manor house (destroyed in 1941), which was the residence of writer Lady Gregory (1852–1932) a friend of W B Yeats and supporter of the Irish literary revival. What has remained is a magnificent cedar-lined avenue and the Autograph Tree, a copper beech with a trunk that shows the carved initials of writers, amongst them George Bernard Shaw, W B Yeats and Sean O'Casey.

Coole Park

The Coole Park Interpretative Centre has information on the flora and fauna of the park and a portrait collection of Lady Gregory and her literary friends.

3km/2 miles north of Gort, off the N 18 to Galway, lies Kiltartan. here the blind poet Rafferty is said to have fallen in love with Máire ni hEidhie, »the Beauty of Ballylee«. W.B. Yeats wrote »My country is Kiltartan Cross, my countrymen Kiltartan's poor«. The **Kiltartan Gregory Museum** presents the works of Lady Augusta Gregory in the old schoolhouse dating from 1892.

❶ Easter–Sept daily 10am–5pm, July and Aug until 6pm; free admission; www.coolepark.ie

June–Aug daily 10am–6pm, at other times only Sun 1–5pm; admission 3 €

*Thoor Ballylee Amidst picturesque river scenery, 7km/4.5 miles north of Gort, stands Thoor Ballylee, a 16th-century four-storey keep. The poet William Butler Yeats (▶Famous People) bought and restored the tower, living there from 1921 to 1929, as shown by a stone plaque with his verses. The tower houses a museum with Yeats memorabilia and first editions of his works. Like Coole Park, Thoor Ballylee is a stop on the ***Yeats Trail** (www.discoverireland.ie/yeatstrail).

❶ May–Sept Mon–Sat 9.30am–5pm; admission 6 €

The strong medieval tower house Thoor Ballylee

Southwest of Gort, on the R460, the ruins of the former monastic site of **Kilmacduagh** nestle in green pastures on a lake, with the Burren as a backdrop. The round tower is 34m/112ft high and leans at an angle, 60cm/2ft out of perpendicular. Its entrance, at a height of 7.80m/26ft, can only be reached via stairs. Next to the tower stands the Cathedral (12th/15th century) with nave, choir and transepts. In the northern transept, look out for some interesting traditional representations of the Crucifixion. To the right of the cathedral stands St John's Church. Of all the other smaller churches, O'Heyne's Church in the northwestern corner is the most beautiful: animal and plant motifs adorn the pillars of its chancel arch. Across the road, opposite the cathedral, is St Mary's Church.

Grand & Royal Canals

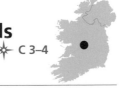

✦ C 3–4

Republic of Ireland, Central South
Information: iwai.ie

The Grand Canal is an important recreation area popular with amateur skippers. On the canal banks, mingle with anglers and people out for a walk.

The 130km/80-mile canal leads right through the province of Lein- **Grand Canal**
ster, connecting Dublin Bay with the ▶Shannon and Barrow rivers.
It was built between 1756 and 1804; further branches were added
in the 19th century. Barges with heavy loads used the canal up to
1960, when commercial transport on the linking canals was ended.
The differences in elevation are overcome by 52 locks in total.
(Boats must not be over 18.5m/60ft long, 3.9m/12ft wide, have a
draught over 1.2m/4ft or a height above water level over 2.75m/9ft).
Every boat coming through the canal has to have a name or number, and the highest permissible speed is 8mph/5kmh. Keep to the
right and overtake on the left; the locks may only be passed in daylight. Boats can be hired at several towns along the canal. To obtain
a guide with descriptions of the canal, contact the Waterways Visitor Centre in Dublin (▶ p.324) or download it from www.iwai.ie/
publications.

Like the Grand Canal, the Royal Canal starts its 146km/91-mile jour- **Royal Canal**
ney in ▶Dublin and also connects Dublin Bay with the ▶Shannon and
Barrow rivers. It runs further north than the Grand Canal, meeting
the river above Lough Ree. There are 47 locks. After a planning and
preparatory period of over 30 years, building work on the Royal Canal began in 1792. In 1817, the link with the Shannon was established, as well as canals connecting nearby towns, which resulted in
a significant increase in cargo and passenger transport. However,
towards the end of the 19th century, there was an inexorable decline
in the amount of cargo and number of passengers and, in 1961, the
Royal Canal was officially closed to commercial shipping. Today, the
Royal Canal Amenity Group strives to preserve the canal as cultural
heritage and a recreation area.

The Royal Canal is **rewarding for boating holiday**s. The dimen- **Boats and**
sions of the boats are determined by the smallest of the lock cham- **anglers**

bers: 22.9m/75ft long and 4m/13ft wide, permitting a draught of 1.4m/4.5 ft. The lowest bridge has a height of 3.05m/10ft. In the Royal Canal, anglers can hope for bream, roach, red-eye, tench, pike and the occasional trout. Canal guides and maps are available from the Ireland Waterways Association at the Waterways Visitor Centre in Dublin (▶ p.324) or downloaded from www.iwai.ie.

Horn Head (Corrán Binne)

✳ A 4

Republic of Ireland, province: Ulster
County: Donegal

Horn Head is the tip of a peninsula jutting out into the Atlantic in the far north of the country. A scenic highlight!

Birders' paradise with a view
The N56 leads to the beautifully located holiday resort of Dunfanaghy, a good base for trips to Horn Head and the surroundings. Dunfanaghy has a harbour (Port-na-Blagh), an 18-hole golf links and fine sandy beaches. The Dunfanaghy Workhouse Heritage Centre on the southwestern edge of town has exhibitions on the New Lake (next to it) and the life of *Wee Hannah*, a tale of hard work and hunger. A hike along the western coast of the peninsula to the actual **Horn Head** is especially recommended: The point falls steeply 180m/590ft down to sea, with the ocean stretching into infinity beyond small islands and promontories, whilst the view inland offers mountain ranges, with Mount Muckish and Mount Errigal in the background. Driving straight across the peninsula towards the point, the best views of the cliffs can be had from the east from Traghlisk Point.

❶ Mon–Fri 10am–4pm, Sat and Sun until 5.30pm; admission to exhibitions 4.50 €; www.dunfanaghyworkhouse.ie

Ards Peninsula
Southeast of Marble Hill,Ards Peninsula has a Capuchin monastery. The grounds and park may be visited by appointment. The area of the peninsula jutting into Sheep Haven Bay is a wild bird sanctuary and stretches across the northern coast of the ▶Ards Peninsula. South of the monastery, on another peninsula, the ruined **Doe Castle**, a four-storey building within a turreted yard, dates back to the 16th century. The churchyard holds the graves of many leading Donegal families.

Creeslough
Some 10km/6 miles south of Dunfanaghy lies **Creeslough**, with picturesque Duntally Bridge and a waterfall. Look out for the modern church of St Michael's.

* Inishowen Peninsula (Inis Eoghain)

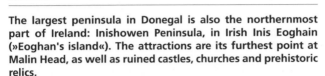

※ A 4/5

Republic of Ireland, province: Ulster
County: Donegal
Information: www.visitinishowen.com

The largest peninsula in Donegal is also the northernmost part of Ireland: Inishowen Peninsula, in Irish Inis Eoghain (»Eoghan's island«). The attractions are its furthest point at Malin Head, as well as ruined castles, churches and prehistoric relics.

Largest of Donegal's northern peninsulas

On its western side, the inlet of Lough Swilly leads far inland, whilst to the east, the bay of Lough Foyle forms the border with Northern Ireland as an inland lake. To the north, the open ocean embraces the coastline of Malin Head. A signposted route (Inis Eoghain 100) leads 160km/100 miles around the peninsula, though this may be shortened by cutting through inland.

Buncrana

The main town in the region, with 3,750 inhabitants, is Buncrana. This pleasant holiday resort owes its popularity mainly to the 5km/3-mile Lisfannon Beach on the eastern shores of Lough Swilly (www.visitbuncrana.com). The well-preserved **O'Doherty's Keep**(14th to 17th century) is an architecturally simple structure in a pretty location on the water. Beyond the bridge, the manor house of Buncrana Castle is unfortunately falling into disrepair. Also of interest is the restored **Tullyarvan Mill** Tullyarvan Mill on the edge of Buncrana (heading for Dunree Head), housing an art exhibition, a textile museum, a small arts and crafts shop and a hostel. Find out about the history of the place, its flora and fauna as well as the mill and the linen industry. Exhibitions are held here, and, on summer evenings, cultural events with traditional Irish music take place. ❶ Tullyarvan Mill: tel. 074 936 16 13; double room 40 €; www.tullyarvanmill.com

Sights south of Buncrana

On Lough Swilly, 6km/3.5 miles south of here, lies the village of **Fahan**. In the churchyard of the former monastery, look for an early cross slab dating back to the 8th century: two standing figures can be seen on the side of the cross shaft, the cross itself is covered in exquisite interlacing. On one of the short sides (the northern one), look for a Greek inscription – rare in Early Christian Ireland.
Some 3km/2 miles further on, the path branches off towards **Inch Island**, connected with the mainland and famous for the many bird species living here. The way south passes Grianán of Aileách.

Drive around Inishowen Peninsula

From Buncrana, take the byroad going northwest to **Dunree Head**; at Fort Dunree, 6km/3.5 miles down the road, consider a visit to the **Guns of Dunree Military Museum**. Videos explain the history of the fort and the region, including the landing of Wolfe Tone on this coast during the rebellion of 1798.

Carry on via the breathtakingly steep **Gap of Mamore pass** (with a gradient of up to 30%!). Its strange beauty is best appreciated by driving it from south to north. At the end of the pass, Dunaff Head awaits, with a stunning view. The cliffs here are **great for climbers**. Carry on, via Clonmany to **Ballyliffin**, popular with visitors because of its 3km/2-mile Pollan Beach. Jutting up at the northern tip of the Doagh Peninsula, the scenic ruins of Carrickabrahey Castle lie right by the sea. The **Doagh Famine Village**, ten minutes by car from Ballyliffin, is devoted to the famine of the 1840s and Irish customs such as the funeral wake.

Next stop is **Carndonagh** (pop 2,540), a little town with a tradition of shirt manufacture and breweries. Opposite the church stand three early Christian monuments, amongst them the 7th-century St Patrick's Cross, one of the earliest in Ireland. The cross shape is still only suggested, the lower part shows a human figure with outstretched arms, and smaller figures standing at its side. The back of the cross is decorated with interlacing and another figure. To the right and the left of the cross, look out for standing stones adorned with reliefs, showing David with the harp and a bird and a man with two bells, amongst others. Further monuments can be found in the churchyard.

Drive north for another 5km/3 miles. The road passes Malin, from where the R242 leads past the pretty country house of Malin Hall (1758) towards **Malin Head**, with a splendid view of the neighbouring cliffs! A short walk (1km/0.5 miles) leads west to Hell's Hole, a narrow and deep rock cavern offering a great natural spectacle at high tide. Southeast from Malin Head towards Glengad Head, cliffs stretch for many miles – rising to 240m/787ft above the sea. The angling centre of Culdaff lies south of these cliffs.

After another 3km/2 miles, in **Clonca**, look out for a ruined church with a remarkable if badly weathered high cross (with representations of the miracle of the loaves and fishes and St Peter fishing) and a finely carved gravestone. There are further historical remains in the area: the Bocan Stone Circle to the east and a group of high crosses in Carrowmore, to the southwest.

The R238 leads to **Moville**, a holiday resort on Lough Foyle, once a port on the transatlantic route. Approx. 4km/2.5 miles to the northwest, **Greencastle**, has the ruins of a large castle, built in 1305. Nearby stands a Martello tower, erected in 1810 (today a hotel). The themes of the Maritime Museum by the harbour are the local fisheries and Irish emigration. The attached planetarium presents astronomy with a laser show and rock music. In the nearby **Cairn Visitor**

Trawbreaga Bay near Inishowen

Centre in Drumaweir, the singer-songwriter Patsy Cavanagh takes visitors through Irish history from early days to the coming of Christianity and the Vikings. Plays are staged here in summer.

Drive northeast on the R241 to reach **Inishowen Head**. From here, another splendid stretch of cliffs stretches northwest, with views across to Northern Ireland. This and the attractive valley of Glenagiveny make the area popular with tourists. Some 0.5km/500yd north of **Muff** a path turns off to the left towards the fine Ardmore Gallan, a heavily decorated Bronze Age stone. At the junction of the R238 and the N13, the modern St Aengus Church is a round structure with a strip of windows and curved tent roof topped by a glass pyramid. This conspicuous building is said to be influenced by the shape of the Grianán of Aileach, only 4km/2.5 miles further south. Near Muff, the Catholic Iosas Centre in Derryvane provides tranquillity for contemplation with a 6-hectare/15-acre Celtic Prayer Garden dedicated to Irish saints, and a reconstruction of the cell of St Columba.

Guns of Dunree Military Museum: June–Sept Mon–Sat 10.30am–6pm, Sun 1–6pm, at other times Mon–Fri 10.30am–4.30pm, Sat and Sun 1–6pm; admission 5 €; www.dunree.pro.ie

Doagh Famine Museum: Easter–Sept Mon–Sat 9.30am–5.30pm, Nov–Dec 9.15am–5.30pm; admission 7.50 €; www.doaghfaminevillage.com

Maritime Museum: Easter–Sept Mon–Sat 9.30am–5.30pm, Sun 12 noon–5.30pm; admission 5 €, with planetarium 10 €; www.inishowenmaritime.com

Cairn Visitor Centre: April–Oct daily 11am–6pm; free admission, donation requested; www.thecairncentre.com

Iosas Centre: Mon–Thu 9am–5pm, Fri 9am–4pm, Sat and Sun 3–5pm; donation requested; www.columbacommunity.com

*Grianán of Aileach   The Grianán of Aileach (Grianán means »palace of the sun«) is a round **stone fort** dating back to early Christian times. It commands an elevated position, surrounded by three concentric earth walls. The fort's windowless wall, built without the use of mortar, is 5m/16ft high and, at its foot, 4m/13ft thick. It encloses a grassy space accessed via a low passage. Small chambers were laid out inside the wall. It is not known when this site was built; between the 5th and the 12th centuries however, it was the seat of the Kings of Ulster. Razed in the 12th century, the fort was restored at the end of the 19th century, then again between 2011 and 2007. A 150-year-old stone church in Burt beneath the monument houses the **Grianán Ailigh Visitor Centre** (tel. 074 680 80, not always open). ***View** The walls of the ring fort afford **panoramic views** across the green, undulating hillscape, from Lough Swilly to the Fanad Peninsula.

* Kells (Ceanannus Mór)

— C 5

Republic of Ireland, province: Leinster
County: Meath
Population: 5,890
Information: tel. 046 924 88 56

Kells was once an important centre of early Christian culture. Today, the town still holds some remnants of medieval times.

Hearing the name of the town, most people think first of all of the famous Book of Kells, a jewel of Irish book illumination. The Gospel manuscript, stolen in 1006, is today kept in the library of Trinity College in ►Dublin (►MARCO POLO Insight p. 68). Visitors can at least see a facsimile edition in the **Kells Heritage Centre** in the old courthouse. As early as the 6th century, St Columba founded an ecclesiastical site here. In the 9th century, monks from Iona in Scotland, fleeing the Vikings, came here. In subsequent centuries, the monastery was plundered and re-established several times. The town, fortified by the Normans, hung on to its position up to the dissolution of the monastery in 1551. Of the once mighty fortifications, nothing is left today. The ruins of the monastery consist of the round tower and three high crosses. The bell tower of the St Columba's Church (1778) is also medieval.

Small town with important monastery

The eleven medieval and historic buildings of the town can be discovered on a **heritage trail**, and eight plaques provide information.

❶ May–Sept Mon–Sat 10am–5.30pm, Sun 4–6pm, Oct–April Mon–Sat 10am–5pm; admission 4 €; www.meathtourism.ie

The former monastery churchyard is located in the centre of town. It is easy to find: look out for its 30m/100ft 10th-century round tower with five windows. Next to it, the South Cross, probably dating back to the 9th century and dedicated to St Patrick and St Columba, is richly decorated: at the base, a procession of chariots, animal-like creatures and interlacing can be made out. The southern side shows the Fall, Cain and Abel, the three young men in the furnace, above them Daniel in the lion's den, the sacrifice of Isaac (left), St Paul and St Anthony in the desert (right) and David with the harp, as well as the miracle of the loaves and fishes (top). The western side has representations of the Crucifixion and Christ in judgment, David killing the lion and the bear, as well as a number of panels with scrollwork and mythical beasts.

*Round tower & South Cross

The cross and round tower are reminders of Ireland's mystic past

Some 30m/35yd away, the preserved rump of a very large cross features biblical scenes, some of them of ambiguous iconography. The **Market Cross** in the centre of town was made much later. An

inscription says that it was erected in 1688 following a 9th-century model, in the tradition of medieval High Crosses.

*St Columcille's House
Northwest of the South Cross, outside the churchyard walls, stands St Columcille's House. The oratory with its steeply vaulted stone roof possibly dates back to the 10th century. The thick, sloping walls meet at the ridge; a steep ladder leads to the wall of a chamber supporting the roof. The oratory is closed, but can be visited on arrangement with the Kells Heritage Centre.

AROUND KELLS

Loughcrew Cairns
Heading west from Kells for some 20km/12 miles, the R168 and R154 run through the range of hills of Slieve na Calliagh (»mountain of the witch«). On the road between Drumone and Millbrook, the burial ground of Loughcrew is well worth visiting. Around 30 passage graves lie on two neighbouring elevations, only some of them featuring discernible burial chambers. Of particular interest is Cairn T in the eastern group. Measuring 36m/118ft in diameter, it houses a large chamber with side chambers, as well as decorated stone blocks. From up here, there is a wonderful sweeping view over the fertile plains of Meath. The key is available from the excellent coffee shop of Loughcrew House and Gardens.

The gardens, with large sculptures by Ann Maldon Hugh, can be visited on three-hour guided tours (3 €). The activities at the adventure centre are zip-lining, archery and climbing (admission from 30 €). There is also an annual Loughcree opera weekend in late June (www.loughcrew.com).
❶ Loughcrew Cairns: guided tours end of May to Aug daily 10am–6pm; free admission

Hill of Lloyd
The only inland lighthouse in Ireland, built in 1791 by the Earl of Bective, lies on a hill with a view of five counties. The ascent must be booked in the Kells Heritage Centre (tel. 046 924 78 40). In **Castlekieran** the memory of St Ciarán's is preserved. **Ciarán's Church** He was a hermit who moved from Kells to the banks of the Blackwater River in the 8th century. Three simple high crosses, an early Christian tombstone and a holy well are to be seen.

Mullagh
In Mullagh the **St Kilians Heritage Centre** is dedicated to the life and martyrdom of the apostle of Franconia (now a region of Bavaria). Kilian was born in Mullagh in 640 and died in Würzburg around 689. The Würzburg Glosses, dating from about 750, are regarded as the earliest extant Irish manuscript. There is a display about the Ogham alphabet (▶MARCO POLO Insight p.35)
❶ Easter–Oct Tue–Fri 10am–6pm, Sat and Sun 2–6pm; admission 3 €

Kildare (Cill Dara)

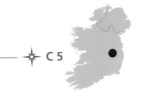

✴ C 5

Republic of Ireland, province: Leinster
County: Kildare
Population: 8,410
Information: www.kildare.ie

Brigid of Kildare (453–521), revered as Ireland's second patron saint alongside St Patrick, founded her famous double monastery for monks and nuns here, under the shared supervision of an abbot and a nun.

The eternal flame that was kept burning by the nuns only went out at the dissolution of the monastery in the 16th century. On 1 February 2006 (St Brigid's Day), President Mary McAleese unveiled the St Brigid's Flame Monument on the marketplace. In 2012 the **Kildare Town Heritage Centre** in the 18th-century Market House was even visited by the Dalai Lama, who then meditated in the cathedral. A heritage trail leads visitors to the sights of the town.
❶ May–Sept Mon–Sat 10am–1pm, 2–5pm; free admission; www.kildare.ie

Famous monastery

A reminder of the glorious past of the town is St Brigid's Cathedral. Dating from 1223, the cathedral was restored several times, most recently in 1875–96. Of the medieval tombs inside, the most interesting is the tomb of Fitzgerald of Lackagh (died 1575). On the north side of the cathedral are the foundations of the ancient **St Brigid's Fire Temple**.
❶ May–Sept Mon–Sat 10am–1pm, 2–5pm; donation requested

St Brigid's Cathedral

In Tully, on the southern edge of Kildare, note on the left the ruins of the Black Abbey and on the right the path to St Brigid 's Well, where there is a bronze sculpture of the saint by Anette McCormack. The road on the left heads to the Irish National Stud). a 20-minute walk from the visitor centre leads to the ****Japanese Gardens**, laid out at the beginning of the 20th century by Japanese gardeners, using plants imported specially for the purpose. The 20 stations of the Way of Life were designed by the landscape gardeners to symbolize life's path from the cradle to the grave. Leave through the Gateway to Eternity. Don't miss a guided tour of the National Stud – many famous race horses were born here. The stud was founded around 1900 by the Scotsman William Hall-Walker, who used eccentric breeding methods: stallions and mares were mated according to their star signs, and every foal was given its own horoscope. If this did not please the manager, the foal would be put up for sale. In 1915 Hall-Walker gave his stud to the English government, and in 1943 it passed to the Irish

**Irish National Stud

state. Walking around the grounds, look out for the valuable breeding stallions, in spring and early summer, the breeding mares enjoying the pastures with their foals, or a saddle-maker and a blacksmith at work. Rocks and water are the themes of **St Fiachra's Garden**. The Irish Horse Museum, documenting the history of the horse from the Bronze Age to the present day. One exhibit on display is the skeleton of Arkle, one of the most famous Irish racehorses.

To the east of the stud, in the plain of the same name, lies the world-famous race course **The Curragh**, where all five Irish classic races are held here, the Derby since 1866.

Irish National Stud: mid-Feb to Nov daily 9.30am–6pm; tours daily 12.30, 2, 4pm; admission 12.50 €; http://irishnationalstud.ie

AROUND KILDARE

Hill of Allen
The top of the Hill of Allen, 8km/5 miles north of town on the R415 used to be the site of a castle belonging to the Kings of Leinster. Now, a tower offers a commanding view of the surrounding countryside.

Old Kilcullen
To the east, on the River Liffey – the bridge dates back to 1319 – lies the small town of Kilcullen. 3km/2 miles to the south, in Old Kilcullen, the remains of a monastery founded by St Patrick are still visible: fragments of a high cross and a round tower. **Dun Ailinne** Between Kilcullen and Old Kilcullen, to the west of the N78, lies **Dun Ailinne** hill fort, once the residence of the kings of Leinster.

Kilkee (Cill Chaoi)

✴ **D 2**

Republic of Ireland, province: Munster
County: Clare
Population: 1,020
Information: www.kilkee.ie

Kilkee is a pleasant family resort in the west of Ireland, which rose to fame as a diving centre. When the property bubble burst, many empty holiday homes remained here.

Pretty coastal town
Lying on a semi-circular bay with a long sandy beach, Kilkee is shielded against the Atlantic Ocean by the Duggerna Rocks. Head west along the beach to pass some impressive rock formations – dominated by the 60m/200ft Lookout Hill. On a clear day, there are good views from here, but take care at the edge of the cliffs!

In 2006 the Hollywood star Russell Crowe unveiled a statue of the Irish actor and film director **Richard Harris** (1930–2002), known for example for play Albus Dumbledore in the first two Harry Potter films.

AROUND KILKEE

Southeast of Kilkee lies the market town and port of Kilrush (pop. 2,700). Kilrush Creek Marina, 3km/2 miles south from here, on the mouth of the River Shannon, has good moorings and is a useful supply stop for yachts, which may be chartered here too. Pack a picnic and take a walk under the old trees of Kilrush Wood, east of town. The main attraction is the **Vandeleur Walled Garden**. The Kilrush Creek Adventure Centre at the marina runs sailing and canoeing courses, and the **Shannon Dolphin Centre** offers dolphin-watching trips. In Moyasta, train fans can visit the **West Clare Railway & Heritage Centre** to learn about railway history.

Kilrush

Vandeleur Walled Garden: April–Sept Mon–Fri 10am–5pm, Sat and Sun 12 noon–5pm, Oct–March Mon–Fri 9.30am–4.30pm; free admission; www.vandeleurwalledgarden.ie
Shannon Dolphin Centre: April–Oct; ticket 22 €; www.discoverdolphins.ie
West Clare Railway & Heritage Centre: April–Sept daily 12 noon–5pm; admission 8 €; www.westclarerailway.ie

From Kilrush, a ferry goes across to Scattery Island; pick up some information from the **Scattery Island Centre** on Merchants Quay. Until 1978, the island measuring just under 1 sq km/0.4 sq miles was inhabited; today, the village is in ruins. However, the island can look back on an important ecclesiastical past, starting with St Senan's founding of a monastery in the 6th century. The monastery's heyday was in the 14th and 15th century; it was destroyed during the reign of Elizabeth I.

Scattery Island

The round tower, with a height of 35m/115ft one of the highest in Ireland, can be seen from afar. An unusual feature is the entrance door at ground level. To the east stands a cathedral, to the north a 12th-century Romanesque church, and to the southeast, an early Christian church with medieval extensions.

Scattery Island Centre: June–Aug daily 10am–6pm; free admission

The N67 ends at Killimer, from where you can take a car ferry over the mouth of the Shannon to Tarbert (near ▶Ballybunion). The ferry saves a detour around the mouth of the River Fergus and the Shannon of about 90km/56 miles.

Killimer

❶ Ticket for car and passengers 18 €; www.shannonferries.com

From Kilkee to Loop Head   A recommended drive starts from Kilkee on a minor road southwest along the coast, past Fooagh to Fooagh Point, with its holy well and spectacular rock scenery of tunnels, caves and cliffs. Via the peninsula, the road leads to **Carrigaholt**, where the ruins of a tall, slender 15th-century tower house standing above the harbour are worth seeing. The castle yard is well preserved too. The village has a language college teaching Irish. Drive west along a scenic route to **Loop Head**, with its lighthouse and stunning views. The cliffs just offshore are Diarmaid's and Grainne's Rock.

★★ Kilkenny (Cill Chainnigh)

✦ **D 4**

Republic of Ireland, province: Leinster
County: Kilkenny
Population: 22,200

Kilkenny, without a doubt the most beautiful inland town, is also called »Marble City«. Indeed, polished Kilkenny limestone is everywhere, looking like the blackest marble.

Medieval inland city   The city lies in the southeast of Ireland on the banks of the peat-brown River Nore. Winding streets and lanes lend Kilkenny a special charm, rows of pretty Georgian houses add elegance. Over the last centuries, extensive restoration works have been carried out on the historic fabric, so that today, the overall impression is of a medieval city. Since times immemorial, Kilkenny has been divided into three districts: Irishtown, with the cathedral as a landmark, High Town, dominated by Kilkenny Castle, and, on the other side of the River Nore, the eastern district, with St John's Priory. The Kilkenny Design Centre enjoys an excellent reputation all over Ireland and has in recent years been highly influential, setting new trends in high-end Irish produce and packaging design. Many of the craftspeople and artists living in the city try to benefit from the prestige of this institution. A farmers market takes place on Thursday mornings on the Parade, while the Market Yard has been home to a country market on Fridays and Saturdays for over 50 years. For gourmets there is the Kilkenny Food Trail (www.trailkilkenny.ie) through the town and county, for cyclists the Kilkenny Cycling Trail, for lovers of the arts an annual festival in August with dance, theatre, classical music and visual arts (www.kilkennyarts.ie).

History   It was St Canice who built a church here in the 6th century. In pre-Norman times, Kilkenny was the seat of the kings of Ossory, later falling to the Ormondes. In the 14th century, parliaments convened

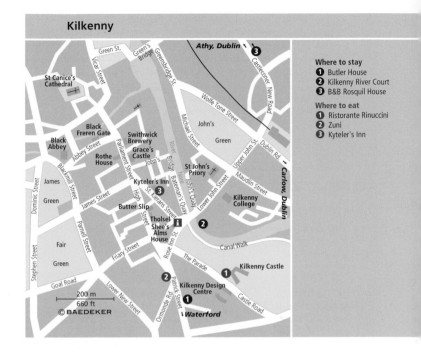

Kilkenny

Athy, Dublin ❸

Green St.
Vicar Street
Green's Bridge
Greensbridge St.
St Canice's Cathedral
Castlecomer New Road
Wolfe Tone Street
Black Freren Gate
Michael Street
John's
Green
Black Abbey
Swithwick Brewery
Grace's Castle
Abbey Street
Parliament Street
Rothe House
River Bridge
Bateman's Quay
John's
St John's Priory
Upper John St.
Dublin Rd.
Carlow, Dublin
Blackmill Street
James
Green
James Street
Kyteler's Inn ❸
St. Kieran's Street
High Street
John's Quay
Lower John Street
Maudlin Street
Dominic Street
Butter Slip
Kilkenny College
Parnell Street
Tholsel
Shee's Alms House ❷
Stephen Street
Fair
Green
Friary Street
Rose Inn St.
The Parade
Canal Walk
Kilkenny Castle ❶
Goal Road
Lower New Street
Ormonde Rd.
Patrick Street
Kilkenny Design Centre ❶
Castle Road
❷
200 m
660 ft
© BAEDEKER
Waterford

Where to stay
❶ Butler House
❷ Kilkenny River Court
❸ B&B Rosquil House

Where to eat
❶ Ristorante Rinuccini
❷ Zuni
❸ Kyteler's Inn

here several times. The infamous parliament of 1366 issued by decree the Statutes of Kilkenny: no Anglo-Norman was allowed to marry an Irishwoman, take on Irish customs, speak Irish or wear Irish clothing. The Irish, on the other hand, were not allowed to live in a walled town. Though rigidly implemented, the laws were not able to stop the mixing of Anglo-Normans and Irish. From 1642 to 1648, the city was the seat of the Confederation of Kilkenny, an association of Old Irish and Anglo-Irish Catholics as an independent parliament. However, this assembly split, and the Anglo-Irish came to an agreement with the English. In 1650, Cromwell took the city, granting the besieged an honourable withdrawal.

SIGHTS IN KILKENNY

The Norman fortress occupies a commanding position above the River Nore amidst the flowerbeds of a large park and is one of the most famous castles in the country. William de Marshal started building the castle on this site, which already had a wooden tower, in

*Kilkenny Castle

the 13th century. From 1391 to 1931, the property, which was repeatedly altered over the course of the centuries, was the residence of the Butler family. Some of the former formal reception rooms have been restored. Most attractive is the Long Gallery, with a fine tapestry and a splendid vault painted with Celtic and pre-Raphaelite motifs. The gallery has been extended to show portraits of some members of the Butler family. The Butler Gallery is considered one of the most important Irish art galleries outside Dublin.

❶ Oct–April 10am–4.30pm or longer, May–Sept 10am–5.30pm; free admission; www.kilkennycastle.ie, www.butlergallerycom

Kilkenny

INFORMATION
Shee Alms House
Rose Inn Street
Tel. (0 56) 775 15 00
www.kilkennytourism.ie

WHERE TO EAT
Ristorante Rinuccini €€€€
1 The Parade
Tel. (0 56) 7 76 15 75
www.rinuccini.com
Named after the 17th-century archbishop, a »bon vivant« and ambassador of the Holy See in Ireland, this is a family-run restaurant with classic Italian cuisine.

Zuni €€€€
26 Patrick Street
Tel. (0 56) 7 72 39 99
www.zuni.ie
The chic modern design in leather and dark wood draws the rich and beautiful into this former theatre. Daring, generous and varied dishes are served with a smile. The attached hotel has 13 rooms.

Kyteler's Inn €€
Kieran Street
Tel. (0 56) 772 10 64
www.kytelers.ie

This historic pub serves international dishes, with an emphasis on fresh produce. Worth seeing!

WHERE TO STAY
Butler House €€€€
16 Patrick Street
Tel. (0 56) 7 76 57 07
www.butler.ie
13 rooms and suites
This Georgian building, once the residence of the Earls of Ormond, has been refurbished to a contemporary style and equipped with all modern amenities.

Kilkenny River Court €€€
The Bridge, John Street
Tel. (0 56) 772 33 88
www.rivervourtshotel.com
90 rooms
Modern rooms with traditional colour schemes, fine views of the river.

B&B Rosquil House €€   **Insider Tip**
Castlecorner Roadt
Tel. (0 56) 7 72 17 14
www.rosquilhouse.com
7 en-suite rooms
Irish hospitality and an excellent breakfast. A self-catering apartment is also available..

From President Street, Irishtown Bridge and St Canice's Steps (1614) lead to one of the most beautiful cathedrals in Ireland, St Canice's Cathedral. The church seen today was begun around 1251 on the foundations of an earlier building and completed in 1280. The low, sturdy 14th-century tower and the walls of the side aisles, transept and clerestory are crenellated. The interior has kept its spacious light-filled character despite various restorations (most recently in 1863–1864). Numerous fine tombs survive, amongst them in the northern side aisle that of Henry de Ponto (the oldest, dating back to 1285) and Edmund Purcell (1549). The latter is remarkable because of the **representation of a living cockerel in the cook pot**, an image sometimes found on Irish sculptures. In the choir, look for the tombs of the Bishop of Ledrede (1360) and Bishop Rothe, in the southern transept the tomb of the eighth Earl of Ormonde and his wife (1539) and, in the southern side aisle, those of Viscount Mountgarrett in knight's armour, Bishop Walsh (1585), as well as one with a lady wearing a traditional Irish garment. The black-marble St Ciaráns Chair in the northern transept and a 12th-century baptismal font in the nave are also worthy of note. Near the southern transept, in the

*St Canice's Cathedral

Kilkenny Castle goes back to the Middle Ages

grounds of an early Christian cemetery, stands a round tower of around 30m/100ft height, built between 700 and 1000. The tower offers fine views of the city and surroundings, but the staircase is very narrow and steep!

❶ April, May and Sept daily 10am–1pm, 2–5pm, June–Aug daily 9am–6pm, Oct–March 10am–1pm, 2–4pm; close Sun morning all year admission 4 €; www.stcanicecathedral.com

Black Abbey   Black Abbey was formerly part of a Dominican monastery founded in 1225, so it was not the stones that gave the monastery its name, but the monks' black habits. The southern transept and the tower date mainly from the 14th and 15th centuries. Inside, look out for the medieval alabaster sculpture of the Holy Trinity and a roughly carved oak wooden figure of St Dominic.

❶ Daily 8am–7pm; donation requested

*Rothe   Rothe House (1594–1610) in Parliament Street is a merchant's house
House   built in the Elizabethan style, with two inner courtyards. In the hall, antique oak furniture, paintings and items of clothing are on display. The building also houses a museum, where the antlers of a giant deer, an extinct species are on show in the Phelan Room. A historic garden lies behind the house.

❶ April–Oct Mon–Sat 10.30am – 5pm, Sun 3–5pm, Nov–March Mon–Sat 10.30am–4.30pm; admission 4.80 €; http://rothehouse.com

Smithwick's   Heading south from Parliament Street, cross the small Bregagh River,
Brewery   the border between Irishtown and High Town. Directly to the left, in the grounds of Smithwick's Brewery, the remains of St Francis' Friary (founded around 1232) are still visible. It was around that time that the fine seven-light east window was made. Smithwick's is the oldest brewery in Ireland – even without considering the friary, where beer was probably made centuries ago. Beer lovers may take part in a guided tour of the brewery, with a tasting session afterwards.

❶ Tue–Sat 12.30, 1, 3, 3.30pm; ticket 10 €; www.smithwicks.ie

Black Freren   To the right, on Abbey Street, stands a gate of the old town fortifica-
Gate   tions, Black Freren Gate. To the left, on Parliament Street, look out for the courthouse, erected on the ruins of 13th-century Grace's Castle. At the corner of Bateman's Quay and St Kieran's Street, a monument commemorates the Confederation Hall, where parliament convened in 1642–49. St Kieran's Street leads to the oldest house in Kilkenny, Kyteler's Inn.

From Butter   Some 70m/80yd further on, a narrow lane connects St Kieran's with
Slip to Jona-   High Street. The Butter Slip owes its name to the butter stalls that
than Swift   used to be set up here. The town's insignia and annals reaching back

to the year 1230 are kept in the Tholsel (1761) on High Street, today's town hall. The tourist information office is located in the former Shee Alms House in Rose Inn Street, founded in 1582 by Sir Richard Shee as a hospital for the poor and in use up to 1895. Opposite Kilkenny Castle (Castle Ward), the Kilkenny Design Centre studios are housed in the former stables, offering a broad range of high-quality crafts (textiles, jewellery, glass, ceramics, etc). Take the opportunity to watch the craftspeople, whose work is sold all over Ireland, at work. **Kilkenny College** The new **National Craft Gallery** in

> **Insider Tip**
> **MARCO POLO TIP**
> *Kyteler's Inn*
>
> To meet nice people and eat well in the process, head for the popular Kyteler's Inn (Kieran Street). This house however, has a dark past: in the 14th century, a certain Alice Kyteler is said to have lived here, drawing suspicion by outliving four husbands. Mrs Kyteler was able to escape being convicted as a witch by fleeing the town. Consequently, it was her old maidservant who ended up being burnt as a scapegoat at the stake.

the Crescent Building, designed by Orna Hanly, cements the reputation of Kilkenny as a centre of design. On the other side of the river, **Kilkenny College** is the successor of St John's College, founded in 1666, which was attended by Jonathan Swift and George Berkeley. Today, it serves as County Hall. Nearby stand the ruins of the 13th century St John's Priory. The arrival of Cromwell's army spelt disaster for its famous fine windows.

❶ Tue–Sat 12.30, 1, 3, 3.30pm; ticket 10 €; www.smithwicks.ie

AROUND KILKENNY

A byroad leads to Dunmore Cave, situated 10km/6 miles north of Kilkenny. The visitor centre above the entrance to the cave shows the finds unearthed there during excavations: bones, coins, and simple tools, amongst other things. Many of the exhibits date back to the 10th century. In 928, some 40 people hiding from the Vikings in Dunmore Cave were discovered and brutally slaughtered. One of the most impressive formations in the limestone cave is a stalagmite measuring over 6m/19ft called the Market Cross.   ***Dunmore Cave**

❶ Only guided tours, mid-March to mid-June daily 9.30am–5pm, mid-June to mid-Sept 9.30am–6.30pm, mid-Sept to mid-March 9.30am–5pm, Nov to mid-March close Mon and Tue; admission 3 €

Some 7km/4.5 miles east of Kilkenny, a small road branching left off the N10 leads to the privately-owned 15th-century Clara Castle, a well-preserved tower house with six storeys. After 2km/1.2 miles, the R702 turns off to the right towards Gowran (pop 480) with its interesting parish church (c1275); its tower has been incorporated into the   **Towards Gowran**

Inistioge nestles in delightful countryside

19th-century church. Inside, look for fine lancet arches and pillars of black marble, as well as some exquisitely wrought sculptures and tombs (14th–17th century).

Via Kilfane to Thomastown

Carry on south on the N9, passing the lovely park and waterfall of Kilfane Glen, to reach, after another 2km/1.2 miles, the village of Kilfane . It is worth getting out of the car at the church and visit the over life-size effigy of the knight Thomas e Cantwell on his 13th-century tomb. Take the byroad to the R703 leading to Graiguenamanagh on the Barrow River. In the town, look out for the former **Duiske Cistercian Abbey**. The churchyard south of the choir has two small granite high crosses with representations of biblical themes as well as ornaments. Follow the N9 south from Kilfane for 4km/2.5 miles to Thomastown. Worth seeing here are a ruined 13th-century church, as well as the high altar in the Catholic parish church, which originally stood in the former abbey church of Jerpoint (see below).

*Inistioge

Picturesque Inistioge (pop. 270) lies on the wooded shores of the River Nore, spanned here by a pretty 18th-century bridge. The village has been used as a backdrop for Hollywood films such as *Widow's Peak* (1993). Of the Augustinian abbey, founded in 1210, little remains, but there is a lovely hike from the village up to Brandon Hill (511m/1,676ft), with a cairn and a stone circle at the summit, rewarded by a magnificent view over the valleys of the Barrow and Nore Rivers. Another nice idea for a trip is Woodstock Park on Mount Alto, 1km/0.5 miles south of Inistioge, a wonderful area for strolls and picnics. At the foot of the mountain, look out for a small pottery selling beautiful ceramics in pastel shades.

The monastic ruins of Jerpoint Abbey, some 3km/2 miles southwest of Thomastown, are amongst the most beautiful in Ireland. Founded in 1158, Jerpoint Abbey was Cistercian from 1180 up to its dissolution in 1540. The Cistercian influence is visible: the church with aisles, transept and apse is joined to the south by the cloister and, to its side, the monastic buildings, of which only the sacristy and chapter house on the eastern side survive. In compliance with the rules of the Cistercian order, the imposing 15th-century tower stands above the crossing. As the tower is in danger of collapsing, it is no longer possible to climb it. The nave is divided into areas for brothers and lay brothers. The church has fine tombs, e. g. of Bishop O'Dulany of Ossory (died 1202), with striking rows of carved weepers on their plinths. In the cloister, look out for the impressive figurative relief sculptures standing between the twin columns in the arcading. These were carved by master stone mason Rory O'Tunney, probably between 1501 and 1552. Allegedly, the church of St Nicholas west of the abbey holds the grave of St Nicholas. It is said that after the crusades, the knights of Jerpoint brought his body from Myra, in what is today Turkey, to bury it here. The saint's grave is marked by a broken stone slab with the engraved image of a monk.

**Jerpoint Abbey

❶ March–Sept daily 9am–5.30pm, Oct 9am–5pm, Nov 9.30am–4pm; admission 3 €

Kells, not to be confused with the former monastery of the same name in the north of the Republic, preserves the extensive ruins of a fortified Augustine monastery founded in 1193. Dating from the 14th and 15th century, they form a most impressive

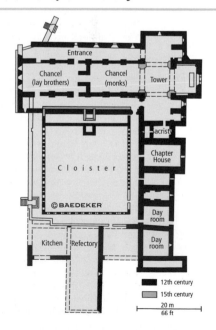

Jerpoint Abbey

Entrance

Chancel (lay brothers)

Chancel (monks)

Tower

Sacristy

Chapter House

C l o i s t e r

©BAEDEKER

Day room

Day room

Kitchen | Refectory

■ 12th century
▨ 15th century

20 m
66 ft

group of medieval buildings. The church with nave, transept, choir and Lady Chapel has a crossing tower as well as two other towers, one of which probably served as the prior's residence. To the south, the remains of the convent buildings abut a courtyard guarded by walls and two towers. The extensive area to the south of the courtyard is similarly fortified by five towers.

Kilree, a 3km/2-mile drive south from Kells via a small byroad, also preserves the remains of a monastery: a 29m/95-ft round tower (without a cap) and a badly weathered high cross, possibly dating from the 9th century. The cross marks the grave of High King Niall Caille, who is supposed to have drowned nearby. As he was not a Christian, his last resting place is outside the church boundaries.

Some 10km/6 miles west of Kilree, on the N76, lies the market town of **Callan**. Before reaching the town, the road passes the Callan Famine Graveyard, commemorating the victims of the Great Famine in Ireland, but also of the famines in Bangladesh (1974) and Angola (1994). Callan still preserves some historic buildings, amongst them the remains of a 15th-century Augustinian friary and the 16th-century St Mary's Church. The carefully restored Rice House gives an idea of what a typical late 18th-century farm house looked like.

Drive south from Callan for 8km/5 miles to reach **Killamery**. Here, the heavily weathered decoration of a 9th-century High Cross shows a line of chariots, a hunting scene, David with the Harp and other biblical scenes, as well as numerous geometrical patterns and animal-like creatures.

West of Kilkenny Northwest of Kilkenny, the R693 leads to Freshford. The western gable of the local church (1730) comprises the fine Romanesque doorway of an earlier church. Beyond the boundary, already in County Tipperary, lie the ruins of ***Kilcooly Abbey**, founded in 1182 as a daughter house of the Cistercian abbey of Jerpoint. The entrance is on the western side of the estate. The church was built between 1445 and 1470 on the site of the previous building and contains numerous sculptures. Between the southern transept and the sacristy, look out for the choir screens decorated with carved relief figures: there is the Crucifixion, St Christopher and a bishop, a mermaid holding a mirror, followed by two fish, as well as the arms of the Butler family. Of the tombs in the choir, the most interesting is the reclining figure of Knight Piers Fitz Oge Butler. The sarcophagus shows reliefs of saints and Early Church Fathers carved as weepers. The master stone mason Rory O'Tunney created these figures and tombs around 1526. Also look out for the two seats on the crossing piers at the end of the nave, as well as the tomb of Abbot Philip (died 1463) in front of the altar. Amongst the ruins of the monastery, the circular vaulted dovecote stands out. Scenes for the film *Excalibur* about the legend of King Arthur were shot at Kilcooley Abbey.

Killaloe (Cill Dalua)

D 3

Republic of Ireland, province: Munster
County: Clare
Population: 1,290

Killaloe is a water sports centre and also a meeting point for numerous cabin-cruise skippers. Restaurants, pubs and shops have joined the many boat hire companies.

This small town lies at the spot where the Shannon leaves long Lough Derg to make its way through the Arra Mountains and Slieve Bernagh towards the plain of Limerick.

Town between the waters

Killaloe's **St Flannan's Cathedral** was built in 1185 on the site of an older church, incorporating its Romanesque doorway. Next to it stands an extraordinary stone, with an inscription in both Viking runes and Ogham inscriptions: »Pray for Thorgrim, who made this stone.« In the cathedral grounds, 12th-century St Flannan's Oratory is a small Romanesque church with a fine doorway and a well-preserved stone roof. Also of interest is **St Molua's Oratory** near the Catholic parish church. Dating from the 9th or 10th century, it was transferred here in 1929 from an island in the Shannon when the planned raising of the water level to serve local power stations threatened to flood it. The **Brian Ború Heritage Centre**, housed in the tourist information building, describes the history of the town the life of Brian Ború, a high king of Ireland who was born in Killaloe.

A walk through time

Killaloe

INFORMATION
Lock Keepers House, Ballina Bridge
Tel. (0 61) 37 68 66
Open: April–Oct
www.discoverkillaloe.com

❶ End of April to mid-Sept daily 10am–5pm; admission 3.35 €; www.shannonheritage.com

AROUND KILLALOE

Stretching out to the north of the town, Lough Derg is the largest of the Shannon lakes, with 67 islets. The boundary between the counties Clare and Tipperary runs right through the lake. A scenic road (R463) follows its western shore, past the scant remains of the once large fort of Beal Ború that gave its name to the famous King Brian Ború.

Lough Derg

Tuamgraney   On the western bank of the lake, the church of Tuamgraney is said to be the oldest Irish church still in use – parts of the building date back to the 10th or 11th century. The small head high up on the east gable represents St Cronan, founder of the first monastery here (around AD 550). Information on the region's history provides the **East Clare Heritage Centre**, which also organizes trips to Holy Island (10 €).
 Mon–Fri 9.30am–5pm; 3 €; http://westclareheritage.com

Holy Island   The fastest way to get to Holy Island (also called Inishcealtra) is from the angling centre of Mountshannon. In the 7th century, St Caimin founded a monastery on the island, and pilgrims and penitents came here up until the end of the 17th century. Today, Holy Island is a lonely spot with five churches, a round tower, an anchorite cell and churchyard.

Killarney (Cill Airne)

—————————————————— ✳ **D 2**

Republic of Ireland, province: Munster
County: Kerry
Population: 7,300

Blessed with magnificent lakes stretching to the south and east, known as Killarney Area, the town is a popular holiday destination.

Long traditi-on of tourism   As early as 1750, Lord Kenmare initiated a tourist infrastructure in the town; by the 19th century, Killarney was an essential destination, for wealthy English travellers.

St Mary's Cathedral   The Catholic St Mary's Cathedral, near the entrance to Killarney National Park, was built in the mid-19th century in the neo-Gothic Early English Style after plans by A W Pugin. During the Famine, the church served as a refuge for many of the local poor; today still, a huge tree marks a mass grave where women and children were laid to rest. The cathedral has a spire 85m/280ft in height, fine screens of Caen stone in the choir and the vault of the Kenmare family, benefactors of this church, in the Lady Chapel.

✶✶ KILLARNEY AREA

Famous for its beautiful scenery, this area is one of the biggest tourist attractions in Ireland. In an area rich in scenic ruins, the three Lakes of Killarney National Park are the main draw: Lower Lake (Lough

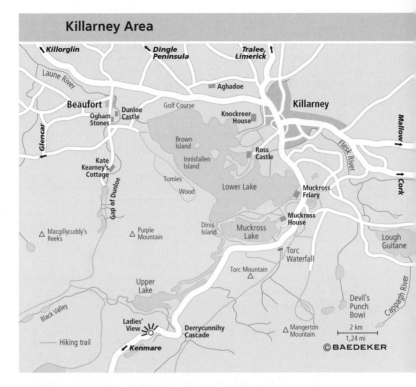

Killarney Area

Killorglin • Dingle Peninsula • Tralee, Limerick
Laune River
Aghadoe
Beaufort
Ogham Stones
Dunloe Castle
Golf Course
Knockreer House
Killarney
Glencar
Brown Island
Ross Castle
Mallow
Kate Kearney's Cottage
Innisfallen Island
Flesk River
Cork
Gap of Dunloe
Tomies
Wood
Lower Lake
Muckross Friary
Macgillycuddy's Reeks
Purple Mountain
Dinis Island
Muckross Lake
Muckross House
Lough Guitane
Torc Waterfall
Torc Mountain
Upper Lake
Devil's Punch Bowl
Cappagh River
Black Valley
Ladies' View
Derrycunnihy Cascade
Mangerton Mountain
2 km
1,24 mi
Hiking trail
Kenmare
© BAEDEKER

Leane), immediately southeast of Killarney is the largest lake, separated by a promontory from Muckross Lake (Middle Lake). A narrow
waterway connects both with Upper Lake, the smallest of the three.
The lake scenery framed by mountains and hills enchants through its
ever-changing display of light and colour. Thanks to the mild climate,
the shores feature a dense cover of luxuriant forest, with oak, arbutus,
bamboo, and giant ferns, amongst many others. In the early summer,
high foxglove shrubs line the roads, and colourful rhododendrons,
as tall as trees, cover the slopes.

There are several ways to explore the lakes, either on your own, for
example by hiring a bike and riding the **Killarney Cycling Trail**, or
using a local tour operator. Most visitors take advantage of the offers
for a package with a jaunting car (open carriage; www.killarneyjaunt-
ingcars.com), pony and boat. Routes go to Kate Kearney's Cottage,
Ross Castle and the Gap of Dunloe. Or take a relaxing cruise on the
MV Lady of Killarney. Kerry Climbing organizes walking and climb-

Tours

Killarney

INFORMATION
Beech Road
Tel. (0 64) 663 1633
www.killarney-insight.com

WHERE TO EAT
Gaby's Seafood Restaurant €€€€
27 High Street
Tel. (0 64) 663 25 19
Closed Sun
Thanks to its lobster and salmon, this expensive restaurant is a top address in the area, offering a three-course set menu.

Robertino's €€€
High Street
Tel. (0 64) 663 49 66
www.robertinosrestaurant.com
Classic Italian dishes cooked according to the principles of Good Food Ireland. The wine list is good, and the early bird menu up to 7.30pm reasonably priced.

WHERE TO STAY
Earls Court House Hotel €€€€
Corner of Woodlawn/Muckross Road
Tel. (0 64) 663 40 09
www.killarney-earlscourt.ie
30 rooms and suites
Ray, Emer and the team really look after their guests in a high-class ambience.

Linden House Hotel €€€
Muckross Road
Tel. (0 64) 663 54 30
www.victoriahousehotel.com
35 rooms
An elegant Victorian hotel with a good restaurant and the Ivy Room bar. Good special offers including dinner and for families.

Gleann Fia Country House €€ Insider Tip
Lower Coolcorcoran, Kilcummin Roadt
Tel. (0 64) 663 50 35
www.gleannfia.com
20 rooms
The O'Connors spoil their guests with free tea and coffee in the Honor Bar and an open fireplace. There is a big breakfast buffet, the Sun Room for listening to music and a fine view of Tommies Mountain.

The lakes around Killarney are wonderful fishing grounds

ing expeditions (www.kerryclimbing.ie). Bus trips are on offer from Dero Tours (www.derostours.com). Trips with Killarney Guided Walk are highly recommended (www.killarneyguidedwalks.com).

Killarney National Park

Killarney National Park covers an area of 10,000 ha/25,000 acres. The nature reserve encompasses Lower Lake, Muckross Lake und Upper Lake including the shore line. The centrepiece is the Bourne Vincent Memorial Park around Muckross House, given to the nation by the family in 1932. Various signposted walking trails lead through the park, famous for its oak woods and red deer.

Located west of the centre of Killarney, in a garden a few minutes' walk from the cathedral, **Knockreer House** is worth a visit. Situated on a promontory in Lough Leane, **Ross Castle** is a late 15th-century fortress, preserving the tower with rounded turrets at the centre of the fortification. A prophecy said that the castle could only be conquered through an attack by water. In 1652, Cromwell's general Ludlow had a large boat brought over and set up in the lower lake in order to bombard the castle from there. The defenders, thinking the prophecy was coming true, surrendered.

From the pier at Ross Castle, row across to quiet **Innisfallen Island**, to visit the remains of a monastery. This is the site where, in the early 13th century, the Annals of Innisfallen were written, today kept in the Bodleian Library in Oxford. The small 12th-century church on the northeastern shore was built from red sandstone. With its cover of mountain ash, ash, yew and holly trees, the island is a good example of the local forest habitat.

At the heart of the national park stands **Muckross House** (1843), a beautiful Victorian villa and one of the best-known stately homes in Ireland. The elegantly furnished rooms are a reflection of the lifestyle of the landed gentry. In the basement of the building, various workshops for traditional craftspeople have been established: a smithy, a weaver's and a pottery. The gardens around Muckross House are famous for their beauty and the splendour of their flowers, in particular the azaleas and rhododendron bushes, as well as for the extensive water garden and rockery. A craft shop, a garden restaurant and the visitor centre for the national park are in the house.

Killarney National Park: April, May, Oct daily 8am–6pm, June–Sept until 7pm, Nov–March until 5pm; free admission; www.killarneynationalpark.ie
Ross Castle: early March–end of Oct daily 9.30am–5.45pm; admission 4 €
Muckross House and Gardens: July and Aug daily 9am–7pm, Sept to June daily 9am–5.30pm; admission to house and garden 7.50 € (including Traditional Farms 12.50 €)

Muckross Traditional Farms

To the east of the manor house, these three traditional farms, run according to the old ways of working the land, offer a trip back in time. Have a chat with the farmer and his wife whilst they go about their

Miles of beauty: the rocky valley and its small lakes

daily chores in the house, in the field or tending the animals. From Muckross House, a path leads around the northern shore of Muckross Lake to the Meeting of the Waters (see below). Splendidly situated in a green setting, ruined 15th-century ***Muckross Abbey** is one of the best-preserved Franciscan abbeys in the country. The only Franciscan tower in Ireland was added after the church was built. The cloister, with an old yew tree at its centre, as well as the adjacent buildings survive complete. There is a splendid view of the lake from the upper parts of the monastery. The monks were driven out by Cromwell's supporters in 1652. Admission is free.

Muckross Traditional Farms: March, April and Oct Sat and Sun 1–6pm, May–Sept daily 1–6pm, June–Aug 10am–6pm; admission 7.50 €, with Muckross House 12.50 €

*Gap of Dunloe   A hike through the , to the west of Lower Lake, guarantees attractive scenery. This rocky defile separates the Macgillycuddy's Reeks

(▶Ring of Kerry) from Purple Mountain (822m/2,697ft), rising up to the east, and its northern foothills. By car, the best way to get to the valley is via the R562, leading around the Lower Lake. There is parking at Kate Kearney's Cottage. Visitors who prefer not to hike through the valley (it is a walk of around 4km/2.5 miles up to the top) may hire a pony or a jaunting car. Five small lakes are fed by a fast-flowing small river. According to legend, St Patrick banished all snakes into the uppermost one, Serpent Lake. The bulky rocks on either side of the valley make for good echoes. From the top (239m/784ft), there is a splendid view of mountains, valleys and lakes in all shades of green, the yellow and brown of the plants and the red of the sandstone.

Continue walking on the northern shore of Muckross Lough with its strange limestone rocks, and cross Brickeen Bridge over to **Dinis Island** for the best view of the **Meeting of the Waters**, where Upper Lake, Muckross Lake and Lough Leane converge. Boat hire companies advertise trips on all three lakes. The road leads around the lake to the N71, running through the park between the shore and Torc Mountain (530m/1,739ft).

On the eastern side of the mountain, the Torc River's attractive **Torc Waterfall** plunges down over an 18m/60ft sandstone precipice. The locals call the lake where the river rises the »Devil's Punch Bowl«. The path up **Mangerton Mountain** (827m/2,713ft) also leads past here. From its summit, enjoy a breathtaking view over mountains near and far, lakes, valleys and inlets – at its most impressive with clouds casting big shadows and squalls of rain drifting across the countryside.

Further up, on the Kenmare road, make sure to stop at ***Ladies' View,** which owes its name to the fact that **Queen Victoria** took a break here with her ladies-in-waiting to admire the panorama. Continue towards Kenmare, passing Molly's Gap, a pass reaching a height of 275m/902ft.

Enjoy another extraordinary view from the ***Aghadoe Heights,** to the north of Lower Lake on a little hill to the right of the R562. In Aghadoe, the ruined monastery (open to the public) has an Ogham stone incorporated into the southern wall of the church. To the southwest of the church stand the remains of a round 13th-century castle. The hill above offers a sweeping view over the lakes and hills: from the Paps (685m/2,247ft) in the southeast to Mangerton Mountain (840m/2,756ft), and all the way to Carrantuohill (1040m/3,412ft) in the southwest.

A nice idea is to take a walk through Tomies Wood (circular trail: approx. 7km/4.5 miles). From the western side of the Lower Lake, the view is delightful.

Tomies Wood

Killybegs (Na Cealla Beaga)

✳ B 3

Republic of Ireland, province: Ulster
County: Donegal
Population: 1,300
Information: www.visitkillybegs.com

Alongside Greencastle and Inishowen, Killybegs, on the southern coast of Donegal, is one of the main fishing ports in the country. Here Donegal Bay forms a natural harbour, cutting deep inland.

Fishing port

This small town is home to both the fish-processing and the sail-making industry. Don't miss the arrival of the fishing trawlers and the unloading of the catch. The town also has a carpet-maker working in the tradition of the Donegal Carpet Factory, which exported its famous products to places like Buckingham Palace, Dublin Castle, the Vatican and the Oval Office of the White House.

Maritime & Heritage Centre

The former carpet factory on Fintra Road is now home to the Maritime & Heritage Centre, where visitors see the largest hand loom in the world and a demonstration of carpet knotting. The main attraction is the Bridge Simulator, an opportunity to take virtual control of a fishing boat and master the perils of the high seas.

❶ Mon–Fri 10am–6pm, July and Aug also Sat, Sun 1–5pm; admission 5 €; www.visitkillybegs.com

AROUND KILLYBEGS

Dunkineely

Some 8km/5 miles east of Killybegs, Dunkineely is the start of a road 8km/5 miles out to sea to St John's Point, leading past a ruined castle on a narrow promontory, with excellent fishing grounds and good beaches.

Kilcar

The picturesque village of Kilcar, west of Killybegs, is famous for hand-woven tweed. Donegal Yarns (www.donegalyarns.com) and **Studio Donegal** in The Glebe Mill sell high-quality material. The cliffs and caves south of here, at Muckross Head, are accessible at low tide.

Studio Donegal: Mon–Fri 9am–5.30pm, May–Oct also Sat 9.30am–5pm; www.studiodonegal.ie

The breathtaking cliffs of Slieve League

Another 4km/2.5 miles inland lies Carrick, above the spot where the Glen River flows into scenic Teelin Bay. It is well worth taking a detour to Slieve League. To reach the highest sea cliffs in Europe, with a height of 590m/1,936ft, take the car to Teelin. From there, the narrow road carries on to Bunglass Point (3km/2 miles southwest). The **Slieve League Cliffs Centre** has a good café, a shop and an art gallery, runs archaeological tours, boat and kayak tours, and provides weather forecasts. Bunglass Point is the beginning of the **One Man's Path**, which is only recommended for sure-footed walkers with a good head for heights. The ridge leads some 4km/2.5 miles past steep slopes up to the summit of Slieve League. The path is not marked, but can be made out fairly easily. Less experienced hikers should take the **Old Man's Path**, signposted from Teelin village. The time needed is approx. 1.5 to 2 hours for both paths, with a height differential of just under 400m/1,300ft. Both paths require more or less the same degree of fitness and sturdy shoes.

Slieve League Cliffs Centre: March–Nov daily 10.30am–5.30pm; free admission; http://slieveleaguecliffs.ie

*Slieve League

* Kinsale (Ceann Saile)

✳ E 3

Republic of Ireland, province: Munster
County: Cork
Population: 4,890

To this day, Kinsale has preserved some of its 18th-century charm. Narrow lanes with colourful houses and the picturesque harbour give the town an almost Mediterranean feel.

Gourmet capital on the southwestern coast

This destination lies above the broad estuary of the Bandon River. Its harbour, 500 years an major point of import for wine and other goods from Europe, is today only used for fishing (mackerel) and the well-equipped marina. In order to serve its international sailing clientele, numerous good restaurants, wine bars and gourmet shops have established themselves in Kinsale (http://food.kinsale.ie). The annual gourmet festival is famous (►MARCO POLO Insight, p.106). The best view of the town can be had from Compass Hill (southwest of the town centre) or from the road leading to Charles Fort.

History

From 1602 onwards, Kinsale was an English town, the Irish were not allowed to live here until the end of the 18th century. The harbour used to be an important naval port: in 1601, a Spanish fleet brought several thousands of men here to join the Irish in fighting the English. They had to surrender, however. A consequence of this decisive victory of the English was the Flight of the Earls to central Europe, sealing Ireland's dependence on England. According to legend, a certain Alexander Selkirk sailed from this harbour in the early 18th century, only to be shipwrecked and stranded on a desert island. Selkirk's fate allegedly gave Daniel Defoe the idea for his novel *Robinson Crusoe*. The atmospheric Man Friday restaurant in the Scilly district refers to this (www.manfridaykinsale.ie). William Penn, founder of the US state of Pennsylvania, was also born in Kinsale.

St Multose Church

St Multose Church is the most remarkable building in town. Built in the 12th century and altered several times, it serves today as parish church. The tower with its Romanesque door is on the northwestern side. The statue above the western door shows St Multose, who is credited with founding the monastery that once stood on this site. Inside the church there is an interesting collection of 17th-century tombs and a medieval baptismal font.

Desmond Castle

In Cork Street stands a well-preserved tower house called French Prison or Desmond Castle, dating back to the 15th century. Used in 1601 by the Spanish forces as their headquarters and in the early 19th

Kinsale

INFORMATION
Cork Kerry Tourism Office
Pier Road
Tel. (0 21) 477 22 34
www.kinsale.ie

WHERE TO EAT
Fishy Fishy €€€
On the Pier
Tel. (0 21) 470 04 15
www.fishyfishy.ie
Martin Shanahan is celebrated as the best seafood chef in Ireland. His books are sold at the counter, and in summer guests dine in the garden.

Max's €€€ **Insider Tip**
48 Main Street
Tel. (0 21) 477 24 43
www.maxs.ie
The cuisine marries French and Irish influences in a cosy atmosphere. Oliver Queva is famous for his sauces and seafood. Don't miss the Irish cheese-board. The fixed three-course menu and the early bird offer help to keep the bill down.

WHERE TO STAY
Trident €€€€
World's End
Tel. (0 21) 477 93 00
http://tridenthotel.com
64 rooms and 11 suites
Friendly service right by the harbour, with an excellent restaurant and bar food in the Wharf Tavern.

Actons €€€
Pier Road
Tel. (0 21) 477 99 000
www.actonshotelkinsale.com
73 rooms
The Captain's Table is the excellent hotel restaurant; a large spa is opposite.

---

century as a prison for French soldiers, the tower today houses a small wine museum, highlighting Kinsale former role in the wine trade.

The Court House (1590, extended in 1703) was the scene of the first investigations into the sinking of the Lusitania by a German U-boat off Kinsale in 1915. The museum illuminates this event, the maritime history of Kinsale, and the Battle of Kinsale in 1601. It also preserves the memory of the **Kinsale Giant**, Patrick Cotter O'Brien (1760–1806), who is said to have been eight foot and three inches tall (2.47m) at the age of 18. He was exhibited in a freak show in London, and his shoes are on display in the museum.

Kinsale Regional Museum

❶ Sat 10am–5pm, Sun 2–5pm; free admission

Head for Summer Cove, 3km/2 miles south of town, on the eastern side of the harbour, to visit Charles Fort (1677). The outer defences of the star-shaped well-preserved fort are 12m/40ft high. On the southwestern corner stands a lighthouse, and the enclosure holds the

Charles Fort

Kinsale has an almost southern European atmosphere

ruins of 19th-century barracks. On the opposite side of the harbour a similar structure catches the eye: James Fort.

❶ Daily 10am–6pm, Nov to mid-March until 5pm; closed Mon from Dec to mid-March; admission 4 €

Ringfinnan Garden of Remembrance The garden commemorates Michael Judge, the chaplain of the New York Fire Department, an Irish American and one of the 343 firefighters who died on 9/11 2001.

AROUND KINSALE

Ballinspittle Take the R600 southwest from Kinsale to the village of Ballinspittle, dominated by the Ballycateen Ring Fort with its three deep ditches and an overall diameter of 120m/130yd. The name Ballinspittle refers to a long-lost medieval hospital, which was probably a foundation of the Knights Templar. Further south, **Old Head of Kinsale** the **Old Head of Kinsale** juts far out into the sea: a ruined castle and a lighthouse, set in spectacular cliff scenery.

Bandon From Kilbrittain (pop. 200), the R603 leads to Bandon, where there is good trout fishing. The town was founded in 1608 for English settlers. Not least because of this, Bandon's parish church, Kilbrogan Church, built in 1610, was one of the first Protestant churches in Ireland.

Letterkenny (Leitir Ceanainn)

✳ **B 4**

Republic of Ireland, province: Ulster
County: Donegal
Population: 19,580
Information: www.letterkennyguide.com

Letterkenny, in the furthest northwest of Ireland, is the main town in County Donegal and an ideal base for exploring northern Donegal. The town lies on the banks of the River Swilly, close to where it flows into Lough Swilly.

The symbol of the town, stretching alongside the O'Cannons hills, is the tower of St Eunan's Cathedral (1901), with Celtic-style carvings and stained glass. The **County Museum** was established in a building that was originally used as a poorhouse, and later by the local authorities. The exhibits highlight the history, archaeology and geology of Donegal, as well as the county's past inhabitants' way of life. The **Regional Cultural Centre** is the focus of the arts in the area (www.donegalculture.com).

Sights

County Museum: Mon–Fri 9am–12.30pm, 1–4.30pm, Sat, Sun 1–4.30pm; free admission

Letterkenny
INFORMATION
Derry Road
Tel. (0 74) 211 60

AROUND LETTERKENNY

Further northwest, Rathmelton (or Ramelton, pop. 1,090) is a meeting place for anglers with a pretty harbour, framed by Georgian houses. Don't miss the ruins of Tullyaughnish Church, with Romanesque carvings on the eastern wall. In the 17th-century **Old Warehouses** it is worth looking at the exhibition on the TV series The Hanging Gale about the Great Famine, which was filmed here.

Rathmelton

❶ Mid-June to Sept daily 10am–6pm; free admission

In the village of Newmills, 6km/3.5 miles southwest of Letterkenny, the Newmills Corn & Flax Mills visitor centre has information on the processing of corn and flax. (Opening times: mid-June–Sept daily 10am–6.30pm). A stroll along the river leads to the former cottage of a flax thresher and a village blacksmith.

Newmills Corn & Flax Mills

❶ June–Aug Mon–Fri 9.30am–7pm; admission 4 €

Colmcille Heritage Centre The Colmcille Heritage Centre in Gartan, 17km/11 miles north-west of Letterkenny, is dedicated to the life, work and times of St Columba the Elder (Colm Cille). On the way there, signposts show the way to the ruins of Colmcille Abbey and the saint's birthplace.

❶ May–Sept Mon–Sat 10.30am–5pm, Sun 1.30–5pm; admission 3 €; www.colmcilleheritagecentre.ie

*Glebe House In 1953, the English painter and art collector Derek Hill bought the splendid **Glebe House** on the shore of Lough Gartan. Glebe House used to be a rectory, and later a hotel. Today, it is Hill's remarkable art collection that attracts most visitors.

The focus of the 300 paintings and drawings is on art of the 19th and 20th centuries (Degas, Renoir, Picasso, Yeats, Kokoschka, amongst others), but the works by »naive« Tory painters promoted by Hill are worth seeing too. The converted stables are used for changing exhibitions

❶ Easter and end of May to Sept Sat–Thu 11am–6.30pm, July and Aug daily 11am–6.30pm; admission 3 €

*Glenveagh National Park West of Lough Gartan lies the **Glenveagh National Park**. The entrance and visitor centre are situated on the northern shore of Lough Beagh and can be accessed via the R251. With a surface area of 100 sq km/40 sq miles, the national park was founded in 1986. At its centre, Lough Beagh is surrounded by impressive mountain and bog scenery.

From the visitor centre, there is a shuttle bus to Glenveagh Castle, 3km/2 miles away, private cars being banned from the national park. The castle, built in 1870 in neo-Gothic style, stands in magnificent, Mediterranean-looking parkland. Don't miss the herb garden.

❶ Visitor centre: daily 9am–6pm, Nov–Feb daily until 7pm; castle daily 10am–5pm; admission to park and visitor centre free; tours and garden tours from 5 €; www.glenveaghnationalpark.ie

Kilmacrenan 11km/7 miles north of Letterkenny lies Kilmacrenan. Situated near the bridge, **Lurgyvale Thatched Cottage** is worth a visit. The kitchen offers tea and scones with home-made jam. On Thursday evenings, there is traditional music with singing and dancing, and in the summer, visitors can have an introduction to traditional crafts. Drive some 3km/2 miles further west to see the Rock of Doon, a remarkable flattened rock that was once the coronation site of the O'Donnell kings. The climb is rewarded with panoramic views across bog scenery. Pilgrims also visit the »holy well« for its curative powers.

Lurgyvale Thatched Cottage: Easter–Sept daily 10am–7pm

Limerick (Luimneach)

✦ D 3

Republic of Ireland, province: Munster
County: Limerick
Population: 57,100

Abroad, the name »Limerick« is mainly associated with the famous five-line humorous verse (and more recently, with Frank Mc Court's best-selling memoirs *Angela's Ashes*, hardly ever with the fourth-largest Irish city, in the southwest of the country.

Several main through roads and railway lines meet here, Shannon Airport is only 24km/15 miles away, and Limerick also has a fairly busy if not very large port. Over the past decades, the establishment of modern branches of industry (optical, electronic, and medical

Hub at the mouth of the Shannon

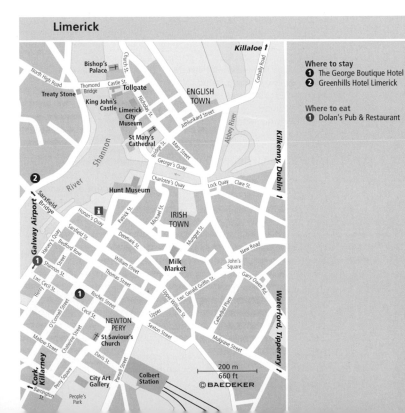

Limerick

Where to stay
❶ The George Boutique Hotel
❷ Greenhills Hotel Limerick

Where to eat
❶ Dolan's Pub & Restaurant

Limerick

INFORMATION
Arthur's Quay
Tel. (0 61) 31 75 22
www.limerick.ie

WHERE TO EAT
❶ Dolan's Pub and Restaurant €€
3 Dock Road
Tel. (0 61) 31 44 83
www.dolanspub.com
Two open-air areas, a good wine list, regular live music, breakfast served at weekends.

WHERE TO STAY
❶ The George Boutique Hotel €€€
O'Connell Street

Tel. (0 61) 46 04 00
www.thegeorgeboutiquehotel.com
124 rooms
The most central hotel in town. Try to get a room on the 7th floor for the view. The George Bar & Restaurant is excellent.

❷ Greenhills Hotel Limerick €€
Ennis Road, Northwest
Tel. (0 61) 45 30 33
www.greenhillsgroup.com
60 rooms
Modern hotel, with all amenities. The restaurant's speciality is lamb (reared at the hotel's farm).

technology) has raised Limerick's profile as the home of industries. There are also corn mills and tobacco-processing companies, as well as factories producing textiles, cement and steel cable. Despite this, unemployment is relatively high and the overall standard of living low. Enormous efforts are being made to promote tourism in this area.

History　In the 9th century, the Vikings established a base at the »bare place«, as the translation of the city's Irish name suggests. From here, they undertook the raids inland and were only driven out by the famous king BrianBorú. Later, Anglo-Normans and Irish alternated as rulers of Limerick. In 1210, King John had a castle and a bridge built. Over the following centuries the city became more powerful and sided with the English. In the 17th century, Limerick was besieged and captured several times, for the last time in 1691. 10,000 Irish soldiers were granted an honourable retreat after bravely defending Limerick, by a treaty signed by King William III himself. However, the English parliament refused to ratify the treaty, not recognizing the religious freedom enshrined in the treaty. The soldiers went to France and joined Louis XIV's army. Over the course of the following decades, tens of thousands of Irishmen served as soldiers in France and Spain.

Limericks　The origins of the five-line verse are uncertain. In all probability it actually came from England. Sometimes the name »Limerick« is also traced back to an Irish 19th-century song, describing in various stanzas the adventures of the inhabitants of various Irish cities. The first limerick to appear in print was published in a Canadian newspaper in 1880.

SIGHTS IN LIMERICK

The **Milk Market** on Cornmarket Row, especially on Saturdays, is one of Limerick's great attractions. To get to know the varied architecture of the town, join one of Noel Curtain's **walking tours** following the trail of Frank McCourt's book *Angela's Ashes*. The main sights are to be found in English Town.

Milk Market: Fri 10am–4pm, Sat 8am–4pm, Sun 11am–4pm; www.milkmarketlimerick.ie
Walking tour: daily 2.30pm, from tourist office; 10 €; bookings tel. 087 235 1339

St Mary's Cathedral

The Protestant St Mary's Cathedral, near Matthew Bridge, was built at the end of the 12th century, under Donal Mór O'Brien, last king of Munster. The western doorway dates from this time. The main parts of the church, however, are 15th century. The magnificent oak choir stalls were carved in 1489; its 23 misericords, decorated with imaginatively wrought creatures, make the choir unique in Ireland. Also look out for the tombs, and **climb the tower** (36m/118ft) for a wonderful view.

The bell-ringers practise on Monday evenings, and sometimes allow visitors to try their hand. The **cathedral choir** gives regular concerts (tickets tel. 086 171 57 91).

St Mary's Cathedral: Mon–Fri 9.30am–4.30pm; admission 2 €; www.cathedral.limerick.anglican.org
Tower tours: from St Mary's Action Centre, daily 11am and 2pm

King John's Castle

Situated on the river banks, impressive 13th-century **King John's Castle** rises above the Shannon. No expense was spared in the restoration of the pentagonal fortress consisting of a main block, three round corner towers, a bastion and a twin-towered gatehouse marred by later additions. Today, parts of the site are used for exhibitions, with recreated scenes bringing to life the history of Ireland and the city. In the **Limerick City Museum**, the history of the town since the Stone Age is presented, with excavated Norman houses and fortifications. The best view of the imposing castle is to be had from the other side of the river, the site of the **Treaty Stone** where the Treaty of Limerick is said to have been signed in 1691. Pass the 18th-century Bishop's Palace and the old tollgate before crossing the river via Thomond Bridge.

King John's Castle dominates the river

King John's Castle: April–Sept daily 9.30am–5.30pm, Oct–March daily 9.30am–4.30pm; admission 9 €
Limerick City Museum: Tue–Sat 10am–1pm, 2.15–5pm; free admission; www.limerickcity.ie/citymuseum

*Hunt Museum The former Custom House today houses the excellent collection of the art historian John Hunt. The founder of the Craggaunowen Project (►Craggaunowen Castle, Ennis) collected nearly 2,000 pieces, mainly medieval liturgical artefacts from the European mainland, but also Irish finds from the Bronze Age and early Christian times. In their significance for medieval Irish art, the Hunt Museum exhibits are second only to the National Museum in Dublin.
❶ Mon– Sat 10am–5pm, Sun 2–5pm; admission 5 €; www.huntmuseum.com

Sarsfield Bridge (1824–35) over the Shannon is a **copy of Pont Neuilly** in Paris. Sarsfield Street leads to the part of town called New-town Pery.

Sarsfield Bridge

Southwest of Irish Town extend the districts of the more recent ex-pansion of the city. Today, the heart of the city is O'Connell Street, with the Daniel O'Connell Monument rising up at its end. In 1829, O'Connell successfully fought for religious freedom for Catholics in Ireland. Note some fine Georgian houses with their colourful doors in Mallow Street, with People's Park at its eastern end. **St Saviour's Dominican Church** In **St Saviour's Dominican Church**, the statue of Our Lady and the surprisingly modern-looking stained-glass win-dows are worth seeing. It is said that the statue was gifted to the Do-minicans in 1640 by a Limerick man. **Art Gallery** Limerick's **City Art Gallery** is situated in the People's Park. On display are works by in-ternational and Irish artists, such as Jack Butler Yeats and Sean Keat-ing.

Newtown Pery

The Belltable Arts Centre in O'Connell Street is a venue for theatre, dance, music and comedy (www.belltable.ie) and for the national **Fresh Film** festival for film makers under the age of 18 (www.fresh-filmfestival.net).

Belltable Arts Centre

❶ City Art Gallery: Mon, Wed, Fri 10am–5.30pm, Tue 11am–5.30pm, Thu 10am–8.30pm, Sat 10am–5pm, Sun 12 noon–5pm; free admission; http:// gallery.limerick.ie

AROUND LIMERICK

Some 20km/12 miles east of Limerick, at the foot of the Slievefelim Mountains, lies Moroe village, with the Benedictine monastery of Glenstal Abbey, founded in 1927 amidst extensive parkland.

Moroe

At Holycross, 25km/16 miles south of Limerick, don't miss this most interesting **site of prehistoric excavations**. In the last century, dur-ing drainage works on the lake it was discovered that its banks had been inhabited as far back as Neolithic times. Numerous finds are on display at the visitor centre on the lake, whilst models, graphics and audiovisuals in the Lough Gur Stone Age Centre give background information about the site. Walking around the extensive area, the monuments you see include: no. 4 – a wedge-shaped passage tomb (approx. 2000 BC); no. 7 – an 8th-century stone fort; no. 8 – an early Christian oval stone fort; no. 12 – a Stone Age burial site, a double wall with a standing stone (menhir) at its centre; no. 16 – a burial mound with a circle of standing stones (approx. 1500 BC); no. 17 – a fine double stone circle (which has not been dated with certainty),

*Lough Gur Stone Age Centre

A grave at the Lough Gur Heritage Centre

with an earth wall and ditch; no. 22 – a small stone circle with large blocks; no. 23 – a crannóg, originally an artificial island, now connected to the shore; no. 28 – an impressive stone circle (approx. 2000 BC), a place of worship with an almost monumental entrance. In the area, also look for the medieval Bourchier's Castle (16th century), Black Castle (14th century) as well as the ruins of the 17th-century New Church.

❶ Easter to late Sept Mon–Fri 10am–5pm, Sat and Sun 12 noon–6pm; admission 5 €; www.loughgur.com

Kilmallock and around

Kilmallock, 34 km/21 miles south of Limerick on the R512, is a long-established rural town. Parts of the 15th-century Collegiate Church of Saints Peter and Paul date from the 13th century (round tower), and there are some handsome funeral monuments. The 14th-century King's Castle and Blossom's Gate in Emmet Street bear witness to the significance of the town in the Middle Ages. The **town museum** shows a model of Kilmallock as it would have looked in 1600, and a small collection of exhibits shows what life was like in this region in the 19th and 20th centuries. To the north stand the ruins of a Dominican priory (13–15th century) with a church displaying good samples of stone masonry. The five-light east window, as well as tombs in the chancel, are worth seeing. The tower (27m/89ft) is supported by narrow bays.

Approx. 10km/6 miles to the southeast, **Kilfinane** lies at the foot of the Ballyhoura Mountains. Kilfinane has a particularly large motte, from the top of which you have a splendid view of the countryside around. In the scenic southwest side valley of Glenosheen, two avenues lead past unusual gatekeeper's lodges to 19th-century **Castle Oliver**, complete with crenellations, towers and bastions. This is the alleged birthplace of Marie Gilbert, also known as Lola Montez, the famous mistress of King Ludwig I of Bavaria. The **Ballyhoura Heritage Information Centre** provides an introduction to the region which has 97km/60 miles of mountain-bike trails and lots of good walking, including the 90km/56-mile Ballyhoura Way.

❶ Town museum: daily 11am–3pm; free admission

Ballyhoura Heritage Information Centre: Mon–Fri 9am–5.30pm; admission free; http://visitballyhoura.com

From Kilmallock, the R518 and R520 lead west to the lively market town of Newcastle West (32km/20 miles southwest of Limerick). The ruins of a castle founded by the Knights Templar in the centre of town date from the 12th century. 8km/5 miles south of Newcastle West, you will come across Glenquin Castle, a well-preserved tower house, dating from the 15th century, with six storeys. Built from red sandstone in the Scottish Baronial style, it is now an eight-room luxury hotel (www.castleoliver.ie) with a wine cellar where 55,000 bottles are stored. **Newcastle West**

Drive west from Limerick on the N69 to see some interesting ruins: after 4km/2.5 miles Mungret Abbey, a monastery school that was once of some prominence, and 6km/3.5 miles further on, the 15/16th-century Carrigogunnell Castle, built on a rock. From here, enjoy a beautiful view of the Shannon and the surrounding area. Kildimo has the remains of a small 13th-century Knights Templar church as well as a parish church, dating from 1705. Carrying on, 12th century Killulta Church appears on top of a hill; look out for the triangular window. **Towards Askeaton**

From Kilcornan village, you can go for walks in **Coillte Forest Park** (Curraghchase Forest Park), for instance to what remains of 18th-century Curraghchase House. The **Celtic Park & Gardens** features copies of important Irish monuments and has a rose garden. Children appreciate the horses, sheep, deer, and poultry.

Celtic Park & Gardens: mid-March to Oct daily 9.30am–6pm; admission 6 €

In Askeaton, on the River Deel, the ruins of 15th-century Desmond Castle rise on a rocky islet in the river near the bridge. The castle features a tower house and a banqueting hall (9x27m/30x89ft), with pretty windows, blind arcades and a vault. On the eastern bank of the **Askeaton** river, the 15th-century Franciscan friary still has a few well-preserved buildings. The church has some beautiful windows and a fine cloister with twelve marble lancet arches, containing a representation of St Francis. The refectory and other rooms also survive.

On to Foynes & Glin
Drive on for 11km/7 miles to reach the sea harbour of Foynes, situated in a scenic position, on the mouth of the Shannon. During WW II, Foynes was a focal point for the entire North Atlantic passenger air traffic. The **Foynes Flying Boat Museum** takes visitors back to this time, with the original terminal building, the radio and weather room, a full size replica of a Boeing 314 Clipper which were used by Pan Am and BOAC as well as photographs showing the first flying boats used on the Atlantic route.

13km/8 miles further west, 19th-century Hamilton's Tower rises above Glin harbour. Outside the village, **Glin Castle** has been in the possession of the Knights of Glin for 700 years, and they have been living here in an unbroken line for the same length of time. The rooms inside the castle, built in Georgian neo-Gothic style, are worth seeing, with elegant stucco ceilings (staircase, hall, library), as well as Irish furniture from the 18th century, and family portraits (18th–20th century). Guided tours are available (tel. 068 341 73).

Foynes Flying Boat Museum: mid-March to May daily 9am–5pm, June–Sept until 6pm; admission 11 €; www.flyingboatmuseum.com

Lismore (Lios Mór)

✦ **D 4**

Republic of Ireland, province: Munster
County: Waterford
Population: 1,370
Information: www.discoverlismore.com

Lismore is a village near the southern coast of Ireland. Situated on the broad River Blackwater, Lismore hugs the foot of the Knockmealdown Mountains.

A place of scholarship
There was a monastery on this site as early as the 7th century; its school was famed for its scholarship. King Alfred the Great of England is said to have studied here in the 9th century.

Lismore Castle
Lismore Castle, perched magnificently on a high rock, was probably built in the 12th century, on the site of a monastery, by the later King John. It was a bishop's residence for four centuries and was later briefly leased to Sir Walter Raleigh. In 1602, the castle passed into the hands of Richard Boyle, later Earl of Cork. His son Robert Boyle

(1627–91), a famous natural scientist (Boyle's Law on the pressure and volume of gas), was born here. Today, the castle belongs to the Duke of Devonshire. It was expanded several times during the 19th century, and it was during those works that significant finds were made: the 15th-century Book of Lismore, as well as the Lismore Cross; today, both may be admired in the National Museum in Dublin. Lismore Castle is not open to the public, but the gardens may be visited.

The west wing houses an **art gallery**, which is used, sometimes in conjunction with the gardens, for an annual exhibition of modern art by international artists. The gallery also promotes Irish and local artists, whose work is displayed in **St Carthage Hall** in Chapel Street in Lismorre.

Gardens: March–Sept daily 11am–4.45pm; admission 8 €, including art gallery; wwwlismorecastle.com

Lismore Castle Arts: April Sat and Sun 11.30am–5.30pm, May–Sept daily 11.30am–5.30pm; admission 8 €; www.lismorecastlearts.ie

St Carthage Hall: May–Oct Fri–Sun 3–6pm, free admission

St Carthage's Cathedral

St Carthage's Cathedral was built in the 17th century by Richard Boyle, using parts of a 13th-century church (the chancel arch and the window in the southern transept). Look out for the tomb of the MacGrath family (1557), with representations of the Crucifixion, an Ecce Homo scene, several saints and apostles, as well as ancient tombstones in the western wall of the nave.

❶ Daily from 7am (Mass), donation requested

Lismore Heritage Centre

An multimedia show in the **Lismore Heritage Centre** brings to life the history of the town and prominent persons associated with it such as Robert Boyle and Sir Walter Raleigh. This is the starting point for daily tours of the town (ticket 5.50 €). A farmers market takes place in Castel Avenue.

Heritage Centre: Mon–Fri 9.30am–5.30pm, April–Oct also Sat 10am–5pm, Sun 12 noon–5pm; admission 4.80 €

Lismore Farmers Market: mid–March to end of Nov every Sat 9.30am–4.30pm

AROUND LISMORE

Cappoquin

East of Lismore, where the River Blackwater turns southwards, lies the scenic fishing town of Cappoquin. The tides reach all the way to here. A few miles further north, in the hills, the Trappist Mount Melleray Abbey was built in 1833. Accommodation can be had in the guest quarters

❶ www.mountmellerayabbey.org.

Affane   At Affane, 2km/1 mile south of Cappoquin, look for a large Georgian manor house where Sir Walter Raleigh (1552–1618) planted **the first cherry trees in the British Isles**. He was also the first to cultivate potatoes and tobacco in Ireland. Near Villierstown (south of Affane), Dromana Gate is a curious gatehouse in a style reminiscent of Indian architecture.

Longford (An Longfort)
✦ **C 4**

Republic of Ireland, province: Leinster
County: Longford
Population: 9,600

Longford, to the northeast of Lough Ree in the centre of Ireland, is a traffic hub, with interesting places to visit in the area.

Sports centre   The main town of Longford County offers plenty of leisure activities: golf, tennis, fishing and hunting; horse and greyhound races are held here too. A farmers market is eld every Friday on Market Square.

AROUND LONGFORD

Carrig Glass Manor   Heading north-east from Longford on the R194, after 6km/3.5 miles look out for Carrig Glass Manor. This private manor house was built in 1837 by Thomas Lefroy, said to have been a friend of Jane Austen's in her youth. Allegedly, Lefroy was **the model for Mr Darcy**, one of the main characters in *Pride and Prejudice*. The house has furniture and paintings from the 18th century, and is now a four-star hotel (www.carriglass.ie).

Granard   In the angling town of Granard a country market is held on Friday mornings. Nearby is the largest motte in Ireland (12th century) . Some 4km/2.5 miles to the east, starting at Lough Kinale and running 10km/6 miles northwest to Lough Gowna, stretches a part of Black Pig's Dyke. This defensive structure consists of a series of **earthwork walls for the protection of overland routes** and runs straight through the north of Ireland (►Cavan, Around). The individual sections were built between 300 BC and AD 300. Here, the wall is up to 6m/20ft high, and at its base 9m/30ft strong, with a ditch to each side.

Longford

INFORMATION
Market Square
Tel. (0 43) 334 2577
www.longfordtourism.ie

The Corlea Trackway Visitor Centre (15km/9 miles from Longford, 3km/2 miles from Kenagh) is dedicated to the Bog Road, a road of wooden planks from the Iron Age. The trackway was built across the boggy landscape near the Shannon in 148 BC and is said to be the longest of its kind in Europe. In recent years, a stretch of 18m/60ft length has been excavated and is now on display in an air-conditioned room. An exhibition explains the conditions at the time when the Bog Road was built and the work of the archaeologists; there is an interesting film too.

Corlea Trackway

❶ April–Sept daily 10am–6pm; free admission

South of Longford, **Edgeworthstown** boasts the manor house where the novelist Maria Edgeworth (1767–1849) was born. Famous colleagues such as Walter Scott and William Wordsworth came to stay here. On the way to Ballymahon, take a short detour off to the right to the pretty **Ardagh Heritage Village**, with the small St Mel's Church, allegedly founded by St Patrick. The Ardagh Heritage & Creativity Centre in the old schoolhouse has an exhibition on the village.

Towards Ballymahon

Take the R392 again in a northwesterly direction to Lanesborough on the Shannon, which flows into Lough Ree here. Both the river and the lake have great fishing (trout). Lanesborough is also a popular stop for boat trips on the ▶Shannon. The power station near the town, on the eastern shore, runs on peat. The island of **Inchcleraun** in Lough Ree preserves the ruins of an ancient monastery.

Lough Ree

Lough Corrib · Lough Mask

✴ C 2

Republic of Ireland, province: Connacht
County: Galway, Mayo
Information: www.oughterardtourism.com

At over 45km/28 miles long, Lough Corrib in the west of Ireland, north of Galway Bay, is the largest lake in the Republic; in some places, however, it is only a few hundred yards.

The scenery around the lake is varied: plains to the east, hills to the west, and to the north, the mountains of Connemara can be spied on the horizon. The green banks with occasional clumps of trees and pastures form hundreds of small bays, promontories and peninsulas that seem to blend into rows of tiny islands. The region is ideal for

*Lough Corrib

boating and a **paradise for fishermen**. Many water fowl live here, such as pochards, coots and gulls. To the north, subterranean rivers connect Lough Corrib with Lough Mask; the former emptying into the sea via the River Corrib. From ▶Galway, pleasure boats leave in the summer for ▶Cong.

SIGHTS AROUND THE LAKES

Aughnanure Castle

Heading northwest from ▶ Galway, the road leads first to Moycullen, a good fishing base, and, past Ross Lake, soon reaches **Aughnanure Castle** (1500), jutting up from a rocky island. The six-storey tower house features two corner oriels of the type typical for the western Irish and Scottish defensive style. Each of the two courtyards is flanked by a round tower.

● April to mid-Oct daily 9.30am–6pm; admission 3 €;
www.heritageireland.ie

Oughterard

After a few miles, the road reaches Oughterard. The town, often called »Gateway to Connemara«, lies snugly in a green setting on the shore of the Owenriff River (plenty of fish here), and is well-known in angling circles. On the other hand, the numerous accommodation options and restaurants also attract tourists looking for other kind of relaxations. Here the **Glengowla Mines**, 19th-century silver and lead mines, can be visited on guided tours that run every 20 minutes.

● March to mid-Nov daily 10am–6pm; admission 10 €;
www.glengowlamines.ie

Inchagoill

From Oughterard or ▶Cong, take a boat to go across to picturesque Inchagoill island (from Cong on the Isle of Inisfree daily at 2.45pm, 20 €, from Oughterard Wed –Mon at 12 noon on the Corrib Queen, 28 €), to see the remains of two churches. The smaller one dates from the 5th century, the larger structure, dating from the 12th century, is considered a good example of Hiberno-Romanesque style. A 75cm/30-inch obelisk nearby marks a burial site. Its inscription »Lie Luguaedon macci Menueh« (stone of Luguaedon, son of Menueh) is taken to refer to the nephew and helmsman of the Irish apostle.

Cornamona

The narrow road along the northern shore of is a dead end. To drive around the lake, use the N59. From the road intersection at Maam Cross (▶Connemara), take the R336 north to Maam Bridge. From there, the L101 running east leads to the scenic fishing village of Cornamona, a good base for walking and climbing in Joyce's Country. From here, visit Castle Kirke with 12th-century Hen's Castle. An island in Lough Nafooey is nearly completely occupied by the ruins of a massive tower.

Trees in blossom on the banks of Lough Corrib

After a drive of 8km/5-mile in parts hugging the lake, stop at Clon-bur, on the isthmus between Loug Mask und Lough Corrib. There is a fantastic view from Mount Gable to the west of the village. To just drive around Lough Corrib, follow the road east and drive via ▶Cong to Ballinrobe.

Clonbur

As the road sweeps around Lough Mask, drive on the pretty side road from Clonbur to the village of Tuar Mhic Éadaigh (Toormakeady), past the atmospheric mountain lake which appears, depending on the weather, either sombre or brightly luminous. From here onwards, the road is signposted as »Lough Mask Drive«.

Lough Nafooey

North of Partry, on the isthmus between Lough Mask and Lough Carra, off the N84, stands Ballintubber Abbey. It was founded in 1216 by the king of Connacht near the site where St Patrick had founded a church as early as 441, coming down from Croagh Patrick (▶West-port). Despite the havoc wrought by Cromwell's army, mass has been celebrated here regularly to this day. Look for a skilfully wrought tomb in the sacristy. The church and cloister were restored in the 1960s. This is the starting point for the 35km/22-mile **pilgrimage up**

*Ballintubber Abbey

Ireland's holy mountain **Croagh Patrick**, which can be seen rising in the distance through the arcades of the cloister.

❶ Daily 9am–midnight, donation requested; www.ballintubberabbey.ie

Lough Carra   The road from Ballintubber to Ballinrobe runs across the isthmus between Lough Mask and Lough Carra. The lakes are connected by a subterranean river. A cairn on a small island in the emerald-green Lough Carra marks the grave of the poet and novelist George Moore (1852–1933, *The Lake*).

Only 11km/7 miles away, **Ballinrobe**, on the Robe River, is also called the »fishing capital of the West«. Some 10km/6 miles south of Ballinrobe, a little side road near the eastern shore of Lough Mask leads to the park of **Lough Mask Estate**. Separated only by a narrow channel from the park lies the island of **Inishmaine**, on which the ruins of a small 13th-century Augustinian abbey still stand; its cruciform church features remarkable stone masonry work depicting animals and foliage.

? MARCO ⊕ POLO INSIGHT

The First Boycott

On Lough Mask Estate resided, at the end of the 19th century, Captain Charles Cunningham Boycott (1832–97), the English agent of the landowner Lord Erne, who treated his Irish tenants badly. With the encouragement of the Irish Land League, the locals refused to work for him or sell him anything. To bring in the potato harvest, workers from the northern counties were hired and given military protection at great cost. This passive resistance drove the Captain back to England, having given his name to the form of protest known today as a »boycott«.

---

*Ross Abbey   The Franciscan abbey that is correctly known as **Ross Errilly Friary** has extensive ruins that are worth seeing. Founded in 1351, the friary stayed in the possession of the monks till 1753. Most of the parts that still survive today, such as the tower and the southern transept, date from the 16th century. To the north of the cloister with its magnificent arcades lies a second courtyard, around which are arranged several utility rooms: a kitchen with water basin for fish, an oven in the mill room, as well as a refectory with recesses for Bible readings. All in all, this is **one of the best-preserved ruins** of a Franciscan friary in Ireland.

Tuam   From Headford, make a detour to the market town of Tuam, only a few kilometres further east. Tuam is a good fishing centre and was, for a long time, a place of great significance for the church. Today still, it is the seat of a Catholic archbishop as well as an Irish-Anglican bishop. The 19th-century Protestant St Mary's Cathedral on Galway Road has a barrel-vault choir with nice sculptures on the chancel arch and east window; both belonged to the original church (12th–14th century). Also worth seeing are the carved shaft of a 12th-century high cross and the Baroque choir stalls. A little to the northeast lies **Dunmore**, an ancient settlement with the ruins of a castle and an abbey. From Tuam, take the R347 **Knockmoy** and the N63 (direction of Roscommon) to the ruins of the former Cistercian abbey of **Knockmoy** (founded in 1190), picturesquely situated on a small lake. On the northern wall of the choir, look out for some **medieval frescoes** (c1400), which are rare in Ireland. Only the black contours are left, showing Christ in the act of blessing, the Martyrdom of St Sebastian and a scene from the legend of the Three Dead and Three Living Kings. Below the three dead kings, the inscription reads: »We have been as you are, you shall be as we are.«

Ross Abbey

Some 8km/5 miles south of Headford, a little road turns off right towards **Annaghdown**, which has some interesting monastic ruins. Parts of Annaghdown Abbey date from the 12th century, the main church and the monastery building were only built 300 years later.

Lough Neagh (Loch nEathach)

✦ B 5

Northern Ireland, province: Ulster
Counties: Antrim, Derry and Armagh
Information: www.discoverloughneagh.com

Covering 388 sq km/150 sq miles, 32km/20 miles long and up to 16km/10 miles wide, Lough Neagh is the largest inland lake in the British Isles. The borders of counties Antrim, Derry and Armagh run right through it.

Birds and fish Six rivers flow into this lake, situated approx. 20km/12 miles west of Belfast. The banks of Lough Neagh have been settled since prehistoric times, and with the lake being so rich in fish, the surrounding area is one of the most important habitats for **many different species of birds** in western Europe. Around 100,000 wild birds come here to spend the winter. The lake is known most of all for its eels; up to 10 tons are caught here every year. There is some fish-processing industry here, a large part of the catch is exported. There is no road around the island, nor a decent footpath. The banks are low, covered in vegetation and marshy in places. Leisure facilities, such as the yacht harbours at Oxford Island and Ballyronan, have been set up.

SIGHTS AROUND LOUGH NEAGH

Lough Neagh Discovery Centre The **Lough Neagh Discovery Centre** on Oxford Island (Co. Armagh) uses videos and an exhibition to introduce visitors to the history of the lake, placing special emphasis on the indigenous flora and fauna. There are some nice hiking trails, as well as boat tours to the islands in Lough Neagh. The **Craigavon Museum** in Waterside House between the discovery centre and the marina houses the 6,000-volume Wilson Library, dedicated to local history, including an extensive collection of Quaker and Methodist literature. In front of the house the barque Enterprise, built in 1900, is moored.

Lough Neagh Discovery Centre: Mon–Fri 9am–5pm, Sat and Sun 10am–5pm, Easter–Sept Sun until 6pm; free admission; www.oxfordisland.com
Craigavon Museum: Mon–Fri 10am–1pm, 2–4pm, May to Sept also Sat; free admission; www.discovercraigavon.com

? *Battle of the Giants*

MARCO POLO INSIGHT

Legend has it that Lough Neagh was created by Finn MacCool, as was Giant's Causeway. One day Finn MacCool, pursuing a Scottish giant, grabbed a lump of soil and tossed it at him. Unfortunately, the Scot managed to escape, but the hole that stayed behind where MacCool had lifted the lump filled up with water, creating Lough Neagh, whilst the lump fell into the sea, creating the Isle of Man.

Antrim (pop. 20,000), which gave the county its name, lies at the mouth of Six Mile Water. Burned down in 1649 by General Monro, in 1798 the town successfully resisted an attack by the United Irishmen. Few old buildings remain, amongst them the court, built in 1762. Belfast International Airport is only 6km/3.5 miles away. Over the centuries, Antrim Castle (1622) was burned down and rebuilt several times. Now all that is left are the castle gardens, laid out by Le Nôtre, creator of the gardens in Versailles, France.

One mile northeast of the town, in Steeple Park, look for a strong and well-preserved round tower, over 27m/88ft high. The Market House of 1726 is home to the tourist information centre (www.antrim.gov. uk).

From Antrim, drive north to Ballymena, a town (pop. 28,000) that is often described as the heart of the Protestant »Bible belt«. The complex called **The Braid** combines the town hall, tourist information centre, an arts centre and the **Mid Antrim Museum**, devoted to local history and outstanding special exhibitions.

Ballymena

The actor Liam Neeson, who shot to worldwide fame with his title role in *Schindler's List* (1992), was born here.

Arts centre: Mon–Fri 10am–10pm; Sat 10am–4pm
Mid Antrim Museum: Mon–Fri 10am–5pm, Sat 10am–4pm; free admission; www.thebraid.com

Protestants from Moravia (in today's Czech Republic) settled in the area around Gracehill (pop. 680, www.gracehillvillage.org), 2km/1.2 miles west, in the mid-18th century, where they continued to live according to their faith, following the strict principles that had made them the target of persecution in their home country. Two entrances lead into their church, one for men and one for women. The cemetery is also segregated by gender. Near Cullybacky, **Arthur Cottage** 6km/3.5 miles west of Ballymena, stood the home of the ancestors of Chester Alan Arthur, 21st president of the United States of America. The former family home can be visited and, in the summer months, actors in period costume explain how bread was baked and quilts sown in the olden days (limited opening times: tel. (028) 2563 5010.

Gracehill

In the small town of Hillsborough (pop. 24,000), southwest of Belfast, at the end of Main Street, the impressive **Hillsborough Castle** catches the eye. In the years 1923–73 it was the residence of the governor of Northern Ireland. From May to August the castle and gardens can be viewed as part of a guided tour (tel. 028 9268 9406, www.nio.gov. uk). At the foot of the hill, the neo-Gothic St Malachy's Church with its two 18th-century organs is worth a visit.

Hillsborough

It is well worth visiting the tourist information centre on the southern edge of the small town of Banbridge (200 Newry Road). There is an excellent café and an art gallery in honour of **F.E. McWilliam**, whose sculptor's studio can be seen. South of Lough Neagh, the small town of Banbridge is the start of the **Brontë Homeland Drive**, stretching along the valley River Bann valley toward Rathfriland, 16km/10 miles further south. The best starting point for a tour is the Brontë Interpretative Centre in Drumballyroney. The father of the

Banbridge

MARCO●POLO TIP

! *Irish Linen Tour* **Insider Tip**

In Banbridge, book a place on the Irish Linen Tour, including the Irish Linen Centre in Lisburn (see photo), a flax farm in Dromore and a working linen mill. If you don't want to do the whole tour, pick up some information from the long-established Ferguson Linen Centre (Scarva Road, Mon–Thu 9am–12.30pm, 1.15–4.30pm Fri 9am–12.15pm admission 6 £; www.fergusonsirishlinen.com).

Brontë sisters, Patrick Brontë, was born here, teaching for a long time at the local school and preaching in the neighbouring church. The locals are convinced that the gloomy atmosphere described in Emily Brontë's *Wuthering Heights* was inspired by her father's tales. A signposted path leads to the remains of the extremely humble Brontë Birthplace.

The theme at the **Scarva Visitor Centre** is the 200-year-old Newry Canal. The **towpath from Newry to Portadown** is now a walking and bike trail. (www.nationalcyclenetwork.org.uk). Megalithic remains nearby such as the **Cloughmore Standing Stone** are also worth a visit.

F.E. McWilliam Gallery and Studio: Mon–Sat 10am–5pm, June–Aug also Sun 1–5pm; free admission; wwwfemcwilliam.com

Brontë Homeland Interpretative Centre: Easter to end of Aug Fri–Sun 12 noon–4.30pm; free admission; www.banbridge.gov.uk

Take the M1 towards Dungannon, driving around Lough Neagh along its southern bank. From there, good detours could lead to The Argory, Ardress House (both ▶Armagh) or **Peatlands Park Peatlands Park,** which is popular with children. Here they can learn about peat and the bog garden, with its typical plants, such as the sundew, one of two indigenous carnivorous plants. A miniature open train used in the past to transport peat gives a 15-minute tour of the place, past two lakes, a small forest and an orchard. At the end of July, the annual Bog Day features a bog snorkelling competition.

❶ March–May and Oct daily 9am–7pm, June–Sept until 9pm, Nov–Feb until 4.30pm; visitor centre March–May and Oct Sat and Sun 1–5pm, June–Sep daily 10am–5pm, Nov–Feb Sun 12 noon–4pm; free admission; www.doeni.gov.uk/niea

Dungannon Dungannon (pop. 11,150), a market and industrial town, was the seat of the O'Neills from the 13th to the early 17th century. The police station on the marketplace with its unusual design was originally intended for the Khyber Pass in Afghanistan. The lake in Dungannon Park, much favoured by campers and caravanners, also attracts anglers. The **Linen Green Designer Village** in a former linen weaving plant sells upmarket fashion items, while a heritage centre illuminates the history of the industry.

The **Benburb Valley Heritage Centre,** 14km/9 miles south of Dungannon in an old weaving shed on the Ulster Canal, tells of the Battle of Benburb in 1646 and the weaving industry. Near Castlecaulfield to the west of Dungannon (approx. 6km/3.5 miles), the **Parkanaur Forest Park** has walking trails and a herd of fallow deer, said to be **the oldest herd in Ireland** and originating in a gift by Queen Elizabeth I, in 1595. Only a few miles further north, at the village of **Dunaghmore**, look for Donaghmore High Cross, put together from two individual pieces. The biblical scenes depicted here are similar to the ones seen on the Ardboe Cross (see below).

Linen Green Designer Village: Mon–Sat 9.30am–5.30pm; free admission; www.thelinengreen.co.uk

Benburb Valley Heritage Centre: Easter–Sept daily 10am–5pm; admission 2 £

Following the road around Lough Neagh, the A29 leads to Cookstown where, until recently, Catholic and Protestant areas were strictly segregated and guarded. For a look at Tullaghoge Fort first, take a right turn onto the B520 just before reaching Cookstown. The fort used to be the burial place of the O'Hagans and the 11th-century **coronation site of the kings of Ulster**. East of Cookstown, on the shore of Lough Neagh, look for the 4m/13ft **Ardboe Cross** on the site of a 6th-century monastery. Despite its weathered state, this is considered one of the most beautiful high crosses in Ulster. Its 22 panels show on the eastern side scenes from the Old Testament (Adam and Eve, the Sacrifice of Isaac, etc.) and on the northern side, scenes from the New Testament (the Adoration of the Magi, Jesus' Entrance into Jerusalem, the Crucifixion, etc.). Close by, visit Coyle's Cottage, a 300-year-old fisherman's hut.

Cookstown

6km/3.5 miles west of Cookstown off the A505, right past Kildress Church,Wellbrook Beetling Mill lies in a pretty wooded valley on the bank of the Ballinderry. In the mill, the last part of the process of linen manufacturing is explained. »**Beetling**« is how the lustrous sheen is achieved, the hard fabric being hammered and passed through (heated) rollers. Between the 18th and the 20th century, linen manufacture was the most important industry in Ulster. Wellbrook alone had six mills; its wooden hammers were powered by water.

Wellbrook Beetling Mill

❶ end of March to end of June and Sept Sat and Sun 2–6pm; July–Aug daily 2–6pm; admission 4 £

Ireland's Bogs

Almost a fifth of the surface area of rainy Ireland is covered by bog. Most of this is blanket bog and fen, but raised bog exists in the Midlands. This fascinating landscape is intensively exploited for economic purposes, and holds many surprises.

▶ **How bogs are created**

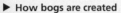

- Water
- Dense underlayer
- Lake sediment
- Reed and sedge peat
- Waterlogged woodland (carr)
- Raised peat bog

A

Bogs are created when the ground is permanently waterlogged due to rain, springs or standing ground water. The lack of oxygen means that dead vegetation does not decompose but builds a layer of peat. This peat is used, especially in Ireland, Finland and Russia, as fuel and for gardens.

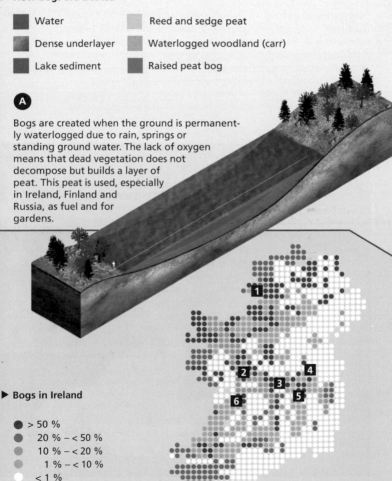

▶ **Bogs in Ireland**

- > 50 %
- 20 % – < 50 %
- 10 % – < 20 %
- 1 % – < 10 %
- < 1 %

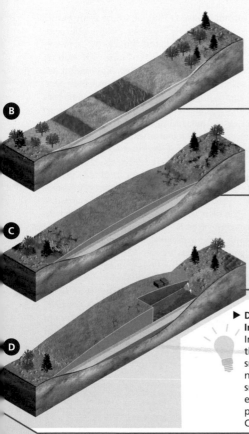

Blanket bog is formed partly by ground water. Its layers of peat are between 2m/6ft and 7m/23ft thick. A distinction is made between Atlantic blanket bog on the west coast and mountain bog on areas above 200m/650ft.

The water supply for raised bog comes mainly from rain. Usually this form is a secondary bog associated with existing bogland.

Raised bog forms thick layers of peat, sometimes up to 12m/40ft deep. It rises towards the centre in the shape of a dome.

▶ **Does peat play a part in Irish whiskey?**
In many Scottish whiskies, drying the malt over a peat fire lends a smoky taste. Irish whiskey is normally smoother, without a smoky tang, but there are exceptions: the Cooley Distillery produces a peated malt called Connemara.

Bog bodies
Finds of bog bodies appear in the headlines regularly. The low oxygen, acidic environment of the bog dissolves bones but preserves soft tissue.

1 Meenybraddan Woman (A.D. 1500-1600)
2 Gallagh Man (400-200 B.C.)
3 Bog body of Tumbeagh (A.D. 1300-1600)
4 Clonycavan Man (400-200 B.C.)
5 Old Croghan Man (350-175 B.C.)
6 Stoneyisland Man (3320–3220 B.C.)

▶ **Electricity generation in Ireland (2013)**

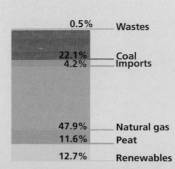

0.5% Wastes
22.1% Coal
4.2% Imports
47.9% Natural gas
11.6% Peat
12.7% Renewables

Springhill House Also impressive is **Springhill House** (1795), an estate some 8km/5 miles northeast of Cookstown. There is beautiful antique oak furniture, but the library, the armoury and the large costume collection are equally fascinating. Not one but two ghosts are said to haunt the premises at night. The gardens and park are very fine. Heading north, don't miss **Maghera Old Church**. There was a monastery here as early as the 6th century, but it was raided by the Vikings in 832. The most interesting features of the ruined church (10th/12th century) are the motifs on the door jambs and the crucifixion scene on the lintel. The eye-catching stone pillar in the churchyard decorated with a carved cross is said to mark the grave of St Lurach, the original founder of the monastery.

> **!** *Scenery and Stone Circles* **Insider Tip**
>
> MARCO ⊕ POLO TIP
>
> The Sperrin Mountains are a designated Area of Outstanding Natural Beauty. To the south of them, the Beaghmore Stone Circles are extensive monuments, some of them with a diameter of over 40m/130ft.

❶ Springhill House: mid-March to mid-June Thu–Sun 12 noon–5pm, July–Aug daily 12 noon–5pm, Sept only Sat and Sun 12 noon–4pm; admission to house and park 6 £

Loughrea (Baile Locha Riach)

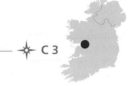

⁎ C 3

Republic of Ireland, province: Connacht
County: Galway
Population: 5,060

Up-and-coming Loughrea got its Irish name Baile Locha Riach (»town on the grey lake«) from the small lake to the southeast.

St Brenda's Cathedral The most interesting building in town is St Brenda's Cathedral, with some very fine windows showing the **development of Irish stained glass in the 20th century**. In addition, there are further good examples of modern art, such as a cycle showing the Stations of the Cross. The devices for a 30-minute audio-tour of the cathedral can be hired from the parish office in Barrack Street. The small Clonfert Diocesan Museum in Abbey Street can be visited in summer. It possesses the oldest wooden statue in Ireland, the Kilcorban Madonna dating from 1180.

Parish office: Mon–Fri 9.30am–1pm, 2–5.30pm; tel. 091 84 12 12; www.loughreacathedral.ie

AROUND LOUGHREA

Some 6km/3.5 miles north of town, on the R350 near Bullaun, look   ***Turoe Stone**
for the 3rd century Turoe Stone, an oval block of granite, some
90cm/3ft high, with a smooth lower quarter and a meander pattern
above. The rounded upper half is decorated with a curvilinear relief
ornament typical of the **Celtic La Tène period**. Originally, the stone
stood beside a prehistoric ring fort, and was used for ritual purposes.

From Loughrea, drive southeast along Lough Rea and take a half left   **Towards**
turn at Carrowkeel, to get (via Duniry) to Pallas. The imposing 16th-   **Portumna**
century castle, which has hardly suffered any damage over the centuries, is open to visitors. Around 30km/20 miles southeast of
Loughrea, at the northern end of Lough Derg and at the mouth of the
Shannon, lies Portumna, a good base for golfing, fishing, sailing and
rowing (there is a new marina). In the state-owned Portumna Forest
Park just out of town visit **Portumna Castle**, a large structure dating
from 1618 and fortified by corner towers, and the Dominican friary,
the ruins of a monastery, consisting of a church with beautiful eastern
window and monastic buildings.
❶ Portumna Castle: April–Sept daily 9.30am–6pm; admission 3 €

Taking the R349 or R348 northwest to Athenry, the scenery gradu-   **Athenry**
ally becomes more rocky and bare. Until the late 16th century, the
little town of Athenry was fairly important; it still preserves many
medieval buildings. Athenry Castle (1235–50) consists of a ruined
gabled tower standing within the remains of outer walls with two
corner turrets. Of a Dominican friary, founded in 1241 and much
altered and destroyed many times, only the ruined church remains,
containing a number of funerary monuments. Of the market cross,
only the base and the top part survive, showing figurative carvings of
the Crucifixion and the Virgin with Child. Remains of the medieval
fortifications, probably from the early 14th century, mark the boundaries of the old town; the tower-like north gate is well-preserved.

Monaghan (Muineachán)
✴ B 5

Republic of Ireland, province: Ulster
County: Monaghan
Population: 7,450

**Only 8km/5 miles from the border with Northern Ireland, Mo-
naghan is the administrative and agricultural centre of the
county of the same name.**

Monaghan

INFORMATION
Market House
Tel. (0 47) 8 11 22
Open: June–Sept
www.monaghantourism.com

WHERE TO STAY
Four Seasons ££££
Coolshannagh
Tel. (0 47) 8 18 88
www.4seasonshotel.ie
Relax in style at the fireplace in the bar, in the restaurant with a good dinner, in the pool, or in the hotel sauna. The Kids Centre gives stressed parents some time out.

A town with history
The Ulster Canal, connecting Belfast with the western coast of Ireland, runs right through the town. Today it is a fairly neglected waterway. There was a settlement here as early as the 9th century, whilst today's Monaghan dates from the 18th and 19th centuries.

Sights
Near the neo-Gothic parish church of St Patrick's look for the pretty Courthouse (1829) containing the excellent County Museum and a small art gallery. On Market Place, the small elegant structure of the Market House catches the eye, built in 1792 in the classical style. A farmers market is held on Friday mornings. On Old Cross Square stands the slightly earlier Old Infirmary Building of 1768, and not far from there, the market cross (1714). The neo-Gothic St Macartan's Cathedral with its slender spire is a local landmark in the south of Monaghan. Convent Lake, with its crannóg, lies at the end of Park Street on the other side of the canal. Most art treasures in Ireland are held in the National Museum in Dublin. A rare exception is the highlight in the County Museum: the bronze processional Crogher Cross, 85cm/2ft 9in high and dating from the 14th century.

❶ County Museum: Mon–Fri 11am–5pm, Sat 12 noon–5pm; free admission; www.monaghan.ie/museum

AROUND MONAGHAN

Glaslough
Take the R185 north out of Monaghan for 11km/7 miles to the picturesque village of Glaslough. At the edge of the village begins the extensive park of Leslie Castle, built in the second half of the 19th century and now a luxury hotel.

Lough Muckno
To the southeast of Monaghan lies Castleblayney. Beside it, Lough Muckno, the largest and most beautiful of the Monaghan lakes, offers good fishing. 20km/12 miles further south, a cooperative in Carrick-

macross produces high-quality lace, sold at the local Lace Gallery on Market Square (www.mcarrickmacrosslace.ie).

West of Monaghan, directly on the border with Northern Ireland Clones (pop. 1,920) was founded by St Tigernach. The famous **crochet lace of Clones** is still made by hand today, examples are shown in the Clones Lace Gallery in the Ulster Canals Stores. On the main square (The Diamond), a 4.5m/15ft high cross dating from the 10th century is decorated with scenes from the Bible. The cemetery has a round tower (23m/75ft) and a house-shaped shrine with remarkable finials. Not far from there, in another churchyard, stands the 12th-century ruined abbey church. The abbey was originally founded by St Tigernach in the early 6th century. Both cemeteries have several interesting tombstones from the 17th and 18th centuries.

Clones

★★ # Monasterboice (Mainistir Bhuithe)

✦ C 5

Republic of Ireland, province: Leinster
County: Louth

The remarkable high crosses of Monasterboice make it one of the most important sights in Ireland. The monastery was founded in the 5th century by St Buite, a pupil of St Patrick.

Happily, the ruins of the medieval monastic enclosure may be visited in peace and quiet; there is no visitor centre, nor that many tourists. The ruins lie right within a cemetery on the east coast of Ireland (free admission), reached via the R168. In 1097, valuable manuscripts perished when the round tower burned out. The old cemetery preserves two churches, a round tower, three high crosses, two early tomb slabs and a sundial of uncertain age. The entrance of the round tower (33m/108ft), which is missing its cap, lies 1.8m/6ft above ground. For safety reasons, it is no longer accessible.

Medieval monastery

The most impressive high cross is Muireadach's Cross (Southern Cross), standing near the entrance. This is one of the most beautiful in Ireland and was named after the donor whose name is inscribed on the western side of the cross. Until recently, it was assumed that this was Muireadach II, who died in 922. New research has shown that the cross was made as early as the first half of the 9th century, in the time of the first abbot, who died at Monasterboice in 844. The 5.1m/17ft monolithic cross is adorned on all sides by **detailed and**

★★ Muireadach's Cross

skilfully carved reliefs. The scenes, mostly depicted on square panels, are to be read from the bottom up. On the eastern side, look for Adam and Eve, Cain and Abel, David and Goliath, Moses Striking the Rock, the Adoration of the Magi, Christ in Judgment and Archangel Michael Weighing the Souls. The top, carved in the shape of a shrine, depicts the meeting of the hermit saints Paul and Anthony in the desert. The western side shows the Capture of Christ, Doubting Thomas, Christ with SS Peter and Paul, the Crucifixion, and a scene that experts have not been able to interpret. The northern side shows again Paul and Anthony, the Flagellation, the Hand of God and interlacing motifs. The southern side depicts the Flight to Egypt, Pontius Pilate, and more interlacing, whilst the base shows hunters and animals, interlacing and fretwork.

Unusually high at 6.45m/21ft, and also richly carved, is the Tall Cross (or Western Cross). Of the 22 panels, only a few can be made out properly. On the eastern side, look for representations of David Killing the Lion, the Sacrifice of Isaac, the Three Young Men in the Furnace, the Capture of Christ, the Ascension, and St Michael with the Devil. The western side depicts Soldiers Guarding the Tomb of Christ, the Baptism, the Mocking of Christ, the Kiss of Judas, and the Crucifixion. | ***Tall Cross**

Of the northern cross at the edge of the churchyard only the top and a piece of the shaft are preserved. | **North Cross**

* Mourne Mountains (Na Beanna Boirche)

— ✳ B 5/6

Northern Ireland, province: Ulster
County: Down
Information: www.mournelive.com

»Where the Mountains o' Mourne sweep down to the sea« – this well-known folk song has made the Mourne Mountains the most famous in Ireland. The Mourne Heritage Trail goes around the range, which is traversed by a single road, the B27 from Kilkeel to Hilltown.

They cover an area 24km/15 miles long and 13km/8 miles wide. The mountain range owes its characteristic shape to its 12 rounded peaks, | **Soft hill scenery in Northern Ireland**

The majestic crosses of Monasterboice

rising to the east to a height of up to 610m/2001ft. A popular but **difficult hiking trail** leads from Newcastle to Slieve Donard, passing the Mourne Wall, erected in the early 20th century to protect the two reservoirs in Silent Valley.

Legananny Dolmen

Some 35km/22 miles north of Newcastle, still in the Mourne Mountains, look for the Legananny Dolmen (►Around Downpatrick) rising up; this is one of the most beautiful and most photographed sights in the country.

Newcastle

Newcastle (pop. 7,450) has been a popular holiday resort since the 19th century, with pretty beaches and a promenade. This coastal town is also known for its close proximity to the famous Royal County Down Club golf course. Holidaymakers can have fun in the Tropicana leisure pool. The little town makes a great base for exploring the Mourne Mountains. There are three parks nearby, as well as several trails for walking, hiking or horseriding.

Donard Park at the southern edge of town is a good starting point for climbing Slieve Donard (849m/2,795ft), the highest of the Mourne mountains. From here, the view stretches all the way to the Isle of Man, the whole of County Down and Strangford Lough with its landmark Scrabo Tower. To the north lie the hills of ►Belfast, to the northwest, ►Lough Neagh can be made out. From the parking lot at Bloody Bridge, near Newcastle, the climb normally takes an afternoon. Around 3km/2 miles northeast of town, alongside the northern slopes of the Mournes, stretches the extensive **Tollymore Forest Park**. The 18th-century country seat has a conspicuous Gothic gateway. At summer weekends there are guided tours, and the Tollymore Outdoor Centre offers hiking, climbing and kayaking courses. There is also a campsite.

By Castlewellan village, further to the northeast, the 450ha/1,100-acre **Castlewellan Forest Park** is a good place to hire a boat, go fishing or hiking. It contains a Peace Maze, with a bell to be rung by all who find their way to the middle. The arboretum, laid out in 1740, has many rare shrubs and trees. **Funny Farm Adventures** in Castlewellan creates a **maize maze** with a new motto every year. Other attractions for children here include go-karting, farm animals and trampolining. Outside the park, Mount Pleasant Horse Trekking Centre offers hacks for beginners and experienced riders (www.mountpleasantcentre.com).

❶ Tollymore Forest Park: daily 10am until dusk; free admission, car 4.50 £ per day; www.nidirect.gov.uk/forests
Castlewellan Forest Park: daily 10am until dusk; free admission, car 4.50 £ per day; www.nidirect.gov.uk/forests
Maize Maze: July–Aug Mon–Sat 10.30am–6pm; admission 4.50 £; www.funnyfarmadventures.co.uk

The **coastal road** leading south from Newcastle goes uphill, providing views out to sea on the left and, to the right, of the ever-changing backdrop of the Mourne Mountains, with its many rare plants. The sleepy-looking villages along the road live from fishing and agriculture. Annalong, Kilkeel, Rostrevor and Warrenpoint make a good stop-off point. From here, several side roads lead to the reservoirs of Silent Valley and the wild scenery around Spelga Dam. In the 18th century, the coastal stretch from Newcastle to the lit-

View of the Mourne Mountains

tle village of Greencastle was infamous for smuggling; today, there are many old lookouts used by the coastal guard. High above the entrance to Carlingford Lough, 13th-century **Green Castle Green Castle, Rostrevor** sits on a rocky ledge.

Some 12km/7.5 miles further west, **Rostrevor**, the most beautiful village in the Mourne Mountains, hugs Carlingford Lough. This **Victorian holiday resort** owes its reputation to its colourful houses, Mediterranean vegetation and a pleasant atmosphere. The stretch of road leading from this seaport **Warrenpoint** to Newry is very charming, with castle-like tower houses and ruins. A particularly beautiful place is where the canal meets the sea at the medieval Narrow Water Castle on the one bank, and the round tower of Clonallan Monastery on the other.

The old commercial centre and border town of Newry (pop. 27,400), **Newry** between Dublin and Belfast, was established because of its strategic location at the Gap of the North, the gateway to Ulster. Reaping the rewards of the peace process, the locals have been improving the town and promoting tourism. Newry did not gain a town charter until 2002, on the occasion of the golden jubilee of Queen Elizabeth II. The **Newry and Mourne Museum** in Bagenals Castle has a fine collection ranging from prehistory to the 21st century, including sculpture of the 11th and 12th centuries and the Gelston Clock, made in around 1780 by John Gelston of Newry. Highlights of the contemporary art exhibition are six paintings by Jasper McKinney and a photomontage about the Troubles by Sean Hillen. St Patrick's Church (1578) was the first Anglican church on Irish soil.

❶ Newry and Mourne Museum: Mon–Sat 10am–4.30pm, Sun 1.30–5pm; free admission; www.bagenalscastle.com/museum

Mullet Peninsula

✳ B 2

Republic of Ireland, province: Connacht
County: Mayo

The lonely, boggy Mullet Peninsula, situated in the furthest northwest of Ireland, is sparsely populated and hardly sees any tourists.

Lonely peninsula

The peninsula's nearly barren western coast is exposed to the rough Atlantic weather, whilst the sweeping bays of the eastern side enfold Blacksod Bay, making it appear like a big inland lake. Both coastlines have pretty beaches, in particular at the narrowest point, along Elly Bay in the east. The main town, Belmullet, lies on a narrow strait connecting the Mullet Peninsula with the mainland. Belmullet is a good base for interesting drives along the 25km/16-mile peninsula, as well as to adjoining areas to the north.

Scenic drive

The Mullet Peninsula is dotted with many ruins. Look out for the clifftop fortress at Doonamo Point (7km/4.5 miles northwest of Bel-

On the way to Belmullet

mullet). The wall, 60m/200ft long and up to 5.5m/18ft high, stretches across the neck of the promontory jutting out to sea, enclosing three **beehive huts** as well as a ruined ring fort. In the southernmost part of the peninsula, at Fallmore, stand the ruins of St Dairbhile's Church. The view from the peninsula's southern Blacksod Point, ▶Achill Island to Slievemore Mountain is very fine.

5km/3 miles southeast of Belmullet, take the R314 northeast. From Glenamoy, take a detour to the north to **Benwee Head**, about 16km/10 miles away. The last half mile from Portacloy has to be walked on foot. Massive jagged cliff walls rise up to 257m/843ft out of the sea. A group of seven sea stacks, the Stags of Broadhaven, jut out of the ocean north of Portacloy . **Belderrig** The village of Belderrig has more impressive wild cliff scenery. Alongside Céide Fields (▶Ballina) 8km/5 miles away, this is a second important excavation site. The remains of a settlement excavated at Belderrig are thought to date from c1500 BC. Belderrig is the venue for an annual triathlon event called **Belderrig Bronze Man** (www.bronze-man.com).

Other sights in the area

Mullingar (An Muileann gCearr)

✦ C 4

Republic of Ireland, province: Leinster
County: Westmeath
Population: 20,100
Information: www.countywestmeath.com

Thanks to two large lakes nearby, Lough Owel in the north and Lough Ennell in the south, Mullingar in Westmeath is a popular recreation area. Much of the town is enclosed by the Royal Canal.

This little rural town lies at the centre of a district mainly given over to cattle breeding. Dominating the town, the Catholic ***Cathedral of Christ the King** (1936–39) features wonderful mosaics by the Russian artist Boris Anrep (1883–1969). The portrait of St Anne is said to show the face of the Russian writer Anna Achmatova, with whom Anrep had an affair during the First World War. In the small **ecclesiastical museum** are memorabilia of Sir Oliver Plunkett. The tourist information office occupies the restored Market House, where guided walks and the Belvedere Trail (2.8km/1.6 miles) begin. County Hall houses an arts centre (www.mullingarartscentre.ie).

Between the waters

❶ Church museum: July and Aug Sat and Sun 3–4pm; admission 1.25 £

AROUND MULLINGAR

Towards Castlepollard

The R394 leads north to Castlepollard, passing several lakes. At Crookedwood lies the ruined 15th-century church of Taghmon, with a fortified four-storey tower house. The tower and church nave feature vaulted ceilings. Take a minor road east of Crookedwood for 2km/1.2 miles to the 15th-century St Munna's Church, built in this beautiful location on the site of the 7th-century church dedicated to St Munna. Look out for the **grotesque figure** above the north window! Located 3km/2 miles from Crookedwood, driving west, Multyfarnham has a modern Franciscan college, standing on the site of a former 14th-century monastery with restored church. The Stations of the Cross in the college grounds are life-size. **Tullynally Castle** which has been the residence of the Pakenham family, earls of Longford, since 1655, also belongs to Castlepollard. The romantic castle (18th and 19th centuries) has been altered several times. Closely connected to the estate are the **Duke of Wellington** and **the writer Maria Edgeworth** (▶Longford). The park surrounding Tullynally Castle on the shore of Lough Derravaragh is very attractive.

❶ Tullynally Castle: park and tea room May–Aug Thu–Sun 1–6pm; admission 6 €; castle only for groups; www.tullynallycastle.com

Uisneach Hill

18km/11 miles west of Mullingar north of the R 390 stands **Uisneach Hill** (Hill of Pride), 184m/604ft high. On this hill is the Cat Stone, in Irish Carraig Coithrigi (Rock of Division), where once the five old Irish provinces met. Here in the 2nd century AD King Tuathal is said to have built his palace, which remained the seat of the High Kings of Ireland for 200 years. This place is also said to have been a major site for druidic fire rituals and for the Bealtaine festival at the start of summer.

Fore Abbey

Situated among hills some 4km/2.5 miles east of Castlepollard, the historical village of Fore is the site of a monastery founded by St Fechin in the 7th century. The church (c900) is preserved, along with a high cross in the churchyard and a fortified house, the »anchorite's cell«, with mausoleum. In the 13th century, the monastery was replaced by a Benedictine priory, the ruins of which stand 400m/450yd apart. Of the priory, a church with two tower houses, parts of a cloister and outbuildings are still standing. Close by, in the fields, note two gates of the former village fortification.

Belvedere House and Gardens

Carry on a few miles south of Mullingar on the N52 to Belvedere House and Gardens. The manor house takes its name from the beautiful view of Lough Ennell and was built around 1740 for the newlywed Lord Belfield, the first Earl of Belvedere. He accused his young wife of committing adultery with his brother Arthur – and had both locked away for the rest of their lives. In other respects, his lordship seems to have been equally belligerent, erecting the »Jealous Wall«, to prevent his other brother, George, who lived nearby, from looking in.

❶ March, April, Sept, Oct daily 9.30am–7pm, May–Aug daily 9.30am–8pm, Nov–Feb 9.30am–4.30pm; admission 8 €; www.belvedere–house.ie

Whiskey lovers will enjoy a visit to Locke's Distillery in Kilbeggan, which has held its licence since 1757. After closing down in 1954, a museum of industry was planned, but eventually, in 1987, the place was taken over by the Cooley Distillery who are now maturing their whiskey here the traditional way, in casks. Join a guided tour of the restored distillery to learn how »**pot still whiskey**« is produced. Recently, a winery was added, showcasing the production of Irish sherry.

Locke's Distillery

❶ Kilbeggan Distillery Experience: Nov–March daily 10am–4pm, April–Oct daily 9am–6pm; www.lockesdistillerymuseum.ie

Naas (An Nás)

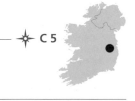

✦ C 5

Republic of Ireland, province: Leinster
County: Kildare
Population: 20,700
Information: www.naas.ie

In early times, the kings of Leinster resided here in the North Mote. Today, Naas, 34km/21 miles southwest of Dublin, is a prosperous industrial town.

The Normans fortified the town, but it was raided in the 14th century. Parts of one of the castles were used in the rectory of the Protestant church. Naas borders the plain of Curragh (►Kildare), famous for **horse breeding**. The town is well known for the horse race on the Punchestown Racecourse 4km/2.5 miles south on the R411.

Town of kings and horses

The town hall dates from 1796 and the **court house**, whose courtroom resembles that of the Old Bailey in London and has therefore often been used for films, from 1807. The three-storey King John's Castle, probably going back to 1206, is the last remaining example of the once numerous fortified houses in Naas. 9km/5.5 miles north of Naas lies Kilteel Castle, founded in the 13th century by the Knights of St John. The gardens of the Georgian country house at **Coolcarrigan** by the Bog of Allen are notable for their rare trees. The estate church has a round tower (1880), leaded glass windows and Gaelic inscriptions inside.

Sights

❶ Coolcarrigan: visits on specific days between March and Oct, 9am-5pm; admission 8 €; www.coolcarrigan.ie

AROUND NAAS

Maynooth The small town of Maynooth (pop. 13,600), around 24km/15 miles northeast, on the Royal Canal, has a branch of the National University of Ireland: St Patrick's College. The institute was established in 1795 in the grounds of an earlier foundation by the English aiming to allow the Irish to train their Catholic clergy in their own country. It is currently the **largest seminary in Ireland and the British Isles**, now also accepting laypeople and women students. The imposing buildings, arranged around courtyards with lawns, date mainly from the 19th century. Note St Joseph's Square with the Gothic Revival façade of St Patrick's House. The President's Arch leads to the college chapel, St Mary's Oratory, with its fine rose window, sculptures and mosaics. The **Bicentenary Garden** was laid out with motifs from the book of Genesis. The highlight of a visit is the **National Science Museum** on the south campus. It displays ecclesiastical and historical items of scientific interest, including old harps, telegraphic instruments by Marconi and items belonging to the natural scientist Nicholas Callan. The yew at the entrance to the college is thought to be the oldest tree in Ireland (12th century). Next to the gateway of the college stand the remains of **Maynooth Castle** (13th–17th century): a tower house, a gate house and parts of a curtain wall. St Patrick's is a papal university (www.maynoothcollege.ie).

National Science Museum: May–Sept Tue and Thu 2–4pm, Sun 2–6pm; donation requested; www.nuim.ie/museum

Leixlip Take the N4 east to Leixlip. The name of the town is taken from the Danish and means »**salmon leap**«. Towering above what has, in recent years, become a dormitory town for Dublin, is Leixlip Castle. A barn about one mile southwest, on private property, which goes by the name of »The Wonderful Barn« is worth seeing. Lady Connolly of Castletown had this conical structure built in 1743, using stone and bricks. Each of its five storeys could be serviced from the outside through hatches; a flight of steps runs in a spiral up to the top.

Castletown House

N

Ground floor

Pompeian Gallery

Kitchen Wing

Dining Room

Entrance Hall

Staircase

Stables Wing

1 Brown Study
2 Red Drawing Room
3 Green Drawing Room
4 Print Room
5 State Bedroom
6 Healy Room
7 Map Room

© BAEDEKER

Castletown House was built in 1722 for the Irish member of Parliament William Connolly by Alessandro Galilei, the central building, approached by a broad flight of steps, consists of three storeys as well as thirteen bays. The wings are connected to the central block by means of quadrant-shaped colonnades. The excellent stucco work inside, the staircase and the Pompeian Gallery are worth seeing. Today, the house is the seat of the **Irish Georgian Society**, which endeavours to preserve as many buildings from the Georgian period as possible.

*Castletown House

❶ Guided tours: mid-March to Oct daily 10am–6pm; admission 4.50 €

The attractions of Straffan, situated 6km/3.5 miles southwest of Celbridge, are a railway museum with steam locomotives and the Lodge Park Walled Garden.

Straffan

❶ June–Aug Wed–Sun 2–6pm; admission 7.50 €;
www.steam-museum.com

Butterflies are free to fly around the tropical greenhouse of Butterfly Farm in Ovidstown; various insects, spiders and reptiles are safely kept behind glass.

Butterfly Farm

❶ June-Aug daily 12 noon–5.30pm, Sat and Sun from 10am; admission 8 €;
www.straffanbutterflyfarm.com

Don't miss the very impressive **standing stone** of Punchestown, standing 5km/3 miles southeast of Naas on Woolpack Road, the medieval road from Dublin to Kilkenny. This menhir is over 7m/23ft high and tapering toward the top. When it toppled in 1931, a Bronze Age burial site was found at its foot. It is over 7m/23ft long and tapers at the top.

Punchestown

On the banks of the ▶Grand Canal, reached via the R409, stands the old Canal Hotel of Robertstown, erected for ship passengers in 1801, at the highest point of the Robertstown Canal. It is now a community centre.

Robertstown

Navan (An Uaimh)

✴ C 5

Republic of Ireland, province:
Leinster
County: Meath

Population: 12,300
Information: tel. 046 909 7060

Navan is the largest town in County Meath. The inventor of the internationally recognized scale measuring wind force, Admiral Sir Francis Beaufort (1774–1857), was born here.

Transport and industry
This little town lies northwest of Dublin in hilly terrain at the confluence of the rivers Boyne and Blackwater. There is a carpet factory here and, nearby, in the direction of Kells, the **largest lead and zinc mine in Europe**: Tara. The large motte on the western edge of Navan is a popular viewpoint.

AROUND NAVAN

Along the N51 towards Slane
Around 2km/1.2 miles northeast of town, in former monastic grounds in **Donaghmore**, stand a well-preserved round tower and a church. This is said to be the site of the first monastery St Patrick founded in Ireland. The 10th-century tower has a **Donaghmore** round-arched entrance door, situated 3.5m/12ft above ground, with a relief of the Crucifixion. The church dates from the 15th century and the churchyard has some early Christian headstones. On a rise further east, **Dunmoe Castle** is visible. Two sides of the rectangular 16th-century keep with round towers survive.

Bective Abbey
South of Navan, take a left turn 1km/0.6 miles past Bective to the 12th-century Cistercian abbey of Bective, a daughter house of Mellifont Abbey (►Drogheda). Some parts of the church, as well as the chapter house, are preserved. The pretty cloister, the tower house and the large hall, possibly a refectory, date from the 15th century, when the monastery was fortified.

Rathmore
Take the N51 west towards Rathmore. The village's ruined 15th-century church has remarkable figurative representations inside. To the left, just off the road towards Athboy, rises the **Hill of Ward** (117m/384ft), an ancient religious and assembly site where Samhain was celebrated.

New Ross (Rhos Mhic Triúin)

✦ D 5

Republic of Ireland, province: Leinster
County: Wexford
Population: 8,150

New Ross, on the steep banks of the River Barrow, is one of the oldest towns in County Wexford. This town in the southeastern corner of Ireland is a base for organized boat trips on the rivers Barrow and Nore.

Narrow, winding streets, occasionally narrow stairways only accessible to pedestrians, still give an idea of the medieval town plan. Small ships enliven the broad river and the port. Of the large early 13th-century St Mary's parish church, only the chancel and transepts remain. In the 19th century, the nave had to give way to a new church. Look out for three delicately mullioned lancet arch windows in the chancel, as well as several medieval tombs. The Tholsel (town hall), built between 1749 and 1804, is a pretty classical building with a domed clock tower. St Michael's Church (1806) is used as an arts centre (www.stmichaelsnewross.com).

In **Priory Court** on The Quay, 15 hand-knotted tapestries measuring approximately 1.80 x 1.40m/6ft x 4ft 6 in tell the dramatic story of Ireland under Norman rule. The designs by Ann Griffin Bernstorff were knotted by 125 volunteers between 1998 and 2011.

❶ May–Oct Mon–Sat 9.30am–5pm; admission 6 €; www.rostapestry.com

AROUND NEW ROSS

A few miles south of New Ross, the 250ha/618-acre ***John F. Kennedy Arboretum** was opened in 1968, with finance provided by Americans of Irish descent in memory of the U.S. president John Fitzgerald Kennedy, whose great-grandfather was born nearby in Dunganstown. 4,500 different kinds of trees and shrubs grow in the grounds, amongst them 500 varieties of rhododendron and 150 different azaleas.

❶ Daily April–Sept 10am–6.30pm, May–Aug 10am–8pm, at other times 10am–5pm; admission 3 €; www.heritageireland.ie

MARCO ⊕ POLO TIP

Dunbrody Emigrant Ship Insider Tip

The SS Dunbrody was a three-master »famine ship« that took emigrants to the New World between 1845 and 1870. A reconstruction moored In the harbour tells its history, with an interactive exhibition that brings to life the conditions aboard those ships. A database on Irish emigration to America allows genealogical research (daily April–Sept 9am–6pm, at other times 9am–5pm; admission 8.50 €; www.dunbrody.com.

New Ross

INFORMATION
Dunbrody Famine Ship
The Quay
Tel. (0 51) 42 18 57
www.dunbrody.com

WHERE TO STAY
Cedar Lodge Hotel €€€€
Carrigbyren, Newbwan (on the N 25)
Tel. (0 51) 42 83 86
www.cedarlodgehotel.ie, 30 rooms
A quietly located four-star hotel with a
high standard of hospitality

Hook Peninsula Continue on the R733 to the Hook Peninsula and **Dunbrody Abbey**, the imposing remains of a 12th-century Cistercian monastery. The austere church has a choir, transepts, a nave and a 15th-century crossing tower. Of the monastic buildings, the library and the chapter house on the east side, the refectory and the kitchen on the south side survive. There is a yew-hedge maze, a cookery school and a visitor centre here. At Arthurstown, **Ballyhack Castle** stands off the road, at the water's edge. The five-storey 15th-century castle with vaulted rooms has been restored and is open to the public.

From Ballyhack, a passenger ferry crosses the broad mouth of the River Barrow to Passage East (www.passageferry.ie). Branch off the R733 past Arthurstown and continue south on a side road to get to the small fishing village of Duncannon, which has a nice sandy beach. On a promontory, a fort guards the mouth of the river.

The road ends at the south of the long peninsula, where on the eastern side **Slade Castle** (15th to 17th century) occupies a picturesque position next to a fishing harbour. ***Hook Head Lighthouse** at the very tip of the peninsula, with its visitor centre, stands on a 700-year-old round keep and may well be the oldest operating lighthouse in the world. Dolphins and whales can sometimes be spotted from here, and boat trips operate.

From Hook Head, take the road back 3km/2 miles north and make a right in Templetown towards **Fethard-on-Sea**, which also has good sandy beaches. In 1169, where the headland of Baginbun extends south out to sea, **the first Normans landed in Ireland**.

Dunbrody Abbey: May to mid-Sept daily 11am–6pm; admission to abbey 3 €, with maze and castle 6 €; www.dunbrodyabbey.com

Ballyhack Castle: mid-June to Aug daily 10.30am–5pm; free admission

Hook Head Lighthouse: daily 9.30am–5pm, May and Sept until 5.30pm, June–Aug until 6pm; admission with guided tour 6 €; http://hookheritage.ie

Omagh (An Omaigh)

B 4

Northern Ireland, province: Ulster
County: Tyrone
Population: 21,400
Information: tel. 028 82 24 78 31

Omagh is known most of all for its open-air museums, the Ulster-American Folk Park and the Ulster History Park.

The place where the Drumragh and Camowen rivers come together is a great base for salmon-fishing. Hikes in the Sperrin Mountains are also recommended. Visitors who enjoy parks can also explore Gortin Glen Forest Park. The **An Creaghán Visitor Centre** on the road to Cookstown is a good information point for cyclists and walkers who are heading for the trails in the Sperrin Mountains. Archaeological finds are on display here.

For active visitors

Omagh was in the news for all the wrong reasons in August 1998, when a car bomb planted by a breakaway group of the IRA killed 31 people and injured another 220, the biggest death toll in a single incident during the Troubles.

AROUND OMAGH

Head out north on the A5 from Omagh for 6km/3.5 miles to reach the **Ulster American Folk Park**. This extensive open-air museum shows the history of emigration from Ulster to the US. The historical reasons behind emigration, the living conditions in the 18th and 19th centuries are portrayed here, as well as the difficult trip across the Atlantic to a fresh start in America. There is a blacksmith's forge, cottages, a Presbyterian meeting house and much more, but particularly impressive are the reconstructed streets as they were in an Ulster village and an American port. Whilst only some 4 million Irish live on the island, **worldwide, around 90 million people are said to have Irish roots**; no less than 15 US presidents are the descendants of Irish immigrants; of those, eleven have their roots in Ulster.

**Ulster American Folk Park

❶ March–Sept Tue–Sun 10am–5pm, Oct–Feb Tue–Fri 10am–4pm, Sat 11am–4pm; admission 8 £

Situated more to the east, Gortin Glen Forest Park may be explored on foot or by car: there is a choice of three walking trails (2–4km/1.2–2.5 miles long); alternatively take a 9km/5.5-mile circular drive through the forest, with a chance of seeing Sitka deer and other wild animals. For a longer walk consider the stretch from Gortin Glen

Gortin Glen Forest Park

After years of famine, Irish emigrants encountered shops in America that were amply stocked with groceries and other goods

Forest Park to the Ulster American Folk Park. The trail, part of the Ulster Way, leads approx. 16km/10 miles along small roads and forest paths. On the way back, it is possible to catch the bus (no. 97). Pick up a trail map from the tourist office in Omagh.

❶ Gortin Glen Forest Park: daily from 10am to dusk; admission for walkers 1 £, for cars 3 £

Strabane Every year, the border village of Strabane, west of the ►Sperrin Mountains, attracts some literary pilgrims following in the footsteps of Brian O'Nolan (aka Flann O'Brien aka Myles na gCopaleen). Flann O'Brien was born in a house on Bowling Green. There is a sculpture trail, including Martin Heron's ***Ambrose the Pig** next to the Alley Theatre, Strabane's answer to the Blarney Stone. It is a reference to the local pig market, to Irish fertility rites and to Flann O'Brien's character of the same name. Touching the pig is said to bring luck. Also of interest is **Gray's Printing Museum** in the former printing workshop where John Dunlop learned the trade. He was the first to print the American Declaration of Independence.

Gray's Printing Museum: Mon–Sat 9am–5pm, Sun until 4pm; admission 3 £

Portlaoise (Port Laoise)

✣ C 4

Republic of Ireland, province: Leinster
County: Laois
Population: 20,150

Nothing remains of the original buildings of the old town of Portlaoise (pronounced »Portleash«), which was destroyed in the 17th century, and most people associate Portlaoise only with the high-security prison for IRA prisoners on the outskirts, off the Dublin road, a fortress protected by barbed wire.

Some 13km/8 miles northeast of town, near Emo village, look for Emo Court manor house. The house was built in the late 18th century for the earls of Portarlington by the famous architect James Gandon. Take a stroll in the park, with yew tree avenues, extensive lawns, rare trees and shrubs. **Emo Court**

❶ Park all year until dusk, free admission; house Easter to end of Sept daily 10am–6pm; admission 3 €; www.heritageireland.ie

Take the N80 east of Portlaoise, passing after 5km/3.1 miles the **Rock of Dunamaise**, a spectacular, somewhat sombre-looking ruined castle (10th–17th century). On the 60m/200-ft ridge, a tower house, bastion walls with turrets, gatehouses, walls and trenches of the old extensive fortification survive. **Around Portlaoise**
The new **Stradbally Steam Museum** (The Green) celebrates the steam engine, whether on rails, the road or in agriculture.
Around 12km/7.5 miles southeast rises the 12th-century, nearly 30m/100-ft round tower, all that is left of a monastery **Timahoe monastery**. The Romanesque doorway is decorated with carved faces.

From Timahoe, drive 13km/8 miles southwest on minor roads to **Abbeyleix**. This pretty little town was established in the 18th century on

Portlaoise

INFORMATION
Laois Tourism
James Fintan Lawlor Avenue
Tel. (057) 867 43 28
www.laoistourism.ie3

WHERE TO STAY
Killeshin Hotel €€€
Dublin Road
Tel. (057) 863 1200
www.thekilleshin.com 87 rooms
This 4-star hotel is a favourite with business travellers and has special offers for families.

the foundations of an earlier monastery, meticulously laid out by Viscount de Vesci. The viscount's family seat, Abbeyleix House (1773), is set in a beautiful park. The old schoolhouse is now the **Abbeyleix Heritage House**, with a small museum. **Heywood Gardens** near Ballinakill, 5km/3 miles south of Abbeyleix, are also worth a visit.

Around Portlaoise

Further south, in Attanagh near Durrow, the **Irish Fly-Fishing & Game Museum** is devoted to 300 years of hunting and fishing. Visitors see the reconstructed rooms of a gamekeeper and a gunmaker, but the main theme is angling. Visits must be arranged with the museum founder Walter Phelan (tel. 057 873 61 12).

The **Famine Workhouse Museum** in Donaghmore west of Portlaoise displays the dormitory, kitchen and other rooms of a workhouse and describes social conditions at the time of the Great Famine.

For information about walking, cycling, riding and golf along the 60km/38-mile **Slieve Bloom Heritage Way**, refer to www.slievebloom.ie

Stradbally Steam Museum: Mon–Fri 9.30am–5pm; admission 5 €; www.heritagehousemuseum.com

Abbeyleix Heritage House: Tue–Sat 9am–5pm; admission 3 €; www.heritagehousemuseum.com

Heywood Gardens: April and Sept daily 8.30am–7pm, May–Aug until 9pm, Oct–March until 5.30pm; free admission

Famine Workhouse Museum: Mon–Fri 11am–5pm; admission 4 €; www.donaghmoremuseum.com

Mountmellick

Mountmellick was founded in the 17th century by Quakers who, in 1677, opened their first school in Ireland on the Owenass River and worked to turn a sleepy little town into »the Irish Manchester«. In the ***Mountmellick Museum**, embroidery and crochet work testifies to their hard work. The shop sells these products. The Quakers established their first cemetery in Rosenallis, at the foot of the Slieve Bloom Mountains.

❶ Mon–Fri 9am–1pm, 2–5pm; admission 5 €; www.mountmellickdevelopment.com

** **Ring of Kerry**

D/E 1/2

Republic of Ireland, province: Munster
County: Kerry   **Information:** tel. 064 6641233

The scenic drive around the Iveragh Peninsula has become famous as the »Ring of Kerry«. The road offers spectacular views of the coast, wild bogs and enchanting hill scenery.

Schedule a whole day to properly enjoy this extraordinarily beautiful landscape dotted with little fishing villages. The circular drive, the **most popular tourist route in Ireland**, starts in Kenmare on the N70 southeast, carries on west via Waterville, and on to Killorglin in the north. Carry on inland on the R562 to Killarney and from there back to Kenmare. The overall distance is 158km/98 miles. If you are planning a detour to Valentia Island in the west, it adds at least 40km/25 miles to the tour.

Most popular tourist route in Ireland

DRIVE AROUND THE RING OF KERRY

The friendly town of Kenmare is situated where the Roughty River flows into the long bay of Kenmare River. High-quality lace is produced here, and the woollen industry also has a good reputation. Today, the main source of revenue is tourism; but whilst much in evidence, tourism has not diminished Kenmare's nostalgic charm. The two main roads of Kenmare form an X. Close by, to the west, on the banks of the River Finnihy, look for the **Druid's Circle**: 15 standing stones with a diameter of 15m/16.4yd and a dolmen at its centre. Kenmare is also for the Ring of Beara, much less known and spectacular in its own way – well worth doing. The Ring of Beara leads around the Beara Peninsula south of Kenmare. (►Beara Peninsula)

*Kenmare

Start the Ring of Kerry from Kenmare initially on the N70 going west, following the bay. On the right-hand side rise the foothills of the Macgillycuddy's Reeks. The church in **Templenoe** dates from 1816. There is a viewpoint with car park at the ruined castle of Dromare. After 6km/3.5 miles, the valley of the **River Blackwater** opens up to the right, where the river plummets through a deep gorge into the sea. Take a little path leading down off the road through dense, nearly tropical vegetation. A little road leads north into the mountains, via a 250m/820ft pass to **Glencar** and Caragh Lake. In **Tahilla** anglers can choose between freshwater fishing and high-sea fishing. Two of the main draws of **Parknasilla** are its scenic location and its year-round mild climate, favouring palm trees, pines, bamboo and jasmine. A bit further inland, situated on a narrow inlet, **Sneem** is a good base for fishing. The Protestant church, which has seen many alterations since its construction in the 16th century, features an original **weather vane in the shape of a salm-**

Ring of Kerry drive

> **MARCO POLO TIP**
>
> ! *Peak season* **Insider Tip**
>
> In peak season the Ring of Kerry can turn into one big traffic jam! It is recommended to start early in the morning in Kenmare – this avoids being stuck behind a coach all day. Coaches start in Killorglin.

The Ring of Kerry, with the mountains on one side, the Atlantic on the other

on. The mountains to the north and west, with a height of up to 660m/2,165ft, are good terrain for hillwalking and climbing.

*Staigue Fort   After approx. 13km/8 miles, a very narrow road turns off to the right at Castlecove. Some 4km/2.5 miles on, a large stone fort of indeterminate date appears on a hill between two valleys. Staigue Fort is a round dry-stone building, 27m/89ft in diameter and over 5m/16ft high, surrounded by a ditch, and with chambers and stairs inside its 4m/13ft walls.

Back at the seashore, enjoy the drive with a view of the many small islands dotting the coast, and turn towards Caherdaniel, which offers opportunities for trout fishing, swimming and surfing. Nearby is a small stone fort.

Caherdaniel

Southwest of Caherdaniel stretches Derrynane National Historic Park. Take the sign-posted nature trail to explore the dunes, with a long sandy beach in front. At low tide, you can go across to tiny off-shore Abbey Island. The manor house was the home of »the Great

*Derrynane National Historic Park

Liberator«, **Daniel O'Connell** (1775–1847). Today, it houses a museum.

❶ April Wed–Sun 10.30am–5pm, May–Sept daily 10.30am–6pm, Oct, Nov, March Wed–Sun 10.30am–5pm; admission 3 €

Lough Currane

The N70 leads up to the Coomakista Pass, rising 210m/690ft above the sea (splendid views!), and down to Ballinskelligs Bay. Lough Currane is to your right. **Church Island**, in this fresh-water lake, has a

ruined 12th-century church with a Romanesque doorway, remains of monks' living quarters, as well as several tombstones with Christian symbols. On the western shore lie the horse-shoe-shaped stone fort of Beenbane and the ruins of a beehive hut with thick walls. **Waterville**, in Irish An Coirean (»little whirlpool«), lies on the small isthmus between Lough Currane and the bay. From here, two minor roads (later becoming one) lead right across the Iveragh Peninsula over the mountains and down to Killorglin, with very few tourists. Well worth doing! The southern route leads past various lakes with plenty of fish.

A sandy beach on the Ring of Kerry

West of Waterville, **Ballinskelligs Bay** has good beaches. Ballinskelligs village lies on the opposite shore. **Coomanaspig Pass** North of Waterville, a road branches off to the left, in the direction of Portmagee. Continue on a narrow side road south towards the **Coomanaspig Pass** (330m/1,083ft) for a magnificent view of the bays and bird islands of this part of the Atlantic. Portmagee bridge (1970) leads across a narrow sound onto bare, rocky **Valentia Island**, which is noted for sea angling. Enjoy a splendid view of the Atlantic shore cliffs from Bray Head, 240m/790ft above the sea. The Valentia Island Ferry sails between Knightstown on the eastern side of the island and Reenard Point on the mainland from April to September between 8.30am and 10.30pm. **The Valentia Heritage Centre** in the schoolhouse of Knightstown has an exhibition about the laying of the first transatlantic cable between 1857 and 1866.

Valentia Heritage Centre: end of April to Sept daily 11am–5.30pm,; admission 3.50 €

*Skellig Experience

A further attraction on Valentia Island is the **Skellig Experience**, near the bridge. The visitor centre has good displays ►Skellig Islands on the life and work of the monks who lived on the islands from the 6th to the 13th century. Another part of the exhibition is dedicated to the local seabirds and the underwater world. There are regular boat trips from Valentia Island out to the islands jutting out of the water like the peaks of a sunken mountain range. The comfortable pleasure boats are only allowed to go around the Skellig Islands – a bird sanctuary since 1987. As the boat trips (usually at 10am) are not

MARCO POLO TIP

! *Ice Cream* ^{Insider} ^{Tip}

Don't miss the ice cream at Valentia Island Farm House, which is made in Kilbeg. In their tiny dairy, Caroline and Joe Daly turn Irish milk into wonderful ice cream flavours using hazelnuts, mangos, mint, pistachios and strawberries.

possible in bad weather, make sure to phone ahead: tel. (066) 947 6306.

❶ March, April, Oct, Nov Mon–Fri 10am–5pm, May–Sept daily 10am–6pm, July and Aug daily until 7pm; admission 5 €; www.skelligexperience.com

The next stop on the Ring of Kerry is Cahirciveen. Opposite the little town, beyond Valentia River, the ruins of 15th-century Ballycarbery Castle can be made out. To the northeast, accessible via a minor road to the left of the N70, lie two ring forts: Cahergall, with a circumference of 32m/105ft, with two stone buildings within the walled enclosure, and Leacanabuaile (9th century) with stairs, chambers and subterranean rooms, on a hill-top. **Cahirciveen**

Carry on northeast on the main road leading uphill through the broad valley of Kells. To the left, Knockadober rises 680m/2,230ft; the peaks of the mountain range to the right are of about similar height. **Valley of Kells**
In between there are beautiful views of the sea and mountains. Running along the foot of Drung Hill, in parts high above the sea, the road leads past an old stagepost. Carry on down to Glenbeigh, accompanied by a magnificent view of Dingle Bay and the Dingle Peninsula.

A small holiday resort in a scenic location, Glenbeigh makes anglers happy, whilst Rossbeigh, 2km/1.2 miles to the west, is the place for beach lovers. **Glenbeigh**

Carry on for 15km/9 miles through moraine terrain to Killorglin. In this little town, the famous **Puck Fair** with horse and cattle market is held. Beyond the salmon-rich River Laune, the road forks. The N70 continues on via Milltown to ►Tralee, with, to the west, the ruins of 13th-century Kilcolman Abbey. The R562 turns off left to the east and continues on the Ring of Kerry along the river. Some **Killorgin**

6km/3.5 miles past the fork in the road stands **Ballymalis Castle**, dating from the 16th century. The picturesque ruins of this four-storey castle lie on the shore, offering a view far across to the Macgillycuddy's Reeks.

Continue on through the lakes of ▶Killarney and, accompanied by splendid views, back towards **Moll's Gap**. A scenic route leads down to Kenmare, the starting point of the drive (Killarney to Kenmare 34km/21 miles).

A DETOUR TO THE MACGILLYCUDDY REEKS

The Macgillycuddy's (pronounced »Maclicuddis«) Reeks, in Irish Na Cruacha Dubha (»the black mountains«), rise from the Iveragh Peninsula, partly wooded, partly bare.

Highest mountains in Ireland

This ancient mountain range formed of red sandstone is the highest in Ireland: **Carrantuohill** (1,040m/3,412ft), Beenkeragh (994m/3,261ft) and Caher (960m/3,149ft). From its two highest peaks, the view stretches for miles: towards Dingle Bay in the northwest, the lakes of Killarney, and the mountains of southern Kerry. The view down to the nearby gorges, green valleys and small shimmering lakes is ample reward for the effort of making the climb.

There are two good **starting points for climbing Carrantuohill**: the youth hostel on the northern slope of the Macgillycuddy's Reeks or a car park nearby (situated approx. one mile from the youth hostel, in the direction of Glencar). The first part of the climb, through Hag's Glen, is also suitable for less experienced hikers and already gives a good idea of the scenery. Hiking up to Lough Callee, the mountain lake in a beautiful location at the end of Hag's Glen, takes about 1.5 hours. The second part of the climb leads via »The Devil's Ladder«. As the name suggests, this should only be attempted by experienced hillwalkers. Schedule another two hours for this.

There is another way of climbing Carrantuohill: from the west, starting from Lough Acoose, a lake beautifully snuggled in the foothills of the mighty mountain. This route also requires some climbing experience.

Impressive scenery in
Macgillycuddy's Reeks

Roscommon (Ros Comáin)

✦ C 3

Republic of Ireland, province: Connacht
County: Roscommon
Population: 5,700

Situated to the north of the town on a hill, the symbol of the town, Roscommon Castle, is a mighty Norman fortress.

Pretty town

Roscommon takes its name from St Coman, who founded a monastery on this site in the 6th century. The Irish name »Ros Comáin« means something like »Forest of Coman«. The Dominican abbey close to this monastery was founded by Felim O'Conor, king of Connacht. A recess in the northern wall of the abbey church (altered in the 15th century) shelters the tomb of the founder (c1290), showing eight armed retainers.

The **County Museum** in the Presbyterian church of 1863 presents such highlights as a sheela-na-gig and a replica of the Cross of Cong. The former court and market house (1763) is now occupied by the Bank of Ireland. Behind it was once the prison, in which, uniquely in Ireland, a female executioner did her work.

County Museum: June–Aug Mon–Sat 10am–5.30pm, Sept–May Mon–Fri 10am–4pm; free admission

AROUND ROSCOMMON

Rathcroghan

Rathcroghan, approx. 23km/14 miles northwest of Roscommon, is said to be the **coronation site of the kings of Connacht**. A mound, probably a passage tomb, is the oldest part of the site. At the centre of a stone ring fort, a standing stone marks what is thought to be the burial place of Dathi, one of the last pagan kings of Ireland. Nearby

Roscommon

INFORMATION
County Museum
The Square
Tel. (0 90) 32 63 42
www.visitroscommon.com

WHERE TO STAY
Abbey Hotel €€€
Galway Road
Tel. (0 90) 6 62 62 40
www.abbeyhotel.ie, 50 rooms
Stylish hotel with special offers for families.

there are more ring forts and Megalithic tombs. The **Celtic Royal Complex** is now a candidate to be a UNESCO World Heritage site. Information is available in the Cruachan Ai Heritage Centre. Visitors can even book a spiritual guided tour from a Druid school for € 50. Ireland's first **mining museum** opened in 2012 in the Arigna Valley, Carrick-on-Shannon. The visitor centre illuminates 400 years of mining history.

The **Claypipe Visitor Centre** in Knockcroghery, south of Roscommon, is of interest not only to smokers. It shows the history of the Irish tobacco pipe, the duidin, and visitors can buy one in the shop.

Cruachan Ai Heritage Centre: Mon–Sat 9am–5pm; admission 5 €
Mining museum: daily 10am–5pm; admission 10 €; www.arignaminingexperience.ie
Claypipe Visitor Centre: May–Sept Mon–Fri 10am–5pm, Sat 12 noon–4pm; free admission; www.oghamwish.com

19km/12 miles northwest of Roscommon in Ballintober stand the **Ballintober** ruins of a castle built by the De Burgh family about 1300 and used as a residence until 1701, with a square ground plan, polygonal towers at the corners of the thick walls and two gate towers. **Clonalis House** is a 19th-century manor house surrounded by a park near the holiday resort Castlerea. The place was once the seat of the O'Conors, who provided several high kings and kings of Connacht. Various documents and exhibits in the house – furnished in Victorian style – serve as reminders of that time. Look out in particular for a copy of the *Brehon Law* and the harp of the blind bard Turlough O'Carolan (1630–1738, ►Carrick-on-Shannon). There is luxurious B & B accommodation here and a restaurant.

Clonalis House: early June to end of Aug Mon–Sat 11am–5pm (only with guided tour); admission 7 €; www.clonalis.com

Roscrea
(Ros Cré)

✦ **D 4**

Republic of Ireland, province: Munster
County: Tipperary
Population: 5,400
Information: www.roscreaonline.ie

The monastic town Roscrea on the banks of the River Bunnow has an interesting historic centre, but its main advantage is its location between Dublin and Limerick, which makes Roscrea a great base for hiking tours in the Slieve Bloom Mountains.

*St Cronan's
Church

Roscrea marks the spot where St Cronan founded a monastery in the 7th century. On the old monastic site, all that is still standing of the 12th-century Romanesque St Cronan's Church is the western façade with an entrance gate and blind arcades. Above the entrance, the figure of a clergyman, probably St Cronan, can be made out. To the north of the church stands a 12th-century high cross, on the other side, a round tower that has lost its conical roof. The 7th-century **Book of Dímma**, written in this monastery, is today kept at Trinity College Dublin.

Roscrea
Heritage
(Castle &
Damer
House)

In Castle Street, note the ruins of 13th-century Roscrea Castle. The castle had strong curtain walls, several towers and an ingenious system of stairs and passages to individual defensive positions. Within the castle walls, Damer House, built in the 18th century, is today used for changing exhibitions. Don't miss the beautifully carved decorations on the stairs. The Heritage Annexe next to Damer House has information on the history of the region.

❶ Mid-April to Sept daily 10am–6pm; admission 4 €

National sheep-shearing championships in Neneagh

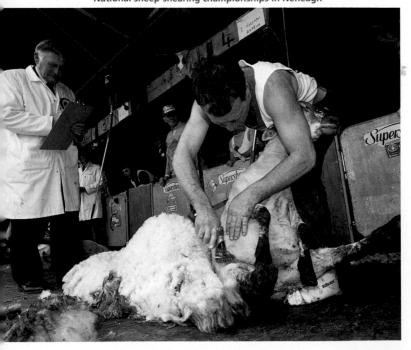

Siç

In Abbey Street, the grounds of the Catholic parish church hold the remains of a 15th-century Franciscan friary: a gate, choir walls and a bell tower, the latter's supporting arches forming the entrance to the modern church.

Franciscan Abbey

Near the golf course, 3km/2 miles east of town, the impressive ruined church of Monaincha (12th and 13th centuries) was part of a monastery founded as early as the 7th century on a boggy island in a lake that was drained in about 1800. As in the case of many Irish lake islands, according to tradition this is an ancient sacred place.

Monaincha

AROUND ROSCREA

About 30km/20 miles southwest of Roscrea, the town of Nenagh (pop 5,500) lies in a fertile plain. The best feature of the town is the keep of Nenagh Castle, built in the early 13th century, a five-storey, round tower (30m/100ft) with walls up to 6m/20ft thick. Of the other towers guarding the Butler family's once pentagonal Norman castle, only one gatehouse tower is left.

Nenagh

A museum has been set up in the former prison, showing cells and an execution room from the 19th century. Using archive material, the museum tells the tragic story of 17 men who were executed.

In the adjoining octagonal **Governor's House**, a classroom, a smithy, a shop and a kitchen have been recreated.

❶ Mon–Fri 9.30am–5pm, May to end of Aug also Sat 10am–5pm; free admission

Rosguill Peninsula

✳ A 4

Republic of Ireland, province: Ulster
County: Donegal

Scenic Rosguill Peninsula is a small peninsula in the far north of Ireland.

The peninsula reaches out between two inlets: Mulroy Bay to the east and Sheep Haven to the west. As in large parts of Donegal, Irish is still the main language here (Gaeltacht). This region is also home to a tweed mill.

Fascinating peninsula

Do follow the famous Atlantic Drive around Rosguill Peninsula. The starting point for this 20km/12-mile tour is Carrigart.

Atlantic Drive

Tranarossan Bay   Also from Carrigart, a narrow road leads uphill north, always hugging the western shores of the bay and, after 6km/3.5 miles, turning off west towards picturesque Tranarossan Bay. The road follows the Atlantic shore for a bit and then winds south, with views of Sheep Haven Bay to Downings, a holiday resort with a nice sandy beach. There is a tweed mill that is open to the public, selling Donegal tweed.

The Rosses (Na Rosa)

A/B 3

Republic of Ireland, province: Ulster
County: Donegal

The many bays of the Rosses on the northwestern coast of Donegal stretch from Gweebarra Bay in the south to Inishfree Bay in the north.

Round trip   Overall, the landscape here is flat coastal land with grey rock, many lakes and small fields delimited by dry walls. Here too, Irish is the main language still (Gaeltacht). The only larger town in this region largely untouched by tourism is Dungloe (pop. 1,180), on the N56. To the southwest are some beautiful cliffs and several caves at Crohy Head. From Dungloe, use either the N56 northeast or a scenic road east leading directly to Gweedore (▶Bloody Foreland). Take the R259 from Dungloe, hugging the Atlantic coast around the Rosses. Staying to the left-hand side, the drive leads along the shore, with good views onto many small islands, and across an isthmus between the sea and Lough Meela. Look out for Rutland Island, with the ruins of a harbour built in 1796 in the sand. Carry on for another 8km/5 miles to **Burtonport** (pop. 280), a fishing town. They say that more **salmon and lobsters** are landed here than in any other harbour in Ireland or the British Isles. Accordingly, several restaurants feature lobster and fresh-off-the boat seafood on the menu. Lying just off the mainland shore, behind some smaller islands, **Arranmore Island** (also called Aran Island,

Field walls characterize the scenery of The Rosse

not to be confused with the ►Aran Islands), is connected to Burton-port by a ferry service (in the summer hourly departures, crossing time approx. 20 min., www.arranmoreferry.com, fare 15 €). Some 500 people live on the island, which measures 13.5 x 5km/8.4 x 3 miles. The main sources of income are fishing and tourism. The island's wild, heather-covered plateau ends at the western coast with cliffs and shore caves, nesting places for numerous sea birds. Further inland lies small Lough Shure, with plenty of rainbow trout. Sandy beaches can be found on the more protected eastern side.

Shannon (River Shannon)

✴ B–D 3/4

Republic of Ireland:

The river Shannon, 370km/230 miles long, rises in County Cavan. With its lakes, tributaries and canals, the Shannon forms an intricate network of waterways, covering a fifth of Ireland's surface.

The Shannon flows through the country's inland limestone plains before emptying into the Atlantic beyond Limerick. With the exception of a few larger towns, the shores of the Shannon are sparsely populated and are often lined by pastures. As there is no industry near the river, the light over the water is particularly clear. This idyllic environment is ideal for relaxing; floating on the longest river in the British Isles in complete tranquillity is one of the most beautiful holiday experiences in Ireland. Apart from a short non-navigable stretch upstream, the gradient up to Killaloe is so low that only six locks have to be traversed along the way.

Longest river in the British Isles

Between Battlebridge (Lough Allan) and Killaloe, the river has good tourist facilities. The Shannon is part of the largest boating area in

Recommended routes

Shannon

INFORMATION
The Inland Waterways Association of Ireland
Shannon Harbour
Tel. Ireland (18 90) 92 4991

Northern Ireland 028 38 32 53 29
www.iwai.ie/nav/shannon.html

Shannon Town
Tel. 061 36 23 19, www.shannon.ie

Europe. A canal disused for over 100 years was restored and now leads from Leitrim, near ►Carrick-on-Shannon, to Lough Erne (►Fermanagh Lakeland) in Northern Ireland, giving 800km/500 miles of continuous waterways! The following tours are recommended, depending on the schedule and where the boat has to be handed over: starting from ►Carrick-on-Shannon, you can explore Lough Key. More interesting, however, is to take the boat through the Lough Allen canal and then along the shores of the lake of the same name. Going in a southerly direction brings you to Lough Boderg; from here a detour explores the only partly navigable Mountain River. The canalized stretch via Lough Bofin downstream to Lough Ree, with Hare Island, also offers plenty of variety. To the north of ►Athlone the route also reaches Lough Ree. Most visitors will probably want to take the boat south to make a quick detour to the famous monastic settlement of ►Clonmacnoise, which can also be accessed from Banagher (►Birr). Lough Derg, with its pretty moorings at Garrykennedy, can also be reached from ►Killaloe. Unfortunately, the moorings are often full. Be careful on the two largest lakes in the Shannon area, Lough Ree, near Athlone, and Lough Derg, near Killaloe. Sudden winds can whip up a strong swell!

* FROM NORTH TO SOUTH ON THE SHANNON

Lough Allen Drumshanbo village is situated at the southern tip of Lough Allen. Every year in June, during the popular **Drumshanbo Festival of Irish Traditional Music, Song and Dance**, the cabin cruisers stack up to a depth of several rows at the moorings. A nice idea is a bike tour around the lake on the 48km/30-mile, signposted Leitrim Scenic Lakeland Tour. The **Kingfisher Cycling Trail**, partly suitable only for mountainbikes (www.kingfishercycletrail.com), connects with further trails from Drumshanbo.

Carrick-on-Shannon Coming from ►Carrick-on-Shannon, most boats first head for the upper reaches of the river, or the Boyle River and its lakes. Don't miss pretty Lough Key (near the town of ►Boyle) with its wooded islands. Lough Key Forest Park, in the grounds of a former manor house, of-

The idyllic Shannon at Shannonbridge

fers strolls on forest trails or in the bog garden, a restaurant and the opportunity to do some shopping (www.loughkey.ie).

Going downstream from Carrick-on-Shannon, pass the Jamestown Canal with its lock. From here, consider a detour to Drumsna and Jamestown. Pass the lock to head for picturesque Lough Boderg, from where a narrow channel through the reeds leads to the lonely Carranadoe Lakes, a paradise for bird lovers and anglers. There is a pretty little harbour, with mooring space for only a limited number of boats however, near Dromod, on Lough Bofin. The next stop, a bit further south, is Roosky with its quay.

Lough Boderg, Lough Bofin & Lough Forbes

Continue on between wooded river banks to Lough Forbes and, past the mouth of the Royal Canal, on to Termonbarry with its large lock. From Termonbarry (or Cloondara opposite), visit Strokestown and ▶Longford . Further downstream, the extensive bogs are exploited by the Irish peat board Bord na Móna. At Lanesborough, a bridge with nine arches spans the Shannon.

Termonbarry, Lanesborough

Shannon · River Shannon

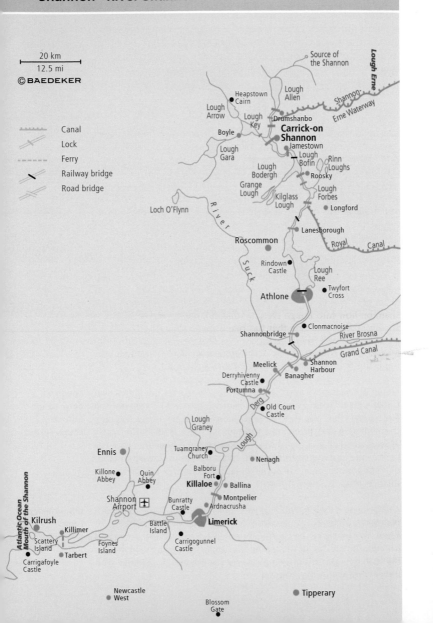

20 km
12.5 mi
©BAEDEKER

Canal
Lock
Ferry
Railway bridge
Road bridge

Source of
the Shannon
Lough Erne
Lough
Allen
Shannon-
Erne Waterway
Heapstown
Cairn
Lough
Arrow
Lough
Key
Drumshanbo
**Carrick-on-
Shannon**
Boyle
Jamestown
Lough
Gara
Lough
Bofin
Rinn
Loughs
Lough
Bodergh
Roosky
Grange
Lough
Kilglass
Lough
Lough
Forbes
Loch O'Flynn
River
Suck
● Longford
Lanesborough
Royal
Canal
Roscommon
Rindown
Castle
Lough
Ree
Athlone
Twyfort
Cross
Clonmacnoise
Shannonbridge
River Brosna
Grand Canal
Meelick
Shannon
Harbour
Derryhivenny
Castle
Banagher
Portumna
Derg
Old Court
Castle
Lough
Graney
Lough
Ennis
Tuamgraney
Church
● Nenagh
Killone
Abbey
Quin
Abbey
Balboru
Fort
Killaloe
● Ballina
Shannon
Airport
Bunratty
Castle
Montpelier
Ardnacrusha
Atlantic Ocean
Mouth of the Shannon
Kilrush
Killaloe
Battle
Island
Limerick
Scattery
Island
Foynes
Island
Carrigogunnel
Castle
Tarbert
Carrigafoyle
Castle
Newcastle
West
Blossom
Gate
● Tipperary

Here, the banks open up to the massive Lough Ree (»Lake of the   **Lough Ree**
Kings«). Several islands, such as Inchbofin, Inishturk and In-
chmore, have remains of early Christian monastic settlements. It
is said that Inchclearaun (also called »Quaker Island«, after a
19th-century inhabitant of the Quaker faith), is the place where
Clothra, sister of Queen Maeve, was killed by a slingshot from the
shore.

To the south of ►Athlone and after passing through its lock, the
river meanders through fairly flat countryside, until the towers of
►Clonmacnoise appear on the horizon. Arriving by water is the
most beautiful way to approach the ruins of this monastic town.

At Shannonbridge (pop. 200), an old bridge with sixteen arches
spans the river. By the bridge are also remains of fortifications from
Napoleonic times, with the excellent **Old Fort Restaurant** (www.
theoldfortrestaurant.com).

On Curleys Island between Shannonbridge and Clonmacnoise
stood the legendary fort **Snámh Dá Éan** (swim two birds), where
St Patrick is said to have crossed the river. The place provided inspiration for Flann O'Brien's novel *At Swim Two Birds*. Shannon
Harbour was used in the past as the starting point for a boat trip on
the ►Grand Canal to Dublin. The ruins of the buildings from that
time give an idea of Regency-period elegance.

Below Shannon Harbour, the river widens, touching the old towns of   **Lough Derg**
Banagher (►Birr) and Portumna (►Loughrea). Only then does the
Shannon flow into Lough Derg (►Killaloe), the largest of the many
Shannon lakes, and one that has many small islets. The landscape
changes now: the banks become more fertile, and there are more
farm houses and settlements. The southern tip of Lough Derg is surrounded by hills, whilst mountain ranges of very old red sandstone
mark the horizon to both sides.

Killaloe (►p.405) is not only known for its many interesting antiqui-   **Killaloe**
ties, but also for its yacht and motorboat marina. Killaloe is Ireland's
waterskiing capital. For those who hired their boat, Killaloe is the end
of the waterway. Boat owners are free to carry on. However, **the following stretch can be difficult and risky**. Whilst up to this point,
the Shannon flows unhurriedly, over the next 29km/18 miles, the
river develops a steep gradient.

Ardnacrusha is the site of Ireland's first and largest **hydroelectric**   **Ardnacrusha**
station, producing some 350 million kilowatt hours of electricity
every year. In the huge lock chambers, the boats are lifted or lowered
over 30m/100ft. Of particular interest in the hydroelectric station is
the »fish ladder«, lifting salmon and other fish up to the level of the
upper canal within three hours.

Limerick Limerick (▶p.419), with docks and moorings for ships weighing up to 10,000t, extends mainly along the Shannon's southern shore. Soon, on the right-hand bank of the river, close to Limerick, Shannon International Airport ▶Enniscomes into view. From here, the river broadens out to a width of nearly 100km/60 miles across, before eventually flowing into the Atlantic in a funnel-shaped estuary. Between Tarbert in County Kerry and Killimer in County Clare, a car ferry operates across the river (▶Kilkee).

** Skellig Islands (Oileáin na Scealaga)

✦ E 1

Republic of Ireland, province: Munster
County: Kerry

For many visitors to Ireland, a trip to the Skelligs, two small rocky islands some 14km/9 miles west of the Iveragh Peninsula off the southwestern coast of Ireland, is an absolute highlight of the journey.

Small rocky islands off the southwestern coast However, you should have fairly good sea legs and be sure-footed. When the sea is rough, **the crossing can be choppy** and visitors should be at ease walking on rocks and stone steps. In order to protect Skellig Michael – the only island that it is possible to visit – **the number of visitors is limited**.
In high summer it is a good idea to book the boat trip at least two days ahead. Boats leave between mid-May and October from Portmagee, Cahirciveen, Ballinskelligs and Derrynane (▶Ring of Kerry). See www.skelligexperience.com/skellig-boats.html for further information.

*Skellig Michael The largest of the islands, the UNESCO World Heritage site Skellig Michael, has the remains of a monastic settlement. St Finan is credited with its foundation in the 6th century. Steps hewn into the rock (Stairway to Heaven) lead to a saddle between two rocky peaks (the highest: 217m/713ft).
At the monastic settlement, a guide greets the visitors and gives a short introduction to the history of Skellig Michael, before allowing visitors to explore the remains of the monastic buildings (on artificially created small terraces below the lower rocky pyramid) at their own pace. The six beehive huts are circular outside and rectangular inside; there are also two stone boat-shaped oratories (6th–9th century). Below those, the remains of a church (12th-

The »stairways to heaven« at Skellig Michael

century?) can be made out. The site also comprises a few little gardens, a well, tombstones, the remains of a sundial and enclosure walls bordering the abyss. Up to the 13th century, a community of 13 monks lived on the islands. As there is no well on Skellig Michael, they had to work hard to collect water in two small reservoirs. Later, many more pilgrims came here to perform a penance, climbing the highest point of the island to kiss the ancient stone standing upright in the rock. From 1820 to 1987 there was a permanent lighthouse keeper on Skellig Michael. In 2007 the Irish long-distance swimmer Robert Bohane became the first person to swim between Skellig Island and Portmagee, taking 6.5 hours.

Jagged Little Skellig is a bird sanctuary and cannot be visited. Many **Little Skellig** boats, however, go around the island to give their passengers the chance to see the birds (and sometimes seals too). Don't forget to bring binoculars! The most common bird here is the gannet. With over 20,000 pairs, the colony on Little Skellig is said to be the **second-largest gannet population in the world**. Seeing a cloud of birds lift, drift apart and descend again is an optically and acoustically overwhelming experience.

Skibbereen (Sciobairín)

E 2

Republic of Ireland, province: Munster
County: Cork
Population: 2,670   **Information:** www.skibbereen.ie

Occupying a charming position on the River Ilen, the market town of Skibbereen is one of the main towns of County Cork.

The fishing harbour Skibbereen, near the southern tip of Ireland, makes a good touring base. This lively and friendly little town, founded in the 17th century by English settlers, attracts visitors to the Skibbereen Arts Festival (www.skibbereenartsfestival.com) and a food festival (www.atasteofwestcork.com).

In the Old Gasworks in Upper Bridge Street, the exhibitions in the **Skibbereen Heritage Centre** are devoted to the famine of the 1840s and the nature of Lough Hyne (Lough Ine), 5km/3 miles away. There are also detailed descriptions of the sights along the Skibbereen Way that leads through the town.

❶ Skibbereen Heritage Centre: mid-March to mid-May, mid-Sept to Oct Tue –Sat 10am –6pm, end of May to Sept also Mon; admission 6 €; www. skibbheritage.com

AROUND SKIBBEREEN

Towards Castletown-shend

The R596 leads southeast to Castletownshend, passing, after half a mile, the ***Liss Ard Gardens** . This is an area of around 16ha/40 acres with forest, flower meadows and little lakes on the banks of Lough Abisdealy. This was the place chosen by the German Veith Turske to create a natural, but also magical garden. The Crater here was made by the American artist James Turrell. The luxurious **Liss Ard Lake Lodge** has accommodated stars of the music world including Oasis, Patti Smith, Lou Reed, Van Morrison and Nick Cave. On the southwesterly edge of Castletownshend, the R596 leads to **Drishane House**, home of the 19th-century writers **Edith Somerville and Violet Martin**, who published their stories using the name Somerville & Ross. A small museum commemorates them. To the northwest, mighty Knockdrum Fort features a 3m/10ft-thick stone ring wall.

Liss Ard Gardens: April–Nov daily 10am–5pm; free admission; Crater only with a booked guided tour, tel. 028 400 00, admission 5 €; www. lissardresort.com

Drishane House: daily 11am–3pm at Easter, in May, mid-June to mid-July and end of August: see www.drishane.com for exact dates; admission 10 €

Leave Skibbereen in a southwesterly direction on the R595 to reach, after about 5km/3 miles, **Creagh Gardens**. In this romantic park right on the water's edge, look for camellias, magnolias, ferns and lilies, as well as many rare plants. The friendly holiday resort of Baltimore, which has a sailing school and is well-known for its fishing. Just offshore, **Sherkin Island** acts like a breakwater protecting the harbour. The island has the ruins of a castle and a 15th-century Franciscan friary. Further out lies **Clear Island**; its 150 inhabitants have preserved much of the old traditions alongside tourism. Irish is still spoken, and there are two colleges teaching Irish. The ruins of a 12th-century church and an old stone pillar with a carved cross are evidence of early Christian settlement.

Admire stunning cliff scenery at **Fastnet Rock**, the southernmost point of Ireland. There are boat services to both islands from Baltimore, and in the summer from Schull too. On the drive back to Skibbereen, a minor road running east passes the clear saltwater lake of **Lough Ine**. Take a signposted path up to Hill Top (just under 20 minutes from the picnic area) to enjoy a fantastic view of the lake, as well as the sea, with its off-shore islands.

Towards Baltimore

❶ Creagh Gardens: April–Sept daily 10am–6pm; admission 5 €

In the artists village of **Ballydehop** (pop. 840), a bronze monument has been erected to the world champion wrestler of 1935, Danny Manony. It is worth stopping to look at Main Street here. There are old copper mines around the small town of **Skull**. Hiking up 400m/1,300ft **Mount Gabriel** is fairly hard work, but the effort is rewarded by a great 360° view. It is definitely worth **Crookhaven** driving on to Crookhaven, with its sheltered seaport. A narrow path leads to **Mizen Head**; its highest point (230m/755ft) offers a great view of the Atlantic coast.

Westwards to Mizen Head

✴ Sligo (Sligeach)

✴ B 3

Republic of Ireland, province: Connacht
County: Sligo
Population: 19,450

On the banks of the wide Garavogue River, connecting Lough Gill with the Atlantic, lies the charming town of Sligo.

Sligo, in Irish Sligeach (»river of the shells«), is the main town in the northwest of Ireland and an important traffic hub at end of the railway line from Dublin, and thus the **northernmost railway station** in the country. In and around Sligo, there is a lot to remind visitors

The town of Yeats

of the poet William Butler Yeats (▶Famous People), who lived here for a while. Every year on 13 June Yeats Day is celebrated.

Arts and entertainment
Work by 15 craftspeople is on sale in many shops under the label **Made in Sligo** (www.madeinsligo.ie). Experimental drama is staged by the **Blue Raincoat Theatre** in the Factory Performance Space in Lower Quay Street (www.blueraincoat.com), and traditional Irish works are performed at the Hawk's Well Theatre in Temple Street (www.hawkswell.com).

SIGHTS IN SLIGO

*The Model
The showcase attraction at Sligo's mall is the The Model, Ireland's leading centre for contemporary art, home to the Niland Collection and a first-class visitor centre in a building of 1862 that has been extended. Here an exhibition about Jack Butler Yeats (1872–1957), the brother of the Nobel laureate of 1935, William Butler Yeats, and their father John Yeats can be seen.
❶ Tue–Sat 12 noon–5.30pm, Sun 12 noon–5pm; free admission; www.themodel.ie

Sligo County Museum
On Stephen Street, north of the Garavogue River, visit the Sligo County Museum. The museum shows exhibits from pre-Christian times to the beginning of the Second World War, but the main draw is of course the **Yeats Room**, part ofv the Yeats Trail and dedicated to Sligo's great writer. On display are first editions of his works, man-

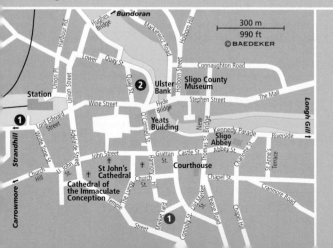

Sligo

Where to stay
❶ Sligo Southern Hotel
❷ Sligo City

Where to eat
❶ Montmartre

uscripts, letters and photographs of the Yeats family. The art gallery in the uppermost floor shows works by various Irish painters, including paintings by Jack Butler Yeats, the poet's brother. They say he was unable to paint anything without putting a bit of Sligo into it.

❶ Sligo County Museum: Tue–Sat 9.30am–12.30pm, 2–4.50pm, Oct–April only mornings; free admission

From the County Museum, cross a bridge to reach the southern bank of the river. Stay to the left to visit the oldest buildings in town: the church, cloister and monastic buildings of *Sligo Abbey. The Dominican friary was founded in 1253 by Maurice Fitzgerald and rebuilt in 1416 after a fire. The abbey suffered further damage during the Tyrone War in 1595 and once more during the troubles of the 1640s, but remained occupied until the 18th century. The church has a double nave;

> **MARCO POLO TIP** ⊕
>
> *Quirke's sculptures* **Insider Tip**
>
> How do fairies, giants and other mythical figures come into being? At Quirke's Sculptures in Wine Street watch how simple chunky wooden logs and blocks are turned into works of art, carefully carved and inspired by Irish legends and folk tales. Of course these archaic-looking figures are also for sale – an unusual, if not cheap souvenir. Tel. 071 914 26 24

the choir dates from the time of the original foundation, whilst the transept is 16th-century. Look out for the canopied tomb of Cormack O'Crean (1506) on the northern wall of the nave with a crucifixion scene and additional bas-relief figures. Also note for the O'Conor Sligo Monument (1624) on the southern wall. The sacristy and 13th-century chapter house abut the pretty 15th-century cloister, three sides of which are still standing.

❶ April to mid-Oct daily 10am–6pm, mid–Oct to early Nov Fri–Sun 9.30am–4.30pm; admission 3 €

Churches
In John Street stands the Protestant St John's Church, built in 1812 in the neo-Gothic style, on Temple Street the Catholic St John's Cathedral, built in 1869–74 in the neo-Romanesque style. These are the two main churches in town.

Yeats Memorial Building
Every year, the courses of the Yeats International Summer School are held in the Yeats (Memorial) Building on Hyde Bridge. The rest of the year, changing exhibitions and a film about Yeats can be seen.

❶ Mon–Fri 10am–5pm; free admission; www.yeats–sligo.com

EXCURSIONS AROUND SLIGO

Drive around Lough Gill
To the east of town, scenic Lough Gill stretches for approx. 8km/5 miles; the lake is rich in salmon, trout and pike. Take a leisurely drive

Sligo

INFORMATION
Tourist Information Office, Temple Street
Tel. (071) 916 12 01
www.sligotourism.ie

WHERE TO EAT
❶ *Montmartre* €€€
1 Market Yard
Tel. (071) 9 16 99 01
www.montmartrerestaurant.ie
Closed Sun and Mon
The friendly staff of this restaurant serve
dishes influenced by French cuisine, e.g.
duck breast served with red cabbage
and lentil ragout. A reasonably priced
three-course menu is served up to 7pm.

WHERE TO STAY
❶ *Sligo Southern Hotel* €€€€
Strand Hill Road
Tel. (071) 9 16 2101
www.sligosouthernhotel.com, 98 rooms
Swimming pool, Jacuzzi, sauna and
gym, as well as Finnegan's Bar and the
cosy, excellent Garden Restaurant.

❷ *Sligo City* €€€
Quay Street
Tel. (071) 9 14 40 00
www.sligocityhotel.com
Situated in the heart of Sligo in the pe-
destrian zone, with the low-cost Quays
Bar & Restaurant .

around the lake (37km/23 miles) or, equally rewarding, take a **boat trip on the lake**, joined, in the summer, take a boat trip from Parke's Castle on the Rose of Innisfree (www.roseofinnisfree.com) or with Lough Gill Tours (www.loughgilltours.com). For an excellent view of the lake and its islets head for Dooney Rock, which Yeats immortalized in *The Fiddler of Dooney*. Innisfree Island, near the southern shore, is also the subject of one of Yeats' poems.

Creevelea Abbey
From the R287, Creevelea Abbey drive east towards Dromahair and the ruins of the Franciscan abbey of Creevelea, founded in 1508, before the order was banned in Ireland. On the northern side of the monastery are some features on the pillars, amongst them St Francis with the stigmata and preaching to the birds.

*Parke's Castle
Picturesque Parke's Castle is situated on the eastern bank of the lake. The castle is a three-storey rectangular structure with a large 17th-century courtyard. The unfurnished fortified manor house has been lavishly restored and may be visited. In the yard, the remnants of an earlier defensive structure have been excavated. A little further on, a small road branches off to the right in the direction of Manorhamilton. Park the car after 3km/2 miles and walk to the impressive mound grave named **Deer Park Court Cairn**, with three chambers (c3000 BC), lying on a wooded hill with a wonderful view of the lake.
On a peninsula between the lake's northwestern tip and the Garavogue River stands **Hazelwood House**, a handsome small manor

house, built in 1731 in the Palladian style, the starting point for a nature trail and a sculpture trail.

Parke's Castle: April to mid–Sept daily 10am–6pm; admission 3 €

Leave Sligo via Church Hill and follow the road for 5km/3 miles to reach **the largest cluster of megalithic graves in Ireland**, the passage-tomb cemetery of Carrowmore. Archaeologists have found some 60 tombs here, many of which are, however, destroyed or damaged. Most are a combination of passage grave and dolmen, with the oldest dating from between 3000 and 2500 BC.

Carrowmore

❶ April to mid-Oct daily 10am–6pm; admission 3 €

Knocknarea mountain lies some 7km/4.5 miles west of Sligo. It is well worth the climb (30–40 min.), and not just because of the views. At the top sits a massive cairn, 11m/36ft high and over 60m/200ft in diameter. A megalithic grave (approx. 2500 BC) is supposed to be under the cairn, and it is assumed that the **legendary Queen Maeve of Connacht was buried here**.

Knocknarea Cairn

Strandhill, 8km/5 miles west of Sligo near the airport, is a resort with excellent sandy beaches. The powerful swell makes Strandhill very popular with surfers. At low tide you can wade across to small Coney Island. Don't miss a visit to the **Voya Seaweed Baths** for an organic treatment (from 25 €; www.voyaseaweedbaths.com.

Strandhill

The seaside resort Rosses Point, with its 18-hole championship links and sheltered sandy beaches, is also popular with holiday visitors.

Rosses Point

NORTH OF SLIGO

The grandfather of the writer William Butler Yeats (▶Famous People) was for many years parish priest at Drumcliff Church, 10km/6 miles north of Sligo. Yeats died 1939 in France, but had requested a grave in Drumcliff in his will, and was buried in the churchyard in front of the church. His headstone has **Yeats' Grave** the following epitaph, composed by the poet himself: »Cast a cold Eye / On Life, on Death / Horseman, pass by!«. Along the footpath to the church, look out for a **high cross, erected around AD 1000**. Its east face depicts Adam and Eve, Cain and Abel, Daniel in the Lion's Den and Christ in Glory. The west face of the cross shows Christ Driving the Vendors out of the Temple, two figures and the Crucifixion. The rest of the cross is decorated with mythical beasts and ornamental interlacing. North of the village, **Benbulben** table mountain (517m/1,696ft) rises abruptly out of the plain. This weird natural formation features in many folk tales and stories. It was here that Queen Maeve and the

Drumcliff

Benbulben has a conspicuous shape

hero of Ulster, CuChulainn, fought for possession of mighty bulls, and Diarmaid bled to death following his fight with the wild boar of Benbulben. However, a historical event also took place on the slopes of the mountain: the »Battle of the Books« of Cuildrevne (561), which resulted in Columba the Elder's exile.

Glencar Lough A pretty area for exploring is Glencar Lough, a few miles east of Drumcliff. At the eastern side of the lake, the waterfall in the middle of all that green is very romantic.

Inishmurray From Grange village, north of Drumcliff, a by-road leads west to Streedagh. There is sometimes the possibility for foot passengers to join a boat to Inishmurray island (another access is from Mullaghmore, see below). The island, 7km/4.5 miles west of Streedagh was inhabited well into the 20th century. There is a particularly **well-preserved early Christian monastic site** here. Founded in the early 6th century by St Molaise, the monastery was abandoned 300 years later following plundering attacks. The remains give a good idea of

how this kind of monastery then looked: a circular wall, 3–4m/10–13ft tall, with five entrances, around an enclosure in the shape of a pear, divided into four areas of different sizes. The enclosure holds various churches and huts: the Men's Church, the small Teach Molaise prayer house, the Church of the Fire, a beehive hut and blocks of masonry, like open-air altars. On top of one of those, look for the five famous **Cursing Stones**, round speckled stones used to place effective curses on enemies. Strewn all over the island are memorial stones and prayer stations that the pilgrims had to complete in a prescribed order. St Patrick's Memorial offers a particularly beautiful view of the mainland (http://inishmurray.com).

At Streedagh Beach, only a few miles on, the Spanish Armada Memorial commemorates 6 September 1588, when three ships were wrecked here. The disaster cost 1,200 lives, 300 people were saved. From Cliffoney, a minor road leads past Classiebawn Castle to the **Mullaghmore** peninsula, with a protected sandy beach, a harbour for boaters and opportunity for deep-sea angling. The Beach Hotel

Streedagh Beach

can arrange trips to Inishmurray Island (www.beachhotelmullagh more.com).

*Creevykeel At Creevykeel, near Cliffoney village, stands an impressive **court tomb**, one of the most beautiful in the whole of Ireland. A wedge-shaped stone wall encloses an open court, behind which lies a double burial chamber, with two more burial chambers and the remains of a third behind it. The site dates back at least 4,500 years.

SOUTH AND EAST OF SLIGO

Collooney 13km/8 miles south of Sligo, Collooney village lies on the Owenmore River, with the pretty 18th-century Markree Castle in the middle distance.

Around Lough Arrow To explore the area around Lough Arrow, some 28km/17 miles southeast of Sligo, turn east off the N4 at Castlebaldwin; this road leads to the large Heapstown Cairn (probably a passage tomb) and then on to a small and **strange lake**. With a diameter of around 300m/1,000ft, Lough Nasuil holds some 1 million litres/26 million gallons of water. In 1933, the lough suddenly ran dry and stayed dry for three weeks, only to fill up again later, just as fast. To the south, 16th-century Ballindoon Friary in its pretty lakeside location is a pleasant place to stop. After around 10km/6 miles you meet the N4 again at Ballinafad.

> MARCO POLO TIP
>
> *Yeats Country* **Insider Tip**
>
> Whether or not you are interested in the works of W B Yeats, the drive through the Sligo landscape is beautiful – past a sandy coastline and spectacular rocks, through forests and along lakes and rivers. Just follow the signs with the quill ...

Carrowkeel passage tomb cemetery Some 5km/3 miles north of Ballinafad, look out for the **passage tomb cemetery of Carrowkeel**, on a lonely hilltop in the Bricklieve Mountains. The site consists of 14 cairns that are all circular (with one exception), but inside show different types of chambers. It is thought that they were built around 3400–3100 BC. In the area below the tombs are remnants of 50 round stone huts, maybe the living quarters of the people who built these tombs.

Lough Key Scenic site Follow the N4 in the direction of Dublin to reach a wonderful viewpoint for Lough Key, on the border between the Counties Sligo and Roscommon. Across the road stands the imposing statue of The Gaelic Chieftain, commemorating the battle at Curlew Mountains in 1599. In Ballymore, 9km/5.5 miles further north stands an ivy-clad ruined castle with six round towers. From being constructed to being razed (c1300–c1700), Ballymote Castle was much contested.

Sperrin Mountains

———————————————— ✦ **B 4/5**

Northern Ireland, province: Ulster
Counties: Tyrone and Derry

The Sperrin Mountains (up to 670m/2,198ft) are a little-known haven for walkers and fishermen in the northeast of Tyrone. Here you can walk for hours without meeting a single soul.

Covered in bog and heather, the Sperrin Mountains northwest of ▶Lough Neagh are criss-crossed by an intricate network of brooks and small roads. The area, stretching across some 65km/40 miles between the towns of Strabane, Dungiven, Magherafelt and Newtownards, is very sparsely populated. Part of the mountain range extends south towards ▶Omagh. Alongside the walking and fishing (salmon and trout), the area is good for biking, horse-riding and golfing.

Lonely scenery

On the southeastern edge of the Sperrin Mountains, 10km/6 miles northwest of Dungannon on the A505 (signposted), look out for the Beaghmore Stone Circles, seven mysterious **stone circles and cairns** dating from the Bronze Age. The site consists of further prehistoric monuments: twelve circular cairns as well as ten stone rows and other fragments, possibly parts of ancient collapsed stone walls. They were discovered during peat digging and it is assumed that the peat hides more stone testimony to ancient times.

*Beaghmore Stone Circles

> **!** *Family fun* **Insider Tip**
>
> MARCO ⊕ POLO TIP
>
> Warm up with a cup of tea in the café of Sperrin Heritage Centre and, weather permitting, try your luck panning for gold in the nearby brook – great fun!

Directly behind the **Sperrin Heritage Centre** in Cranagh, approx. 20km/12 miles northwest of Cookstown via the B162 and the B47, rises Mount Sawel (678m/2,2224ft). Displays and interactive animation show some of the history of the region, its environmental issues, as well as the **gold** found nearby, and exhibits on the influence of the local landscape on literature. If you are looking specifically for information on walking trails, this is the place, as the Ulster Way passes nearby.

● Easter–Oct Mon–Fri 11.30am–5.30pm, Sat 11.30am–6pm, Sun 2–6pm; admission 3 £

Somewhat easier to reach is the An Creagán Visitor Centre, about half-way between Cookstown and Omagh on the A505. Here too, an exhibition explains the countryside and its people to visitors. There is information on walking trails and bike hire. In addition, a broad

An Creagán Visitor Centre

cultural programme stretches from Irish traditions such as music, storytelling, dance and crafts, to language classes, talks on history and archaeology, and guided walks.

❶ April–Sept daily 11am–5pm, Oct–March daily 11am–4.30pm; free admission; www.an-creagan.com

Tara (Teamhair)

✳ C 5

Republic of Ireland, province: Leinster
County: Meath

As a ritual site associated with the goddess Maeve, the Hill of Tara lay at the centre of the Irish-Celtic world, but the site already had religious significance in prehistoric times.

A spiritual place

Northwest of Dublin, take a left into a small side road at Tara village. The road leads slightly uphill to the famous mountain, from where you can see far out to the north and west. From the 3rd century onwards, Tara was the seat of lower-ranking priest kings, and later of the **High Kings of Ireland**. Every three years they held public gatherings here where laws were passed and disputes amongst the tribes were settled. With the spread of Christianity, Tara lost its significance as a site of worship, but stayed the seat of the High Kings until it was abandoned in 1022. The region had to wait until 1843 for its next major event, when Daniel O'Connell made a speech during one of his mammoth meetings campaigning for **Catholic emancipation** in Ireland.

*Hill of Tara

Walking across the Hill of Tara today, you only see flat grassy mounds. The ancient tombs and their ring-shaped earth walls can only be made out from the air. The impressive structures built in Celtic times from wood or wattle-and-daub are said to have had gates decorated with precious stones and inside were said to be furnished with tools made of gold and bronze. Of all of this, nothing has survived.In order to get an impression of Tara's significance, watch the »Tara: Meeting Place of Heroes« video in the Tara Visitor Centre, housed in the former Protestant Church, the starting point in summer for recommended 40-minute tours that bring the mythology and history of the come to life.

End of May to mid-Sept daily 10am–6pm; admission 3 €

Royal Enclosure

The central area of the site, the Royal Enclosure of the Irish High Kings, is surrounded by a large wall. Roughly at the centre of the enclosure stand the two walls of Cormac's House and the Royal Seat. In the past, the **Stone of Destiny** (Lia Fáil), the coronation stone, is said to have stood near Cormac's House. According to legend, the stone would roar when the right king was standing on it. Today, there is a memorial stone for the rebels fallen in 1798 on Tara on that site, erroneously called »coronation stone«. To the north of the royal court, look for the Mound of the Hostages. In this passage tomb, dating from 1800 BC, the burnt remains of 40 humans were discovered. It is said that on ascending the throne, the kings of Tara took hostages from high-ranking families in their kingdom to ensure their loyalty. After their death – certainly not always of natural causes – the hostages were buried in this mound.

To the north, the royal courtyard abuts the Ráth of the Synods fort, dating from the 2nd to 4th centuries. Fortified at one time by a circular wall, this dwelling was partly destroyed in the early 20th century by over-zealous hunters of the **Ark of the Covenant** described in the Old Testament. Further to the north, two walls (30m/100ft apart) run parallel for some 180m/200yd, with a dip in the centre. Traditionally, these walls have been called the **banqueting hall**. An early representation shows the dining table in the wooden structure, and the seating order of the guests of the High King, according to their status and profession. Archaeologists think, however, that the walls might have formed a ceremonial entrance to a ritual site. To the west, there are two more earth walls that probably served as ritual sites: first **Gráinne's Fort**, and next to it the **Sloping Trenches**.

Ráth of the Synods fort

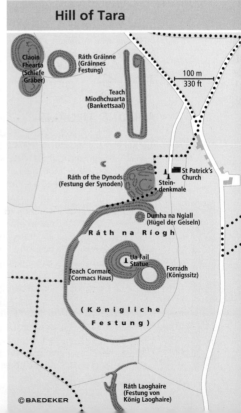

AROUND TARA

Some 800m/0.5 miles to the south, another hill is occupied by **Fort Ráth Maeve**. The fort with a diameter of 220m/722ft is surrounded by a wall and a ditch, but nothing remains other than this embankment. The name refers to the legendary **goddess Maeve**, queen of the fairies and also a warrior queen who features in the cycle of Ulster myths.

Thurles (Durlas)

✦ D 4

Republic of Ireland, province: Munster
County: Tipperary
Population: 7,930

The old diocesan town of Thurles, 22km/14 miles north of Cashel, is the seat of the archdiocese of Cashel and Emly, though not only religious discipline is important here. Sport has also always found great support.

A cathedral with an Italian touch

The keep of 12th-century Bridge Castle stands by the bridge over the Suir, and the smaller keep of the 15th-century Black Castle stands on the square. The cathedral, built in the Lombard Romanesque style in 1865–72, contains a 17th-century Baroque high altar by Andrea Pozzo originally from the Il Gesù church in Rome. In the chapel for the dead lies the tomb of Archbishop Croke (1824–1902), a great supporter of Irish independence. Among other things, he sponsored the **Gaelic Athletic Association** (GAA), founded in 1884, which is one of the largest amateur sporting associations in Europe today. The GAA stadium in Dublin, which has the status of a national shrine, is named after him. There is a small bird sanctuary on the island in the River Suir.

AROUND THURLES

*Holy Cross Abbey

The former Cistercian abbey of Holy Cross (13th–15th century) lies 6km/3.5 miles south of Thurles, on the right bank of the River Suir. Founded as early as 1168, the monastery was a much visited pilgrimage site because it owned a splinter from the cross of Christ. The restored church has two transepts and a mighty crossing tower built above. The 15th-century choir, with its east window and stone seats decorated with coats of arms, is particularly beautiful. The choir vaults, the transepts and crossing are also noteworthy. In the northern transept **a fresco** – so rare for Ireland – has survived in part: a hunting scene with three hunters, a dog and stag are shown in brown, red and green. Between the two chapels in the southern transept there is a construction of pillars and arches, which was presumably used to exhibit the relic. From there a staircase leads to the upper storey of the monastic chambers.

The chapter house on the east side of the cloister is not open to the public. The refectory on the south side has been destroyed.

❶ Holy Cross **Abbey**: May–Sept Mon–Fri 11.30am–5.30pm, Sun 3–5pm, Oct–April only Fri 10.30–11.30am, Sun 3–5pm; donation requested; www. holycrossabbey.ie

Around 5km/3 miles north-west of Holy Cross stands 16th-century Ballynahow Castle, one of Ireland's rare round keeps. Two of the original five vaulted ceilings survive. | **Ballynahow Castle**

Tipperary (Tiobraid Árann)

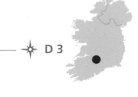

✴ **D 3**

Republic of Ireland, province: Munster
County: Tipperary
Population: 5,310

Here in the Golden Vale, where the pastures are richest and the harvests most generous, lies Tipperary, capital of the county of the same name.

The town became famous for the song *It's a long way to Tipperary*, which was sung by British troops at the beginning of the 20th century and which entered the standard canon of English music at the beginning of the First World War. Jack Judge, the English author of the song written in 1912, never went to Ireland, but his grandparents came from Tipperary. Little survives of the old town. Of note is the choir arch in the 13th-century monastic church and the ruins of the primary school. Exhibits on the War of Independence (1919–21) can be seen in a small exhibition at the eastern end of Main Street. | **Industrial and market town**

AROUND TIPPERARY

About 9km/5.5 miles east on the N74 stands the ruin of Thomastown Castle, which was built in the 17th century and extended in the neo-Gothic style around 1812. Father **Theobald Matthew**, a famous promoter of abstinence from alcohol, was born here in 1790. ▶Cork. | **Thomastown Castle**

Turn right before crossing the bridge to reach the ruins of Ireland's largest medieval abbey, Athassel Priory (13th–15th century). It was founded for Augustinian monks by William de Burgh. The priory was in use until the dissolution of the monasteries in the mid-16th | ***Athassel Priory** century, when the lands were given to the Earl of Ormonde. The remains cover an area of 1.6ha/4 acres. The church is 65m/70yd long, with a choir, an imposing crossing tower, and a nave with aisles. Almost nothing survives of the cloister. All around are ranged the numerous convent buildings enclosed by a high wall. Once there was a bridge by the gate house, where it was possible to cross into the monastery from outside. There was a town here up until the middle of the 14th century, of which nothing has survived.

Tralee (Trá Lí)

 ✳ **D 2**

Republic of Ireland, province: Munster
County: Kerry
Population: approx. 23,690

Tralee is not only the most important urban centre in the large county of Kerry, but also where the most beautiful Irish-born girl in the whole world is voted the »Rose of Tralee«.

Worthwhile stop In spite of its relatively small population, Tralee, Trá Lí in Irish (»bay of the river Lee«), offers enough to make a one or two-day stop worthwhile. For most visitors, however, Tralee is the gateway to the historically rich ▶Dingle Peninsula, and the starting point for a tour of the famous ▶Ring of Kerry. The town is a regional centre for services and shopping, and site of the headquarters of the **Kerry Group dairy conglomerate**, founded in 1974, which exports products under the brand name of »Kerrygold«. Nothing survives from the old town because Tralee was burnt down by occupying forces in 1643 and 1691, to leave nothing for the enemy. There are however a few Georgian houses in the centre.

*Kerry the Kingdom Museum »**Kerry the Kingdom**« encompasses three attractions at the Ashe Memorial Hall: »Kerry in Colour« is a slide show that introduces the visitor to the scenic beauty of the region. The »Treasures of the Kingdom« museum shows the most significant archaeological exhibits and art pieces and brings to life the county's history **from the Stone Age to the present** with recreated scenarios; at the »Geraldine Experience«, eleven time-travelling vehicles take the visitor through the Tralee of 1450, complete with authentically recreated streets and squares. An effort is even made to replicate the sounds and smells of the era. This attraction is named after the Desmond Geraldines, one of the leading Norman families that ruled Tralee and the surrounding area.
❶ June–Aug daily 9.30am–5.30pm, Sept–May Tue–Sat 9.30am–5pm; admission 5 €; www.kerrymuseum.ie

The Siamsa Tíre Theatre at Tralee maintains Celtic heritage

Siamsa Tíre

The Siamsa Tíre Theatre was built in the style of an Irish stone fort near the Ashe Memorial Hall. It is a **national folk theatre** dedicated to the preservation of Celtic culture and language. The programme is made up of music, dance and theatre (performances at 2pm and 8.30pm, www.siamsatire.com).

Blennerville Windmill and Steam Train

A **narrow-gauge railway** operated on the route between Tralee and Dingle from 1891 to 1953. It has been revived and travels from Tralee to the restored Blennerville Windmill at hourly intervals from May to September, a distance of around 3km/2 miles. By car, the windmill can be reached on the R559 leading to Dingle. The Blennerville Windmill was built in 1800 and in service until 1880. It has been restored and the visitor can watch as the great mill stones grind wheat to flour. A multimedia show gives further insights into the history of the mill. As Blennerville Quay was an important departure point for emigrants, an exhibition is dedicated to the emigration waves of past centuries.

❶ June–Aug daily 9am–6pm, April, May, Sept, Oct daily 9.30am–5.30pm; admission 5 €

Tralee

INFORMATION
Ashe Memorial Hall
Denny Street
Tel. (0 66) 7 12 12 88
www.corkkerry.ie

WHERE TO STAY   *Insider Tip*
Ballyseede Castle €€€€
Southeast

Tel. (0 66) 7 12 57 99
www.ballyseedecastle.com, 23 rooms
Those with a passion for old castles
can stay the night at Ballyseede Castle.
Its history goes back to the 15th century. Two restaurants, O`Connell and
the Stone Room, drinks in the Library
Bar.

Aqua Dome   Near the Steam Railway Station stands the Aqua Dome where an impressive waterworld with slides and wave pools, saunas and steam
baths.
❶ Winter Mon–Fri 10am–10pm, Sat–Sun 11am–8pm, summer Mon–Fri
10am–10pm, Sat and Sun 10am–9pm; admission 15 €;
www.aquadome.ie

AROUND TRALEE

Ardfert   Drive 8km/5 miles northwest on the R551 to reach Ardfert, whose
grounds boast significant remains of old buildings. **Saint Brendan**
(483–578), born in neighbouring Fenit, founded a monastery here.
The associated cluster of churches by the cemetery includes the
castle-like cathedral (around 1250); the beautiful west porch and
blind arcading of a previous Norman building (12th century) were
used in its construction. The Gothic choir window and the lancet
windows in the south wall are especially successful.
The nave of the small Norman church **Temple na Hoe** can be found
to the northwest, as well as remains of the 15th-century Temple na
Griffin.
A few hundred metres to the east stand the ruins of a Franciscan
monastery (13th-15th century), with circular columns and a beautiful south window in the church.

Kerry Head   Jutting out into the Atlantic, Kerry Head awaits past the quiet holiday
resort of Ballyheige, situated further north on the R551. With a bit of
luck, **six-sided quartz crystals** from the Kerry mountains can be
found here, but Ballyheige's popularity stems from Banna Beach to
the south. This is where in 1916 Sir Roger Casement (▶Famous People) had himself set down from a German U-boat to take part in the
Easter Rising.

Crag Cave lies around 20km/12 miles east of Tralee. This impressive stalactite cavern was only systematically investigated in 1981, when it was established that this cave system is actually one of the largest in Ireland and almost 4km/2.5 miles long.

*Crag Cave

❶ April–Dec daily 10am–6pm, Jan–March Fri–Sun 10am–6pm; tours several times daily; admission 12 €; www.cragcave.com

Trim (Baile Átha Troim)
✠ C 5

Republic of Ireland, province: Leinster
County: Meath
Population: 8,270
Information: Tel. (0 46) 943 7227

The pretty, quiet town of Trim has a great past, and film-makers (*Braveheart*) like to use the spectacular castle as a backdrop.

Hugh de Lacy, a vassal of Henry II, built a castle in the year 1172 precisely opposite the spot where Saint Patrick (▶Baedeker Special, p.34) founded a monastery in the fifth century. The castle changed hands several times and during the 14th century, the entire settlement was fortified with walls and gates. Several parliaments were held here in the 15th century. In 1649 the town fell to Cromwell. The film *The Power & the Glory* which can be viewed at **Trim Visitor Centre**, offers a good historical overview.

Small town with a great past

❶ Trim Visitor Centre: Mon–Fri 9.30am–5.30pm, Sat–Sun 12 noon–5.30pm; admission free, multimedia show 3.20 €; www. meath.ie

Information panels at Trim Castle explain what life was like in the past

In the town centre on the south shore of the Boyne, the magnificent fortifications of ***Trim Castle** rise up. It covers a surface area of about 1.2 ha/3 acres, which makes it the **largest of Ireland's castles from the Norman era**. The square keep is situated on the highest point in the middle of the site, with four small towers rising above it on the four corners of the main building, and fortified by four projecting towers, of which only three survive. In this way a design in the shape of the cross was formed. A wall fortified with (only partially surviving) semi-circular towers and a moat enclosed the grounds. A drawbridge was used at the tower gate on the south side. The Trim Castle Hotel is part of the complex (www.trimcastlehotel.com).

❶ Mid-March to Sept daily 10am–6pm, Oct 9.30am–5,30pm, Nov to mid-March Sat and Sun 9.30am–5pm; admission incl./excl. Tower 4/3 €

Yellow Steeple

Today, the landmark of Trim is the Yellow Steeple, which is the all that remains of an Augustinian monastery on a bare elevation above the river. The almost 40m/130ft tower stood at the north side of the church. The 12th-century Augustinian abbey of St Mary's had been restored in 1368, and in 1415 parts of it were turned into an imposing manor house, which became knon by the name of Talbot's Castle. Later a school was housed here, at which Arthur Wellesley (1769 –1852), later the Duke of Wellington, was taught. A little further south from the Yellow Steeple (near the shore of the river) stands **Sheep Gate**, the two-storey ruin of the only town gate still to be seen today.

Black Friary, Maudlins Cemetery

The relics of the 13th-century Black Friary to the north are interesting, and so is the beautiful bronze statue of *Our Lady of Trim* in Maudlins Cemetery, at the other end of town. The statue of the Virgin Mary was made after the design of a wooden statue said to have once been at St Mary's Abbey.

Newton Trim

Barely a mile downriver, east of Trim, the ruins of Newton Trim standing by an old bridge once were a monastery dedicated to Saint Peter and Saint Paul. Only the choir, crossing and part of the nave survive of this once very large 13th-century cathedral, built for the bishop of Meath. To the south, a few remains of the monastic buildings can still be seen. To the east stands a smaller 13th-century church with a notable **double tomb** from the late 16th century.

Tullamore (Tulach Mór)

✦ C 4

Republic of Ireland, province: Leinster
County: Offaly
Population: 14,360
Information: www.midirelandtourism.ie

The most important town in the County of Offaly is well-known among whiskey lovers and lies almost exactly in the centre of Ireland.

From the 1950s the famous Tullamore Dew and Irish Malt Whiskey Liqueur were produced here. Now they are made by William Grant & Sons in Midleton, County Cork. Tullamore, Tulach Mór in Irish (»great gathering hill«), served as the terminus of the ▶Dublin Grand Canal until 1804, and experienced a boom as a centre for distilleries and breweries. In 1790 however, when Tullamore was still fairly small, the explosion caused by a large hot air balloon crashing destroyed most of the buildings.

Former centre of whiskey production

The main attraction in the town is the Tullamore Dew Heritage Centre in an old warehouse at Bury Quay. Of course the focus is on whiskey production, but a **Living History Museum** also shows how people used to live and work, and highlights a few key moments in the history of the town, which, in around 1620, consisted merely of a castle, a windmill and a few huts. The strong drinks can be sampled at the end of the tour.

*Tullamore Dew Heritage Centre

❶ Mon–Sat 9.30am–6pm, Sun 11.30am–5pm; admission 8 €; www.tullamoredewvisitorcentre.com

To the west of the centre, Charleville Castle, with its turrets and spires, seems like a Gothic folly. It was built for William Bury, later Lord Tullamore, at the turn of the 18th century, designed by Francis Johnston, one of Ireland's most famous architects, and has not been changed since then. A highlight is the dining room, furnished by Sir William Morris. The castle is said to be haunted, and the park, where some of the oldest oak trees in Ireland stand, to have been a dwelling of druids.

Charleville Castle

❶ Tours by arrangement, tel. 057 932 30 39; admission 8 €; http://charlevillecastle.ie

On the N52 bypass, the sculptor **Maurice Harron** has placed four figures that symbolize learning and sanctity. In the boggy Lough Boora Parklands, an area of 80,000ha/300 sq miles south of Tullamore, large-scale works concerned with the nature and industrial heritage of the boglands have been placed in a 40ha/100-acre sculpture park.

Lough Boora Parklands

❶ Open all year, free admission; www.sculptureintheparklands.com

AROUND TULLAMORE

A little north of Tullamore, in Durrow, there was once a monastery founded by Saint Columba in the 6th century. It became famous through the **Book of Durrow** which can now be admired in Trinity College Dublin. It was written and illuminated in the 7th century. A 10th-century high cross also survives, adorned with fine figurative

Durrow

carving. The east side shows the sacrifice of Isaac: Christ in glory, to his left, David playing the harp, and to his right, David slaying the lion. On the west side, one can see the Soldiers guarding the tomb of Christ, as well as the flagellation, the arrest and the crucifixion of Christ.

Edenderry   East of Tullamore lies the picturesque little town of Edenderry (pop. 6,980). 7km/4.5 miles north stand the ruins of Carrickoris Castle, which used to belong to the O'Connor family and was the site of a massacre in the year 1305. In 1325, in penance for his father's crime, John de Bermingham had the small abbey of Monasteroris built for the Franciscans, 3km/2 miles to the northwest.

★ Waterford (Port Lairge)

✦ **D 4**

Republic of Ireland, province: Munster
County: Waterford
Population: 51,100

Waterford, founded by Vikings in 835 and later expanded by the Anglo-Normans, became into a significant port due to its location.

Port in the southeast   Waterford remained an **English stronghold** up to the 19th century, a position that was firmly established after Henry VII granted the town the motto of »Urbs intacta manet Waterfordia« (»Waterford remains untouched«) in 1487. Twice before that date the inhabitants had stood firm against rival pretenders to the throne. After Cromwell and his troops unsuccessfully laid siege to Waterford in 1649, the town was taken the following year. Many houses in the centre still date from the time around 1800, when the glass industry experienced its heyday in Waterford. There are many Georgian houses, especially on the Mall. In 2004 the old Viking harbour was rediscovered.

SIGHTS IN WATERFORD

Town walls   Waterford, the **oldest town in Ireland**, got its impressive town walls during the time of its foundation by the Vikings and its expansion under King John. Parts of them can still be seen in the Palace Garden by the theatre. In addition, several towers survive, such as the Half Moon Tower (Patrick Street), the Watch Tower near Railway Square, and Reginald's Tower.

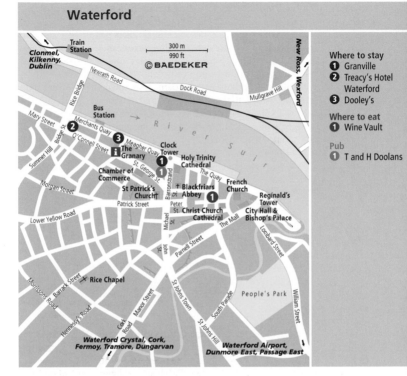

Waterford

Where to stay
❶ Granville
❷ Treacy's Hotel Waterford
❸ Dooley's

Where to eat
❶ Wine Vault

Pub
❶ T and H Doolans

The impressive round Reginald's Tower stands at the point where Parade Quay makes a sharp bend into the Mall. It is said to have already been part of an old Viking fortification from 1003. In reality, however, the tower in its present shape appears to be the remains of a 13th-century Norman construction. Behind the 3m/10ft-thick walls lies the interesting **town museum**.

***Reginald's Tower**

❶ June to mid-Sept daily 10am–6pm, mid-Sept to May daily 10am–5pm, mid-Sept to early March closed Mon and Tue; admission 3 €

On the wide Mall, next to the town hall from 1788, is the Victorian Royal Theatre, dating from 1876, where part of the municipal art collection can be viewed in the foyer (www.theatreroyal.ie). In this building the Café Royal has a fine view of the gardens of a beautiful town house, the ***Bishop's Palace**, built by Richard Castle (or Cassels), one of the major architects of 18th-century Ireland, who designed Leinster House and the Rotunda Hospital in Dublin as well as Powerscourt House (see p. xxx) and Westport House (see p. xxx).

The Mall

Waterford Museum of Treasures With high-tech exhibits, the museum in the restored Bishop's Palace illustrates the history of Waterford from 1700 up to the 1970s and presents some special items, including Viking brooches, superbly adorned Norman crosses, relics and a glass decanter from 1790. The medieval collection is housed in the undercroft of Choristers' Hall in Greyfriar Street opposite the cathedral. The Great Charter Roll of 1372, 4m/13ft long, can be seen here. Also in Greyfriars Street is the **Waterford Municipal Gallery**, in the old Methodist church. It is also worth visiting the **Garter Lane Arts Centre** in the former Quaker assembly house in O'Connell Street. It accommodates a theatre and dance studio (http://garterlane.ie).

Waterford Treasures: June–Aug Mon–Sat 9am–6pm, Sun 11am–5pm, Sept–May Mon–Sat 10am–5pm, Sun 11am–5pm; admission 7 €; www.waterfordtreasures.com

Waterford Municipal Art Gallery: Tue–Sat 11am–5pm; free admission; www.waterfordtreasures.com

Waterford

INFORMATION
South East Tourism
Tel. (0 51) 87 57 88
www.waterfordtourism.com
www.discoverwaterfordcity.ie

WHERE TO EAT
❶ *Wine Vault* €€€
High Street
Tel. (0 51) 85 37 77
www.winevaultfinewines.com
The restaurant with its wine shop and cellar is housed in a customs warehouse dating from the 15th century. The wide-ranging menu includes good fish dishes, and the owner cultivates his own vines near Waterford.

❷ *T and H Doolans* €€   *Insider Tip*
George's Street
Tel. (0 51) 84 15 04
One of the oldest pubs in Ireland, offering traditional music. The house speciality is Guinness with oysters.

WHERE TO STAY
❶ *Granville* €€€€
The Quay
Tel. (0 51) 30 55 55
www.granville-hotel.ie
100 rooms and suites
This hotel dating from the early 19th century once hosted Charles Stewart Parnell. The Bianconi Restaurant has a good early-bird menu.

❸ *Dooley's* €€€
The Quay
Tel. (0 51) 87 35 31
www.dooleys-hotel.ie 113 rooms.
Third-generation family-run business with a restaurant and bar.

❷ *Treacy's Hotel Waterford* €€€
91 Merchants Quay
Tel. (0 51) 87 72 22
www.treacyshotelwaterford.com
170 rooms
With Timbertoe's Bar and Crocker's Restaurant, leisure centre, beauty spa and pool.

Behind the town hall stands Christ Church Cathedral. A spacious interior contains two interesting tombs: the Rice Monument (1469) and the Fitzgerald Monument, made of Carrara marble. Continuing from here along Greyfriars Street, the remains of **French Church** stand on the right. Its origins reach right back to the foundation of a monastery in the year 1240. The nave was used as a poor house and hospital from the 17th to the 19th century, while the choir was used as a church by Huguenot immigrants.

Christ Church Cathedral

❶ June–Sept Mon–Fri 9am–6pm, Sat 10am–4pm, Oct Mon–Fri 10am–5pm, Sat 10am–4pm; free admission, donation requested; www.christchurchwaterford.com

> **MARCO POLO** TIP
>
> **Insider Tip**
>
> *House of Waterford Crystal*
>
> At this attraction on The Mall, visitors can take a one-hour tour to learn about the production of crystal glass and take home a souvenir from the shop (shop Mon–Sat 9.30am–5pm or longer, March–Oct also on Sun; tours Mon–Sat 9.30am–3.15pm or longer; admission 12 €; www.waterfordvisitor-centre.com.

In 1996 the Catholic missionary Edmund Ignatius Rice (1762–1844) was beatified. The museum in the heritage centre is devoted to social conditions in the 19th century. The grave of Rice is in the new chapel, its inscription in the Ogham alphabet. The bakery in Barrack Street with which he provided for poor children is also in the care of the heritage centre.

Edmund Rice Heritage Centre

❶ Chapel daily 7am–6pm, museum Mon–Fri 9am–5pm, Sat 10am–2pm; admission 5 €; www.edmundrice.ie

AROUND WATERFORD

A good 10km/6 miles east of town, on the R683, lies Passage East, where the River Suir flows into the bay of Waterford Harbour. A car ferry crosses here to Ballyhack (www.passageferry.ie). Strongbow landed here with 1,200 men in 1170 before taking Waterford.

Passage East

Back roads lead from Passage East to Dunmore East, which lies at the southern end of Waterford harbour. It is a pretty resort situated on a rise, complete with yacht harbour, beach and a rich selection of leisure activities.

Dunmore East

A detour of 4km/2.5 miles on minor roads in a westerly direction is an opportunity to see the beautiful Knockeen Dolmen, presumed to be 4,000 years old. After about 13km/8 miles, the main road reaches the popular family resort of Tramore (pop. 10,330), with its attractive sandy beach, 5km/3 miles long. The biggest surfing school in Ireland is based here. When the weather is bad, go swimming in the Splashworld **water park** (www.splashworld.ie).

Towards Tramore

Copper Coast Geopark Between Tramore and Dungarvan lies the Copper Coast Geopark, where geology and mining history in Knoackmahon and Tankardstown in the 19th century are presented. This 25km/16-mile stretch of coast also boasts eight beaches. A geological garden at Bunmahon explains the geology of the region. Visitors can go walking, hire kayaks and take trips to the outlying Ireland, while the Copper Coast Mini Farm caters for children.
❶ Copper Coast Experience: free admission; www.coppercoastpark.com

Portlaw Drive upriver along the Suir from Waterford, initially heading west on the N25 and then in a north-westerly direction on the R680, to the former Quaker town of **Portlaw**, reached after about a mile. Its tanneries make up the greatest part of Irish leather production. To the north-west lies **Curraghmore Park**. The mansion of the Marquess of Waterford stands amidst the magnificent estate, which also includes a shell house created with shells brought from all over the world by sailors. ❶ Curraghmore: Easter to mid-Oct Tue–Tue and 1st/3rd Sunday in the month 10am–4pm; admission from 5 €; www.curraghmorehouse.ie

✶ Westport (Cathair na Mart)

✦ C 2

Republic of Ireland, province: Connacht
County: Mayo
Population: 6,060

For many, Westport is one of Ireland's prettiest places. Thanks to the abundance of fish in Clew Bay, it has also developed into a popular centre for sea fishing.

Pretty coastal town on Clew Bay The narrow Carrowbeg River runs along the middle of the main road, the Mall, lined by lime trees and spanned by charming old bridges. At the southern end of the Mall lies an attractively designed square called the Octagon, where a statue of Saint Patrick depicts the saint entangled in snakes. Designed for the Earl of Altamont by the English architect James Wyatt in 1780, the town was an important centre of trade before the arrival of the railway.

✶Westport House The entrance to Westport House on Westport Quay is reached by following the main road south from the Octagon square. Built by Richard Cassels in 1730–34 and extended by James Wyatt, the seat of the Marquess of Sligo is **among Ireland's most interesting manor houses**, even though little survives of the original interior. There are family portraits in the Long Gallery, and the dining room is decorated with stucco. Upstairs, landscape paintings depict scenes from the local area. Downstairs, a shopping arcade rather lacking in style has been installed. The beautiful park, designed in the English style, tempts visitors with unusual water features that make use of the tides. Children love the **Pirate Adventure Park**.

Westport House: end of March to June and Sept daily 10am–4pm, July–Aug daily 10am–6pm, Sept–Dec Sat, Sun 10am–4pm; admission 12.50 €; www.westporthouse.ie

Pirate Adventure Park: Easter and May Sun 11am–6pm, June Mon–Fri 10am–3pm, Sat and Sun 11am–6pm, July and Aug daily 11am–6pm; admission 20 €; www.westporthouse.ie

Also on Westport Quay, near the manor house, Clew Bay Heritage Centre has interesting exhibits and information on the region's history. Guided tours of the town start from The Clock on Bridge Street.

Clew Bay Heritage Centre

❶ Mon–Fri 10.30am–2pm, June–Sept until 5pm, July and Aug also Sun 3–5pm, town guided tours July and Aug Wed 11am; admission 3 €; www.westportheritage.com

In summer flowers adorn the bridge on The Mall

Westport

INFORMATION
James Street (The Mall)
Tel. (0 98) 2 57 11
http://westporttourism.com

WHERE TO EAT
Quay Cottage €€€
Harbour (by the entrance to Westport House)
Tel. (0 98) 2 64 12
www.quaycottage.com
Fans of ships and all things nautical will feel at home in little Quay Cottage. The speciality is fish dishes of course, but the vegetarian menu is not to be sniffed at either.

J.J. O'Malley's €€€
Bridge Street
www.jjomalleys.ie
Tel. (0 98) 2 64 12
Not only young people meet in this establishment, which serves dishes from Mexico, Italy, India and Thailand.

PUBS
The Clock Tavern
High Street
Tel. (0 98) 268 70
www.theclocktavern.ie
This lively pub is possibly the best in Westport, with live music from Friday to Sunday.

Matt Molloy's €€ **Insider Tip**
Bridge Street
Tel. (0 98) 2 66 55
www.mattmolloy.ie
This belongs to the »Chieftains« flute player Matt Molloy. When he is around, he sometimes joins in with the music sessions.

WHERE TO STAY
Westport €€€€
The Demesne, Newport Road
Tel. (0 98) 2 51 22
www.hotelwestport.ie
123 rooms, 6 suites
Home of the Ocean Spirit Spa & Leisure Centre, as well as a good restaurant. Attracts families, e.g. with story-telling evenings on Sundays. Also a venue for murder mystery weekends.

Westport Woods €€€€
Quay Road
Tel. (0 98) 2 58 11
iwww.westportwoodshotel.com
The Beach Health Club & Spa with its 18m/60ft pool, Lakeview Restaurant, children's playground, tennis courts and evening entertainment are among the advantages of this house in a peaceful location.

Just a few miles west of Murrish stands the National Famine Memorial by John Behan. The artist designed it in the shape of a »coffin ship«, one of the notorious ships on which **the survival chances of emigrants were very slim**.

National Famine Memorial

AROUND WESTPORT

Ireland's **holy mountain** Croagh Patrick (753m/2471ft), rises suddenly out of the shore landscape south-west of Westport. The climb can be made from a car park on the R335, at Murrisk. A small road initially leads to the white statue of Saint Patrick, and then goes up via a steep slope covered in quartz scree (good walking shoes are needed). To reach the summit via the exhausting path requires a good two hours, but it is worth the effort, not least for the constantly expanding horizon. From right at the top, Clew Bay with its many little islands can be seen to the north, stretching away to the heights of the Curraun Peninsula and even further, to Nephin mountain, especially atmospheric at sunset. To the south, it is even possible to see the Twelve Bens of Connemara beyond the Mweelrea Mountains. Each year on the last Sunday of July, there is a pilgrimage up the mountain to commemorate the forty days of penance that Saint Patrick is supposed to have undergone here in the year 441. There is a

*Croagh Patrick

Croagh Patrick, Ireland's holy mountain

chapel on its flat summit, where a service is always held on the day. Many pilgrims perform this pilgrimage barefoot, and the discarded shoes can be seen along the path. For more details refer to the **Cro-agh Patrick Visitor Centre**.

❶ March–Oct daily 10am–6pm, July and Aug longer if required; free admission; www.croagh–patrick.com

Louisburgh   The fishing village of Louisburgh, Cluain Cearbán (»Kerwan's Mead-ow«) in Irish, is especially popular with visitors due to its beautiful surrounding countryside. The plain, traversed by many rivers rich in fish, is enfolded by mountains, and the coast is lined by cliffs and beautiful beaches. To the north-east, the viewpoint of Old Head juts out into the bay. In the Granuaile Visitor Centre visitors can learn all about the **legendary pirate Grace O'Malley**. Historical documents, castle and ship models tell of her life and of the Great Famine.

❶ All year Mon–Fri 10am–4pm; admission 4 €

*Doo Lough Valley   The R335 leads from Louisburgh through the beautiful Doo Lough Valley, also known as the Valley of Delphi (►Connemara), though the road climbs gradually up towards Doo Lough (»dark lake«) until suddenly, the lonely lake opens up, with the Mwellrea Mountains be-hind. Salmon and trout can be caught here. When the sun is shining, the landscape appears bright green, though everything is cloaked in an opaque grey when fog banks draw in from the Atlantic. The cross by the side of the road recalls a tragedy that occurred during the Famine (1845–49): 600 men, women and children set off from Lou-isburgh to Delphi Lodge to ask the then owner for food. He refused them, however, and 400 people died of hunger and cold during the return journey.

Killeen, Killadoon   A minor road heading south-west from Louisburgh leads to the Car-rownisky River as well as to Killeen and Killadoon. The two isolated villages have a wonderful view towards the sea and beautiful beaches.

Clare Island   The quiet holiday paradise of mountainous Clare Island lies off the coast, to the north-west. The island, still inhabited by 140 people, can be reached from Roonagh Quay, from where two companies operate small ferries (www.clareislandferry.com). Boats also run to Inishturk Island and Achill Island. During the 16th century, Clare Island be-longed to the legendary Grace O'Malley, and the castle on the small harbour is said to have been built by her. About 2.5km/1.5 miles south-west of the harbour stand the ruins of Saint Bridget's Church, dating from around 1500. Medieval frescoes displaying strange hy-brid creatures of man and beast can be seen in the choir. The only character that is definitely recognizable is the Archangel Michael holding the scales of the day of judgment.

The Pirate Queen

Probably no other woman earned the love of the Irish people as much as the »Pirate Queen« Grace O'Malley (1530–1603). Songs and legends claim her as the first Irish patriot.

The head of the O'Malley clan and ruler over **Clew Bay near Westport** was the only child and thus the sole inheritor of Owen Dubhdarra (»the Black Oak«). The O'Malleys' livelihood depended on the sea: selling fish and piracy put food on the table. At an early age, Grace stepped into the footsteps of her father and, at nine years' old, successfully pestered him into allowing her to learn the trades of the sea. Her first marriage to Donal »of the Battles«, next in line as chieftain of the O'Flaherty clan, and the birth of three children, initially confined her to dry land. When Grace took to the sea again, her trading, pirating and war expeditions added more to the family's coffers than her husband. Soon, the O'Flahertys accepted her as the real clan leader. After the death of her husband, Grace returned to the family home and, in 1566, was elected the **first female head of the O'Malley clan**. Her second marriage was a strategic one, giving her domination over the whole of Clew Bay. Celtic law gave her the opportunity to release her husband from the marriage after one year but hang on to his possessions.

Meeting Elizabeth I

With her **20 boats and 6,000 men**, Grace O'Malley soon dominated large parts of the west coast of Ireland, becoming the scourge of all merchant ships crossing the Atlantic. Getting on the wrong side of the Pirate Queen was not a good idea: when her lover was murdered, she destroyed the murderer's whole clan. The only power to best hers was England, which, under Elizabeth I, was increasingly laying claim to Ireland. Grace O'Malley gave in to the superior force, paying tribute to the English Queen, which allowed her to hang on to her possession as a fiefdom. In 1593 she travelled to London in order to ask Queen Elizabeth I in person for the release of her imprisoned son. It was this action in particular that made the »Pirate Queen« and feared clan chieftain into a legendary Robin Hood character and heroine of Irish freedom.

Rockfleet Castle was a favoured residence of Grace O'Malley

Inishturk Island Inishturk Island can also be reached from Roonagh Quay via Inishbofin (www.clareislandferry.com). Nature lovers will enjoy the beaches, beautiful walking trails and interesting plant and animal life here.

Newport and around Newport is especially popular for the sea fishing in Clew Bay and trout fishing in the surrounding lakes. The landscape is characterized by numerous drumlins (Ice Age deposits). Other islands in Clew Bay are also the remains of these gravel and sand hills that have sunk into the sea. **Burrishoole Abbey** North of Newport, situated on a quiet ocean bay, the imposing ruins of the former Dominican **monastery of Burrishoole** (15th century) can be found. The cloister and several memorial slabs have survived well. **Rockfleet Castle** Just a few miles further west, left of the N59, the 15th century **Rockfleet Castle** – also known as Carrigahooley – stands on an ocean inlet. The four-storey keep with its single corner tower belonged to Grace O'Malley (►MARCO POLO Insight, p.509). 12km/7.5 miles further on, in **Mulrany**, fuchsias, rhododendron and Mediterranean shrubs grow in profusion in the mild climate. There is a golf course here and tennis courts.

> **!** **MARCO ⊕ POLO TIP**
>
> *The Art of Black Pudding* **Insider Tip**
>
> The butcher Kelly's of Newport (17 Main Street) is famous for its black and white pudding, and has won the gold medal of the fraternity of black pudding makers, held in Normandy, for its black pudding in the shape of a pint of Guinness (www.kellysbutchers.com)

Wexford (Loch Garman)

✣ **D 5**

Republic of Ireland, province: Leinster
County: Wexford
Population: 20,070

Situated on the most south-easterly tip of Ireland, Wexford has a pretty quaint town centre with narrow winding streets typical of the settlements established by the Norman conquerors.

Lively town By the end of the 19th century, the previously flourishing port had silted up noticeably. In former times, the town lived mostly from agriculture, but today it is industry (the manufacture of farming equipment, among others) that defines economic life. Wexford is a lively town with pretty pubs and a colourful art and cultural scene, as well

Wexford

INFORMATION
Kilrane Office
Rosslare Harbour
Tel. (0 53) 916 11 55

WHERE TO STAY
Whites Hotel €€€
George Street

Tel. (0 53) 912 23 11
www.whitesofwexford.ie
Situated in the historic centre, the hotel
is housed in a building from the late
18th century. It has a fitness club, a restaurant with an outdoor terrace and the
Library Bar.

as being linguistically unique: the **Yola dialect** of earlier inhabitants
still colours the pronunciation of several words.

SIGHTS OF WEXFORD

The local tourist office can be found on the semi-circular Crescent **Crescent**
Quay. This is also the site of a statue (given by the American govern- **Quay**
ment) of John Barry (1745–1803), who fought in the American War
of Independence and is regarded as the **father of the US navy**.

At the junction between Quay Street and Main Street, a small square **Bullring**
is known as the Bullring, where the guild of butchers staged bull-
baiting twice a year between 1621 and 1770. The square was restored
to commemorate the uprising of 1798.

Westgate Tower is the only surviving city gate; once there were five. **Westgate**
Built in the 13th century, it was once a customs checkpoint. In the **Centre**
Coach House on Spawell Road, the **Westgate Heritage Centre** presents a one-hour audio-visual show on the town's history.
❶ April and Sept Mon–Fri 10am–5pm, May–Aug Mon–Fri 10am–6pm, Sat
and Sun 12 noon–6pm; admission 7 €

Next door stand the ruins of Selskar Abbey, founded in the 12th cen- **Selskar**
tury and destroyed by Cromwell's troops in 1649. A tower and parts **Abbey**
of the 15th-century St Selskar Church survive.

St Iberius Church was built south of the Bullring on North Main **St Iberius**
Street in 1760, on the site of several earlier buildings. The best way to **Church**
savour the beautiful interior is during one of the summer lunchtime
concerts, held every Wednesday at 1pm.
Lunchtime concerts 10 €, evening concerts 15 €, booking tel. 053 224 00;
www.musicforwexford.ie

AROUND WEXFORD

**Irish National Heritage Park

The Irish National Heritage Park was laid out in swampy landscape near Ferrycarrig. In the grounds of the open air museum **9,000 years of Irish history** are brought to life in recreations of settlements and buildings. Among others, there are dolmens, a stone circle, a Viking settlement complete with long boat, an early Christian monastery, as well as a round tower. There is also a nature trail.

❶ Daily 9.30am–5.30pm, May–Aug until 6.30pm; admission 9 €; www.inhp.com

Wildfowl Reserve

3km/2 miles outside the town, the **Wildfowl Reserve** is bordered by the broad bay of Wexford Harbour. Thousands of geese overwinter in the large sanctuary, and in summer there are swans, ducks and 42 other bird species. Nearby at Raven Point, waders and ravens can be observed. To the north lie the dune-protected beaches of ***Curracloe Beach**, which served as a film set for the D-Day landings in Normandy in the film *Saving Private Ryan*. Excursions are organized from the visitor centre.

❶ Daily 9am–5pm; free admission; www.wexfordwildfowlreserve.ie

*Johnstown Castle and Irish Agricultural Museum

In a southerly direction, leaving Wexford for Rosslare, take a right on a signposted road to Johnstown Castle. It was built in neo-Gothic style in the second half of the 19th century using the remains of a castle dating from Norman times. The entrance hall can be visited,

9,000 years of history in the Irish National Heritage Park

and a stroll around the park with artificial ponds and 200 different trees and shrubs is very pleasant. The national agricultural museum has been installed in the farm buildings.

❶ Park daily 9am–4.30pm, in summer until 5.30pm; museum Mon–Fri 9am–5pm, Sat and Sun 11am–5pm, Nov–March until 4pm; admission to museum and garden 8 €; www.irishagrimuseum.ie

Yola Farmstead Folk Park is located south of Wexford, on the road to the port of Rosslare. It comprises a **reconstructed Irish village complete with 19th-century windmill**. A craftwork shop offers gifts to take home, and the Heritage Centre allows visitors to research their family histories.

❶ March, April and Nov Mon–Fri 10am–4.30pm, May–Oct daily 10am–6pm; admission 6 €

Yola Farmstead Folk Park

North of Wexford, near Gorey, the Gravity Forest Adventure Park has climbing walls, zip wires and similar challenges for young and old.

❶ Only at weekends 11.15am–5.15pm and by arrangement, tel. 053 947 48 49; admission 24 €, individual attractions 9.60 € each; www.gravityforest-park.ie

Gravity Forest Adventure Park

Rosslare, one of the sunniest and driest places in Ireland, is reached on the N25. A wide bay offers several miles of sand and pebble beaches. The well-known ferry port lies at the southern end of the bay. **Rosslare Harbour** is the point of arrival for connections from Fishguard (Wales) and Le Havre (France). Almost all passenger ferry traffic from the European mainland is dealt with here. South of Rosslare Harbour, a narrow strip of land separates **Lady's Island Lake** from the sea. An island in the lake is connected to the mainland by a dam. The ruins of a monastery and 12th-century Norman castle can be seen on the island. The place is visited by pilgrims (www.ourladysisland.ie).

15th-century **Rathmacknee Castle**, reached by turning left off the N25 onto the R739, gives a convincing idea of what Irish castles of the 15th and 16th centuries looked like. Further along, the R739 leads to Kilmore and Kilmore Quay, a picturesque fishing centre off the beaten track at Forlorn Point.

Rosslare

From here, consider a trip to the cliff islands of Saltee Islands (Little and Great Saltee Island). **One of Europe's largest bird sanctuaries**, with over 350 species living here, including cormorants, puffins, razorbills, and northern gannet, this is a little-known place to visit. Great Saltee, like the other islands, is privately owned and accessible to visitors only between 11am and 4.30pm. Boat trips from Kilmore Quay lasting 90 minutes take account of these times (tel. 053 912 96 84, www.salteeislands.info).

Saltee Islands

Wicklow (Cill Mhantáin)

✦ **D 5**

Republic of Ireland, province: Leinster
County: Wicklow
Population: 10,360

The Vikings made use of the advantageous position of Wicklow's harbour. They settled at the 5th-century monastic centre of St Mantan and called it »Wykingio«.

Beach base for mountain excursions Wicklow stretches from the sea to the lower reaches of the Wicklow Mountains. The River Vartry flows into the Irish Sea here, after forming a narrow inland water stretching for 3km/2 miles.

Black Castle Black Castle (12th century) once protected the old narrow streets of the town. Standing on a cliff promontory to the east, the Norman castle was frequently embattled up to the 17th century. The remains of a Franciscan monastery in the parish garden date from the 13th century. The 18th-century parish church has a beautiful Romanesque porch. The most interesting place to visit, however, is **Wicklow's Historic Gaol**. The former prison deals with the history of the penal system.

❶ Mon–Sat 10.30am–4.30pm, night tours on last Friday in the month 7pm; admission 7.30 €, tour 15 €; www.wicklowshistoricgaol.com

AROUND WICKLOW

Wicklow Head The viewpoint of Wicklow Head (83m/272ft high) lies about 3km/1.8 miles south-east of Wicklow. The two lighthouses started operation

Wicklow

INFORMATION
Rialto House, Fitzwilliam Square
Tel. (04 04) 6 91 17
www.visitwicklow.ie

WHERE TO STAY
Grand Hotel
Abbey Street

Tel. (04 04) 6 73 37
www.grandhotel.ie
33 rooms
The Grand Hotel is once again resplendent, and has the recommended Almondo Restaurant (www.almondo.ie) was well as Wynnes Bar. There is a tour to Glendalough at 11.35am.

in 1781. Further south, the Silver Strand reaches all the way to **Mizen Head**, site of a world-class golf course, via Brittas Bay.

Ashford, attractively situated on the River Vartry, is reached via Rathnew on the R750 and the N11 heading out of Wicklow in a northwesterly direction. This is where Mount Usher Gardens spread out on the shores of the river. Originally designed as a small garden of no more than half a hectare/1.2 acres by Edmond Walpole in 1868, this garden landscape of exceptional beauty and rare trees, shrubs and sub-tropical plants now covers approx. 8ha/20 acres. It continues to be in private hands.

*Mount Usher Gardens

About **5,000 different species of plants** thrive in the romantic park landscape, providing an overwhelming palette of colour in May and the beginning of June, during the flowering of the azaleas and rhododendrons.

❶ March to end of Oct daily 10am–6pm; admission 7.50 €; www.mountushergardens.ie

Further up the Vartry Valley, a landscape feature worth seeing is the Devil's Glen. Water shoots through the densely verdant walls of a deep gorge before falling 30m/100ft into a rock basin known as The Devil's Punchbowl. Beautiful views of this natural spectacle are provided by well-maintained footpaths.

Devil's Glen

* Wicklow Mountains

✳ C/D 5

Republic of Ireland, province: Leinster
County: Wicklow

The Wicklow Mountains are an appealing mountain landscape of dark lakes and brown and purple speckled hills. Their peaks are often shaped like sugar cones and sometimes cloaked in wisps of fog.

Bog alternates with heather and deciduous forests with pine forest. The granite mountains begin south of Dublin and continue south through the county of Wicklow for a distance of around 60km/40 miles. To the east, they run towards the Irish Sea, to the west, they finish in the plain traversed by the River Barrow.

»The Garden of Ireland«

There are only two passes, Sally Gap and Wicklow Gap, that offer the possibility of crossing the mountains from east to west. Right up until the 18th century, the **inaccessible upland valleys** were a safe haven for the persecuted, outlawed and criminals. After the revolts of

Sally Gap, Wicklow Gap

the 1890s, the British built the Military Road in order to keep better control of the region.

A good starting point for hiking tours is the visitor centre at Upper Lake in ►Glendalough.

Upper Lake

❶ May–Sept 10am–5.30pm, otherwise Sat and Sun 10am–4pm; tel. information 0404 454 25; free admission; www.wicklowmountainsnational-park.ie

A DRIVE THROUGH THE WICKLOW MOUNTAINS

The drive from Rathfarnham (►Dublin) goes uphill towards the south. Half to the right, Kippure Mountain (767m/2517ft) and its radio mast can be seen and, looking back, there is a beautiful view towards Dublin. The R115 continues onwards to the south, passing two small lakes and crossing a highland bog.

From Rath- farnham to Laragh

From Sally Gap (505m/1641 feet), the road leads south through bare bog land, crossing several rivers that rise from the eastern flanks of the high mountains to the right (Gravate, Duff Hill and Mullagh-cleevaun). **Laragh** is eventually reached via the road passing a water-fall in the boulder-lined valley of Glenmacnass; the waterfall is best seen from the valley side.

Sally Gap

The R756 climbs in a westerly direction, past the famous monastic settlement of ►Glendalough, and back into the mountains towards **Wicklow Gap** (486m/1595 ft), located between the mountains Tonelagee to the north and Camaderry to the south. The latter lies in **Glendalough Forest Park**; the road following the park's borders. About 4km/2.5 miles past the top of the pass, a small road turns off to the right for Glenbringe youth hostel, located in an isolated valley basin. After a further 6km/3.5 miles, a road turns half right towards the north and **Poulaphuca Lake**, also known as Lacken Reservoir. Covering about 2,000ha/5,000 acres, it serves Dublin's electrical and water needs.
About 2km/1.2 miles south of Hollywood, reached by the R756, a stone circle of indeterminate age near Athgreany is known as **The Piper's Stones**. Beyond the circle stands a lone stone: the piper.

From Laragh to Dublin

North of Hollywood on the N81, the reservoir is reached once again, and after 6km/3.5 miles Russborough House, the seat of the Beit fam-ily. It was built by Richard Cassels and Francis Bindon in 1740–50, in

*Russ-borough House

**The waterfall at Powerscourt Gardens
in the Wicklow Mountains has a drop of 130m/430ft**

the Palladian style. The main building includes colonnades, wings and a large flight of steps. The interior contains good stucco work by Francini, as well as the **Beit Art Collection**, with works by Goya, Rubens, Velázquez and Vermeer, as well as Irish silver. 5,000 3D glass negatives taken on the journeys around the world of Sir Alfred Beit are also on display. There is a maze in the garden, a café and accommodation in the west wing.

❶ Mid–March–April and Oct Sat and Sun 10am–6pm, May–Sept daily, guided tours each hour; admission to house 10 €, 3D exhibition 6 €, maze 3 €; http//russboroughhouse.ie

Detour into Glenmalure Valley and to Lugnaquilla Mountain	Continuing south on the former Military Road from Laragh, after 2km/1.2 miles, the road turns right towards the mountains again, climbing up to a height of 386m/1266ft before leading down into the valley of Glenmalure. The terrain of Glenmalure Valley is frequently described as dark and haunting, but the **scenic impressions of this isolated region** are unique. At the hamlet of Drumgoff, at a small crossroads, a right turn soon leads to a car park, a starting point for Lugnaquilla Mountain (943m/3093ft). The 17km/10.5-mile footpath is not signposted, and the height to be climbed is about 800m/2,600 feet.
From Laragh to the Great Sugarloaf	The R755 leads south-east from Laragh through the exquisitely beautiful landscape of the **Vale of Clara**, along the Avenmore River towards Rathdrum. The Avondale Forest Park (▶Arklow) lies to the south. Turn off the R752 (leading to Wicklow) north onto the N11, to reach (▶Mount Usher Gardens) Ashford. The R764, heading inland, passes the large Vartry Reservoir. At pretty Roundwood, change onto the R755 heading north. Further along the road, the **Great Sugar Loaf** (501m/1,644ft) rises up above the upland plain. It can be climbed from a large car park at the southern base of the mountain which, with a height difference of around 210m/690ft, takes about 45 minutes. A further stop along this road worth making is ▶Enniskerry, and the magnificent **Powerscourt Gardens** nearby. From Enniskerry, the R117 leads back to Dublin (15km/9 miles).

LONG-DISTANCE FOOTPATH

Wicklow Way	The Wicklow Way long-distance footpath, **126km/79 miles long**, leads south from Marlay Park (County Dublin: car park, bus service from Dublin) to Clonegal (County Carlow). There are car parks within range of the footpath, making it possible to walk individual sections of the route. The first part leads along the eastern flank of the mountains and ends at the R759 at Luggala, between Sally Gap and Roundwood at Lough Tay. Continuing from Luggala, through the

valley of Glanmacnass in the direction of Laragh, the path turns west and then south-west in the direction of Moyne via Drumgoff and Aghavannagh. The last section leads south from Moyne to Clonegal, past the Ballycumber Hills and other ranges via Tinahely and Shillelagh. Leaving the region of the Wicklow Mountains, it is possible to continue walking from Clonegal to Graiguenamanagh in County Kilkenny on the South Leinster Way (40km/25miles). More details can be found on an information leaflet available from the Irish Tourist Board (The Wicklow and South Leinster Way) and at www.wicklowway.com.

Youghal (Eochaill)

✳ E 4

Republic of Ireland, province: Munster
County: Cork
Population: 6,000

Youghal (pron. »yawl«) is a historic market and fishing town in the south of Ireland. The Blackwater River widens to a lake and thus forms a safe harbour before running into the sea.

Youghal, Eochail in Irish (»yew forest«), was a thriving town from the 13th century until 1579, when it was destroyed by the rebellious Earl of Desmond. Towards the end of the 16th century, Sir Walter Raleigh governed Youghal, later it was Richard Boyle. In 1649, the town fell to Cromwell, who made it the headquarter for his campaigns in Ireland. To the west of the historic town centre, the 15th/16th-century walls and towers of the well-preserved town fortifications sweep towards the south-east for a distance of about 600m/650yd. Many houses in the town centre date from the 18th and 19th centuries. The main street runs parallel to the shores of the Blackwater River. Today, Youghal is a popular bathing resort due to its sandy beaches, 8km/5 miles long and all awarded the Blue Flag. Memories of John Huston's **filming of *Moby Dick***, with Gregory Peck as Captain Ahab, remain, and the town is also known for the original patterns of its traditionally produced needle lace, known as »Youghal Point«. | **Cromwell's headquarters**

Coming from the north, North Abbey, the ruins of a Dominican monastery founded in 1268, stands surrounded by a cemetery to the right of the main street. On North Main Street, note the Red House, a Dutch-style building. Several streets further on, William Street leads right to the collegiate church of St Mary, with its freestanding tower. It was built in the early 13th century and rebuilt several times after that. Worth seeing in the interior are the oak carvings in the | **From the Middle Ages to today**

Fishing boats in the harbour at Youghal

nave, the baptismal font and various tombs, including the tomb of Richard Boyle in the southern transept (1619). Northeast of the parish church stands Myrtle Grove, an imposing Elizabethan manor house that used to belong to **Sir Walter Raleigh**. The five-storey **Clockgate Tower** at the southern end of Main Street, which was built to replace an old town gate in 1771, served as the municipal prison until 1837 and is home to a small museum today. **Fox's Lane Folk Museum** in Tyntes Castle exhibits traditional household goods from the 18th century.

❶ Fox's Lane Folk Park Museum: June–Sept Tue–Sat 10am–1pm, 2–6pm; admission 4 €; http://tynttescastle.com/fox

AROUND YOUGHAL

Molana Abbey Drive north on the N25, then head along the western shores of the Blackwater River and pass the ruins of Rinncru Abbey and Templemichael Castle to reach the destroyed abbey of Molana, an extremely picturesque group of church and monastic buildings located on the river.

Youghal

INFORMATION
Youghal Heritage Visitor Centre
Market Place
Tel. (0 24) 2 01 70
www.youghal.ie

WHERE TO STAY
The Walter Raleigh Hotel €€€
O'Brien Place
Tel. (0 24) 9 20 11
www.walterraleighhotel.com, 38 rooms
A view of the harbour and sea, traditio-
nal Irish food in the Parkview Restaurant
and Atlantic Lounge Bar.

To the west of Youghal, 12km/7.5 miles away, the round keep of 13th-century Inchiquin Castle is visible from the N25 near Killeagh. The road continues on to Castlemartyr, with its remains of 15th-century Seneshal's Castle. About 10km/6 miles further on, Midleton is a busy market town and commercial centre with a pretty 18th-century Market House and a church built after designs by the Pain brothers in the 19th century.

Towards Midleton

Midleton is a culinary centre, home to the best-known cookery school in Ireland, the Ballymaloe Cookery School (www.cookingisfun.ie). The main sight is the **Jameson Heritage Centre**, installed in a mill house that was built in the 18th century. From 1825 to 1975, there was a working whiskey distillery here. Various models, demonstrations and exhibits give an overview of whiskey distillation.

Midleton

❶ Jameson Heritage Centre: daily 10am–1pm, 2.15–5.30pm; admission 13 €, whiskey tasting 20 €; www.tours.jamesonwhiskey.com

PRACTICAL INFORMATION

What a postcard costs, the speed limit on Ireland's roads, what you need to know about public transport. Find out before you go!

Arrival · Before the Journey

GETTING THERE

By air There is a huge number of connections from airports in the United Kingdom and North America to destinations in Ireland. Here is a selection of non-stop flights.

United Kingdom: British Airways (London Heathrow to Dublin), Aer Lingus (Heathrow or Gatwick – Dublin, Heathrow to Cork, Heathrow to Shannon, Manchester to Dublin, Birmingham to Dublin, Glasgow to Dublin), Cityjet (London City to Dublin), Citywing (Gloucester and Blackpool to Belfast), easyjet (Liverpool/Edinburgh/Manchester/Bristol/London/Edinburgh to Belfast), flybe (Cardiff to Cork, Exeter to Dublin, Glasgow to Belfast), Ryanair (Liverpool to Cork, London Stansted – Kerry, East Midlands to Knock, Manchester to Shannon, Dublin to Leeds to Bradford, Newcastle and many other destinations).

North America: Aer Lingus (New York JFK to Dublin, Chicago to Dublin and Shannon, San Francisco to Dublin) Delta (New York and Atlanta to Dublin, New York to Shannon, Orlando to Belfast), United Airlines (Chicago to Dublin, Newark to Dublin) US Airways (Chicago to Dublin), Air Canada and Air Transat (Toronto to Dublin).

Aer Lingus
www.aerlingus.com

American Airlines
www.americanairlines.ie

Air Canada
www.aircanada.com

British Airways
www.britishairways.com

Cityjet/Citywing
www.cityjet.com, www.citywing.com

Delta Air Lines
www.delta.com

Easyjet
www.easyjet.com

Flybe
www.flybe.com

Ryanair
www.ryanair.com

US Airways
www.usair.com

BY CAR AND FERRY

By car and ferry There is a ferry service to Ireland from several British ports. It is advisable to book the crossing in advance.

Car ferries, bus and rail

FERRIES FROM BRITAIN
*Campbeltown (Scotland)– Bally-
castle (Northern Ireland)*
approx. 1.5 hrs: Kintyre Express.
Passenger service between Easter and end
of September, www.kintyreexpress.com

*Cairnryan (Scotland) – Belfast
(Northern Ireland)*
2hrs 15min: Stena Line

*Cairnryan (Scotland) – Larne
(Northern Ireland)*
2hrs: P and O

Fishguard (Wales)–Rosslare
3.5–4hrs: Stena Line

Holyhead (Wales)–Dublin
2 hrs; Irish Ferries

Holyhead (Wales)–Dublin
3 hrs 15 min; Stena Line

Liverpool–Dublin
8hr: P and O

*Liverpool – Belfast (Northern
Ireland)*
8 hrs: Stena Line

Pembroke (Wales)–Rosslare
4hrs: Irish Ferries

FERRY COMPANIES
Irish Ferries
Ireland: tel. 0818 300 400
www.irishferries.com
UK: tel. 08717 300 400

P and O
Tel. (0 21) 4277801
www.poferries.com
UK bookings: tel. 0800 130 0030
Ireland 1 686 9467

Stena Line
Ireland: tel. (01) 907 5555
UK: Tel. 08447 70 70 70
www.stenaline.com

COACH
Bus travel to Ireland
Bus Éireann/Eurolines: tel. (0 1) 8 366111
https://eurolines.buseireann.ie.
Reservations in UK: tel. 08717 818 177.

RAIL
National Rail
Tel. (0845) 48 4950
www.nationalrail.co.uk

*Irish Rail
(Iarnród Eireann)*
Tel. (1850) 366222
www.irishrail.ie

BY COACH AND RAIL

Taking the train to Ireland is expensive and takes a long time. Visitors
opting for this mode of transport have to travel to Holyhead (in
Wales), the terminal for ferries to Dublin or Rosslare. Coach trips
through Ireland are offered by various companies. The Eurolines bus
service connects Ireland to British destinations.

TRAVEL DOCUMENTS

Travel documents
Entry to the Republic of Ireland and Northern Ireland is normally granted to travellers holding a full passport, with the following exceptions: for British citizens some form of photo identification is needed, for other EU citizens an identity card suffices.

National driving licences and insurance papers should be carried and are recognised in both the Republic of Ireland and Northern Ireland. Be sure to carry the International Insurance Card or »Green Card«. Vehicles must carry an EU sticker or the relevant blue oval country sticker.

Pets
Import permissions are required for dogs and cats and a six-month quarantine is mandatory, though it is waived for arrivals from England as long as British import conditions have been met.

Customs for EU citizens
Personal effects and goods can normally travel without customs duty within the EU, though there are limits. For example, the individual limit for people aged 17 and over is 800 cigarettes, 10 bottles of spirits and 90 bottles of wine.

Customs for non-EU citizens
For travellers from outside the European Union the limits for individuals aged 17 and over are set at 200 cigarettes or 100 cigarillos, or 50 cigars or 250gr of loose tobacco and for alcohol at two bottles of wine and one bottle of spirits. (This applies both to the Republic of Ireland and Northern Ireland).

TRAVEL INSURANCE

Medical insurance
British and other EU citizens are entitled to free emergency medical care in hospitals and with general practitioners. Make sure to carry the EHIC (European Health Insurance Card), which replaces the old E111 forms and can be picked up from post offices or applied for online (www.ehic.org.uk). Emergency services are usually free, but US, Canadian, etc. citizens may have to pay for some medical services and reclaim at home with their health insurance provider. It is worth checking the details of your travel insurance policy.

Electricity

Visitors from outside the British Isles require adaptors to use the Irish and British three-pin plugs. The Republic of Ireland's electricity functions on 220 volt, with a frequency of 50 hertz. Northern Ireland functions on 240 volt, also with a 50 hertz frequency.

Emergency

CAR ASSISTANCE

In the case of a breakdown contact the nearest garage or one of the automobile clubs mentioned below. In the case of hired cars always contact the hire firm in the first instance. In the case of accidents resulting in personal injury the police must always be informed at once.

Emergency service contact numbers

EMERGENCY IN IRELAND
Free in all of Ireland
Tel. 999 or 112 in the Republic of Ireland, 999 in Northern Ireland (police, fire brigade, ambulance and sea rescue)

Irish Tourist Assistance Service
Tel. 01890 36 57 00.
Help in case of theft and accidents.

BREAKDOWN ASSISTANCE
Breakdown Assistance
Tel. 1800667788 (free of charge)

Northern Ireland
Automobile Association (AA)
Tel. (0800) 887766
www.theaa.com
Royal Automobile Club (RAC)
Tel. (0800) 828282
www.rac.co.uk

Etiquette and Customs in Ireland

Greetings

The standard greeting formula is »how are you« and signifies nothing more than »hello«. The speaker certainly does not expect a full report of your day or week, but a simple »how are you« in return.

Smoking Prohibited

Smoking in Irish pubs and restaurants has been prohibited since 2004, and anyone who ignores this law risks a fine of up to £1500.

Invitations

The Irish are a sociable nation, famous for their **hospitality**. There is usually no point in declining an invitation out of politeness. Yet the Irish can be quite shy as guests, so if you have Irish people visiting, you may have to insist several times before they will help themselves to tea and cakes. Generally, courtesy dictates that you offer at least a cup of tea when inviting somebody to the house. Note that

Irish time-keeping has its own rules. For example, if you invite people to your house for 8pm, you can be sure they will not arrive before 8.30pm or even later, and any time arrangements accompanied by the phrase »ish« after the time specified are definite agreements to an unspecified later hour. For example, a suggestion to meet »at 8ish« in the evening guarantees that no one will be there on the dot of 8pm.

Humour The Irish love to make fun and are not shy of using the popular sport of »slagging« with foreigners either. **Slagging** is never meant to be malicious so please don't take this light-hearted banter the wrong way. Humour is expected and visitors do well to join in the spirit of fun intended.

Travelling The **weather** in Ireland is always an important conversation topic with the locals and you should always come prepared for rain on excursions.

Directions All travel directions should be treated with care. In addition to the often unsatisfactory and even misleading road signs in rural areas, many locals appear to have a problem with **giving directions**. Often they either confuse the traveller with well-meant but highly complicated instructions, or they send you off just anywhere, with the advice to ask again later, because they don't want to admit ignorance.

Queueing Queueing is standard procedure in Ireland and normal at bus stops, in supermarkets and at cashpoints at the weekend. Queue-jumping is frowned upon.

Fun To enjoy »the craic« (pronounced »crack«) basically means to have fun. The story goes that two Irishmen in America wanted to have some »craic«, so they approached a policeman and asked him for some, whereupon he immediately arrested them for soliciting crack cocaine.

Health

Visitors from outside the EU should take out health insurance when visiting Ireland. EU citizens can claim treatment using their EHIC card.

Pharmacies in Ireland and Northern Ireland are usually open Mon–Fri 9am–6pm and Saturday 9am–1pm. In the larger cities of Northern Ireland, a 24-hour pharmacy service exists.

Information

THE REPUBLIC OF IRELAND
Tourism Ireland
5th Floor, Bishop's Square
Redmond's Hill, Dublin 2
Tel. (01) 476 34 00
www.ireland.com,
www.discoverireland.ie

NORTHERN IRELAND
Tourism Ireland
Beresford House
2 Beresford Road
Coleraine BT52 1GE
Tel. (028) 70 35 92 00
www.ireland.com,
www.discovernorthernireland.com

EMBASSIES · CONSULATES
IN USA
Ireland
Embassy of Ireland
2234 Massachusetts Ave. NW
Washington, DC 20008
Tel (202) 2 4623939
www.dfa.ie/irish-embassy/USA

Consulate General of Ireland,
New York Ireland House
345 Park Avenue 17th Floor
New York, NY 10154
Tel. (212) 3192555
https://www.dfa.ie/newyork/

Consulate General of Ireland
100 Pine St, 33rd Floor
San Francisco, CA 94111
Tel. (415) 392 4214
https://www.dfa.ie/sanfrancisco/

Northern Ireland
British Embassy

3100 Massachusetts Avenue
Washington DC, 20008
Tel. (202) 5886500
www.gov.uk/government/world/
organisations/british-embassy-
washington

IN CANADA
Ireland
Embassy of Ireland
Suite 1105
130 Albert Street
Ottawa K1P 5G4 Ontario
Tel. (01) 6 132336281

IN AUSTRALIA
Ireland
Embassy of Ireland
20 Arkana Street
Yarralumla
ACT 2600
Tel. (02) 62 14 0000
www.dfa.ie/irish-embassy/australia/

IN NEW ZEALAND
Ireland
Consulate General of Ireland
Tower One, 205 Queen Street
Auckland
Tel. (09) 9 919 7450
www.ireland.co.nz/

REPUBLIC OF IRELAND
EMBASSIES
Britain
British Embassy Dublin
29 Merrion Road
Ballsbridge, Dublin 4
Tel. (01) 20537 00
www.britishembassy.ie

USA
Embassy of the United States
42 Elgin Road
Ballsbridge Dublin 4, Ireland
Tel. (01) 668 8777
https://ie.usembassy.gov/

Canada
Canadian Embassy
7–8 Wilton Terrace, Dublin 2
Tel. (01) 234 4000
www.geo.international.gc.ca/ireland-irlande

Australia
Australian Embassy Ireland
/th Floor, Fitzwilton House
Wilton Terrace, Dublin 2
Tel. (01) 6 645300

New Zealand
Contact the High Commission in London
(see below).

IN NORTHERN IRELAND/UK
USA
US Consulate General
Danesfort House
223 Stranmillis Road
Belfast BT9 5GR
Tel. (028) 90386100
www.london.usembassy.gov

Canadian High Commission
Macdonald House
38 Grosvenor Street
London W1K 4AA
Tel. (020) 72586506
www.canada.org.uk

Australian High Commission
Australia House
Strand, London WC2B 4LA
Tel. +44 (20) 737943 34
http://uk.embassy.gov.au/

New Zealand High Commission
New Zealand House
80 Haymarket
London SW1Y 4TQ
Tel. +44 (20) 79308422
www.nzembassy.com/uk

INTERNET INFORMATION
www.discoverireland.com
Website of the Irish Tourist Board »Fáilte Ireland«; check this for information on entry requirements, accommodation and travelling within the whole island of Ireland.

www.discovernorthernireland.com
Website of the Northern Irish Tourist Board. Information and attractive pages.

www.eventguide.ie
Events, entertainment, concerts, cinema programmes.

www.visitdublin.com
Online guide to Dublin.

http://irishdancingdirectory.com/
All about Irish dance, from show dates, dress makers, to contacts of dance schools for Irish Dance all over the world.

www.gaelchultur.com
Irish-language classes in Dublin and Cork.

www.irish-music.net
Lots of information and links.

www.ireland-information.com
North American web pages with tourist information and tips on ancestor research.

Language

English is the most commonly used language throughout Ireland, though visitors might have difficulties with some words originating in Gaelic. The **Gaelic alphabet** has a few less letters than its Latin counterpart; k, v, w, x, y and z are missing. Other letters have orthographic differences. For example, an accent on a letter indicates emphasis. A recommended English-Irish dictionary **dictionary** (Eng: dictionary, Irish: foclóir) is published by the Talbot Press Ltd. in the Republic of Ireland, with many distinct words and geographical names, as well as information on grammar. It has been updated several times.

IRISH LANGUAGE COURSES

For an overview of Irish language courses, contact the tourist boards or see www.irishlanguage.net.

Literature

Binchy, Maeve: Circle of Friends. Dublin: Arrow 2006. In her books, the best-selling popular novelist describes daily life in Ireland with a keen eye and warm heart, with the plot often revolving around friendships between young women, town and country, love and innocence. — *Novels, short stories*

McCabe, Patrick: The Butcher Boy. London: Picador 1993. An unsettling read, though fascinating in its language and dramatic vibrancy, about the life of a murderer from the Irish provinces who, in everything he did, was only looking for love. Neil Jordan made the novel into a successful film

McNamee, Eoin: Resurrection Man. London: Faber & Faber 2004. The story of recent conflicts in Belfast, narrated succinctly and poetically as a man becomes a member of a Protestant terror organization. Also available as a film noir on DVD.

Eds. John Somer/John J. Daly. New York: New Irish Writing. Anchor 2000. A collection of stories by authors as diverse as Elizabeth Bowen, John Banville, Joseph O'Connor and Anne Enright – a treasure trove of the legendary Irish storytelling with a contemporary twist.

O'Brien, Flann: The Best of Myles. London: Harper Perennial 2007. Under the pseudonym of Myles na gCopaleen, from 1940 to his death in 1966, Flann O'Brien gave the readers of his column for the Irish Times advice on all the vital questions of life; from bureaucracy to booze and unforgettable Dublin vignettes, this is a hilarious read.

Biographies, journals

McCourt, Frank: Angela's Ashes. London: HarperPerennial 2005. This bestselling memoir, telling the story of an impoverished childhood in Limerick, was made into a successful film.

Sayers, Peig: An Old Woman's Reflections. Oxford Paperbacks 1977. Fisherwoman Peig Sayers describing her life on the bleak Blasket Islands, this has become a classic of Irish storytelling.

Dames, Michael: Mythic Ireland. London: Thames and Hudson 1996. An archaeologist's engaging illustrated exploration of Ireland's sacred locations, legends and mythological figures.

McCarthy, Pete: Mc Carthy's Bar: A Journey of Discovery in Ireland. London: Hodder & Stoughton 2000 The late Anglo-Irish writer's hilarious exploration of the country, through visiting all bars bearing his family name on a quest to find his Irish roots, is not without deep undertones.

Hawks, Tony: Round Ireland with a Fridge. London: Ebury Press 1999/New York: St. Martin's Griffin 2001. The story of a drunken bet to hike around Ireland with a fridge, told with a comedian's skill.

Non-fiction

Arnold, Bruce: Irish Art. London: Thames & Hudson 1995. Compact and beautifully illustrated overview of Irish art from the Celtic era up to the late 1970s.

Feeney, Brian: O'Brien Pocket History of the Troubles. Dublin: O'Brien 2007. The Northern Ireland conflict – where does it come from, who are the main players, and what might the future hold? Revised edition of a clear and non-partisan overview of a complex issue, published in a breakthrough year for the peace process.

Somerville, Alexander: Letters from Ireland during the Famine of 1847. Ed. K D Snell. Dublin: Irish Academic Press 1995. An engaging read based on the dispatches of a journalist who travelled in Ireland during the Great Hunger.

Irish Fairy Tales

Stephens, James: Classic fairytales from the Emerald Isle, available as an e-book on www.gutenberg.org/etext/2892.

Sterry, Paul: Complete Irish Wildlife. London: Collins 2004. In-depth photoguide of the country's flora and fauna.

Parkinson, Siobhán: Cows Are Vegetarians. Dublin: O'Brien 2002. The story of city girl Michelle's eventful visit to her country cousin Sinéad is an engaging children's variation on the classic theme of town versus country, or »Dub« versus »culchies«.

Young readers

Media

The main daily papers are the Irish Independent and Irish Times, in Northern Ireland the Irish News, as well as the Belfast Newsletter and the Belfast Telegraph. Irish editions of the British papers are also sold, and English-language papers from outside Ireland are readily available.

Newspapers

Many TV channels can be received. The long-established broadcasters in the Republic of Ireland are RTE One and Two, TV3 Ireland and TV4. In Northern Ireland the BBC with its regional programme and UTV, the Ulster channel of ITV, are broadcast along with many other options.

TVany

Money

The euro has been the only acceptable currency in the Republic of Ireland since 1 January 2002.

Republic of Ireland

In Northern Ireland the working currency is the pound sterling (£), divided in 100 pence (one penny or pence). There are bank notes to the value of £5, £10, £20 und £50. Coins come in denominations of £1 and £2, as well as one pence, two pence, five pence, and ten, 20 and 50 pence.

Northern Ireland

EU citizens are allowed to bring (and take out) an unlimited amount of EU currency to the Republic of Ireland and Northern Ireland.

Customs

Standard international cards, such as Visa, Euro-/Mastercard, and American Express can be used almost everywhere.

Credit cards

EXCHANGE RATES
€ 1 = £ 0.82   £ 1 = € 1.20
€1 = US$ 1.10   US$ 1 = € 0.90

EXCHANGE RATES
NORTHERN IRELAND
£ 1 = US$ 1.33   US$ 1 = £ 0.75

WHAT DOES IT COST?
3-course menu: from 35 €
Simple meal: from 15 €
Cup of coffee: from 2 €
Pint of Guinness: from 4 €
Basic room: from 40 €
Hire car: from 40 € per day

Post and Communications

Post

In the **Republic of Ireland** letter boxes and postal service vehicles are painted green. Stamps can be purchased at post offices, at machines and in some newspaper kiosks. The standard rate for a letter or card under 50g is 55 cents within Ireland (including Northern Ireland), and 78 cents to Great Britain, Europe and worldwide. In **Northern Ireland**, letter boxes and postal service vehicles are red. British stamps and rates are required here, which means letters and cards up to 20g to the rest of the UK require a 55p stamp, for other countries £ 1.05. **Post Offices** are open from 9am to 5.30pm, Monday to Friday, and from until 5pm on Saturdays (in Northern Ireland until 12.30pm on Saturdays).

Telephones

Telephone boxes in the Republic of Ireland are grey or green and white. In Northern Ireland, they are red or metal with plexiglass. Public telephones accept coins or alternatively phone cards, which can be purchased at newspaper kiosks. Check with your mobile phone **Mobile phones** provider for the cost of using mobile services while travelling. Directory inquiries: call 1 18 50 (www.118.ie).

DIALLING CODES
To the Republic of Ireland
Tel 0 0353

To Northern Ireland
from outside UK: tel. 0 48
from the UK (area code): tel. 028

To the UK
Tel 0044

To the US and Canada
Tel 00 1

Prices and Discounts

Visitor attractions

Some visitor attractions are free, but occasionally very steep entrance fees are charged, even for churches. For those planning on visiting several cultural heritage sights in Ireland it might be worth buying the **National Heritage Card**, which gives access to over 100 attractions, including Dublin Castle, Rock of Cashel, Newgrange and others. The card is valid for one year and can be purchased in almost all of Ireland's tourist centres for € 25 per adult, € 60 for families (www.heritageireland.ie). On the first Wednesday in the month, most attractions run by the Office of Public Works (OPW) open free of charge. The National Trust (www.nationaltrust.org.uk) in Northern Ireland maintains over sixty buildings or areas of outstanding natural beauty, including Castle Ward, Giant's Causeway and Strangford Lough Wildlife Reserve. Members of the National Trust are entitled to free entrance to all their properties. Annual membership for adults over 26 costs £ 63, for those under 26 £ 31.50.

The Dublin Pass provides free admission to many sights, discounts at other places, a 24-hour ticket for a hop-on/hop-off bus tour and transfer to the airport (www.dublinpass.ie). It is valid for 1, 2, 3 or 5 days at various prices.

This pass gives its holder free use of public transport, including line 600 from George Best City Airport but not line 300 to Belfast International Airport, and discounts of up to 55% on admission prices and tours. It is available from the Belfast Visitor Centre and online at www.gotobel-fast.com. It is valid for 1 day (£ 6.50), 2 days (£ 11) or 3 days (£ 14).

Transport

BY CAR

The network of motorways in the Republic of Ireland is undergoing expansion, for example with the Atlantic Corridor, which will link Letterkenny with Waterford via Sligo, Galway, Limerick and Cork. Tolls are charged on some motorways, for example the M 1 (Dublin to Dundalk), part of the M 4 (Dublin to Kinengad), the M 6 (Dublin to Galway) and the M 7 from Naas to Limerick . The main routes are designated either as national roads (»N«) or regional roads (»R«). Many roads are extremely narrow, but usually have very little traffic. However, as visibility on many roads is difficult and the roads themselves often in less than perfect condition, driving can be a slow business. The road network in Northern Ireland is good. There are motorways (»M«) near Belfast, as well as long distance country roads designated as A (major) and B (minor) roads.

Road network in the Republic of Ireland

Driving is on the left in the whole of Ireland, and overtaking on the right. If not indicated otherwise, however, the rule of »right has priority« still applies. On the numerous roundabouts, traffic already on the roundabout has priority.

Apart from driving on the left, more or less the same rules apply in Ireland as for the rest of Europe, including the obligatory use of safety belts and helmets (for motorcycles). In general, road signs match international norms.

Traffic regulations

Speed restrictions In both the Republic of Ireland and Northern Ireland a speed restriction of 30mph/48kmh applies in built-up areas. On country roads it is 60mph/97kmh; and on motorways the maximum speed allowed is 70mph/113kmh.

Alcohol levels In both the Republic the maximum level of alcohol permitted while driving is 0.5 g of alcohol per litre of blood, in Northern Ireland 0.5 g.

Parking restrictions Parking is prohibited on roads signposted with »NO WAITING« signs. Continuous double yellow lines by the side of the road mean 'no parking', and a single yellow line indicates parking is permitted

Hire cars The minimum age for hiring a car varies between 21 and 25. Most car hire firms expect you to have had your licence for at least one year.

RAIL
Irish Rail
From abroad:
Tel +353 1 8 36 62 22
Republic of Ireland:
Tel 1850 36 62 22
www.irishrail.ie

BUS
Irish Bus
www.buseireann.ie
Tel 01 8 36 61 11

Ulsterbus/Translink
Tel 028 90 66 66 30
www.translink.co.uk

RENTAL CARS
Car Rental Council of Ireland
Tel 01 6 76 16 90
www.carrentalcouncil.ie
Representative trade organisation for the car rental industry in Ireland

AVIS
Republic of Ireland:
Tel 01 6 05 75 00
Northern Ireland:
Tel 084 45 44 60 36
www.avis.ie

Budget
Republic of Ireland:
Tel 01 8 44 51 50
Belfast/Northern Ireland: Tel 028 90 23 07 00
www.budget.ie

Hertz
Republic of Ireland:
Tel 01 8 44 54 66
Belfast/Northern Ireland:
Tel 028 94 42 25 33
www.hertz.ie

Thrifty Car Rental
Tel 01 8 44 19 50
www.thrifty.ie

BREAKDOWN ASSISTANCE
Automobile Association (AA)
Republic of Ireland:
Tel 1800 66 77 88
Northern Ireland:
Tel 0800 88 77 66

Royal Automobile Club (RAC)
Northern Ireland:
Tel 0800 82 82 82

BY RAIL AND BUS

Ireland does not have much of a rail network and only the larger towns are connected by train. The Dublin Area Rapid Transport (DART) connects coastal areas around the capital. The Explorer rail pass permits journeys on five days within a 15-day period for € 160. The bus network is extensive and also significantly cheaper than rail travel. Various ticket types, including family returns and monthly returns, are on offer. A special tourist ticket called Open Road serves journeys on the Wild Atlantic Way between Donegal and Cork, with unlimited hop-on/hop-off travel on three days out of six for € 60 (www.buseireann.ie).

BY AIR

There are four international airports in the Republic of Ireland (Dublin, Cork, Shannon and Knock), and one at Belfast in Northern Ireland (Aldergrove). The regional airports at Galway, Killarney (Farranfore), Waterford, Sligo, Derry and Londonderry, are mostly used by smaller internal carriers and private aircraft. Aer Lingus is the state airline, which flies both regional and international routes.

Airports

Time

All Ireland uses Western European Time (WET), meaning in summer it is one hour ahead of Greenwich Mean Time (GMT), and the same as GMT at other times.

Travellers with Disabilities

The Irish Tourist Board can provide a comprehensive list of accommodation suitable for travellers with disabilities ▶Information (www.discoverireland.com, see Plan your visit, facts, disabled travellers). With the relevant identification card all disabled travellers can park for free at any parking metre in Ireland.

Weights and Measures

Ireland uses the metric system. Only the »pint« remains current, though other old measures are also often used.

WEIGHTS AND MEASURES
Length Measures
1 inch = 2.54cm
1 foot = 30.48cm
1 yard = 91.44cm
1 mile = 1.61km

Liquids and Weights
1 pint (pt) = 0.568 l
1 gallon (gal) = 4.546 l
1 ounce (oz) = 28.35g
1 pound (lb) = 453.59g

When to Go

The tourist season generally runs between the end of March and the end of October. The warmest months are July and August, so this is often the best time for a beach holiday, though in many places you will have to compete with large crowds. May and June offer the best chance of sunny days, while autumn is also a pleasant time for a holiday to Ireland, as the weather during the months of September and October is often mild and relatively dry. Ireland lies in an area of mild southwesterly winds which is influenced by the warm waters of the **Gulf Stream**. Its island nature favours a relatively stable climate, with cool summers and mild winters, though the Atlantic currents ensure **the weather is very changeable** so rain gear should always be carried. Rainy days regularly end with a brightening sky towards evening and rainbows can often be seen. Snow rarely falls in Ireland and when it does, it only settles on high ground in hilly areas, and even there it does not lie for long. Seasonal temperature variations are small. During the coldest months, in January and February, temperatures range between 4 °C/39°F in the northeast and 7 °C/45°F in the southwest, while the warmest months of July and August enjoy an average temperature of 14–16 °C/57–61°F. Temperatures of 25 °C/77°F and above are rarely reached. The southeast of the country enjoys the most sunshine, while the west of the island is directly influenced by Atlantic winds, and heavy showers often pelt the coastal mountains. On average there are 250 rainy days in western Ireland, with 3000mm/120in of precipitation, while Dublin, on the sheltered east coast, only has 190 rainy days on average, with a precipitation of only 750mm/30in. Air humidity is relatively high in the whole country.

See the following websites for weather information: www.met.ie and www.metoffice.gov.uk

Index

List of Maps and Illustrations

Photo Credits

Agentur Bilderberg: Wolfgang Fuchs 12
akg-images: U3 (right), 38, 53, 69, 88
Baedeker-Archiv: 113, 114, 134, 355
Bildagentur Huber: Mehlig 44,
    S. Torrione 108, Tom Mackie 110,
    Fantuz 156, Ripani Massimo 244, Spila
    Riccardo 389
Borowski: 384, 472
DuMont Bildarchiv/Olaf Meinhardt: U8,
    6 (below), 7 (centre), 70, 73, 140, 196,
    209, 314, 335, 399, 413, 416, 512
DuMont Bildarchiv/Jörg Modrow:
    U2, 3 (right below), 4 (centre),
    5 (below), 8, 9, 14, 19, 31, 60, 81, 82,
    149, 159, 166, 194, 226, 227 (above
    left), 233, 316, 339, 340, 343, 358,
    364, 376, 381, 410, 462/463, 464, 495,
    507, 516
Fotolia: alswart 117 (below)
getty images: Religious Images/UIG
    3 (left below), Gamma-Rapho/Chip
    Hires 57, Oliver Strewe 111, Conleth
    Mc Kernan 102, Laurence Monneret
    98, Dave G. Kelly 120, Fox Photos 131,
    Stephen Saks 424, Religious Images/
    UIG 444, Santino Patanè 486/487
GlowImages: 42, 116 (above), 248, 371,
    391, 436
Interfoto: 48, 219
iStockphoto: Xavier Arnau 16, thierry
    Maffeis 24
Kuttig: 11, 251
laif: Berthold Steinhilber 4 (below),
    Hemispheres/John Frumm 85, laif/
    Miquel Gonzalez U2, 92, Christian
    Kerber 96, Ralf Kreuels 124, Hollandse
    Hoogte 322, laif/Samuel Zuder 522
laif/Hartmut Krinitz: 3 (left above), 6
    (above), 39, 63, 65 (below and above

right), 163, 191, 217, 231, 262, 265,
    268, 294, 431, 470, 479, 509, 520
LOOK-foto: H. & D. Zielske 27, age
    fotostock 94
mauritius images: ib/Martin Siepmann 7
    (below), age 25, ib/Martin Siepmann
    116 (below), 118 (below), age 173,
    Robert Harding 287
Merten: 227 (below), 293, 357
picture-alliance: dpa U4, 7 (above), 55,
    chromorange 117 (above), empics 101,
    dpa 321, 346, Roy Rainford 422
Jürgen Sorges: 106, 309
Stahn: 227 (above right), 243 (above
    right)
Beate Szerelmy: 1, 28, 56, 65 (above
    left), 200, 213, 234, 238, 250, 277, 278,
    297, 349, 447, 448, 458, 475, 497
Tourism Ireland: Chris Hill U3 (above),
    U7, Brian Morrison 2, Chris Hill 3 (left
    centre), 4 (above), Roger Kinkead 5
    (above), Holger Leue 5 (centre), Pho-
    tographic Library 66, St. Patricks Fes-
    tival 104, James Fennell 123, Chris Hill
    127, 136, Brian Morrison 178, Chris
    Hill 205, Failte Ireland 220, Chris Hill
    255, Northern Ireland Tourist Board
    284/285, Holger Leue 312, Tony Pleav-
    in 328/329, Photographic Library 362,
    Nutan 367, Jonathan Hession 402,
    Eoghan Kavanagh 408, Abbie Trayler-
    Smith 455, Photographic Library 466
Vario Images: Design pics 118 (above),
    Irish Image Collection 184, 222, 300,
    505
Widmann: 243 (above left and below)
Cover photo: DuMont Bildarchiv/POlaf
    Meinhardt

Publisher's Information

1st Edition 2017
Worldwide Distribution: Marco Polo
Travel Publishing Ltd
Pinewood, Chineham Business Park
Crockford Lane, Chineham
Basingstoke, Hampshire RG24 8AL,
United Kingdom.

Photos, illlustrations, maps::
171 photos, 44 maps and and illustra-
tions, one large map
Text:
Beate Szerelmy; with contributions by
Birgit Borowski, Achim Bourmer, Rainer
Eisenschmid, Dr. Peter Harbison, Odin
Hug, Wilhelm Jensen, Dieter Luippold,
Dr. Hedwig Nosbers, Matthias Öhler, Bri-
an Reynolds, Jürgen Sorges, Dina Stahn,
Jürgen Stumpp und Dr. Margit Wagner
Editing:
John Sykes, Robert Taylor
Translation: John Sykes, David An-
dersen, Barbara Schmidt-Runkel, Robert
Taylor
Cartography:
Klaus-Peter Lawall, Unterensingen;
MAIRDUMONT Ostfildern (large map)
3D illustrations:
jangled nerves, Stuttgart
Infographics:
Golden Section Graphics GmbH, Berlin
Design:
independent Medien-Design, Munich
Editor-in-chief:
Rainer Eisenschmid, Mairdumont

Ostfildern

Printed in China

Despite all of our authors' thorough
research, errors can creep in. The pub-
lishers do not accept any liability for thi
Whether you want to praise, alert us to
errors or give us a personal tip Please
contact us by email or post:

MARCO POLO Travel Publishing Ltd
Pinewood, Chineham Business Park
Crockford Lane, Chineham
Basingstoke, Hampshire RG24 8AL
United Kingdom
Email: sales@marcopolouk.com

FSC
www.fsc.org
MIX
Paper from
responsible sources
FSC® C011918

MARCO POLO

HANDBOOKS

 ANDALUCÍA

 BALI

 BARCELONA

 BERLIN

DRESDEN

 DUBAI

 FLORIDA

 GRAN CANARIA

 ICELAND

 IRELAND

 LONDON

 NEW YORK

 NEW ZEALAND

 PARIS

 PRAGUE

 ROME

TUSCANY

  VENICE

www.marco-polo.com

Irish Curiosities

Not only the Guinness Book of Records shows that the Irish do some strange things. But what do they have in common with the Scots, and why did an Irishman walk all the way across the country?

►Record breakers

The Guinness Book of Records saw the light of day for the first time in 1955, in Ireland of course. The managing director of the Guinness brewery, Sir Hugh Beaver, had the idea. Since then many Irish people have set unusual records. In 2011 a student from Cork peeled and ate seven bananas in 60 seconds. John McGuire shaved 60 heads in a single hour in Dublin in 2010. And between 19th and 21st September 1983, Roberta Brown and Lorraine McCourt covered 71 miles on the catwalk in Parke's Hotel, Dublin.

►Thrifty Scots? No, an Irish skinflint

In 2011 Michael O'Leary, boss of the budget airline Ryanair, announced that in future his planes, with 189 seats, would have only one toilet. The point of this space-saving was to fit in an extra six seats.

►The genuine and the plastic Irish

A hibernophile is someone who loves Ireland and its culture. This is often the case with people who have Irish roots. By contrast there are also hibernophobes. The Irish themselves criticize the so-called »plastic Paddy«, someone who does not come from the Emerald Isle but who imitates old-fashioned stereotypes of supposedly Irish behaviour.

►Honesty is the best policy

In 2012 Ireland's oldest public library, Archbishop Marsh's Library in Dublin, got back a book that had been missing for over 100 years. The 500-year-old volume, which was not for lending, turned up in a second-hand shop after a house clearance. The person who found this treasure bought it and returned it to the library, absolutely refusing to accept a reward.

►String them up

After the Siege of Kinsale in 1601–02, Elizabeth I issued an order to Lord Barrymore to hang all Irish harpists and destroy their instruments, as their playing had encouraged the Irish soldiers.

►Run, Paul, run!

On 1st January 2010 an new version of the Defamation Act came into force in Ireland: blasphemy can be punished with a fine of up to € 25,000. Paul Gill protested against the new law by walking across the whole of Ireland. His walk from Mizen Head to Malin Head took 25 days. So far, the feat has failed to change the law.